Environmental Psychology for Design

fb

Environmental Psychology for Design

Second Edition

DAK Kopec, Ph.D., MCHES, IDEC
Radford University

Fairchild Books
New York

Executive Director & General Manager: Michael Schluter
Executive Editor: Olga T. Kontzias
Assistant Acquisitions Editor: Amanda Breccia
Development Editor: Rob Phelps
Associate Art Director: Sarah Silberg
Production Director: Ginger Hillman
Associate Production Editor: Linda Feldman
Project Manager: Jeff Hoffman
Copyeditor: Susan Hobbs
Ancillaries Editor: Amy Butler
Associate Director of Sales: Melanie Sankel
Cover Design: Andrea Lau
Cover Art: © Russell Kord/Alamy
Text Design: Ed Hamel
Page Layout: Mary Neal Meador
Photo Research: Alexandra Rossomando
Illustrations: Precision Graphics

Library of Congress Catalog Card Number: 2011930772
ISBN: 978-1-60901-141-3
GST R 133004424

Printed in Canada

TP14

Table of Contents

Extended Contents

If it weren't for all of the dynamic students and exceptional mentors who have come into my life, a book like this could not be possible. For this reason, I would like to dedicate this book to all of you who continue to teach and inspire me.

Preface

to the Second Edition

Environments built for human habitation must be carefully designed to fulfill the needs of the intended occupants. A collaborative approach between designers and environmental psychologists can create an artistic statement as well as satisfy the needs and preferences of the intended users. This allows designers, environmental psychologists, and occupants to reach a consensus of opinion. While this might seem obvious to some, there was once a time when humans saw themselves as separate from the natural world. We looked for solutions to our problems in education, social services, rules and laws, and chemical intervention. Today, more and more people realize that environmental modification can be a viable and more sustainable solution to several of our physical and social woes. This realization comes at a time when the world's population spends the vast majority of a lifetime inside various built environments. We live, learn, work, shop, and recreate within the built environment; and when we are outside, we spend a considerable amount of time surrounded by man-made structures. Although several fields address environmental modification, environmental psychology is well positioned to study the psychosocial responses to the human condition in relation to the built environment.

Designers (architects, industrial designers, interior designers, landscape architects) are among the leading professionals who plan, design, and develop our built environment. These professionals have shown increasing awareness of the role of the built environment in relation to the human condition. This is evidenced by the programmatic accreditation boards of the Council for Interior Design Accreditation (CIDA) and the National Architectural Accrediting Board

(NAAB) and professional societies such as the U.S. Green Building Council (USGBC) that include environment and behavior criteria as a performance measure. Unfortunately, the attention to detail and use of qualified environment and behavior professionals during the design process remain inconsistent and viewed as not necessary by many within the general populace. This is a trend that is changing and is likely to continue to change as societies become more enlightened.

BRINGING ENVIRONMENTAL PSYCHOLOGY INTO THE DESIGN FIELDS

The core focus of the first and second editions of *Environmental Psychology for Design* is on the practice and principles of environmental psychology as they pertain to the design fields. The writing is specifically geared to the student of design and the practicing designer. Its intent is to bridge the gap between theory and practice so that designers are better equipped to critically analyze and to think comprehensively when designing the built environment. Through brief discussions of scientific research, philosophical perspectives, and illustrations of design in practice, this book incorporates fundamental environmental psychology concepts into the practice of the design fields.

ORGANIZATION OF THE SECOND EDITION

The second edition of *Environmental Psychology for Design* is a continuation of content, research, and principles of the Joel Polsky Prize–winning first edition. The second edition has taken all of the excellent aspects of the first edition and made them more comprehensive and user-friendly. The second edition is divided into 16 chapters. Chapter 1 introduces the fundamentals of environmental psychology while Chapters 2 through 6 build upon this introduction by illustrating how psychology, biology, and social science impact our built environment and how our environment, in turn, affects us. Chapters 7 through 9 address our environmental needs from infancy through childhood and adolescence and into our elder years, taking into account both universal design and multicultural perspectives. Chapters 10 through 16 apply both the fundamentals of environmental psychology from the early chapters and the human factors explored in the middle chapters to a broad spectrum of residential, commercial, and community and neighborhood design.

Pedagogical Features

Each chapter begins with a quote that sets the tone of the chapter for the reader. These quotes are followed by an outline of the chapter's contents and learning objectives and a concise introduction of the principles and concepts discussed throughout the chapter. Key terms are bolded throughout the text, listed at the end of the chapter, and defined again in a Glossary at the end of the book, where a robust list of references

can also be found. Each chapter ends with a Conclusion that summarizes key chapter points followed by Studio Activities, Discussion Questions, and Learning Activities.

The second edition also offers more new features, such as Web Links that direct readers to related web sites; Sustainability Connections that offer thought-provoking examples for designers to consider how their work affects global ecology or the balance of nature; Cultural Connections that provide design considerations pertaining to influences based on social identity, gender, age, economics, customs, religious beliefs, and traditions; and Expert Spotlights, in which leading design academicians, many of whom also have thriving practices, share their insights into the content of each chapter.

WRITTEN FOR CREATIVE AND VISUAL THINKERS

Design students are visual and creative. Often they have difficulty understanding discussions of multiple research studies. This book discusses in a meaningful and practical way environmental concepts, issues, and resolutions. It includes the fundamental principles that are grounded in research conducted within the design and social science fields that guide environmental psychology, and it examines various factors that influence human behaviors within the built environment.

Acknowledgments

A special thanks to ASID, the University of Minnesota, and Caren Martin for the production and maintenance of the extremely valuable website /www.informedesign.umn.edu. This website provides excellent and easy-to-use information that can benefit all designers.

I would like to thank Edith Sinclair and Julia Cota who helped me to identify and develop discussion questions, activities, and web sites that have the greatest meaning for students. I want to extend a special thanks to those at Fairchild Books who made both editions possible—especially to Executive Editor Olga Kontzias, who is a phenomenal person and a tremendous asset to her authors; to Development Editor Robert Phelps, who stayed with me and guided the manuscript through the editorial stages; to Sarah Silberg, who managed and polished the art; and to Noah Schwartzberg, who helped make the instructor's guide diverse, fun, and of value to new instructors. I truly enjoy working with the Fairchild team because you all make it easy and fun, and you all have a great sense of humor!

I would also like to thank the following colleagues, selected by Fairchild Books, for their thoughtful reviews

of both the first and second editions—for the first edition: Jan Best, Design Institute of San Diego; Robert Bechtel, University of Arizona; Dan Beert, Bellevue Community College; Duncan Case, University of Nebraska; Naz Kaya, University of Georgia; Katrina Lewis, Kansas State University; Setha Low, City University of New York; Joan McLain-Kark, Virginia Tech; Jack Nasar, Ohio State University; and Suzanne Scott, University of Wisconsin; and for the second edition: Robert R. Bell, Jr., Miami University; Lindsay A. Clark, Kansas State University, Department of Interior Architecture and Product Design; Connie Dyar, Illinois State University; Sheila Flener, Western Kentucky University; David Michael Lieb, New England Art Institute; Debra Sutterfield, Iowa State University; and Ann Thakur, California State University–Northridge.

Finally I want to acknowledge and thank all of my colleagues who contributed to this book by offering their expert comments. I love my profession, and you all make teaching and writing an enjoyable experience!

01

An Introduction to Environmental Psychology

Man is the only animal for whom his own existence is a problem which he has to solve.

—Erich Fromm

The human-environment relationship is symbiotic in that the environment influences our behaviors and we in turn influence the environment. Whether due to fear, necessity, or naturally occurring challenges such as droughts, floods, and extreme temperatures, we have adapted to a variety of environmental conditions that then lead to changes within the environment. Early humans examined weather patterns, interpreted animal behaviors, and identified fertile soils, among various other efforts in order to increase their understanding of the natural world. Many of these efforts were among the first of our environmental studies. The results of these early studies prompted human responses, such as stockpiling food and water, seeking shelter and high ground, and planting and harvesting crops.

HUMAN BEHAVIOR AND THE ENVIRONMENT: WHICH CAME FIRST?

Beginning at about 10,000 BCE, humans moved from the natural world of trees, bushes, and savannahs to a world constructed by fellow humans (Scarre & Renfrew, 1995). Once we humans surrendered a nomadic lifestyle, we began the practice of environmental modification, in which we altered our surroundings to better suit our needs. Examples include the infill of wetlands, irrigation to make dry land yield crops, and the creation of lakes by damming rivers. However, human intervention does not occur without consequence. In the 1930s over-farming of the prairie lands in the United States combined with a lack of rain created the Dust Bowl, in which the topsoil literally blew away (Figure 1.1).

More recently we have seen myriad diseases arise from treating animals as a commodity. For example, we never had the swine flu virus until

1

[**Figure 1.1**] Overfarming combined with severe drought conditions led much of the nutrient-rich topsoil to blow away, resulting in the Dust Bowl of the 1930s in U.S. prairie lands. © Everett Collection Inc. / Alamy

[**Figure 1.2**] Western society relies upon the built environment to satisfy needs for shelter. However, there are some people throughout the world who still live nomadic lifestyles, and the concept of home is more about a territorial expanse than a structure. © Barry Lewis / Alamy

[**Table 1.1**] Human Interaction with the Environment

Culture	Orientation	Explanation
African	Harmony	The goal is for everyone to get something. When out of balance, such as in conditions of extreme poverty, people will try to bring about harmony, which is how poaching is justified.
Asian	Resolution	Rule-oriented culture with a strong sense of black/white, yes/no, and right/wrong orientation. The need to eat, for example, leads to the resolution that everything is consumable and therefore valued only for consumption.
Eastern & Western European	Blame	Nothing just happens; therefore, someone or something is always to blame; and blame demands punishment or alteration to prevent an action from reoccurring.
Traditional Native American	Balance	The world is composed of many different forces that must be continually balanced. There is not hierarchy within life or events, just the constant struggle for equilibrium.
Latin	Mixed	This culture is a blend of European and traditional native American, which means that the culture strives for balance but is encumbered by the European disposition for blame. This conflict is dealt with by a strong belief in a supreme being's interference as a means of bringing balance.

China started to farm duck and swine together. A virus common to ducks was transmitted to swine, where it mutated to a point that it now affects humans. Each year a new flu virus is introduced into the population. In the early twenty-first century Great Britain was plagued with a disease originating from cattle, called *mad cow*. Each of these conditions resulted from human intervention and manipulation of life's natural order.

As a product of nature, humans are inextricably woven into the fabric of our environments, and we affect those environments just as they affect us. Different cultures approach their role within the world and their relation to other life forms from different perspectives. Each perspective, however, will bring about a consequence.

Over the millennia most human societies have, in essence, evolved from small groups of nomadic hunter-gatherer clans into villages and, finally, into cities. There is evidence in some parts of the world today of the way humans used to live. The Mongolians and some Eskimos (Figure 1.2), for example, continue to live a traditional nomadic lifestyle. Nomadic lifestyles are inherently the most sustainable way of life because the tribe's people do not exhaust an area of its natural resources, thereby allowing those resources to replenish themselves.

In the past 100 years alone, much of humanity's relationship to the various environments we occupy has undergone more radical changes than ever before.

We spend most of our time inside, we make products that linger within the environment, and many of our small cities rival the largest ancient cities. For example, the population of the modern city of Bakersfield, California, is roughly equivalent to that of the great ancient city of Rome (250,000). Thus, with the continued advancements of humanity, we are constantly going where our ancestors have never been in terms of population growth and what is required to support that growth. And, many experts agree that the global human population has exceeded the Earth's capacity to sustain life (see Table 1.1).

Human technological advances have overcome many of nature's laws including Darwin's idea of natural selection. The various forms of technology that have been a boon to humanity have also influenced our evolution. World-renowned physicist Stephen Hawking, for example, was afflicted with Amyotrophic Lateral Sclerosis (ALS), commonly known as Lou Gehrig's Disease, at age 22. Had he contracted this disease back in 1900, he would have most likely died in his twenties. Today, however, Stephen Hawking continues to live a productive life and is able to do so with the assistance of modern technologies.

While these technologies have enabled the world to benefit from people such as Stephen Hawking, we now have the capability to keep people alive longer, diagnose, and treat congenital illness in the fetal stage. We can also provide infertile couples with options to procreate. Modern technologies have allowed for high-yield food production, the recombination of chemicals for the production of pharmaceuticals, and methods for early detection of diseases. These advancements have translated to increased populations and increased personal expectations. Although these changes may seem benign, the unintended consequences include increased crowding and decreased personal space within many of our public and private environments such as schools, hospitals, and neighborhoods (Figures 1.3a–c).

Our symbiotic relationship with the environment causes researchers to struggle with the timeless question of which came first: the behavior or the environment. Box 1.1, "Cause and Effect," illustrates the cause-and-effect relationship between humans and their surroundings.

[**Figure 1.3a**] Western societies now spend approximately 90 percent of their time inside of the built environment. ©81a / Alamy

[**Figure 1.3b**] There are few places where a person can escape the signs and symptoms of human attempts to dominate the planet. © View Stock / Alamy

[**Figure 1.3c**] Increased population has engendered the largest cities in human history. © Greg Balfour Evans / Alamy

Imagine yourself chewing gum as you walk down the street. You want to spit it out, but you see no trashcans. The absence of a trashcan in the environment causes you to wonder what to do with your gum: swallow it or spit it onto the ground. Ultimately you spit the gum onto the ground—a behavioral action—and you have now influenced the environment by littering. One could argue that it is within our nature to spit out the gum. However, it was social conditioning against littering that caused you to think about your action. Ultimately, however, it was the absence of the trashcan that caused conflict within you.

In another scenario, you spit the gum onto the ground but you unknowingly step on the gum when you have to turn around.

You then track that gum into a friend's house making a mess on their floor. Your friend reacts with hostility, so you take offense and storm out of the house. In this situation a chain of unfortunate events began to unfold all because of something missing from the environment. This absence, coupled with your emotional disposition and your friend's emotional response, led to a chain reaction.

Source: Reyes, N. (2005). Interior designer, practicing in San Diego, CA

[**Figure 1.4**] Today, hospital emergency rooms, school classrooms, and a host of other public places experience high levels of crowding, which leads to inadequate care, substandard services, and negative personal experiences. © Sally and Richard Greenhill / Alamy

We must, however, remember to avoid attributing an **effect** (result) entirely to a single cause because social and biological factors also contribute to an effect. In the chewing gum scenario in "Cause and Effect," it was the absence of a trashcan that started the sequence of events; but it is also the disposition of the interacting people that caused the situation to precipitate. All we can say for certain is that the absence of the trashcan led to gum being spit onto the ground and subsequently tracked into a home. The interplay between the two people as a result of this event will depend on each individual person. As this simplified example illustrates, it is important to avoid engaging in **deterministic behaviors** (i.e., acting on the notion that preceding events and conditions determine every succeeding event). Evans (2004) corroborated this position when he linked environmental conditions to social manifestations that influence social conditions.

The field of environmental psychology is one that embraces multiple factors and rejects the single-variable approach. Although some fields such as Western medicine and social services rely on a single or *purist* approach, environmental psychology is *multimodal*: It utilizes both social and physical science perspectives, and views human-environment behaviors as deriving from a combination of social, cultural, and biological factors. Thus, the premise behind the research and practice of environmental psychology is a holistic thought process that considers biological, social, and environmental causal agents (Figure 1.4).

Within Western societies, physicians often use medications and surgery while counselors or therapists use methods of introspection and behavior modification to solve issues. Some of the *biological factors* that influence our behaviors might be a result of absorption and secretion of neurochemicals or hormones within our brain or other regions of our body. The *social factors* that might influence beliefs and subsequent actions might derive from our unique cultural, religious, social, and/or personal experiences. In many instances we mimic the behaviors that we have observed from our families or peer groups. Environmental psychologists not only consider these biological and sociological influences, but they also use methods of environmental modification and design to enhance preferred actions and reduce undesirable behaviors.

Environmental psychology can solve problems related to the principles of learning, motivation, perception, attitude formation, and social interaction, to name a few. Environmental psychologists are poised to explain why humans engage in particular behaviors in relation to their environments. For the purposes of this book, the disciplines that can benefit the most from this work include architecture, interior design, and landscape design. "Designers need to consider how buildings affect the people using them by understanding both how design influences people and how we can modify the design to facilitate the function for which the setting is intended" (Bell, Greene, Fisher, & Baum, 2001).

GOVERNING PERSPECTIVES IN PSYCHOLOGY

Psychology has many governing perspectives from which different professionals subscribe. Although there are too many perspectives to discuss here, there are a few that a person must understand in order to understand where environmental psychology gains much of its information.

Beginning with *neurobiology*, the body of science that presupposes our actions, behaviors, and preferences result from genetics and our biological composition. There are other psychologists who contend that our actions are based on situations where we have learned, through either positive or negative outcomes, which behaviors we want to repeat and which ones we want to avoid. The *sociocultural* aspect within psychology is based on learning and behavioral perspectives. The difference is in social interactions within the family or society. Gender roles, valuing the elderly, and moral values are all examples of sociocultural influences on behavior. By about age eight we begin to think for ourselves and form our own thoughts and opinions. Cognitive psychologists study the way in which we process information and how that information effects our emotions, behavior, and physiology. The branch of psychology that is most often of interest to designers is the *humanistic* perspective. This perspective emphasizes subjective meaning and a concern for positive growth rather than pathology (cause and effect). Its combined rejection of deterministic thoughts along with subjective postulations allows for the greatest freedom of interpretation for the designer (see Table 1.2).

Within design, we can differentiate between the psychological perspectives by thinking of *cognition* as the process of figuring something out, *humanistic* as one's desire to match his/her perceived self with the way in which he/she is perceived in the world, and *neurobiology* as one's compulsion to do or be a certain way because it is in his/her nature. The perspectives of learning/behavioral and sociocultural are very similar, but where they differ is in *influence*. People might learn that they get better grades when they study with music playing in the background. The sociocultural perspectives are lessons learned through society. An example might be that a new mother brings her crying infant to a restaurant and the host makes her wait a long time for a table. Then, when the new mother sits down with her crying child, other patrons give her disapproving looks. The young

mother eventually learns that it is socially inappropriate to bring a crying infant into a restaurant. Unlike the first case in which learning occurred through trial and error, learning taking place in this latter case is based on societal norms and the aggregate group reactions to the new mother.

Because no one perspective is more correct than another, the field of environmental psychology tends to incorporate multiple perspectives into a holistic analysis.

Contemporary psychologists tend to view each of the different perspectives as complimentary. An environmental psychologist, because of the multivariable **paradigm** (theoretical framework) characteristic of this field, would view this situation in stages and incorporate each of the five perspectives while analyzing the aggregate of behaviors in response to the environment. The environmental psychologist would then analyze the design of the building with an understanding of how the people will respond in an emergency in order to identify designs that would promote specific life-saving behaviors and facilitate people evacuating the building safely.

Of the different psychological perspectives, *neurobiology* is the most consistent because it is based on physical science. This means that an action can be performed multiple times and continue to yield similar results. In the design fields, physical science stemming from neurobiological perspectives has tremendous implications. Neurochemical secretion, absorption, and interaction that are attributed to environmental design and conditions provide the impetus for certain behaviors. For example, the **neurotransmitter** (neural chemical) serotonin is associated with mood. The body's natural response to overstimulation is to absorb serotonin as a means of coping; however, this absorption can cause too little serotonin to be present in the brain, which can lead to depression.

An environmental modification for an over-stimulated person may include reducing environmental stimuli by decreasing lighting levels in the home and limiting visual complexity by reducing the number of items such as knick-knacks, artwork, and reading material.

In contrast, the social sciences are based on the social world and systems—culture, religious beliefs, and **traditions**—and tend to study the social perspectives that lead to certain outcomes. The social sciences are not as precise as the physical sciences because human interactions are not uniform and social trends are fluid; however, they do provide a high probability of accuracy. Human beliefs and notions change with the passage of time; for example, during the Victorian era, people behaved and dressed more conservatively than they did during the roaring twenties.

Such social trends make it difficult for social scientists to make absolute statements; they can predict with some certainty how most of the population will respond but cannot

[**Table 1.2**] Psychological Perspectives

Perspective	Design Considerations	Illustration
Neurobiology	Our actions are hardwired as a result of neurological or biological activity, and therefore our behaviors result from both our genetic makeup and our physiological reactions to our environments. For example, because external stressors, such as noise, can stimulate the secretion of adrenaline, which causes a faster heart rate and increased blood pressure, many people need to control the occurrence and levels of these stressors within their environments. © AGStockUSA / Alamy	
Learning/ Behavioral	Our future behaviors are dictated by what we learn from past experiences of pleasure or pain. For example, by touching a hot stove burner and discovering that burner = hot = pain, we learn to avoid contact with stove burners. © Najlah Feanny / Corbis	
Sociocultural	Social conditions, such as status, gender norms, and expectations, operate in conjunction with cultural traits, such as ethnicity, heritage, and tradition, to produce certain behaviors. Fathers often teach their sons social morality so that their sons can grow up to be productive citizens. © Encore / Alamy	
Cognitive	The process by which an organism gains knowledge or becomes aware of events or objects in its environment and uses that knowledge for comprehension and problem solving develops as a result of the relationship organisms have with their environment. This includes the processes people use to think, decide, and learn. For example, any children who want something can usually figure out which parent to approach and how to ask. © Hill Street Studios / Blend Images / Corbis	
Humanistic	Based on the notions of free will (the idea that we control our own destinies) and the desire for self-actualization (the idea that we aspire for more than basic survival). Its main premise is that a person's primary motivation in life is to fulfill his or her potential. For example a person might seek personal improvement through self-help books. © Pauline St. Denis / Corbis	

state that every person will absolutely respond in a given way. Design is highly contingent on social evolution and on scientific research into perceptions, preferences, interpretations, and worldviews that must be constantly examined to provide designs that will be embraced by the general populace.

A home with both formal and informal living rooms was considered highly desirable in the 1960s and 1970s but is much less so today. This typifies how design trends evolve over time and emphasizes the importance of social science as a collaborative component of design.

CONFLICTING VIEWS WITHIN PSYCHOLOGY

Just as there are multiple perspectives from which psychologists examine phenomena, there are also conflicting viewpoints that are constantly being examined and challenged. Some of these include the underlying causes of given phenomena, which are often polarizing in nature. These underlying viewpoints include:

- Nature versus nurture
- Person versus situation
- Stability versus change
- Diversity versus universality
- Mind versus body

The conflicting views between a single individual versus a situation assign cause to either the individual person or to a given situation. Imagine a person losing his/her temper while at the airport or grocery store. The very idea of a person losing his/her temper within such an environment is generally socially unacceptable, and we thus ascribe blame to the person. However, in ordinary situations that same person may be kind and gentle, and it was the situation that caused him or her to move from rational thoughts to irrational behaviors. As designers we cannot compensate for individual mental defects (the person). We, however, can influence situations through space planning such as wider walkways, larger bathrooms, and the availability of accommodations such as ample seating and lighting, ensuring adequate resources such as multiple check stands, and the use of redundant sources to acquire information such as boards stating, "your wait time is estimated to be 15 minutes."

The conflict between nature versus nurture assigns cause as being either a genetic predisposition or the result of social forces. Following the previously mentioned situation, the nature perspective would contend that the person lost his/her temper because of some genetic predisposition to anger and hostility. The nurture perspective assumes that the person lost his/her temper because he/she had never been taught anger management, or that the person learned at a young age that the loss of one's temper would yield positive results. The nature-nurture debate is a slippery slope because of the implications. Consider that if we are nothing more than the sum of our genetic codes, what we are really saying is that we have no control over our behaviors.

Stability versus change is a conflict between the belief that human behaviors are relatively stable throughout successive generations versus constantly changing and adapting. The notion that women *have always* and *will always want* to nurture and care for children is an example of a stability perspective. Change, on the other hand, is the idea that our behaviors continually adapt and evolve. This idea suggests that it is possible for men to become more nurturing while women become more aggressive. Within design, we can see that while styles change throughout the years, gender spatial preferences generally remain stable. Male preferences for higher ceilings and greater visual access have remained fairly stable, and women still prefer greater complexity and spatial versatility within their environments.

The conflict between diversity and universality is the idea that people are either fundamentally different or the same. Those who subscribe to *diversity* view all people as being unique and diverse whereas those who ascribe to *universality* consider all humans as being fundamentally the same. From a design perspective, diversity means that every person will have a unique and individualist design style. Conversely, universality suggests that people will share common denominators such as the preferences for a view to the outdoors.

The last conflict to be discussed is mind versus body. The conflict arises from beliefs that behaviors are either psychological or biological. The idea that all people need to feel loved is psychological since love is an emotion. However, scientists have proven that the absence of love can lead to less developed regions of the brain. In this way, love then becomes a biological need. In design, the notion of safety from a psychological construct helps people to feel more at ease. However, one's belief that he/she is not safe can lead to stress-related illnesses, including sleep deprivation, elevated heart rate, and other similar reactions.

Again, rather than subscribe to one or the other of these paradigms, many within environmental psychology concede that each has merit and can account for our needs and wants within design.

A person may be responsible for his/her actions, but the environmental or social situation can also incite a behavior. This is partly because the person has been placed in a situation where his/her body is secreting high levels of adrenalin because he/she has learned that there is no viable alternative to the solution. This person may or may not always respond with hostility when presented with similar situations. The person may change the way he/she thinks about the situation, but the fact that it continues to be an annoyance to the person will not change. Because people are diverse, not all people will respond in the same way. However, the situation will most likely be universally interpreted as being frustrating. How the situation is handled will depend upon the mind, but repeated exposure to the situation will likely affect the body by way of increased stress.

HISTORY OF ENVIRONMENTAL FACTORS WITHIN PSYCHOLOGY

The principles of observation and assessment—that is, observing the role of stimuli and tracking the subsequent reaction—are at the core of every science. However, even today most social science fields, including the various disciplines of psychology, tend to neglect the role of the environment when considering behavioral responses. This wasn't always the case; a great number of social science fields carried out by many of the early studies documented the effects of environmental phenomena. Psychologists in the 1800s examined the effects of environmental perception as related to light, sound, weight, and pressure, among other variables, on learning and behavior (Bell et al., 2001). A 1916 study examined how external distractions affected work performance (Morgan, 1916). These pioneer studies were soon followed by another that examined the influence of workers' hours and the effects of ventilation on their productivity (Vernon, 1919). In 1929, an influential study examined the relationship between where in a classroom students sat compared to the grades they earned (Griffith, 1929).

Among the most famous analyses conducted of the human–environment relationship were the 1924–1932 Hawthorne studies, which analyzed the effects of lighting on workers' performances (Snow, 1927) (Figure 1.5). The researchers involved in these studies hypothesized that increased lighting in the room would correlate with increased worker production. To test this premise, the researchers placed a group of workers in a room where they performed their job duties. Each day, the researchers brightened the room by using a higher-wattage light bulb. As hypothesized, worker performance increased with brighter lighting; however, to crosscheck their results, the researchers decided to decrease the brightness, the idea being that worker production should decrease with lower lighting levels. This did not happen; instead, worker production continued to increase as a result of other variables. Because of these findings, many scientists regarded the Hawthorne studies as a failure. However, these studies taught us the importance of controls (referred to as the Hawthorne Effect) in research, and they produced the following three important findings:

1. The effect of the physical environment is buffered by perceptions, beliefs, preferences, experiences, and personality (i.e., a new bulb must be an improvement; consequently, the workers perceived that this must be a better environment).
2. One environmental variable turned out to be more important than the subtler variations (i.e., the employees who were selected for the study felt that they were *special*).
3. The physical environment changed the social dynamics (i.e., the study room layout facilitated more social contact among the workers; thus they were "happier").

These results are important for designers because they illustrate the importance of environmental variables. Theoretically, designers should be able to increase worker performance simply by making workers believe that their environment is better than others, making employees believe that the organization values them and sees them as being special, and providing appropriate measures to meet the space-planning needs.

The Hawthorne study, along with other early studies, illustrated that the environment we occupy dramatically influences how we perceive the world around us, how we see ourselves in relation to the greater social hierarchy, and how the environment affects our social behaviors. Understanding this symbiotic relationship is essential to an environmental psychologist.

Egon Brunswik, considered by many to be the founder of environmental psychology, is credited with using this term first in 1943 to describe the field of human–environment relations (Brunswik, 1943). Other researchers who have contributed to the study of the human–environment relationship come from the fields of behavioral geography and urban sociology. Kurt Lewin, a social ecologist, regarded the environment as a significant variable in the determination of behaviors and is credited with the idea of integrating information obtained from research with that of social practices, otherwise known as *action research*

[**Figure 1.5**] A study, which lasted from 1924 to 1932, at the Western Electric Hawthorne Works facility in Cicero, Illinois, was designed to analyze the effects of various working conditions on production. One of the conditions they tested was lighting levels. However, they found that no matter what they tested, the production went up. The answer was simple—the test subjects felt special and responded to this feeling. © Trinity Mirror / Mirrorpix / Alamy

(Lewin, 1943). Another notable contributor to the study of human–environment relations was Roger Barker, who is widely regarded as an ecological psychologist. Barker and his colleagues formed the Midwest Psychological Field Station in Oskaloosa, Kansas, in 1947. They observed that two children in the same place behaved more similarly than one child in two places and concluded that the surrounding environment exerted a great deal of control over behavior. Eventually, Barker and his colleagues would document this phenomenon, ultimately concluding that our environments create behavior settings.

Other important names in environmental psychology include Abraham Maslow, William Ittelson, and Harold Proshansky. Maslow conducted a study with photographs of people and found that observers responded more positively to the people photographed when the observers were in beautiful rooms and more negatively when the observers

were in ugly rooms (Maslow, and Mintz, 1956). Although this research may seem trivial, when we consider the behaviors that likely manifest from a positive environmental experience, we may theorize that beautiful environments evoke happy or pleasant feelings whereas ugly rooms evoke annoyance or discomfort. This kind of information could go a long way to increasing customer satisfaction in many government and institutional environments. Ittelson and Proshansky not only conducted extensive research relative to theory, methodology, and application in real-world settings, but also developed the first Ph.D. program in environmental psychology in 1968 at the City University of New York (CUNY), which awarded the first doctorate in environmental psychology in 1975. The 1974 text, titled *Introduction to Environmental Psychology*, written with Leanne Rivlin and Gary Winkel, was the first textbook in this new field.

The work of these early environmental psychologists serves to highlight not only the incredible impact buildings, interior spaces, and landscape have on us, but also the capacity humans have to understand that taking care of our physical environments is the same as taking care of ourselves—in other words, environmental consciousness.

DEFINING THE PROFESSION

Ideas and concepts relative to the effects of the built environment on humans have been popularized within mass media. However descriptive titles such as *design psychology* and *design therapy* are used to describe work that has been traditionally associated with environmental psychology. In many ways the title *design psychology* is a more precise term to describe an area of expertise within the broader field of environmental psychology. Notwithstanding, the American Psychological Association (APA), the governing body of psychological sciences, has yet to acknowledge design psychology as professional division within the psychology field.

Professional associations such as the American Psychological Association, American Society of Interior Designers (ASID), or the American Institute of Architects (AIA) develop governing guidelines that lead their respective professions. They do this by establishing baseline competencies and ethical standards among professionals within their fields. When a new title, such as design psychology, is contrived, there is no way of knowing the level of competence that a person using such a title brings with him/her. Hence, current or former therapists desiring a career change might reinvent themselves as designers without any formal design education and thus are unaware of important building codes and municipal regulations. Likewise, designers might want to expand their business by adding the dimension of psychology or human health and behaviors to their list of services with only limited formal education in psychology, and even less in biology or more specifically neurobiology. As such, many will not completely understand individual conditions in which the environment could threaten one's quality of life. One of the neurobiological issues of concern is the exposure to sunlight. Morning sunlight, for example, has more bands of blue light, which are associated with calmness and the absorption of melatonin. Conversely, evening sunlight has more bands of red, which are associated with excitatory responses. Hence, people with psychological disorders such as Alzheimer's disease, schizophrenia, and bipolar disorders can be influenced by sunlight (Gillie, 2004). From a behavior perspective, we can expect people to be more alert and generally in a more positive mood within homes that have kitchens oriented to the east to capture the morning light. From a design perspective, we can lose this beneficial effect when ultra violet (UV) filtering windows are used, or if window treatments prevent the flow of this full spectrum sunlight.

In a hypothetical situation, a designer might create a building with operable windows in an attempt to make a building more "sustainable." However, after three months of occupancy, many employees are complaining of asthma-like symptoms. The designer comes back assuming that the issue is occupational asthma and brings in several plants known to help mitigate the off-gassing of carpets and building materials (environmental toxins). The designer also tells the occupants to keep their windows open for longer periods of time in order to better flush-out the environment. Then, one day an employee suffers such a severe asthma attack that he/she is rushed off to the emergency room. Further analysis revealed that this person suffered from allergic asthma and the additional plants coupled with the open windows that faced a pine tree forest created a potentially dangerous situation for this employee. The employee, who had to be hospitalized overnight, sues his/her employer who in turn, sues the licensed designer because the designer should have brought in a professional consultant when analyzing the site and attempting to address an issue of concern.

Likewise, the courts are starting to hold licensed designers liable for their designs when those designs compromise human health and safety. Hence, it behooves the design professional to seek out professional guidance in those areas where he/she lacks a firm knowledge base. Throughout this book, *sustainability connections* have been added to the specific environments under discussion as a means of thought-provoking examples of the plethora of considerations designers must be aware of in any given setting, space, or building.

Formal education isn't the only way to acquire knowledge; it can also be attained through apprenticeships, as well as self-teachings. What's important about nontraditional education methods, such as apprenticeships, is that the knowledge must be acquired from reputable sources such as a designer who is a licensed architect or certified by the National Council for Interior Design Qualification (NCIDQ). When it comes to issues of physical or psychological health and safety; licensed medical doctors, licensed psychologists, or those who have been certified by the National Commission for Health Education Credentialing (NCHEC) should be consulted. It is important to understand however, that when a person is licensed or certified in a specific area, that does not equate to

[**Figures 1.6a and b**] Grandparents have different requirements of their homes than do young gay couples. As such, designers must get to know their clients and without judgment develop the best and most appropriate environment for people. a: © Ocean / Corbis; b: © Rainer Elstermann / Corbis

omnipotence and other experts should be sought out as part of the design process. It is equally important that those who are self-taught use peer-reviewed textbooks and not rely solely on books intended for mass media. Granted, mass media or *popular press* books tend to be easier to read, but the information lacks authentication.

Mass media has facilitated a growing interest among the general population on the way our built environment can affect people's lives. However, this format offers only sound bites or a brief overview of the total available knowledge. The environmental psychology field, along with design professions, must take the necessary steps to provide meaningful education to those who have been enticed by popular media. Currently, environmental psychology is the only recognized academic disciple that bridges design and psychology.

ENVIRONMENTAL PSYCHOLOGY TODAY

Environmental psychologists study a range of issues related to the human–environment experience and, as a result, can predict with some certainty many emotional and physical reactions to environmental attributes. They analyze environmental cues that contribute to perceptions about a community, including:

- infrastructure quality
- the condition of city-owned buildings
- the types and condition of local businesses
- the availability and maintenance of green spaces
- owner-to-renter ratios

Other cues come from advertising methods, placement, and the messages themselves. For example, signs on poles or roofs along a commercial street indicate a drive-through community; signs situated just above head level along sidewalks indicate that it is walkable. Advertising messages indicate behaviors within a community and can inspire stereotypical or negative images when limited to certain areas; however, distributing the same ads equally throughout the community invalidates the image. For instance, the parents of teenage girls may decide to not buy a home in an area plastered with anti-teen-pregnancy campaign ads because the ads might invoke a site-specific judgmental reaction: "Our daughters would be at risk in this neighborhood." But if those ads were all over town, the parents would tend to consider teen pregnancy as a common concern rather than a site-specific concern.

Large-scale gathering areas, such as corporate offices, schools, and resorts, are ideal settings for analyzing the environment to identify factors that contribute to or detract from desired behaviors. For example, the occupants of corporate offices who use cubicle spaces or open office plans tend to exhibit greater levels of stress, lower productivity, and higher turnover rates than do occupants of offices with private work spaces. Environmental psychologists examine not only components related to the physical attributes, such as lighting, room size, acoustics, ancillary rooms (lunchrooms or lounges), wall and floor coverings, placement of work/study stations and equipment, and the use of color, but also the various relationships among employees, supervisors, and management to analyze the links between behaviors and outcomes. For home environments, environmental psychologists analyze occupant desires and behaviors to develop homes that facilitate those activities (Figures 1.6a and b).

Environmental psychology is especially important in the initial planning and development of residential properties.

For example, if a home's adult occupants work 9-to-5 jobs, the worst position for the kitchen is southwest; the occupants are already stressed from the day's activities, the evening sun adds glare and heat while they prepare dinner, and cooking adds to the heat of the room. These combined factors create in the occupants an agitated state and a greater propensity for verbal hostility. Environmental psychology can serve to create supportive environments for people challenged by physical, psychological, and age-related illnesses and injuries, and the stress and anxiety related to daily life or end-of-life issues, as those detailed in subsequent chapters.

Academic Programs and Post Educational Opportunities

For many in the mainstream population, the discipline of environmental psychology is virtually unknown. This is partly because no proactive media campaigns educate the public about the field, its research focus, or the importance of these studies to the human race. Also, only a handful of schools in the United States offer stand-alone degrees in environmental psychology, and the vast majority of students who matriculate with a degree find themselves in academia because the degree is available almost exclusively at the graduate level. Generally, only a small percentage of students who graduate with a degree in environmental psychology move on to work in the field, either for a design firm or for themselves as independent consultants. Because the discipline itself is quite broad with currently only a few opportunities for higher education, individual interests within the field further separate those individuals who study environmental psychology.

Most institutions house their environmental psychology courses in the schools of architecture, design, psychology, human or social ecology, or arts and sciences. This limits the uniformity of what is taught within the field; a clinical psychologist will teach an environmental psychology course differently from an architect. It is important that practicing designers appreciate that each approach is valuable because it contributes a different perspective to the total body of knowledge. Not all environmental psychologists share an interest in a particular area of specialization, but they do share the belief that the environment plays a crucial role in human behavior. The American Psychological Association (APA) recognizes environmental psychology under Division 34, *Population and Environmental Psychology* (American Psychological Association, 2003). Its website lists the following areas of research interest:

- human response to built and natural settings
- impact of technological and natural hazards
- environmental perception and cognition
- design and planning issues

For people who enter the fields of environmental and behavioral psychology, common subspecialties or concentrations include, but are not limited to, the following:

- diversity, exclusion, and the environment
- housing issues and policy
- the meanings and experiences of the home and homelessness
- conflicts and contradictions in urban planning
- neighborhood and community participation
- open space planning and use
- human mobility and transportation
- design, use, and evaluation of public institutions
- participatory research and design
- gender and space
- political ecology and development
- environmental justice
- supportive environments for people with disabilities
- elderly people and the environment

The scope and practices of the environmental psychology field have a direct and symbiotic relationship with the design industries. But the field itself studies the human–environment relationship on three levels of analysis (Gifford, 2002) as follows:

1. Fundamental psychological processes of perception, cognition, and personality as they filter and structure each individual's experience of the environment
2. Social management of space related to personal space, territoriality, crowding, and privacy
3. The effect of the physical setting on complex but common behaviors in everyday life (such as working, learning, and participating in daily activities in the home or community) and our relationship with the natural world

Environmental psychology may be defined as the study of symbiotic relationships between humans and their environments. It is this *holistic* approach that separates environmental psychologists from other professionals within the fields of design and social science.

Practical Applications

Because environmental psychology is a science that examines human behaviors in relation to their environment, much of the research has broad practical applicability within the human experience. In 1954, Maslow unveiled a model depicting a hierarchy of needs, based on natural instincts present in all animals (Figure 1.7).

Almost from its inception, the model has come under scrutiny, with critics claiming that it lacks a scientific basis,

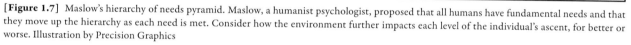

[Figure 1.7] Maslow's hierarchy of needs pyramid. Maslow, a humanist psychologist, proposed that all humans have fundamental needs and that they move up the hierarchy as each need is met. Consider how the environment further impacts each level of the individual's ascent, for better or worse. Illustration by Precision Graphics

an integrated conceptual structure, and supportive research evidence and that the concepts lack validity. Maslow, a humanist psychologist, proposed that all humans have fundamental needs and that they move up the hierarchy as each need is met. When an individual's environment is not "right" or appropriate for his/her needs (and many times this is the case), he/she will not proceed up the hierarchy; and this failure to advance causes psychological and emotional dysfunction.

If we were to accept Maslow's notion of the hierarchy of needs, along with the premise that the environment serves no other purpose than to fulfill hedonistic desires, the traditional human–environment relationship would be at the top of the pyramid as an aspect of *self-actualization*. However, human–environment research proves that our environments have a tremendous impact on how we feel, respond, and cope in daily life. Because the environment plays an intricate role in the overall physiological health and responses of the human psyche, concern for our surroundings is a component not only of self-actualization but also of safety and of physiological needs.

For example, a child who feels crowded and vulnerable within an environment may experience child-related stress (Jewett & Peterson, 1997). Feelings of crowding can lead to the fight-or-flight response, which is characterized by sympathetic nervous system activation that secretes chemicals into the bloodstream and mobilizes a behavioral response (Taylor et al., 2000). If a child is repeatedly subjected to such a response due to an environmental condition, a physician may prescribe medication, and a counselor or therapist may pursue behavior-modification techniques; however, an environmental psychologist, using the methods most compatible with natural human behaviors and responses, will modify the child's environment by eliminating sources of stimulation in the child's environment as the first step.

Human–environment interactions are based on our psychological processes in relation to our surroundings. Our environments are made up of physical stimuli (noise, light, and temperature), physical structures (dimensions, furniture, and hallways), and symbolic artifacts (the meaning or image of a setting). The fundamental psychological processes of **arousal**, **overload**, **affect**, **adaptation**, and **personal control** are integral to human–environment interactions.

- **Arousal** can be defined as excitement or stimulation to action or physiological readiness for activity.
- **Overload** is the negative mental state that results from excessive stimulation and arousal.
- **Affect** encompasses emotional reactions to the environment.
- **Adaptation** describes the process of adjustment to environmental conditions.
- **Personal control** is the ability to control an environment or a situation.

These interactions lead to outcomes that fall into categories of performance, interpersonal relationships, satisfaction, and health or stress. The positive relationship between human performance and the attention given to the individual, as well as the effects of room size and external stimuli such as noise, affect performance. For example, if a teacher pays more attention to student X, student X should do better in school. However, this one-dimensional approach assumes that variable Y (the teacher's attention) influences human performance, which equals the behavioral output. The field of environmental psychology has evolved to approach behavioral science research in a multidimensional manner. This means that student X, when factored with situation Y and personality Z: may develop behavioral response XYZ. In other words, if a teacher gives added attention to a student who has (1) eaten a proper breakfast, (2) received enough sleep, and (3) is not stressed at home, and (4) we decrease the density within the classroom, (5) increase natural full-spectrum lighting, and 6) decrease external stimuli such as noise, then the student's academic performance will be optimized. The level of optimization, however, is contingent on all of these factors.

Practical Applications for Designers

Use these resources, activities, and discussion questions to help you identify, synthesize, and retain this chapter's core information. These tools are designed to complement the resources you'll find in this book's companion Study Guide.

SUMMING IT UP

Our symbiotic relationship with the environment causes researchers to struggle with the timeless question of Which came first: the behavior or the environment? The premise behind the research and practice of environmental psychology is a holistic thought process that considers biological, social, and environmental causal agents. Environmental psychologists not only consider these biological and sociological influences, but they also use methods of environmental modification and design to enhance preferred actions and reduce undesirable behaviors.

Within design, we can differentiate between the psychological perspectives by thinking of *cognition* as the process of figuring something out, *humanistic* as one's desire to match his/her perceived self with the way in which he/she is perceived in the world, and *neurobiology* as one's compulsion to do or behave a certain way because it is in his/her nature. Social sciences are based on the social world and systems (e.g., culture, religious beliefs, traditions) and tend to study the social perspectives that lead to certain outcomes.

Understanding the importance of including multiple disciplines into design is essential. Gone are the days when one person can possibly know everything. Currently, environmental psychology is the only recognized academic disciple that bridges design and psychology. The environment plays an intricate role in the overall physiological health and the responses of the human psyche—concern for our surroundings is a component not only of self-actualization but also of safety and of physiological needs.

You can also refer to this textbook's companion Study Guide for a comprehensive list of Summary Points.

Enhancing Quality of Life Through Design

Denise A. Guerin, Ph.D., FIDEC, FASID, IIDA, University of Minnesota

Holism. Interdisciplinary. Collaboration. Wicked problems. Interaction among the parts. All of these terms seem to ask us to think about what we, as designers, must know to solve problems in ways that support and enhance people's quality of life. And all of these terms seem to point in the direction of the synthesis of the parts into a cohesive whole—i.e., the many knowledge areas, some of which are outside the designers' body of knowledge—that must be considered to not only enhance people's lives but keep them out of harm's way. Furthermore, these terms imply that our work processes may be changing in the future—even as we speak. The amount and diversity of knowledge that are required to solve today's complex design problems call on designers to know more than ever before about a wider number of topics, with deeper understanding, and when to find other knowledgeable people to bring onto the team.

What can be helpful to guide us in our identification and application of knowledge is the idea that a theory about design and human behavior can actually become an ordering system or a framework upon which to place knowledge, make decisions, and measure outcomes. In fact, that is exactly how theories are supposed to work; they define the constructs or structure of the knowledge and the relationships among all the knowledge areas or parts. How simple! Yet most designers are woefully unprepared to use a theoretical framework to identify project parameters, evaluate design options, make decisions upon which solutions are determined, and measure the results of the design outcome. We tend to limit ourselves to the notion of design theory; that is, the principles of design as applied to the elements of design such as the principle of balance as applied to the element of volume. This is only one part of the designer's body of knowledge. There is more—so much more.

Interior designers are educated to identify problems and solutions that improve the human condition and protect people's lives. With the increasing emphasis on evidence-based design, or evidence-informed design, it is timely to focus on educating designers to underpin their design decisions with the constructs of theories that explain human behavior. We must consider each design solution as a simple hypothesis, a prediction that the solution will work. Understanding theories about design and human behavior can increase the probability that our prediction will work. This is the method new designers will use to optimize the design of environments that support people's behaviors, activities, cultures, and norms and prevent harm from coming to them in the spaces in which they lead their daily lives.

- **adaptation**
- **affect**
- **arousal**
- **deterministic behaviors**
- **effect**
- **neurotransmitter**
- **overload**
- **paradigm**
- **personal control**
- **tradition**

All Psych Online: The Virtual Psychology Classroom (http://allpsych.com)

American Academy of Neurology (http://www.aan.com)

American Psychological Association (APA), select "Glossary of Psychological Terms" (http://psychologymatters.apa.org)

Association for Humanistic Psychology (www.ahpweb.org)

BBC's Mind Changers series, "The Hawthorne Effect" (www.bbc.co.uk/programmes/b00lv0wx)

Center for Human Environments (CHE) sponsored City University of New York (http://web.gc.cuny.edu/che/)

InformeDesign sponsored by the University of Minnesota (www.informedesign.umn.edu/)

International Association for People-Environment Studies (http://iaps.scix.net)

National Commission for Health Education Credentialing (NCHEC) www.nchec.org

Research Design Connections (www.researchdesignconnections.com)

Smithsonian Encyclopedia (www.si.edu/Encyclopedia_SI/History_and_Culture)

Society for Environmental Graphic Design (www.segd.org)

United Nations Environment Programme (www.unep.org)

U.S. Environmental Protection Agency's National Center for Environmental Research (www.epa.gov/ncer)

U.S. Green Building Council (USGBC) (www.usgbc.org)

U.S. National Library of Medicine, PubMed (www.pubmed.gov)

Postapocalyptic World

Design Problem Statement
A gamma ray storm from outer space just hit the planet and wiped out all electronic devices (e.g., cars, phones, computers) on the planet. Civilization has regressed to warring tribal villages that compete for basic resources. Using only trash found from around your school, create a model of an inhabitable village that has some color scheme or building attribute that distinguishes your village from others.

Directions
Step One: Identify cultures that built and abandoned villages (e.g., those of Canadian Eskimos or Mongolian tribes), and that developed temporary villages that could be assembled and disassembled, and temporary villages that simply reverted back to the landscape.

Step Two: Identify the pros and cons of each village type along with the building configuration (i.e., tee pee versus yurt versus hut).

Step Three: Identify and justify your village type.

Step Four: Build your village.

Deliverables: Village model. Written and/or oral presentation.

Observation and Assessment

Observe one's surroundings as a means to identify design needs.

Directions
Step One: With a camera walk around your community and photograph common environmental conditions that can be influenced with design (for example, you may note that a lot of snow builds up during the winter months).

Step Two: Develop chains of logic from the photos (for example, photo deep snow mound). The chain of logic would look like this: Deep snow mounds = snow being tracked inside. Snow on wood floors = wet wood = warped floorboards.

Step Three: From the chain of logic deduce a solution (for example, inside the doorway will be a 3′ x 2′ polished concrete inlay where people can come inside to take their shoes off without getting the wet snow on the wood floor).

Step Four: Develop a sketch of what the proposed design solution would look like.

Deliverables: Using ten different photos showing ten different issues, students will develop ten chains of logic. Ten solutions to the issues presented earlier with ten sketches showing the design intervention.

1. Considering how the environment influences our behaviors and we in turn influence the environment, discuss how applying this perspective into design would benefit the design process.

2. Discuss reasons why a thorough understanding of culture should be analyzed and understood before the consideration of a design project. Do you think it's important that a cultural analysis be conducted and implemented in the design process? If so, explain your opinion.

3. Consider your daily routine and analyze one aspect of it from three different psychological perspectives (cognitive, humanistic, learning or behavioral, neurobiological, or sociocultural). For example, you wake up to music rather than an alarm sound, or you *must* have a cup of coffee to begin your day.

4. Discuss the benefits of having an architect with environmental psychology understanding working in the design of a space versus an architect without knowledge on the subject. What differences in design do you think there would be? Would one design be more comfortable than the other, or would there be a small difference between the two?

5. Discuss reasons why an environmental psychologist with a background in architecture may take a different approach to analyzing an environment than would a designer with no background in environmental psychology.

1. Research events in which we have modified our living environment by altering our surroundings to better suit our needs.

2. Observe a site where people need to perform some sort of work. Evaluate the environment and document people's behaviors. Point out what you would modify in the environment to facilitate the task.

3. Research examples of social trends our society has embraced from the past to the present. Explain how these events exemplify the evolution of human social trends.

4. Develop your own examples for all the conflicting viewpoints that are constantly being examined and challenged by psychologists.

5. Research two design projects—one done by a designer with environmental psychology background and the other by a designer who didn't have the same skills. Observe the two designs, and evaluate both the positive and negative impacts of the designs. Describe the benefits of applying the use of environmental psychology into design.

02 Foundational Theories of Environmental Psychology

Perhaps one of the most outstanding weaknesses of contemporary psychological theory is the relative neglect of the environment by many of the most influential theoretical viewpoints.

—Isidor Chein

Environmental psychology is one of the few sciences recognized in the United States that exclusively examines the relationship between humans and their environments. Unfortunately, the environment is often neglected as a *cause* of human behaviors. Perhaps one reason is because we seek to remedy physical and social issues that we do not completely understand from perspectives such as biological or cognitive functions. In many respects we have long been able to dominate our environments, but medicine and the human psyche are still relative enigmas. Therefore, when we encounter socially deviant behaviors, we unfortunately tend to seek the cause within those fields in which we do not have all the answers. As designers of the built environment we must consider the environment as a co-variable, and reject the **magic bullet approach,** which is the simple deduction of A + B = C. Put another way, if a person gets a headache, he/she often solves the problem with a pill rather than looking at social conditions or the physical environment as a causal factor to prevent the headache from occurring in the first place (i.e., is the individual under stress or is there excessive glare from a window?).

When addressing the human–environment relationship, environmental psychologists will often speak in terms of *theories* as a way to help them conceptualize the human–environment relationship. These theoretical concepts by themselves do not provide answers, but rather help guide the research process. Research then generates the knowledge, which then informs the application of design solutions. This chapter explores various theories that help explain the human–environment relationship and environmental

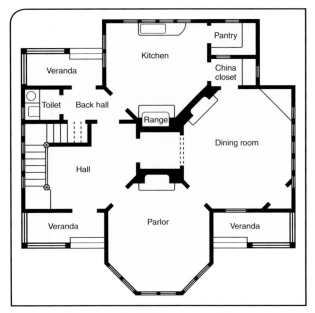

[**Figure 2.1**] Notice in this highly segmented floor plan how the kitchen, dining room, and living room (parlor) are separated from each other. This was common in nineteenth- and early twentieth-century homes. Illustration by Precision Graphics

perception. These theories are applied throughout the text as a means of developing thoughtful design, which can be evaluated in relation to occupant profiles, differences in climates, and other factors that lead to differences in perceptions, cognitions, and behaviors.

ENVIRONMENTAL PSYCHOLOGY TODAY

Environmental psychology is rooted in scientific methods related to the acquisition of theory, pursuit of knowledge, and practical application. In the minds of many practitioners, however, theory and knowledge can become blurred, and many theories are passed along as if they were knowledge, rather than ideas to guide research. Knowledge is the truth that has been obtained from research. Think of a matador waving a red cape to entice a bull to charge. The theory that the color red invokes the bull's aggression was generally accepted until research proved that most animals are color-blind and that the movements of the cape are what caused the bull's arousal. However, matadors continue to use red capes because of other important variables affecting the practice: culture (the values, norms, and artifacts of a group of people) and tradition (a custom or practice that has been passed down from generation to generation). Humans tend to embrace these variables until they prove harmful or inconvenient; in other words, they will maintain cultural

and traditional behaviors as long as the results are not negative to their health and well-being.

Although practice can be based on theory, researchers who contribute to the practice of environmental psychology are obligated to pursue scientific truths. But change is always a constant in the dynamic human–environment relationship. Whenever life is involved in the research process, the end result will eventually change because people change. Consider architectural preferences. The predominating New England home in the 1700s was highly segmented (it had many small rooms), but its main feature was that the kitchen was blocked from general view by a door (see Figure 2.1).

Contemporary studies indicate that women who work outside the home prefer kitchens that are open to the dining and living rooms (Seligman, 1992). Therefore, research conducted in the 1700s would yield very different *truths* from identical research conducted in the late twentieth and early twenty-first centuries.

Incorporating the practice of environmental psychology within the design fields offers unique opportunities. Designers can make use of tools such as user needs assessments, known within the design fields as **predesign research (PDR)**, to evaluate a client's requirements prior to design, construction, or occupancy. Early needs assessments were conducted primarily by academicians who focused on settings such as housing, college dorms, and residential institutions (Barker, 1968). An occupancy evaluation (assessment conducted during occupation) is another useful tool that was developed as a result of research by social scientists, designers, and planners interested in understanding the users' experiences within the buildings (Gifford, 2002). Evaluating a future development for the intended user is not a novel idea; many architects have adopted it, calling it *behavior-based architectural programming,* and in medicine and psychology the same formative evaluation is called an *intake assessment.* Research methods include reviewing current literature, observing similar populations in similar environments, surveying individuals via personal interviews or written surveys, and developing focus groups. When this preliminary research has been factored in, the completed development tends to have fewer problems. Ideally, a needs assessment should be augmented by an occupancy evaluation of a similar environment. As a final evaluation of the project, **a postoccupancy evaluation (POE)** should be performed to assess the human–environment relationship because design ideas and concepts may not be applicable in an actual setting, and a POE can determine if the occupants have modified the environment in a way that negatively affects the build-

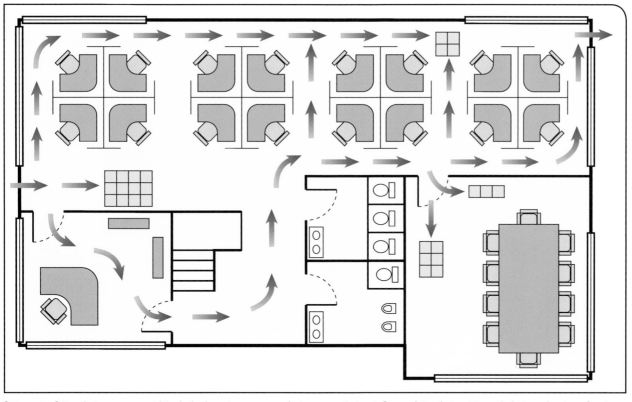

[**Figure 2.2**] Ventilation systems within the built environment are design to maximize airflow and circulation. Through the introduction of environmental accessories, designers can inadvertently block that airflow. Hence, caution should be used when space planning so as to not impede airflow and circulation. Illustration by Precision Graphics

ing's performance. For example, an office's air circulation may be blocked if the employees were to pile storage boxes atop strategically placed furnishings (see Figure 2.2).

Environmental psychologists are trained to use the methods and tools necessary for quick and cost-effective needs assessments and to follow-up with a POE to verify if user needs were adequately addressed; in this manner, environmental psychologists can help architects, city planners, and interior and landscape designers to develop environments best suited to the specific needs of the users. The POE evaluates an overall product and is usually the final phase of the design process, enabling the designer to learn from previous mistakes and ensure better plans for future projects. The scenario described in "Needs Assessment (Pre-Design Research)" illustrates the value of a user needs assessment or pre-design research (see Box 2.1).

Because environmental psychologists are uniquely trained and qualified to understand the thoughts and emotional processes that produce or shape human desires, they can help people understand the differences between temporary and long-standing needs. They also ascertain the primary,

secondary, and tertiary functions of an environment so that it can be designed to fulfill human needs. Some methods an environmental psychologist might employ include taking an individual on a tour of various buildings in the area, encouraging a person to visit similar environments as the one desired, and introducing issues that will arise in the future if the person proceeds with initial choices. Design parties and brainstorming sessions similar to a design **charette** are other effective methods to find out what people want from their environments. For example, the environmental needs of a secretary will differ from the needs of an executive. A design party hosting all of the intended occupants can help the environmental psychologists determine occupant needs and convey those needs to the architect, interior, or landscape designer. A design party works well because discussions are more relaxed and casual creating an environment in which occupants are willing to communicate more freely.

The outcome for the design firm is greater client satisfaction over a longer period of time because this process will linger in the client's mind. It is also common for satisfied clients to bring more referrals.

BOX 2.1 NEEDS ASSESSMENT (PRE-DESIGN RESEARCH)

Scenario

A business executive who has been transferred to New England commissions a design firm to build her new home. The designer conducts a needs assessment to ascertain the executive's desires—a Spanish-style villa complete with a courtyard for entertaining, high ceilings, tile floors, and so on (Box Figure 2.1). Realizing the design's impracticality in such a harsh environment, the designer then tries to suggest an alternative design style, but the executive insists that such a villa has been a dream since childhood. Further investigation reveals that the executive, born and raised in Southern California, has the design styles of that region as a primary point of reference and is drawing upon that which is most familiar and comfortable to her.

This scenario raises three issues, all of which the designer must discuss with the client. First, the executive has had insufficient time to acclimate to and embrace her new environment. Second, her feelings of insecurity about the unfamiliar surroundings are the source of her attempts to create a comfort zone. Third, a Spanish-style home will be an issue in the winter. As the executive gets to know the new environment, her design preferences will slowly change. She will start to embrace the New England style, want to fit in more with her new surroundings, and eschew the extra costs associated with architecture inappropriate to the New England climate.

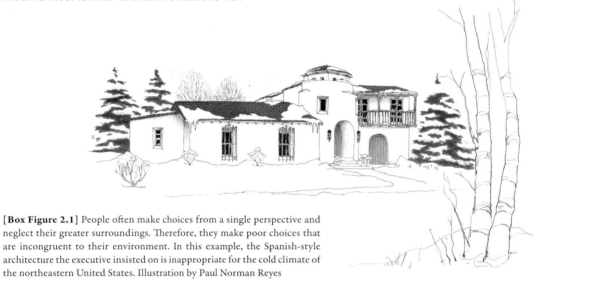

[**Box Figure 2.1**] People often make choices from a single perspective and neglect their greater surroundings. Therefore, they make poor choices that are incongruent to their environment. In this example, the Spanish-style architecture the executive insisted on is inappropriate for the cold climate of the northeastern United States. Illustration by Paul Norman Reyes

THEORIES OF THE HUMAN– ENVIRONMENT RELATIONSHIP

Much of the research conducted on the human–environment relationship has been based on four major theories:

- integration (also called *integral*)
- stimulation
- control
- behavior-setting

The integration theory maintains that a combination of design features will influence people to behave and act in the most appropriate manners. Stimulation theory, by some accounts, has the broadest and most diverse implications related to environments. Consider the differing stimulation needs of a casino and that of a surgical recovery ward: The casino benefits from maximized environmental stimulation, whereas the surgical recovery ward does not. Stimulation theory overlaps with control and behavior-setting theories. Most built environments have controls—some of which have more than others; for example, prisons. Designs that support behavior settings also establish **behavioral controls,** such as automatically being quiet and refraining from other potentially disturbing behaviors in a library. The way humans behave in other environments depends on social controls, as described by social learning theories, which claim that we learn socially acceptable actions and behaviors by observing others.

Social Learning Theories

Social or **observational learning** theories differ from human–environment theories because they declare that we learn first by observing others and then eventually by reproducing those actions. Social learning theory emphasizes the following three precepts (Rotter, 1982; Rotter, Chance, & Phares, 1972):

1. People are intrinsically motivated to seek reinforcement, such as positive stimulation and avoid unpleasant stimulation.
2. Personality represents an interaction of the individual with the environment (for example, the stimuli that a person is aware of and responds to) and it is a relatively stable framework for responding to situations in a particular way.
3. To understand behavior, we must first consider an individual's life history and learning experiences as well as the environment because our subjective interpretation of the environment determines our behavior.

Albert Bandura, another proponent of the social learning theory (Bandura, 1977, 1986), agreed that personality is an interaction among the environment, behavior, and the person's psychological processes—and that the environment and a person's behavior affect each other (a concept called **reciprocal determinism**). However, Bandura's theory also stressed the importance of observational learning or *modeling* as a primary means of obtaining reinforcement. This is because we humans generally observe, process, and imitate the behaviors, attitudes, and emotional reactions of other people to gain approval, acceptance, or reward. Behavior modeling is intrinsic to all **behavior settings** (physical or psychological environments that elicit or support certain patterns of behavior that are based on the environmental design and learned as a result of **operant conditioning**. Operant conditioning is the social process that teaches and reinforces acceptable/desirable behaviors). Behavior modeling is fundamental to child development, is widely used in training programs, and is crucial to the success of commercial advertising, including marketing displays (by promoting an idea such as, "If I buy that car, then I will be popular too"). When we as a society accept deviant behaviors such as graffiti by calling it art, we then send the mixed message that role modeling deviant behaviors is also acceptable.

Integration (Integral) Theories

Robert Gifford uses the term **integral theories** to describe a group of models used to understand the complexity of the human–environment relationship (Gifford, 2002). Isidor Chein's integral framework (Chein, 1954) described the following five major elements that work in harmony to facilitate a particular behavior:

1. *Global environment.* Generalized characteristics of an environment.
2. *Instigators.* Stimuli which trigger particular behaviors.
3. *Goal objects and noxients.* Situations which cause satisfaction or produce unpleasantness.
4. *Supports and constraints.* Environmental aspects that facilitate or restrict.
5. *Directors.* Features that tell us where to go and what to do.

Understanding a person's environment in this context will allow for a greater understanding of his/her behavior (Gifford, 2002).

Also considered to be part of the integration theories are interactional, transactional, and organismic theories. The **interactional theory,** the simplest form of integration theory, declares that people and the environment are separate entities that are constantly interacting (Gifford, 2002). It is based on **deterministic** ideas; in other words, it is based on the philosophical notion that circumstances have an absolute causal relationship to certain events. Many people subscribe to a system of **separatism** that presupposes that one entity must dominate another. An example of an interactional event might be a city-owned vacant lot in an urban setting. The logic is simple, vacant lot equals lost revenue for the city. The solution is an infill project. However, that vacant lot could have been a significant play area for neighborhood children, and with an infill project the children will be forced to play someplace else, which could include the streets or in front of businesses (Figure 2.3). The point is that the vacant lot likely represents much more to others than the single "lost revenue" identifier; it could have meaning and thus be saved for future community purposes.

This idea leads to **transactional theory.** This is a level of inquiry that concentrates on the patterns of relationships

[**Figure 2.3**] In a simple interactional relationship, one might deduce that a vacant lot equals lost tax revenue. In a transactional relationship, the vacant lot may give back to the city by way of providing a place for children to engage in constructive play. © Joseph Sohm / Visions of America / Corbis

and contends that the human–environment relationship is mutually supportive. In the previous example, a transactional approach would look at the benefits of the city's vacant lot as a means of supporting the community by providing a place for kids to hang out. The idea is that the environment affects the user just as the user affects the environment.

The **organismic theory** (Wapner, 1981) takes the whole human–environment relationship a step further by looking at how the social, societal, and individual characteristics intertwine with the environment in a complex symbiosis. The organismic theory recognizes multiple contributing factors (e.g., people's experiences that day, their current health, their state of mind, and the mood or disposition of others around them), which combine with the environment to induce a particular behavior. In the previous example, the presence of the vacant lot may keep children out of trouble yet cause the city losses in tax revenues; but it may provide open space for neighborhood gatherings, thus promoting neighborhood solidarity. The point is that the vacant lot has many positive and negative attributes that manifest differently depending upon other factors, such as the community constituency, the actual location of the lot, and the time of year. It is important to note that design can influence environmental behaviors. To illustrate: A person's recycling *behavior* can be influenced by the convenient presence of recycling bins, but the bins themselves cannot address the *motivation* to recycle.

Control Theories

Having a sense of control over our world and our place in it is crucial to our well-being. Some forms of control involve one person's control over another such as in prisons. Another form of control is over his/her environment, such as how one adorns the interior of their home. In some situations, people control other people's ability to control their environment. An example of this is when a supervisor forbids an employee to change the temperature of his/her workspace, or a hospital staff determines who can enter a patient's room and for how long the visitor may stay and visit the patient.

Hence, in these examples, the employee or patient may feel disempowered because he/she has little social or environmental control. James Averil suggested that we have three types of control over our environments:

1. *Behavioral control.* The ability to change the environmental event.
2. *Cognitive control.* The ability to change the way in which we think of an environment.
3. *Decisional control.* The ability to choose a response.

There is also primary and secondary control, primary control being overt in a given situation, and secondary control being more accommodating to the reality of a given situation (Weisz, Rothbaum, & Blackburn, 1984). An example of a primary control for a person who is unhappy with the temperature in an office setting is to change the thermal controls. If this is not an option, the person can opt for secondary control by either wearing more or less clothing. However, corporate dress codes may preclude secondary controls (i.e., employees are typically not allowed to wear sleeveless shirts or expose their bare legs or toes while in the office). The solution for designers is to afford as much primary control for building occupants as possible.

SUSTAINABILITY CONNECTION 2.1

Individual workstation temperature controls not only save on energy consumption but also allow each employee a level of personal control over his/her thermal comfort and spatial air quality.

Personal control within an environment relates to both our freedom of action and the level and type of stimulation to which we are subjected; moreover, our actual or perceived influence or control over our environments directly affects our feelings within and about it. Most people have the ability to adapt to various levels of stimulation, have more actual control in certain settings than in others (e.g., at home as opposed to at work), and attempt to establish personal control using the psychological mechanisms of personal space and territoriality (Altman, 1975). When this ability is compromised—for example, when we feel that our freedom is constrained, or even anticipate a restricting factor, and when we exceed our threshold—we usually try to reassert control over the situation or setting, a phenomenon referred to as **psychological reactance** or simply *reactance* (Brehm, 1966). However, when people believe they cannot control distressing factors within their environments, or they experience repeated failed efforts to establish or regain control, they may create physical or psychological barriers (i.e., engage in social withdrawal behaviors) and eventually give up, succumbing to *learned helplessness* (Seligman, 1992). Learned helplessness results from being put in a situation where there is no possibility of escape from harm or pain. Eventually, the person succumbs to fatalism and resignation: the person is powerless and decides there is no point in trying to improve the situation.

Behavior-Setting Theories

Some behaviors are considered appropriate in certain environments but not in others (e.g., it is socially acceptable to dress and act provocatively at a nightclub but not at a house of worship). Roger Barker (1968) conceived the behavior-setting theory, which he defined as public places or occasions that evoke particular patterns of behaviors. The theory proposes that behavior must be studied in its natural context. These behavior settings are small-scale social systems composed of people and physical objects arranged in such a way as to carry out routine actions within a specified time and place. Examples include public places such as schools, theaters, nightclubs, and places of worship, as well as occasions that shape behaviors, such as graduations, weddings, and funerals.

Through operant conditioning (the use of consequences to modify the occurrence and form of behavior), we learn at an early age the behaviors expected of us within various environments and act accordingly.

Thus, we can say that certain environments bring about specific behaviors. An important behavior-setting theory perspective is that of **synomorphy,** the principle that physical and social aspects of an environment should fit together (Gifford, 2002). However, behavior settings are not permanent and evolve according to the support and constraints of society over time (Wicker, 1987). For example, during the Soviet regime in Russia (which opposed the practice of religion) many ancient churches were converted to bathhouses, gymnasiums, warehouses, and so on. However, the activities associated with bathhouses and gymnasiums are contrary to the activities associated with churches, thus the building and activities lacked synomorphy.

Most behavior settings are public environments that contain the following three components:

- Physical properties
- Social components
- Environmental settings

A novice designer attempting to develop a behavior setting through design alone would be fulfilling only one of Barker's criteria if he/she did not consider the social components or the environmental setting. In this case, the designer would be engaging in a concept known as **architectural determinism** (Bell et al., 2001), which is a direct and absolute relationship between the designed environment and a particular behavior. Many academicians do not subscribe to architectural determinism—which, at an extreme level, contends that it is the environment alone that causes behavior X—but certain design components of an overall environment do serve as learned-behavior cues. For example, a picture of a holy icon may or may not signify a holy site, but the picture commands respect from those who worship that icon. It should be noted, however, that many social workers and public health agencies operate on the premise of social/educational determinism; meaning that social services and/or education can have a direct effect on behavior. This ideology is equally flawed.

Neurobiological research may one day firmly establish *architectural determinism* as the cause of certain behaviors. For example, casinos, cruise ships, and disorderly neighborhoods are all environments in which our senses are bombarded with environmental stimuli, prompting our natural human desire to minimize the stimulation. If we do so by ingesting a neurological depressant such as alcohol, has the environment created a situation that promotes alcoholism? Research shows that behaviors can indeed be activated by *environmental cues* without conscious thought (Bargh, Lombardi, & Higgins, 1988). The behavior manifested is often unconscious, and the person is unaware of the potential influence of the stimulus in shaping his/her behavior. Because people differ in their everyday motivations, differences arise over time in the same way that unconscious behaviors manifest. Clearly, more research is needed to assess the ethical implications of developing environments that elicit or instigate certain behaviors.

Stimulation Theories

Every living thing on earth reacts to sensory stimulation. **Stimulation theories** serve to conceptualize and explain the environment as a source of sensory information derived from sight, sound, touch, taste, and smell (Wohlwill, 1966). At a chocolate factory, for example, a line worker may call upon each of the five senses in relation to the production of chocolate candy. He/she would be surrounded by an assortment of visual stimuli, as well as the numerous sounds of machinery and production, the various chocolate smells, the feel of individual candies, and the taste of an occasional morsel (for quality control purposes, of course). Whereas this factory affects all five senses, most environments stimulate only sight, sound, and smell. Examining the different levels of sensory information deriving from an environment enables us to assess that environment's level of stimulation.

Each of our five senses can be overstimulated (hyperstimulated) or understimulated (hypostimulated). An important concept to understand is that of **threshold,** the point at which too much or too little stimulation is available. At one end of the threshold spectrum is the absolute minimal intensity of stimulus we can perceive and at the other is the maximum amount of stimulation we can cope with effectively. When accustomed to a certain level of stimuli, we will no longer consciously notice it until it changes. Our level of perception will often dictate how much the stimulation must change before it is noticed.

The **Weber Fechner Law** states that as we get "used to" a level of stimuli, we will need a greater intensity of that stimulus in order for us to notice a change. For designers, we can use this concept when we want people to pay attention to something of importance. To accomplish this goal, we would bring down the level of stimulation associated with other scenes involved in an experience. Hence, our attention is directed to the more stimulating and captivating scene. For example, if the designer wanted to draw attention to a particular exhibit in a museum, he/she might use neutral colored backdrops for all the displays except the display of importance. For this area he/she might use a deeply saturated color for the backdrop. The difference (contrasting values) in the backdrops according to the Weber Fechner Law will cause people to notice the display.

SUSTAINABILITY CONNECTION 2.2

Although many people associate issues involving the health of our planet with objects and human artifacts (e.g., industrial waste, trash, toxic chemicals, burning fossil fuels), the primary cause can be linked to *human behavior* (Koger & Scott, 2007) and *motive* (do people "get used to" being gluttonous or not conserving resources?). Psychologists together with environmental scientists can take a more proactive approach to educating the next generation and contributing to reducing the negative impacts of environmentally dangerous human motives and behavior.

Related theories that help to explain the relationship between stimulation and human behaviors include the arousal perspective, environmental load or overstimulation, and adaptation. According to the **arousal perspective,** the environment itself causes an automatic physiological response such as increased heart rate, blood pressure, respiration, adrenaline (epinephrine) secretion, and neural activity within the brain. In this way, architectural determinism does play a role in environmental design. Arousal has been described as being somewhere along a continuum between sleep and excitement (Berlyne, 1960). In the cliché, "It sparked my curiosity (or imagination or interest)," the "spark" is *arousal*, which prompts the person to pursue the next step (satisfying that curiosity). The level of arousal we experience is often directly correlated to the level of stimulation provided by the environment. An excited child is overaroused, and a bored child is underaroused. Optimum arousal is an important factor in successful learning and productivity. Whereas overarousal can lead to cognitive chaos ("I have so many ideas flooding my head that I don't know where to start"), underarousal can lead to inaction ("My mind is blank, and I don't know where to start") or even apathy ("I can't think, and I don't care"). Simply stated, arousal is a component of the human psyche and is depen-

dent on stimulation. Design cannot affect arousal directly, but it can serve to modify stimulation levels that affect arousal. The terms *overstimulation* and **environmental load** are often used interchangeably. This concept assumes that humans have a limited ability to process incoming information; and in many cases when they experience too much information, it leads to *overload* (Kaplan & Kaplan, 1982a; Milgram, 1970). However, just as we can be overstimulated, we can also be understimulated. Anxiety and other psychological problems can occur when individuals are deprived of sensory stimuli (Zubek, 1969). Although there is much controversy about the effects of understimulation, at least one study suggests a negative connection between understimulation and the development of children (Sapolsky, 1997). When considering environmental load, designers must be knowledgeable about the greater environment in relation to lesser ones. For example, children attending a preschool in New York City are likely to be subjected to high amounts of urban clamor and, therefore, may benefit from a lower level of stimulation in their school environment, whereas children attending a preschool in rural Maine will likely require a variety of environmental stimuli in their school setting because their greater environment presents low levels of stimulation.

The **adaptation level theory** states that as a person becomes accustomed to a component or variable within an environment, its influence will be reduced. The survival mechanism of the human psyche can adapt to a wide variety of stimulation levels, but there are both positive and negative implications. If a person's optimal level of stimulation is high, when thrust into average levels of stimulation he/she will experience the negative effects of understimulation and vice versa. To illustrate this point, think of two business executives, one from New York City and the other from Spokane, who have relocated to San Diego and are experiencing the negative effects of stress but for different reasons. The former New Yorker desires more intensity, which is why the "laid-back" environment of San Diego becomes a source of stress. However, the Spokane native is used to a more conservative style and slower pace of life than that which exists in San Diego, thus it would be considered a faster-paced environment thereby becoming a source of stress. Although these people experienced stress related to over- and understimulation differently, the adaptation level theory states that over time both will adapt to the stimulation levels of their new environment.

The adaptation level theory can be applied to preferences in design styles. Imagine the reaction of Catherine the Great of Russia if she were to find herself in a Frank Lloyd Wright home (Figures 2.4a and b). How would she perceive the design? Considering the opulent display of wealth and

[**Figures 2.4a and b**] For Catherine the Great, the (*above*) Hermitage was created to be a high-stimulus environment, whereas she would likely find (*right*) Frank Lloyd Wright's Guggenheim Museum in New York City a comparatively low-stimulus environment. According to adaption theory, Catherine the Great could grow to appreciate Wright's simplicity while he would grow to appreciate the complexity of the Hermitage. © Pictorium / Alamy

artistry in both of the royal estates, the Hermitage and Summer Palace, she would probably view Wright's clean lines and blending of design materials with the environment as boring and mundane. However, in time she might adapt to a different way of thinking and eventually change her thoughts regarding the design style.

Attention restoration theory, developed by Rachel and Stephen Kaplan (Gifford, 2002), is based on concepts related to voluntary and involuntary attention. This theory maintains that situations requiring mental effort cause us to engage in **directed attention** (voluntary, intention- or goal-based attention), which requires more exertion over time. Like overworked muscles, directed attention can fail, thus creating **attentional deficit,** or an inability to concentrate (i.e., we need more time and energy to understand, retain, and recall information). Recovery requires rest, but excessive attentional fatigue may not be restorable by sleep. A periodic episode of **effortless attention**, which is the involuntary interest-based attention, such as a walk in the woods or along the beach, serves as a powerful and effective means to restoring attention capacity. The word *effortless* is crucial; navigating a crowded beach where a person must avoid hazards in the sand and surf requires directed attention. When we need physical, psychological, and energy restoration, we are drawn to nature, and the presence of nature in our environment has a profound effect on reducing levels of stress, thereby helping to restore attentional capacity (Ulrich, 1979, 1984, 1986, 1987; Ulrich et. al, 1991). The attention restoration theory asserts that **restorative experiences** occur in settings where we can function primarily in the involuntary mode (i.e., when we can observe or surround ourselves with stimuli that are involuntarily interesting).

Arousal, environmental load, and adaptation—three aspects of stimulation theories—interact dynamically. Consider a man who has spent his whole life in a high-stimulus environment. He has not only adapted to a high level of stimulation, but also probably finds it arousing and pleasurable; therefore, it would take a great deal of stimulation to overload him, but he also would be very susceptible to stress related to understimulation. Understanding how stimulation affects each individual and the source of that stimulation is important for design professionals. People who are overstimulated in the workplace will probably desire homes with few environmental stimuli (see Figure 2.5); people who thrive on stimulation will probably want high-stimulus homes as an adjunct to their high-stimulus careers; and people who are understimulated by their careers may want higher levels of stimulation in their homes. There are differing aspects of stimulation that affect the design process. By understanding these fundamental psychological processes and their behavioral outcomes, designers can enhance the environment.

THEORIES OF ENVIRONMENTAL PERCEPTION

The human–environment experience is complex, and researchers have attempted to explain the relationship from various perspectives to better comprehend how individuals perceive their environments.

Brunswik's Probabilistic Lens Model

Egon Brunswik is among a group of researchers termed **functionalists** (Bell et al., 2001). Brunswik, as all functionalists, theorized that the environment contains an abundance of cues and that perceivers (people) must be able to make sense of the most important ones if they are to function effectively. His probabilistic lens model (Brunswik,

[**Figure 2.5**] Minimalist design styles often lack complexity. The lack of complexity within an environment can often be perceived as being cold and boring. Conversely, in an overpopulated and complicated world, a home environment that is spacious and devoid of complexity may be very appealing. © Robert Harding Picture Library Ltd / Alamy

1943, 1956) is a theoretical framework that considers the human–environment relationship holistically and can be used to analyze subjective interpretations of an environment's beauty or usefulness.

Brunswik considered the process of perception as being similar to a lens through which stimuli are perceived and become focused; however, in the lens model, environmental cues have only a certain probability of being useful (a concept called **probabilism**). The probabilistic lens model uses sets of predetermined objective criteria that lead to **actual** beauty and a different set of subjective (judgment-based) criteria that lead to **perceived** beauty.

Brunswik's theory differentiates between distal cues, which are characteristics of the setting, and proximal cues, which are the observer's subjective impressions. It relies on the concept of *ecological validity,* that is, the relationship between an environment and its cues that leads to an accurate perception of the environment. Because our understanding of an environment is affected by our perceptions of and familiarity with its individual components, Brunswik suggests that problems arise when we encounter environments that contain components or patterns that are unfamiliar to us. In these environments, we may come to incorrect conclusions, for example, about size, height, color, or angle.

The lens model further suggests that observers infer personality judgments about occupants based on environmental cues. The accuracy of those judgments is based on *cue validity*—whether the cue provides good information—and *cue utilization*—how the observer weights the cues (Gosling, Ko, Mannarelli, and Morris, 2002). Going back to the earlier example, how would you characterize a person who prefers a pink sitting room with flowers on the coffee table and scented with perfume? For most of us, pink suggests an environment belonging to a woman with strong feminine characteristics. However, depending on the *cue validity* and *cue utilization,* that conclusion may be incorrect.

Gibson's Affordances

James J. Gibson's *affordance* is a perspective that takes an ecological approach to perception. It suggests that rather than perceiving individual features within an environment, we organize those features into recognizable patterns based on the arrangements of cues that provide immediate perceptual information (Gibson, 1976, 1979). He further suggests that humans (among other organisms) actively explore their environments and perceive objects in a variety of ways. As such, we experience different objects differently; the functional properties of those objects as they are encountered are termed *affordances.* In Gibson's theory, the world is composed of substances, surfaces, and textures, the arrangement of which provides cognitive affordances, or instantly recognizable functions, of environmental features.

In contrast to Brunswik, Gibson believes that rather than perceiving individual features or cues, humans respond to an ecologically structured environment. We do this by examining environments for those components that are useful or meaningful to us. For example, a flower garden may afford a quiet place to meditate, a source for freshly cut flowers, and a place to work; it also affords many insects with a home and a source for food. Many architects and designers strive to create environments that afford more than shelter. They attempt to develop environments that suit the unique needs of individuals while considering issues of sustainability, conserving the earth's natural resources, as well as cultural aspects (neighborhood support and community connections).

Although many design elements afford instantly recognizable functions, some environmental components are so similar that cognitive processes (the act recalling what has been learned or is known) are needed for people to make sense of what they are seeing (Kaplan and Kaplan, 1982a). For example, a tired child who is touring a museum with her father may sit on an antique chair because she perceives it as a good surface for sitting and knows that it will afford her rest. According to Gibson's affordances, the child is correct. However, the father knows from the chair's appearance and placement that it is on display and not intended for use. His child, not yet properly socialized to understand this environmental cue, does not make the same cognitive connection.

CULTURAL CONNECTION 2.1

Our world is seemingly getting smaller with the ease of travel because now people from around the globe can travel to places their ancestors never could. Where distance is no longer a deterrent to experiencing another country, language may still create a separation. In the situation of the child and the chair on display in the museum, the "language barrier" can be reduced by the designer's adding an additional *environmental cue.* Adding a bench near the displayed chair would highlight the differences between the seat to sit upon and the chair on display by way of contrasting environmental information.

Berlyne's Collative Properties

Daniel Berlyne was one of the first psychologists to develop a model of aesthetics. His theory states that we respond to aesthetics based on their collative stimulus properties—that is, properties such as novelty, complexity, incongruity, and surprise that elicit comparative or investigative responses, which in turn cause perceptual conflict with other present or past stimuli (Berlyne, 1971, 1974).

- *Novelty* is anything new, an innovative idea, or something used in a different way. For example, a few years ago in South America, I first saw glass bottles built into a physical structure much as glass block is used.
- *Incongruity* refers to design features that seem out of place or out of context. Designers sometimes violate neighborhood congruity by incorporating modern buildings into neighborhoods dominated by early twentieth-century styles, or confuse incongruity, which is perceived negatively, with novelty, which is perceived positively.
- *Complexity* refers to the variety of items in the environment. Many old world designs, for example, are extremely complex compared to many of the designs of today.
- *Surprise* reveals the unexpected, such as a home built around a large tree or a bathtub situated in a great room.

These properties are sometimes referred to as *collative properties,* meaning that they create a perceptual conflict; how we resolve that conflict leads to an aesthetic evaluation.

Berlyne believed that these properties influence the perceiver's aesthetic judgments through the following two psychological dimensions:

- *Hedonic tone* refers to those design elements, such as multiple gold-plated showerheads, that serve no purpose other than to provide beauty and artistic pleasure.

- *Uncertainty-arousal* refers to subjective uncertainty; that is, simultaneous feelings of excitement and discomfort evoked by environments that seem both complex and simple or ordered and chaotic.

Berlyne's collative properties cannot be applied without an understanding of a person's attitude, or predisposition, toward what is being perceived. Our attitudes are often rooted in our **worldview,** a perspective or philosophy that incorporates a general belief. Because such beliefs are often held by a certain culture or generation, a group of people may hold a similar attitude. For example, the attitude of many Asian people toward a particular building or location is based on their worldview that *Chi* or *qi* (life energy) must be allowed to flow smoothly.

CULTURAL CONNECTION 2.2

A *worldview* is a deep-seated set of values originating in familial nurturing and cultural experiences all culminating into fundamental beliefs about the nature of things. A *perspective* is an opinion or a point of view on how things look from your current position in life. A perspective can change with new information whereas a worldview cannot; it is quite literally—all you stand for and believe.

Differences in attitude and worldviews have important consequences for design. For example, a garden complete with pathways constructed within a residence as part of the overall design may be perceived as novel by some observers, surprising by others, incongruent with others' expectations of home décor, and highly complex, and most who view it will probably consider it hedonistic.

Berlyne also examines the distinction between diversive and specific exploration. Diversive exploration occurs when a person is understimulated and seeks arousing stimuli in the environment. For example, a person who finds an environment too quiet may respond by turning up the stereo. Specific exploration occurs when a person is aroused by a particular stimulus and investigates it to reduce the uncertainty or to satisfy the curiosity of arousal. This is the case when a person hears water and explores the environment in search of the source.

Pleasure–Arousal–Dominance Hypothesis

Albert Mehrabian and James A. Russell postulated that humans have three primary emotional responses to an environment—pleasure (positive feelings), arousal (excitement or challenge), and dominance (control over the setting or situation)—based on the perspective that emotion is a mediator between our environments and personalities (preexisting influences) and our behavior (outcome) (Mehrabian and Russell, 1974). Russell later rejected dominance as a primary

response; his modified pleasure-arousal hypothesis (Gosling et al., 2003) claims that we are most attracted to settings that are *moderately* arousing and *maximally* pleasurable, but that, in unpleasant environments, moderately arousing settings are the *least* desirable.

Russell's revised model is represented by a circumplex (i.e., a circular ordering or pattern of environmental evaluations) consisting of polarized emotional dimensions: arousing–not arousing and pleasurable–not pleasurable. Using this model, an observer can evaluate an environment by plotting its characteristics along each of the continuums.

Variables that affect a person's response to these dimensions include, but are not limited to, environmental factors (light, temperature, and objects or cues) and individual personality characteristics (introvert–extrovert and internal–external locus of control). The interaction of environmental and personal variables manifests in emotions, which affect work performance, interpersonal relations, and other behaviors.

The studies of Russell, Mehrabian, and others indicate that the emotional impact of an environment is systematically related to behavior in it. Because the opposite of dominance is vulnerability (which leads to uncertainty), the original **pleasure–arousal–dominance hypothesis** is wholly applicable to environmental design because people need to feel they have at least some measure of control over their circumstances (Russell, Ward, & Pratt, 1981). Meeting all three emotional needs will result in user or consumer satisfaction, particularly within the retail, service, and hospitality industries.

Kaplan and Kaplan Preference Framework

Based on the idea that people prefer scenes that are engaging and involving rather than simple or boring, Stephen and Rachel Kaplan (Kaplan & Kaplan, 1982a) devised a theoretical framework to organize environmental preferences according to four elements: coherence, legibility, complexity, and mystery.

- *Coherence* (making sense) refers to the way that objects in a scene come together to form some sort of understandable context. For example, a room with a fireplace, cushioned seating, a coffee table, and ambient lighting is immediately recognizable as a living room and therefore is a coherent space. A home office that doubles as a guest room but looks like a storage area, however, is an incoherent space.
- *Legibility* (the promise of making sense) refers to the level at which an individual is able to understand or categorize the scene and the objects within it. Legibility can be affected by items that serve dual or obscure purposes, such as a faux book hiding a treasured keepsake on a bookshelf.

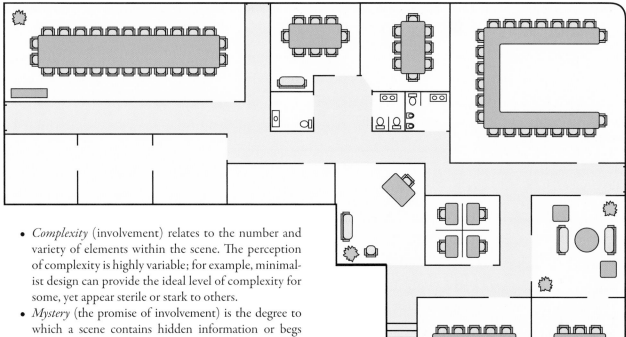

- *Complexity* (involvement) relates to the number and variety of elements within the scene. The perception of complexity is highly variable; for example, minimalist design can provide the ideal level of complexity for some, yet appear sterile or stark to others.
- *Mystery* (the promise of involvement) is the degree to which a scene contains hidden information or begs exploration. Victorian architecture was bursting with features designed to pique a viewer's curiosity and invite investigation; most homes incorporated elaborate carvings and ironwork, built-in buffets, cabinets, and closets situated in obscure places, and even hidden rooms and corridors. Secret and special places often beckon to the child in all of us, and we gravitate to coves, nooks, and even intriguing sounds and smells to explore. However, Berlyne (1960) suggested that mystery brings about uncertainty, and too much uncertainty evokes fear. Uncertainty coupled with knowledge that it will be safe brings about arousal (i.e., a funhouse is scary but it is fun because we know it is safe). But when we know too much, it is no longer arousing and no longer fun.

Lynch's Elements of Legibility

Kevin Lynch, working with the city of Boston's planning department in the late 1950s, conceived of five predominating qualities or elements of a city that enhance its legibility to the average person: paths, edges, districts, nodes, and landmarks. As built environments become increasingly larger, many have become communities within communities (airports, malls, resort hotels, and cruise ships are all communities within communities, or microcommunities), and Lynch's elements of legibility can be applied to the built environment in general.

- *Paths* are channels that people use as they travel from one area to another; examples include walkways, roads, and transit lines.

[**Figure 2.6**] In this floor plan we can see that hallways serve as the paths, the edges are the walls, and the districts are the various conference rooms with the nodes being the restrooms and workspaces. The landmarks are the reception area and lounge because they are easily identifiable and a point to travel to and from. Illustration by Precision Graphics

- *Edges,* such as shorelines and fences, preclude travel and appear to be boundaries.
- *Districts,* the largest elements, are regions having a particular character that people can readily identify: commercial, residential, artistic, and so on.
- *Nodes* are well-known points within the environment to and from which people travel; they are often places where paths converge, such as a bank of elevators, information desk or an airport.
- *Landmarks,* easily seen and singular components within an environment, are used for location orientation and are often found within districts and nodes, such as clock towers, large statues or church steeples.

In his classic book *The Image of the City,* Lynch stated, "Districts are structured with nodes, defined by edges, penetrated by paths, and sprinkled with landmarks. Elements regularly overlap and pierce one another" (Lynch, 1960; Figure 2.6).

Theory	Major Premise
Social learning theory	Determines that we learn by first observing others and eventually reproducing their actions
Integration (integral) theory	Elements of the environment work in harmony to facilitate a particular behavior
Control theory	Group of theories that address behavioral constraints and a person's perceived control over his or her actions and behaviors
Behavior-setting theory	Public places or settings evoke particular patterns of behavior
Stimulation theory	Environment is a source of sensory information (stimuli) that leads to arousal
Attention restoration theory	Mental fatigue is caused by excessive directed attention, and attentional capacity can be restored by engaging in effortless attention
Probabilistic lens model	Stimuli from the environment become focused through our perceptions
Affordances	The world is composed of substances, surfaces, and textures, the arrangement of which provides instantly recognizable function (i.e., affordance) of environmental features
Collative properties	We respond to aesthetics based on their collative stimulus properties (i.e., properties that elicit comparative or investigative responses and cause perceptual conflict with other present or past stimuli)
Pleasure–arousal–dominance hypothesis	Three primary emotional responses are translated to positive feelings, excitement or challenge, and control over the setting or situation; later modified to use a circumplex model, with pleasure and arousal as the two main axes
Preference model	People prefer engaging scenes to boring scenes
Elements of legibility	Five predominating qualities (i.e., elements) enhance its legibility to the average person

OVERLAPPING THEORIES, MODELS, AND PERSPECTIVES

Theories, models, and perspectives offer ways to approach or evaluate the design process. The designed environment often calls for the use of multiple theories, models, or perspectives. For example, if we were to design a hospital in the United States we would need to gain an understanding of established societal norms (social learning theory) such as expected privacy levels. We would also want to understand the interrelationship between the different areas within the hospital (integral theories) and the design elements that lead

Key Concepts	Relevance for Design
Reciprocal determinism, modeling	Encourages an understanding of established societal norms
Global environment, instigators, goal objects and noxients, supports and constraints, directors	Offers a holistic approach to design
Psychological reactance	Suggests that design elements lead to perceptions of control
Operant conditioning, interactional theory	Emphasizes that design is an important component of a setting, that contributes to certain behaviors
Threshold, arousal, environmental load, overload, adaptation level	Holds that design styles can lead to over- or understimulation
Directed (i.e., voluntary) attention, attentional deficit, effortless (i.e., involuntary) attention, restorative experiences	Include views of green spaces for effortless attention within environments demanding much directed attention
Distal and proximal cues leading to cue validity and cue utility	Emphasizes the perceptual relationship between design and the human observer
Environmental layout, contextual cues, direct perception	Highlights perceptual influences of design styles and probable dual uses of designs
Novelty, incongruity, complexity, surprise, hedonic tone, uncertainty-arousal	Claims that the joint nature of design elements merge to develop one overall impression
Pleasure, arousal	Offers a method to evaluate environmental designs
Coherence, legibility, complexity, mystery	Offers a method for designing engaging environments
Paths, edges, districts, nodes, landmarks	Offers a method to enhance an environment's legibility

to perceptions of control (control theories). Table 2.1 shows the different theories, models, and perspectives. Review them, and imagine the different and overlapping ways each can be used in the design of such facilities as malls, nursing homes, schools, and hospitals.

Practical Applications for Designers

Use these resources, activities, and discussion questions to help you identify, synthesize, and retain this chapter's core information. These tools are designed to complement the resources you'll find in this book's companion Study Guide.

SUMMING IT UP

Environmental psychology is one of the few sciences recognized in the United States that exclusively examines the relationship between humans and their environments. Environmental psychologists make use of tools such as user needs assessments, known within the design fields as pre-design research (PDR), to evaluate a client's requirements prior to design, construction, or occupancy. Because they are uniquely trained and qualified to understand the thoughts and emotional processes that produce or shape human desires, environmental psychologists can help people understand the differences between temporary and long-standing needs.

Environmental psychology includes a multidisciplinary approach to understanding not only the human behavioral response—but the human motive as well. Theories in the human–environment relationship aid the process of understanding the users long before a design is created. They include: integration (also called *integral*), stimulation, control, and behavior-setting. Theories that help to explain the stimulation–human behavior relationship include: the arousal perspective, environmental load or overstimulation, and adaptation. Theories of environmental perception (how individuals perceive their environments) include: Brunswik's Probabilistic Lens Model, Gibson's Affordances, Berlyne's Collative Properties, Pleasure–Arousal–Dominance Hypothesis, Kaplan and Kaplan Preference Framework and Lynch's Elements of Legibility.

You can also refer to this textbook's companion Study Guide for a comprehensive list of Summary Points.

EXPERT SPOTLIGHT 2.1

The Role of Theory in Architectural Design

Chris Ford, M.Arch.,
University of Nebraska Lincoln

Artists are primarily dependent upon creative thinking in order to solve aesthetic problems of their own making.

Scientists are primarily dependent upon analytical thinking in order to solve scientific problems that exist outside of themselves. If artists and scientists anchor two ends of a figurative spectrum, then designers would occupy the conceptual midpoint between the two, in terms of both disciplinary interest and operation. Designers are equally dependent upon both creative and analytical thinking, and their thinking oscillates as they yield creative solutions for problems framed outside of themselves. This running difference among artists, designers, and scientists is simplified in order both to quickly illuminate the major differences between them and to situate the role that designers play in larger society.

Whereas design methodology addresses the analytical and objective aspects of design thinking, then design theory addresses its creative and subjective aspects. At the height of architectural design methodology in the late 1960s and 1970s, methodologists successfully confused the role of theory in design by championing prescribed methods of design that subverted subjectivity to more heavily emphasize objectivity. Today, it is important to recognize that the act of design requires both objective and subjective thinking.

A design theory emerges from one's personal expectation for how design decisions *ought* to be made. Having a personal expectation is necessary due to the emptiness present at the crux of every architectural design problem—the origin for architecture "has no presence: It is a verbal noun, an attitude; it has no internal ability to generate form out of the void." (Jones and Pfau, 1987). Despite what some design methodologists have previously argued, architectural solutions have never truly been the summation of intrinsic constraints such as Site, Program, User, Budget, or Schedule. Despite finding congruencies with a designer's subjective design theory, these constraints are creatively vacant for establishing any specific expectation for architecture, whether it be functional or aesthetic in nature. At best, these constraints are *informative* toward defining an architectural design problem and possess no capacity to assist the *decisive* thinking process about forthcoming solutions.

A review of architectural history (which could also include the design histories of landscape, industrial, textile, and graphic design) reveals that theory is central to every act of design. For most designers, the creation of a theory occurs at a local, personal level, and the emerging theory is formulated within one's own experience of engaging design problems. Whereas design theory has become its own form of scholarship and is sometimes studied for its own sake, it is important to recognize that the most celebrated contributors to design theory are themselves distinguished design practitioners. Among these include Vitruvius, Gottfried Semper, Viollet Le-Duc, Walter Gropius, Le Corbusier, Frank Lloyd Wright, and Juhani Pallasmaa. For these designers, an actionable theory emerges from the repetitive yet polemically subjective act of design. In turn, the fullness of this externalized theory provides designers with a helpful intellectual tool, which narrows their search for a final solution.

- **actual**
- **adaptation level theory**
- **architectural determinism**
- **arousal perspective**
- **attention restoration theory (ART)**
- **attentional deficit**
- **behavior setting**
- **behavioral controls**
- **charette**
- **determinism**
- **directed attention**
- **effortless attention**
- **environmental load**
- **functionalists**
- **integration (integral) theories**
- **interactional theory**
- **magic bullet approach**
- **operant conditioning**
- **organismic theory**
- **perceived**
- **pleasure–arousal–dominance hypothesis**
- **postoccupancy evaluation (POE)**
- **predesign research (PDR)**
- **probabilism**
- **psychological reactance**
- **reciprocal determinism**
- **restorative experience**
- **separatism**
- **social or observational learning theory**
- **stimulation theory**
- **synomorphy**
- **threshold**
- **transactional theory**
- **Weber Fechner Law**
- **worldview**

WEB LINKS

The Brunswick Society, select "Notes and Essays" (www.brunswik.org, select "Notes & Essays")

Center for Spatially Integrated Social Science, for more on Kevin Lynch and other spatial innovators (www.csiss.org)

Changing Minds, select "Theories" for more on learned helplessness (www.changingminds.org)

"Defensible Space: Deterring Crime and Building Community" (for more on broken window theory), by Henry Cisneros, former U.S. Secretary of Housing and Urban Development: (www.books.google.com) or (www.hud.gov)

Environmental Protection Agency, search for "pharmaceutical contaminates" (www.epa.gov/)

Her Home, on women-centric designs (http://womancentrichomebuilder.com/)

Mental Health Matters, select "Research" for more on psychological theories (www.mental-health-matters.com)

Post Occupancy Evaluation sample (www.smg.ac.uk/documents/POEBrochureFinal06.pdf)

STUDIO ACTIVITY 2.1

Social Learning Theory

Design Problem Statement
To produce innovative techniques when designing an airport based on Bandura's social learning theory.

Because of social learning theory, we know that red means stop, yellow means caution, and green means go. Using these colors as visual cues, develop an airport terminal, food court, and security area.

Directions
Step One: List common programming attributes of an airport.

Step Two: Draft a floor plan of a hypothetical airport (make sure to include all of the items listed in number one).

Step Three: Analyze the different areas to determine which should appear as red, yellow, or green.

Step Four: Using a transparent medium over your floor plan, identify the red, yellow, and green areas, and justify your rationale.

Step Five: Identify ways that each of those areas could be designed to include the respective color. (Hint: directional signs might be illuminated in the respective color.)

Deliverables
1. List of programming attributes.

2. Floor plan of a hypothetical airport with an overlay showing different areas as red, yellow, and green.

3. One-page paper explaining why you assigned a specific color to a given area. (For example, security might be given the color red because everyone proceeding to a terminal must stop in this area.)

4. A perspective rendering of one area showing how the use of red, yellow, or green were incorporated into the overall design scheme.

STUDIO ACTIVITY 2.2

Attention Restoration Theory

Design Problem Statement
To develop the design of a museum based on Kaplan and Kaplan's Attention Restoration Theory.

Keeping in mind a museum's main purpose to house a collection of artifacts, how can the planning and design process of a museum be organized based on the four elements proposed by Kaplan and Kaplan's Preference Model?

Directions
Step One: List different areas of a museum along with the physical features required in these areas (for example, display or exhibition areas that require natural or artificial lighting).

Step Two: Identify and demonstrate aspects of the scenes that help to facilitate or attract the visitor's attention.

Step Three: Discuss the importance of restorative experiences as part of a museum's success.

Step Four: Identify locations within the museum that could be of use for restorative experiences.

Step Five: Demonstrate what an area dedicated to restoration might look like.

Deliverables

1. Programming list of spaces contained within an average museum.

2. Diagramed perspective of one display area that demonstrates design attributes intended to captivate and retain a patron's attention.

3. One-page paper discussing the importance of attention restoration experiences within a museum environment.

4. Perspective rendering of a space designed to facilitate a restorative experience.

DISCUSSION QUESTIONS

1. Describe what makes environmental psychologists uniquely trained and qualified to assist designers in determining the occupant's needs.

2. Analyze a variety of spaces that you frequently spend time in; describe how the human–environment relationship theories apply; and explain the importance of correctly implementing them in design.

3. Discuss ways in which the social learning theories can be implemented into design of a more productive and stimulating architecture, interior, and landscape design.

4. Discuss *architectural determinism* in terms of your own experience. Can you provide any true examples, or can all of your experiences be traced back to *operant conditioning*? How do your cognitive experiences affect your perception of this concept?

5. How would you describe the interior design of your school according to Lynch's elements of legibility?

LEARNING ACTIVITIES

1. Visit three different types of places for evaluation purposes. Observe and write down the different kind of stimulation each of the sites projects, and describe how and what human–environment relationship theories apply.

2. Research public spaces that meet the behavioral setting component requirements, and point out specific facts about the design that relate to the behavioral setting components.

3. Consider the term *architectural determinism* and give examples of "good use" and "bad use" of the term. Explain your opinion of each of the examples and express your concerns, if any.

4. Visit a new and unfamiliar site to explore; take a few friends with you.

5. Analyze Brunswik's theory from the concept of ecological validity. Record your observations of the area, describing the size, height, color, or angles of what you observe. Share your findings with others and compare conclusions. Are they similar or different, correct or incorrect?

03

Psychobiology of Behavior

The great tragedy of science—the slaying of a beautiful hypothesis by an ugly fact.

—Thomas Huxley

Environmental psychology, a collaborative field of study, draws upon research generated from the social and physical sciences. Recent scientific advances have enabled us to delve deeper into our neurobiological responses as well as various environments and environmental components. Thus, science could provide evidence to explain reactions related to the secretion, absorption, and interaction of neurochemicals as they relate to environmental variables such as lighting, color, and odor. Understanding the effects of the environment may enable us to predict more precisely human behavioral responses to certain environments. If we can comprehend our neurobiological responses to the environment, we can identify where "nature" begins and ends and where "nurture" begins, augments nature, or vice versa.

Comprehending the effects of the environment on humans requires us to first understand that people interact with the world around them on three different levels: physical, social, and biological. The *physical responses* consist of all elements within an environment, including the atmosphere (e.g., temperature, humidity, lighting). How we behave or react within the environment is often directly related to *social responses* stemming from our upbringing (i.e., family, education, and religious affiliations). *Biological responses* include examples such as shivering in a cold room, allergic reactions to certain substances, and congenital defects caused by environmental pollutants.

Unfortunately, with the exception of researchers who purposely study the human–environment relationship, many researchers continue to look exclusively at social situations when investigating the effects of the environment on humans. The physical environment is often a contributing factor, as evidenced by the relationship between teen smoking and the proximity of cigarette advertising to schools.

BEHAVIORAL NEUROSCIENCE: THE BIOLOGY OF SENSATION

To fully comprehend how our brain obtains, interprets, and reacts to stimuli, we need to first understand the biology of sensation. From this knowledge, designers of the built environment can then begin to better understand the relationship between humans, designed spaces, and environmental sensations. Then, and only then, can we initiate evidence-based design practices with the intention of enhancing the experiential qualities of the built environment.

Much of the past and current psychological research focuses on social phenomena (i.e., culture, social learning, gender norms) that effect behaviors. However, within psychology there are a group of researchers who concentrate on the neurobiological aspects of human behaviors. The American Psychological Association (APA) lists this area of specialty as Division 6: Behavioral Neuroscience and Comparative Psychology. The APA states that, "behavioral neuroscientists study the brain in relation to behavior, its evolution, functions, abnormalities, and repair, as well as its interactions with the immune system, cardiovascular system, and energy regulation systems" (APA, n.d.).

Along with the field of psychology, studying the interrelationships between neurons, neurochemicals, and hormones on behaviors is the up-and-coming field of neuroscience. This relatively young field is dedicated to the exclusive study of the brain. **Neuroscience,** as defined by the Society for Neuroscience (SFN), is the study of the entire nervous system including the brain, spinal cord, and networks of sensory nerve cells, or neurons (SFN, 2006.). Whether it is the neurobiological research obtained from psychology or research obtained from neuroscience, the common denominator is that the results derive from the scientific inquiry into neural impulses, chemical, and hormonal interplay, and the predetermined outcomes caused by genetics.

The study of the brain and affiliated nervous system often yields research with a high degree of reliability. However, brain and nervous system research is still relatively new, and thus research is concentrated to the description of how the human brain functions normally, the development and maintenance of the nervous system, and ways to prevent or cure neurological and psychiatric disorders (SFN, 2006). According to the SFN (2006), neuroscience research is conducted on:

- Aging
- Brain development
- Learning and memory
- Movement
- Molecules, cells, and genes responsible for nervous system functioning
- Neurological and psychiatric disorders
- Sensation and perception
- Sleep
- Stress

BRAIN PHYSIOLOGY AND BEHAVIOR

Imaging studies of our brain show that the neural basis of spatial location and navigation occurs in the right **hippocampus**. Through magnetic resonance imaging (MRI) or functional magnetic resonance imaging (fMRI) tests we have been able to see the activation of the right **caudate nucleus** of the **basal ganglia** when a person moves (Maguire et al., 2000). In a study where the research subject was asked to find his/her way through a simulated urban environment the MRI was able to record the activation of special "place cells" and "direction cells" located in the brain's hippocampus. Corroborating this research was a study using MRI images of London taxi drivers. These images showed a correlation between the length of time a person spent as a taxi driver with the degree of redistribution of gray matter from the anterior (front) to the posterior (back) part of the right hippocampus (Maguire et al., 2000). The hippocampus is the region of the brain known to be involved in spatial localization.

Other studies have shown that damage to the right parietal lobe's **angular gyrus** and **supra-marginal gyrus** may cause problems in our ability to use space (e.g., difficulty in dressing, problems orienting within a space, trouble drawing figures in 3D, neglect of the body's entire left side). Likewise, lesions in the right hemisphere's parietal lobe, which could result from Alzheimer's disease, among other causes, negatively affect spatial comprehension. In one study, researchers discovered that patients with macular degeneration (a disorder of the eye common to older people) unconsciously focus their vision by using other parts of their retina as a means to compensate for their loss of central vision. They further found that the person's brain seems to compensate for this action by reorganizing its neural connections (Georgia Tech, 2008)

Looming

Another way that science has been able to show a neural environmental connection is through a biological defensive reaction called **looming**, which happens when people or objects quickly enlarge. The objects are perceived by the viewer as moving toward him/her instead of just growing in size. Large expansive movements and exaggerated gestures can thus evoke an automatic (instinctive) defensive reaction. As a result, humans as young as 14 days old avoid large objects that move—it is as if they perceive danger from the object (Figure 3.1). This is important information for designers for two reasons. The first is so designers can avoid including such objects in nurseries and in the environments of young children. The second reason is because many people with advanced stages of Alzheimer's disease often revert to instinctual behaviors, which include this fearful response to looming.

Architecture of the Brain

Although the brain is an organ responsible for mechanical functions and chemical interactions, it is also responsible for our sense of self. In this way we can say that the brain is a "psychological organ," which gives rise to mental processes and experiences. As an organ, however, the brain is composed of tissues that form different regions. Each region has specific functions that when combined, lead to our cognitive experience (Figure 3.2). These different regions include:

Occipital lobe. This lobe is located at the back of the head, and its primary functions are related to different aspects of vision such as the understanding of shape, color, and motion.

Temporal lobes. These lobes are located on each side of the head, just in front of the ears and slightly below the temples. Their many functions include the storage of visual memories, processing sound, and comprehending language.

Parietal lobe. This lobe is situated at the top (center/rear) of the head. This lobe is where spatial locations

[**Figure 3.1**] As adults, we see large stuffed toys as de facto guardians, as represented here with a large Winnie the Pooh. To an infant, a toddler, or an older person with Alzheimer's disease, these large objects can inspire a natural fear response. © FURLONG PHOTOGRAPHY / Alamy

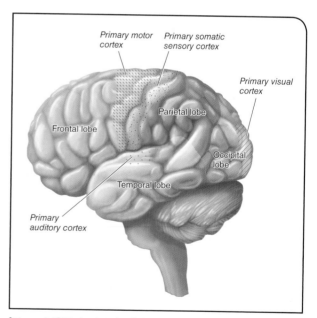

[**Figure 3.2**] The brain is divided into four primary lobes that have specific responsibilities related to who we are and how we interpret the world. Illustration by Precision Graphics

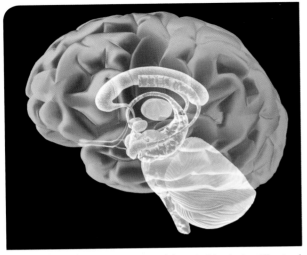

[**Figure 3.3**] The amygdala is part of the primitive brain. All animal life has an amygdala, and its primary role is to initiate a fight or flight response. A goal of good design is to limit the activation of the amygdala during an emergency situation. © DocCheck Medical Services GmbH / Alamy

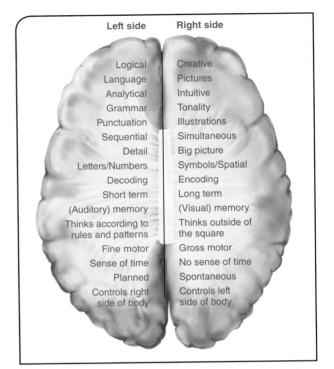

[**Figure 3.4**] Both sides of the brain are responsible for different functions, but it is the joint nature of the two sides that truly allows us to excel in either art or science. Illustration by Precision Graphics

are processed, where our capacity to maintain attention occurs, and where we are able to perform motor control functions.

Frontal lobe. This lobe is what many believe separates humans from other mammals. It is located behind the forehead, and it is where planning, memory search, motor control, reasoning, emotions, and other functions take place.

Another important part of the brain is the **amygdala** (Figure 3.3). This is a small sub-cortical structure that is part of the primitive **limbic system**. It is deep within the brain near the brain stem. The amygdala plays a key role in emotional memories and the stress response (also called the *fight-or-flight response,* it is an automatic response to stress that is perceived to be a survival threat) and the conditioned fear response, influencing emotion and behavior in response to neurochemical triggers. A person with a damaged amygdala will likely remember the details of an event, but he/she will not recall the emotions that accompanied the event.

Left Side, Right Side: What's the Difference?
Among popular culture, the left side of the brain is often regarded as analytic and verbal, whereas the right side of the brain is responsible for perceptions and intuition. Studies reveal that the left side of the brain is better than the right at determining whether an object is above or below another object (Hellige & Michimata, 1989). Likewise, the right side of the brain is better at some aspects of language such as raising the pitch of

one's voice at the end of a question (inflection) or understanding humor (Bihrle, Brownell, Powelson, & Gardner, 1986; Brownell, Michel, Powelson, & Gardner, 1983).

Research has also shown that the left hemisphere is where many aspects of language are formed, whereas the right temporal lobe plays an important part in the recognition of overall shapes (Ivry & Robertson, 1998). This is why we encounter such cognitive confusions as illustrated in Figure 3.6 . On the other hand, the frontal lobe of the cerebral cortex and both hemispheres of the hippocampus are particularly active during memory recall of factual information such as building codes, rhymes that help with sequential order, or specific names of designers. Notwithstanding, researchers contend that the abilities of the brain's right and left hemispheres differ very little in terms of their overall capabilities (Hellige, 1993), and that all behavior is, presumably, in some way represented in brain physiology (Gifford, 2002; Figure 3.4). The question thus remains, whether or not and how much, the brain's physiology, neurochemical secretions, and structures change as a result of a person's physical and social environment.

Plasticity: Making the Connections for Wayfinding
The human brain has a high degree of **plasticity**, which means that it is highly adaptive. Many of the pathways and neural connections result from an individual's experience (Figures

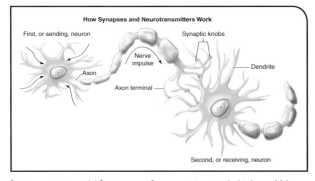

How Synapses and Neurotransmitters Work

First, or sending, neuron

Synaptic knobs

Nerve impulse

Axon

Dendrite

Axon terminal

Second, or receiving, neuron

[**Figures 3.5a and b**] As we perform certain acts (which could be as simple as merely "taking in" the world around us) we form more and more neural connections. These connections grow stronger with repetition. However, they begin to weaken when we no longer use them and thus the connections decay. *top*: © Jamie Grill / Lake Images / Corbis; *bottom*: Illustration by Precision Graphics

3.5a and b). This is an important concept because it goes directly with wayfinding. We get used to similar spaces being next to each other and ingress/egress points being in certain locations. This means that we have strong neural synaptic formations associated with ingress/egress locations, for example, at the front of a store. When this norm is violated, the individual is more likely to experience disorientation because weaker neural connections are called upon. This can be an aspect of interest, a source of frustration, or pose a dangerous situation depending on the circumstance. The Winchester Mystery House in Northern California is a great example. It has doors that lead nowhere, stairs that suddenly end, and secret passages as the only ingress/egress points. In short, this house can be likened to a maze in which our existing neural connections may or may not assist us in finding our way through this house.

Plasticity is not limited to only the young; evidence has revealed that in some regions, the adult brain is also able to create new neurons (Gould, Reeves, Graziano, & Gross, 1999). Hence, as we interact with the environment, neural connections are being established, and those connections will remain as long as they are used. If we cease to use established neural connections, those connections will be

severed through a process call **pruning** (Cowan, Fawcett, & O'Leary, 1984; Huttenlocher, 2002). Studies of amputees (Ramachandran & Rogers-Ramachandran, 2008) revealed that parts of the brain once dedicated to sensory detection of a missing appendage are often taken over by surrounding parts of the brain leading to phantom sensations in the missing appendage.

Through a basic understanding of the brain, designers can better grasp how a particular design may be processed by a variety of end users. For example, a client may have been in a bad car accident in which his/her left parietal lobe sustained injury. A family member may seek out a designer to help make the home more accommodating for the injured person. The designer knows that this lobe is responsible for spatial locations and attention and motor control, and understands that the left side of brain determines whether an object is above or below another object. With this knowledge the designer can then proceed to develop a design that is more unique to the individual user. Among some of the design suggestions might be rounding out walls so that when the person accidentally bumps into them there is less chance of injury that could be sustained from knife-edge corners. Another example might be limiting items from coffee tables such as water-filled vases, which the person might inadvertently knock over as he/she reaches across the table. Along these lines, a designer will want to maintain clear pathways to reduce spatial navigation around items such as furnishings.

BIOLOGICAL SENSATION

For the majority of people, the ability to detect sensation is contingent upon *thresholds*. The first is called the **absolute threshold**, which is the minimum level of stimulation needed to detect a particular stimulus 50 percent of the time. For example, the absolute threshold for sound would be the lowest possible volume of a sound that could be detected half of the time in which the sound is generated. The second threshold is called the **difference threshold**, which is the least amount of difference between two stimuli that one can detect 50 percent of the time. An example here might be the placement of two color swatches side by side; however, each swatch would have a slightly different hue. The difference threshold is the ability to see the differences between two very similar colors 50 percent of the time. Other examples of approximate absolute thresholds include:

- 50 percent of the time, a person will be able to see a candle flame from 30 miles away on a clear, dark night.
- 50 percent of the time a person will be able to hear the tick of a watch when it is 20 feet away in a very quiet space.

- 50 percent of the time a person will be able to smell one drop of perfume that has spread throughout an average-sized three-room apartment (Morris & Maistro, 2006).

Thresholds can differ depending on factors such as individual sensory acuity, prior exposure, and **ambient** conditions. These sensory thresholds are important in design because a person may experience difficulties discerning the difference between two textures, may not see the difference between two similar colors, or may not hear an intended sound that has been masked by surrounding noise. Conversely, a person may have hyperawareness to sensation under normal circumstances, or a biological condition such as autism (see Box 3.1, "Autism") that causes sensory detection to be chaotic and erratic. For those who are acutely aware of sensation, their absolute threshold is much higher. This means that the individual may be able to detect differences in texture, color, and sound that you as the designer cannot detect. As such, understanding these thresholds and the client's ability to distinguish between similar but different sensations becomes an important part of understanding a client's needs.

BOX 3.1 AUTISM

A 2007 Centers for Disease Control report found that 1 in 150 children in the United States has an autism spectrum disorder (ASD), and the Autism Society of America estimates that 1.5 million people in the United States and their families are now affected by autism (ASA, 2007).

Unlike the average person who integrates multiple sensations concurrently in order to understand the world, the autistic person experiences difficulties with the detection of sensory stimuli. The result is that the autistic person tends to experience sensation in either a hyper- or hypo-sensory state. For example, a cozy living room may elicit feelings of warmth to the average person. However, the autistic person might interpret the sensation of velvet upholstery on a sofa as prickly and painful. Likewise, whereas most people find the scent from a vanilla candle as soothing and pleasurable, the autistic person might perceive the scent as so strong and pungent that it initiates a gag reflex. This erratic and inconsistent detection of sensory detection can cause the autistic person to interpret soft lighting as being excessively bright, or the sound cascading water in a small fountain as deafening. Likewise, each of the aforementioned stimuli could also go undetected because the autistic person's senses are understimulated.

Source: Yavorcik, C. (December 30, 2008). Make a Change Today! Retrieved from http://support.autism–society.org/site/News2?page=NewsArticle&id=12477

COGNITIVE CONCEPTIONS OF THE ENVIRONMENT

Reinforcing the idea that we think through the conduit of vision, Karon Oliver defines environmental cognition as "the way we perceive, think about, and make sense of our environment" (Oliver, 2002). Through Oliver's definition, we can establish that we as a species predominantly use the sense of vision to conceive thoughts and ideas related to our environments. Pallasmaa (2005) poses the argument that humans, designers in particular, are "ocularcentric," and suggests that architects need the combined sensory input from our ability to touch, smell, see, hear, and in some cases taste in order to gain true vision. Indeed, if Pallasmaa is referring to environmental cognition and a higher level of thought, then his supposition is correct—but is cognition vision? Those in the fields of arts and design might argue "yes," but those in the fields of biology and psychology would argue "no." This emphasis on vision perhaps explains why it can be so catastrophic when a sighted person loses his/her ability to see. The world as he/she has come to understand it is no longer present. However, many have argued that the visually impaired person is able to experience the world in its truest form and thus those with sight could benefit from the visually impaired.

Albert Ames Jr. demonstrated in 1946 that a sighted person looking into a room could arrive at erroneous conclusions (Wade & Swanston, 1991). He demonstrated this through a specially constructed room that, due to size and shape constancy, looks normal. However, the room's walls and windows were not square, but instead trapezoidal. Also, he placed one corner of the back wall farther away from the observer than the other corner. Therefore, when two people stand in the different corners of the room, one person appears small while the other appears tall. The illusion generated by the Ames room can be explained by the lack of cues that we normally rely upon to determine three-dimensional shape constancy (Dorward & Day, 1997). Recall Brunswick's Lens Model from Chapter 2 where visual cues only have a certain probability of being perceived accurately. In the Ames room the visual cues may be interpreted as being accurate, but they are not.

Within the field of psychology there is a law that states one cannot change what one has formed an association with. Hence, if you associate with your visual reality, as most people do, these associations are difficult to change (Figure 3.6).

Even when we close our eyes, we conjure images of a space as we remember, or expect, that space to be. For the person who has lost his/her sight at an early age or who was born without sight, there is no visual reality. The physical world then takes on another reality of deeper understanding, which in many instances is more pure. In studies, researchers have found that people with severe visual disabilities can detect air currents and thermal conditions from windows, doors, and ventilation ducts, which can then serve as a method for navigation and wayfinding (Hall, 1969). For example, Hall described a group of visually impaired people who relied upon the heat radiating from a brick wall located on a certain street as a landmark for wayfinding. Similarly, the blind are often able to detect subtle differences among a group of objects with varying textures such as shells (Goldstein, 2002). It is this highly developed acuity of the person's remaining senses that enable him/her to read with his/her hands. Therefore, we can say that a person who cannot see the world through sight will perceive and experience the world through a different set of criteria and hence, understand it differently. Also their difference threshold for their other senses becomes much lower thus enabling them to detect subtle differences that others may not detect. In short, the person who relies upon his or her sight to understand the world will incorrectly perceive the Ames Room; but the person who has no sight, because he or she relies on enhanced auditory sensations will not be deceived by the room's optical illusion.

NEUROCHEMICALS AND HORMONES

Along with the physical structure of the brain, several important chemicals are needed to facilitate the transmission of impulses among the brain's neural pathways. Among these are **neurochemicals**, which consist of:

- **Neurotransmitters** send signals from one neuron to another.
- **Neuromodulators** alter the effect of neurotransmitters.

A way to think of these neurochemicals is to consider a neurotransmitter as the chemical that opens a door, whereas the neuromodulator shuts the door. **Hormones** are chemical substances produced by our glands and act as neuromodulators.

In many ways, neuromodulators, hormones, and neurotransmitters operate in a symbiotic manner. For example, when the body initiates a stress response, cortisol (a hormone) is released in cooperation with catecholamines (neurotransmitter).

Substances introduced into the body such as carbon monoxide and nitric oxide (toxic air pollutants produced by combustion engines and power plants) act as neurotransmitters and neuromodulators within the brain (Barañano et al., 2000). Other substances that act on neurotransmitters and neuromodulators include a wide variety of drugs. Depending upon the chemical composition, the effects of drugs on the brain can either be an increase or decrease in the effectiveness of neural activity. Some pharmaceuticals activate certain neural receptors while others increase the amount of neurotransmitters. Examples of drugs used to increase the levels of neurotransmitters are those used to treat depression. These are a class of pharmaceuticals called selective serotonin reuptake inhibitors (SSRIs). They work by blocking the body's absorption of the neurotransmitter serotonin thus keeping serotonin levels within the brain elevated. According to the National Center for Health Statistics, within the United States, (2006) about 10 percent of women and 4 percent of men older than 18 take an antidepressant.

Acetylcholine is a chemical stimulant found in the brain and throughout the entire nervous system. In the brain, acetylcholine causes excitement and anticipatory actions; in the body, it causes muscle fibers to contract (tense up) in anticipation of an event. This is called the fight-or-flight response. Acetylcholine is quickly synthesized after

[**Figure 3.6**] Is this an image of a saxophone player or an image of a young woman? It is not until someone else points out the alternative perspective that we are able to see. In this way, our vision has the capacity to deceive or mislead us. Illustration by Precision Graphics

fulfilling its intended function; if not, it can be destructive to nerve fibers throughout the system. Conversely, a shortage of acetylcholine can also negatively affect the body. For example, a shortage of acetylcholine in the brain has been associated with the onset of Alzheimer's disease; it is thought that sufferers may experience a degeneration of cells that produce acetylcholine.

Catecholamines, a group of neurochemicals composed of naturally occurring compounds, serve as hormones, neurotransmitters, or both within the **sympathetic nervous system**, the branch of the autonomic nervous system that is responsible for breathing, circulation, and digestion. As with other neurotransmitters, catecholamines are released at nerve endings and facilitate signals from the nerve cells to other cells within the sympathetic nervous system. **Epinephrine** (commonly referred to as **adrenaline**), **norepinephrine** (also called **noradrenaline**), and **dopamine** are all catecholamines. Norepinephrine, which is almost identical in structure to epinephrine, is released into the bloodstream from the adrenal gland under sympathetic activation and, along with acetylcholine, mobilizes the body's resources in response to a stressful event (the fight-or-flight response). The sympathetic nervous system functions in response to short-term stress, which is why norepinephrine and epinephrine are often referred to as stress hormones; they increase both heart rate and blood pressure. As mentioned, cortisol is also a stress hormone. These substances prepare the body to react to emergencies such as pain, fatigue, and shock.

Norepinephrine, dopamine, and serotonin are also associated with mood. Dopamine is necessary for the synthesis of epinephrine, which affects the activity of neural synapses. A deficiency of dopamine is thought to be responsible for the symptoms of Parkinson's disease, which is characterized by uncontrolled shaking.

Serotonin is a chemical that regulates appetite, mood, sexual desire, and sleep; in simple terms, low levels of serotonin are directly related to lower moods and depression. Inadequate serotonin levels compromise the signals between brain cells, and this often results in depression and anxiety. Unfiltered sunlight plays a role in the absorption of serotonin, and other research suggests that tightly sealed office buildings, in conjunction with air-conditioning units, decrease levels of serotonin and norepinephrine, which leads to greater stress and depression (Lambert, Reid, Kay, Jennings, & Esler, 2003). Tightly sealed buildings with recirculated air also cause an imbalance of **ions**, oxygen and carbon dioxide levels, or increased **ozone** levels. Ions are particles that are positive or negative electrically charged. Too many positive ions can result in anxiety while too many negative ions can cause depression. Ozone is a colorless gas with a strong oxidizing agent that can be produced by the use of electrical equipment. Too much ozone is associated with coughing, congestion, wheezing, shortness of breath, and chest pain. People with asthma, bronchitis, heart disease, and emphysema often find their condition worsens with high levels of ozone. Also, breathing ozone may increase the risk of getting certain lung diseases.

Endogenous cannabinoids are neuromodulators that influence the activity of a sending neuron (Wilson & Nicoll, 2002). Note the similarities between the words cannabis and cannabinoid. Cannabis is another word for marijuana, which stimulates neural receptors. The cannabinoids affect specific locations on neurons, which then affect certain activities such as the perception of pain, as well as concentration and attention (Kreitzer & Regehr, 2001; Sanudo-Pena et al., 2000). **Melatonin** is sometimes called the *Dracula of hormones*: Only when darkness occurs can the **pineal gland** (Figure 3.7) produce melatonin and release it into the bloodstream.

When melatonin levels rise sharply in the blood stream (usually around 9:00 p.m.), we begin to feel less alert as sleep beckons us. Melatonin levels normally stay elevated for about 12 hours before they return to barely detectable daytime lows (usually by around 9:00 a.m.). Bright light directly inhibits the release of melatonin, which the pineal gland cannot produce unless the person is in a dimly lit environment. Both sunlight

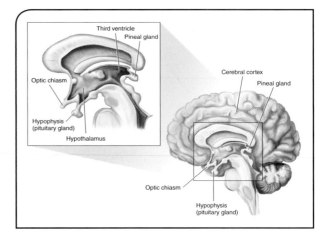

[**Figure 3.7**] The pineal gland secretes melatonin and communicates information about environmental lighting to various parts of the body. Melatonin helps the body to establish necessary biological rhythms. Illustration by Precision Graphics

and artificial indoor lighting are bright enough to prevent the release of melatonin and promote insomnia. When daylight or artificial light is inadequate, the natural suppression of melatonin production fails to occur. The result is often feelings of depression and sleepiness (Lewy, Bauer, Cutler, et al., 1998). Melatonin has a direct relationship to our circadian rhythms. These rhythms regulate our body's internal clock and inform us when we should sleep and when we should wake up. The circadian rhythms are established by light hitting the retina and then being transmitted to the hypothalamus. Emergency personnel, healthcare workers, and other professionals who provide 24-hour service must have ample access to bright lighting for them to remain alert.

Because high melatonin levels cause drowsiness, whereas low melatonin levels are related to a state of alertness (Edwards & Torcellini, 2002; Veitch & McColl, 1993), designers should learn about their client's sleeping patterns before deciding upon window treatments or even floor configurations. For example, a person who has no problem falling and staying asleep may benefit from window treatments that are more translucent. On the other hand, a person who has difficulty sleeping may benefit from heavier or "black-out" window treatments.

CULTURAL CONNECTION 3.1

The culture of acute sleep deprivation is common among groups such as truck drivers, college students, designers, medical staff, and military personnel. The belief that "all-nighters" are productive, and that resisting the sensation to sleep because it is an activity that one can do without is extremely flawed. In these modern times, a large segment of western society claims to be getting less than five hours of sleep per night. With the invention of artificial light came the first wave of "burning the midnight oil," followed by the light bulb when 24-hour establishments came into being. In these modern times, with televisions, cell phones, game systems, and computers to keep us awake and busy all night, it is not difficult to explain the ensuing side effects of sleep deprivation: irritability, emotional instability, and hyperactivity. Perhaps the recent increases in the phenomena of human aggression such as road rage, work and school shootings, and the advent of complex disorders such as attention deficit hyperactivity disorder (ADHD) and attention deficit disorder (ADD) can be linked to generations of increasingly *exhausted* people.

Understanding the effects of neurotransmitters and hormones on learning and behaviors is an important start when understanding how we perceive and respond to our environments. With modern medical advancements and new technologies, we are seeing fewer infants dying within the first few years of life, fewer people dying as a result of accidents or injuries, and fewer people dying from a first heart attack or stroke. However, we are also seeing more cases of cognitive disorders such as autism and Parkinson's and Alzheimer's diseases. This means that modern designers are expected to know of the various ailments that could affect the usability of a variety of environments.

STRESS AND BEHAVIOR

The World Health Organization defines health not only as the absence of disease and infirmity, but also as a state of optimal physical, mental, and social well-being. Designers must assume the responsibility of ensuring that the occupants for whom they create environments can maintain optimum health. Incidents of injury and illness often result from the human–environment relationship simply because the environment is a causal factor. This fact emphasizes the interrelationship between the design fields and human health. Fear of injury or victimization related to the environment typically results from a combination of personal experiences, peer influences, and media messages and can be either real or imagined. For example, the exposed corners of walls that meet at right angles present a real risk for broken toes, facial injuries, and minor concussions, but riding in a glass elevator along the exterior of a high-rise could stimulate an irrational fear of falling. Imagined threats are often, but not always, a result of irrational fears (**phobias**); although they are very real to the individual, they are highly unlikely in normal circumstances.

Because many older designs focused almost exclusively on artistic and aesthetic qualities, older buildings often fail to protect their occupants from exposure to risk factors or disease-causing organisms. For example, poorly ventilated high-density housing increases the rate of communicable diseases and facilitates the degeneration of mental health (Marion, 2003). Numerous studies indicate that the leading causes of death for children in developed countries are injuries sustained from biological and environmental sources and psychological and physical reactions to stress. Clearly, health on both the physical and psychological levels is affected by the environment.

STRESS AND STRESSORS

Stress is a psychological or physiological response to a stimulus or stressor. Our daily stress levels derive from a variety of situations, whether social (e.g., an employer's unrealistic demands), physical (e.g., trying to concentrate in an open office setting), or biological and chemical (e.g., carpet fumes that cause nausea, headaches, fatigue), all of which affect our responses. Human stress can be caused by internal or external sources (Gunnar & Barr, 1998). External stressors include variables from the physical environment, such as noise, temperature, crowding, and over- or understimulation. Internal stressors include interpersonal conflict or violence, disorganized daily life, or a combination of these. However, both types of stress can build over time and manifest as physical ailments. For example, traditional gender roles for men encourage stoic responses to physical and emotional pain. However, just because a man does not complain doesn't mean that he doesn't experience pain or stress. Instead, the likely reaction will be an ulcer, a heart attack, or a stroke. The stressor itself must be examined to determine if the stressful episode is acute or chronic. An acute stressor is sudden, intense, and short-lived; a chronic stressor is ongoing or recurring and has the most significant and detrimental effects, such as having a home located near smokestacks (Gunnar & Barr, 1998; Lombroso & Sapolsky, 1998).

Stress itself does not cause injury or illness, but how we respond to it can, especially over time. Bioemotional reactions to stressful environments can result in a wide range of physiological responses (including increased activity in the heart, stomach, intestines, and endocrine glands), which can result in stress-related illnesses such as increased heart rate, high blood pressure, ulcers, and migraine headaches. Behavioral responses to stress include aggression, withdrawal, and compulsion, and in extreme cases lead to violence, delusions, or psychosis. The effects of stress "outlive" the stressor: Our physical and psychological responses continue even after the stressful event or experience has ended (Campbell, 1983). Medical experts declare that if the body must continually cope with particular stressors over a long period of time, the circulatory, cardiovascular, gastrointestinal, and hormonal (glandular) systems may suffer permanent damage.

Environmental sources of psychological distress include air, odor, and noise pollution as well as the perception of being at risk. Stressors such as odors, heat, noise, and crowding are often referred to as **ambient stressors** (Arnsten, 1998) because they are chronic, nonurgent, physically perceptible, and limited to a particular environment. Chronic environmental stressors (e.g., feeling unsafe in our homes or neighborhoods) slowly wear away our abilities to cope. A stressor's ambience or chronicity is determined by its frequency and its impact on a person's level of stress. For example, one person may find the scent of a candle factory to be a perpetual annoyance (chronic stressor), whereas another may enjoy all but one or two distinct fragrances (ambient stressors).

COGNITIVE DISORDERS

Cognitive disabilities are often accompanied by self-doubt, with regard to self-competence. This insecurity often manifests with symptoms of the disability becoming more pronounced. Consider this phenomenon to be similar to *test anxiety*. Students might know all of the answers for an exam, but in the testing environment, they lose their ability to recall the information. Try as they will, their minds close down and prohibit them from performing successfully on the exam. To counteract this type of insecurity with design, designers will want to reduce ambient environmental stressors. For example, movement detected from one's peripheral vision, or ambient noises may be the triggers for the anxiety. The designer's job then becomes to identify ways to use design as a means to reduce those events from occurring.

A similar stress response is to become paralyzed in an emergency or to become *immobilized by fear*. For example, to help facilitate evacuation during emergency situations, designers should consider easy-to-see, instantly recognizable, and redundant wayfinding mechanisms. Also, they will want to lower social density by increasing the width of pathways thereby alleviating perceptions of crowding, which can also cause someone to panic. Designers can also include a multitude of wayfinding methods into the overall design through the use of ample signage that uses both large and easy-to-see lettering in combination with pictographs. They can use landmarks that include varying architectural details, landscaping, and public art (e.g., water fountains, statues, sculptures), and they can incorporate color-matching methods into the design (i.e., matching the floor or wall color to areas of significance).

Learning Disabilities

The topic of disabilities will be discussed in greater detail in Chapter 9, but the least understood and often dismissed are disabilities associated with *cognitive processing*. In such cases, a person's brain either has lost its ability to interpret incoming stimuli, or interprets incoming stimuli differently than the majority of the population. Often times these disabilities are not discovered until school, when a child is placed into a learning environment. In this situation the child with a processing deficit struggles and is often thought of as "slow." Learning disabilities, in particular, are defined by the *Diagnostic and Statistical Manual of Mental Disorders* (DSM-IV, 1994) [the psychologist's handbook]) as being lower achievement on standardized tests in reading, mathematics, or written expression. Overall, learning disabilities refer to a broad range of brain-related abnormalities that persistently interfere with an individual's ability to learn, process, and use new information such as reading impairment (dyslexia), delayed maturation, clumsiness, hyperactivity, and perceptual disorganization.

Learning disabilities are more common than one would expect, and many prominent figures such as Agatha Christie, Albert Einstein, and George Washington suffered from various learning disabilities. In fact, some of Thomas Edison's teachers thought he suffered from a mental illness (Sagmiller, 2000).

Some estimates suggest that approximately one in five people within the United States is affected by a disorder of the brain. Jans, Stoddard & Kraus, (2004) state that of all the children affected with a processing deficit, more than half are boys. Within the array of learning disabilities are individuals who have **dyslexia** and **dysgraphia**, and attention disorders like **attention deficit hyperactivity disorder (ADHD)**.

For many people with cognitive disabilities, the built environment rarely serves as a barrier (Wilcoff & Abed, 1994); however, as our built environment become larger, issues of wayfinding and navigation may become more pronounced. The challenge with learning disabilities for the designer is that the needs of individual users are diverse, and the disability cannot be mimicked in order to identify solutions. This is because it is common for individuals with cognitive disabilities to have deficits in one area but exhibit typical skills, or even advanced skills, in other areas. A designer can easily put himself/herself in a wheelchair and move about an environment; likewise, he/she can put on a blindfold or soundproof headset to gain some understanding of how a person who is blind or deaf interprets the world. With a learning disability, the manifestation and severity differs from person to person, and it is nearly impossible to replicate the world as the affected person understands it. Therefore, the designer's responsibility is to gain as thorough an understanding of the different cognitive disabilities as possible.

Designers can accommodate the learning disabled person through a variety of environmental modifications. One suggestion for those with cognitive disabilities that make them especially sensitive to sound might be to replace open-office cubicles with reconfigurable floor to ceiling glass offices along one wall.

In these spaces the learning disabled can listen to information (if audio data is more easily processed) from a computer or from a tape recorder. Also, this quiet and distraction-free space can allow the employee or student to dictate information into voice-processing software, or into a recorder for transcription. Another suggestion for the visual learner might be the use of large computer monitors. This way he/she can view words in a larger font, which can reduce the transposition of numbers or letters.

Alzheimer's and Parkinson's Disease

Alzheimer's and Parkinson's disease are two cognitive disorders that are typically age-related. It is estimated that dementia of the Alzheimer's type (DAT) will affect up to 16 million Americans by 2050 (Alzheimer's Association, 2004). Currently, about 5 to 10 percent of people who are age 65 and older have DAT, an incurable condition that affects the nervous system by reducing cognitive abilities and increasing spatial disorientation (Passini, Rainville, Marchand, &

Joanette, 1998). After Alzheimer's disease, Parkinson disease is the most common neurodegenerative disease in the United States. Approximately 1.5 million Americans are affected by Parkinson's disease, with about 60,000 new cases appearing each year (Avicena, n.d.). Approximately 90 to 95 percent of those who develop Parkinson's disease do so after the age of 60. The remaining 5 to 10 percent, referred to as "young onset" patients, develop symptoms before the age of 40. Parkinson's disease is related to the lack of dopamine in the brain, and it presents itself with muscular rigidity and tremors along with cognitive processing challenges. Alzheimer's and Parkinson's disease will be discussed more thoroughly in Chapter 8.

Cognitive impairments include Alzheimer's and Parkinson's disease as well as those who are born with or acquire a mental deficiency. There are several forms of mental deficiencies: genetic, such as Down syndrome; prenatal neglect, such as fetal alcohol syndrome; or environmental, such as heavy metal poisoning (toxicity). The results of these conditions include declined cognitive functioning, lower levels of intelligence, and limitations in daily living skills.

Mental Deficiencies

Mental deficiencies typically show up in childhood or adolescence and affect approximately 3 percent of the general population (Olendorf, Jeryan, & Boyden, 1999). The *DSM-IV* lists four levels of mental deficiency in terms of severity: mild, moderate, severe, and profound (Table 3.1).

Decreased cognitive functioning has been linked to decreased response time when avoiding obstacles; tripping over objects is a frequent cause of falls and accidental injury. Therefore, when designing interior environments for those who have cognitive impairments, designers should consider the longer reaction times for occupants as well as the different ways in which designs can be interpreted. Designers should also avoid architectural features that can serve as obstacles (Chen, et. al., 1996). Large signs and dry erase boards can be incorporated into designs to serve as safety reminders (e.g., "Remember to turn the stove off"), as well as a large daily calendar, clock with large numbers, and a night-light to help minimize disorientation. Because people with cognitive impairments seem to respond better to routines, clocks that chime on the hour or cuckoo clocks might help the person to remain oriented and provide a sense of order and routine (Figure 3.8).

Designers should also consider the inclusion of timers on electrical equipment to help prevent accidental fire, and alarms placed on doors to signal other family members of unwanted ingress and egress.

Designers should avoid the use of bright and highly contrasting colors (except for signs) because they can appear three-dimensional and therefore lead to problems of balance and mobility. Marking a residence with the occupant's

[**Table 3.1**] Classification and Description of Mental Deficiencies

Classification	Description
Mild	This classification makes up the majority of persons affected by mental deficiency. These people typically acquire only the intellectual skills common to a sixth grader, and many can live on their own.
Moderate	People with moderate mental deficiency can live and work within the community in a supervised environment. Many will need to reside within a group home.
Severe	These individuals might be able to care for themselves to some degree, but they will require the assistance of others. Most live in group homes where assistance can be easily accessed and provided.
Profound	These people's condition is often caused by a neurological disorder and thus requires a high degree of structure and supervision.

[**Figure 3.8**] Including subtle reminders related to orientation—such as time of day, one's given location, and what one should be doing—are important environmental supports for the person with cognitive impairments. This clock has two features that assist with orientation. The first is the clock's hourly chime; the second is the orientation pictograph of day or night above the clock face, helping the person to remain oriented to the daily a.m./p.m. rotation. © Flat Earth / www.fotosearch.com

personality has been shown to bolster self-esteem (Eshelman & Evans, 2002). Consider modifying the cognitively impaired person's environments so they can better adjust to their lives (Rabins, 1989), as this behavioral approach is essentially the only "treatment" that will benefit sufferers. Also, to assist the people who require institutionalization because of their cognitive impairment, buildings should be arranged in simple continuous configurations that allow for wandering, help to prevent disorientation, and control access to areas that could be dangerous.

For people who suffer from cognitive deficiencies that directly affect intellectual growth and development, the world is filled with many possibilities. Recall the example of a child interpreting a chair in a museum that is on display as simply a place to sit and rest. The same holds true for many with mental impairments. Red berries may be seen as a source of food, not as poisonous; an electrical outlet might be seen as a keyhole, not a source of an electrical shock; and a person in a mirror may not be seen as a reflection, but rather as a playmate. With these and many other concerns, it is important that designers understand as much as possible about his/her client's condition and how it manifests for that person.

Autism

People who suffer from various levels of mental deficiencies experience diminished capacities in all developmental pathways (e.g., motor, social, communication) in unison, which means that all of the pathways continue to function in coordination—just at lower performance levels. This is not true for the person affected with autism; he/she will be advanced in selected areas of development such as auditory recall, and not so advanced in another area of development such as knowing when and where to place an emphasis on certain words when communicating (Ritvo, 2005). This results in a diminished ability to understand how different sensory stimuli come together. A person suffering from autism perceives sensations, such as sight, sound, smell, and pain, as incoherent fragments. In general, the autistic person will tend to gravitate toward visual and tactile stimuli and will experience the most distress from auditory stimuli. In short, a person without autism will automatically integrate different sensations into a single meaningful experience; the person with autism cannot do this.

Some estimates state that one out of every 150 children is diagnosed with some degree on the *autistic spectrum*, and that the condition affects males four times more than females (Mostafa, 2008). The word *spectrum* is used in conjunction with autism because those afflicted with the disorder present a range of disabilities that affect social relationships, communication, and imagination to a varying extent (Autism Society, 2008). The proper title is **autism spectrum disorder (ASD)**.

The person with ASD often experiences difficulty with multiple-sensory stimulation, such as the sound of a person's voice while a train is rolling down the tracks off in the distance or concentrating on a story while beads of perspiration drip down his/her face. The person with ASD often experiences great difficulty screening out irrelevant sensory stimuli. Likewise, he/she is unable to integrate multiple stimuli into one coherent meaning. Instead, he/she is likely to be very sensitive to specific sensations, and completely oblivious to others. For example, a person may be telling the autistic person a story about trains and rather than incorporate the sounds of the train rolling down the track into a singular experience, thereby providing greater meaning to the story, the person with ASD might interpret the two sensory stimuli as being separate and thus distracting.

Because ASD is a spectral disorder, individuals experience sensations differently and have difficulty understanding and cataloguing these sensations. For this reason, the built environment can be a source of frustration, fear, and anxiety (Mostafa, 2008). The disconnection between two or more sensations allows the person with ASD to better compartmentalize incoming information, which thus imbues him/her with superior memory and recall. For example, many people with ASD can instantly and accurately identify the two letters that surround any letter in the alphabet. This is because they can recall the whole image of the alphabet and not each letter in relation to another. The person with ASD understands visual images as a whole and nonsequentially. In design, we use natural ordering such as a bathroom placed near a location that serves food and beverage, but not directly adjacent. This logic may be lost on a person with ASD who would likely respond to an environment

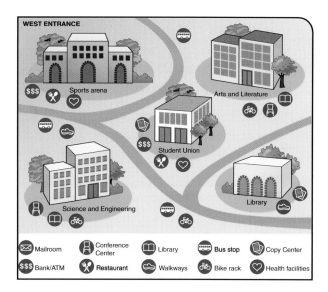

[**Figure 3.9**] A person with autism spectrum disorder (ASD) understands visual images as a whole, not as separate pieces. This means that a person with ASD might respond better to a rendered map of the environment in totality. Illustration by Precision Graphics

better by looking at a rendered map or picture of the environment in its totality (Figure 3.9). This method of recall enables the person with ASD to possess an uncanny ability to detect and identify subtle differences in an object or detail within the environment, which is why many children with ASD seem to find pleasure in identifying similarities and differences as well as highlighting differences so that they are more explicit (van Rijn & Stappers, 2008).

It is interesting to note that 85 percent of the rods and cones in the eye of a person with ASD allow for greater visual acuity, thereby making colors appear more intense (Paron-Wildes, 2008). For example, a child with a hypersensitivity to the color red may perceive the color as a bright fluorescent color and may react disruptively in search of a visual field with less stimulating colors (Paron-Wildes, 2008). This may be a reason why traditional lighting in public spaces can be a source of irritation for some people with ASD. For others, they are able to cope for a period of time, but eventually the sensory stimulation exceeds the individual's coping threshold. The many sources of disconnected stimulation that a person with ASD receives can be so overwhelming that many find it difficult to make sense of their surroundings. For example, people with ASD might be extremely sensitive to sound. They are often able to hear an ambulance siren well before it is audible to the nonautistic person (Kern et al., 2006). The problem is that when the siren goes off near the person with ASD, the sound can be painfully loud.

The natural reaction to perceptual chaos is the desire to create order, and many people with ASD will make this a central focus of their daily routine (van Rijn & Stappers, 2008). This may explain a preference that children with ASD have for toys they can organize, such as the game "memory" or jigsaw puzzles (van Rijn & Stappers, 2008), or Lego building blocks in which they can arrange or create objects in isolation.

CULTURAL CONNECTION 3.2

The autism rights movement (ARM) encourages society to accept autism not as a disease or a disorder but as a different way of thinking—as a different way of being human. Proponents understand and respond to autism as a natural genetic *adaptation* of the human

> STABLE IPREDICTABLE ENVIRONMENT
>
> ELEMENTS THAT PROVIDE DIRECT FEEDBACK
>
> CONTROL

---

to them. Preferences may include a stable and predictable environment, a degree of control over their environments, and minimizing sudden or dramatic changes (Cohen & Volkmar, 1997), such as suddenly turning the lights on after watching television in the dark. In this case, lights on a dimmer switch will allow for gradual increases in illumination.

To help people with ASD get used to changes within environmental stimuli, designers can include elements that provide direct feedback. Through repetition the person can begin to predict the effects of their actions. The key is to allow the person to generate the effect. For example, one person with ASD might prefer color, so a cause (pushing a button) could be related to the effect (generation of color). However, caution should be exercised to include only cause-and-effect elements that best match the person with ASD's preferred sensation (e.g., sight, sound, touch). There are some studies that suggest individuals with ASD relate better to robots with artificial intelligence than to other humans (Mondak, 2000). The thought is that the artificial intelligence eliminates the unpredictability of human emotional responses, and the robot's reactions are more controllable (Murray, 1997).

Practical Applications for Designers

Use these resources, activities, and discussion questions to help you identify, synthesize, and retain this chapter's core information. These tools are designed to complement the resources you'll find in this book's companion Study Guide.

SUMMING IT UP

Recent scientific advances have enabled the field of environmental psychology to delve deeper into the environment versus human behavior through neurobiological responses. Environmental psychologists consider the aggregate of the physical, social, and biological factors of the overall environmental experience. The APA states that, "behavioral neuroscientists study the brain in relation to behavior, its evolution, functions, abnormalities, and repair, as well as its interactions with the immune system, cardiovascular system, and energy regulation systems" (APA, n.d.). From this knowledge, designers of the built environment can then begin to better understand the relationship between humans, designed spaces, and environmental sensations.

The built environment can be a source of frustration, fear, and anxiety for people with different cognitive functions. Environmental designers must find out as much as possible about the users (their conditions and environmental-cognitive preferences) prior to designing spaces for them.

You can also refer to this textbook's companion Study Guide for a comprehensive list of Summary Points.

EXPERT SPOTLIGHT 3.1

Phenomenology and Meaning in Design

Jo Ann Asher Thompson, Ph.D., FIDEC, FIIDA, Washington State University, Spokane

According to the Stanford Library of Philosophy, phenomenology is "the study of structures of consciousness as experienced from the first-person point of view. The central structure of an experience is its intentionality, its being directed toward something, as it is an experience of or about some object." Put more simplistically, phenomenology is the study of various "phenomena" and how individuals experience such phenomena (i.e., how things [objects] appear, how these are experienced, and what meanings are attached to these objects through human experiences). Phenomenological design research is qualitative in nature and examines various subjective experiences based on an individual or first person physical encounter and/or interaction with objects and their sensory properties.

Further examination of the concept of phenomenology tells us that it is about "lived" experiences and what it means to be "human" on a daily basis. How people perceive, behave, and interact with phenomena (objects/things) is core to phenomenological research and exploration. Design research means integrating the theoretical and philosophically reflective practices with pragmatic everyday design problems situated in the project, process, or product. This definition of design research fits well with those who argue that design and the creation of knowledge are both intensely human acts—the meaning of which is dependent upon the utility and cultural location or "situatedness" of the environment or artifact. Design research for interior designers is dependent upon the "situatedness" of the people within the environment.

Interior design deals with spaces in which people routinely live, work, and play. Continual examination and re-examination of how individuals perceive the spaces and interior artifacts we design and specify is an essential role of every interior designer. If artifacts are defined as "objects that are produced or shaped by human craft; a product of human conception or agency," then each designed interior space is itself an artifact—a humanly created object produced to satisfy a particular experience or behavior.

When built, an interior environment accommodates a variety of artifacts (furnishings and accessories) that have meaning and purpose for the people who occupy that environment. Thus it is that with each project, interior designers must put themselves in the shoes of the clients and try to understand the world of these potential occupants through their eyes and their experiences—in other words, from a phenomenological perspective. The importance of understanding how people experience space and the meanings that people attach to artifacts should not be underestimated in the design of our built environment. For example, in housing for the elderly, critical concepts such as *sense of place* and connectivity to family can be reinforced through the spatial layout and display of artifacts brought from "home." So it is that with each project, be it residential or commercial, interior designers must continually examine how space and its elements inspire, support, or sustain human behaviors and experiences.

KEY TERMS

- **absolute threshold**
- **acetylcholine**
- **adrenaline**
- **ambient**
- **ambient stressors**
- **amygdala**
- **angular gyrus**
- **attention deficit hyperactivity disorder (ADHD)**
- **autism spectrum disorder (ASD)**
- **basal ganglia**
- **catecholamines**
- **caudate nucleus**
- **difference threshold**
- **dopamine**
- **dysgraphia**
- **dyslexia**
- **endogenous cannabinoids**
- **epinephrine**
- **hippocampus**
- **hormones**
- **ions**
- **limbic system**
- **looming**
- **melatonin**
- **neurochemicals**
- **neuromodulators**
- **neuroscience**
- **neurotransmitters**
- **noradrenaline**
- **norepinephrine**
- **ozone**
- **phobias**
- **pineal gland**
- **plasticity**
- **pruning**
- **supra-marginal gyrus**
- **sympathetic nervous system**

WEB LINKS

The Autistic Self Advocacy Network (http://www.autisticadvocacy.org)

Harvard Medical School, Division of Sleep Medicine (http://sleep.med.harvard.edu/)

National Center for Learning Disabilities (http://www.ncld.org)

Organization for Autism Research (http://www.researchautism.org)

The Secret Life of the Brain, PBS series Web site, including a 3-D interactive model of a human brain (http://www.pbs.org/wnet/brain)

Society for Neuroscience (http://www.sfn.org)

Looming

Design Problem Statement

You have been hired by a Hollywood studio to design a frightening set for young people. You have decided to make the theme of your set looming, either by generating a rendered perspective of a room or main street in a town or by building a model of a town.

Issue: In this exercise, you must identify five different ways to include looming into the design.

Purpose: To explore the different manifestations of looming within the built environment as a means of negating or enhancing the effect.

Deliverable

A diagramed rendering or model along with a justification paper stating what measures you included in the rendering or model and why you anticipate those measures to work (i.e., the use of contrasting colors enhances the perception of three-dimensionality so the yellow angled wall will appear as though it is protruding farther out than it is in reality, thereby enhancing the looming effect).

Circadian Rhythm and Melatonin

Situation

You have been commissioned to build a hotel in Saint Petersburg, Russia. Because of where Saint Petersburg is latitudinally, the sun is out for only a short time in the winter and out for nearly 22 hours in the summer.

Issue: Sunlight affects circadian rhythms and causes melatonin to be either released into the body in darkness or absorbed in bright light. Business people will be coming to this hotel from all over the world, many of whom will suffer from jet lag.

Purpose: Develop a hotel where people's circadian rhythms can remain in balance and their jet lag can be minimized.

Deliverable

A diagramed rendering or model along with a justification paper stating what design measures you included to address the issues and how you anticipate those measures will work to satisfy the issue.

1. What is needed for us to initiate evidence-based design practices, with the intention of enhancing the experiential qualities of the built environment?

2. What are the different regions within the brain that lead to our cognitive experience?

3. By understanding the basic functions of the brain, what are some design suggestions a designer can use to develop a design that is unique to the individual user?

4. What are good design strategies that can be implemented to avoid creating tightly sealed buildings and avoid an imbalance of ions, oxygen, and carbon dioxide levels, or increased ozone levels? And why is it important to avoid designing these types of toxic environments?

5. What are some design strategies that should be considered when working with clients who have problematic sleeping patterns? And why should the designer learn about the client's sleeping patterns before completing the design?

1. Considering the plasticity of the brain in relation to its ability to create new neurons as we interact with the environment, design a space that implements this knowledge and devise a strategically interactive design that would allow for brain growth.

2. Envision a situation where you need to work with a client who has encountered trauma to the brain. How would you use your knowledge of the basic understanding of the brain to better understand the particular design needed to suit your client? What are some suggestions you would implement in the design, based on our example?

3. Design the ultimate working office space. What stress factors would you eliminate through good architectural design? What external stress factors would you eliminate to make the space the most comfortable and productive working environment?

4. Considering how exposure to mild or moderate uncontrollable stress impairs the prefrontal cortical processes, put yourself in a loud and stressful environment and try to get work done. Record your stress reaction to the environment and note the moments where your memory becomes impaired.

5. Design an environment for a person with a learning disability. What design responsibilities should be considered for the design?

04

Sensation and Perception

There can be no knowledge without emotion. We may be aware of a truth, yet until we have felt its force, it is not ours. To the cognition of the brain must be added the experience of the soul.

—Arnold Bennett

Many humans see natural environments as stockpiles of raw material to fulfill their wants and needs (Merchant, 1993; Oelschlaeger, 1991). This statement can be considered not only physically, referring to natural resources such as water, wood, and oil, but also metaphorically as sights, sounds, smells, and tactile sensations. Sensory stimulation is something all life requires, and in many ways the world around us provides the raw materials for our brain to interpret and organize **sensation**. This interpretation and organization leads to a perception that helps us know and remember a particular environment. Of course what we will know or remember depends greatly on the aggregation of raw stimuli that has been filtered and processed by our brain. Perception is the process of creating meaningful patterns from the raw sensory information.

Perception, the first phase in our overall thought process, involves the interpretation of sensations. **Cognition**, the second phase, is the way that information and knowledge comes to be known, through the actions of perception, reasoning, or intuition. Cognition is the way in which we think, learn, form memories, and make decisions.

PERCEPTION

Sensation and perception are two distinct steps in the course of acquiring and processing information. Although perception is the interpretation of incoming sensory information, it is influenced by a variety of factors (e.g.,

[**Figure 4.1**] If there are no reference points, a person looking from end to end of this airport hallway may not perceive it to be as long as it actually is. Many connector hallways can be as long as a city block. © Jon Arnold Images Ltd / Alamy

the type and level of the stimulus as well as a person's past experiences, level of attention to detail, readiness to respond, level of motivation, current emotional state). Research has found that people derive as much, if not more, of their perception of distance and movement from visual cues despite independent and sometimes contradictory nonvisual cues (Harris, L. R., Jenkin, & Zikovitz, 2000). When visual cues are absent, occupants often misjudge both how far away something is and how far they have traveled. Specifically, in large-scale environments such as airports and convention centers people tend to overestimate short distances—especially when little or no visual information is provided—and underestimate long distances, people become less aware of their movements within a space if there is an abundance of visual information (Sun, Campos, Young, Chan, & Ellard, 2004). This means that we are less able to experience the environment with our other senses. (Figure 4.1)

CULTURAL CONNECTION 4.1

Cognitive information management, in terms of understanding and cataloging of the world around us, has taken on an added complexity since the advent of the personal computer. Initially, most people used computers as glorified word processors, calculators, or gaming systems. In today's world, the personal computer has quite nearly become an external portion of the human brain. Computer culture has turned to machines and software to take on the roles of memory storage, language processor (i.e., spell check, grammar check), perception (virtual worlds), interpersonal communication (email), and socialization (network sites and chat rooms); therefore, researchers in the cognitive sciences have themselves turned to the computer to better understand human cognitive information management. Simply put, researchers have reason to believe that how individuals organize their "file folders and icons" on their computers is exactly how they organize information in their minds.

In comparison to our other senses, vision occupies the largest portion of our brain (Bear, Connors, & Paradiso, 2002). It's also responsible for just over two-thirds of the total nerve fibers within our central nervous system (Lawson, 2001). Because of evolution, only primates have the ability to distinguish between a multitude of colors, which may have resulted from a need to differentiate among various fruits and berries (Jacobs, 2005), and to understand the environment from a three-dimensional perspective (Haines, 2003). This includes the perception of depth, motion, and speed.

After our sensory organs gather stimuli, the brain interprets that information. As the brain continues to receive and organize the incoming information into patterns of understanding, we move beyond perception into the cognition phase. Within our brain we have cells that enable us to *make sense* of visual stimuli. These cells include:

- **Simple cells**, which respond to a line presented only at a certain angle or orientation
- **Complex cells**, which coordinate information from a group of simple cells
- **Hypercomplex cells**, which respond to complex stimulus features

Perception and Design

As one of the most influential psychological variables affecting design, perception can also be one of the most frustrating human attributes because of its highly subjective nature and myriad variables that affect interpretation. Most individuals will interpret an object or scene in the same manner, regardless of distance, angle, or brightness; however, selective attention allows them to focus on select stimuli and screen out others. Understanding how people perceive their environments is vital to the design process. The goal of a designer is to develop a design with as much perceptual consistency as possible. If the end product is not what the client had in mind, then it is likely that the designer did not understand how the client sees the world.

Simply stated, perception is the interpretation of incoming sensory information, and is influenced by a variety of factors (e.g., the type and level of the stimulus as well as a person's past experiences, level of attention to detail, readiness to respond, level of motivation, and current emotional state). When sensory organs gather stimuli, the brain interprets that information through the process we know as perception. As the brain continues to receive and organize the incoming information into patterns of understanding, we move beyond perception to cognition. In this manner, perception consists of various elements of sensation organized into patterns that result in cognition. The functional perspective of standard perceptual theory claims that certain patterns of features or cues give us direct and immediate perceptions of an environment; however, some experts believe that we perceive individual features, and others believe that we perceive patterns.

Process of Perception

As suggested above, a **perceptual set** is the sum of one's assumptions and beliefs that leads to a predetermined expectation with regard to the perception of certain objects or characteristics within particular contexts. This perceptual set can be so influential that people will sometimes develop **perceptual expectancies** (perceptions dependant upon their previous experiences) based entirely on a context (Kosslyn and Rosenberg, 2005). Many people who relocate from mainland regions to islands often encounter conflict between their perceptual expectations that island life is always fun and easy. However, the reality is that people have to work in order to pay their bills and that the money they make doesn't go as far because the cost of living tends to be higher. This is a contrast between perceptual expectations and reality.

Another component of perception is **perceptual consistency**, which is based on size, shape, brightness, and color. We tend to perceive objects as unchanging, regardless of changes within the sensory stimulation. To illustrate, objects that we have encountered are often perceived as the same size regardless of the distance from which they are viewed; they also appear as the same shape from whatever angle they are viewed. A building in the distance, for example, appears much smaller than it is in reality. Because we know how big a building is, we impose our cognitive reality onto the scene. This is one reason why many people find it difficult to do perspective drawings (Figure 4.2). Additionally, an object will retain a constant lightness even though its illumination varies, and familiar objects will retain their color despite changes in sensory information. These size, shape, brightness, and color constancies are important because they help us to understand better and relate to the world.

Some experts believe that we perceive individual features while others believe that we perceive patterns. One of the ways a designer can influence perception is by capitalizing on **selective attention**. This is an innate human process where we tend to focus on one attribute within a scene and neglect other less important aspects.

Designers can incorporate select stimuli to attract and prompt an individual to focus his/her attention upon a particular feature or aspect of the design. Whereas this method can be used to enhance the perception of a space, design professionals should strive to create perceptual consistency within environments because there are many ways in which people's perceptions differ. Perceptual consistency basically means that there are core aspects and attributes that distinguish, for

[**Figure 4.2**] Perspective drawing can be a challenge because we wrestle with what we know to be true versus what it is that we are truly seeing. In this child's drawing of a house, note the relative sizes of various objects. © 81a / Alamy

example, a church from a restaurant. If a church is designed with the perceptual set common to a restaurant, it will lose perceptual consistency and the person will have difficulty understanding and recalling details of the environment. The fact that the church looks like a restaurant may be intriguing enough for people to remember, but the more subtle details that create the perceptual set will likely be forgotten. To achieve perceptual consistency, the designer can use color, objects, and various design techniques; but these must be congruent with how a person understands the world, which is why culture and personality are important variables in the design process.

Perceptual Responses

How much and to what degree we direct our attention is an important concept in understanding perception. Research suggests that we select a relatively small, manageable portion of the available information on which to focus our attention. Further, we either focus on specific details or vast expanses within that portion of the environment, and we will more readily notice the comforts or discomforts within as well as any new feature or scene in an environment (Gifford, 2002). For example, in a waiting room we will either focus our attention on a single painting or see the overall design (theme) without particularly noticing the artwork. Along the same lines, a simplified view of a classic psychophysics principle, the Weber-Fechner law, states that as we **habituate** (get used to) a particular stimulus, the level of intensity of a new stimulus must be greater or proportionate to the current stimulus for the new to be perceived as different (Sommer, 1973). Without change in the environment, we run the risk of developing

environmental numbness and not taking particular notice of an environment until some feature grabs our attention (Gifford, 1976). Environmental numbness can be potentially dangerous because it can cause us to overlook problems or hazards. It can, however, be prevented by consciously redirecting our perceptions and cognitions within those environments that we cannot alter, as well as periodically updating or refreshing our personal spaces.

SUSTAINABILITY CONNECTION 4.1

A study was done in 1976 to measure environmental numbness in 34 university-level experimental psychology students as they were secretly observed while in their classroom. The researchers intentionally designed the classroom to be extremely uncomfortable and nearly impossible to move about. In some cases the researchers put only six inches between table and chair for someone to pass between. The students were observed for one week yielding to unnecessary barriers and squeezing past furniture in the course of getting their work done without so much as moving a table two inches (Gifford, 1976). To accept and not change or modify the placement of the furniture to make it more comfortable or even remotely complain that the classroom was inhospitable was discussed as a form of environmental numbness and perhaps even learned helplessness. As an interesting note, the following week the students were informed of their involvement in the study and were asked "why" they did not change their environment. Not one of the 34 students remembered there being a problem in the arrangement of the room.

Gibson provides a useful perspective: his holistic **ecological perception theory** states that instead of perceiving individual components of an environment, we organize all of those components into recognizable patterns. This suggests that much of our information is directly and immediately conveyed by perceptual patterns without higher-brain processing; that is, people notice and respond to meaning that already exists in an ecologically structured environment (Gibson, 1979). For example, through popular media we have come to regard the combination of graffiti, barred windows, and pawnbrokers' shops as being an unsafe environment. It is not the actual barred windows or graffiti in their singularity that convey the message that an environment is unsafe, but rather the aggregate of the scene compared with similar combinations that we have experienced in the past.

Attitude

Attitude is made up of a mental and neural state of readiness to respond, organized perspectives that have been established through experience, and feelings that exert a directive or dynamic influence on behavior (Allport, 1961). Our attitude or predisposition strongly influences our perception and tends to follow the values of an era and vice versa (Bell, Greene, Fisher, & Baum, 2001). For example, during the 1960s the general attitude toward design favored simplicity and synthetic materials, whereas present-day attitudes favor economical and easily assembled designs (Figures 4.3a and b). Again, many external factors such as culture and tradition, as well as internal factors such as personality, have a strong influence on attitude formation. For example, a person with a strong personality can override cultural attitudes that were instilled throughout his/her life. Hence, he/she is freer to appreciate the many differences encountered throughout life.

STIMULUS RESPONSE

Associations have no basis in biology; however, because of social learning, an association can evoke both a cognitive and biological response. For example, a person who has never been exposed to a gun is not likely to have a response to one pointed at his/her head. Conversely, a person who knows the destructive power of guns will likely experience the psychological response of panic followed by the physiological response of increased heart rate, high blood pressure, and accelerated breathing. Therefore, we can say that in most circumstances, stimulation without an association is nothing more than raw data. For many people, such as those who are blind, this process is limited and can lead to a lack of or compromised sensory detection. Studies from "feral children" have shown that our interpretation and understanding of raw data is a learned process. Victor (the wild child from France) and "Genie" (the girl who was locked in her room until age 13) seemed to be impervious to cold temperatures (Candland, 1995; Curtiss, 1977). The question in these cases is whether or not the children detected cold sensations or interpreted that sensation differently. Many children seem impervious to the cold, which is evidenced by their willingness to jump and play in cold water or stay outside for hours playing in the snow. As we grow older, our tolerances for the cold seem to decrease, and we are more hesitant to enter cold environments.

Human associations to experience follow three types of sensory responses (Malnar & Vodvarka, 2004):

1. **A response is dictated by prior knowledge**. When a toddler is familiar with a family dog, it will often point to other animals and say "dog" simply because the new animal shares similar characteristics such as walking on four legs, being furry, or having a tail. This demonstrates the comprehensive nature of our cognition. That is to say, when we try to make sense of something new, we first attempt to associate the new information with existing knowledge. From a design perspective,

[**Figures 4.3a and b**] Two chairs from two eras. What can we say about the attitudes and predispositions of people from the 1960s (*left*) versus people from 2010 (*right*) based on design choices such as color, shape, form, and texture? © a: ImageState / Alamy; b: © Fancy / Alamy

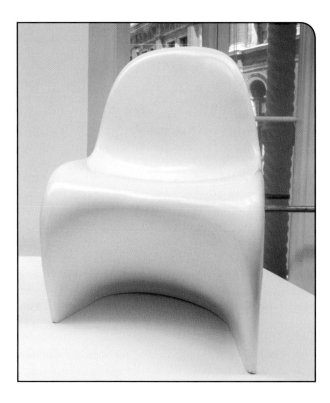

the use of a coffee table and dining table may be used interchangeably for a younger adult. As the person matures, the rules of society regarding the dining table as the only place to consume food becomes more firmly entrenched. As such, designers can expect that children and younger people will engage in multiple uses for furnishings that share similar characteristics whereas older adults will be more likely to assign specific uses to specific furnishings.

2. **A response to a stimulus is based on one's memory pertaining to a significant time or place**. An example of this could be the smell of cinnamon. Because cinnamon is a popular baking ingredient, particularly during the winter months, many Westerners have developed positive associations with this scent to winter holidays. In some parts of the world cinnamon is used very little or not at all. For these populations, the smell of cinnamon has little or no association and, therefore, does not evoke the same feelings (Chrea, et al., 2004). In design we can infuse certain scents within different environments to help facilitate positive associations. For example, the smell of coconut or piña colada could be used in a beach resort, the scent of roses and chocolate in a romantic bed and breakfast, or the aroma of cookies and coffee at a ski lodge.

3. **The stimulus causes a physiological reaction.** An example of this could be wincing away or retraction upon the infliction of pain. When a person inadvertently grabs the hot handle of a pan he/she will almost immediately jerk his/her hand away from the offending object. A physiological reaction could also result from a prior experience such as being locked in a small room. For the person who was once locked in a closet as a child, the mere sight of a small area such as an elevator could evoke physiological responses related to fear. A simple remedy in this situation would be to use illusions to make the space appear larger than it is in reality.

Along with stimulus associations, the human brain interprets and ranks stimulation according to prior knowledge and our interpretations of priority. To illustrate this point, few stimuli are more important than a speeding car in our immediate path. The ability to detect, process, and then prioritize a response to a multitude of stimulation simultaneously is crucial to survival. For instance, imagine if one were to take the time to swat away a fly sitting on his/her pant leg rather than jumping out of the path of the speeding car. But, because the speeding car poses the greater threat, the irritation of the fly becomes unimportant and may go unnoticed. From a design perspective, a person may screen out important stimuli because it gets deemed as unimportant. An example might be

[**Figure 4.4**] During emergencies people tend to focus on large macro cues as opposed to subtle cues. Having a door blend into the wall could thus create a dangerous situation during an emergency. © Fancy / Alamy

a doorway that blends into a wall (Figure 4.4). This doorway may go undetected during an emergency because the brain screens out the subtle visual cues indicating the door. During times of great distress, one of the physiological reactions we experience is the dilation of our pupils so that we can maximize our field of vision while the sensations detected by the remainder of our senses go unnoticed (Goldstein, 2002). If you have ever been in a fistfight, try to recall what it felt like during the actual time that the other person's fist hit your face, or try to recall the sounds that you heard during the fight. For most of us, we will screen out the immediate pain and sounds as we concentrate our attentions to the actual fight. This ability to ignore or screen out the less important stimuli during a crisis situation is what makes the brain such a wonderful and complex system, and that ability affects the way we perceive and interact within a complex environment.

Some sensations become so interwoven with a previous experience that the stimulus itself can result in a series of feelings and behaviors. Consider the sensations that you would experience during a horrific car accident. A week later, when you get released from the hospital, you notice that you feel anxious each time you get into a car; your muscles tense, palms become sweaty, pupils dilate, and heart rate increases. In this situation, you were in a car when the accident occurred; therefore, you associate the car with the negative experience. Perhaps the most famous example of a physical response being caused by an associative trigger is that of Pavlov's dog. In the 1890s, the Russian scientist Pavlov had been studying the effects of saliva on the digestive system. However, he noticed that his dogs would begin salivating before they were fed. After he noticed this phenomenon, he shifted the focus of his experiments to the physiological response observed within the dogs. He would sound a tone and then feed the dogs a treat. After a few repetitions, the sound of the tone alone would trigger a salivation response despite the fact that no food was present. It was not only the sound that triggered the response in the dogs. After using the same method, Pavlov triggered responses by turning on a light, touching the dogs' legs, and even showing them a picture of a circle (Myers, 2003). This response is not limited to dogs; it can also occur in humans. Imagine, for example, taking a bite out of a lemon wedge and having the tart juice flow into your mouth. The thought of the sour flavor alone often triggers salivation. This is called a **stimulus response**, which was coined by John Broadus Watson in his 1925 paper, *Psychology as the Behaviorist Sees It*. According to this theory, behavior can be explained as a response to a set of stimuli. Although much of the theory has fallen out of popularity, it continues to have a profound influence, particularly within design and the built environment and with regard to tradition and prestige.

The development of the stimulus response is thought to date back to our first ancestors who lived on the African plains. Humans, like all other animals, not only relied upon their senses, but also on the memories associated with certain sensations for survival (Rossano, 2003). The most primitive of our senses is the ability to smell, which is evidenced by the olfactory centers (smell) being one of the first areas to develop in a fetus. It is this sense that enables a newborn to detect its mother and easily locate her breast. Likewise, the olfactory centers are thought to have evolved concurrently with our ability to remember and feel emotion, which explains the direct connection between scent, memory, and emotion that continues within all of us. Scent, by all accounts, is more strongly associated with memory than any of our other senses and, as such, can trigger memories that we might have thought were long forgotten (The Sense of Smell Institute, 1996).

SUBLIMINAL PERCEPTION

Within the human body, we have specialized features that are designed to gather information about our environment and then transmit that information to our brains for processing. The brain can process about 400 billion bits of information per second, however, our conscious mind can only process about two thousands bits (Neddermeyer, 2005). This means that most of the information we receive is recorded and responded to at a subconscious level. The term *subliminal* implies that sensory information can be received and processed in the brain without conscious thought (Velmans, 1996). Essentially, perception occurs whenever a stimulus is presented *below* the threshold of awareness, and these stimuli influence our thoughts, feelings, or actions

(Kazdin, 2000). Conversely, when information occurs *above* the threshold of awareness, we call this **supraliminal**. The first uses of subliminal messages were in the form of whisper therapy. The therapist would whisper suggestions for behavior modification to the patient. Messages can be conveyed in a number of forms, ranging from audio to visual, and even olfactory. Whereas we often find subliminal messages in visual media such as print and television advertising, some messages are concealed in the physical features of design.

In the 1970s, Wilson Bryan Key wrote books such as *Subliminal Seduction* and *Media Sexploitation* in which he claimed subliminal sexual symbols or objects are often used to entice consumers to buy and use various products and services. Key claimed that because words (or images) were only perceived at an unconscious level, they can elicit sexual arousal, which would make a product more attractive. However, there is no evidence that embedded subliminal messages are effective for influencing consumers' decisions (Kazdin, 2000).

The topic of subliminal messages has been hotly debated for almost a century. Many contend that it is an unethical method of manipulation; others say that it is a perfectly acceptable medium. During the early 1970s, media coverage and discussion of subliminal messaging in advertising resulted in fear and paranoia among the general population. The concern was so great that the Federal Communications Commission (FCC) held hearings, which led the FCC to declare subliminal messaging in advertising to be "contrary to public interest." For example, some believe if they listen to certain music with subliminal messages promoting weight loss that their eating habits will change for the better. In instances such as this, researchers are unclear if it's the subliminal messaging that works, or if the person changed his/her eating habits simply because he/she was ready to make the commitment. Despite the numerous research studies focusing on whether or not subliminal messages directly affect human behaviors, the findings are largely subjective and difficult to interpret (Harris, Brown, & Werner, 1996). Morris and Maisto (2006) contend that the vast majority of research demonstrates little to no effect on human behaviors as a direct result of subliminal messages.

James Vicary, who was a market researcher, conducted an infamous study on subliminal messaging in 1957. He claimed that over a six-week period, 45,699 patrons at a movie theater in Fort Lee, New Jersey, were shown two advertising messages, "Eat Popcorn" and "Drink Coca-Cola," while watching the film *Picnic*. The messages were flashed for 3/1000 of a second once every five seconds. The messages' were so short that the audience never consciously perceived them. Vicary claimed that over a six-week period, sales of popcorn rose 57.7 percent and sales of Coca-Cola rose 18.1 percent. Despite the fact that Vicary never released the details of his study, his claims were often accepted as fact. However, in 1962 during an interview with *Advertising Age*, Vicary admitted that the original study was fabricated (Kazdin, 2000).

SUSTAINABILITY CONNECTION 4.2

A new social-political movement called ecofeminism contends there are similarities among the domination and abuse of nature, the devaluing and degradation of the feminine orientation, and global anthropocentric values. Simply put (yet admittedly over generalized), the premise of the ecofeminism movement is that the world and its resources are simultaneously seen as the gifts of *Mother Nature* and that by way of feminine association, it is not acceptable to assault, abuse, and essentially mistreat her for economic gain. This premise is compounded by attempting to change people's minds on the valuation and care of all things *non-human*.

In today's modern built environment, the use of sensory stimuli has been raised to an art form. Business and marketing professionals tantalize the public with erotic images that present a host of messages to the brain on both a conscious and unconscious level. The majority of subliminal messaging that we encounter are in visual form, and often symbolic, or plainly visible (ClassRoomTools, 2002). However, some messages can be so cleverly embedded that the message or image may not be easily discovered. Subliminal messages can occur within visual and auditory media. Auditory messages are most often found in music recordings. However, the messages aren't detectable to the conscious mind until the music in question is slowed down, sped up, or played in reverse. The process of including messages in music is called "backmasking," which can be either intentional or unintentional. Intentional backmasking occurs when a verbal message is recorded in reverse and then superimposed on an existing musical passage. People may not listen specifically to what is being heard; however, it is possible that we process the information. This is demonstrated by our ability to hear our names spoken even though we are engaged in deep concentration (Du Plessis, 2005). To illustrate this point, consider being engaged in a highly focused conversation with another person while dining at a restaurant. For the most part, we will screen out other stimuli as we focus on the conversation at hand. Then, through the numerous other conversations, the ambient noise from dishes and silverware, and our own intense concentration a phrase such as "both the president and vice president of the United States were assassinated" is spoken. Because of the important roles that these two people have in North American society our brain will shift focus from our intense conversation in order to hear the information that our brain deems as being more impor-

tant. Hence, even though humans are constantly bombarded with multiple stimuli, we do possess the superior ability to subconsciously prioritize and attend to important matters while filtering and screening out peripheral information that is regarded as unimportant (Du Plessis, 2005).

ILLUSIONS

Subliminal messages and illusions might be regarded as interchangeable. The difference is that subliminal messages are just that, messages being communicated. Illusions, on the other hand, are more about perceptual conflict. This occurs when the brain is tricked into believing one thing while reality is different. One way to create the illusion of youth and beauty is to lower the lighting levels and use lighting that casts a pink hue. Another way to create an illusion is to manipulate normative standards such as the width of a chair seat. A wider chair seat can lead a person to feel thinner whereas a narrower seat can make a person feel wider. We can see this kind of comparison to normative standards illustrated in phrases such as, "I feel so tall in this room," or "this chair makes me feel like child." By and large, an illusion is created by forcing a person to focus on a specific set of variables while ignoring others.

Overall, there are two basic types of illusions: physical illusions, such as the bent appearance of a stick when placed half way into water; and perceptual illusions, which occur because a stimulus contains misleading cues. An example of a perceptual illusion is the use of an oversized chair to make a room seem smaller. However, because illusions are a part of perception, the human element can affect them through:

1. *Motivation*. People often perceive what they want.
2. *Expectations*. People often perceive what they believe they ought to perceive.
3. *Cognitive style*. People often perceive what they have typically perceived in the past.
4. *Experience and culture*. People often misperceive what they have not perceived before.
5. *Personality*. People have different personalities, which often filter our perceptions.

Visual illusions occur when we use a variety of sensory cues to create perceptual experiences that do not actually exist. The context, or lack of context, can lead to an illusion. The brain is able to interpret stimuli by calling upon previous information. If there is no context or supporting information from which to understand a given stimulus, however, the brain will do its best to interpret the stimulus, which often leads to erroneous conclusions; hence, an illusion. A seemingly near-empty restaurant conveys the message that the food or service must not be good. Conversely, a busy restaurant is often regarded as a good place to eat. In both of these situations we assign value without context. A near empty restaurant on a Wednesday evening won't carry the same meaning as a near empty restaurant in the heart of a thriving community on a Saturday night. Context then enables us to sort through stimuli to help us make sense of it. Words are another example of how an illusion can be created through the auditory channels. The word "decay" if spelled phonetically it would appear as *d-e-e-k-a-y*. Likewise, the initials D.K. would be spelled phonetically as *d-e-e-k-a-y*. Thus the word "decay" spoken with no context could be interpreted as someone's initials (D.K.), or rotting material (decay). Incoming sensory stimuli therefore require context in order for us to interpret meaning successfully. However, there are some who are skilled with words and context manipulation and thus have the ability to generate a wide range of illusions.

Professionals within the design fields are unique from many other professions because we are often asked to create illusions such as making a room appear larger or brighter than it is in actuality. However, without an understanding of how illusions work, one can inadvertently create an illusion—thus, a potentially hazardous situation. For example, the illusion of movement can be caused by mixed signals effecting the **lateral inhibition** of vision. In essence, our eye and brain have special mechanisms for seeing edges clearly. These mechanisms allow us to see sharp boundaries between objects (e.g., a person or a building) and the background. Lateral inhibition is the mechanism that we use to sharpen edges. It works by the eye's light-sensitive receptors switching their neighboring receptors off. This makes an edge look more pronounced. This switching on and off can give the illusion of movement, which can be a fun

experience in a funhouse or science museum, but a devastating experience if accidentally created in a nursing home, on a flight of stairs, or in a hospital.

Illusions can also result from the way in which our brain obtains and sequences information. In one instance, we process stimuli from the bottom up; in other instances, we process information from the top down. Sometimes, these two processes happen concurrently. However, bottom up processing is initiated by stimulus input, and top down processing is guided by knowledge, expectations, or beliefs.

Illusions are a fundamental part of design and have been used throughout human history. For example, the ancient Greeks built their temples so that the roof was slanted in order to give the illusion that the temple was actually standing straight. They also designed the columns of their buildings to bulge so that they would look perfectly proportioned from a distance (Figure 4.5). We also use illusions to make items appear larger or smaller, more or less spacious, and more or less elegant. It is important for designers to understand and implement illusions in ways that enhance an environment and reduce the potential for accidental illusions that could potentially harm an occupant or end user.

ANTHROPOMORPHIZING

The term **anthropomorphizing** means to attribute human qualities to nonhuman items. Designers have often looked to the human form for inspiration and because of the high probability of the design to be perceived favorably by the general populace. This attraction to the human form begins

[**Figure 4.5**] The façade of Celsus Library in Ephesus shows a two-story gallery accentuated by curved and triangular pediments supported by a double-decker layer of paired columns. The center columns have larger capitals and rafters than those on the end. This gives the illusion that the columns are farther apart than they really are. The podium beneath the columns slopes slightly down at the edges to contribute to the illusion. © David Ball / Alamy

as early as infancy where studies have shown that infants are innately attracted to the symmetric, top-down shape of an inverted triangle (Simion, Valenza, Cassia, Turati, & Umiltà, 2002). Because of this symmetrical top-down preference, one can also begin to see the relevance of the Gestalt laws of symmetry, continuity, and proximity in action. Rather than seeing independent characteristics, we perceive the whole as an ecologically structured image and then ascribe meaning.

Anthropomorphism can be found in nearly every incarnation of design. In industrial design we see it applied to the front of cars; in interior design it is applied to the configuration of furnishings; and in architecture we see it in common building configurations. One reason why designers might be attracted to anthropomorphism is because they often identify the idea of form with the expression of art. Thus the practice of anthropomorphizing in various designs such as electrical outlets, lighting fixtures, and counter top configurations take on expressive qualities.

Why and to what degree we anthropomorphize is a subject of great debate within social sciences. Within art and design the issues of whether or not to anthropomorphize and whether or not anthropomorphizing diminishes art are constant topics of dispute. Many artists adopt the imperial view that anthropomorphizing diminishes the value of design and see it as a rudimentary or "beginner's" work. Developers and contractors, on the other hand, continue the practice because they know that anthropomorphized designs sell faster and have a broader market appeal.

There are a host of theories that attempt to explain our attractions to anthropomorphized design; these include familiarity, comfort, social, best-bet, object-subject interchangeability, phenomenological intersubjectivity, and command and control (DiSalvo & Gemperlem, 2003). The **familiarity theory** is based on a cognitive motivation to understand the world, but we must do it from a point of reference that we already know and understand (Guthrie, 1997). **Comfort theory** states that we find comfort in a world that is reminiscent of *us*. In essence this theory views humans as species centric; we want the world to be and look like us (Guthrie, 1997). The **best-bet theory** is about stacking the odds in our favor; the idea is that we find confidence in a world that is humanlike (Guthrie, 1997).

DiSalvo and Gemperlem (2003) developed **social theory** as a means to explain psychological discussions of attributing value and social consequence. The idea is that we can be neglectful and abusive to everything not human.

Through anthropomorphizing, we develop social bonds with nonhuman entities (objects and other life forms)—thus ensuring that we care and protect those things. Related to this theory is **object-subject interchangeability**. The premise of this theory suggests that people attribute mean-

ing to other people and objects in the construction, adaptation, and maintenance of the self. The concept of phenomenological intersubjectivity argues that anthropomorphism is a pragmatic response to objects in order to make sense of them (Jackson, 2002). **Command and control** theories state that anthropomorphism is used to explain relationships with (and exert authority over) objects. Its premise is that humans view themselves as superior to everything else on the planet (see Table 4.1).

The act of anthropomorphizing extends beyond human features to include human characteristics such as moral judgment (good or bad) and gender. Some designs are intended to look evil or bad whereas others are intended to look good and wholesome.

Evolutionary ideas suggest that males are compelled to protect women and children. To do this, men respond to rounder features, larger eyes, redder lips, and softer skin—

[**Table 4.1**] Theories to Explain Anthropomorphism

Theory	Reason Being
Familiarity	We use ourselves as a point of reference to understand objects and events.
Comfort	We derive security from being around objects and events that are reminiscent of other humans.
Best-Bet	In a world full of probabilities, we believe that events are in our favor when we deal with events and objects that are similar to ourselves.
Social	We act more socially responsible and caring to those items and objects that have similar attributes as humans.
Object-Subject Interchangeability	People attribute meaning to other people and objects in the construction, adaptation, and maintenance of who they perceive themselves to be.
Phenomenological Intersubjectivity	We require a pragmatic response to objects in order to make sense of them (a point of reference).
Command Control	We exert control over relationships between humans, objects, and events.

Adapted from: DiSalvo, C., and Gemperle, F. (2003). *From seduction to fulfillment: The uses of anthropomorphic form in design: Designing pleasurable products and interfaces.* Pittsburgh, PA: ACM Press.

features common to girls, boys, and women. Some experts theorize that feminine features symbolize weakness and vulnerability and thus require protection. Conversely, masculine features, which include squared brow and jaw lines, smaller eyes, rougher skin and less noticeable orifices, symbolize strength and protection.

Because of anthropomorphizing, we use these features to ascribe gender to objects such as automobiles and buildings (Figures 4.6a and b). Unfortunately, because we are still predominately a sexist society, those entities with strong masculine features tend to be regarded more favorably, while those imbued with feminine characteristics as being inferior. Consider for example the Porsche Boxster versus the Porsche Cayman. The Boxster has been dubbed a "chick" car while the Cayman is considered a "manly" car (MotorTrend, 2008). Now consider the price differential. A 2008 Porsche Boxster can range from $45,800 to $55,200 whereas the 2008 Porsche Cayman can cost between $59,100 to $69,900. This pricing differential can be seen throughout Western civilization where the "feminine characteristics" (e.g., jobs, such as nurse versus physician; objects, such as Porsche Boxster versus Cayman; animals, such as poodle versus pit bull) command less monetary value and social respect.

We also see masculine and feminine traits expressed in shapes. A restroom sign for example might take the shape of a triangle to represent the female body with broader hips and the upside down triangle to represent the male body with broader shoulders. We see these generalizations mimicked in such items as furniture and echoed throughout the interior design.

Within design our mission is to create designs that go beyond Gibson's ideas of cognitive affordances and develop designs that tantalize our cognitive, cultural, emotional, and social expectations. The anthropomorphic form accomplishes this task by imbuing objects with symbolism and expressionism, and commanding an emotional response (i.e., how does this room *feel?*) from us. However, because of cultural values and the ascription of gender to these objects, a provocative design may be underscored simply because it contains feminine features.

[**Figures 4.6a and b**] Notice the arches with more prominent windows in the (*left*) Chrysler Building. These feminine features are contrary to the smaller masculine and rectilinear lines of the (*above*) Empire State Building. a: © SERDAR / Alamy; b: © BL Images Ltd / Alamy

Another form of perception that is important to the design professional is Gestalt perception. Psychologists who follow Gestalt theories of perception study the ways in which people organize and select from the vast array of stimuli presented to them. In short, Gestalt theories contend that the whole is greater than the sum of its parts. In design we can see this theory played out in everyday life whether it is in a room or across a city skyline. What determines if the design of a room is successful is the way each of the individual pieces comes together (i.e., the wrong color sofa, improperly placed sofa, or wrong sofa style can ruin the design of the entire room).

The word *Gestalt* originates from Austria and Germany, and it refers to the way things are put together. Gestalt theory evolved from associative theory at the end of the nineteenth century as a way to explain perception (Kearsley, 1998). Max Wertheimer, Wolfgang Kohler, and Kurt Koffka are regarded as the founders of Gestalt theory, although they focused on different aspects of the theory. Wertheimer analyzed Gestalt theory in relation to problem solving and suggested that the parts of a problem should be examined as a whole and in relation to the situation (Kearsley, 1998). He also developed the idea of "Pragnanz" (the German word for "precision"), which states that when ideas, concepts, or sensory stimuli are understood as wholes, minimal energy is needed for understanding. Unlike Wertheimer, Koffka examined Gestalt theories as they related to applied and child psychology. This work led him to conclude that infants first experience the environment and situations around them as an organized whole. They look for relationships between stimuli and responses and then learn them as larger units rather than as simple stimulus-responses. This is important because it helps explain why environmental congruence and attention to adjacencies are so important.

Gestalt psychology contends that we are innately driven to experience the world around us in a regular, orderly, simplified, and symmetrical manner (Boeree, 1998–2004). Gestalt psychologists will reject a reductionist approach to perception, which is common to an associative theorist (one who analyzes a person's perception part by part and aggregates that information to draw a conclusion), because they assert that it is the interplay between the parts that creates perception (Bell et al., 2001). Therefore, to analyze how a subject perceives a bowl of fruit, a reductionist researcher would determine how the subject perceives each piece of fruit and the bowl separately, whereas a Gestalt researcher would analyze a subject's perception of the whole scene. Some researchers question Gestalt's role in perception

research (Goldstein, 1999), although it does explain why different people perceive a scene differently. For example, the average person tends to prefer symmetry because of the balance in appearance, whereas designers tend to prefer asymmetry because of the artistry. It also explains how design can be used as a means of creating illusions (e.g., making items look larger, more spacious, or more illuminated than they are in actuality; Bell et al., 2001).

Environmental perception is the human awareness and understanding of the environment in a general sense (Whyte, 1977). It is based on our experiences and psychological variables that are not part of our simple sensations, such as prior experiences and enculturation. Because of overlapping ideologies related to prior experiences and enculturation, Gestalt ideas and concepts have had the greatest influence on current design practices of any other school of thought (Lang, 1987). Because humans are primarily visual by nature (Gifford & Ng, 1983), perception is heavily influenced by what a person sees as well as by other cues originating from sound, smell, and touch. Therefore, perception as a whole is greater than the sum of its parts, which is the premise behind Gestalt theories. When viewing the "whole," the mind no longer sees the individual parts, but rather only the aggregate of the whole along with the thoughts and feelings associated with that whole. This is why you have likely heard people say phrases such as, "I don't like it. . . . I'm not sure why, but I simply don't like it."

Through the grouping of stimuli, Gestalt theorists can lead to the development of organized wholes, and thus produce different views. These organized wholes then translate into the Gestalt Laws of Perception, which include the laws of Proximity, Closure, Symmetry, Continuity, and Similarity.

Law of Proximity

The Law of Proximity states that objects or shapes that are close to one another form groups (Moore, 1993). Despite myriad differences in color, shape, and size, the individual will cluster the individual pieces to come up with a broader category. We can see this Gestalt law in the organization of a community where individual homes are clustered together into a neighborhood. How the individual components are grouped together will influence how they will be perceived.

As designers, we want to be careful of adjacencies because of the Law of Proximity. For example, artists often have their own unique style; but if work from two artists who share a similar styles are placed near each other in a gallery, the entire group of art will likely be attributed to a single artist by the novice observer. To counteract this assumption, similar pieces should be placed apart and with contrary styles in between them we can also use the law of proximity to our advantage when we want to cluster dissimilar items together to form a meaning. A sofa that differs from a chair that differs from an ottoman can be arranged together in a living room to create the "living room furniture."

Law of Closure

The Law of Closure states that we seek completeness in our perceptual fields. As such, our mind fills in missing pieces of information in order to close gaps. This occurs in communication where a person lacks sufficient information to draw correct conclusions, as well as other forms of sensory stimuli. In design this law has been used to enhance artistic appeal. Examples include wall prints that have been divided into multiple sections, or tile mosaics. We know that the separate pieces of the painting or mosaic are part of one larger image so we perceive that image even without its missing pieces.

Law of Symmetry

The Law of Symmetry states that humans seek balance. Without symmetry, the mind will seek out that which it deems as missing. As such, an asymmetrical image will force the individual to think about what he/she is seeing. This law has two important considerations for the designer. In one sense, we are likely to alter an image in our mind in order to create symmetry.

We in design can force the observer to take notice of another design attribute by using asymmetry. For example, rather than incorporate two similar end tables, a lounge section of a sofa, a potted plant, or a freestanding lamp can provide symmetry to a single end table. This asymmetry draws our attention to the two separate and independent pieces, but also allows us to perceive the scene as one image.

The concept of *figure-ground* is part of symmetry that outlines the ability of one aspect of the stimuli to stand apart from its background. In this relationship there is an opposite such as white on black, or a downbeat opposite to an up beat that is heard with music. Consider the image of the saxophone player or woman's face in Figure 3.6. One person might see the musician whereas another may see the face. According to the idea of *multistability* (or multistable perception) there are two ways from which to interpret incoming stimuli. In design, this might translate to what a person sees as his/her focal point.

Law of Continuity

The Law of Continuity states that people continue shapes beyond their ending points (Moore, 1993). This means that people will need good direction in order to comprehend a scene. Much of design stems from basic geometry, and thus the law of continuity can be used to enhance a design such as the case of Chicago's Twin Towers.

Law of Similarity

The Law of Similarity states that objects that appear to be similar will be grouped together in the mind of the individual. Similarities can range in shape, color, or size. Within the interior environment, a study and home office can been seen as interchangeable because of the law of similarity. However, in accordance with strict definitions, a study is a place where one would read, engage in self-improvement, or learn something of interest. A home office, on the other hand, would be a place where one would complete a task or perform duties associated with work

In many respects we want designs to create linkages to the larger context. A sprawling resort, for example, will want its customers to know that they can expect the same high quality service in a restaurant that shares the same property but is not attached to the hotel. Hence, the grouping together of dissimilar services in an individual's mind can be achieved through shared design features. Conversely, in large-scale housing developments, the law of similarity can wreak havoc on the person who is new to an area. Like being in a forest where all of the trees begin to look alike, a mass housing track with multiple homes of a similarity will easily lose their individuality.

Gestalt concepts are applicable not only to visual images but also to human cognition. If a person were to experience an event that does not quite make sense, for example, that person would tend to remember it in a way that has meaning, regardless of the accuracy of that meaning. Likewise, we usually do not recall a particular environment in isolation, but rather in relation to its surroundings. For example, the image of a red apple in a person's mind would likely be conceived in some sort of setting, such as on a tree, on a table, or in a bowl, but not in its singularity simply floating in blackness (see Figures 4.7a and b).

COGNITIVE INTERPRETATIONS

One of the many functions of the brain is to enable us to catalogue and make sense of the world. The understanding that derives from this process then leads to cognitive thought, which is based on **association** (Banich, 2004). To illustrate, consider that most people associate bathrooms with a high degree of privacy. Because of this association, it is unlikely that a person in a public bathroom stall would ask a stranger in the next stall for the time. This is because the sensations derived from the physical environment (sight, smell, sound, and touch) of a public bathroom have become associated with privacy, and we learned through social learning that we should not violate the other person's privacy.

Broadly defined, *cognition* is the process of thinking, knowing, or mentally processing information. It is the ability and process that encompass memory, attention, perception, action, problem solving, and mental imagery. However, because different functions of the brain occur in different hemispheres, conflict in cognitive abilities can occur. Figure 4.8 is an example where the right side of the brain tries to say the color but the left side wants to read the word. This leads to conflict in the brain, which can be exacerbated when one feels apprehensive or nervous.

In design we have to be careful not to promote cognitive conflict, which could occur, for example, with the development of wayfinding signs. A person could be parked on Level 3 Red, but the sign is written with a green font. Hence, a person might recall his/her parking level to be Level 3 Green.

Environmental cognition is a more specific concept that refers to how people understand, diagnose, and interact with the environment. Much of cognitive theory contends that solutions to problems are based on rules that are either not necessarily understood but promise a solution or are understood but do not guarantee a solution. Some researchers maintain that environmental cognition is simply the way in which we acquire, store, organize, and recall information about locations, distances, and arrangements.

Spatial cognition is a specialized thinking process that helps humans navigate through their environments. Most people do this by forming **cognitive maps,** pictorial and semantic (i.e., language) mental images of how places are arranged. As we move through these spaces, items within the spaces are often regarded as having volume and depth.

[**Figures 4.7a and b**] Many photographers understand the way the human mind interprets objects and scenes, which may explain why it is relatively easy to find Renzo Piano's work in the context of its surroundings, whereas much of Frank Gehry's work appears in isolation. In these two photos, notice how (*left*) Renzo Piano's work blends with its surroundings at his Tjibaou Cultural Centre in Noumea, New Caledonia, but (*below*) Gehry's Walt Disney Concert Hall conflicts with its surroundings in downtown Los Angeles. a: © Angelo Hornak / Alamy; b: © Spencer Grant / Alamy

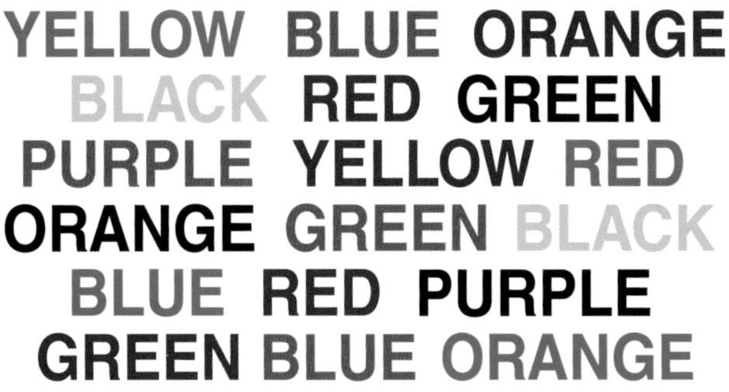

**YELLOW BLUE ORANGE
BLACK RED GREEN
PURPLE YELLOW RED
ORANGE GREEN BLACK
BLUE RED PURPLE
GREEN BLUE ORANGE**

[**Figure 4.8**] Try to say the color of the font for each word quickly (i.e., the first is green). Illustration by Precision Graphics

Gibson argues that as the observer moves through space, there is a flow of stimulation on the retinas that leads to a better understanding of the three-dimensional nature of our world. In other words, Gibson believes that we do not really have depth perception in the strictest sense of the word. Instead, our visual senses are stimulated by our movements through environments. This means that although we cannot see depth, we can understand the spatial relationships among things by the way they are arranged and how they change as we move through the environment.

It is debatable whether we see depth or simply understand the spatial relationship between our bodies and other objects, and the relationship between two or more bodies and multiple objects. However, as we proceed through environments, we do so by creating images in our minds. Some people find their way by identifying landmarks and others by using written directions, whereas those who are born sightless create cognitive maps based primarily on physical contact.

Nonspatial environmental cognition is a mental model of how we conceptualize ideas and concepts (e.g., categorizing local restaurants according to food, price, location, and so on). Critics (e.g., food, fashion, film, literary, design) capitalize on this form of cognition, which provides them with their means of categorizing information.

As a factor in the client–designer relationship, attitude consists of three psychological components: cognitive (thinking), affective (feeling), and behavioral (doing). These components are based on **cognitive truths,** beliefs held to be true about a particular instance, object, or situation. For example, if you know that ceramic tile floors feel cold to bare feet, this cognitive truth will generate an effective reaction to cold tile, which will lead to a behavioral response based on your cognitive truth. Therefore, a client to whom cold tile is unpleasant may forbid the use of tile anywhere in the home whereas a client who finds it refreshing may insist on tiling an entire bathroom suite.

Practical Applications for Designers

Use these resources, activities, and discussion questions to help you identify, synthesize, and retain this chapter's core information. These tools are designed to complement the resources you'll find in this book's companion Study Guide.

SUMMING IT UP

Perception involves the interpretation of sensations. Cognition is the way in which we think, learn, form memories, and make decisions. Perception is interpretation; understanding how people perceive their environments is vital to the design process. Interpretation is based on the perceiver's past experiences, level of attention to detail, readiness to respond, level of motivation, and current emotional state.

Sensation is our sensory organs gathering *stimuli*. Perception is the conversion of stimuli into *information*. Through the use of selective attention and perceptual consistency, designers can create and enhance spaces for users.

Humans possess the superior ability to subconsciously prioritize and attend to important matters while filtering and screening out peripheral information that is regarded as unimportant. Subliminal perception is messages being communicated to the human brain on a barely perceptible sensory threshold. Illusions, on the other hand, are more about perceptual conflict—tricking the eye. It is important for designers to understand and implement illusions in ways that enhance an environment and reduce the potential for accidental illusions that could harm an occupant.

An innate attraction to the human form begins as early as infancy; this is referred to as anthropomorphizing, meaning to attribute human qualities to nonhuman items. A host of theories attempt to explain our attractions to anthropomorphized design, which include familiarity, comfort, social, best-bet, object subject interchangeability, phenomenological intersubjectivity, and command and control.

Gestalt theories contend that the whole is greater than the sum of its parts. Gestalt Laws include the laws of Perception, Proximity, Closure, Continuity, and Similarity.

Architecture for Autism

Magda Mostafa, Ph.D.,
The American University in Cairo

In recent decades autism has reached, what many experts say are, epidemic numbers. Recent statistics vary depending on diagnostic techniques and criteria, but an estimated 1 in every 110 children fall within the range of Autism Spectrum Disorder (ASD). These incidences are regardless of sociocultural and economic aspects, with a 4:1 prevalence of males over females (ADDM, 2009). A developmental disorder with a range of degrees, from mild to severe, ASD is characterized by delayed speech and communication difficulties, challenges with social interaction, repetitive behavior, and apparent withdrawal and introversion. This final characteristic is what gave the disorder its name, from the Greek word *autos,* in 1943.

The key to designing for autism is to look at architecture as a sensory environment and a source of controllable stimulation, such as spatial organization, acoustics, texture, color, pattern, and lighting. Being a disorder intrinsically linked to sensory processing, autistic users can benefit from specific design concepts and standards developed through research over the past years using the "sensory design" model (Mostafa, M., 2008). These concepts and standards include:

Sensory Zoning

Possibly the most important aspect of designing for autism, sensory zoning requires a departure from traditional functional zoning toward an approach that organizes spaces in accordance with their required sensory stimulus levels. This approach categorizes spaces into areas of high stimulus, such as bathrooms, kitchens, and playgrounds, and low stimulus, such as bedrooms, offices, and study areas; then sensory zoning organizes them using proximity or segregation, accordingly.

Compartmentalization

Working on a single space (rather than an entire building or a particular level), compartmentalization allows single functional spaces to again be zoned according to their sensory stimulation level. Additionally, research has shown that by controlling and limiting the number of activities conducted, and accordingly sources of sensory stimulation found, in a single space, the more conducive that environment is for autistic users.

Spatial Sequencing and One-Way Circulation

By capitalizing on autistic users' adherence to routine, spaces can be organized using one-way circulation to correspond, as much as possible, to the routine organization of activities throughout a typical day. For example, classrooms can be organized according to the daily schedule in a school, or residential spaces organized according to the daily routines of getting ready for work and retiring at the end of the day, in a seamless sequence with no sensory distractions along the circulation path.

Use of Transition Zones

When spatial sequencing must be interrupted, as is inevitable, it is recommended that transition zones be used. Placed as nodes between zones of different sensory levels, i.e., from high stimulus to low stimulus zones, these neutral spaces allow for sensory readjustment and preparation for the change to a different level of stimulation.

Use of "Escape Spaces"

Research has shown that the simple provision of a small, sensory-neutral space, physically and visually separate from the space at hand, greatly improves various positive behavioral indicators in autistic individuals, such as attention span, response time, and general temperament. These spaces may be as simple as a partitioned corner with cushions and other desirable sensory objects, such as brushes, sand paper, mobiles, music, and lights. Such spaces provide a chance for autistic individuals to recalibrate themselves when they have been over-stimulated, allowing them to correct any sensory imbalance with the removal or addition of the necessary sensory stimulus.

Graduated Acoustical Treatment

One of the most influential aspects of the built environment on autistic behavior, acoustics should be appropriately managed and controlled. This is particularly the case in areas requiring low stimulus, such as classrooms, study areas, bedrooms, etc. Such treatments however, should not be universal to avoid the "greenhouse" effect of creating a completely acoustically controlled environment, outside of which the autistic user fails to function; therefore, acoustical treatment should be used at the minimum level required for each space, graduating from space to space.

Safety and Durability

Given the unique range of autistic behavior, which may include self injury, particular attention should be given to the durability and safety of various finishes, fixtures, and equipment.

Despite its overwhelming prevalence, and with the exception of a handful of research projects, autism has yet to be incorporated into the architectural design process through codes and standards to a level equivalent to that of other special needs. It is this researcher's hope and goal to strive toward remedying this and to continue to develop strategies for environments designed using the "sensory design" model, an approach which was first developed for autism but has shown to be applicable to us all, and to our need for more sensitive environments.

References

Autism and Developmental Disabilities Monitoring (ADDM) Network, Center for Disease Control (CDC). (2009). *Prevalence of autism spectrum disorders in multiple areas of the United States, 2004 and 2006.* Retrieved from http://www.cdc.gov/ncbddd/autism/states/ADDMCommunityReport2009.pdf

Mostafa, M. (2006). *An architecture for autism—A new dimension in school design.* A paper presented and published in the conference proceedings of the Second World Autism Congress, Cape Town, South Africa, October/November 2006.

Mostafa, M. (2006, Autumn). Enabling architecture. *Communication Magazine* [National Autistic Society, UK], *40*(3).

Mostafa, M. (2006). *Let them be heard: Appropriate acoustics for autism—Special needs school design.* A paper presented and published in conference proceedings of the ArchCairo International Conference "Appropriating Architecture and Taming Urbanism in the Decades of Transformation." Cairo, 2006.

Mostafa, M. (2008). An architecture for autism: Concepts of design intervention for the autistic user. *International Journal of Architectural Research, 2*(1), 189–211. Retrieved from http://archnet.org/gws/IJAR/8821/

Mostafa, M. (2010). Housing adaptation for adults with autistic spectrum disorder. *Open House International, 35*(1).

Additional information for architects can be found at the National Autistic Society, UK. http://www.autism.org.uk/nas/jsp/polopoly.jsp?d=1562 and http://www.autism.org.uk/nas/jsp/polopoly.jsp?d=2171

KEY TERMS

- **anthropomorphizing**
- **association**
- **attitude**
- **best-bet theory**
- **cognition**
- **cognitive map**
- **cognitive truth**
- **comfort theory**
- **command and control**
- **complex cells**
- **ecological perception theory**
- **environmental cognition**
- **environmental numbness**
- **environmental perception**
- **familiarity theory**
- **habituate**
- **hypercomplex cells**
- **lateral inhibition**
- **nonspatial environmental cognition**
- **object-subject interchangeability**
- **perception**
- **perceptual consistency**
- **perceptual expectancies**
- **perceptual set**
- **selective attention**
- **sensation**
- **simple cells**
- **social theory**
- **spatial cognition**
- **stimulus response**
- **supraliminal**

WEB LINKS

Anthropomorphism.org (Carnegie Mellon University) (www.anthropomorphism.org)

Ecofem.com (www.ecofem.org)

Encyclopedia of Psychology, for additional links on sensation and perception (http://www.psychology.org/links/Environment_Behavior_Relationships/Sensation_and_Perception)

Graphic examples of Gestalt principles, scroll down to "G" for Gestalt (http://graphicdesign.spokanefalls.edu/tutorials)

International Journal of Aromatherapy (www.elsevier.com)

Rensselaer Polytechnic Institute, for examples of perceptual illusions (www.cogworks.cogsci.rpi.edu/cogpsy/illusions.html)

Resources for Personal Information Management (http://pim.ischool.washington.edu/)

Sensing Architecture, for articles on the application of Gestalt principles in the built environment (http://www.sensingarchitecture.com/index.php?s=Gestalt)

STUDIO ACTIVITY 4.1

Subliminal Design

Design Problem Statement
You have been hired to design a high school gymnasium for a local private school. The funding is coming from the Coca-Cola Company, and they are insistent that the gymnasium should subliminally sell their product. You have been chosen from a number of designers to create a design that does not contain the Coca-Cola name, but represents the company in as many ways as possible. You have been given a program list of the needs by the school; however your true client is Coca-Cola.

Directions
Step One: Create a diagrammatic map representing the Coca-Cola Company's marketing strategies and what they represent without using words (i.e., use graphics, colors, and images). Keep in mind the demographic that you are designing for will not recognize the marketing history; therefore keep your research to within the last five to ten years.

Step Two: After the completion of your diagram, begin to design the gymnasium for full programmatic functionality, however, subtly use the Coca-Cola forms, graphics, and images to guide you in creating circulation and form.

Step Three: Create three renderings of your design, a full set of design drawings, and build a 3/16" scale model illustrating the gymnasium.

Use your diagram to help guide you in material choices and textures. Use as many marketing schemes as possible without using the Coca-Cola name or overtly selling the company in your design (i.e., the gym should not be 100 percent "Coca-Cola" red!).

Added Optional Step: As a fun, nonscientific study, present your drawings to a neighborhood group or some other group not associated with this class. When you do this, place a cooler of Pepsi next to a cooler of Coca-Cola and look to see if your design inspired people to select Coke over Pepsi.

Anthropomorphizing

Design Problem Statement
To demonstrate the numerous ways that anthropomorphizing is used throughout art and design.

Tools
- Scissors
- Glue or tape
- Poster board
- A few art and design magazines

Directions
Step One: Flip through the pages of the magazines and identify the various incarnations of the two-eyes, one-nose triangulation. Cut out these images and place them onto the poster board to form a collage.

Step Two: When completed, display your poster somewhere in your studio space. Then walk around and look at other people's posters and identify the most unique incarnations of anthropomorphizing.

Step Three: Discuss how often you found anthropomorphizing and whether you believe it compromises the design process or enhances it.

Deliverable
One 3 x 5 collage of anthropomorphizing used within art and design.

DISCUSSION QUESTIONS

1. Find examples where *perception* could be used to influence a decision in the design process of site selection to trim selection. How can you use this information to prepare a client to consider a broader range of options?

2. Consider *phenomenology* in the interview process of a client. Your intent is to make the space meaningful to them. What questions would you ask your client, so that your design better suits their needs?

3. Observe the general design of art galleries. What *sensory* design perspectives do you think would be implemented in the design? And explain why you think they would be pertinent applications?

4. Evaluate the human built environment and the effects of a successful design, which allow for the development of humanity to flourish in it. Consider how a right-brained person would intend to design the world as opposed to a left-brained person. Explain the importance of utilizing a designer who can incorporate a balanced approach in design in order to create the feeling of an ultimate built environment.

5. Explain the importance of including people in renderings of the built environment. How do you think it benefits the understanding of the overall design, or do you think it is not necessarily important?

LEARNING ACTIVITIES

1. Discuss ways *perception* can be influenced and consider them in relation to the design process, from site selection to trim selection. How can you prepare clients to consider a broader range of options?

2. Devise a scenario in which sensation, perception, memory, and cognition all take place. Create your example in a way that could potentially happen in real life. Be descriptive.

3. Using the Gestalt Laws of Perception, create your own illustrations for each law.

4. Discuss ways in which subliminal messaging could be used in the design of buildings and homes to positively influence their occupants environments?

5. Discuss possible benefits and drawbacks of using illusions in the design of a public space. How could the use of illusions make a positive impact in the design? And explain the importance of understanding the effects of illusions before applying them into the design.

05 The Human Condition

In sex we have the source of man's true connection with the cosmos and of his servile dependence. The categories of sex, male and female, are cosmic categories, not merely anthropological categories.

—Nicolai A. Berdyaev

The human experience in relation to the built environment is an evolving process that began with early hunter-gatherers adapting to the environments they inhabited. Much of these adaptive qualities were divided according to gender and gender roles. The general theory is that ancient males were expected to hunt and defend the village while women were expected to gather food and care for the children. These respective roles led to differing perspectives on similar experiences. Many argue that within our genetic code lay the basis for some of our basic preferences. One of these preferences is our attraction to the human face. We superimpose common masculine and feminine attributes onto design.

Our perceptions are also influenced by our individual personalities, which serve to mitigate absolute adherence to gender norms. However, when we consider masculine and feminine characteristics, we must do so in terms of *personality* and not genitalia. Many females are competitive and action-oriented (conventionally thought of as masculine characteristics) and many males are collaborative and nurturing (conventionally thought of as feminine characteristics). Through a better understanding of an individual's predispositions, we can better design for that person.

Memory is the process of acquiring information, retaining that information, and then retrieving that information at a later time. To get a basic idea of how sensation, perception, memory, and cognition work, consider the scenario portrayed in Box 5.1, "Sensations, Perception, Memory, and Cognition."

BOX 5.1 SENSATION, PERCEPTION, MEMORY, AND COGNITION

A realtor has an old, abandoned listing that he is trying desperately to sell. He takes all of his clients by this house. With the exception of lighting, temperature, and a few random sounds, each person the realtor takes to the house will be exposed to same sensory stimuli. How each person will interpret and catalog those sensations will be fairly unique. Some people may view the house as being grotesque or even haunted; some may be excited by the challenge of renovation; and still others may disregard the structure completely and concentrate on the land. Such judgments are based on a person's perceptions, which have been influenced by past memories, which then lead to a cognitive reaction.

[**Box Figure 5.1**] Photographers often capture images of despair, as if these images epitomize the human condition. Likewise, many romanticize notions of living in and rehabilitating homes that have been neglected for many years. In this way, beauty is tied to the meaning the individual attributes to the image. © Version One / Alamy

EVOLUTION AND GENDER

With human evolution, we have come to rely on our sense of vision more than any other sense (Park, 1999). The dominance of this sensory organ differs from that of other mammals such as dogs and dolphins. Dogs rely heavily on their sense of smell and thus have the ability to discern a great deal from an environment simply by detecting the different aromas. Dolphins rely predominantly on their ability to detect sound. Although humans are not able to differentiate between a wide variety of smells as dogs have the ability to do, nor can we discern between the wide varieties of sounds like dolphins, we can see in color and, like all primates, we see in three dimensions (Park, 1999). To illustrate this point,

consider that the human visual processing centers consume approximately one third of our entire brain (Ortiz, 2004).

With the evolution of humans, some of our senses have become less important and have therefore become less acute. In some cases, the brain's interpretation of specific sensations is detected and catalogued almost exclusively on a subconscious level. Scent is one of these senses. Consider the smell of pheromones. In other terrestrial mammals, the aroma derived from pheromones is so consuming that the behaviors of these animals change dramatically. In humans, we no longer consciously detect the scent of pheromones; instead they affect us on a subconscious or instinctual level. Many studies have shown that men and women evaluate each other by scent. Men are attracted to scents that indicate fertility; women are attracted to scents that indicate a robust immune system (Rossano, 2003). Because modern humans are no longer as dependent on all our senses equally, people with deficiencies in one or more of their sensations, such as blindness or deafness, are able to function relatively effectively through the heightened development of their remaining senses. Likewise, because of the profound ability of our sensations to influence our behaviors, many researchers and artists alike strive to influence human perception through a subtle triggering of one or more of our senses. The fragrance industry, for example, attempts to develop scents that incite positive responses to the person wearing a particular aroma.

Gender Roles

Males are generally seen as the stronger sex because they tend to have more muscle mass than women. In ancient hunter-gatherer societies, males were expected to hunt animals whereas women gathered edible vegetation (e.g., fruits, vegetables, roots). Primitive men were often regarded as aggressive, competitive hunter-warriors whose primary gender role was to kill animals for food and protect the community. In these groups, males formed close relationships only as groups of invaders to conquer others or as teams of hunter-gatherers to bring in a potential meal. In the safety of their village they often competed among themselves for the choicest cuts of meat, the enemies' weapons, or the most desirable females.

Hunting usually took place on open savannahs and plains with expansive views and few physical obstacles to navigate or obstruct weapons in flight; males traveled wide ranges and dispersed to strategic positions where they silently waited in isolation or in pairs. Because their primary role was to kill, they had to be able to screen out distracting stimuli—after all, when chasing down a meal or an enemy, they needed to be highly focused on the task at hand. This may explain the results of a study in which men outperformed women when doing mental arithmetic (a strategy-based activity) under noisy conditions (Gulian & Thomas, 1986). Males were simply better at screening (i.e., ignoring) distracting sounds while engaged in a task.

Primitive women were seen as breeder-nurturers who worked with and cared for others close to home. The **ethic of care theory** evolved from this role. It claims that it is in a women's nature to focus on sustaining relationships and taking care of others' needs. It is supposed that primitive females had to be able to manage a myriad of tasks within limited areas, which may explain why modern females tend to approach high-density settings more cooperatively than males (Karlin, Epstein, & Aiello, 1978; Taylor, 1988). They also are more tolerant to other people, mainly children, invading their personal space.

Women formed small groups to forage for vegetation within forests and jungles; these dense and complex environments limited peripheral and distance views, and hence promoted verbal communication (which additionally served to deter potential predators). Females had to multitask because they were responsible for childbearing and nurturing (offspring were usually either in, on, or near the mother's body); maintaining cooking fires, providing shelter, clothing, and healthcare; and performing other duties shared with other females in the community.

Gender and Perception

For whatever reason, modern men and women continue to perceive, interpret, and describe their environments differently. This may be because the human psyche has evolved more slowly than human technology; therefore, both sexes continue, at least to some extent, to behave and regard the environment according to primal instincts. Although current research is inconsistent with regard to gender differences in high-density conditions, traditional research suggests that males and females react as they do because socialization teaches females to be affiliative (i.e., able to connect with others, socially cohesive) and males to be competitive (Crawford & Unger, 2000; Deaux & LaFrance, 1998) and independent. Socialization of gender roles, however, is still based on the theoretical primary gender roles of early humans.

Within the environmental context, we can see that females tend to prefer collaboration and avoid direct competition (Chapman, 2000; Fiore, 1999; Rosser, 1985; Sanders, Koch, & Urso, 1997). This is not to say that females do not engage in indirect competition. They also tend to enjoy activities that support and facilitate socially relevant communication (Sanders, Koch, & Urso, 1997). Unlike men who prefer low spatial density, females tend to be adversely affected by the absence of multiple people (Freedman, Levy, Buchanan, & Price, 1972). This may help to explain many women's will-

ingness to assist a person in need while in complex settings; males tend only to offer assistance in simple settings (Amato, 1981). Another example is women's willingness to sit closer to people who look either happy or sad; again, males tend to respond only to those who look happy.

Males tend to avoid situations that promote "debate" and/or "discussion" (Welty & Puck, 2001). This may be a result of males being result- and action-oriented. Hence, discussions and debate may be interpreted as a call to action. Males also require more personal space and consistently claim larger territories than do women. This may be one reason why women seem to cope with high-density situations and perceptions of crowding better than men (Aiello, Epstein, & Karlin, 1975). Interestingly, this need for more personal space can be seen as early as five years old (Lomranz, Shapiro, Choresk, & Gilat, 1975), and it is also more apparent when males are in a room with low ceilings (Savinar, 1975).

In much of society there are professions and environments that continue to be dominated by one gender. Masculinity and femininity are often associated with genitalia; but the reality is that a male might have strong feminine personality characteristics, and the same holds true for women having strong masculine traits. Hence, when designing for a specific gender orientation such as a firehouse or a beauty salon, the designer must move beyond simple thoughts regarding gender and genitals and consider gender in terms of a personality predisposition. (Personality will be discussed later in this chapter.)

The terms masculinity and femininity are also used to describe culture values in terms of assertiveness or socially supportive actions.

CULTURAL CONNECTION 5.1

To get a better idea of how masculinity and femininity are used as a descriptor, consider Japanese and Latin American preferences for values of assertiveness, task-orientation, and achievement. There tend to be rigid gender roles in these cultures (Hofstede, 2001). Conversely, the cultures of Scandinavia, Thailand, and Portugal value cooperation and relationship solidarity, which are by Western standards feminine traits. Hence, associations with gender vary greatly across cultures, which mean traits considered masculine in one culture might be considered feminine in another (Hofstede, 2001).

Gender and Space

The degree to which instinct, genetic memory, or socialization is responsible for gender behaviors, especially at an early age, is open for debate. In a study of kindergartners and first graders, boys preferred simpler and larger settings to girls (Cohen & Trostle, 1990). As boys mature, their personal space requirements appear to increase more than girls', and these space requirements continue to grow until early adulthood, when they stabilize (Hayduk, 1985). A study of males and females, from ages 5 to 18 years, suggested that older boys used larger interpersonal distances more than older girls; but among the younger children, there were no gender-based personal space differentials (Bell, Greene, Fisher, & Baum, 2001). However, other researchers found that by the age of four, boys will keep greater distances from other boys than from girls, and the girls will not change their distances from other girls (Goldstein, 2002; Figure 5.1).

Numerous studies have shown that, generally, pairs of males maintain greater interpersonal distance than female pairs, and male–female pairs maintain the least distance; but this depends on both the social relationship and the culture (e.g., males in Latino cultures maintain much less interpersonal distance than Northern European males; Tannis & Dabbs, 1975). In general, women seem to feel more comfortable at closer distances than men (Ashton, Shaw, & Worsham, 1980). This confirms several studies that have shown a decrease in male comfort levels when their interpersonal distances shrink, whereas the comfort level of women declines when interpersonal distances increase (Fehrman, 1987; Smith, 2003; Valdez & Mehrabian, 1994). However, Vrugt & Kerkstra (1984) noted that when strangers interact, the interpersonal distance between women is smaller than it is for a woman and a man.

[**Figure 5.1**] Notice how the males are fairly evenly dispersed and do not sit close to each other, whereas the females have no issue sitting next to each other, or sitting next to a male. © Fancy / Alamy

In general, women tend to stand closer than men when talking among friends. Understanding these gender differences can help us design spaces where everyone is able to behave appropriately in social situations that include both men and women as well as boys and girls. Interestingly, an experiment of men and women in an elevator revealed that men prefer to stand next to strangers who do not make eye contact despite the presence or absence of a smile. Women, on the other hand, preferred to approach someone who made eye contact and smiled (Vrugt & Kerkstra 1984). People on elevators try to minimize personal space violation by minimizing their body movements, avoiding eye contact and refraining from loud conversations.

These primal gender roles may help to explain why men respond with more aggression than women in long-term, high-density situations, such as incarceration. For example, when a Mississippi prison experienced a 30-percent reduction in the inmate population, inmate physical assaults decreased by about 60 percent; and later, when the population increased by 19 percent, assaults increased by 36 percent (Cox, Paulus, & McCain, 1984).

PERSONALITY

The personality traits that we possess are unique attributes that generally define who we are. Scientists continue to debate the importance of nature versus nurture and whether personality can be affected by environmental influences that a person encounters as he/she develops into an adult. In one study of twins, researchers found that personality traits seem to be innate (exhibited throughout the life span; Harris, 1998). Other researchers contend that various environmental factors influence personality by shaping skills, values, attitudes, and identities. This suggests that the opportunities presented by different environments predict, to some degree, the manifestation of personality traits (McCrae & Costa, 1999). For example, a person born with an outgoing, social personality can have that trait suppressed by long-term exposure to a crowded environment. How and why certain personality traits do or do not manifest is important insofar as certain traits may be supported or discouraged through environmental modification.

Personality and Design

From a design perspective, we can see that personality traits are often expressed through the quantity and types of artifacts found within a built environment as well as the overall environmental style; the assumption is that individuals develop environments that reflect and reinforce who they perceive themselves to be (Gosling et al., 2003). In many respects, the first cues that an outsider can gain about a person's emotions, feelings, and moods are the color choices they select to adorn themselves or their personal spaces. Consider a person who selects bright contrasting colors for their home as opposed to muted neutrals. Overall, humans strive to create environments that best satisfy their personality and emotional needs, whether or not that environment is supportive of other people within that space. Few of us realize that through the creation of a particular environment—a casual one versus a highly structured one, for example—we shape our offspring's personalities and futures through the symbolic order or disorder that we create.

Designers who strive to understand their clients' personalities are more likely to engage in communication, which will enable them to develop the most appropriate designs and thus better meet their clients' needs. There are many methods to determine personality traits. Two of the most well-known are the Big Five Inventory and the Myers-Briggs Type Indicator.

The Big Five Inventory

The **Big Five Inventory (BFI)** was developed by Oliver John, who discovered through statistical analyses how different personality traits can be linked together to define certain human qualities. The Big Five was a result of analyses of traits that tend to co-occur in the population (John & Srivastava, 1999). For example, *affectionate* and *kind* are both traits associated with being agreeable, but a person can be kind without being affectionate. Because each human is unique, variations occur; however, statistical studies show that most people who are kind are also affectionate, explaining the reason for the broader factor of "agreeable." The key to understanding the Big Five dimensions is to recognize that they are purposely broad and that each dimension consists of more specific traits. Here are the BFI broad dimensions (John & Srivastava, 1999).

- *Extraversion* (sometimes called *surgency*) encompasses specific traits such as talkativeness, energy, and assertiveness.
- *Agreeableness* includes traits such as sympathy, kindness, and affection.
- *Conscientiousness* includes being organized, thorough, and able to make plans.
- *Neuroticism* (sometimes reversed and called *emotional stability*) is characterized by traits such as tension, moodiness, and anxiety.
- *Openness to new experiences* (sometimes called *intellect* or *culture*) includes having wide interests and being imaginative and insightful.

The Myers-Briggs Type Indicator

Katharine Briggs and Isabel Briggs Myers developed the **Myers-Briggs Type Indicator** (**MBTI**) by expanding on personality types developed by Carl Jung (a pioneering psychologist) to include a judging–perceiving function. The resulting 4 primary personality dichotomies converge to create 16 possible personality profiles. Each of the four dichotomies—introvert–extrovert, sensory–intuitive, judger–perceiver, and thinker–feeler—are identified, which is how they end up with personality profiles such as INTP (i.e., introvert–intuitive–thinker–perceiver), ENFJ (i.e., extrovert–intuitive–feeler–judger), and so on. However, for our purposes, we can scale each of the categories according to extremes. Using a 0–10 scale for the introvert–extrovert component, clients are asked where they would rank themselves; a self-ranking of seven, for example, would indicate a person who is more extroverted than introverted.

Introvert–Extravert The personality component of Introvert–Extravert relates to a person being either outgoing or reserved. People with extroverted personalities tend to have high energy levels, prefer to multitask, and like to be around other people. They also tend to talk more than listen, act before thinking, and can be easily distracted. Those with introverted personalities tend to be quiet thinkers, prefer being in a supportive role where attention is not focused on them, and appear to be reserved. They enjoy time alone, prefer to focus on one task at a time, and possess great capacity for concentration.

People with extroverted personalities tend to prefer physical closeness to others and often use open furniture arrangements, whereas those with introverted personalities tend to use closed arrangements (and chairs as opposed to sofas) that establish distances appropriate to their comfort zones. Extroverts like to be near other people and do not allow furniture to separate them, whereas introverts prefer the safety of separation. In larger social gatherings, extroverts prefer group seating that facilitates greater contact and interaction, and introverts appreciate single seats and unobstructed paths that allow free mobility and easy escape.

Sensory–Intuitive People who are sensors usually focus on the details rather than the big picture. They embrace practicality, are aware of the finer points and subtleties, remember significant attributes and comments, and view life as a step-by-step process; they are pragmatic, live in the here and now, and tend to trust actual experience. Intuitive people are more creative in their thought processes, prefer their environments to be more complicated, are inventive in their ideas, and consider future implications. They focus on big-picture potential, trust their instincts, and enjoy learning.

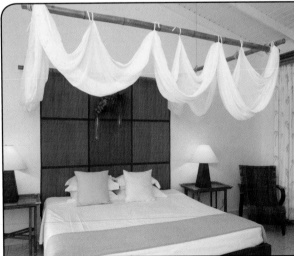

[**Figures 5.2a and b**] Which of these environments do you find to be more representative of how you see yourself? Note the more traditional design that contains authentic pieces that all serve a function on the sensory side. In contrast, the intuitive side is more whimsical and contains elements that serve no function other than fun. *top*: © Arco Images GmbH / Alamy; *bottom*: © Michael Ventura / Alamy

Sensing clients will likely scrutinize the functional aspects of design, be more concerned with budget issues, and probably want a cost-benefit analysis of proposed designs. Intuitive clients will likely desire more complex designs, embrace the creative exploration of ideas and concepts, and view designs in their entirety as opposed to their individual components (see Figures 5.2a and b).

Thinker–Feeler Thinkers tend to be reserved, draw their conclusions from objective facts, and respond best to rational nonarbitrary arguments; they are usually honest and direct, value honesty and fairness, and are motivated by end results. Thinkers are also inclined to be business oriented in that they view design in terms of cost-benefit ratios. They also see more flaws and often argue or debate issues. Feelers, on the contrary, often make decisions based on personal values and how they feel at the time; they appear to be warm and friendly and tend to be diplomatic and tactful. Feelers tend to value harmony, take issues personally, and avoid conflict.

Clients who rank high in either disposition can be somewhat challenging. Thinkers will demand extensive research and will question a designer's decisions whereas feelers will be less aggressive because they respect and value the professional and will seek to avoid friction. Feelers tend to make emotional rather than carefully considered decisions, and thus will rely heavily on a designer's ability to ask the right questions and read between the lines (see Figures 5.3a and b).

Judger–Perceiver Judgers are inclined to be more serious and conventional in their preferred design styles. Such people tend not to mix work with social activities. They expect dedication and will not respond well to delays; they make decisions fairly easily but also value rules and order over creativity. Perceivers tend to be more playful and unconventional. They value the freedom of spontaneity and like to keep their options open; therefore, they usually have difficulty making and adhering to decisions. They can be oblivious to time and schedules and value creativity, especially when it goes against the norm.

Judgers can pose a challenge for design professionals because not only do they tend to watch deadlines, hold designers to their projected schedules, and have little tolerance for delays, but also they have a very traditional or conventional style from which they don't usually deviate. They often regard designers and planners as the hired help and will avoid casual social interaction. Perceivers, conversely, tend to embrace creativity and innovation in the design process and desire more social interaction. However, explicit communication is crucial; if unchecked they can accumulate numerous change orders and will ultimately feel betrayed by the cost increases resulting from those orders (see Figures 5.4a and b).

[**Figures 5.3a and b**] Which of the two photos better exemplifies your ideal environment? The thinker views design from practicality and is aware of its importance in making an impression. However, he or she is not likely to justify spending a lot, so the design must be up-to-date, but still affordable and functional for daily activities. Conversely the feeler will have many items that have significant meaning. For this person, design is not so much about a beautiful image but rather the meaning behind the various artifacts. *below*: © Built images / Alamy; *right*: © Ashley Morrison / Alamy

[**Figures 5.4a and b**] Which of the two closets better reflects your bedroom closet? Judgers are often perfectionists and prefer absolute order all of the time. Perceivers tend to be more organic and allow situations and events to evolve without trying to control them. *above*: © paolo negri / Alamy; *right*: © UpperCut Images / Alamy

[Table 5.1] Components of Personality and Associated Design Preference

Personality Type	Personality Trait	Design Preferences
Introvert (I)	Guarded	Desires safe haven or privacy. Prefers closed furniture arrangements.
Extrovert (E)	Social	Desires interaction or stimulation. Prefers open furniture arrangements.
Sensory (S)	Detail-oriented	Embraces practicality. Will scrutinize details and functionality of design.
Intuitive (N)	Instinctual	Prefers complex creative environments. Is guided by gut feelings.
Thinker (T)	Rational	Views design in terms of cost-benefit ratio and demands extensive research.
Feeler (F)	Harmonious	Values harmony, respects professionals, but will rely heavily on designer's ability to ask the right questions and read between the lines.
Judger (J)	Demanding	Has high expectations and conventional design preferences.
Perceiver (P)	Unconventional	Values uniqueness and innovation but may have difficulty making and sticking with decisions.

Table 5.1 summarizes design preferences according to the primary components of personality. It is important to note however, that personality is not an all or nothing trait. As humans, our personalities vary in degrees as well as evolve with age. Rarely are people always to one extreme or the other within these personality traits. Instead, we all move throughout the spectrum. Should a person identify with the number four on the judger perceiver scale it is likely that he/she will want to feel in control of the design and its progression. However, it is important not to stereotype a person with these personality traits, but rather to use the traits as a guide to better interact with and serve the client.

Designing for Screeners Versus Nonscreeners

Our ability to screen out unwanted environmental stimuli (e.g., noise, glare, odor) depends on how we respond to various distractions that arrive in different patterns. People who are less affected by a stimulus are considered to possess greater screening abilities, whereas those who are bothered or annoyed by a stimulus are thought to be nonscreeners. Nonscreeners are inclined to be much more sensitive to and affected by their environments than screeners. The implications are clearly more profound with clients who are nonscreeners; however, just because screeners can filter out negative environmental factors does not mean that they

are unaffected by them. Therefore, with both screeners and nonscreeners, it is important for designers to consider the quantity of stimulation in the environment as well as the level or the degree of stimulation from each source. Because the nonscreener will be most affected by stimuli, understanding the different environmental uses and individual preferences will be important to the success of a design.

All life forms are affected by numerous sources of stimulation within their environments. The five senses—taste, touch, sound, smell, and sight—transmit these stimuli to the brain. Negotiating among various and often competing stimuli is the brain's job. In this way, the brain functions as an information manager. However, when too much stimulation or information is provided, our brains cannot adequately filter and sort through everything. By analyzing the surrounding environments, designers can either increase or decrease levels of stimulation with their designs to meet their clients' needs and desires (see Chapter 2).

PERSONAL SPACE

The idea of personal space is actually an *inter*personal phenomenon; it does not exist without interaction with others. Humans, like most animals, subconsciously use consistent inter-organism spacing to regulate basic biological processes such as mating and food gathering (Gifford, 2002). How-ever, personal space tolerances can ebb and flow depending on various factors related to how we feel.

We tend to tolerate or allow closer interpersonal distances when we feel strong, secure, or safe. Conversely, we tend to require more interpersonal space when we feel weak, insecure, or at risk.

Similar to facial expressions, gestures, and postures, the amount of space we place between others or objects and ourselves affects our behaviors. This spacing is governed by cultural rules and biological boundaries. Therefore, we can say that personal space is a subjective experience.

Although most of us are familiar with the concept of a fixed, invisible comfort zone or buffer that surrounds an individual, personal space is essentially a portable, flexible territory relative to other people and things (see Figure 5.5).

According to *social learning theories,* personal space is culturally acquired over time and results from a combination of a person's history and others' behavioral reinforcement; in other words, personal space is a learned behavior (Cox, Paulus, & McCain, 1984). Baxter (1970) suggested that we learn what is considered acceptable interpersonal spaces by imitating others in our culture. He studied the interpersonal space differences among three cultures and found that Mexican Americans had the shortest distances followed by white Americans, and then Black Americans. In Japan, where social densities are high, one may hand prow (i.e., face the palm-edge of one hand vertically forward in front of the nose), and bow the head slightly, as a symbol of apology for crossing between two people, or intruding into another's space while moving through a crowded room. In this case the hand acts like the prow of a ship cutting through water (Morris, 1994).

Spacing mechanisms used in design serve to help maintain an individual's sense of personal space. In architecture, walls, windows, statuary, pillars, and varying floor heights serve to assist in the management of personal space. In interior design, end tables, chairs with armrests, and potted plants can help to increase perceived boundaries and interpersonal distances as well as furniture and layout. The size of tables, for example can regulate how close one chair is from another. With increased status comes increased awarded personal space. Consider airline seats in first class versus coach and the width of desks for presidents and CEOs.

Affiliative-conflict theory as proposed by Argyle and Dean suggests that we simultaneously want to be closer to and farther from others and that we use interpersonal distance to balance these conflicting desires (Sebba & Churchman, 1983). Eric Knowles (1983) provides clarity to this approach-avoidance behavior by suggesting that even our most rewarding relationships involve avoidance tendencies (i.e., no matter

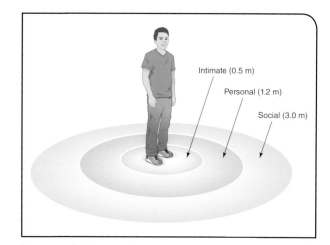

[**Figure 5.5**] Observing the average distance between others and our-selves is one way to determine what kind of relationship is occurring. Just over a foot and half away indicates an intimate encounter. Almost four feet away indicates a personal encounter and about 10 feet away indicates a social acquaintance. Illustration by Precision Graphics

how much we love our partner, sometimes we just want to be alone). Interpersonal discomfort results when there is a discrepancy between our approach and avoidance tendencies (Nasar, 1994). During typical social interactions, we tend to believe that we are either closer to or farther from others than we actually are and that others occupy more of our personal space than we occupy theirs (Gifford, 1983). We are less tolerant of closer distances when the lighting levels are lower (Adams & Zuckerman, 1991); we seem to need more space when we are in corners as compared with the centers of rooms (Tannis & Dabbs, 1975); and we tend to prefer more personal space when we are indoors than we do when we are outside (Cochran, Hale, & Hissam, 1984). In other words, we seem to require more personal space when there is or appears to be less physical space.

Personal space is an important factor in design because it directly affects how people will judge an environment. This holds true even in situations that seem relatively benign such as the spacing of urinals in bathrooms. Even though the spacing of urinals, for example, may be over-looked in the design, the distance between urinals is so important that when placed too close, men will select every other urinal. Thus the attempt of incorporating more urinals becomes a reason for fewer urinals used. Personal space itself is a factor of proximity within Western cultures, but within many Eastern cultures it is about social rules. Put another way, personal space is about the physical distance between two or more people, or from an object (e.g., chair). In many Eastern cultures, personal space is more about eye contact and visual invasion (e.g., people watching others is socially unacceptable).

Some studies suggest that within Western cultures, personal space zones are so important that when we are too close or too far from another person, our personal comfort levels are adversely affected (Scott, 1984) and we will usually compensate by taking a step backward or forward. This natural tendency can also communicate a lot about us during social situations. The term **power distance** is used to describe the degree of difference and acceptance of unequal power between people (Hofstede, 2001). From a cultural perspective, many find comfort with **high power distance** that ascribes superiority to those with a certain social status (e.g., celebrities, politicians, business executives). This high social status can be a result of race, age, education, personal achievements, celebrity status, family background, and a multitude of other factors. Cultures with **low power distance** tend to assume equality among people and focus more on earned status than ascribed status (Hofstede, 2001).

Within the United States, Canada, and Australia, multiculturalism has led to a lack of uniformity in terms of power distance, which can be a source of frustration for other cultures when attempting to form business collaborations or negotiations. Notwithstanding, the cultural norm within the United States, Canada, and Australia is to afford more personal space to individuals whom we perceive as holding greater status (Gifford, 2002). If a person responds by taking a step closer to us, the subliminal message is that they view themselves as our equal. However, the greater the difference in status or condition, the greater distance we are expected to keep (Aiello, Thompson, & Brodzinsky, 1983). This social norm applies not only to one's social status but also to power, dominance, familiarity, and physical ability and appearance.

Norms for personal space requirements differ between cultures and, to some degree, educational and income levels. An intrusion of personal space by another person can therefore incite positive or negative arousal, which affects the social relationship. A business relationship between two people might change from professional to romantic, or it can lead to alienation of one person. There are many ways to violate someone's personal space, includ-

[**Table 5.2**] Hall's Interpersonal Distance Zones

Personal Space Zone	Description	
Intimate (0–18")	Kept by two or more people who share a strong bond (e.g., lovers, close friends, family members).	Little can be accomplished at this distance because vision is minimal, which means that we would have to rely more on our sense of smell and touch. We tend not to get this close to people we are not intimate with, and usually we try to escape if we do.
Personal (18"–4')	Used by casual friends or people with close social contacts (e.g., friendly acquaintances, same-department coworkers, members of clubs or like organizations).	At this distance, touch is minimal (except perhaps when shaking hands), and vision and hearing become important. This is the distance we use to interact with friends. Within this range, normal conversations can take place easily. We might allow strangers into the outer limits, but we reserve the inner limits strictly for friends.
Social (4'–12')	Maintained by people who know of one another but do not really know one another to come together for a common purpose (e.g., friends of friends, casual acquaintances, fellow employees from other departments).	This distance includes formal social interactions such as business meetings, interviews, or customer-merchant interactions.
Public (12'–25')	Used by people whose only association is being in the same place at the same time. In public situations we usually prefer keeping as much space as possible between ourselves and the strangers around us, and when this distance is violated, we often start to feel crowded (e.g., two people waiting for a train on the same platform).	At this distance there is little detail involved in communication. A public speaker (e.g., actor, politician) communicates only one way with an audience.

ing physical invasion, eavesdropping, staring or watching without permission, playing loud music, and reeking of perfume or body odor. Designers need to understand the relationships between individual personal space zones and accommodate and support those social norms with the design of the built environment.

Personal Space and Communication

Research on how we communicate in private and public spaces began with studies of animal behavior (ethology) and territoriality in the nineteenth and early twentieth centuries. In 1969 Edward Hall concluded from studies that Americans hold four interpersonal distances in their social interactions: intimate (0 to 18 inches), personal (18 inches to 4 feet), social (4 to 12 feet), and public (12 to 25 feet) (Fisher & Byrne, 1975). Hall noted that different cultures set distinctive norms for closeness in various behaviors (e.g., speaking, business, courting) and that standing too close or too far away can lead to misunderstandings and even to culture shock (see Table 5.2).

Robert Sommer's studies demonstrate the importance of both distance and angle of orientation in cooperative and competitive interactions: Individuals in competitive settings chose to sit farther apart using direct orientation (face-to-face seating), whereas those in cooperative settings sat closer together using indirect orientation (side-by-side seating) (Hewitt & Henley, 1987).

Angulation

Angular body postures reveal how we relate to, or how much we care about, the people with whom we interact. The more squarely aligned we are with the person with whom we are interacting indicates our level of admiration and respect we feel toward that person. Our dislike and lack of respect for a person is indicated by how much we angle our body away from the other person. Angulations equate to further distances, and thus larger interpersonal space zones. This means that if person A approaches person B and does not acknowledge person B's level of respect that he/she believes is appropriate, then person B will angle his/her body away from person A as a means of increasing personal space distances and, perhaps, in an attempt to communicate this discomfort with body language. Degree of angulation can range from 0 (directly facing) to 180 degrees (turning one's back). Interestingly, young boys will often create a greater angular distance with adult strangers than girls will (Stern & Bender, 1974).

Unlike seating arrangements where face-to-face interactions generally indicate competition, standing face-to-face is generally related to cooperation. Conversely, two people standing with their bodies angled away from each other generally means competition or disagreement (Blum, 1988). When the situation is for pleasure and/or between two people courting, face-to-face interaction signifies cooperation; and two friends sitting side-by-side at a bar or nightclub indicates competition (Severy, Forsyth, & Wagner, 1979). Hence, personal space, body language, and other non-verbal communication are highly variable and context specific. The designer should understand the intended use of a space and then understand how people will be occupying, moving about, and interacting within that space.

TERRITORIALITY

Although inherent in all animal species, territoriality is difficult to define. For our purposes, it can be explained, according to the work of Julian Edney, as that which involves the possession and defense of physical space, as well as the exclusiveness of use, marking, personalization, and identity (as a reflection of the self) of that space by the occupant or user (Edney, 1974). In most civilizations, territories serve to organize human behaviors so that acts of violence, aggression, and overt domination are reduced.

Territories provide individuals with reliable access to the social contacts they need; through the use of **organizers** (e.g., directional signs, fences, edging), mutually acceptable ground rules are established and social behaviors can be transacted without confusion. When we are "on our own turf," we feel more secure and expect to be able to control or dominate an intruder. The level of dominance is closely associated with the amount and quality of a territory. For example, when a friend comes into your home, it is expected that you will control the distribution of food and beverages. Social rules reinforce territorial boundaries, but as competition for resources increase so too will territorial behaviors by those with established territories, as well as territorial infringement by individuals who struggle to obtain resources. If food is a scarce commodity, you may be more reluctant to offer it to a guest, who may be more likely to risk territorial infringement in search of it.

Most animals mark their territories (i.e., place an object or substance to indicate territorial intention or control); for example, a dog marks an object or area with urine, whereas a moviegoer marks a theater seat by placing a personal belonging on it. In an interesting study of motorist behaviors regarding parking spaces at an Atlanta mall, researchers found that motorists who occupy a parking spot will instinctively defend it from a person waiting to assume the spot by taking more time to leave the spot (Ruback & Juieng, 1997). As part of our socialization, we have been conditioned to recognize numerous signs and symbols indicating "territoriality."

[**Figure 5.6**] Plants in a public space can easily belong to an individual who is marking his or her space within the public venue thereby giving them value beyond the aesthetic. © amana images inc. / Alamy

Not all territorial markers are clear to all parties, however. For example, not everyone is aware that many older people will prop a chair against a table to symbolize their claim to a particular seat. Humans often mark their territories through **personalization** in ways that represent some aspect of their identities (e.g., vanity license plates on cars, family photos in office cubicles).

Some research indicates that "female" markers may be less effective than "male" markers (e.g., scarves versus sport coats) for territorial defense. This suggests that a male's territory is less likely to be invaded than a female's (Haber, 1980; Shaffer & Sadowski, 1975). This may be due to primordial notions of dominance and submission. The concept of territorial marking can be integrated into the design of a built environment in overt or subtle ways. An overt example would be inscribing a person's name into a concrete walkway; a more subtle way might be a nondescript personal item such as a plant placed in a public space (see Figure 5.6).

Types of Territories

Different territories meet different needs. Territories as personal spaces can be thought of as being primary, secondary, or public. **Primary territories** are spaces that are generally owned by individuals or primary groups and are

[**Figure 5.7**] Some territories are public and can be used by those in good standing with social rules. Once two or more people occupy a specific territory, it becomes an interactional territory. These territories are also controlled and defended like any other territory. © Martin Barraud / Alamy

controlled on a relatively permanent basis. The psychological importance of a primary territory to its occupants is always high. **Secondary territories** are less important than primary spaces; they are usually not owned by the occupants, and possess only moderate significance to them. Psychological control of these territories is less essential to the current occupants and is likely to change or be shared with others. **Public territories** are open to anyone in good standing within the community and occupants cannot expect to have much control. A person's home is a primary territory, the workplace is a secondary territory, and a public park is public territory. **Interactional territories** are temporarily controlled by a group of interacting individuals. There is usually little overt marking of these territories, yet entry into them is often perceived as interference. For example, groups of students often use library conference rooms as places to discuss group projects or for study groups; although no one student or group owns the room, should another student or group enter while the others occupy it, a conflict may arise (Figure 5.7).

Territories can be permanent, temporary, or temporarily permanent. Whereas a home is a permanent territory, the guest room would be a temporary territory for out-of-town friends. Likewise, a rented apartment is a temporarily permanent territory for tenants (although the tenants don't own the building, no one can enter that territory without their permission as long as they pay their rent).

Territorial Infringement

Conflict and aggression can result when territories have high-perceived value or when territorial boundaries are unclear. Territorial infringements can be classified as invasion, violation, and contamination. **Territorial invasion** occurs when an outsider physically enters a territory with the intention of taking control of it. On a macro level, territorial invasion occurs when countries invade other countries; at a micro level, it occurs when gangs invade other gangs' turfs. Invasion need not be violent; members of blended families often feel invaded when forced to share their primary territories with new parents or siblings. **Territorial violation** is a temporary incursion into someone else's territory. The violator's goal is usually not ownership, but rather annoyance, harm, or power. For example, a territorial violation occurs when a child sneaks into and rummages through an older sibling's room. **Territorial contamination** is the intentional fouling of someone else's territory. Vandalism, graffiti, stink bombs, and excessive noise are only a few examples of territorial contamination.

Rita and Mike had been dating for a little more than a year when he asked her to marry him. The two were wed six months later. Given that she lived in a three-bedroom house with her two daughters, ages 6 and 4, and he lived with his 13-year-old daughter in a two-bedroom apartment, it made sense for Mike to move in with Rita.

Rita decided to move her six-year-old into the four-year-old's bedroom (Box Figure 5.2) so that Mike's daughter could have a room of her own. Over the next couple of months the six-year-old started acting out her emotions by deliberately scattering her belongings around the house and even started to write on the walls. She probably felt invaded by Mike and even more so by his daughter; not only did she now have to share her mother and her home, but also her bedroom. A designer might have done best to have included the six-year-old in a brainstorming activity to determine how she could gain control over her new territory. He/she might hang drawstring draperies from ceiling to floor so the six-year-old could enjoy privacy while sharing a room with her sister. Because each child would surely feel somewhat disoriented by the merge, each child could then select wall art for the dining room. The six-year-old, having lost the most, could be allowed to select the piece that would serve as the room's focal point.

By understanding the role of territoriality, particularly in a primary territory setting, designers can assist in reinforcing a person's sense of belonging and ownership. In this case, the designer could help the child establish territorial boundaries and reassert her place in the family by allowing her to select a piece of art that represented her sense of identity, which then would serve as a focal point in the design.

[**Box Figure 5.2**] When two children are suddenly asked to share a room, they may feel as if they have experienced territorial invasion, particularly if one child has to move into a second child's room. A soft wall such as this will help the first child believe he or she is still in control of a portion of the original territory. © Elizabeth Whiting and Associates / Alamy

PRIVACY

Irwin Altman defined privacy as the selective control over another's access to our physical body, our groups, or our environments (Altman, 1975). Privacy involves more than just control of physical access; our visual, acoustical, olfactory, or informational privacy can also be infringed upon. There are many different interpretations of privacy because of people's needs to regulate their access to others; and their abilities to express those needs are influenced by their culture, personalities, gender, experiences, and stage of life. For example, young children need much less privacy than adolescents. Generally, our privacy needs vary according to the social situations in which we find ourselves.

Alan Westin (1967) described four aspects of privacy: solitude, intimacy, anonymity, and reserve.

- *Solitude* refers to the state of being alone, free from physical invasion. Although most people associate privacy with solitude, solitude doesn't always equate with privacy; for example, many elderly people live alone not to ensure their privacy but because they *are* alone. Darhl Pedersen (1982) distinguished solitude as the state of being alone among others (e.g., in the Swiss Family Robinson, the family members are alone on the island after their shipwreck) and *isolation* as the state of being alone with no others nearby (e.g., Robinson Crusoe, the early years, when he sets out alone, with no other company).
- *Intimacy* refers to group privacy and emotional bonds (e.g., lovers who want to be alone together). Whereas solitude refers to physical invasion, intimacy deals with visual and auditory invasion (e.g., a young couple showing their affection for each other in public may become annoyed with someone who stares at and makes comments about them). Pedersen (1982) described two psychologically distinct forms: *intimacy with friends* and *intimacy with family*. The level and type of intimacy obtained from each form is highly contingent on a person's gender, culture, and stage of life. For example, adolescents are more likely to share intimate thoughts with a friend and reveal intimate vulnerabilities to a family member.
- *Anonymity,* the state of being invisible or unknown to others, is a form of privacy commonly lost by celebrities and others who want to be among others but do not want to personally interact with or be identified by them.
- *Reserve* refers to the distance people create between themselves and others by erecting psychological barriers to protect inner thoughts and feelings, in public or

private. Most of us know people about whom we can say, "I've known them for years, but I really don't know anything *about* them."

Our notions of privacy depend greatly on our cultural backgrounds, socioeconomic levels, personalities, and the prevailing social norms and behaviors. To some, privacy is a behavioral expectation, while to others it is a personal value, preference, or need. Altman considered privacy to be central among human behavior processes related to space and noted four interpersonal control mechanisms by which people regulate their privacy: *personal space, territory, verbal behavior*, and *nonverbal behavior* (Altman, 1975). Westin described four essential functions of privacy: to regulate or protect communication, facilitate a sense of control, allow the integration of information about ourselves and our relationships, and allow emotional release (Westin, 1967). Pedersen contended that privacy is a basic human need with six further functions: uninterrupted contemplation, rejuvenation, creative expression, recovery, concealment of self, and concealment of illicit activities (Pedersen, 1982). Gifford and Price noted that privacy affects how we learn to adapt to space and is important during our development as children (Gifford & Price, 1979). Drawing upon these ideas, we may deduce that people who are deprived of adequate privacy (e.g., institutionalized persons) can feel they lack control over their lives; this can lead to lack of autonomy, learned dependence upon others, and learned helplessness.

Privacy is controlled through verbal, nonverbal, cognitive, environmental, temporal, and cultural mechanisms (Harris, Brown, & Werner, 1996). It is also be controlled by economics (see Figure 5.8). The wealthy can easily exclude "others" most of the time, and many middle-income families who opt to live in gated communities can minimize door-to-door solicitors; but lower-income and especially poor people often struggle to maintain social and physical privacy if they reside in dense multifamily housing or shelters.

Designers of the built environment are obliged not only to identify their clients' individual privacy needs but also to design according to those needs. For example, designing a home involves identifying the owner's notions and expectations of privacy, whereas designing a workplace setting requires a broader approach to meet the needs of current and future employees.

Design professionals can ensure their clients' desired levels of privacy via city-planning initiatives. These include, for example, transforming through-streets into dead ends; landscape initiatives, such as the use of hedge lines and strategically placed bushes or trees; architectural initiatives, such as the incorporation of porches, photosensitive windows, and good insulation; and interior design initiatives (in the work-in *groupthink* (the "mob mentality"). Emotional intensity can reach such a frenzied state that the emotions themselves become unstable. (Think of this in terms of being so happy or so angry that you burst into tears.) In a crowd of sports fans, for example, we see personal space boundaries shrink as the enthusiasm becomes contagious. In these situations the group is highly suggestible; people tend to behave not as individuals but rather as elements of the crowd. An emotion that is shared by the crowd can escalate to a state of frenzy that overwhelms the entire group—a condition that has resulted in the trampling deaths of people at nightclubs, concerts, and political gatherings throughout human history. Designers can incorporate safety features into buildings or facilities that will help law enforcement defuse mobs. Such examples include creating a stronger stimulus than that which caused the mob scene (e.g., very bright lights with a loud sound), but one that doesn't cause a diversion that may feed the frenzy (e.g., a sprinkler system that may effectively break up a crowd but also may create pandemonium and a stampede as people seek escape).

Interestingly, in laboratory settings, men respond more negatively to high-density situations than women (i.e., men's moods, attitudes toward others, and social behaviors are more hostile); however, in field studies, men often cope with high-density situations by leaving the environment.

It, therefore, appears that women handle the stress of high-density situations better when there is no easy way out (Aiello et al., 1983; Gifford, 2002). Both genders are more tolerant of invasions of personal space by females than by males (Fisher & Byrne, 1975; Hewitt & Henley, 1987), but one study revealed that gender influenced personal space only when age, race, and the other person's gender came into play (Severy et al., 1979).

Understanding the different ways in which males and females interpret and respond to high-density situations can help designers to better accommodate the needs of each gender. With the exception of public restrooms, most environments are open to both males and females and should, therefore, be designed for the group that will be most affected. For example, to accommodate men's increased perception of high density and crowding, spaces that are intended for numerous people should have multiple entry and exit points along with oversized or double doors. Likewise, the space-planning process should ensure that spacing between solid walls and furnishings is large enough to accommodate multiple *personal space* zones. Other methods of reducing perceived *spatial density* include making the space appear larger, such as increasing the level of natural light and incorporating mirrors, higher ceilings, and large unobstructed windows.

Population density does not determine **crowding.** Crowding is a subjective term that refers to a psychologically

[**Figure 5.8**] Many people throughout the world feel compelled to build mini fortresses to ensure their safety. In this compound we can see two sets of walls and doors that a visitor must pass through. © William Robinson / Alamy

place), such the use of "occupied/vacant" signs on restroom doors, furniture arrangements that increase or decrease conversational privacy, and special wall textures (e.g., transparent, translucent, opaque).

CROWDING AND DENSITY

Crowds are large, temporary groups of often-emotional individuals. We tend to regard crowds in terms of negative consequences (consider the destructiveness of a lynch mob or riotous sports fans or concertgoers), but the excitement of a crowd can be infectious and can help even the staunchest curmudgeon to have fun and release inner tension. A crowd's key characteristics include the anonymity and suggestibility of its members, and the unpredictability of the group's behavior (Weller, 1985). Emotions are intensified and amplified within crowds; as individual arousal increases, so does the group's, and people start to lose their individuality and engage

or emotionally based feeling that we experience when we perceive ourselves as being physically constrained in some way or that other people are interfering with us (Bell et al., 2001). This typically happens to us when we feel that there are too many people in too little space. Briefly, **density** is the mathematic ratio of individuals to a specific area, whereas *crowding* cannot be measured or calculated. **Social density** is created by a varied number of individuals occupying a fixed amount of space, whereas **spatial density** is created by a fixed number of individuals occupying different-sized spaces.

SUSTAINABILITY CONNECTION 5.1

Many hospital patients feel a need for more space between themselves and strangers. Consider the vulnerable position many patients in their weakened states are in when they arrive at a hospital—flat on their backs, weak, broken, or otherwise unable to sustain comfortable distances from strangers. Now think of the numerous studies suggesting that windows and views to natural green environments promote healing. Researchers have theorized many reasons why people are positively affected by the presence of a view; perhaps maintaining visual distances while in an impaired condition should be added to the list. If one can look out a window to sustain even an imagined distance when physical distance cannot be had between himself/herself and others, could that not bring about solace as well?

Planners and designers must be aware that perceptions and evaluations of crowding vary according to individual experiences, circumstances, belief systems, and personalities. Different cultures respond differently to high social density.

CULTURAL CONNECTION 5.2

Many Asian cultures tend to have smaller personal space zones due to centuries of high population density. These cultures have adopted social coping mechanisms such as avoiding eye contact and limiting expansive physical gestures. Whereas Asians prefer social barriers to crowding, people from the Mediterranean prefer physical barriers (Nasar & Min, 1984). Although these are only two examples, such cultural nuances can affect a person's idea of crowding.

In most settings, density is relative to proximity (the number and nearness of others). Knowles proposed a proximity concept of social interaction: Theoretically, the effects other people have on an individual will increase with the square root of their number (crowding) and decrease with the square root of their distance (Knowles, 1983).

Three components of crowding are the *situation*, the *emotion* (effect), and the *behavior* produced by the emotion (Gifford, 2002; Montano & Adamopoulos, 1984). The nature and organization of an environment make up the situation; this will evoke an emotional reaction, which if unresolved, will result in a behavioral manifestation. Once we begin feeling the negative pressures of density, our predominating concerns are loss of control, the inability to act toward a particular goal, having a limited number of options, or any combination of these. Imagine you are stuck in traffic and cannot determine the cause or the outcome. Your loss of cognitive control will likely cause you to experience more stress than another driver who can see that an accident down the road has just been cleared away; in this instance, knowledge is the mitigating factor between the situation and the effect (emotional reaction). The inability to act toward your goal is exemplified by being unable to arrive at work on time, which evokes feelings of frustration; here, the situation or environment is causing the effect. Your feeling that you lack control can be exacerbated by your limited options; but whether you choose to breathe deeply and meditate until the traffic clears or drive along the sidewalk—your end reaction is the behavioral response.

High density is a source of physiological arousal and stress, as demonstrated by numerous laboratory and field studies of its effects on skin conductance and perspiration; cardiac functions, including blood pressure; and other stress indicators. High density is often, but not always, a precursor to feelings of crowding. However, a study of prisons found that crowding, not density, was related to psychological stress (Schaeffer, Baum, Paulus, & Gaes, 1988). This is supported by findings that crowding results in psychological stress when perceived control is lower (Lepore, Evans, & Schneider, 1992). Feelings of crowdedness are directly proportional to the level of stress a person feels; increased crowding equals increased stress and vice versa. Therefore, regardless of actual density levels, feeling crowded can negatively affect human health.

Our experience of crowding within an environment depends on our perceived levels of control over it, our purpose for being in it, our expectations of it, and the others sharing it. For example, being in a police holding cell with two other occupants can evoke stronger feelings of crowding than being at an after-Christmas sale event with hundreds of other shoppers. We expect airports and amusement parks to be packed with people and do not usually experience much crowding in these environments; however, we also expect libraries and grocery stores to be relatively empty at certain times, and when they are not we tend to feel more crowded. Studies suggest that feelings of crowding are intensified when people are in an environment with others whom they perceive to be different from themselves (Manning, 1985; Schaeffer & Patterson, 1980). While dining out, an upper-class socialite will likely feel more crowded among working-class individuals at a greasy spoon than among the same number of peers at a chic café of equal size and space.

Feelings of crowding are highly contingent upon the individual's personality factors. For example, people with a strong internal locus of control believe they can control many aspects of their lives and will attempt to control situations presented by crowded environments, which increases their odds of incurring greater levels of stress. In extreme situations, individuals subjected to crowding may engage in behaviors related to learned helplessness. Mood and timing are also important factors (i.e., the less enjoyable a situation, the more crowded we feel; Mueller, 1984). Queuing up in long lines of fellow motorists at the local department of motor vehicles is more stressful than standing in similar lines waiting to buy movie tickets. High social density is a source of emotional arousal, and feelings of crowding are affected by a person's sense of control. Most of us would expect a popular club to be crowded; and when we choose to go dancing amid high social density, we are unlikely to experience feelings of crowding. Research has shown that people who prefer and expect high-density situations respond to them more favorably than people who have no preferences or expectations (Womble & Studebaker, 1981).

Experience can help to alleviate some of the feelings associated with crowding. Consider the extremely dense populations of New York City, Hong Kong, and Mexico City; people who choose to live in such environments are better able to adapt to crowded conditions than those who are locked in by career or personal obligations. Experience may help us cope with crowding in secondary environments (e.g., grocery store, shopping mall), but not in primary ones (e.g., home, workplace; Gifford, 2002). Feelings of crowding can be minimized to some extent through the use of information. In a study resulting from the findings of a *postoccupancy evaluation,* visitors reported significantly reduced perceived crowding, discomfort, anger, and confusion when directional signs were added to a crowded lobby (Wener & Kaminoff 1983). In short, *the perceived,* rather than actual, level of density determines our behavioral responses (Rapoport, 1975).

Although designers have little control over occupancy loads, design can decrease perceptions of space confinement (e.g., by installing mirrors, increasing light levels and ceiling heights), which will, in turn, decrease perceptions of crowding. Brightness (from wall or accent colors, natural or artificial light sources, or combinations of these) leads to less perceived crowding, and sunnier (natural daylight) rooms are perceived to be less crowded than darker rooms

(Mandel, Baron, & Fisher, 1980; Nasar & Min, 1984; Schiffenbauer, 1979). Less crowding is elicited by rectangular rooms than square ones (Desor, 1972), by rooms with well-defined corners as opposed to curved walls (Rotton, 1987) and by rooms with windows and doors (visual escapes). The presence of visual distractions—such as potted plants, wall art, and garden sculptures—leads to more perceived space (Baum & Davis, 1976; Worchel & Teddlie, 1976). A room will be perceived to be more crowded if the furniture is arranged in the center rather than at the sides. (Sinha, Nayyar, & Mukherjee, 1995). **Sociofugal** (facing away) seating arrangements tend to elicit less crowding than those that are **sociopetal** (facing others) (Wener, 1977).

Research has determined that people have spatial needs in both horizontal and vertical dimensions. If available space is limited in one, our spatial needs will increase in the other. The same study also demonstrated that males associate greater ceiling height with less crowding (Savinar, 1975). According to another study, when temperatures rise, so do our perceptions of crowding; users of public transportation reported more crowding when the temperature was high, although the number of passengers on the train remained constant (Ruback & Pandey, 1992).

MEMORY

Memory is a form of cognition that enables us to store information so that we can recall it at a later time. In general, we have short- and long-term memory that some investigators have suggested occurs in three distinct phases:

1. Perception and recording of a stimulus
2. Temporary maintenance of a perception (short-term memory)
3. Encoding into long-term memory

As noted, short-term memory is the temporary maintenance of perception to a specific set of stimuli. Generally speaking, short-term memory can hold as much information as can be repeated or rehearsed in 1.5 to 2 seconds. However, we can increase the amount of information stored within short-term memory by grouping information into meaningful clusters. We often forget information held in our short-term memory because the passage of time causes us to forget (**decay theory**) or because we get additional information that interferes with the memory (**interference theory**). To move information from short-term memory into long-term memory we can either engage in rote rehearsal (simply repeating information over and over) or elaborative rehearsal, which links new information with familiar information that has already been stored. In design, long-term memory is often achieved by linking new information with familiar or established information. For example, we are used to seeing restaurants or cafés adjacent to the lobby of a hotel. As such, when we visit such a place we know where to first look in order to find a restaurant or café.

Long-term memory (LTM) differs from short-term memory (STM) in that it describes information storage that is more permanent. This form of memory can be vast and be retained for many years, and it is strongly associated with meaning. Because long-term memory is a more complex process, there are six different descriptive processes used to define this kind of memory:

1. *Episodic memory*. The portion of long-term memory that stores personally experienced events.
2. *Semantic memory*. The portion of long-term memory that stores general facts and information.
3. *Explicit memory*. Memories that we are aware of, including episodic and semantic memories.
4. *Implicit memory*. Memories for information that either was not intentionally committed to LTM or is retrieved unintentionally from LTM, including procedural and emotional memories.
5. *Procedural memory*. The portion of long-term memory that stores information relating to skills, habits, and other perceptual-motor tasks.
6. *Emotional memory*. Learned emotional responses to various stimuli.

In addition to forms of memory there are differences in the way we remember events. To get a better idea of how memory relates back to design let's examine a sequence of events. On September 11, 2001, two planes collided with the World Trade Center towers in New York City causing the buildings to collapse. Now, several years after many of us can still recall the event. We may have thoughts, feelings, and anxieties tied to that single episode in time, thus forming an episodic memory. Today, if you were in a high-rise that was suddenly hit by a plane you would likely experience a flood of emotions associated with the episodic memory, but your semantic memory would allow you to recall how to exit the building. Explicit memories occur concurrently. As we proceed out of the building, we may recall images of the Trade Center towers collapsing, and we may also recall the quickest path out of the building. Oftentimes we will associate flooring colors or materials and wall colors with an exit path. Our ability to recall the path to the nearest emergency exit that wouldn't have ordinarily been recalled because that path leads only to an emergency exit is an example of implicit memory. This path can be brought to the forefront of implicit memory

by a flashing strobe light. Because we have been through multiple emergency preparation drills and the design path to an exit differs from the design of other spaces, many of us will have developed procedural memories, which then enable us to stay somewhat calm and help a coworker to safety (i.e., we know that we are going the right way to exit the building). Later, when the authorities ask us to recall the event, most of us will do so with much emotion and may even start trembling and crying. This last phase is an example of emotional memory. What is also important to know is that some of the sights, sounds, smells, and other sensations that we encountered as we proceeded to safety will also become part our emotional memory and may evoke emotional responses when we encounter similar sensations in the future.

The **Serial Position Effect** is related to both long- and short-term memory, and can affect the way we recall information. This effect states that when given a list of items to remember, we tend to recall the first and last items in the list better than the items in the middle. This concept is similar to the way we experience design. We tend to remember our first and last impressions of a building or room. The serial position effect is similar to **procedural memory** because it involves the recall of learned skills and actions, such as finding your way out of a building. This function involves a step-by-step process and includes landmarks. The relevance of procedural memory for design also assists with spatial cognition because a person can become familiar with the amount of time, number of steps, and other perceived experiences between two landmarks (i.e., there are 14 steps in most staircases within the United States).

A **schema**, on the other hand, is a mental representation of an object or event that is stored in memory. Schemata provide a framework from which we can catalogue incoming information, and may lead to the formation of stereotypes and inferences. The recall of this memory is often associated with **declarative memory**, which is related to the recalling of facts, rules, concepts, and events, as well as specific stimuli, such as a particular scent, sound, sight, taste, or texture. Schemata and declarative memory are most often associated with feelings; for example, the smell of roses may evoke in people strong memories of their mothers. Planners and designers can increase their clients' levels of satisfaction by creating environments that evoke positive feelings and memories simply by incorporating elements from their clients' declarative memory. However, without careful research, the plan may backfire: Even the most exquisite rose garden would be traumatic for a client who has a strong negative association with roses.

Memory Loss

Our ability to form memories means that we also have the potential for memory loss. Each of us has a different capacity for storing and recalling information. Theories that help explain why we forget include the concept of disuse, which proposes that forgetting occurs because stored information is not used (and may explain why many of us lose our higher math skills once we leave school), and the concept of interference, which suggests that new information is forgotten when old information interferes with the new. However, some memory loss is related to a physiological process called *amnesia,* or occurs as a result of brain cell deterioration related to stroke, cardiovascular disease, or dementia such as Alzheimer's disease. Using design as a means of memory association can help users make appropriate neural connections. For example, placing the commode in the direct line of sight (with the bathroom door open) for a patient with Alzheimer's disease has been shown to reduce episodes of incontinence (Morgan & Stewart, 1998).

Practical Applications for Designers

Use these resources, activities, and discussion questions to help you identify, synthesize, and retain this chapter's core information. These tools are designed to complement the resources you'll find in this book's companion Study Guide.

SUMMING IT UP

The human experience in relation to the built environment is an evolving process that began with early people adapting to the environments they inhabited. Modern men and women continue to perceive, interpret, and describe their environments differently; both sexes continue, at least to some extent, to behave and regard the environment according to primal preferences. The terms masculinity and femininity are also used to describe culture values in terms of assertiveness or social support. Women seem to feel more comfortable with others at closer distances than men; although, when interacting with strangers, the interpersonal distance between women is smaller than it is for a woman and a man.

Personality traits are often expressed through the overall design of and the quantity and types of artifacts found within a built environment; the assumption is that individuals develop environments that reflect and reinforce perceptions of themselves. The Big Five Inventory (BFI) was developed by Oliver John, who discovered through statistical analyses how different personality traits can be linked together to define certain human qualities. Myers-Briggs Type Indicator (MBTI) expands on the personality types developed by Carl Jung to include four primary personality dichotomies that converge in a matrix to create 16 possible personality profiles.

To design with confidence, human spatial behavior should be investigated, and findings or best practices must be implemented. Planners and designers must be aware that perceptions and evaluations of crowding vary according to individual experiences, circumstances, belief systems, and personalities. Research has determined that people have spatial needs in both horizontal and vertical dimensions.

You can also refer to this textbook's companion Study Guide for a comprehensive list of Summary Points.

Gender, Design, and Stress

Kathryn H. Anthony, Ph.D., ACSA, University of Illinois at Urbana-Champaign

Visually striking lobby spaces in offices, museums, hotels, and retail establishments often feature ceremonial stairways with open risers and transparent glass steps or floors that allow passersby underneath to take a sneak peek right up the skirts of women and girls. The New Acropolis Museum in Athens, Greece, which opened in 2009, is one such example. And every day, women who spend hundreds of dollars to see a blockbuster Broadway play spend the entire intermission waiting in long lines for the ladies' room while their male companions zip in and out of the men's room in a flash. When designers create environments like these without taking gender issues into account, certain individuals who inhabit, work in, or visit their buildings experience high levels of stress.

Although we are forced to use them every day, public restroom designs are among the most important spaces where gender concerns have all too often been overlooked. For decades, at major places of assembly such as theaters, sports venues, and transportation hubs, inadequate numbers of toilet stalls result in long lines for ladies' rooms, disadvantaging women, girls, toddlers, and infants. These designs met the minimum requirements dictated by building codes in effect when they were built, but these were simply not enough. Historically, most architects, contractors, engineers, building code officials, and clients rarely contacted women to learn about their restroom needs. Until recently, women were rarely employed in these male-dominated professions nor were they in a position to affect change. By contrast, through the passage of the Americans with Disabilities Act (ADA) in 1990, persons with disabilities were successful in legislating sweeping changes in restroom design nationwide.

People of all ages—especially children, seniors, and persons with special medical conditions—face emergencies when they desperately need a restroom. Waiting to use a restroom causes both psychological and physiological stress for women and men, boys and girls. For women routinely forced to wait, cystitis and other painful urinary tract infections may result. Waiting in line poses special problems for pregnant women who need restrooms more often than usual. The same is true for women during menstruation, which at any time affects about one quarter of all women in their child-bearing years. Waiting can also lead to constipation, abdominal pain, diverticula, and hemorrhoids. Even worse, for anyone who can't make it on time, having an accident is embarrassing and demoralizing.

Ever since California led the way with its first "potty parity" legislation in 1987, at least 21 states and scores of municipalities have passed potty parity laws calling for greater ratios of women's to men's toilets and equal speed of access for women and men. Recently revised plumbing and building codes have called for greater numbers of toilet stalls for women. Yet laws and codes only apply to new construction or existing buildings where major renovations are underway, and most of the older building stock remains untouched.

The design of urinal stalls can also pose special problems for men. "Trough" urinals and rows of urinals with minimal dividers or none at all compromise men's privacy and can result in a medical condition called paruresis, or "shy bladder syndrome," making it impossible for someone to urinate in public if others are within seeing or hearing distance. Some men's room entrances are designed in such a way that when the door is open, passersby in an adjacent hallway can see men standing up to urinate, albeit from behind. This is the case at one university building whose men's room was recently remodeled to meet updated accessibility codes. Male professors who work nearby refuse to use it.

Many men's rooms feature at least one lower urinal, enabling young boys to use it without assistance, promoting their independence. Yet one rarely finds a women's room with child-height toilets, forcing young daughters to depend upon their mothers and grandmothers to lift them. This presents special problems for mothers with multiple children in tow and for mothers who are pregnant. Child-height sinks are almost non-existent in both men's and women's rooms.

As a result of recent legislation and revised building codes, family restrooms are slowly on the rise in new or newly renovated assembly and retail spaces like shopping malls, theaters, airports, and stadiums. Family restrooms are long overdue. They provide safe spaces for parents with opposite-gender children as well as persons needing the assistance of caregivers. Many family restrooms include child-height toilets and sinks along with adult-sized fixtures.

Some innovative public restroom designs feature unisex stalls opening directly to the outdoors, creating gender equity. One of the nation's best is an award-winning facility, Kellogg Park Comfort Station at scenic La Jolla Shores along the Pacific Ocean in San Diego, California. It opened in 2005 and receives two to three million visitors a year. Designed by resident Mary Coakley, along with local architect Dale Naegle, the new restroom and surrounding landscape responds with exceptional sensitivity to gender and family needs. Coakley, a local resident who lived across the street from the beach, spearheaded the movement to replace a deteriorating 1960s restroom plagued by vandalism, crime, and long lines for ladies. Coakley also led the effort to construct a large, artistic lithocrete map adjacent to the restroom showing the nearby La Jolla Canyon underwater park and marine reserve that attracts divers from all over the world, along with an innovative playground design that teaches children about the wonders of the sea. The trio of state-of-the-art restroom design, public art, and playground has now become a popular tourist attraction, a national prototype that can be emulated elsewhere.

To learn more about gender issues in restroom design, consult the web sites of the World Toilet Organization and the American Restroom Association, along with

Anthony and Dufresne (2007) and Greed (2003). For more information about gender issues in design, consult Anthony (2008) and Weisman (1992).

American Restroom Association. Retrieved from http://www.americanrestroom.org

Anthony, K. H. (2008). *Designing for diversity: gender, race, and ethnicity in the architectural profession.* Urbana, IL: University of Illinois Press.

Anthony, K. H., & Dufresne, M. (2007). Potty parity in perspective: Gender and family issues in planning and designing public restrooms. *Journal of Planning Literature, 21,* 267-294.

Greed C. (2003). *Inclusive urban design: Public toilets.* Oxford, UK: Architectural Press.

Weisman, L. K. (1992). *Discrimination by design: A feminist critique of the man-made environment.* Urbana, IL: University of Illinois Press.

World Toilet Organization. (n.d.) World Toilet. Retrieved from: http://www.worldtoilet.org

To learn more about the author, go to http://www.kathrynanthony.net

KEY TERMS

- **affiliative-conflict theory**
- **Big Five Inventory (BFI)**
- **crowding**
- **crowds**
- **decay theory**
- **declarative memory**
- **density**
- **ethic of care theory**
- **high power distance**
- **interactional territories**
- **interference theory**
- **low power distance**
- **Myers-Briggs Type Indicator (MBTI)**
- **organizers**
- **personalization**
- **power distance**
- **primary territories**
- **procedural memory**
- **public territories**
- **schema**
- **secondary territories**
- **Serial Position Effect**
- **social density**
- **sociofugal**
- **sociopetal**
- **spatial density**
- **territorial contamination**
- **territorial invasion**
- **territorial violation**

WEB LINKS

The Center for Evolutionary Psychology (www.psych.ucsb.edu/research/cep)

"Equal prey in prehistoric times," on contrasting archaeological findings and "gender-blind" views on the roles of the sexes in ancient times (www.latrobe.edu.au/bulletin/2008/0208/research4.html)

Journal of Men's Studies (www.mensstudies.com)

The Myers & Briggs Foundation, select www.humanmetrics.com to assess your own personality type (www.myersbriggs.org)

NASA, for research on gender and space, search for "interpersonal distance zones" (www.nasa.gov)

Neuromarketing (www.neurosciencemarketing.com)

Social Psychology Network (www.socialpsychology.org/cognition.htm)

The Srivastava Lab at University of Oregon, on the Big Five Inventory; select "Measuring the Big Five" (www.uoregon.edu/~sanjay)

UC Santa Barbara's Center for Spatially Integrated Social Science (www.csiss.org/classics)

U.S. National Library of Medicine and the National Institutes of Health, Medline Plus (www.nlm.nih.gov/medlineplus/memory.html)

STUDIO ACTIVITY 5.1

Client Profile

Design Problem Statement
You have been asked to redesign the office of a newly elected female district attorney in her late fifties. According to Myers-Briggs Personality Indicator, she is an ESTJ. (Refer to Table 5.1.)

Directions
Step One: Identify common personality characteristics associated with a female in her late fifties with a personality type of ESTJ.

Step Two: From the profile deduce probable office design preferences, and explain why you believe that person would prefer that design.

Step Three: Translate your design ideas into one cohesive design of an office for this woman. Diagram this design with the preferences you identified from the personality profile.

Deliverable
Diagram of the design

Territorial Markers

Design Problem Statement

You have been asked to develop a list of territorial markers used by an assortment of people in the workplace environment.

Issue: Territories have different meanings and levels of control for different people. It is important to ensure adequate provisions for territorial markers should an employee want to exercise their use.

Directions

Step One: Visit a group of similar workplace spaces. Photograph the various uses of territorial markers from office to office. Make sure to distinguish if those markers are permanent or temporary, and whether they were included as part of the original design or if the individual added them.

Step Two: Create a PowerPoint photo essay of the various ways and degrees that territorial markers have been used. Also evaluate the permanence of those markers as well as their effectiveness.

Deliverable

PowerPoint photo essay.

DISCUSSION QUESTIONS

1. Discuss observances regarding the belief that we are either closer to or farther from others than we actually are and that others occupy more of our personal space than we occupy theirs.

2. Discuss how visiting clients in their homes or offices can reveal details about their personal space needs.

3. What is the Big Five Inventory, and what are its broad dimensions?

4. Describe traits that identify both an introverted and extroverted person. Which do you identify closest to?

5. Discuss the differences among Alan Westin's four aspects of *privacy*. How are the different levels of privacy related? Why are all four aspects important for psychological health? Can a designer create spaces for each type of privacy?

LEARNING ACTIVITIES

1. Go on an outdoor trip with friends, both male and female. When socializing closely among each other, note the distances maintained between males and females. Describe all the patterns you observe.

2. Design two restaurants: one that subscribes to the characteristically male sense of personal space and one that subscribes to the female sense. Draw floor plans and highlight specific unique characteristics of each plan, and write a short description comparing and contrasting them.

3. Wait in line at a busy public place (e.g., movie theater, grocery store) and, without purposefully touching anyone, observe what happens when you stand within five to six feet of the person in front of you. What happens when you stand within one foot of them?

4. Visit the lobbies of two multistoried buildings: one spacious and well lit and the other darker and more enclosed. How does the architecture affect the appearance of crowding? How does the architecture affect the way each lobby is used? How does the design appear to affect each building's visitors?

5. Visit a local museum and observe where visitors mingle or relax. Are they in the center of the room; the corners; near entrances or exits; in bright, sunny areas; or in dark, cool spaces? Create a chart of possible locations, photograph or sketch each site, and observe and record the number of individuals who pause to relax or regroup in each one. Define a rest period (e.g., 30 seconds) and count only people who meet that criterion.

06 Information Management

There can be no knowledge without emotion. We may be aware of a truth, yet until we have felt its force, it is not ours. To the cognition of the brain must be added the experience of the soul.

—Arnold Bennett

Some aspects of aesthetics seem to be universal. This includes the ability to see human characteristics and symbolism within design. In many cases, the meaning behind a symbol can be so powerful that it can be placed within an atrocious design and people will still regard it as beautiful. However, it is not the design that they are responding to but rather the symbol. Gender roles and expectations are also heavily influenced by culture and tradition, which are handed down from one generation to the next.

In Western societies, women have been successful in breaking out of their culturally compelled role of staying at home to rear the children. Men, on the other hand, continue to be bound by cultural norms of "what it means to be a man." The number of females who have successfully entered the traditionally male-dominated fields of architecture and medicine supports this assertion. Males, conversely, have not made the same strides into the female-dominated professions of interior design and nursing. Gender roles, however, are only one aspect of culture that needs to be addressed with design. Religion, holiday rituals, and the family are also important aspects of culture. Because the environments that we occupy are a reflection of our personalities, designers can use these characteristics to identify and create a space that is better suited to the individual.

Color is an influencing variable on the perception and judgment of aesthetics. Our ability to perceive and respond to color is based upon a complex visual system that begins with our eyes and ends in our brains. Our eyes are the tools to capture an image; the brain is a processing center that registers and interprets images and then assigns meaning. There are many conflicting views on the relationship between color and the human condition, but the common denominator is that color does affect humans, and it helps us to make sense of our world. In some situations it gives us behavioral clues, whereas in others it represents situations and events. Color is also used in wayfinding—a process we use to help us navigate though complex environments. Wayfinding is made easier through the use of signs, color matching, and other directive devices. We then take that information to form mental images called cognitive maps. These maps help us to understand ourselves in relation to the larger environment.

SENSORY DESIGN

The ability to experience sensation is a basic part of the human condition. For many artists, sensation is an ethereal concept related to one's feelings and how they experience a given situation. Because people experience sensation and stimuli differently, it is difficult to predict with absolute certainty how a set of sensations will be perceived. Wool, for example, has often been prized for warmth, but the scratchy sensation that comes from the fiber can be perceived negatively.

From a scientific perspective, sensation is the way that humans are able to experience and interpret the world. From both the scientific and artistic perspective, sensory detection derives from our ability to see, hear, smell, taste, and feel. Humans rely on sensory perception in order to understand themselves within the context of the physical world, which has been of great interest to both artisans and scientists. In many instances and situations, sensation has come to be synonymous with feelings of pleasure, joy, anger, and sadness. For example, the sight of a tender moment shared by a father and his newborn baby has moved many mothers to tears. In this situation, the biological ability to see evokes an emotional response, which is based on meaning.

Many ancient designers seemed to understand the relationship between human stimulation and the built environment. The stonemasons of Chartres, for example, were able to create one of the world's most beautiful buildings, which has transcended the centuries (Figure 6.1) to tell a story in stone, glass, and light of a time long ago. Although it is assumed within the fields of design that structures such as this were built on intuition, it is likely that the designers were skilled observers who simply recreated attributes that caused pleasure for other people.

Art by its very nature relies heavily upon ideas and concepts that are often abstract and based on intuition. Because it is generally accepted that intuition occurs in the right hemisphere of the brain while the left hemisphere is responsible for logical mathematical thinking, it is not uncommon to ascribe right-brain dominance to designers and artists. However, designers of the built environment must be able to draw

equally from intuition and science in order to successfully develop environments where humans can flourish.

Throughout life we encounter a multitude of environments, some of which stay stored in our memories while others are forgotten. Why we remember one place over another is often the result of memory and emotion, which are tied to one or more of our senses: touch, smell, sight, sound, and taste. Our senses gather data from the environment to be processed by our brain. At a later date, when one or more of our senses detect a similar sensation, the memory of the previous experience is brought to conscious thought.

As we begin to understand the role of our senses in understanding the world, the senses themselves start to be questioned as viable instruments of perception. As humans, we rely heavily on our vision. The ability to see often usurps the other senses, which in turn biases our understanding of the world. People who are blind, for example, experience the world differently than those who can see.

[**Figure 6.1**] Stonemasons of the past built some of the world's most beautiful buildings, probably by being skilled observers who saw attributes that evoked pleasure and happiness and recreated them. Cathédral Notre-Dame de Chartres, Chartres, France. © David R. Fraizier Photolibrary, Inc. / Alamy

AESTHETICS

Humans have come to regard aesthetics and color from different perspectives, including that of regional culture. Just as arctic cultures use dozens of specific terms to describe snow and xeric cultures (people who live in extremely arid climates) have many ways to describe sand, people who are affected by and work with aesthetics seem to be more sensitive to the nuances of color and design. For instance, the world of fashion and design uses many names to describe the color variations of pale red, but to most Western males, pink is pink.

When discussing the relationship between the built environment and human behaviors, the role of color and aesthetics are often among the first topics a lay person will understand and want to discuss further. These are two aspects of environmental psychology that bring about much fascination and result in many disagreements. Aesthetics can be defined as a branch of philosophy that deals with beauty and art. The fundamental premises behind the study of aesthetics are the definitions of what constitutes beauty, the rational and emotional criteria of beauty, and the value of beauty. When it comes to beauty, our judgment of an environment's appeal is highly subjective and influenced by many overlapping and individual factors that include culture, age, gender, and experience.

As with gender roles, aesthetics and color preferences evolve. However, they evolve according to fashion and trends, not out of necessity. Although men and women have evolved to excel at certain everyday chores in terms of physical strength, the role gender plays with regard to aesthetics and color seems to be more closely related to social norms. For the purposes of this text, **aesthetics** may be considered to be the values and expressions that the physical environment can embody and represent. The study of aesthetics in design is an attempt to identify, understand, and create environmental features that lead to positive (pleasurable) responses (Bell, Greene, Fisher, & Baum, 2001).

An overarching theme within the study of aesthetics is the idea of form. The value of the word form, or *forma*, holds such significance to Western ideals that it is one of the few words that remain from the ancient Roman language of Latin. Hence the word form can be seen and heard from as far northeast as Russia to as far southwest as Spain. Albeit, some languages have modified the word's ending such as the omission of the letter "a" in English and the replacement of the letter "a" with the letter "e" in French. Notwithstanding, the meaning of form, forma, and forme remains the same (University of Virginia Library, 2003).

The concepts of art and design are indistinguishable when it comes to aesthetics, and the history of aesthetics reveals an underpinning emphasis on form. *The Dictionary of the History of Ideas* (University of Virginia, 2003) identifies five uses of the word form as it relates to art and aesthetics:

1. The arrangement or order of parts
2. The content and arrangement that evokes the senses
3. The boundary, or colors and contour of an object
4. The conceptual essence of an object, also called "entelechy"
5. The contribution of the mind to the perceived object

From these approaches to aesthetics, the arrangement of color and contour have the propensity to provoke the senses from real or conceptual ideas as the mind forms associations. In this way color and aesthetics are intertwined and mutually interdependent. Color shapes an environment and strongly influences how we interpret and feel about the environments (Smith, 2003). In fact, color is so important to aesthetics that we see some of the earliest evidence of color being used by humans (a powdery red pigment derived from ocher) around 250,000 years ago (Scarre, 1993) in the cave homes of ancient humans (Figure 6.2). But because of aesthetics' joint nature of arrangement, boundaries, and contours, personal meaning, conceptualization, and sensory effects, aesthetics are often difficult, if not impossible, to quantify. Hence, the old adage of "beauty is in the eye of the beholder" is apropos to design.

[**Figure 6.2**] The homes of our ancient ancestors were often caves. These caves were decorated with various etchings and paintings, which demonstrate the importance of color and aesthetics throughout humanity. © Images & Stories / Alamy

BOX 6.1 FORMAL AESTHETICS SURVEY

To measure the beauty of this office according to formal aesthetics, attribute a score of 1 to 5 (with 1 being the lowest and 5 being the highest) within each category; then write your score in the last column and total your scores. A total that is closer to 65 means the room is considered beautiful, a total closer to 39 means it is considered average, and a total lower than 39 means it is considered to be unattractive. Keep in mind that each individual's notion of beauty will differ based on his/her past experiences; whereas one person may find this room very beautiful, another may not.

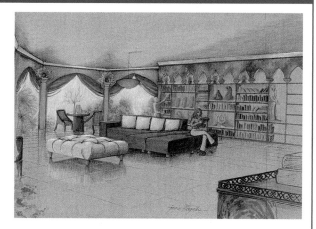

[**Box Figure 6.1**] On entering this room, each individual will perceive each of the aesthetic categories differently. The result will determine whether the environment is preferred. Illustration by Jimma Alegado

Dimensions		
Shape	Does this room have a shape that is appealing for its intended use?	1 2 3 4 5
Proportion	Are items in the room sized so that no single object dominates the scene?	1 2 3 4 5
Scale	Do furnishings and accessories fit the room without looking too large or too small?	1 2 3 4 5
Novelty	Are there elements or components of uniqueness or fascination?	1 2 3 4 5
Illumination	Is lighting sufficient and appropriate for the room?	1 2 3 4 5
Enclosure		
Spaciousness	Does the room give the appearance of having space and not being cluttered?	1 2 3 4 5
Density	Is the floor-to-space ratio ample in relation to objects occupying the room?	1 2 3 4 5
Mystery	Do elements within the room inspire or beg for exploration?	1 2 3 4 5
Complexity		
Visual richness	Are there interesting items to view while maintaining the room's unifying theme?	1 2 3 4 5
Diversity	Are a variety of objects or architectural features present within the room?	1 2 3 4 5
Information rate	Do all aspects of the room register with the viewer at an equal rate?	1 2 3 4 5
Order		
Unity	Is there a unified theme among all parts of the room?	1 2 3 4 5
Clarity	Is the purpose or function of the room and objects obvious?	1 2 3 4 5
Total		

Formal Aesthetics

Within Western cultures the sensory apparatus has been investigated since the beginning of the academe of Ancient Greece. The word *aesthetics*, which relates to the idea of being visually stimulating or pleasing, was derived from the Greek *aethetikos*, which means "of sense perception" (Bloomer and Moore, 1977). From the scientific perspective the purpose of design is to create attractive, pleasant environments that we enjoy. It is essential that planners and designers create environmental features that both elicit pleasurable responses and fulfill functional requirements. Evidence shows that aesthetics can be important in determining behavior (Nasar, 1994); however, aesthetic design considerations may conflict with behavioral considerations. *Pleasant* and *attractive* can be highly subjective terms, as can *function*. Some of the most beautiful structures do not function well, and some of the most functional designs lack aesthetic qualities.

There are differences between physical and psychological aspects of design aesthetics (Lang, 1987; Nasar, 1994). Physical aspects are the focus of **formal aesthetics,** which focus on the following components of design:

1. *Dimensions.* Shape, proportion, scale, novelty, illumination
2. *Enclosure.* Spaciousness, density, mystery
3. *Complexity.* Visual richness, diversity, information rate of environmental stimuli
4. *Order.* Unity and clarity

Symbolic Aesthetics

Formal aesthetics have traditionally depended on the Gestalt theory of perception, (Bell et al., 2001), which hypothesizes that people's perceptions of stimuli affect their responses. **Symbolic aesthetics** complement formal aesthetics by moving beyond the physical world to the intangible world of meaning. Whether denotative (e.g., function, style) or connotative (i.e., implying an association, such as welcoming or forbidding), sources of symbolic aesthetics include the following:

1. *Naturalness.* The level in which natural elements were used in the design
2. *Upkeep.* The level in which designs can be easily maintained
3. *Intensity of use.* The intensity or presence of particular design features
4. *Style.* The overall design arrangement

Gestalt tradition dictates that if two individuals are exposed to an identical stimulus, their reactions to it will be different because their reactions are based on separate past experiences. For example, two people may have been raised in different size homes—one large and one small. When exposed to a midsize home later in life, the person who grew up in the large house will likely view the midsize home as being small, whereas the person who grew up in the small home will likely view the midsize home as being large. Box 6.1 contains a survey form that can be used to evaluate the formal aesthetic qualities of any environment.

SYMBOLS AND ICONOGRAPHY

During the mid-eighteenth century, French philosopher Denis Diderot understood that emotional experience might be heavily based upon association rather than exact reasoning (Bloomer & Moore, 1977). A great poet, for instance, had the ability to relay meaning through the use of metaphor, analogy, and associative memory, which were not the product of any form of classical exact reasoning. In his paradigm of thought, people could develop emotional connections to places and objects based on associative meaning, which is similar to a **stimulus response**.

Symbols and iconography convey meanings that are real or merely the result of designer oversight. However, messages can also work their way into our behavioral manifestations. For example, at one time or another most of us have found ourselves humming, whistling, or playing a catchy slogan over and over in our head, particularly when we are exposed to an associative stimuli. For example, the automobile maker Honda had an ad campaign in the late 1970s that used the jingle, "Honda, we make it simple." This ad was in response to the decadence of the 1960s and 1970s, and it heralded a car that served basic functionality and fuel efficiency. The jingle was so successful that most who were exposed to it still remember the catch phrase, and some even repeat it when exposed to another person who simply says the word, "Honda." In this way we can see messages of social and cultural trends being introduced and reinforced through the designs of the era. Whether it is in the designs of automobiles, buildings, or cityscapes, the uniform message of the later 1970s was simplicity, functionality, and reliability. Today that design message is *green* or sustainability.

Subliminal perception has no direct effect on behaviors, but designers can incorporate subliminal messages in environments that support the mission of the environment. Consider how you feel when you put on those tight pants; most of us will conclude that we have gained weight. Likewise, we often take the liberty of rich desserts when our clothing feels loose. These same principles can be applied to weight loss clinics, or centers that treat anorexia or bulimia. In weight loss clinics the mission is to help people lose weight, but also provide encouragement. Hence, the waiting room of a weight-loss program might have chairs that are narrower to provide a continual reminder to the person of why they are at the weight-loss clinic. When enrolled in a program, the chairs used for group counseling might have larger seats so that the person feels good about small, gradual accomplishments.

Symbolic Representation

Recognizing objects and then using them as a guide for environmental understanding has long been a central focus of human evolution and survival (Kaplan & Kaplan, 1982b). Architectural researchers have identified the interaction between a setting and activity as *place*. Objects and places, therefore, serve as icons or symbolic representations embedded into our personal, social, and cultural identity; thus, they lead to an experience. Jerusalem, for example, is a place that has symbolic meaning to many who follow the Judeo-Christian religions. To understand the meaning behind a location or object involves affective and cognitive processes (Kaplan & Kaplan, 1982b) that converge to form powerful social and cultural understanding with a unified meaning (Pondy, Frost, Morgan, & Dandridge, 1983; Schein, 1990). The meaning ascribed to a location or object can then be explained as an icon or a symbol, which is merely an interpretation.

SUSTAINABILITY CONNECTION 6.1

Designers have the heavy burden of caring for public health, safety, and welfare; and with that goes sustaining the cultural identity of the region. To the general population an object is an object; although an object (such as a picture, building, or statue) becomes a *symbol* when it conceals to all but the "knowing few" a deeper meaning and a larger message. Many groups or communities have their own unspoken language—symbols. Thus, to sustain and promote the mutual relationship between cultural identity and the built environment, designers must engage local people in the design process to ensure the appropriate and adequate use of symbols and design features.

People who encounter icons or symbols assign meaning through their own individual perspectives and recurring experiences. The dollar sign ($), for example, is a symbol associated with U.S. currency. This symbol has many meanings and represents complete ideas such as: money, capitalism, and wealth to Americans and others throughout the world. However, the symbol used to denote the British Pound (£) is less recognizable in the United States and may not represent or hold significant meaning for Americans. The interpretation

of a symbol is therefore dependent upon the group of people and their assigned meaning of it. We can thus say that symbols provide a tangible expression of a shared reality between multiple groups of people (Dandridge, Mitroff, & Joyce, 1980).

Design often contains many symbols that lead to an unspoken mode of communication. This communiqué imparts many messages to include a level and degree of trust and social status, and to some degree it assists in wayfinding.

Consider the following hypothetical situation:

Imagine walking through a set of tall glass doors and into a large office building in the middle of busy city block. As you approach the doors, there is a doorman dressed with a top hat and a jacket with tails. This man opens the door as you approach. The people around you are all carrying some form of leather bag: Some are purses, some computer bags, and others look like brief cases. The people are all wearing suits in shades of black, navy blue, and gray. Inside the tall glass doors is a vast space with a marble floor, a coffee stand, and a little convenience store that sells a little bit of everything. You approach and enter a highly reflective chrome elevator. Inside the elevator soft soothing music is playing in the background. and the people riding the elevator with you are perfumed and manicured. The elevator deposits you on the seventeenth floor. As you step out of the elevator, you see a heavy dark wood door with a brass plate mounted on it. As you enter this door, you see a younger person sitting behind a very large mahogany desk that rests upon a marble floor. The person is a woman who is wearing a suit, matching lipstick, and a cordless headset. Above this woman, mounted on mahogany paneling, is a brass-outlined rendition of what looks to be a blindfolded woman holding a set of scales.

In this example there are several symbols that lead a person to arrive at one set of conclusions over another. These symbols include:

- *Location*. Middle of a busy city block
- *Architecture*. Large building with tall glass doors
- *Amenities*. A doorman in uniform, and types of services in the lobby
- *People*. The clothing people wear and their accessories
- *Interior design*. Heavy woods, marble flooring, reflective chrome elevator
- *Pictographs*. The brass outline of a blindfolded woman holding a set of scales

All of these symbols can be powerful physical indicators of organizational life, and not merely a backdrop from which organizational actions occur. They represent underlying values, assumptions, philosophies, and expectations that serve to influence behavior through associative values and norms; and they provide a framework of reference that facilitates conversation about abstract concepts and captures systems of meaning that integrate emotion, cognition, and behavior into a shared set of codes.

The symbols identified in the previous example were formed through societal norms. There are other sets of symbols that are central to cultural and religious practices. For example, a large mountain such as Mount Rainier in Washington State, a large rock such as Ayers Rock in Australia, or very large trees such as the California Redwoods become viewed with wonder and may take on religious symbolism. In design, we see this kind of awe-inspiring reactions to very tall or extremely large buildings. The Taipai 101 tower in Taiwan stands among the tallest buildings in world and is a significant source of pride for the people of that country. Likewise, Catherine the Great's Hermitage and Summer Palaces are enormous buildings and a source of strength and pride for the Russian people. Borrowing from the concept of *looming*, large objects can appear imposing, frightening (Givens, 1986), and make us feel small. Perhaps this is why large natural attributes take on a special reverence within human societies; the sheer size communicates a unified symbolic understanding of power.

CULTURE AND TRADITION

Culture and diversity are two important components of self-identity that define who we are in the context of the greater population. However, many average North Americans regard diversity solely in terms of ethnicity. As a component of social diversity, culture is an important consideration, but by what means do we define culture? Filipinos, for example, have physical features typically associated with people of Asian descent but mostly follow the Catholic religion. In this way, Filipinos are more *culturally* similar to Latino populations. Both Filipinos and Latinos tend to have large extended families and share religious iconography and a predominantly *external locus of control* (discussed below). However, diversity is more than ethnicity and religion; it is language, gender, and sexual orientation; to a broader extent, it can encompass physical diversities such as amenities and décor.

Anthropologists suggest that people develop and maintain culture as a method of dealing with everyday problems or circumstances. In this way, culture is one way to bring about predictability within the world, to make sense of our surroundings, and to maintain self-preservation. We do this by applying meaning to objects, events, and people—thereby making the world a less mysterious and frightening place. Perhaps one of the most important components of culture is the way in which people function on a daily basis.

This includes how people interact with others, how time affects their attitudes and behaviors, and how they work to resolve conflicts. In short, this is a value system by which we perceive the world. To illustrate this point, consider that culture defines a person's self identity and behaviors based on family structure, societal roles, norms of decorum, religious beliefs, and other influencing aspects of one's life. For many Polynesian Islanders, the family structure is viewed in terms of the mother and father having equal status in decision-making. Likewise, many people from the Filipino culture prefer same-sex healthcare providers when total nudity is involved, especially adult males. Hence, this value system will influence the person's perceptions and subsequent feelings. A Filipino male who is undressed and given a sponge bath by a female nurse may feel like he has lost his dignity and, therefore, may become depressed and withdrawn.

Culture is in many respects the compilation of a community's knowledge, experience, beliefs, values, actions, attitudes, meanings, hierarchies, religion, notions of time, roles, spatial relations, concepts of the universe, and artifacts acquired by a group of people in the course of generations through individual and group striving (Samovar & Baldner, 1998). Some of the common orientations of culture are how one interacts with others, how one perceives oneself in relation to time, and how one views problems and the relationship between the material and spiritual world. For example, as people relate to one another, they may do so from their own perspective, through a relationship that has formed, from a collective perspective of a family or group, or from the collective perspective of a community or tribe (Figure 6.3). As such, we in the design fields need to carefully consider the population constituencies of the various built environments if we are to assist in the promotion of both physical and psychological health, safety, and welfare.

CULTURAL CONNECTION 6.1

Space is an interesting notion for designers to ponder through the lens of other cultures. To a Westerner, *space* implies a location such as one with enclosing walls or the like, whereas in the Navajo culture there is no such concept—space is *movement*. To illustrate: for spatial connotations the Navajo recognize six cardinal points: north, south, east, west, zenith (overhead), and nadir (beneath). Combined with their worldview of "all is in motion" and thereby changing, the Navajo idea of constraining space is foreign and unattainable. Therefore, defining their built environment is unnecessary to them, although defining how one would *move through it* is necessary. With this perspective, designers could create spaces as an exercise in terms of the symbolic meaning of expressing human movement rather than confining it.

[**Figure 6.3**] In many traditional cultures the use of design was a means to convey messages. For many Native American tribes, shapes and colors had meaning and were thus included into many interior features and became a part of the people's history. © Pat Canova / Alamy

Locus of Control

Belief systems are often rooted in the individual's locus of control, which refers to how we view ourselves and opportunities. Individuals who have a strong **external locus of control (ELOC)**, or *externals,* believe that they are controlled by external forces (e.g., fate, luck, chance, powerful others) rather than their own actions. Conversely, those with a strong **internal locus of control (ILOC)**, or *internals,* believe that their actions, choices and pursuits control their destiny. From a design perspective externals tend to prefer larger interpersonal spaces (Heckel & Hiers, 1977), whereas internals tend to tolerate higher-density situations (Verbrugge & Taylor, 1980). Consider this from a control perspective: Internals believe that they can influence outcomes; thus, if their personal space is invaded, they will not hesitate to attempt to regain control of that space or they will simply leave the situation. They are likely to be proactive

throughout the design process and will try to influence future safety and resale value. One study found that internals usually prefer the simplicity and orderliness of straight lines, whereas externals usually prefer more romantic-style buildings with rolling lines and greater detail (Juhasz & Paxson, 1978). Additionally, externals tend to be superstitious and gain support outside of themselves, which is why they tend to have more artifacts—things that make them feel safe (Figure 6.4).

How our locus of control develops depends greatly on the environment of our youth. Internals tend to grow up in families that emphasize effort, education, responsibility, and thinking, whereas externals tend to have lower socio-economic standing, limited access to information, or, in some cases, have been oppressed to the point of developing learned helplessness. The key variable for those with an external locus of control is their perceived inability to influence the outcome of their future.

Religion

The way in which one's personality develops will depend greatly upon his/her cultural values, traditions, and upbringing. Within the world there are approximately ten core religions. Within each of these core religions are a multitude of variations. For example, Christianity is the religion from which Episcopalians, Baptists, and Catholics derive. When we consider the implication of religion on culture and its relationship to diversity, we need to first understand one's cultural disposition regarding the material (tangible) or spiritual (intangible) realm. Those cultures with a material disposition often operate from the paradigm that one must be able to touch and see something for it to exist (Figure 6.5). This belief set is common among the European cultures. Conversely, those cultures that have a spiritual orientation tend to give credence to those elements beyond the human senses and perceptual reality (Kopec, 2007). However, different cultures conceive of spirituality differently. For example, many Asian cultures regard spirituality from the perspective of universal forces, whereas many Native American populations conceive of spirituality through interconnectivity with nature.

Humans by nature are a reference-based species and, therefore, we look to symbols, actions, artifacts, and **mores** (societal practices rather than laws) as points of reference for our cultural affiliation. The symbolism used within different cultures assumes a variety of forms including:

1. *The spoken word (i.e., pronunciation, intensity, and volume).* For example, many Arab cultures tend to speak loudly and pronounce their words forcefully. Conversely, many Asian and Latino cultures tend to

speak softly and with less intensity (Samovar & Porter, 1994).

2. *The written word (e.g., types of lettering, the direction from which the word is read).* For example, traditional Jewish script is read from right to left, while much of Chinese literature is read from top to bottom.

3. *Nonverbal actions (e.g., shaking hands, bowing, eye contact).* For example, eye contact is important in American culture because it indicates honesty and sincerity; however, in Asian cultures maintaining eye contact with someone of a higher social status is considered disrespectful.

Within design there are many objects of affiliation, which include flags, emblems, logos, and religious iconography. The symbols of Australia, for example, are the kangaroo, emu, and Southern Cross constellation (Figure 6.6), whereas the symbol of the gay and lesbian community is the upside-down triangle (pink for gays; black for lesbians).

Color can also be a form of symbolism that transmits information about emotions, feelings, and moods. All countries, states, and provinces mark their identities with colorful dyes affixed to banners, crests, flags, and seals. In fashion, wearing the same color suggests a social tie, such as shared membership in a club, gang, pack, school, sorority, team, or tribe. This grouping or affiliation is a byproduct of the primate's **trichromacy** (Jacobs, 2005), meaning the ability to see color.

Other associations can come from objects of power or status (e.g., automobile, jewelry, artwork, technology). In the political realm, the nuclear bomb is considered a symbol of power, which makes it an item of status. Likewise, the Catholic religion prides itself on being the religion with the largest following. Having the largest population size is the source of status. For many organizations a particular design could be the source of status. The Seattle Space Needle, for example, is a source of status because of its uniqueness. Similarly, because of Frank Gehry's popularity, his avant-garde designs have become a source of status for many cities. Hence, whether a design is good or bad may be irrelevant because the ascribed status may take precedence.

As designers working within a culturally diverse world, we must recognize that culture itself is a complex phenomenon that is highly adaptive, subjective, and likely to evolve. This means that cultures will differ from region to region, from one point in time to another, and across the population's socioeconomic status (SES). What this means for the designer who is charged with the corporate design across a nation or the world is that each design will need to be regarded in its singularity and be adaptable to each location's unique target population.

[**Figure 6.4**] Many people who are religious imbue objects with special spiritual significance. The cross is an important material object within the Christian religion. © Stephen Barnes / Religion / Alamy

[**Figure 6.5**] In this photo we can see the kingdom of God as being larger than life and the people as servants to God. The idea behind the imagery is to remind people that if they are good and lead a God-fearing life they will be welcomed into God's kingdom. © Yadid Levy / Alamy

[**Figure 6.6**] Large groups of people—whether a club or an entire nation—look to symbols for identity and affiliation. The Australian coat of arms and flag serve as unifying symbols for all Australians. Here the coat of arms has been integrated into the design of the Australian Parliament House in Canberra. © Steve Taylor ARPS / Alamy

COLOR

Human perceptions of and reactions to color are, to some extent, dependent on our cultural belief systems. For example, in European cultures, brides wear white and mourners wear black, whereas in Asian cultures, brides wear red and mourners wear white. A study of color preference in Japan found that while *hue* relates more to perceived warmth, *saturation* (regardless of hue) relates most closely to preference (more saturated hues were evaluated as more elegant, more comfortable, and just better); moreover, the study found that *brightness* or *lightness* (regardless of hue) is related to perceptions of how active the room seemed to be—brighter colors were perceived as fresher, lighter, and more cheerful than darker ones (Kunishima & Yanase, 1985).

Within design, color can be described according to three main attributes: hue, saturation, and brightness. It is important to note that although the color of objects are described in terms of hue, lightness, and saturation, light is described in terms of hue, brightness, and saturation. Hence, color quality is dependant on both pigment and lighting.

- *Hue* is the color family or name (such as red, green, or purple) that allows its identification; hue is directly linked to the color's wavelength.
- *Saturation* (also called *chroma*) is a measure of the purity of a color (how sharp or dull it appears) as well as a color's depth or intensity (i.e., its freedom from dilution with white).
- *Brightness* or whiteness (also called *luminance* or *value*) is the shade (darkness) or tint (lightness) of a color relative to its saturation (the degree to which a color reflects light). Its levels of lightness and saturation determine a color's brilliance.

Other aspects that effect the perception of color are textures and materials. Color perception can be affected by the way light interacts with various textures and materials. Fabrics such as velvet, which is thick and deep, tend to look much darker than reflective surfaces of the same hue (Pegler, 1998). Likewise, rough natural textures such as wood and cork cause color to appear darker.

Color and Sight

Color is an important component of sight because it gives better detection of spatial features, highlights specific items, and sets the mood within interior spaces (Bell & Ternus, 2006). However, without light we cannot perceive color (Pegler, 1998) or form, and without the proper use of color and contrast we are unable to accurately perceive our environment.

The effects of color and color patterns on humans appear to be far-reaching. Although red, yellow, and orange are thought to be high-arousal (warm) colors and blue, green, and most violets are considered low-arousal (cool) colors, a color's brilliance can alter its psychological message. Researchers have found that a significant variance in emotional response to color happens not because of the color's hue, but rather its levels of brightness and saturation (Smith, 2003). One study demonstrated that different intensities of the same color affected people's responses: subjects perceived light-green rooms as being less crowded than identical dark-green rooms (Baum & Davis, 1976). This corroborates a study where researchers demonstrated that rooms designed with lighter colors are perceived as more open and spacious (Pelligrini, 1985). Another study identified more cooperative behaviors among children in day care centers where rooms had varied wall color as opposed to uniformity (Persad et al., 1995). Research has also shown a correlation between our perceptions of ambient temperature and the color of our surroundings. For example, a room designed with "cool" accessories (e.g., tile, stainless steel, glass, the color blue) can reduce an observer's perception of the ambient temperature by a few degrees. From the vast and diversified research in this area, we can see that color can be used to create illusions of spaciousness, as an adjunct for the facilitation of certain behaviors, and, through perception, as a mild method of temperature regulation (Figure 6.7).

Neurobiology of Color

Color is a property of light that depends on wavelength (Figure 6.8), and light is a function of energy. Warm colors (i.e., those having longer wavelengths along the electromagnetic spectrum) range from red to yellow; cool colors (i.e., those having shorter wavelengths) range from blue to violet. White sunlight contains the primary colors of light: red, green, and blue. A surface looks white when it reflects all of the light waves that strike it. Black is not a color, but rather a visual effect caused by the absence of light. Surfaces that absorb all light waves *appear* black and convert light waves into heat energy—an important consideration when designing outdoor settings. Color, as we see it, is simply a portion of the spectrum of a light wave that is reflected by a surface. Humans, apes, and monkeys see these colors because we all possess an autosomal gene that encodes a blue light-sensitive pigment and at least two X-linked genes (genes carried on the X chromosome) that encode for red and green pigments (Shyue et al., 1995).

Some studies have shown that how people perceive color may be related to a sex-linked genetic trait. Pardo, Pérez, and Suero (2007) found that men and women had different perceptions of color. This could be a result of biological differences between men and women when detecting the properties of color, or it could be a result of evolutionary demands for color perception and detection. It is thought that primitive women needed to be able to discern between two shades of red berries in order to identify the edible berry, whereas primitive men in the open savanna and direct sunlight (which tends to wash out subtle differences between colors) did not evolve to develop a higher level of color perception.

How Our Eyes Detect Color

The first level of detecting color occurs within the human eye. The eye has three different types of color-sensitive photoreceptors that are sensitive to the primary colors, which is why all other colors can be created from primary colors. We perceive color as a result of light and pigments (the substance that imparts color to another substance). The primary colors of light (red, green, and blue) are the *additive primaries,* used to create *transmissive color.* The primary colors of pigments (cyan, magenta, and yellow) are the *subtractive primaries* (because they absorb or subtract other colors) used to create *reflective color.*

Monochromatism (color blindness) is a condition where a person is unable to perceive the differences between some or all colors. It is often a genetic condition and affects about one tenth of the male population. Color blindness can also occur as a result of chemical exposure as well as damage to the eye, optic nerve, or brain. The genetic manifestations of color blindness can range from the partial or complete loss of function in one or more of the eye's different **cone** systems. Cones are the aspect of the human eye that enables us to see color. Should only one cone system be compromised, **dichromacy** results and the person loses only one range of the color spectrum.

[**Figure 6.7**] Color has the ability to influence not only some of our physiological responses but also our perceptions of temperature and spaciousness. Illustration by Precision Graphics

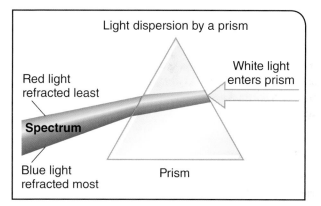

[**Figure 6.8**] Color is a byproduct of light. Without light we have no color. Warmer colors (red through yellow) tend to have higher wavelengths and, as such, experience less refraction. Greens through blue have lower wavelengths and are refracted more. Illustration by Precision Graphics

Red-green color blindness is the most common form of color blindness. It results when the cones that detect and process middle or long wavelengths have been compromised. People with this condition experience difficulties discriminating between reds, yellows, and greens. This can be problematic when driving because traffic lights use the colors red, yellow, and green; but it is a benefit during military combat because men with this disorder can better see others dressed in camouflage. There are other less frequent forms of color blindness. One of these includes the inability to discriminate between blues and yellows. People with this condition view the world in blacks, whites, and shades of gray. Classifications of color blindness include:

- *Protanomaly.* When a person is better able to detect shorter wavelengths. Individuals with this condition are less sensitive to red light, and the color is often mistaken for black.
- *Deuteranomaly.* A mutated form of medium-wavelengths. This causes a reduction in the sensitivity to colors within the green spectrum. This is the most common form of color blindness, and occurs in about 6 percent of the male population. Deuteranomates experience difficulties discriminating between the small differences in colors red, orange, yellow, and green. People with this disorder often make errors when naming the hues in this region because the red wavelengths tend to dominate.
- *Tritanomaly.* A mutated form of the short-wavelengths (blue). This is the rarest form of color blindness. Trichromasy color deficiencies can present equally in both male and female populations.

How Our Brains Adjust Color

The way in which we perceive color is regulated by the visual systems within our brain. The brain has the ability to adjust to varying colors in different illuminations; this is called *chromatic* or *color adaptation*. Color adaptation allows us to balance color signals detected by our eyes as we move through various environments. In this way, our brain continually processes information retrieved by our eyes. In other words, light and color are never completely balanced within an interior space. This means that color may appear more or less saturated depending upon its location and its interaction with light. Without this ability to continually adapt to the different lumens within the environment, most light sources would probably make us sick. For example, if you look at an object's color first under an artificial light source and second under natural daylight, like most people, you will not be able to observe a significant shift in color. However, if you were to photograph the same object under each lighting condition, the color of the object would look different. This occurs in part because our brain acts as a filter and helps us to interpret what we see.

The majority of optic nerve fibers travel from the eye to the very back of the brain, a region called the occipital lobe. However, different parts of the brain are responsible for different parts of vision. The thalamus, for example, responds to form, motion, and color. Other areas such as the V1 are responsible for the interpretation of three-dimensional images and allow us to determine the form and orientation of objects. The V2 area allows us to understand the relationship between form and color.

To illustrate this relationship and its importance to designers, consider the person afflicted with Alzheimer's disease. The disease for many of these people affects the V1 and V2 regions, which means that the person will experience difficulties distinguishing the top of a chair from the floor when the flooring material and the chair seat are similar in color. A person with a well-developed V4 (the area responsible for color) may look at a bowl of fruit and see vibrancies between the different colors whereas a person with a more developed V2 (the area responsible for depth perception) may find greater fascination with the three-dimensional form of the fruit in the bowl (Canter, 1997).

Equally important is the brainstem, which allows for the mechanics of vision, such as the size of the pupil in response to light intensity, and which allows the brain to perceive smooth scans as we shift our gaze across a room or from object to object. This happens because the brain stem fills in the gaps between a series of relatively still images to complete the visual field.

Psychosocial Effects of Color

Color speaks to each of us on an emotional level, but the manner in which color influences human behavior directly is still being investigated. The question of whether our reactions to color have a biological correlation or are merely a by-product of our socialization requires further exploration; for the purpose of design, there appears to be an association both ways because learned responses can cause biological manifestations. For example, imagine that you learned snakes were dangerous when you were a child, and you come face-to-face with one now as an adult. As you approach the reptile, your body will likely respond with a faster heart rate, higher blood pressure, and possibly even fear-induced paralysis. Your biological response was to an environmental element, but your psychological conditioning shaped that biological response.

Many theorists and researchers claim that color acts on the body as well as the mind. Physiological changes occur when we are exposed to certain colors due to a phenomenon called *chromodynamics*. One research team concluded that long wavelength hues are more arousing than short wavelength hues after determining that higher-state anxiety scores were associated with red and yellow as opposed to blue and green. Because anxiety involves displeasure and high arousal, "these findings were consistent with results from studies of physiological reactions to color (demonstrating that red and yellow were more arousing than blue and green) and with studies of color preferences (showing that yellow and yellow-green were less pleasant than blue and green)" (Valdez

[**Table 6.1**] Psychological Effects of Color

Color	Psychological Effect
Red	Stimulates brain wave activity, increases heart rate, increases blood pressure
Pink	Appetite suppressant, relaxes muscles, soothes
Orange	Energizes, stimulates appetite
Yellow	Energizes, relieves depression, improves memory, stimulates appetite
Green	Soothes, mentally and physically relaxes, mitigates depression and anxiety
Blue	Calms, lowers blood pressure, decreases respiration
Violet	Suppresses appetite, inspires the sense of a peaceful environment, helps alleviate migraines
Black	Inspires self-confidence, strength, power
White	Elicits sense of the clean, virginal, and angelic

Adapted from: http://webdesign.about.com/od/colorcharts/l/bl_colorculture.htm

& Mehrabian, 1994). However, another study conducted in a specially constructed learning environment found that higher-level functioning such as math, reading, and motor task performances did not vary significantly in red, blue, or yellow rooms (Fehrman, 1987), suggesting that color affects the involuntary biological systems more than the voluntary biological systems. This suggests that the effects of color are more biological than psychological (Table 6.1).

When we look at an object, our brain determines its color in the context of the surrounding colors. When two very similar colors meet, both appear to wash out and become indistinct because the borders between them are difficult to distinguish and the brain blurs them together. Similarly, bright complementary colors placed next to each other attract attention, but the effect is disconcerting. Looking at such combinations (such as red stripes on a green background) causes a vibrating or pulsing visual effect: The colors appear to pull away from each other, making our eyes feel like they are being shaken. This effect, called *color fatiguing*, occurs as the optic nerve sends confused signals to the brain; hence, the term optical illusions.

The effects of certain colors such as warm and cool colors seem to be more universal than others. Warm colors appear to be closer to us than cool colors, but vivid cool colors can overwhelm light, subtle, warm colors. Using warm colors for foreground and cool colors for background enhances the perception of depth. Cool colors are frequently used for backgrounds to set off smaller areas of warm colors. Used together, cool colors can look clean and crisp, implying status and calmness. However, bright cool colors are more stimulating than light, medium, or dark cool colors.

Color and Environmental Cognition

Research has demonstrated that color is important to the perception of space, building form, wayfinding, ambiance, and image; its relationship to the practice of design can be understood within the four aspects that make up the following theoretical framework (Valdez & Mehrabian, 1994):

1. *Conceptions of designing* (production, retail, experiential, and structural). Color is often used as a method of branding (i.e., identifying a product or service) and serves as a symbol that conveys a message. For example, the bright orange vests worn by public workers and other construction crews have come to symbolize construction work in general, and a popular home-

improvement retailer has capitalized on the color reference of "construction orange."

2. *Place formation and the architectural experience* (relationship of the person to the environment). Color coding enables us to use certain colors to facilitate wayfinding, and we also recognize universal uses of color as symbolic representations. For example, the color "red" means *stop* or *emergency;* in an emergency, we can just search for the color red instead of having to depend upon our higher cognitive skills.

3. *Understanding of the nature of the built environment* (object, product, communication, and social domain). The interiors of most, if not all, Western hospitals in the past were white. Even today, just being inside a structure with white walls and floors can make us feel as if we are in a hospital.

4. *Fashion and styles.* Color is often associated with certain historical periods. For example, the popularity of avocado green, goldenrod, and burnt orange make us recall the early to mid-1970s; likewise, mauve, pink and gray are representational of the early to mid-1980s.

Whether our reaction to color is the result of selected combinations of light waves hitting our retinas and subsequently causing the secretion or reuptake of neurochemicals, a learned response passed from generation to generation, or a combination of these processes remains to be determined by empirical research. Our experience of color is affected by a combination of biological, physiological, psychological, social, and cultural factors; in fact, the manner in which people associate colors is often the most meaningful aspect of visual experience.

WAYFINDING

The process of wayfinding (i.e., navigating to or from a particular destination) may be a function of our biological sex, culture, tradition, and history. Finding our way involves various techniques and skills; some people use reference points such as landmarks, whereas others seem to have a built-in compass. However, an almost universal but incorrect assumption (*ecological fallacy*) holds that men have a better sense of direction than women. Perhaps this is because men were the primary designers of our early built environments and constructed it according to their wayfinding preferences; had women been the first city planners, would the woman's sense of direction be seen as superior? Modern megastructures and concrete jungles have made wayfinding an issue of growing concern and a subject of intense study as scientists and design professionals strive to develop better means and methods to ease navigation and blend into or even enhance surrounding designs.

In modern society, to find our way around an environment, we often make use of color (Figure 6.9). We depend on the technique of color coding and symbolic representations that rely on color (red = stop and green = go) to navigate within the built environment. Although wayfinding may seem like a relatively new phenomenon, it has been a necessary function of humanity since our earliest beginnings. Whether hunting on an open plain or gathering in the dense bush, humans have had to travel away from their homes in search of food and water and therefore had to devise ways to find their way back. The methods that humans used might have included the formation of paths, breaking branches, retracing their tracks, or maybe even using their cardinal senses. Because it is theorized that early men and women had different roles and were subjected to different environments, their methods of wayfinding might have thus evolved differently.

How we find our way in the world is a psychological process that can be highly subjective and individual. To successfully navigate an environment—which changes as we move through it—we must continually acquire, process, reassess, recall, and respond to different stimuli and objects (Abu-Ghazzeh, 1996). Wayfinding, as a process of navigation, consists of three major actions that are generally performed sequentially (Abu-Obeid, 1998; Passini, Pigot, Rainville, & Tetreault, 2000):

1. Deciding what to do and how to do it
2. Moving from decision to action
3. Applying information obtained through sensory input and cognitive processes; in other words, environmental problem solving

How these decisions and processes are categorized in our brains depends on our retrieval methods of cognitive infor-

[**Figure 6.9**] We have often used color for navigation along public transportation routes. Signs appearing in a certain color often corresponded to the color of trains; thus, wayfinding becomes easier. © Michael Dwyer / Alamy

[**Figure 6.10**] Within malls, the food court serves as the central focus and is usually located about 100 yards from one of the anchor stores. People will walk only about 100 yards without stopping, and food courts and anchor stores are likely to cause a person to stop, thus restarting the 100-yard countdown. © Bill Brooks / Alamy

mation, which the built environment can support or constrain. For example, narrow corridors that cannot accommodate traffic flow, lack visual access, and lack reference points all contribute to poor wayfinding.

Scenographic (or picture-based) **representations** and **abstract** (or data-based) **representations** are the two most common ways in which people perceive, comprehend, and store information (Tversky, 2003). Some people map out a route in their heads using visual images or landmarks to orient themselves. Others use such information as actual mileage, **cardinal directions** (the compass directions of north, south, east, and west), and street signs. And, a third group of people use a combination of both picture- and data-based representation.

Cognitive Maps

Understanding how people perceive and conceptualize space is key to helping them interact effectively with an environment. We can measure geometric space, but we must construct a *cognitive map,* or mental image of **navigational space,** the space we move through and explore, which

usually cannot be seen all at once. Cognitive maps are based on sensory information, imagination, and language. In short, our understanding of a space is based on objects within it and their meaning and relationship to us (Fehrman, 1987). We understand the space around us three-dimensionally (based on head–feet, front–back, and left–right axes) and use these directional cues to learn about an environment's spatial arrangement; but our understanding of navigational space is generally two-dimensional and, therefore, subject to conceptual errors (Lawton, 1996). This dichotomy occurs because we learn about spaces as children, three dimensionally, but we recall or imagine space two dimensionally, which helps to explain why design clients strongly prefer models over rendered drawings.

We use cognitive maps as well as the physical objects and elements within a space to locate and reach our destinations (goals) as efficiently as possible. Some people rely heavily on mental floor plans, whereas others rely on orientation or reference points such as landmarks. Research indicates that the number one method of wayfinding by humans is through the use of landmarks (Figure 6.10).

However, wayfinding techniques and abilities appear to differ between men and women. Men rely on reference points, distance estimates, and cardinal directions more than women do, and they exhibit greater confidence in their wayfinding skills (Lawton, 1996; Lawton, Charleston, & Zieles, 1996). This gender difference may be related to levels of anxiety rather than ability (Burns, 1998; Sholl, Acacio, Makar, & Leon, 2000). During childhood, boys are usually allowed to roam farther from home than girls, and experience engenders both ability and confidence (Matthews, 1986a, 1986b). People who question their directional abilities are more likely to experience spatial anxiety (i.e., fear of becoming lost) in a new setting (Lawton, Charleston, & Zieles, 1996; Sholl et al., 2000) and, over time, may come to limit their interactions with the physical environment (Sholl et al., 2000).

Navigation Techniques

The ability to navigate through an environment easily influences our overall perception of it (Passini, Rainville, Marchand, & Joanette, 1998). Greater environmental legibility (the design makes sense) facilitates greater exploration, which leads to greater understanding or at least to a sense of familiarity, all of which promotes greater overall satisfaction with an environment. Wayfinding is made easier through spatial organization, which includes: ordering functions and facilities to create effective circulation (e.g., paths people take) and environmental communication (e.g., architectural and graphic information). Therefore, circulation should be clearly articulated in the spatial organization of a structure so that signage is a secondary means of communication (Weisman, 1981). Without good wayfinding measures built into the design, people will experience difficulties reaching various destinations quickly and efficiently.

Wayfinding Measures

Wayfinding measures that can be built into the design include visual access, architectural delineation, signage, and building layout (Gifford, 2002).

- *Visual access.* Refers to *prospect* or visibility (e.g., clear lines of sight that serve to increase visual access to a destination or reference point), such as half walls, glass partitions, and windows.
- *Architectural delineation.* Refers to the separation of one area from another via architectural elements or features (e.g., thresholds, walls, variations in ceiling height and floor depth).
- *Signage and numbering systems.* Enable us to match displayed codes with the messages or symbolic mean-

ings that we either bring with us (e.g., when we know that a friend occupies a certain hospital room) or obtain from on-site sources (e.g., what we learn from information centers, "you-are-here" maps, or by asking directions).
- *Building layout.* Relates to logical spatial progression and organization (e.g., in a department store, we expect to find women's shoes near women's apparel, not near home appliances).

These mechanisms can be applied to a microenvironment such as a café; but they are equally efficient in larger settings such as hospitals, campuses, malls, office buildings, transit stations, and airports.

Segmentation Bias

People use the psychological construct of **segmentation bias** to cope with long distances. It is estimated that we will walk for only about 100 yards and drive for about 60 minutes before the effort becomes uncomfortable or intolerable. When we have to travel greater distances, we mentally segment or divide the path into smaller, more manageable sections. For example, when driving long distances we segment our route according to the highways (90E for about 35 minutes to the 290N for about 25 minutes to the 190N for about 20 minutes). In large facilities, design can support segmentation biases through the incorporation of sitting areas, changes in flooring material and lighting, and the number and placement of windows.

In design, elaborate wayfinding mechanisms indicate that a structure or environment is not legible enough on its own (Gifford, 2002). The more intricate the floor plan, the more problems people will have with wayfinding (Gärling, Lindberg, & Mantyla, 1983; Moeser, 1988; O'Neil, 1991). One way to mitigate such problems is to increase visual access to the environment (Burns, 1998); many large offices with open floor plans delineate workspaces by dividing the space with partitions that employees can see over. Many people use reference points for orientation purposes (Gärling et al., 1983); in a resort, for example, the lobby, a landmark, or a particular amenity are all reference points. One study recommends the use of floor plans with greater symmetry as well as multiple architectural elements that interact to facilitate wayfinding, noting that such measures are more effective than the use of signage (Allen & Kirasic, 1985).

Multistoried structures with long corridors (e.g., large hotels, cruise ships, hospitals, office and apartment buildings) can seldom use ceiling height to facilitate the wayfinding process. However, we can tell when we have entered an auditorium or ballroom simply because the ceiling has risen. Long corridors and other monotonous paths can appear endless and often lead to confusion in wayfinding, as well as to increase perceived crowding. Design can introduce segmentation bias by incorporating intersections, objects, or color or patterns to help people mentally break up a long monotonous path into more manageable sections.

"You-Are-Here" Maps

A "you-are-here" map is most effective when it matches both the structure and the orientation of the environment—the "you-are-here" symbol should be accurately placed on the map, which itself should be positioned so that users can easily correlate their locations within the environment shown. The map should depict actual sites and landmarks within the setting, and the map's alignment should be the same as the actual setting (e.g., north is north), with the top of the map representing "straight ahead" (Gifford, 2002). However, good signs require considerably less cognitive effort than even good "you-are-here" maps (Gärling et al., 1983).

Signage

Research findings concerning the influence of signage on wayfinding are contradictory and inconclusive (Gärling et al., 1983) perhaps because signs themselves can be illegible due to imprecise wording and lack of detail. Such lack of detail may result from the size constraints of signs, which limit the number of words that can be listed on a sign as well as the illustration detail. Signage is an important form of environmental communication that enhances environmental legibility when properly executed and installed. Words, pictographs (e.g., symbols, logos, images), directional arrows, and numbering systems serve to identify objects and locations and to direct and regulate human activities. Typeface, color(s) and color coding, size, shape, specificity, accuracy, consistency, and visibility all contribute to overall signage legibility. A sign is useful only if it can be clearly seen and understood. For example, displaying the international "No Smoking" symbol will not prevent people from smoking if they cannot see the sign.

CULTURAL CONNECTION 6.2

Throughout the years helping people navigate their surroundings, *wayfinding* has often resulted in excessive signage, arrows, and large informational plaques. Welcome to *waymarking*. The earliest form of waymarking was the delineation of historic or scenic routes for tourists. Perhaps in response to being perpetually lost in new environments or possibly because the technologically savvy adventurers are beginning to make their "mark," waymarking's newest trend in exploration of the global environment involves people armed with Global Positioning Systems (GPS) and digital cameras. These waymarkers document interesting places and things by latitude/longitude coordinates, an image, and a brief description, and then share it with the world through the Internet. With the advent of the GPS, is it perhaps the user who has taken their environment back from designers?

Practical Applications for Designers

Use these resources, activities, and discussion questions to help you identify, synthesize, and retain this chapter's core information. These tools are designed to complement the resources you'll find in this book's companion Study Guide.

SUMMING IT UP

Aesthetics can be defined as a branch of philosophy that deals with beauty and art. The fundamental premises behind the study of aesthetics are the definitions of what constitutes beauty, the rational and emotional criteria of beauty, and the value of beauty. Symbols provide a tangible expression of a shared reality between multiple groups of people.

Diversity is more than ethnicity and religion. It is language, gender, and sexual orientation, and to a broader extent it can also encompass physical diversities, such as amenities and décor. Culture brings about predictability within the world, helps us make sense of our surroundings, and helps us maintain self-preservation by associations with others. Culture is in many respects the compilation of a community's knowledge, experience, beliefs, values, actions, attitudes, meanings, hierarchies, religion, notions of time, roles, spatial relations, concepts of the universe, and artifacts acquired by a group of people.

Color is an influencing variable on the perception and judgment of aesthetics. The arrangement of color and contour have the propensity to evoke conceptual ideas as the mind forms associations. In this way color and aesthetics are intertwined and mutually interdependent. Our experience of color is affected by a combination of biological, physiological, psychological, social, and cultural factors; in fact, the manner in which people associate colors is often the most meaningful aspect of visual experience.

Wayfinding is made easier through the use of signs, color matching, and other directive devices that are the used to form mental images called cognitive maps. Wayfinding measures that can be built into the design include visual access, architectural delineation, signage, and building layout. While wayfinding is an essential function within all of our built environments, security is also a significant factor. Designers must be acutely aware of a multitude of defensible space measures that can be utilized to protect retail and service workers.

You can also refer to this textbook's companion Study Guide for a comprehensive list of Summary Points.

EXPERT SPOTLIGHT 6.1

Color, Security, and Wayfinding

Linda O'Shea, IIDA, LEED AP, IDEC, Kean University

The Problem

Wayfinding in the context of architecture refers to the user experiences of orientation and choosing a path within the built environment—concerns that are paramount for the public's safety and security. An alternative definition of wayfinding, focusing only on the visual aspects comes from J. E. Cutting (1996), who defines it as "how people find their way through cluttered environments with ease and without injury." A successful wayfinding system can solve complex problems of disorientation, which can cause significant stress, especially when trying to evacuate a building in times of emergency or perceived threat. Eliminating disorientation through the design of a wayfinding system that enables building occupants to exit a building safely is an important consideration in design security and supports the design professionals' objective of protecting the health, safety, and welfare of the public.

A good wayfinding system gives strong indicators of where the user is and how one can get to a destination from one's present location, a primary concern when dealing with safety and security issues. Ineffective wayfinding systems are problematic because of valuable time wasted when searching for a desired location, such as an area of refuge, or in times of crisis, such as the evacuation of a building.

Practical Solutions

In terms of safety and security, wayfinding is critical because people need to know the easiest, safest, and fastest way to exit a building safely. When considering safety and security issues within the wayfinding program, it is important to consider the following:

1. Clearly marked building evacuation routes

2. Locations of safe havens (areas of refuge)

3. Exits leading to the outdoors

4. Configuration of the corridor system

5. Adequate light on and around directional signs

6. Placement of signs in areas where people expect to find them

Security zoning is another important consideration when designing an environmental graphics design program from a safety and security perspective. Security zoning allows building users to reach their destination, but prevents them from entering areas where they have no reason to be. Controlling access to specific departments or areas in a building, when appropriate, can screen out unwanted visitors and help employees identify and challenge unauthorized persons. These areas, considered in the initial space planning process, are supported through an effective and organized wayfinding system.

Security zoning commonly uses a varied wayfinding color palette to designate the establishment of three distinct zone types:

1. *Unrestricted zones.* Might include spaces such as lobbies, reception areas, certain personal and administrative offices, and public meeting rooms.

2. *Controlled zones.* Require a valid purpose for entry such as administrative offices, staff dining rooms, security offices, office working areas, and loading docks.

3. *Restricted zones.* Sensitive areas limited to staff and individuals assigned to space within those areas. They include areas such as sensate record storage areas, control rooms, special equipment and other sensitive work areas.

The use of color in security wayfinding programs, based on the Pantone color system, is largely dependent on federal, state, and local codes. An excellent resource to assist the designer in understanding general guidelines; the appropriate use of design elements such as color, text, and graphic layout; as well as requirements for Interior Signage for Code & Life Safety Wayfinding Systems can be found at the Department of Veteran Affairs, VA *Signage Design Guide*: http://www.cfm.va.gov/til/signs/signage01.pdf

A wayfinding program for the built environment that works well in terms of safety and security is one that has been planned as an integrated whole and establishes a clear program that communicates and informs in a direct and simple manner. This is especially important when building occupants require areas of refuge, safe evacuation, and the ability to exit a building rapidly.

Cutting, J. E. (1996). Wayfinding from multiple sources of information, *Journal of Experimental Psychology: Human Perception and Performance, 22,* 1299–1313.

KEY TERMS

- **abstract representation**
- **aesthetics**
- **cardinal directions**
- **cones**
- **dichromacy**
- **external locus of control (ELOC)**
- **formal aesthetics**
- **internal locus of control (ILOC)**
- **monochromatism**
- **mores**
- **navigational space**
- **scenographic representations**
- **segmentation bias**
- **stimulus response**
- **symbolic aesthetics**
- **trichromacy**

WEB LINKS

Colormatters (www.colormatters.com)

Design and Culture (www.designandculture.org/index.php/dc)

Symbols.com, online encyclopedia of Western signs and ideograms (www.symbols.com)

The Mind Science Foundation, listen to "Art and the Brain," by V. S. Ramachandran (www.mindscience.org)

Waymarking.com (www.waymarking.com)

STUDIO ACTIVITY 6.1

Form and Aesthetics

Design Problem Statement
The *Dictionary of the History of Ideas* identifies five uses of the word *form* as it relates to art and aesthetics:

1. The arrangement or order of parts.

2. The content and arrangement that evokes the senses.

3. The boundary, or colors and contour of an object.

4. The conceptual essence of an object, also called "entelechy."

5. The contribution of the mind to the perceived object.

Directions
Step One: Survey design styles contained within three popular design magazines.

Step Two: Cut out photos that exemplify one or more of five uses of the word *form*.

Step Three: On 16 x 20 (or instructor-selected size) foam core, develop a collage using the photos.

Step Four: Diagram the photos so that the observer can focus his or her attention on what you are seeing.

Deliverable
Presentation board that conveys to another observer how you perceive form in the examples.

STUDIO ACTIVITY 6.2

Cultural Preferences

Design Problem Statement
You have been asked to develop an authentic design of the XYZ (you choose) people. This design will be one structure within a city-funded interactive cultural museum. The museum's mission will be to provide an interactive recreational venue for families. Your job is to research

culture XYZ and then develop an authentic design within one of the structures.

Directions
Step One: Identify predominate colors, patterns, shapes, textures, and symbols of your culture.

Step Two: Analyze the different ways in which those color, patterns, shapes, and symbols are used within the culture. (For example, would a cross be hung over a door, to the right of a door, or to the left of a door in a Filipino household?)

Step Three: List important cultural activities that take place throughout a given year and the rooms within a home where those activities take place.

Step Four: Using authentic design, develop a room in your building making sure to allow the design to be interactive with the visitors.

Deliverable
Presentation board that provides examples of different cultural design elements used for the flooring, walls, and fixtures.

DISCUSSION QUESTIONS

1. Why is it important for designers to analyze the surrounding environments of a design?

2. Discuss the different crowding and privacy design directions you would take with a client with an *internal locus of control* versus a client with an *external locus of control.*

3. Discuss directional signage and what aspects can make it illegible, using specific examples from your neighborhood or campus. Consider how someone from a non-English-speaking country might interpret the signs.

4. Describe your method for remembering directions. What steps are involved, and what techniques do you employ? Are your methods stereotypically masculine or feminine?

5. Discuss methods in which design determines circulation and methods by which to ensure that the spatial organization of a structure is self-explanatory.

LEARNING ACTIVITIES

1. Come up with ideas for the design of a public space that implements both *formal aesthetics* and *symbolic aesthetics.* Describe measures you would implement in your design to create a balance of perception in the public's eye of your design. List your ideas and discuss possible scenarios that could arise from your final design. Would you make any changes after your evaluation? If so, what would you change and why?

2. Using the city of Jerusalem, show how each of the six means of cultural transmission of place attachment applies.

3. Contact a local retirement or nursing home and request a social visit with several residents who have complete cognitive functioning. Bring in 12 color samples (available free from a home-improvement store's paint section), ensuring they span the color spectrum and provide a variety of saturation levels. Ask the residents to view each sample separately and respond to each one. Record their responses for each color, making sure to discuss the subjects' reasons, and try to determine if their responses are objective or subjective. Next, repeat the experiment with classmates; compare and contrast their responses to the same colors, noting any differences or similarities due to gender or age.

4. Photograph or sketch ten local signs that are directional or offer information about a place or its use. (Do not use signs with street names because these are labels.) Make sure your images do not show the setting. Show your images to a friend and see how many of the signs he or she can identify out of context.

5. Create a new town. Design a county seat (i.e., include a courthouse, sheriff's department, and the like) for a population of 10,000 people, complete with a city hall, library, parks, and so on. Draw a zoning map that supports people's needs for visual access to open space, environmental communication, and spatial organization. How will people navigate your streets? Will tourists be able to find their way to local shops and attractions easily?

07 Infants, Toddlers, and Childhood

As your baby progresses from one milestone to the next, remember that he doesn't really leave any of them behind. In order to grow and develop to his full potential he must continually build on and strengthen all of the steps that have gone before.

—Stanley I. Greenspan

In the early 1800s, Kaspar Hauser was abandoned as a young child and raised until the age of 17 in a dungeon. Hauser's experience in the dungeon was of relative sensory deprivation. As a result, his emotional, behavioral, and cognitive abilities were grossly underdeveloped (Kitchen, 2001). This is just one of the sad yet important cases of children who were deprived of sensory stimuli either because of abandonment or institutionalization in substandard environments. Over time, we have learned a great deal about the importance of including a variety of stimulation within environments intended for young people. For example, research performed on animals has shown that animals raised in environments rich in sensory stimuli develop brains that are larger, more complex, and possessing greater flexibility (Diamond & Hopson, 1998; Meaney et al., 1988; Plotsky & Meaney, 1993; Uno et al., 1989). There is also a demonstrated 30 percent increase in synaptic density in the cortex of animals raised in environments with significant levels of stimulation versus those raised in sensory deprived environments (Altman and Das, 1964; Bennett et al., 1964). The physical brains of rats raised in enriched environments have been found to be heavier than the brains of rats raised in average environments. The added weight comes from increased blood flow to the cortex (Jones & Greenough, 1996) and a multitude of new neural connections (Black et. al., 2001; Comery et al., 1995; Diamond et al., 1972; Greenough & Chang, 1988; Nelson, 1999; Turner & Greenough, 1985).

[**Figure 7.1**] Infants, toddlers, and children need enriching environments for optimal emotional, intellectual, and physical development. This means that items with bright contrasting colors in numerous shapes and sizes should be included within play spaces to encourage cognitive activity. © imagebroker / Alamy

[**Figure 7.2**] Throughout the world, many cultures still regard the environment from a purely functionalist perspective. Although this perspective was not a problem when we spent the majority of our time outside in nature, our relatively recent movement to the interior world means that we lack the enriching stimulation levels required for optimal development. © Jeremy Sutton-Hibbert / Alamy

Children raised in orphanages versus those placed in foster homes revealed that the attention and nurturing associated with a home environment produced superior emotional, intellectual, and physical development. The results of these studies are what helped to produce the common children's design style that incorporates bright, bold colors and a vast array of toys (Figure 7.1).

In 1973 Dennis published a book about children who were brought up in the orphanages of Lebanon. In essence, what he concludes is that children who grow up within an institutional environment devoid of individual attention, cognitive stimulation, emotional affection, or other forms of physical stimuli showed an average IQ score of 50 by age 16. A score of 50 roughly translates to the cognitive ability of an eight-year-old. Conversely, children adopted by age two showed an average IQ score of 100 by age 16, and children adopted between the ages of two and six years showed an average IQ of 80 (Dennis, 1973). More recent studies in Romania reveal that children raised in orphanages but adopted prior to six months of age have greater intellectual, emotional, and physical improvements after four years than children who were adopted between ages six months and two years (Rutter et al., 1998, 1999; see Figure 7.2).

Studies show that children, infants in particular, require a variety of physical and emotional stimuli and that there is an interactive and symbiotic relationship between individuals and their environments. In short, the physical environment affects the behaviors of all people to some degree. Children stand out as users of the built environment because they develop from completely helpless beings into young adults who have learned how to live within those environments. The manner in which the environment affects children varies by circumstance and is highly contingent on their stage of development. Most experts agree that the primary developmental stages include fetal or prenatal, infant, toddler and preschool, child, preadolescent, and adolescent. At each stage of development there are specific needs and concerns that relate not only to their cognitive development, but also their overall physical and psychological health. Therefore, we must first understand the developmental stages in order to gain insights into their perceptions and thought processes and to understand how various environments affect them.

THE FETUS: OUR FIRST ENVIRONMENT

The first environments that we are exposed to are in the womb. All life develops faster in the womb during the embryonic and fetal stages than at any other time in life. From the moment of conception, the fetus undergoes rapid changes in a relatively short period of time. The fetus will first develop the organs necessary for survival as well as the cognitive capabilities that it will need to survive outside of the womb. These changes are marked by three distinct phases referred to as first, second and third trimesters (Berger, 2006). During these stages, the fetus's first defenses and learning tools will be his/her ability to detect sensation. The five senses (i.e., sight, sound, touch, smell, and taste) begin to develop early in gestation, and researchers believe that the ability to detect sensation at an early age enables the infant to begin experiencing and cataloging the world around him/her. However, it is important to understand that a fetus's environment is made up of the mother's womb and all that she is exposed to (e.g., light and sound). Designing a suitable environment for the expectant mother is, in essence, designing for the offspring; and the mother's exposure to environmental agents—both emotional and physical pollutants—has a direct impact on the fetus. At this stage of development, the fetus's experiences are intertwined with the experiences of his/her mother. Likewise a fetus needs stimulation during gestation in order to become better equipped for detecting the differences between ranges of stimuli that he/she will be exposed to throughout life.

Around eight weeks into gestation, the receptors in the skin that are used to detect sensation begin to develop. Although visual development typically begins a little earlier in gestation (about four weeks), both vision and hearing are the least developed of the senses at the time of birth. In fact, it can take several months, or years, for vision and hearing to reach full development (Children's Hospital Boston, 2005). See Table 7.1 for a brief categorization of youth developmental stages.

The areas of the body that have the most touch receptors are the hands, lips, face, neck, tongue, fingertips, feet, and genital area. At about eight weeks, the touch receptors are the first of the sense organs to develop. The fetus will first become sensitive around the mouth, then the genital area, palms of the hands, soles of the feet, and later the buttocks and stomach (Bilich, 2006). The sensation of touch for the developing fetus is often limited, but many of the fetus's first sensory stimuli from the external world are sensations derived from its mother's experiences. For example, by about 28 weeks a fetus is able to smell and he/she will begin to experience a variety of scents that derive from regional vegetation and favorite scents (e.g., cooking, perfume, candles; Bilich, 2006). By the twenty-sixth week of gestation, a fetus's retinas will be almost fully developed. Despite the fact that the fetus will not be able to see shape and form from within its mother's womb, he/she can detect the difference between light and dark. Some researchers believe that a fetus may be able to see a faint orange glow as light passes through a pregnant woman's flesh during the last weeks of pregnancy. This assumption is affirmed by tests that demonstrate fetuses turning toward a directed light source when that light source is placed onto the woman's stomach. However, because of the lack of visual stimulus within the womb, the connection between the eyes and the visual cortex is unable to form (Berger, 2006). Also during this time, the fetus's eyelids are not fully developed and the retinas are sensitive. This means that a pregnant woman should avoid exposing her stomach to intense bright light because it could damage the developing eye (Bilich, 2006).

Although the fetal ear formation begins at about eight weeks into gestation (Berk, 2006), the fetus won't begin to hear sounds such as his/her mother's heartbeat, digestion, and other bodily noises until about eighteen weeks (Bilich, 2006). At about the twenty-seventh week, the fetus will be able to hear more sophisticated sounds such as its mother's voice and other sounds in its mother's environment (Bilich, 2006). This belief stems from a preponderance of **anecdotal evidence** from pregnant women who report that their babies respond differently to loud noises as opposed to soft and soothing music. Research supports the idea that newborns have some auditory capacities, but the limitations are not fully understood (Werner and Bargones, 1992). For example, some research suggests that newborns are more responsive to higher-pitched voices, thereby demonstrating greater auditory development for this sound range. The ability to detect high-pitched voices over lower-pitched voices may be a hard-wired response to enable the infant to detect its mother, or a result of high-pitched sounds being more apt to transmit through a mother's flesh and amniotic fluid. Hence, exposure to this range of sound would cause this part of the auditory system to be more fully developed than the ability to detect sound of different ranges.

Research shows that infants have an affinity for the language spoken by their mothers, as well as the ability to recognize their mothers' voice (Goldstein, 2002). One study of pregnant women had one group read Dr. Seuss's *The Cat in the Hat* the way the story was written. A second group was asked to read a modified version of the story. They were asked to replace the words *cat* and *hat* with *dog* and *fog* (DeCasper & Spence, 1986). Upon birth, the infants clearly showed a preference for the version of the story they had heard while in utero (Goldstein, 2002), thereby showing that associations between sensation and preference begin early in life.

What this means for the designer is that a stress-free and soothing environment can assist in the development of unborn children. These environments should be suitable for the expectant mother to read to the unborn child; they should include natural scents such as foods, spices, or flowers; and they should contain the ability for soft background music to be played. Other important attributes of this environment should be access to early morning sunlight. This light isn't as bright as sunlight during the remainder of the day, and the fetus will be stimulated not only from the light itself (Bilich, 2006), but also from the warmth of the sun.

Teratogens

Environmental agents called **teratogens** can produce developmental malformations. These agents can be inhaled or absorbed by the mother and thus circulated through her bloodstream to the developing fetus. Teratogenic agents include exterior pollutants, such as pesticides, smoke, and vehicle emissions, as well as interior pollutants such as emissions from floor coverings and furnishings, and levels of cleanliness. Allergen-producing life forms (e.g., molds, pollens, dust mites, cockroaches, and pets) are also considered teratogens because **allergens** are often related to both the incidence and prevalence of asthma (National Institute of Environmental Health Sciences, 1997). Although the correlation between environmental contaminants and developing fetuses is still being researched, the cause-and-effect relationship has been substantiated by many infants who, exposed to cocaine in the womb, tend to be hyperactive and overly sensitive to environmental stimulation, and have extremely low tolerances to being held.

The first step in designing an environment for an expectant mother is to conduct an environmental analysis to assess potential sources of interior and exterior pollution as well as stress levels incurred from the mother's various environments, including work, home, and community. This analysis requires a multimodal approach, beginning with a walk-through analysis of known sources of interior pollution. Pollutants include materials such as water-based acrylic wall paints and indoor sealants, nylon carpeting, vinyl furnishings, and PVC (polyvinyl chloride) floor coverings—which all have negative biological and neurological effects on developing humans (Sakr, Knudsen, Gunnarsen, & Haghighat, 2003)—and the presence of dampness, mildew, mold, dust, and byproducts of certain insects have been linked to the prevalence of asthma (Haynes, Reading, & Gale, 2003; National Institute of Environmental Health Sciences, 1997).

The exterior environment should also be analyzed and evaluated. Items of interest include elevated highways, heavily traveled roads in front of, or alongside the residence.

Motor vehicles are the primary source of air pollutants (e.g., benzene, 1, 3-butadiene, diesel particulate matter, carbon monoxide, reactive organic gases, and oxides of nitrogen) that are associated with multiple health issues (Gunier, Hertz von Behren, & Reynolds, 2003). For example, vehicular exhaust produces lead dust that penetrates the soil, blows into houses (Adgate, et al., 1998) and causes health risks usually associated with cognitive functioning. Therefore, the presence and penetrability of air pollutants need to be analyzed in relation to glazing layers (i.e., single-, double-, or triple-paned windows), quality of insulation, and the presence of foliage that can absorb or block the pollutants.

Finally, a stress assessment is required; using strategic questions to determine which environment has the most stressful agents and whether the primary stressors are internal or external and acute or chronic.

Through an environmental assessment, designers can proactively assist their clients to achieve optimal physical and mental health. When converting a room in a home to a nursery or infant's bedroom, for example, it might be beneficial to plan for low-level soft lighting that will aid parents in locating the infant during the night without the use of bright lights. In this situation the designer will want to add electrical outlets for night-lights and incorporate lights that emit a soft glow; dimmer switches can also be useful to achieve these lower levels of lighting.

After a child has been born, he/she will proceed through many developmental stages. Each of these stages can pass quickly and each requires unique design attributes and features. This can make designing for young people somewhat daunting because it must be flexible in order to accommodate and adjust to each developmental stage (Table 7.1).

[Table 7.1] Development Stages of Youth

Developmental Stage	Predominant Characteristics	Design Recommendations
Prenatal	Beginning from the eighth week after conception to birth; fastest growth period of the child's life.	Reduce the mother's exposure to teratogens and allergens that affect the developing fetus.
Infancy	Primary lesson is cause-and-effect relationships	Include items that respond to an infant's action (e.g., musical instrument or stuffed toy that squeaks when squeezed or spins when hit).
Toddlerhood and Preschooler	Cognitive and gross motor skills develop, and children begin conforming to gender stereotypes.	Use objects that foster gross motor skills and that promote temporal associations (e.g., beginning, middle, and end, or those of other cultures if applicable).
Childhood	Children start to understand what others think, and comprehend that others may see things differently. By age six, children are gender sensitive and want their external worlds to match their perceived gender identities.	Provide places for children to imagine themselves as adults.

Source: Bilich, K. A., http://health.discovery.com/centers/pregnancy/senses/senses.html

SUSTAINABILITY CONNECTION 7.1

As children grow, the adults in their lives should closely monitor their physical and mental development. However *creativity* and *creative thought* appear to be considerably more sustainable and relevant to every aspect of a person's life (e.g., language skills, analytical problem-solving, everyday life). Sadly the latter are often neglected. Fostering creativity is sometimes viewed as adding little value to the demands of life, much like having an education, a job, or survival skills. Child psychologists following the *multivariate approach* maintain that creative thought is the key to higher thought processes and a fully evolved brain. This approach claims intelligence, desire, and environmental factors facilitate the building of creativity and vice versa. That is to say, every healthy brain has three basic features: the ability to think (intelligence), the ability to feel (emotions/ desire), and the potential for creative thoughts (environment). Sometimes a child does not have the freedom to be allowed creative thought, and thus the other two features of the brain may not develop to their full potential. Designers and caregivers should put an emphasis on the sustainable development of *creativity* by providing an environment rich in opportunities for a child to grow: mentally, physically, emotionally, and creatively.

INFANCY AND SENSORY NEURAL DEVELOPMENT

Infancy to adulthood is the second fastest time in which humans develop during the course of their life. Most mammals are nearly fully functional within hours of birth; but the human infant is born with only the basic elements of survival and requires time and stimulation to fully develop. This development occurs in stages that broadly apply to all young people. Infancy is the first developmental stage between birth and one year (Harms, 2006); the years between one and three are often referred to as toddlerhood. After this stage comes the preschool period that include the years between ages three to six (Feldman, 2007). These initial stages are important because it is during this time that we see significant biological and neurological growth, much of which pertains to sensory detection.

The development of the senses requires time and stimulation for optimal acuity. In fact, the only senses that are fully functional at the time of birth are taste, smell (Goldstein, 2002), and touch. Similar to the fetal stage, the infant will undergo many changes as it develops through its first year of life. During this time he/she will be able to taste, smell, detect touch, and to a lesser degree see and hear (Feldman, 2007). With these senses the infant will have a limited capacity to learn about his/her surroundings as development continues. In some cases, such as hearing and sight, full maturity and acuity of sensation will not be reached until just before preadolescence (Goldstein, 2002). For designers of the built environment it is important to understand how our youth develop in order to maximize the child's development within static environments (those that do not undergo significant changes throughout the years) such as schools, playgrounds, and public spaces.

The foundation of development is based upon the following four stages: **sensorimotor**, preoperational, concrete operational, and formal operational (Huitt and Hummel, 2003). These stages of cognitive development are defined as:

1. *Sensorimotor stage (infancy).* A period in which intelligence is demonstrated through motor activity without the use of symbols. It is a stage where knowledge of the world is limited (but developing) because it's based on physical interactions/experiences. In this stage young people acquire *object permanence* (memory), physical development (mobility), and some symbolic (language) abilities.
2. *Preoperational stage (toddler and early childhood).* This period is demonstrated through the use of symbols (language ability increases), and *memory and imagination* are developed. More specifically, the young person tends to be egocentric (i.e., the world is referenced from themselves outward), and thinking is done in a nonlogical, nonreversible manner.
3. *Concrete operational stage (elementary and early adolescence).* This stage is characterized by abstract thinking related to *number, length, liquid, mass, weight, area*, and *volume*. Intelligence is demonstrated through logical and systematic manipulation of symbols related to concrete objects, and operational thinking develops (meaning that mental actions become reversible and egocentrism begins to diminish).
4. *Formal operational stage (adolescence and adulthood).* In this stage, intelligence is demonstrated through the logical use of symbols related to abstract concepts. Early in this developmental period there is a return to egocentric thought. An interesting point is that only approximately 35 percent of high school graduates in industrialized countries reach formal operations, and many people will go through life without ever engaging in formal thought (i.e., maturity).

Jean Piaget was a Swiss psychologist and forerunner in childhood developmental studies. His theory in which the main premises are *assimilation* and *accommodation* is called: "Theory of Cognitive Development." However, new sociological theories of child development challenge Piaget's theories of the development of knowledge, and regard child development as a unique and individual experience that is derived from the family, cultural context, and individual factors that influence the possession of feelings and experiences. Whereas the latter perspective provides a great deal of latitude for the parent, teacher, and any other professional who works with young people directly, Piaget's broader more generalized ideas that every young person is believed to develop in relatively predictable stages is of more use to professionals such as designers who do not have direct day-to-day contact with the individual. Hence, designers of preschools and daycare centers need this more generalized guide to aid them in the creation of environments that accommodate the majority of this demographic.

Sight

The infancy stage, from birth to about one year, is a period marked by rapid developments. Vision and the physical formation of the eye predominantly occur during the first year of life. At birth an infant's vision is extremely poor, and he/she cannot distinguish detail; this early vision has been compared to looking through thick frosted glass (Goldstein, 2002). The infant's perceptual ability is limited to the visual distinction between light and dark and the perception of motion (Nelson & Horowitz, 1987). Our ability to see develops at various developmental stages and designers will need to enhance the visual complexity at each stage (see Figures 7.3a–f).

Infants, however, can detect and are attracted to motion, even though they can't understand or comprehend the meaning or causes of that motion. At about two weeks of age the infant will start to comprehend the sources of motion (Goldstein, 2002), but they won't be able to follow the motion of an object with their eyes until they are two to three months of age. The process of following a moving object with one's eyes is called **tracking**, and this is an important part of child development.

Researchers suspect that although infants do store memories, they have difficulty retrieving them (Rovee-Collier, 2000). This means that motion deriving from a cause-and-effect situation may seem new to them regardless of how many times a situation has been encountered. Experts speculate that the experience is similar to déjà vu or that the association is more of a hardwired response as opposed to a cognitive response. Whereas it is true that infants will form an association between crying and being held, the effect (being held) of the cause (crying), this relationship could be one of instinct (i.e., a hardwired response) or one of déjà vu. Notwithstanding, when given a choice between looking at a familiar stimulus and one that is new, an infant is more likely to look at the new stimulus (Fagan, 1976; Slater, Morison, & Rose, 1983). What this means is that as designers, we need to think creatively in order to keep a stimulus appearing fresh

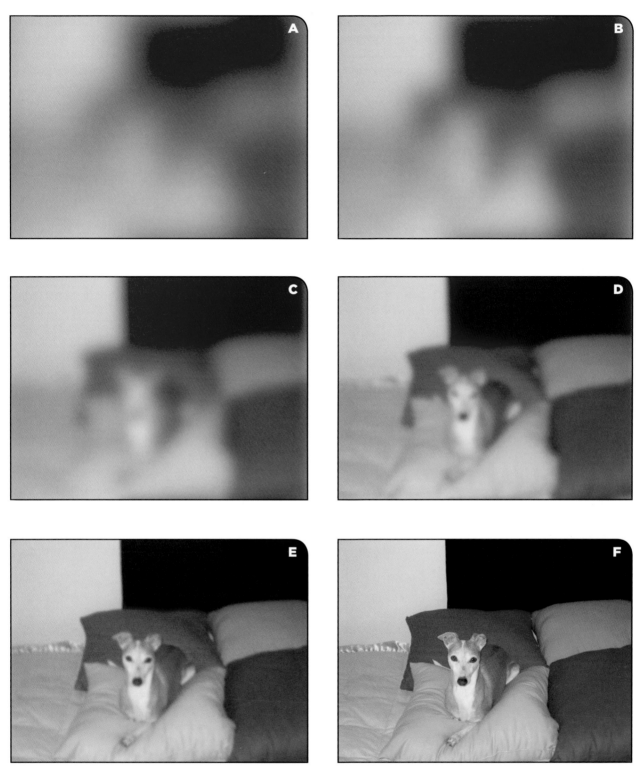

[**Figures 7.3a–f**] Visual development at a distance of 24 inches: (a) newborn, (b) four weeks old, (c) eight weeks old, (d) three months old, (e) six months old, (f) eight years old. Photos by DAK Kopec; image generated and printed with permission of tinyeyes.com

and new. For example, we might incorporate a mobile that is composed of photosensitive Plexiglas or a ceiling treatment that creates various shadow patterns on the walls as the light changes throughout the day. As the lighting levels change throughout the day, the mobile will change color, thereby giving it a new appearance (Kopec & LaCapra, 2008). Likewise, in recent years, there have been advances made in clothing decals. One such advancement includes decals that appear as black and white line work in artificial light, but when exposed to natural light the decal changes from black and white to full color. These types of decals could be incorporated into the wall or ceiling décor so that the appearance changes. Other advantageous environments to expose infants are shaded outdoor areas on calm days where butterflies, the leaves on trees, and other similar items found in nature tend to move slowly and smoothly providing the infant with a variety of slow, smooth-flowing objects to watch.

Whether it is déjà vu or a cause-and-effect relationship, both are important to the development of the brain and the infant's ability to learn. Because infants have a difficult time accurately perceiving the world around them, they need complimentary visual cues to help them identify and comprehend what they see.

Visual stimulation during the early days of development is important, particularly when we consider that sight comprises more than one third of our brain mass, and it takes the longest of all the senses to fully develop. When developing innovative ideas, it will be important to remember that infants only possess the ability to focus on objects at close range (about 8 to 10 inches), which is approximately the distance between the infant and the face of the person holding him/her. The reason for poor vision among infants is because the cells in the retina and fovea of the eye have not yet fully developed, and the optic nerve and visual pathways within the brain have not sufficiently developed to relay the visual massages. The eye relies upon **rods** and **cones** for the detection of light, color, and detail. In short, the rods facilitate vision in low light, and the cones allow us to detect color and detail. Of the two, rods are more developed at the time of birth (Abramov et al., 1982); but the cones of an infant are unable to effectively absorb light. To provide perspective, the adult eye has cone receptors that cover about 68 percent of the fovea, whereas the newborn infant has only about 2 percent. Also, a newborn's eyeball is only about half the size of an adult's and will not reach its full size until about pre-adolescence. Hence, it will take a significant amount of time for the eyes of an infant to mature and the cognitive visual pathways to develop (Atkinson, 2000).

By one month of age, the infant will have about 20/400 to 20/600 vision, which means that he/she must view a stimulus from 20 feet in order to see the same stimulus that a normal adult can see from 400 or 600 feet (Banks & Salapatek, 1978; Dobson & Teller, 1978). At approximately two months, infants will be able to see color across the full color spectrum (Teller, 1998). However, vision will be blurred and will lack clear delineation between similar adjacent colors. This is why it is important to use bright contrasting colors; it helps the infant discern where one color ends and another begins. At three months they are able to follow an object if it moves slowly (Aslin, 1981). The ability to see color and understand depth begins to develop during mid- to late infancy (between 6 and 12 months). This is when mobiles and other colorful three-dimensional toys are an important addition to the child's environment (see Figure 7.4). Also, designers should refrain from using colors of the same color family, such as red and pink next to one another because the colors will blur together.

The use of color in relation to adult-infant interaction establishes early socialization of gender roles, which are developed through language (words, tone, and volume) and the way the child is handled. For example, adults respond differently to an infant based on the colors that surround that infant (e.g., through clothing and environmental décor). If an infant is dressed in the color blue, adults will speak in deeper, stronger tones and hold that infant upright, encouraging it to use gross motor skills. Whereas if an infant is dressed in the color pink, adults tend to speak in higher-pitched and softer voices and cradle that infant in their arms.

[**Figure 7.4**] Between ages 6 to 12 months, infants start to understand depth. To help them with this understanding. it is important to use contrasting colors so that the infant can easily identify each object. © Corbis Flirt / Alamy

No matter how subtle our response to an infant, these early actions form the basis of how that child is expected to behave in later years (Eccles, Jacobs, & Harold, 1990; Witt, 1997).

The behavioral nuances that we direct at infants tend to be passed down from generation to generation through cultural norms, values, and expectations. These behavioral norms can be mirrored in the adornment of infant spaces. For example, a male infant may be surrounded by various sporting scenes or equipment (e.g., a stuffed toy that looks like a basket ball) or by automobile scenes such as a mobile with different racecars. The décor of an infant's space provides adults with visual cues of how they should respond to the child. Some parents prefer not to promote gender specific behaviors and opt to surround their infant with *gender-neutral* scenes such as nature, animals, and colors such as greens, yellows, and oranges. It's important to understand that while our genes define the possibilities for brain circuits, it is our interactions with the environment that lead some connections to persist and others to disappear. Hence, from the way in which we interact with and adorn an infant's environment, we begin the social learning process.

SUSTAINABILITY CONNECTION 7.2

Gender-bias, gender inequality, and sexism are all the same thing: the obvious, concealed, or accepted discrimination or hatred of persons due to their biological sex. Gender equality is a human rights issue as well as a sustainability issue. To develop in a sustainable manner, a community must allow all members (female and male) equal opportunity to grow financially, emotionally, and productively. A diverse pool of *human* resources is always more valuable than a constrained one. Thus, parents, teachers, designers, caregivers, and other potential role models are all strongly encouraged to reject gender-social arrangements, gender-color stereotypes, and imposing outdated gender roles on young children because this behavior restricts human potential of both female and male citizens.

Beginning at about two months of age, infants will show a preference for patterns as opposed to monochromatic or homogenous surfaces (Siegler, Deloache, & Eisenberg, 2006). For the designer this means incorporating patterns into the infant's environment such as patterned wallpaper or a celestial mural on the ceiling. Likewise, it is important to note that studies have shown that infants prefer photos of faces with realistic features as opposed to photos with blank faces (Johnson & Morton, 1991) such as the "smiley face" icon. By about three months of age the infant should be able to distinguish facial expressions, and by four months of age

the infant should begin to judge depth and identify separation of objects (Goldstein, 2002). Then, within the first six to seven months of life, the infant's visual acuity will significantly increase to almost that of adult vision (20/20; Banks & Salapatek, 1978; Cole, Cole, & Lightfoot, 2005; Dobson & Teller, 1978).

Hearing

A second important sensation for a developing infant is the auditory system. Unlike vision, the auditory system is fully developed by the time of birth; however, many newborns are considered hard of hearing (Trehub & Schellenberg, 1995) and have difficulty recognizing some parts of the sound spectrum (Fernald, 2001). This limitation will be corrected within the first few months of life, thereby greatly improving auditory acuity (Tharpe & Ashmead, 2001). By eight months the infant is able to discriminate between different phonemes (e.g., distinct sounds in a language but often not heard by a nonnative speaker), but they lose this ability to distinguish sounds that lack meaning by 12 months (Siegler, Deloache, & Eisenberg, 2006). This means that the introduction of multiple languages should begin at about eight months and continue throughout life, or at least until preadolescence.

After an infant is born, it is important to stimulate his/her hearing by playing an assortment of music and speaking directly to the child. Research supports this assertion by showing a connection between language acquisition and caretakers who speak directly to the child, and a direct connection between music and improved cognitive development. Consonant tones, or rhythmic patterns are much more pleasing to the infant than dissonant tones, or disconnected sounds (Trehub & Schellenberg, 1995). This is why we see infants showing greater preferences for consonant tones (Trainor & Heinmiller, 1998; Zentner, & Kagan, 1996). It has also been suggested that infants find pure sounds to be more preferable than complex sounds, particularly during the first few months of life. For example, parents may want to begin by exposing the infant to only the sounds of drums, and then gradually begin to play music that incorporates another instrument, such as a saxophone. This gradual introduction of musical instruments will help the infant learn to distinguish the differences between sounds and aid in neuropathway development.

Infant Sound Systems and Playlists

One of the design considerations when developing environments for infants and toddlers is the incorporation of a sound system. This system should be able to provide clear and balanced sound for equal entry into the auditory system. The range of sounds that should be available include natural ones, such as those generated by birds, crickets, and frogs, and a variety of different accents and singing voices. For example, books on tape might be played throughout the day. Young children also seem to respond well to melodies or other similar musical forms, and as such, this genre should also be included in the repertoire of sound.

As the child begins to move on his/her own, consider incorporating musical instruments into the child's environment so that he/she can imitate the sounds that have been heard. Likewise, supply toys that bring about various tones and sounds that a child is likely to encounter as he/she grows into an adult; for example, stuffed toys that speak when squeezed.

CULTURAL CONNECTION 7.1

Cultural sounds are the acoustic tones and musical personalities that are prevalent to specific ethnicities. Sometimes called *folk, native,* or *ethnic* music, the sounds created and the instruments used are as varied as the method and tempos for each cultural background. Cultural sounds carry profound and powerful messages. In some cases the instrumental sound alone can immediately conjure up a veritable novel of the culture from which it originates—its ceremonial costumes, mannerisms, customs, and perhaps even their environmental setting.

Take, for example, bagpipes. This unusual instrument has symbolically absorbed the physical characteristics of the Scottish people (e.g., plaid tartans and rugged terrain), and the sound that emanates from it can communicate the collective emotions of Scottish history. The vast majority of folk music commemorates social and political movements and, in that way, becomes the oral history of a people and a time. As the population of the world begins to move and shift beyond the limited migrations of the past, hybrid cultural sounds are evolving to combine traditional sounds of multiple cultures. And new technology is offering the ability for individuals to quite literally carry their cultural sounds with them to new locations.

Touch

The act of touching produces chemical changes in the brain that last a lifetime. These chemical changes enable us to draw conclusions and link sensation with perception. In this way, touch is the most vital sense to all people. It enables us to feel our world as well as helps us to locate where we are in space. Touch also gives us immeasurable amounts of information about our environment such as ambient temperature, textures, and depth. Because tactile sensation stimulates brain activity, one can say that childhood development is activated by touch. For this reason, carefully using textures within the

built environment where children spend a great deal of time, such as pediatric medical facilities, daycare centers, entertainment areas, and schools, is a vital part of the material selection and design choices.

The sense organ that relays information related to touch is the largest organ in the body, the skin. For many years experts believed that infants did not experience pain, and they would often perform minor surgeries, including circumcision, without the use of painkillers. However, recent research has shown that when exposed to pain an infant will perspire, his/her heartbeat will increase, pupils will dilate, and he/she will display facial expressions indicating distress (Jorgensen, 1999; Simons, et al., 2003; Warnock & Sandrin, 2004). We know infants can feel pain; we also know that they can feel other types of sensation including texture, temperature, and touch. Furthermore, many now believe that touch is the most highly developed sense at the time of birth.

An infant will learn about his/her environment by touching objects with his/her hands, fingers and toes, or by touching objects with the lips, tongue, and mouth. Recall from earlier in the chapter that the hands, fingers, and lips are dense with nerve receptors; and, therefore, the detection of touch is among the first experiences that will encourage cognitive development in the newborn infant. During the first few months of an infant's life, he/she will explore the world predominantly through touch receptors located in the mouth and lips (Ruff, 1989; Siegler, Deloache, & Eisenberg, 2006; Figure 7.5). This is one reason why designers should exercise caution not to include small objects that could be swallowed, nor use products from which small pieces could become loose or easily dissembled when creating environments for infants. It's through these different means of touch that the infant learns to understand what he/she sees as well as where he/she is in relation to other objects. As designers it is our responsibility to provide a variety of surfaces, textures, and atmospheres within an infant's environment so that the child can explore and maximize the development of sensory organs and neural connections.

From about four months of age, an infant will gain better control over his/her arms and hands. At this time we start to see infants exploring their world by rubbing their hands and fingers against textured objects, sticking their fingers into the various orifices of things they encounter, and banging an assortment of objects (Siegler, Deloache, & Eisenberg, 2006). It's important to supply an array of tactile surfaces that allow the infant to feel different textures. This can include different fabrics used for bedding, different textured stuffed toys, and different floor coverings. In many cultures, the importance of touch is being explored in great depth, and recent discoveries show that the sensation of touch is the most important sense for early cognitive development (Larner, et al., 2001).

[**Figure 7.5**] Infants often explore their worlds with their mouths, which is why it is important not only to consider the possibility of small parts coming loose but also to consider the contents of paints, varnishes, and stains. © Yan Zverev / Alamy

[**Figure 7.6**] Cause-and-effect relationships are important to cognitive development late in infancy. Cause-and-effect items that can be easily reached, but cannot cause harm, should be incorporated into the infant's primary surroundings. © NorthernExposure / Alamy

Among an infant's primary lessons are cause and effect relationships (Piaget, 1969). Each time an infant witnesses an effect of an action, the brain forms new synapses or neural connections (e.g., when they cry and someone comes, they gain a rudimentary understanding of the relationship between crying and assistance). This is why squeaky toys and mobiles are important in the design of spaces for infants. Because the developmental effect of a mobile is maximized only when the object is low enough for the infant to swat or kick at it, mobiles should be suspended from retractable cords so they can be raised up to accommodate adult interaction and lowered for play. The goal of the designer for this age group is to incorporate as many items as possible that show a direct cause-and-effect relationship (Figure 7.6).

Taste and Smell

Infants are able to discriminate between sweet, sour, and bitter stimuli (Beauchamp et al., 1991), and evidence suggests they will prefer tastes that are sweet and exhibit a dislike for tastes that are sour or bitter (Children's Hospital Boston, 2005). Interestingly, newborn infants do not seem to have the ability to detect salty flavors, or if they do, they do not respond to the taste (Ganchrow, 1995). This preference for certain tastes is likely to be an evolutionary carry-over that aided in the infant's survival. In nature, those items (e.g., certain sticks, berries, roots) that could threaten the life of an infant tend to be either bitter or sour. Hence, in evolutionary terms, it would be advantageous for the fetus to develop the ability to discern between tastes that are sweet, sour, and bitter early in development. In our built environment we have included hazardous materials such as lead paint that tastes sweet. Thousands of young children suffer all sorts of neurological impairments each year as a result of licking or chewing on objects with lead paint.

It's believed that taste and smell are the first learned reactions that occur as a stimulus response—an automatic psychological or physiological response to a particular stimulus. The idea is that the senses of taste and smell are stimulated when the infant is being fed; thereby, the infant learns to recognize the smell of the person who feeds him/her (Goldstein, 2002). This is how the association is made that a particular scent equals food. Likewise, many cognitive theorists believe that babies use their sense of taste as a way for them to understand the world around them (Bee & Boyd, 2003).

Smell and taste are the two senses that have the strongest links to one another. For those who have lost the ability to smell, the taste of food seems to be less flavorful. The sense organs of both taste and smell are the first to develop. This means that before an infant is even born, it will be exposed to various flavors (Bilich, 2006) and scents that cross the amniotic fluid. Because smell is the sense most strongly tied to memory (Goldstein, 2002), humans—like many mammals—rely on it to protect us from predators, help mothers and babies identify each other (Berk, 2006), and distinguish among potentially toxic substances. By learning the differences among scents while still in the fetal stage, the recognition of aromas is cumulative. Likewise, it is important to note that scents are rarely pure, but rather a combination of many smells; and humans seldom forget a smell they have experienced (Goldstein, 2002). It is for this reason that memory retrieval is often triggered when we smell a familiar odor. Like an appreciation for wine, the uncultivated palette may not be able to detect the subtle differences in flavor and aroma between different wines; on the other hand, the person who is continually exposed to different vintages will likely develop the ability to better discern the subtle differences. The same can be said with regard to smells and textures; the more exposure, the better acuity the child will possess as an adult. This is why it is important to consider ways to enhance greater discernment of the child's various senses in their different environments (e.g., home, preschool, recreational centers, and elementary school). Each of these environments is significant in the development of the child's biology and neurology.

Some have suggested that the early development of sensation accomplishes two goals: to respond to caregivers, and to be soothed and comforted (Berger, 2006). In an older study, researchers noticed that when they subjected infants to the smell of chocolate or bananas that the infants' facial expressions relaxed and the infant seemed happier. Conversely, when the same infants were subjected to the odor of rotten eggs they responded by frowning (Steiner, 1979). In more recent studies infants showed, through facial expressions, a preference for sugary aromas and a dislike for garlic or vinegary aromas (Marlier, Schaal, & Soussignan, 1998; Soussignan, Schaal, Marlier, & Jiang, 1997). This means that as infants begin to form their stimulus responses we as designers may be able to affect the response. For this reason it is important for infants, toddlers, and children alike to receive exposure to myriad sights, sounds, smells, tastes, and textures in order to develop sensory acuity.

We can also incorporate sweet smells in a doctor's office to help relax and comfort a child who has come to associate that environment with pain. Or, we can use the natural repulsion that children exhibit toward certain tastes in items that could be potentially dangerous, thereby inhibiting children from accidental harm.

Building Environments That Build Synapses . . . but Safety First

An infant's environment is typically made up of a crib, a bassinet, a playpen, and play objects. To facilitate learning and the formation of new neural synapses, infants should be exposed to objects and situations that show cause-and-effect relationships. However, we have to remember that young people gain their experiences through sensation. In essence, they look for ways to better understand their environment by looking, tasting, smelling, listening, and touching everything they can. This is one reason why designers will want to reduce the presence of cords by incorporating fixtures such as ceiling lights and refraining from the use of cords for window treatments. Cords in an infant or toddler's environment are likely to be pulled, chewed upon, and wrapped around the young person as he/she explores it. When designing nurseries or other places for infants and toddlers it's important for the young person to have an area that allows for the safe exploration of their environment through the use of all of their senses.

Objects that illustrate three-dimensionality will help the infant develop depth perception. Choices and uses of color during early infancy, however, are functions of adult socialization and early formation of gender roles and expectations because infants cannot distinguish color well until after they reach six months of age. Floors should be suitable for crawling and playing. Cushioned cork, rubber, or vinyl is easy to clean; area rugs should be secured to the floor with nonslip adhesive strips. Walls should be washable and suitable for repainting or repapering. If a client's heart is set on wallpaper, suggest a single color or a small-scale print that the client and child will not tire of over time. Also, it's not advisable to paint a young person's sleeping area in bright, primary colors; they are thought to be stimulating (Camgöz, Yener, & Güvenç, 2004) and thus may cause the young person to associate the area with mental and physical activity.

Storage space is an almost limitless design variable; toy boxes, closets, cabinets, baskets, hammocks, and under-bed drawers can store a variety of items while adding to the visual design (see Figure 7.7). Designers must also consider the parents' wishes regarding socialization. If they do not want their children to grow up with gender-related expectations, avoid blues, pinks, and purples, and use more gender-neutral colors such as yellows, greens, oranges, and reds.

Designers need to be aware of sources of stress and injury that could affect infants. Most infants feel stress from external sources such as excess noise and light or bad or strong smells, and these stressors can be either chronic or acute. Infants who as fetuses were exposed to certain drugs (including alcohol) may suffer from internal stress related to addiction and hypersensitivities. Injuries can occur without proper supervision or as a result of poor environmental design. Because infants lack strength and gross motor skills, their inabilities to rescue themselves from potentially hazardous situations—such as being wrapped in too many blankets, being surrounded by stuffed toys that are too large, or getting caught between the bars of a crib—can be fatal.

TODDLERHOOD AND PRESCHOOL YEARS

This developmental stage encompasses children from about one to five years of age. During this period toddlers begin conforming to gender stereotypes; boys start to gravitate toward trucks and building blocks while girls start to gravitate toward dolls and toy tea sets. As designers we want to accommodate these desires, but we must consult with parents about décor because they may want to saturate their children's environments with predetermined gender-oriented artifacts. Parents may opt for gender-neutral wall

coverings, window treatments, and bedding or may want to saturate the toddler's environment with gender-specific items such as sports-themed wallpaper or frilly canopy beds. Although the parents' wishes must be honored, it is the designer's ethical responsibility to inform clients of alternatives without bias.

Mirrors are an important design feature during this stage. As infants develop into toddlers they start to recognize that they are separate entities. Mirrors encourage toddlers to see themselves as individuals (Courage, Edison, & Howe, 2004; Loveland, 1986). Mirrors can help facilitate this understanding because the toddler sees his/her reflections move in unison with his/her movements, yet cannot touch that reflected person. Thus, the mirror also helps to facilitate analytical skills.

At around age two, toddlers enter an egocentric stage where they understand that their thinking is their own (Piaget, 1963; Piaget, 1969). However, they inappropriately assume that others see and experience what they do. For example, because they don't feel pain when they pull on Fido's ears, they assume that Fido doesn't either. Likewise, when they get hurt and run to their parents for comfort,

[**Figure 7.7**] This bedroom set provides many attributes that contribute to the conservation of space, including built-in drawers and shelving, as well as a guest bed for when the child wants to have a sleepover. It is also gender-neutral, providing opportunities for the designer to introduce yellows, greens, oranges, and reds, which do not have the socialization messages associated with blues, pinks, and purples. © Patti McConville / Alamy

they assume that the adults know what happened because it must have happened to them as well. It is at this stage that toddlers engage in behaviors of taking and grabbing as they explore their environments and their limitations and form their concepts of self.

Playrooms and Play Areas

An important consideration when designing environments for children at this stage of development is that while toddlers are still developing cognitive skills, they are also developing gross motor skills. They start to form short-term memories, require many new distractions, and start to project their thoughts onto the world. A playroom with various play areas will help accommodate a child's limited attention span.

A table covered with paper allows toddlers to project their thoughts in a variety of mediums (e.g., crayons, markers, pencils) and helps them to learn about limits while they explore. Games that involve matching colors, shapes, or images facilitate memory enhancement. Because toddlers have difficulties differentiating colors (or smells) until about age three, which is why colors need to be highly contrasting.

Low, padded balance beams or box springs and mattresses at floor level help developing youngsters learn how to use their muscles for balance and coordination. The ability to maintain eye contact with parents or caretakers from any location in the room is crucial to a toddler's exploration of spaces and interaction with peers (Legendre, 2003). The confidence they get from seeing a protector nearby will encourage further exploration, which is how a child learns.

From ages two to four, toddlers recognize the difference between themselves and other people but still cannot comprehend that others may feel, think, or react differently from them (Piaget, 1963, 1969, 1973). For example, three-year-olds who see someone who is angry or sad will assume that whatever makes them feel better will make the other person feel better, too. Toddlers have little understanding of how other living things grow or respond. At this stage they see the world as they would like to see it; therefore, nondescript objects such as empty boxes or broomsticks allow them to foster their imagination.

Art for Toddlers

Toddlers also start to view actions as having a beginning, middle, and an end. Although toddlers have little or no concept of past or future, they respond well to routine, which reinforces their understanding of beginning, middle, and end relationships. Using wall art, mobiles, or other design initiatives to depict progression in a time line of world history or the construction of a historic building promotes the formation of neural connections associated with time, especially when these features are positioned at a toddler's level.

Developing Sophistication Through Design

Between the ages of four and five years, preschoolers explore how to be adults by playing games that mimic adult activities, such as having tea parties or pretending to be firefighters. They still have difficulty with logical spatial deductions such as judging the size of a room or the volume of liquid in a container. This is when children start to project into—and anticipate or dread—the future, for example, getting excited about visiting Grandma or crying in a doctor's waiting room.

The toddler and preschool years are more about sophistication of sensation. When developing playrooms in homes or schools, designers will want to include highly contrasting colors so that children can clearly delineate between one color and another. One vital attribute that will help the child understand separation and delineation is the inclusion of a wall-mounted mirror or some other type of reflecting devise that will not break easily. This will help children develop a concept of themselves as individuals. Along with his delineation should be a segmentation of the space for appropriate behavioral activities: a place to climb and roughhouse, and a place for quiet contemplative activities. This will help the child learn about behavior settings and will promote an understanding of separation and delineation.

One of the important developmental aspects of toddlers is the increased sophistication of cognitive thought. This includes items that facilitate memory, analytical skills, and gross motor and coordination skills. Games played at a table or on the floor are often designed to promote memory and analysis; but toddlers have a difficult time sitting for extended periods of time, so items that promote physical activity should also be included.

CHILDHOOD

The next developmental stage includes the years six to twelve. These are referred to as the middle childhood years, and are often associated with one's projection and self-image. For example, two children may have the same object, but each imagines it to be something different (e.g., a broomstick can be a pony for one child and a motorcycle for the other); and this difference is acceptable. By the age of five, children start to understand what others think, and they comprehend that others may see things differently from them (Piaget, 1969). Five-year-old children are keenly aware of their limitations and envious of the power that adults have (e.g., freedom, choice, strength, and knowledge). Their imaginative and creative play focuses more on adult behaviors and activities as they attempt to grow up as quickly as possible. Ironically, at this age children can often memorize better than adults because they see the world as singular components, whereas most adults see components in relation to other components, a memory process called clustering, and must therefore sift through additional information (Yussen & Santrock, 1982).

This ability to manage multiple thoughts, while diminishing short-term memory, is essential for quick assessments of alternatives in reaction to crises. Designers can assist children to develop their abilities to process multiple thoughts by incorporating places such as clubhouses, tree houses, or other separate areas where children can learn about adult responsibilities by having control over a selected environment. If indoors, these special spaces can be under loft beds, in closets, or in a section of their bedrooms. Such spaces should contain a multitude of toys that have meaning for a child. Young children prefer toys that provide them with enjoyment (this preference lasts longer for boys) and that they can personify (this preference lasts longer for girls) (Dyl & Wapner, 1996). For example, a boy may want a clubhouse that can serve as a spaceship or submarine with toys that support his imaginary place, whereas a girl may want a special space that mimics a kitchen or office with toys that personify her notion of being an adult. Each child will develop attachments to specific objects, and those objects in essence become a part of their notions of self as well as sources of enjoyment and *personification.*

At around age six, children start to reason through simple deductions and superficially analyze situations or circumstances. At this age children are gender sensitive and want their external worlds to match their perceived gender identities. Gender identity and genitalia are not always congruent. Tomboys, for example, have strong "masculine" gender identities: They like to engage in athletic sports, play with trucks, and roughhouse with boys; and they probably will balk at the notion of "girly furniture," much less wear pink. By age seven, Western children take their gender identities very seriously and view male and female roles in strictly black-and-white terms, believing, for example, that boys don't dance and girls don't spit. Although many young girls prefer toy kitchen sets or nurseries and boys prefer toy

spaceships or time machines, designers must remember that children have individual likes and dislikes and that a girl may desire a spaceship and a boy may desire a kitchen. Clearly, the support that we offer our children reflects gender expectations and roles; whereas tomboys are often considered to be cute, society is far less tolerant of boys who exhibit "feminine" preferences.

By age eight, children's brains reach 95 percent of their adult size, and their prefrontal cortexes are sufficiently developed to plan and theorize (Yussen & Santrock, 1982). However, children still have difficulties conceptualizing what has not yet or may never happen; when they are included in the design process, they will need to see renderings to understand the big picture (i.e., see objects in relation to the environment). As children age into preadolescence, the shape of the eyeball changes. This can lead to many teens developing nearsightedness, a condition that will usually improve with age; but many of these teens may require corrective lenses (Berk, 2006).

When properly designed, facilities for children not only encourage cognitive and physical development; they can also encourage desirable behavior characteristics. For example, when a child's mind and body are appropriately stimulated by the environment, there is a greater probability that the child will engage in more positive behaviors because he/she is less likely to experience boredom (Flynn, 2006; White, 2004). Also, designers need to find balance between some risk during the exploration process, which will help in maintaining the interest of the child, but also in ensuring a sense of safety, which will encourage exploration. One method of accomplishing balance between risk and safety is to include transition spaces where the child is given the opportunity to gradually enter new situations. This is important because children are not able to process changing stimuli as quickly as adults (Stoecklin, 1999). For example, providing a small wooden bridge from a walking path to an outdoor play area allows the child visual access to the playground equipment, and it signals a change in activity zones.

Transition zones between different environments are important for the child to assess and prepare for the change. Similarly, because of the diminutive size of children, scale and proportion are often exaggerated in large atriums and lobbies, which can seem disconcerting. Therefore, environments intended for young people such as pediatric hospitals, schools, and other buildings should retain a residential scale and offer welcoming buffer zones from exterior to interior spaces as well as between spaces that change in function.

Children between the ages of five and eight require a variety of environments and objects that will accommodate their imaginations as well as support the active creative play in which they mimic adult behaviors; designers must consider this when designing environments for young people. Children develop attachments to specific objects and places as they explore their notions of self; designers can help to establish favorite places within the home or in children's actual rooms by creating nooks, alcoves, and other small spaces that young children can adopt as play areas and that can be adapted for other uses as they mature. Children at this stage are acutely aware of their place in the world and are both conscious of and sensitive about their gender identities; therefore, they must be consulted when designers are considering gender-specific designs. For example, a boy may not want wallpaper with images of race cars, and a girl may prefer stuffed animals over dolls.

PREADOLESCENCE AND ADOLESCENCE

The last developmental stages are the ages from 8 to 12 and then 12 to 20. These stages are called preadolescence and adolescence respectively. Between ages eight and nine, children start to take responsibility for their own decisions and are capable of independent thought. At this stage in their development, they should be included in the design process so that they can see the relationship between their decisions and the future; however, they will need many pictures to be able to visualize the end results. Because children at this age have not been fully socialized to adult norms, their idea of appealing décor is all their own, and it may vary greatly from that of designers or their parents. By age nine children start to distance themselves from their parents; most of their time is spent with their peers, and they need to be able to control their environment so it conforms to their expectations.

Between ages 10 and 11, gender barriers start to break down, and both genders begin engaging in behaviors previously conceived as gender-specific (e.g., boys cook meals and girls repair bicycles). Eleven is a good age at which to allow children to redecorate their rooms because they can now manage a multitude of thoughts related to colors, shapes, textures, and costs. However, it is important to understand that it is the 11-year-old child who will be the client.

Design for Developing Self-Images

The further children progress into adolescence, the more obsessed they become with the image they portray to the world. This is especially apparent in their choice of costume (e.g., clothing, accessories, jewelry), accoutrements (e.g., electronic equipment, games), and modes of transportation. For adolescents, possessions are often sources of comparisons and friendly competition and can support their status among their peer groups. Cherished possessions are linked to the self, affecting the development and reflection of self-concept (Yussen & Santrock, 1982). Such objects have tremendous

psychological importance in that they help adolescents relate to the social world and support how they want to be personified; therefore, when designing personal spaces for adolescents, consider how to incorporate their special objects.

The nature of attachment to special objects changes as youngsters move through the individuation process, separating themselves emotionally from their primary caretakers, and enter the affiliation stage, in which they begin integrating with others. Preadolescents prefer objects they can control and master, whereas adolescents prefer objects they can acquire and control or contemplate. Boys tend to prefer action or fantasy figures and audiovisual or sports equipment, such as action and mechanical or instrumental objects related to present experience; girls tend to prefer dolls, clothes, and mementos, such as contemplative and interpersonal objects related to past experiences (Dyl & Wapner, 1996). These special objects serve not only to support their notions of their places in the world but also as a means of stress reduction. Many youngsters who are upset will retreat to their rooms and use these objects for comfort and support while psychologically working through the stressful event.

As children move into preadolescence and adolescence, they develop into the people they will become. Throughout this developmental process, they become less concerned with their parents' preferences and care more about their peers' expectations. They also gravitate toward special objects that represent their notions of self and their aspirations for the future. For example, an adolescent or preadolescent may embrace extracurricular activities at school and desire paraphernalia associated with their school (e.g., pennants; old posters advertising a particular event; jackets, hats, or other clothing that promote their school). Friends are also important to adolescents and preadolescents. In design we might include the use of bulletin boards in the adolescents and preadolescents' room so that they can display items of meaning such as a friend's photograph or a movie ticket stub. It is important to understand that the adolescent or preadolescent must embrace the overall design if it is to create a place where he/she can feel safe and secure. Oftentimes, designs will be conceived from their perceived expectations of their peers. If their environments are constructed without their permission and input, it will not hold the psychological value they need; and the design and room will be rejected.

EFFECTS OF STRESS ON YOUTH

Stress can occur from objects or events we encounter or from other individuals. The results of stress on individuals can range from shortened gestation periods to alterations in the brain's chemistry and function, which contribute to lower disease resistance (Lombroso & Sapolsky, 1998). The negative impact of stress on a fetus can lead to premature birth, malformation of fetal brain function, or both (Monk et al., 2000). The effects of stress seem to be more profound in children who are younger than ten years of age, are male, or who experienced prenatal stress. Children who live in poverty or in violent communities or are bullied in school settings are also subject to more external stress than other children (McLoyd, 1998). Children who have lower thresholds for external and internal stimuli find a wider variety of social events and conditions to be negatively stressful as measured by cortisol levels (Stansbury & Harris, 2000).

A child's physical response to stress is usually much more intense than an adult's and involves the entire body. Stress in children often manifests as overt physical reactions, such as crying, sweating palms, running away, aggressive or defensive outbursts, rocking and other self-comforting behaviors, headaches and stomachaches, twirling or pulling the hair, chewing and sucking of thumbs or fingers, biting of skin and fingernails, bed-wetting, and sleep disturbances (Fallin, Wallinga, & Coleman, 2001; Marion, 2003; Stansbury & Harris, 2000). Other signs of stress include depression and avoidance; excessive shyness; hypervigilance; excessive worrying; obsessive interest in objects, routines, and food; persistent, strong concerns about "what comes next"; and excessive clinging (Dacey & Fiore, 2000).

Stress has greater effects on children, particularly those younger than six years, because children are developmentally less capable of thinking about a stressful event in its entirety. They don't have the experience to discern among different possible behaviors in response to a stressful event. They experience difficulty understanding that an event is separate from them and their feelings and that they can change their reactions in response to a change in stimuli (Allen & Marotz, 2003).

One factor in the breaking point of stress for children is that of *threshold,* the point at which a person can no longer psychologically handle additional stress. When a threshold is exceeded, the resulting manifestation is either internal (e.g., learned helplessness, eating disorders, suicide attempts, reclusion) or external (e.g., firing a gun into crowded areas, open hostility to others, random acts of violence). Sources of stress can derive from multiple venues and accumulate in a person's psyche. As stress levels increase during the day, people must spend equal or more time in a stress-free environment to allow those levels to decrease. What goes up must come down. If a person has no access to a stress-free environment or his/her exposure to it is minimal, the stress level will eventually reach the breaking point.

Prolonged exposure to a single stressor can lead to the continued use of coping strategies that may result in entrenched behavior patterns, especially if children perceive their strategies as effective (Kochenderfer-Ladd & Skinner, 2002; Stansbury & Harris, 2000). Stressors often converge, causing a seemingly low-stress event to be perceived very differently by children; the interaction of these stressors can have cumulative and long-lasting effects on children (Stansbury & Harris, 2000). Examining the causes and manifestations of stress in children helps to illustrate the importance of designing stress-free environments and of modifying environments that cause stress.

INJURY AND ILLNESS

Designers must acknowledge the basic law of physics: For every action, there is an equal and opposite reaction. Designers of the built environment have the goal or obligation to alleviate as many safety threats as possible through their design. Additionally, designers must beware of risk factors that their designs may create. When designing homes, one of the first steps is to understand the clients and the clients' particular needs from an environment. Clients who have young children or who are planning to have a family in the near future will need to coordinate with the designer in the selection of materials and also in the actual space planning. For example, parents may insist on getting plantation shutters if a neighbor's child died because of a curtain string. When developing an environment for a child, every designer must be acutely aware of multiple factors that may lead to injury, illness, or both.

Incidents of injury and illness are good examples of the human–environment relationship because the environment is often a causal factor. The probability of accidental injury and victimization can be real (i.e., physical threats to safety) or perceived (i.e., fearful expectations instilled by a blend of personal experience, peer influences, and media messages). Injury is the number one health risk for children younger than 15 years. According to statistics compiled for children ages 12 and younger, each year more than 14 million—1 out of 4—are injured seriously enough to require medical attention, and nearly 92,000 children become permanently disabled (National SAFE KIDS Campaign, 2003). Falls are the leading cause of unintentional injuries. In 2002, 92,500 children younger than 14 were treated in emergency rooms for burn injuries (Figure 7.8). Additionally, in 2002 about 115 youngsters drowned in or around the home (National SAFE KIDS Campaign, 2003); and 206,000 children, mostly boys, were treated in U.S. hospital emergency rooms for toy-related injuries (U.S. Consumer Product Safety Commission, Office of Information and Public Affairs, 2003). The desire to prevent accidents is a basic parental instinct, yet injury is the leading cause of death for children in developed countries, more so for boys than girls (Haynes, Reading, & Gale, 2003).

[**Figure 7.8**] The built environment is riddled with many environmental hazards for young children. This is because young children are curious by nature, which is how they learn. Designers must, therefore, help to keep the environment safe while encouraging exploration. © Angela Hampton Picture Library / Alamy

Preventive Health Design

Allergies and disease prevention are also important considerations for designers. In the United States, allergic asthma affects about 3 million children (8 to 12 percent of all children) and 7 million adults at an estimated cost of $6.2 billion a year. Researchers implicate the increased time youngsters spend indoors and the resulting exposure to carpeting and other materials that hold allergens (National Institute of Environmental Health Sciences, 1997). Scientists recommend not only preventing the growth of mildew and mold in homes by eliminating sources of indoor moisture (e.g., leaky roofs and plumbing), but also encouraging caregivers to increase their awareness of environmental triggers to reduce school absenteeism associated with asthma. More frequent cleaning with a HEPA vacuum cleaner can reduce a child's exposure to allergens, as will removing stuffed animals, rugs, curtains, and lamp shades from an asthmatic child's bedroom (National Institute of Environmental Health Sciences, 1997).

Inactivity among children can adversely affect their ability to cope with stress, and negatively affect their physical and psychological well-being (Stratton, 2000), as well as their social and emotional competence (Malone & Tranter, 2003). Likewise, research shows that increasing a child's physical activity can reduce risk factors for diseases such as diabetes, heart disease, and osteoporosis. Ideally the built environment should support a variety of forms for moderate to vigorous daily exercise (Stratton, 2000).

Unstructured playtime is valuable for the development of children in the first seven to eight years of life. Areas devoted to unstructured play must not only include space for physical activities such as running, jumping, climbing, and swinging, but also allow for and stimulate fantasy play, social dramatic play, sensory and exploratory play, and construction play (building things with material such as sand, gravel, water, or dirt; Scott, 2000). These outdoor spaces must suit children's developmental needs related to both diverse play and learning opportunities (Lindholm, 1995). Green schoolyards and playgrounds, for example, promote physical activity, more creative play (Taylor, Wiley, Kuo, & Sullivan, 1998), and social interaction (Herrington, 1997).

Residential space, place, and privacy preferences and evaluations are important considerations to environmental psychologists, and outdoor spaces are just as valuable as those indoors. Developers often build megahousing complexes made up of fairly large houses on small parcels of land or high-density housing such as condominiums with reduced floor space in their efforts to maximize land use and increase profits (Figure 7.9). Ideally, such projects should at least incorporate recreation areas containing facilities such as basketball courts, soccer fields, and playgrounds; and at most they should include swimming pools, whirlpool baths, and clubhouses. Such amenities, whereas not feasible on most single parcels, are an important factor in the development of children's gross motor and social skills. The physical environment can promote or hinder social relationships that are crucial to personal and community well-being (National Institute of Environmental Health Sciences, 1997), and outdoor spaces with natural landscaping can build a sense of community and facilitate the development of social skills.

Although young people often identify natural settings as their favorite places, those with high fear-expectancies; disgust sensitivities toward insects, dirt, or dampness; or a desire for modern comforts are more likely to prefer manicured outdoor settings to wild land environments (Bixler & Floyd, 1997). Although older adolescents seek affiliation with their peers, they often seek solitary places to relax and gain perspective on events that threaten their self-esteem and sense of place in the world (Korpela, 1992). It is, therefore, important for developers and landscape architects to understand the cultural and developmental norms of the population that intends to inhabit or use a particular development, such as a rooftop recreation area. Also, when developing the site plan for mass housing, it is important to consider multiple developmentally appropriate play areas as opposed to one large play space that will be occupied by all age groups. The different play areas should be themed so that distinct differences can be easily seen (Figure 7.10).

Crowding

Within high-density developments, crowding and privacy can be significant issues of concern. Residential crowding (i.e., number of people living in a specific unit) can negatively affect children's psychological health (Evans, Saegert, & Harris, 2001), and increase both undesirable classroom behaviors and parent–child conflict. Children who experience high residential crowding tend to use less sophisticated speech and be less verbally responsive. Researchers speculate that this may be one reason why children in crowded homes experience delays in cognitive development (Evans, Maxwell, & Hart, 1999). One study found that incidents of child abuse increased significantly when residential density exceeded 1.5 persons per room (Zuravin, 1986). This may be a result of stimulation reaching levels where a parent may not be able to cope.

The violation of a child's need for privacy results in either physical aggression or psychological withdrawal, depending on the child's personality and the length of crowding; children are more susceptible to behavioral disturbances (e.g., aggression, anxiety, depression, hyperactivity) when chronically exposed to excessive high density in the home, in childcare settings, or both (Maxwell, 1996). In sum, children's growth, development, and behavior all suffer in high-density households if there is no means for the child to escape (see Figure 7.11).

In homes where population density is high, it is especially important to provide safe spaces where children can obtain a degree of privacy. A small clubhouse can provide a space in which children can engage in pretend play, contemplate stressful events, or seek temporary *refuge*. In the future, the clubhouse could be converted to a home gym or home office. In smaller homes, the use of oversized tablecloths can be used to allow a child to conceal him/herself under the tables.

Privacy

Bedrooms are personal territories. Children need and desire their own territories not only for self-expression and identification, but also as private places for contemplation and relaxation. The desire for privacy is contingent on developmental stage and concepts of self-identity and self-esteem

[**Figure 7.9**] Many of the mega housing developments that we have seen since the 1990s include large homes on small parcels of land. Although this is an ideal setup for adults who do not have much time to maintain landscaping, young people are forced to spend more time within the built environment. © Skyscan Photolibrary / Alamy

[**Figure 7.10**] Diverse play spaces are important for the formation of analytic skills, coordination, socialization, and exploration. © Alex Sergre / Alamy

(Laufer & Wolfe, 1976; Newell, 1994, 1995). *Personalizing* their private spaces gives young people tangible ways to express their individuality (Rivlin, 1990; Sobel, 1990); children as young as age three prize a room they can personalize and to which they can retreat when they are upset or wish to be alone (Chawla, 1991). However, children have fickle desires that change fairly rapidly, and designs should be inexpensive and easily modified.

[**Figure 7.11**] Many young children will seek out private spaces and look for items that will afford them the ability to build a fort or to temporarily hide from the world. © Michael Ventura / Alamy

Practical Applications for Designers

Use these resources, activities, and discussion questions to help you identify, synthesize, and retain this chapter's core information. These tools are designed to complement the resources you'll find in this book's companion Study Guide.

Environments for human occupation should be rich in sensory stimuli to aid in developing healthy brains and bodies. At about twenty-seven weeks the fetus will be able to hear more sophisticated sounds such as its mother's voice and other sounds in its mother's environment. Once a child has been born, he/she will proceed through many developmental stages: infancy, toddlerhood and preschooler, preadolescence, adolescence, and adulthood. Infancy, the first developmental stage between birth and one year, is associated with the sensorimotor stage. Toddlers span the years between one and three and are often referred to as the preoperational stage. Preschoolers include the years between ages three to six and are associated with the concrete operational stage. Adolescence and adulthood are in the formal operational stage, demonstrated by the logical use of symbols related to abstract concepts.

Child development is predicated on family, cultural context, and individual factors that influence the possession of feelings and experiences. Designers must beware of risk factors that their designs create, such as chances for slips, falls, toxins, and choking hazards for young users. Designers need to find balance between some risk during the exploration process, which will help in maintaining the interest of the child, while also providing a sense of safety, which will encourage exploration.

You can also refer to this textbook's companion Study Guide for a comprehensive list of Summary Points.

Adolescents value the freedom and control that they feel in their solitary places, yet also value places where they can interact socially (Owens, 1988, 1994). A study of Swedish children ages 13 to 17 found that girls preferred private places, whereas boys' preferred public ones (Lieberg, 1994). Girls tend to be more affiliative and as such prefer private environments where they can discuss personal thoughts and feelings with other girls their age. It is through these personal revelations to others that they solidify social bonds and friendships. Boys tend to prefer environments that are more public and allow them to see and be seen. It is through this sense of belonging to something larger than them (the group) that they gain confidence and forge a support system of lasting friendships.

Physical Environment and Child Development

Lorraine E. Maxwell, Ph.D., EDRA, Cornell University

The physical environment plays a critical role in child development. Yet, often when referring to the home or classroom environment, the reference is to the social environment, i.e., the people with whom the child has a relationship. For example, when describing the home or classroom environment, what comes to mind is the relationship between parents and children or teachers and students. However, because all activities occur in a physical place, the physical environment must be considered as well. The physical environment is more than a stage setting for these activities. Attributes of the physical environment directly affect the individual. In addition, the physical environment can affect the quality of the interactions between people.

Noise has a detrimental effect on children. In school settings chronic exposure to noise associated with airports, trains, and road traffic make it difficult for children to pay attention or to focus, especially on difficult or complex tasks. Children's long-term memory is also negatively affected by noise, which makes it difficult to learn. Children in noisy classrooms and those who live in chronically noisy homes consistently perform lower on reading and math achievement measures than their peers in quieter environments. One of the key factors related to the effects of noise is the inability of the individual to control the noise source. Noise originating from road traffic, trains, and airports cannot be easily turned off.

Density is another attribute of the physical environment that has particular consequences for children. For example, large class sizes are associated with lower achievement scores on standardized tests and behavior problems; but the amount of space, or spatial density, available in the classroom is also important. Less space per child is associated with lower reading scores and behavior problems. Some children withdraw from interacting with their classmates in crowded classrooms. Children, especially boys, living in crowded homes are more likely to have behavior problems in school. Parents may also be less responsive to their children in a crowded home. In other words, density can affect the way parents and children and teachers and students interact with each other.

The physical environment plays a role in how children feel about themselves. It can help children feel competent, it can boost their self-esteem, or it can give negative messages. The self-esteem of elementary school-age children is related to the amount of personalization in the classroom.

Deteriorated school buildings are associated with higher student absentee rates. Minority and low-income high school students notice that their schools are more likely to be deteriorated than the schools in white, higher-income neighborhoods. School buildings can also promote a sense of pride and ownership among children and adolescents when student artwork is permanently displayed.

The physical environment is not neutral or a stage setting. The quality of the physical environment is as important as the social environment in the lives of children. It can affect the nature of the social relationships that they have with their peers and with the adults in their lives.

KEY TERMS

- **allergen**
- **anecdotal evidence**
- **cones**
- **rods**
- **sensorimotor**
- **teratogen**
- **tracking**

WEB LINKS

The Association for Prenatal and Perinatal Psychology and Health, select "life before birth" (www.birthpsychology.com

Barnard Center for Toddler Development (www.barnard.columbia.edu/toddlers)

Helpguide (www.helpguide.org)

Jean Piaget Society (http://www.piaget.org)

The Monell Center (www.monell.org)

The National Parks Service's Natural Sounds Program, visit the Sound Gallery and links to other public "sound libraries" (www.nature.nps.gov/naturalsounds)

The Smith-Kettlewell Eye Research Institute, select "vision for non-scientists" (www.ski.org)

United Nations Development Programme of Women's Empowerment (www.undp.org/women)

U.S. Environmental Protection Agency's "Indoor Air Pollution: An Introduction for Health Professionals" (www.epa.gov/iaq/pubs/hpguide.html)

STUDIO ACTIVITY 7.1

Interactive Wall

Design Problem Statement
Develop an interactive wall for a two-year-old (male or female, you decide).

Issue: Toddlers require a diverse set of stimuli and cause-and-effect situations to help them develop neural connections. However, these stimuli and cause-and-effect situations must increase in complexity as a child grows. How will you address physical and cognitive growth within the design of this wall?

Directions
Step One: Identify the elements that will be contained within this wall and the purpose each element will serve. Remember to include a diverse array of elements.

Step Two: Build a mock-up of this wall with each element to scale.

Deliverables
A model of a room showing the interactive wall along with a paper describing each of the design elements as well as their intended outcome for the cognitive growth of this child.

STUDIO ACTIVITY 7.2

Teen Centers

Design Problem Statement
You have been asked to build a teen center in a suburban neighborhood. Your population constituency is diverse in terms of race and ethnicity. The goal of this teen center is to promote greater interpersonal and intercultural understanding.

Issue: People naturally self-segregate and certain people, based on their age, cultural preferences, racial biases, or gender, gravitate to certain design styles and/or color choices and patterns. How can one designer develop a teen center that appeals to all teens regardless of gender, culture, or ethnicity?

Directions
Step One: Identify common design elements that appeal to majority of teens (provable). These elements include shape, lighting, color, patterns, and more.

Step Two: Identify common features of a teen center that would appeal to the majority of teens regardless of gender, culture, or ethnicity.

Step Three: Develop a rendered floor plan of a teen center complete with individual rooms (if there are any) and services, such as a snack bar, etc.

Deliverables
A rendered floor plan of a teen center along with a paper describing the design elements and why they have mass appeal to the target population as well as ways that the design can contribute to intercultural understandings and promote unity.

DISCUSSION QUESTIONS

1. Describe important attributes that should be implemented into the design of an expectant mother's environment. Give examples of how these attributes impact the unborn child.

2. As designers, why is it important to understand how our youth develops?

3. When does an infant's social learning process begin, and what environmental conditions trigger this response?

4. What is important to consider when designing a room for a toddler? What stages of development should the design enhance? Give examples of good design techniques for a toddler's environment.

5. Why is it important to understand that preadolescents and adolescents must be able to embrace the overall design of their space, and what measures can be taken to ensure a successful design?

LEARNING ACTIVITIES

1. Design a thorough environmental analysis for the home of an expectant mother. Address all the environmental issues that could arise within the interior and exterior of the home in order to better suit the unborn.

2. Design a room for an infant. Use a variety of surfaces, textures, and atmospheres within the infants' environment.

3. Design a questionnaire for a client who has a toddler. What essential questions should you ask regarding the design of the toddlers' space? What would you consider in the design to make it suitable to the developmental needs of the toddler?

4. Design the ultimate playing area for children. Integrate into it both male and female characteristics, and include spaces that encourage cognitive and physical development. Ensure a sense of safety to allow for exploration.

5. Describe an interview process for the design of a room for a preadolescent or adolescent. What questions would you ask, and what information would you acquire to ensure the space is accepted and embraced? Consider the adolescent as your client.

08 The Elderly Population

Old age is no place for sissies.

—Bette Davis

Accessibility, utility, and safety are important considerations in every built environment, particularly for environments used by people whose abilities are impaired by age, disease, or genetic issues. When many people hear the words *disabled* or *handicapped,* the first image they conjure is of a person in a wheelchair. However, many disabilities affect not only those who are developmentally or physically challenged but also many in the geriatric population who, like the disabled population, have a range of abilities, as well as significant impairments, such as Alzheimer's and Parkinson's disease (Kopec, 2007). We must, therefore, pay extra attention to the design of environments intended for the elderly population.

As we age, all of our abilities (e.g., sensory detection, cognitive acuity, balance, motor skills) decline (Rogers, Meyer, Walker, & Fisk, 1998). Motor and cognitive limitations influence every aspect of an elderly person's daily life and determine the amount and type of activities in which they can participate. The older person's mind and body react and function slower as part of the normal aging process, and he/she experiences a decline in one or more of the five senses. Many older people also experience difficulty staying asleep, performing simple movements, acts of coordination and balance, and processing simple mental activities. Attention, problem solving, and general anxiety have a strong relationship to accidents; and the elderly may be more prone to tripping when contradictory or changing verbal and visual information are presented simultaneously (Persad et al., 1995).

Given the developmental realities associated with the aging process, it is important to design environments where older people can physically and mentally flourish. This is not always an easy task because each person ages differently and has varying degrees of abilities. In this chapter we discuss the elderly population in terms of common illnesses and disorders, and how we can develop environments that better serve their needs.

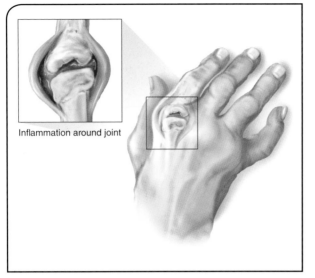

[**Figure 8.1**] Arthritis is a condition that can lead to joint malformations. When this happens in the hands, the person loses dexterity and strength, which impedes his/her ability to perform tasks requiring fine motor skills, such as manipulating coins and keys. Illustration by Precision Graphics

THE GERIATRIC POPULATION

During the twentieth century, the U.S. population under the age of 65 tripled, and those 65 and older increased by a factor of 11 (Aging in the Know, 2005). This means that our older population is growing much faster than our younger population, and that our society is aging in general. The actual number of senior citizens in the United States grew from 3.1 million in 1900 to 33.2 million by 1994, and it is anticipated that by the year 2050, the population over age 65 will exceed 80 million. This roughly translates to about one out of every five Americans, or 20 percent of the total population (Aging in the Know, 2005), will be senior citizens.

Developmental Characteristics

When a person reaches the age of 65, there is a 50 percent chance that he/she will live another 20 years (Clark & Quinn, 2002; Hardy, 2002; Kinsella & Velkoff, 2001). As a person ages, he/she must come to terms with the incongruence between memories of what he/she could once do with the reality of his/her present physical capabilities. Oftentimes these people will have full mental acuity and clear memories of their once-independent lifestyles, so the sense of having a young mind trapped in a frail old body can provoke feelings of anger, despair, and helplessness. Likewise, progressing from a lifetime of self-sufficiency and relative freedom to not being able to perform simple routine

activities of daily living (ADLs)—routine functional tasks (e.g., driving, cooking, reading, getting up from a chair, taking a stroll, bathing, grooming, dressing, or even eating)—can be frustrating to the point of severely damaging an older person's self-esteem. For example, many everyday items, such as vending machines, can be problematic for the elderly person with arthritis because many lack the manual dexterity required to insert coins and bills (Figure 8.1). This, coupled with cognitive decline and memory loss, can lead to anxiety as the person is forced to acknowledge all that he/she has lost with age (Dark-Freudeman, West, & Viverito, 2006). Living with these limitations can be psychologically debilitating, particularly when a person's ability to function is further impeded by the environment.

From a developmental perspective, the aging process can be broken down into two types: primary and secondary. Primary aging typically entails the natural loss of basic functions. Examples include a decline in eyesight, decreased short-term memory capabilities, and difficulty identifying and recalling certain words. Secondary aging typically results from chronic conditions from lifestyle choices (Kempler, 2005). The natural aging process can also result in neurochemical and anatomical changes in the brain, which can increase the risk of dementia. The Centers for Disease Control (2006), estimates that 88 percent of people over age 65 have at least one chronic health condition. Chronic diseases are generally not prevented by vaccines or cured by medication because most of these diseases are created through unhealthy behaviors such as tobacco use, alcohol abuse, lack of physical activity, and poor eating habits.

To a great extent, the major chronic disease killers (e.g., heart disease [HD], cancer, stroke, diabetes) are an extension of what elderly people do or not do in their everyday life. It is not clear where primary aging effects end and secondary begin.

The elderly population is further divided into two developmental classifications: young-old and oldest old. The young-old are people who are in their sixties and seventies. Many of the young-old are financially stable and lack major health issues. Conversely, the oldest-old are people in their eighties and above. This population tends to be financially challenged, and many suffer from multiple health issues (Belsky, 2007). In general, people over the age of 65 are affected by chronic and age-related conditions that negatively affect ADLs. These conditions include decreases in musculoskeletal strength, decline in motor skills, and diminished cognitive capabilities (Belsky, 2007).

The *oldest old* make up one of the fastest-growing population segments within industrialized nations (Figure 8.2). Social factors (e.g., family, friends, caregivers) can pro-

[**Figure 8.2**] In the past we expected the oldest old to be hidden away behind closed doors. Today many are living active and fulfilling lives and can continue to do so as long as we design environments that support their abilities. © Oxford Picture Library / Alamy

vide emotional support and physical assistance; but living in a culture in which youth is prized for its productivity, while old age is dishonored and often regarded as burdensome, can have devastating psychological effects, including feelings of worthlessness. Adding to these realities are the dominant medical approaches to aging, which view it as a curable condition. Face-lifts, joint replacements, and an assortment of pills—all address the symptoms of aging but ignore the social, environmental, and quality-of-life needs of the oldest old (Schwarz, 1997).

Mastering Environmental Challenges

Designers and caregivers alike should provide the means for the oldest old to adapt, identify, and utilize psychosocial resources in order to help them compensate for a decline in their physical health. A longitudinal study found that oldest old individuals who were living independently and with better perceived health and mastery over their environment displayed greater stability in ADL functions. These researchers also found that age, marital status, grip strength, and actual—as opposed to perceived—mastery were significant predictors of mobility status after four years (Femia,

Zarit, & Johansson, 1997). Of course ADL functioning is dependent not only on age, but also on individual physical, psychological, and social characteristics, and environments that promote a sense of mastery over challenging situations. Mastery thus helps to prevent passive and dependent behaviors, which are preludes to an assortment of disabilities and perhaps institutionalization. Other researchers found that although older adults experience difficulties with new technology, they are eager to learn how to use technology that will enrich their lives and help them to remain independent (Rogers, Meyer, Walker, & Fisk, 1998). Designers, therefore, should not be afraid to consider new technologies that will help the older person retain mastery over his/her environment as a means of promoting independence and self-confidence (Figure 8.3).

When a person's mastery over his/her environment declines, the person is likely to lose much of his/her independence and autonomy, which in turn affects his/her self-esteem (Baker, Stephens, & Hill, 2002). Implementing compensatory and adaptive strategies can create positive perceptions that lead to feelings of power, self-sufficiency, and mastery (i.e., autonomy). Designers can alleviate some of the

[**Figure 8.3**] Several new technologies have been developed that can help the older person retain mastery over his/her environments. Whereas it is true that cognitive processing does decline with age, many older people are eager to learn. These technologies offer a way for older people to retain their skills without placing themselves in harm's way. The people in this photo are playing Wii baseball. © Adrian Sherratt / Alamy

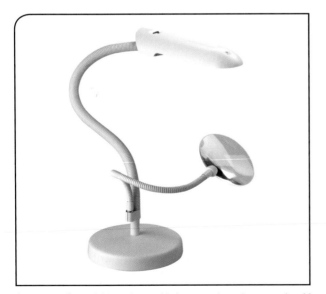

[**Figure 8.4**] Bendable and movable lamps such as this not only add to a room's ambience, but also the highly directed light can be aimed at a menu, thereby allowing an older person to better read the menu's contents. © Mouse in the House / Alamy

obstacles through simple design attributes, such as adding grab bars in elevators, making aisles in retail environments wider, and providing small-task lighting in restaurants that the guests can brighten if they choose (Figure 8.4).

Autonomy-Supportive Environments

People's perception of autonomy has been shown to be a crucial factor in the development of intrinsic motivation. Autonomy-supportive events are defined as those that encourage the process of choice and the experience of self-determination. Autonomy support is associated with positive emotions, higher self-esteem, greater intrinsic motivation, greater interest, better conceptual learning, more cognitive flexibility, greater persistence of behavior change, more trust, and better physical and psychological health. It is also associated with less pressure, tension, and aggression than *controlled support* (Deci & Ryan, 1987); which is support that is dependent on others. We can therefore say that autonomy-supportive environments can promote positive or desired outcomes because they encourage choice and promote the experience of self-determination.

SUSTAINABILITY CONNECTION 8.1

In an effort to maintain balance within a community, designers must consider mixed-income, mixed-age, and mixed-use developments preferable over single-use endeavors. For example, a development such as City Heights Square in San Diego includes residential, retail, office, and healthcare—all within one convenient city block. The housing was designed especially for fixed-income seniors 62 and over. The connected 5,348-square-foot pocket park services the offices, retail, and ground floor medical clinic. As a part of the collaboration to support the older adults living in the community, services offered include meals, counseling, and legal assistance. As our population ages and technological advances give greater autonomy to older adults, it is thought that developments such as this one will become commonplace.

Helplessness is a central construct of personal control (Seligman, 1992). Personal control is stabilized through autonomy-supportive environments; hence, protracted *learned helplessness* brings about depression. Learned helplessness can develop when a person is repeatedly put into a position where there is no possibility of success; eventually, the person responds by doing nothing—in the belief that he/she is powerless to improve the situation. Helplessness is a useful predictor of depression, low achievement, and poor physical health (Seligman, 1992). There are numerous reports of the sudden deaths of men and women of various ages, backgrounds, and levels of health; all had no discernible pathological cause (confirmed via autopsy), reported prior to death feelings of overwhelming helplessness and hopelessness (Seligman, 1992). There are many studies that provide evidence in support of the idea that independence interferes with future learning of dependence. In other words, a person may simply give up and die, but such a fate is by no means inevitable and can be prevented by measures that include the implementation of autonomy-supportive design.

Some of the autonomy-supportive concerns identified by the elderly population include having well-defined but different needs, and achieving and maintaining independence. Designers can best serve physically challenged people by identifying their clients' specific needs and ADLs, and by working with them to create environments that support their clients' feelings of autonomy. A study was conducted to determine if older adults with chronic illness or disabilities used different strategies to adapt to everyday activities and how these strategies affected feelings of independence, dependence, helplessness, emotional reactivity, and coping ability. The study subjects demonstrated a wide range of coping strategies to self-manage their disabilities. These strategies include the following:

- Giving up or restricting an activity or performing it less frequently
- Optimization (i.e., spending more time on an activity, planning an activity to avoid problems, using movement to avoid pain or stiffness, and resting periodically)
- Compensation (i.e., substitution, modification, or use of furniture or equipment for assistance)
- Accepting help from others (Gignac, Cott, & Badley, 2000)

Because older adults greatly fear losing their independence, the negative psychological impact is inherent in their coping strategies, all of which are associated with feelings of dependence and helplessness, loss of independence, and lower coping efficacy. Optimization techniques also heighten emotional reactivity or a person's response to an event. To maintain an active and independent lifestyle, older adults must be able to perform daily activities such as bathing, eating, and taking medications without active external support from others (Rogers, Meyer, Walker, & Fisk, 1998; Figure 8.5).

Multiple factors contribute to successful aging, including eating a healthy diet, getting adequate sleep and exercise, participating in a social network, engaging in enjoyable activities and projects, and feeling as though one has a purpose. All of these contribute to one's attitude and predisposition to aging. People who accept the aging process as an integral

[**Figure 8.5**] Pets require daily activities such as being fed, taken for walks, bathed, and brushed out. Several studies have shown that these activities go a long way to making older people feel good and providing them with a sense of purpose. © Marmaduke St. John / Alamy

part of the life cycle with unique characteristics (Schwarz, 1997) are more likely to remain vital and active; those who cannot may literally give up on life.

CULTURAL CONNECTION 8.1

Retirement and aging are not the end of life; by the standards of many cultures, it is merely a time when the role and purpose of the older adult changes. For example, Japanese society holds their elderly in high regard and looks to their elders to care for the younger generation, while the middle generation earns the family income. Members of Russian society seek out their elders for advice and guidance. Nigerian tradition accords their eldest the responsibility for the group's legal and moral decisions. The most consistent role across the cultures is that elders are entrusted with instructing the younger generation on their traditions, customs, and values. Some of this is seen in the United States, where in 2009 the average age of justices on the Supreme Court, the highest court in the land, was 68. Giving elders new responsibilities to the family and/or community has been shown to enhance the immune system and quality of life for older adults—due in large part to the elderly having a continued *purpose* for life, *joy* in being productive, and *happiness* through social contact.

Designers can best contribute to residential environments for the elderly by supporting their personal expressions of identity and helping to facilitate *place attachment* through interior features (Eshelman & Evans, 2002). Researchers advocate providing visual spatial cues (i.e., objects or elements in the space) in environments used or occupied by older adults to help them maintain balance—noting, however, that such cues can become compromised when a person is moving (e.g., walking) or when an environment itself moves (e.g., going up an escalator). When an individual's balance becomes unstable it may take longer for him/her to regain control, particularly when visual cues continue to move (e.g., standing on a moving bus, walking down stairs, riding a moving sidewalk at an airport) (Sundermeier, Woollacott, Jensen, & Moore, 1996).

When designing for the elderly, designers will want to include elements that compensate for the physical and energy limitations of the elderly. Many older adults require easily accessible storage because they have trouble reaching into upper wall cabinets and the lower shelves of base cabinets or refrigerators. Moreover, they do not cook extensively, cannot use the back burners on stoves safely, and prefer to use smaller appliances (e.g., microwaves, toaster ovens, electric slow cookers; Boschetti, 1995). Consider incorporating an L-shaped kitchen layout that provides a corner where people with limited stamina can lean and a small work triangle (the area between the refrigerator, sink, and oven or range) to reduce the effort involved in meal preparation (Boschetti, 1995; Figure 8.6).

Design should also provide both storage and display areas for personal objects, memorabilia, and heirlooms, which can evoke pleasant feelings and symbolize the self and specific memories for older individuals who may depend on those objects for their well-being (Boschetti, 1995). One researcher, citing earlier findings that possessions can trigger memories that give *meaning* to a home and reinforce self-identity, also found that *place attachment* is more likely to occur when personal artifacts are incorporated into an otherwise anonymous space where they can be seen and touched. This researcher recommended using personal possession criteria in design programs to determine how individuals feel about their personal possessions (Boschetti, 1995). Personal possession criteria: clients (not designers) must rate the "specialness" of their own belongings because some people may not want to be reminded of their past experiences or lost youth.

[**Figure 8.6**] This kitchen layout provides several opportunities to lean against a counter. Notice that a person need only take one or two steps to reach another rest spot. Also notice the chairs that provide ideal places to rest along one side of the counter. © 2009, Mike Watson Images Limited

An increased aging population coupled with many debilitating social phenomena such as single parenting, drug and alcohol addiction, and lack of a living wage has created a unique social situation whereby today, many older people must also act as the primary caregivers to young children. For example, more than six million children—approximately 1 in 12—live in households headed by their grandparents. In many of these homes (approximately 2.4 million), it is the grandparents who assume the primary responsibility for the children's needs, and without either of the child's parents present (AARP Foundation, 2007; Figure 8.7). This can present difficulties for the older person who is likely to experience a 38.8 percent decrease in activity levels by the age of 65 and 56 percent decline by the age of 85 (Center for Inclusive Design and Environmental Access, 2001).

Recognizing the diminished abilities that comes with age along with the need for young children to develop motor skills can pose a unique challenge for the designer. In such cases, the designer will need to include toys that are bright and contrast with the flooring and furnishings so that they can be easily seen by the older person and child. Also, wherever possible, including soft squishy materials for toys such as puzzles and building blocks allows the grandparent who accidentally steps on the toy to right himself/herself before a fall occurs.

Currently, more than 50 percent of the U.S. population is characterized as having some form of diminished physical ability, 49 million older people have at least one physical disability, and approximately 10 percent of the population has more than one limitation in their abilities. Findings show that as a person reaches the age of 65, his/her likelihood of experiencing an accident leading to a disability increases by more than 50 percent. Among those who are aged 70 or older, 79 percent had one or more of seven chronic conditions (Aging in the Know, 2005):

- Sensory deficits
- Arthritis
- High blood pressure
- Heart disease
- Diabetes
- Lung diseases
- Stroke
- Cancer

Most have impaired mobility or dexterity, including 37 million with arthritis.

Heart disease (HD) is the leading cause of death among persons 65 or older; about 33 percent of deaths occur in this age group (Van Houtven et al., 2008). Common HDs

[**Figure 8.7**] Since 1990 there has been nearly a 30 percent increase in the number of children being raised by grandparents. The 2000 census data shows that more than 4.5 million children live in 2.4 million grandparent-headed households. © Kevin Dodge / Corbis

include adult congenital HD, coronary artery disease commonly caused by atherosclerosis and high cholesterol, bradycardia, angina pectoris (angina), arrhythmia (dysrhythmia), cardiomyopathy, congestive heart failure, heart attack (myocardial infarction), high blood pressure (hypertension), and valvular HD. High blood pressure is an inherent risk factor for developing HD, and it is very common among senior citizens. Approximately 50 percent of the people between the ages of 65 and 74 are affected by high blood pressure. One research study found that high cholesterol within 35 percent of men and 60 percent of women age 65 or older (Beaglehole & Jackson, 1991) leads to high blood pressure.

To address HD and high blood pressure in design, the key is to reduce emotional and physical stress. Emotional stress often comes from others, or from one's frustration at not being able to complete a task that could once be performed fairly easily. Physical stress might come from labor-intensive movements such as cleaning high windows where the task is not only difficult but also requires the person doing the washing to perform the task with arms above his/her head. This causes the person's heart rate to increase, thereby increasing the potential for a heart attack. When designing a home for an older person, it is important to limit any design features that are up high and/or require excessive maintenance or cleaning (Figure 8.8). When those features exist, the designer should look at ways to reduce the maintenance associated with that feature.

Stroke is the third leading cause of death among people ages 65 and over, and the condition affects two to three million

[**Figure 8.8**] High windows such as these are unsafe for older people because many cannot afford to have someone clean them and will often attempt to do so by themselves. Raising the arms over the head to perform a task such as cleaning the windows increases the heart rate. For a person with heart disease, this could result in a heart attack. © JC Photography / Alamy

[**Figure 8.9**] People with chronic lung diseases often require the use of oxygen tanks; however, this medical device has specific design requirements that must be followed in order to prevent the highly flammable gas from igniting. © Corbis Super RF / Alamy

elderly people annually. The most deadly type of stroke is caused by cerebrovascular disease (Van Houtven et al., 2008). Some of the underlying conditions that lead to stroke include atherosclerosis, atrial fibrillation, hypertension, dyslipidemia, and diabetes. Warning signs are sudden weakness, difficulty speaking, sudden loss of vision, and severe unusual headaches or dizziness (Weir, 2005). The causes of stroke are thought to be related to certain air pollutants—lead, ozone, and other forms of airborne particulate matter (Kettunen et al., 2007).

From a design perspective, it is important to locate retirement and nursing homes away from heavily traveled roads and raised freeways. This is because pollutants from combustion engines drift into the residential areas, and many have been associated with health conditions. Landscaping and house plants are also important features that a designer will want to include in the designs because plants play a key role in filtering and cleaning the air and also have many psychological benefits. For those who have suffered and survived a stroke, many are left with partial paralysis and some damage to their brain functioning. This can be devastating and lead people to look at what they don't have versus what they still have. As such, designers should develop designs that show people what they can do as opposed to designs that highlight what a person cannot do. This concept ties directly into *universal design* and *aging in place* principles. Aging in place is a concept that is similar to universal design, the premise being that homes should be flexible and adaptable to accommodate changes that occur as part of the normal aging process. Research has shown that people who are allowed to remain in their homes do better both physically and psychologically than do people who are forced to relocate.

Chronic lung disease is a group of illnesses that affect one's ability to breathe and are characterized by continuous shortness of breath. These illnesses include asthma, emphysema and chronic obstructive pulmonary disease (COPD), lung cancer, and chronic lower respiratory disease. Research has shown a direct connection between environmental contaminants and the onset of certain chronic lung diseases such as lung cancer. Asbestos, radon (Van Houtven et al., 2008), tobacco smoke, an assortment of particulate matter, and excessive ozone produced by many common types of office equipment have all been linked to chronic lung disease. Lung cancer, in particular, has the second highest prevalence within the elderly population ages 65 and older. In total, chronic lung diseases are the fourth leading cause of death within the elderly population. Those who have one or more chronic lung diseases often require special equipment such as oxygen tanks, which have specific safety instruction that must be followed; its highly flammable gas can cause materials that burn to ignite faster and burn more easily, thereby taking on an explosion-like appearance (Figure 8.9).

When designing spaces for people who suffer from a chronic lung disease and require the use of oxygen, make sure that primary sitting and sleeping spaces are at least eight feet away from significant heat sources such as an electric radiator, fireplace, or kitchen stove. Also, avoid the use of candles, incense, or other devices that require a flame. Because of issues related to static electricity, designers should also avoid the use of wool, nylon, or synthetic fabrics for the bedding, window treatments, furniture upholstery, and carpeting as they have the potential to provide a catalyst for a fire. Cottons and leathers are the best materials. Finally make sure to incorporate a variety of fire extinguishers throughout the environment so that one is never too far away. The addition of residential fire-sprinkler systems also reduce the risk of dying in a home fire by 82 percent.

Arthritis and related conditions such as osteoporosis are the leading cause of disability in the United States, and they affect nearly 43 million Americans. Within the broad classification of "arthritis" there are more than 100 types with different causes, symptoms, and manifestations. The most common are osteoarthritis, rheumatoid arthritis, and gout.

The word "arthritis" means "joint inflammation," and although there is presently no cure, some experts recommend regular exercise as a means of reducing joint pain and stiffness through the building of strong muscles around the joints and increasing flexibility and endurance.

For those who live with one or more forms of arthritis, getting up and down from chairs, climbing stairs, and using keys can be a painful and daunting task.

With arthritis comes a great deal of chronic pain, fatigue, and limited range of motion, which can lead to strong negative emotions. Designers will want to address the physical aspects of arthritis through principles of universal design and aging in place. To help people cope with chronic pain, designers can reduce travel distances within the home, create distractions, and lower environmental stimulation. A highly stimulating environment will often provoke people to pay closer attention to details, including how one feels. Low-stimulus environments tend to promote relaxation and lesser awareness to one's surroundings. When designing for pain, however, the best way to design is through psychological immersion. The idea here is to focus the person's attentions away from his/her pain and onto something else. One simple example might be a media center within the home (Figure 8.10). Large screens and surround sound can help the person become completely focused on the media show, which could be a movie or a virtual trip through a rainforest, and not focus on their pain.

[**Figure 8.10**] Provide situations that envelope the individual so that he or she is unable to think of the pain. Large screen televisions or handheld devices that can be used up close force the individual to direct his/her attention to the screen. Surround sound systems bring sound from all directions, thus helping the person to become immersed into a given story or atmosphere. By distracting attention away from the pain, the person's perception of that pain will be decreased. © David P. Hall / Corbis

NEURAL DISORDERS

Many of the age-related disorders that affect the brain come from disease. In 1817, a British physician by the name of James Parkinson described a disorder in which people would move sluggishly and with a shuffling gait. He also noted that the affected people's hands would shake, or their limbs periodically seemed stiff, as if they were frozen. Today we call this disorder Parkinson's disease, and roughly a half a million Americans suffer from it. Alzheimer's disease is another disorder that affects the brain by causing it to atrophy. Some believe that this disease can result from a shortage of the neurotransmitter, acetocolyne. This shortage could be a result of genetic or environmental factors, or a combination of both. The primary symptoms associated with Alzheimer's disease include a reduction in cognitive abilities and increased spatial disorientation (Passini, Rainville, Marchand, & Joanette, 1998). Some estimates suggest that the disease will affect up to 16 million Americans by the year 2050 (Alzheimer's Association, 2004).

Parkinson's Disease

Parkinson's disease is a condition where the neurons in the brain responsible for producing the neurotransmitter dopamine become impaired or die (Parkinson's Disease Foundation, n.d.). Dopamine is needed for smooth control and coordination of voluntary muscle groups. The symptoms associated with Parkinson's disease typically develop after 80 percent of the dopamine-producing cells have ceased to function. Researchers suspect that the cause of Parkinson's disease reflects a combination of genetic factors coupled with exposure to certain environmental toxins.

Research has shown that people with Parkinson's disease often have abnormal basil ganglia (a subcortical structure located on the outer sides of the thalami, which depends on the neurotransmitter dopamine; dopamine is discussed in Chapter 3). However, in the person afflicted with Parkinson's disease, many of the cells that produce dopamine die,

[**Figure 8.11**] Chairs that allow a person to grip the arms, brass railings for people to grip while waiting in long lines, and large cabinet and control knobs that people can grip, all help to reduce the tremors that are commonly associated with Parkinson's disease. Notice in the image that grab bars are in the shower, by the commode, and on the side of the wash basin. ©Corbis Premium RF/Alamy

thereby causing a deficiency. The basil ganglia's functions include the planning and production of movement (Rhawn, 2002), as well as some types of learning, development of a habit, and the connection of a stimulus with a response.

The most common symptoms of Parkinson's disease include tremors, rigidity, and bradykinesia (slowed ability to start and continue movements, and impaired ability to adjust the body's position). Many of the secondary symptoms include speech changes, loss of facial expression, micrographia (small, cramped handwriting), difficulty swallowing, drooling, pain, dementia or confusion, memory difficulties and slowed thinking, fatigue and aching, and loss of energy.

Because tremors are more likely to occur when muscles are relaxed, many patients with Parkinson's disease prefer to grip or hold onto something. This is important within design because designers can use chairs with armrests that can be gripped, include rails or grab bars where people are forced to stand in line, and include items with large knobs that can be more easily grasped when a person experiences tremors (Figure 8.11).

Additionally, designers should consider placing grab bars at key locations, such as hallways, bathrooms, and along outdoor paths. They should also be aware that rigidity can greatly decrease an individual's range of motion to the point where lifting a hand over the head to reach for something can be problematic. Mechanical storage shelves that raise and lower will reduce the need to bend down low or reach up high.

Dementia of the Alzheimer's Type

Dementia of the Alzheimer's type (DAT) is a disease that affects the nervous system. Of the current elderly population who are aged 65 and older, between 5 to 10 percent are in one of three stages of DAT: mild, moderate, or severe. The cognitive degeneration that occurs with DAT is generally associated with memory loss, confusion, language problems, lack of identity, emotional and personality changes, sleep and sexual disorders, and disruptive behaviors (Rabins, 1989; Zeisel, 2000). Many experience an inability to interpret visual cues, memory loss, confusion, wandering, loss of identity, and emotional regression. As the disease progresses, all sense of time and place are lost, and activities of daily living such as eating, dressing, and bathing become negatively affected. During the final stages of DAT, symptoms increase to include atypical motor and verbal activity, hallucinations, incontinence, agitation and irritability, aggression and violence, social withdrawal, and wandering (Day & Calkins, 2002). Many people with DAT mentally regress to the level similar to that of a young child. This regression can lead the individual to use a native language and engage in earlier cultural behaviors (Valle, 1989). Much

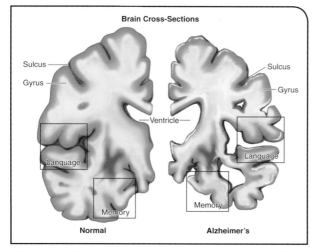

Brain Cross-Sections

Sulcus — Gyrus — Ventricle — Language — Memory

Sulcus — Gyrus — Language — Memory

Normal   Alzheimer's

[**Figure 8.12**] From this illustration, one can see that the overall brain size decreases with Alzheimer's disease, and sections of the brain dedicated to memory, language, and other cognitive functions have disappeared. Illustration by Precision Graphics

of these behaviors will depend upon each individual's level and degree of cultural adaptation, and to what extent the person has integrated the new culture into his/her identity (Kopec, 2007). Eventually, the symptoms associated with DAT become so unbearable that many families find it necessary to institutionalize their loved one.

As cognitive degeneration progresses to the later stages, symptoms generally manifest at a faster rate. With DAT, specific structural changes occur within the brain, which renders cells incapable of transmitting nerve signals to neural cells throughout the brain (Figure 8.12). As the number of these damaged cells increases, the symptoms become more pronounced.

DAT sufferers who are aware of their impairment and deterioration often respond with feelings of helplessness and depression (Brannon & Feist, 1997). An important variable in the disease's progression is the person's degree of privacy, particularly as it relates to the control and freedom of choice regarding accessibility to body and mind (Morgan & Stewart, 1998). For designers, it is important to incorporate methods into the overall design that help facilitate visual privacy at minimum and complete privacy whenever possible (without limiting the medical staff's need for safety surveillance of patients). Privacy is a fundamental human need that when taken away, can bring about learned helplessness and depression.

Symptoms of DAT depend greatly on the stage of the disease, as well as the person's unique circumstances. Depending on these circumstances, the speed of cognitive decline along with the presence of volatile behavioral episodes associated with over-stimulation can vary. This

means that designers must exercise caution when planning lighting levels, including different plants that produce aromatic scents, and introducing the presence of different sounds (tone and volume; see Box 8.1, "Sound Reduction"). The result of these kinds of stimuli often manifest as confusion, disorientation, and agitation.

BOX 8.1 SOUND REDUCTION

For many people who suffer from cognitive disorders, whether it is attention deficit disorder or Alzheimer's disease, noise and extraneous sound reduction is an important part of developing a supportive environment. The most cost-effective way to reduce sound transmission between rooms is to create thicker walls with multiple air cavities. This can be done by:

1. Placing thick drops of caulking along the studs where the drywall is attached

2. Attaching drywall with screws so fewer holes are made in the drywall

3. Placing a second layer of drywall and making sure to create a thin air pocket between the two sheets of drywall by placing several drops of caulking on the first panel of drywall and sandwiching the caulking with the second panel of dry wall

Of course, there are manufactured materials designed for sound reduction; but they may not be available or are cost prohibitive, so research should be done on the part of the designer.

Adapted from: Soundproofing 101. Retrieved from http://www.soundproofing101.com/soundproofing_3.htm

One of the most challenging decisions for family members to make is when to place a loved one into an institution such as a nursing home or other type of long-term care facility. Families can delay this decision by having their home environments designed to be more compatible with DAT symptom manifestation (Passini et al., 1998). Currently, there are many projects that are looking into ways that an environment can be adapted so that a person with Alzheimer's disease can remain living at home for a longer period of time (Figure 8.13).

Designers should keep in mind, however, that DAT sufferers have different environmental needs than do other older adults, and they are less able to adapt to environmental stress (Morgan, & Stewart, 1998). They often find it hard to stay asleep, and some may wander throughout the night (Brannon & Feist, 1997). Designers will want to avoid the use of direct and concentrated light as well as inadequate

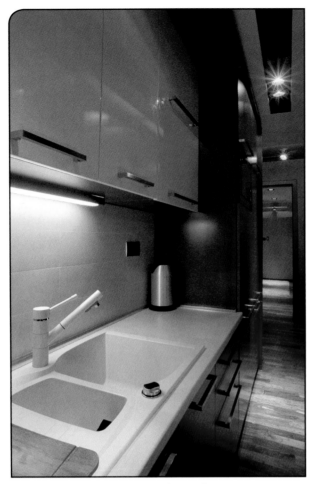

[**Figure 8.13**] A prototype of the *ambient kitchen* is being developed at Newcastle University in an effort to bring digital technology into the home. Sensors placed within cupboards, drawers, and appliances relay messages to a central computer so this computer knows exactly what a person is doing at any given time. If the computer suspects that the individual has become confused (as might be the case of a person with Alzheimer's disease), it has the capacity to project written reminders of what to do next on the closest wall. In many ways, this kind of technology can assist many people with early stages DAT to remain in their homes for a longer period of time. © Dejan Krsmanovic / Alamy

When designing an environment intended for a person with DAT, designers need to consider some of the more prominent behavioral manifestations that accompany the disease (see Table 8.1). These behavior manifestations include:

- *Catastrophic reactions.* Commonly seen as sudden and extreme emotional or physical outbursts, designers should exclude items that could be thrown, broken (glass or ceramic vases), or protrude from a wall (coat hooks, three-dimensional art, or protruding light switches).

- *Picking.* This behavioral condition compels the patient to remove small items, bit by bit. Designers will want to avoid the use of wallpaper, woven cloth upholstery where a thread could become loose, upholstery with edge piping, and shag carpeting that could develop a snag.

- *Reflections.* The potential of seeing oneself or another's reflection can be very disturbing to the dementia patient. Recall that one symptom of DAT is the regression to an earlier time. Hence, it is possible that the person experiences errors between reality, self-image, and a relationship to the passage of time. Simply put, they may not recognize themselves, and this incongruence can be disturbing. Designers will want to limit their use of reflective items such as mirrors, foils, and polished metals. Likewise, they will want to use nonreflective glass in picture frames, and put coverings on high-gloss surfaces.

- *Rummaging.* This is an insatiable need to search. The search could be limited to one's own room, but often encompasses all areas within the environment. When an item of interest has been found, the person is likely to hide it someplace else. Designers will want to allow for this need to search and thus strategically place items around the environment where they can be searched out as well as hidden. Examples include the placement of a desk with drawers in a hallway, bookshelves, and cubby spaces with doors. Additionally, dangerous or private spaces should be fitted with locks to prevent access by the person with DAT.

- *Sundowning.* This is a phenomenon that manifests as agitation, heightened confusion, or unusual behavior during late afternoon or early evening. In this situation, it is best to limit western-exposure windows; however, scientists are unsure of what causes sundowning. It may be related to a change in light waves, neurochemical levels, circadian rhythms, a combination of all, or none.

- *Visual cliffing.* This is an inability to differentiate between colors and textures. For example, a dark mat in front of a door may appear to be a deep hole. The

lighting of primary pathways in the event that the person wanders about during the night.

During daytime hours, it is important to promote autonomy, which can be done by facilitating spatial orientation and wayfinding. A person's ability to reach his/her desired destination is a critical therapeutic attribute within design (Passini et al., 1998) because it helps to foster feelings of autonomy and mastery, which affects perceived quality of life (Passini et al., 2000). In this way, design can directly influence the emotional disposition of the Alzheimer's patient, which then influences the disease's progression.

[Table 8.1] Common DAT Behaviors and Design Suggestions

Behaviors	Design Suggestion
Catastrophic reactions	Develop space plans that allow for the easy escape of caregivers or other patients in the event that a patient experiences a catastrophic reaction. For example, incorporate open furniture design.
Picking	Avoid patterns containing specks, sparkles, or realistic representations of flowers or fruit. This includes floor and wall coverings, upholstery, window treatments, and other fabrics.
Reflections	Limit the use of reflective materials such as polished metals, mirrors, and large non-segmented panes of glass throughout the home or facility.
Rummaging	Include lockable storage spaces for valuables, potentially dangerous items, and employee work areas. Also, include furnishings with a variety of options to rummage and hide objects throughout the facility.
Sundowning	Regulate the light levels throughout the facility, including natural light levels (i.e., as the natural light diminishes, artificial light is increased). Likewise, the designer will want to provide a means of adjusting the lighting levels in order to mimic the day/night environment, especially on overcast days.
Visual cliffing	Avoid the combined use of light and dark colors along floor and wall surfaces. This includes wall art placed upon a wall with a contrasting color.

presence of this perceived "hole" might prompt the resident to attempt jumping over it, thus risking a fall and serious injury, or to stop suddenly, which often results in falls, a phenomenon known as **stalling**.

In one study, people with DAT fell more frequently than those with Parkinson's disease and twice as often as healthy adults (Chong, Horak, Frank, & Kaye, 1999). Those who suffer from Parkinson's disease exhibit balance problems across all test situations, thereby indicating general balance problems. Falls by people with DAT seem to be more related to poor motor (body) control. The person was simply unable to process and control information gained from the senses.

The illusion of **visual cliffing** can have positive as well as negative consequences for older people. The DAT patient might perceive a dark mat in front of an ingress or egress point as something like a castle moat. This can serve as a restraint by preventing the patient from inadvertently wandering outside of the facility. From the design perspective, visual cliffing can be a problem not only with flooring but also with wall surfaces, such as when a dark-colored wall appears to be an empty space. Designers, therefore, need to

avoid the use of dark colors paired with light colors such as black and white tiled flooring, or using dark pieces of art on a light colored wall surface. Also, designers need to be aware of lighting and shadows so that an inadvertent shadow is not cast upon a floor or wall surface.

Designers can help to ensure the most appropriate environments for client-relevant activities in both a primary role (e.g., environmental design and facility adaptation) and a complementary role (e.g., the design of communication and restraint systems). DAT affects behavioral, emotional, and cognitive functioning (Day & Cohen, 2000) particularly memory (Cohen & Weisman, 1991), as well as physical functions, often to the point where sufferers can no longer control their bodily functions (Passini et al., 1998). Incidents of incontinence are acutely distressing to both patients and caregivers (Brannon & Feist, 1997). One way that designers can support sufferers' sense of personal control is by strategically positioning—and clearly marking—toilet facilities.

Institutionalization is often inevitable for most people with moderate to severe DAT (especially those who wander). However, being institutionalized can be equally devastating to the person. Because people who suffer from Alzheimer's disease usually do best in familiar surroundings it is important to incorporate familiar furnishings in similar positions as they were arranged in the home. Notwithstanding, some of the negative effects of institutionalization include, but are not limited to, compromised physical freedoms to move about as one wishes, psychological damage related to a lack of privacy and knowing that one is in the last stage of life, and restricted communication stemming from anger, depression, or medications (Passini et al., 2000).

As is the case for most people, the transition from an environment associated with familiarity and privacy into one of unfamiliarity and higher density induces feelings of insecurity and fear. Numerous studies indicate that institutionalized people have higher mortality rates than those who receive care in their home environment. However, researchers have found that residents who had better cognitive and physical functioning, expressive language, and less agitation experienced more overall decline one year after being admitted into a long-term care facility (Chappell & Reid, 2000). These findings suggests that the transition itself accelerates patient decline, and those who decline less are usually at a point in which there isn't much further to go.

CULTURAL CONNECTION 8.2

The process of dying is a personal and complex event. Moving from one's home of perhaps many years to a medical institution is a sign the elderly can take to mean "the beginning of the end." How a person approaches his/her impending death is closely tied to religious affiliation, ethnic background, family connection, and culture. The elderly who perceive their lives to be full of meaning and purpose have experienced less fear and anxiety moving into the last phase of their life. Spirituality and close family ties have also been found to decrease depression and anger in aged individuals. Some cultures expend extraordinary life-prolonging measures for their loved ones, and still others support and comfort their loved one as they await together the passage of the elder. Designers will need to understand and respect the beliefs and customs of their clients and their extended family to accommodate the process of death and dying.

Designers might consider modifying dementia patients' environments so they can better adjust to their lives (Rabins, 1989), as this behavioral approach is, essentially, the only "treatment" that will benefit sufferers. A paradigm shift in treatment is occurring as more is discovered about dementia of the Alzheimer's type, and researchers are studying how the designed environment supports the unaffected abilities of dementia patients (Zeisel, 2000). In many ways, the impact of design for dementia sufferers spreads far beyond serving the needs of cognitively impaired individuals, and provides support for all residents of long-term care facilities (Day & Cohen, 2000). Those in the early and middle stages of DAT, for example, can still make decisions based on environmental information and routine sets of behavior (Passini et al., 1998), and appropriate designs can help to slow the disease's progression (Morgan & Stewart, 1998).

Environmental design can greatly benefit people who suffer from various forms of dementia, especially when implemented to aid both patient and caregiver. These designs should be developed and implemented in a way that best mitigates, and maximizes the management of symptom manifestation (Day & Cohen, 2000). When designing institutions for DAT patients, designers should allow for environmental markings that are representative of the occupant's personality. This accommodation has been shown to bolster self-esteem (Eshelman & Evans, 2002). Other design concepts include recognizing the importance of the physical environment, including sunlight and fresh air; improving patient quality of life while mitigating problematic behaviors; and providing interior and exterior environments that are diverse, user-appropriate, and that minimize sensory overstimulation. From a facilities perspective, building designs should include special care units specifically dedicated to Alzheimer's patients. These units should have simple building configurations that provide smaller residentially scaled spaces such as kitchen areas, outdoor spaces, natural views, and landmarks. These spaces should allow for personalized touches by the patients in order to provide cues for patient orientation.

Research has also identified the following crucial components for designers to consider when designing facilities for people who suffer from DAT (Chappell & Reid, 2000):

1. Use or nonuse of restraints (physical and chemical)
2. Flexible care routines (client-relevant activities)
3. Specialized environmental design
4. Facility adaptation

These components can help to ensure the most appropriate environments for client-relevant activities in both a primary role (e.g., environmental design and facility adaptation) and a complementary role (e.g., the design of communication and restraint systems).

FACILITIES FOR THE ELDERLY

Ideally, it is the designers' job to help facilitate older people remaining in their homes as long as possible. Not only does this help seniors feel more in control of their own destiny, but older people also contribute significantly to the community by providing "eyes on the street," serving as a source for many oral traditions, and often helping with community maintenance.

In addition, it can be much more cost effective to help people remain in their homes. Some estimates state that nursing home care currently costs the U.S. government $100 billion a year, and other long-term care costs more than $150 billion per year. This translates to roughly twice the amount it costs to support independent living (Confino-Rehder, 2008). Terminology of the different types of long-term care facilities includes: *long-term care facilities, continuing care facilities,* and *special care units.*

Long-term Care Facilities

Long-term care facilities, also called nursing or convalescent homes, serve as residences for individuals whose chronic conditions require routine medical care or assistance (i.e., those who, living on their own, pose a threat or hazard to themselves or others). Becoming ill and requiring frequent hospital stays are a part of advanced age for many in the elderly population; however, leaving one's home for a long-term care facility represents life's final stage before death. This relocation is profoundly stressful for older adults because of its association with the loss of mobility, possessions, social relationships (Lutgendorf et al., 1999), and independence. This is partly due to the transition from a place with many memories to one with none. Overall, a lack of control, whether real or imagined, can decrease a person's capacity to concentrate and increase a person's tendency to report physical symptoms (Brannon & Feist, 1997).

The residents of most long-term care facilities are generally elderly people, but such facilities can also accommodate younger patients. The unfortunate truth regarding long-term care settings for the elderly is the cultural labeling of such facilities as "warehouses" for the elderly. Many of the residents of these facilities feel "put away to die." Hence, tremendous guilt often consumes family members for not being able to care for their loved ones, and many of the residents adopt the sick role that leads to learned helplessness and an exacerbation of physical and/or mental deterioration.

The roots of long-term care in the United States can be traced to facilities called poorhouses, almshouses, poor farms, county infirmaries, asylums, or county homes. These were in essence human storage facilities that were fraught with abuse, abominable living conditions, and a host of human rights violations. Many poor houses of the 1700s and 1800s resembled prisons more than homes. Residents were referred to as "inmates," and they were required to wear a uniform, ask permission to come and go, and were mandated to perform menial labor. Poor houses not only housed the elderly and those in financial hardship, they also became

repositories for society's undesirables. This meant that many elderly were forced to share living and sleeping quarters with petty thieves, alcoholics, and the mentally ill. The result of this cohabitation often manifested in physical injuries to the elderly and fear for their personal safety (Kopec, 2007).

Creating a Sense of Familiarity and Security

In more recent times, the design of long-term care facilities resembled the stark and sterile appearance of hospitals. Modern design trends, however, strive to balance the clinical needs of healthcare with a softer more home-like atmosphere. As part of this change, designers have modified the nurses' station, which was once designed to be the focal point and also served to establish a power hierarchy between employees and residents. In modern designs, the nurses' station has been replaced with a large statue or some other item that serves as the focal point, and the main lobby area now looks more like a hotel lobby or, in some cases, a living room. Additionally, we see the use of green spaces being incorporated into the overall design. Courtyards, greenhouses, and plants distributed throughout the facility enhance the environment's livability, while serving as a **restorative environment**, or a place for relaxation.

Although federal and state regulations, intended to prevent the mistreatment of elderly people while controlling costs, have dictated minimum and maximum requirements for long-term care facility design since 1954, such facilities still suffer from the stigma of being considered poorhouses for the elderly and from the elder-abuse scandals of the 1970s (Schwarz, 1997). However, this is changing in light of research showing that institutionalized elderly people have a higher risk of depression and death within institutional-type settings (Sumaya, Rienzi, Deegan, & Moss, 2001). Those who leave home to stay in healthcare environments, whether for days or years, must be selective as to the size and quantity of personal possessions they can or may bring to the limited space of a hospital room. Patients and their well-meaning loved ones often transport a collection of personal objects to the new residence with the hope of fostering perceptions of familiarity. However, a familiar but disorganized display of meaningful yet unrelated artifacts can serve to accentuate the alien environment (Eshelman & Evans, 2002). In many cases, simple interior components with a homelike aesthetic (e.g., small-scale furnishings, wall coverings, lighting fixtures) can serve to create a sense of familiarity and security (Eshelman & Evans, 2002).

An initial study of institutionalized elderly demonstrated that autonomous residents experienced improved overall well-being (Langer & Rodin, 1976); the follow-up study of the same residents 18 months later found those individuals to be healthier than their peers who did not receive autonomy-support (Rodin & Langer, 1977). Additional studies demonstrated that some of the oldest old can remain stable over time, that psychosocial factors play a critical role in improving or maintaining health, and that a sense of dependence and a lack of control—typical within long-term care facility environments—contribute to physical decline (Boschetti, 1995). Long-term care facilities should, therefore, be designed to encourage feelings of usefulness and independence.

Some design examples include the use of materials, finishes, lighting, furnishings, and decorative objects that serve to create a more residential atmosphere (Passini et al., 2000). Linking artwork to familiar life events can create more resident interest, but be careful not to use items that dementia patients might perceive as toys (Dickinson & McLain-Kark, 1996). In the same sense, it is important to secure artwork with locks or adhesives; and, when possible, anchor furniture so that patients experiencing vertigo (dizziness) can reach for support without fear of the furniture moving. Also consider creating dedicated space and fixed furniture layouts for eating, sleeping, and leisure activities because rearrangement can cause confusion (Passini et al., 2000).

Private areas for residents that can be personalized (e.g., bedrooms, sitting rooms, small areas within a common space) have the potential to help trigger residents' memories and facilitate calmness (Zeisel, 2000), as well as indoor and outdoor spaces for residents to engage in physical activity. Research shows that people who remain active into advanced old age (Day & Cohen, 2000) do better psychologically and physically. Providing facilities for shared, festive meals can benefit residents who lack other opportunities for social interaction (Day & Cohen, 2000). Contributing to this is the use of culturally supportive design elements that focus on activities and relationships with a social and physical context and are easily understood by dementia patients (Day & Cohen, 2000). To help patients distinguish their spaces from others', allow patients to personalize their rooms, especially directly inside and outside of the entries; combine signage with patients' names and photographs of their younger selves; and vary the color of individual doors and frames (Passini et al., 2000).

Continuing Care Retirement Communities

Continuing care retirement communities provide independent-living apartments, assisted-living facilities, and skilled nursing facilities within campus-like environments, which allow residents to "age in place" as their health deteriorates. Such institutions provide both homes and workplaces for residents and have become increasingly popular over the past 50 years. Their popularity is expected to continue

meeting the needs as the *baby boomer* generation ages. Both long-term care facilities and continuing care retirement communities provide assistance for residents who need help with activities of daily living. Some healthcare facilities accommodate different patient populations with specific needs in separate **special care units (SCUs)** that provide, for example, emergency, orthopedic, and rehabilitation services within a single building or complex. Other patient-specific healthcare environments include **Alzheimer's units or behavioral health facilities**, and **hospices** for terminally ill patients.

Understanding the specific purposes of different facilities is crucial to effective design because each plan, scheme, and feature must support the overall function of the facility as well as the requirements of the individuals who occupy it.

MOVEMENT AND MOBILITY

One's range of movement and mobility naturally become more challenging as we grow older. Exercise at a level appropriate to each individual is a key part of maintaining a healthy lifestyle. Nevertheless, designers must be aware of certain conditions and risks involving movement and mobility that go hand in hand with the aging process.

Wandering

Special care units often house people with DAT because of their unique needs and behaviors. One of these behaviors is a desire to wander—a behavior that inadvertently places them at risk. Healthcare environments designed to accommodate such patients must, therefore, address the special safety and behavioral needs of this population. Many experts contend that wandering is a form of restless behavior often engaged in by very young, very old, and cognitively impaired people. In a study of patients with DAT, a wide range of wandering behavior was observed at all levels of impairment, indicating that wandering in these patients is not caused solely by cognitive decline. Subjects who were less cognitively impaired, depressed, and functionally impaired seemed to wander less; and no gender, ethnicity, age, or living-situation differences in wandering behavior were identified (Logsdon et al., 1998). Four different pattern types can categorize those who do wander: *direct*, *random*, *pacing*, and *lapping* (Dickinson & McLain-Kark, 1996).

The act of wandering can cause various problems related to health, safety, and social order, especially within healthcare facilities housing dementia patients. Some facilities still physically or chemically restrain their wandering residents, but the current trend is to alter living environments to help accommodate wandering (Dickinson & McLain-Kark, 1996) and to prevent accidental wandering off site. Adjusting design to accommodate wandering can keep residents safe while providing an environment that they can continue to explore freely, encouraging independence, a sense of well being, and exercise.

Why dementia patients wander is unclear; they may be unaware of their actions or become lost even if the environment is familiar to them. When they start out to do something, they may forget what they were doing, where they were going, or where they are. The resulting wandering may be a byproduct of that forgetfulness. One study reports that up to 40 percent of residents in SCUs wander, and the investigators further suggest several reasons for this behavior: Residents seek to relieve boredom or stress, escape the facility, escape social interaction, or simply follow others (Dickinson & McLain-Kark, 1996). In many cases, the wandering process itself seems to have a calming affect and reduces agitation and verbal disturbances (Passini et al., 2000). Wandering can be beneficial for some patients by providing an opportunity for exercise, stress reduction, and filling unstructured time; but unsafe exiting is a serious problem for those suffering from dementia.

Planning Spaces for Wanderers

Many researchers advocate developing spaces that allow wandering to occur, contending that this will not only decrease the need for staff oversight and search parties but also increase perceived freedom for patients (Passini et al., 1998; Passini et al., 2000). Others recommend providing rooms, spaces, and facilities for activities and social interaction to engage those who wander due to a lack of environmental stimulation (Logsdon et al., 1998); creating continuous paths that do not lead to a dead end and that maintain social or visual areas of interest along them; and providing visual and sensory stimulation along these "wandering paths" to encourage users to stop and interact with the environment (Dickinson & McLain-Kark, 1996).

When designing facilities for cognitively impaired patients, keep in mind that endless corridors will accommodate "lapping" wanderers, but should not dead-end into nodes. Interior courtyards provide outdoor space from which residents cannot wander away, and circular paths minimize disorientation and fear of getting lost (Passini et al., 2000). Such design features encourage meaningful walks instead of wandering (Zeisel, 2000). Recent research indicates that paths that travel through garden areas or even along corridors with much shadowing or mottling (i.e., lacking visual penetration) seem to have a calming effect on dementia sufferers (Zeisel, 1995).

Wandering paths and endless corridors should pass through activity areas to encourage social interaction and participation in scheduled activities and to reduce the staff time dedicated to watching and locating patients. Facility exits must be visible but must not attract dementia patients. Consider placing exits away from wandering paths so they do not become destinations for wanderers and camouflaging exits (Dickinson & McLain-Kark, 1996). Placing visual barriers in front of exits helps prevent escapes by dementia patients (Cohen & Weissman, 1991). However, designers should be aware that some design elements might increase a person's fear of falling. Some of these elements include angles, distances, and surface textures. Also, railings and other supports should be provided along the wandering paths to help stabilize a person who experiences periodic balance problems (Chong, Horak, Frank, & Kaye, 1999).

Falls

The difficulties associated with advanced age are often compounded by greater risk and incidence of injury, physical or mental illness, or a combination. As part of the aging process, internal bodily systems that maintain balance deteriorate (and some completely fail). This change results in greater dependence on visual cues to maintain balance (Sundermier, Woollacott, Jensen, & Moore, 1996). Changes in the body cause older people to be more susceptible to falls, which can then have a debilitating effect on the individual's psyche because they fear falling.

Thirty percent of people age 65 years and older fall each year in the United States. These falls are the leading cause of injuries, hospital admissions for trauma, and death due to injury. Participants in one research study reported that the mere fear of falling could cause a person to avoid everyday activities such as going outdoors when the conditions might be slippery or even reaching overhead for a desired item indoors (Lachman et al., 1998). One reason why older people are more prone to fall has to do with the biomechanics of aging. When young people become unstable they move their ankles to retain their balance, but older people move their hips (the heaviest bones in the body), which alters their center of gravity thus causing them to fall. Movement of the hip to regain balance is a sign of diminished postural control (Sundermeier et al., 1996).

When we are younger our visual acuity is sharper and the degree of contrast needed to distinguish between different objects is minimal. As we age, the ability to differentiate between colors decreases (see Chapter 10), and many older people require a higher degree of contrast to notice differences between colors. One study found that by age 75 a person would need twice as much contrast to see as well as a younger person, and by age 90, that same person will require three times as much contrast (Brabyn et al., 2000). Hence, pastel colors from the cooler end of the spectrum (blues, greens, or purples) are very hard for the older person to delineate. For many, these colors all appear gray. This is an important consideration for designers, particularly as it applies to changes in elevations where a potential fall might occur. Although older people require more contrast between colors, it is important that designers also avoid creating too much contrast (i.e., black and white, black and yellow), particularly within patterns, which could lead to a three-dimensional illusion (see Chapter 4).

One study demonstrated that not only color detection and direct vision decline with age, but also **peripheral vision** (outer part of the field of vision), depth perception, and adaptations to changes in light levels (Brabyn et al., 2000). The researchers noted that contrast impairments not only impede reading ability, but are problematic when detecting curbs or stairs. Compounding the issue is that many older people experience attention impairments during low-light, low-contrast, and glare conditions. This impairs their reaction and response time during crisis moments.

As the overall population ages, the percentage of impaired people is likely to grow due to the increased incidence of age-related diseases such as macular degeneration, glaucoma, and cataracts (Baker, Stephens, & Hill, 2002; see Chapter 9), and osteoporosis, osteoarthritis, and a host of other chronic illnesses that have replaced the once deadly infectious diseases. This shift from infectious diseases to age-related chronic conditions will have important implications for designers and planners. Designers will need to consider visually impaired older people by increasing lighting levels and contrast, avoiding sudden changes in lighting levels (e.g., in building entrances) and avoiding the use of washed-out colors in interiors, signage, and environmental markers (Brabyn et al., 2000). They will also need to be more aware of the physical capabilities of the older population and plan for more lever style handles and strategically locate areas for rest.

HEALING GARDENS AND OTHER LIVING SPACES

Design features should include elements found in nature, and possibly include "healing gardens" within the design. Spaces such as these provide patients and family members with a sanctuary and relief from confinement. Some studies have shown that some patients choose to sit quietly amid the greenery, whereas others pursue gardening activities (Zeisel, 2000). One research team noted that gardens help to reduce stress by providing places for individual reflection and psychological restoration for both staff and patients. This team recommends that gardens be incorporated along primary pathways (e.g., facilities located in temperate climates could have gardens between buildings; in colder regions, greenhouses could be utilized) and notes

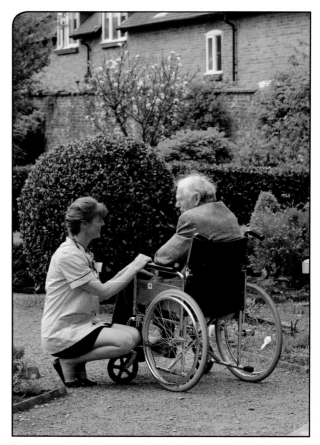

[**Figure 8.14**] Including nature into facilities occupied by the elderly helps to promote social activities and promotes a stress-reducing environment. © Peter Titmuss / Alamy

that healing gardens provide screened-off areas for privacy, wheelchair access, support for patients' equipment (e.g., IV stands, oxygen tanks), and plants with soothing scents, such as herbs and edible flowers (Whitehouse et al., 2001; see Figure 8.14). Note, however, that facilities housing dementia patients need to incorporate security precautions to prevent patients from wandering off, and to make sure that vegetation is not poisonous.

SUSTAINABILITY CONNECTION 8.2

Not every flower is edible. A small sampling of the types of herbs and flowering plants that are fine for human consumption include lavender, thyme, dill, cilantro, day lily, squash blossom, nasturtiums, chives, English daisy, dandelions, basil, and marigolds. Designers should also be cautious of not inundating a small garden with flowering plants without some thought to the introduction of insects and maintenance.

Soothing Environments

Whenever possible designers should incorporate nature into a facility's interior by using plants and other natural elements, as well as windows framing natural gardens outside. Indoor gardens containing features appropriate to the patient population and complementary sensory stimulation, such as water features, colorful surfaces (Whitehouse et al., 2001), and *music streams* (a constant flow of pleasurable, musical background noise), can also be very beneficial to psychological and physical health and help reduce stress associated with the facility for patients, visitors, as well as for staff members. Designers will also want to allow visual access to the natural, outside world for bedridden patients to promote their health and maximize their feelings of security (Leventhal-Stern et al., 2003; Ulrich, 1984).

When designing facilities that have corridors and individual living spaces, make sure to include niches or other exhibit areas by the entryways to the individual living spaces. Patients can use these niches to display personal memorabilia in an organized way (Eshelman & Evans, 2002). These features provide a way for patients to communicate to others what is important to them; they provide the patients and visitors with an activity (like window displays; they can be changed out) and go a long way in reminding staff that they are caring for people who were once vital contributors to society. According to healthcare staff and family members, designers should also plan patient rooms so that toilets can be seen from the patients' bed. This visual cue seems to help reduce episodes of incontinence (Morgan & Stewart, 1999); for the same reason, place clearly marked and visible public toilet facilities near group activity areas.

Safety and Comfort

Other design recommendations include the provision of generous lighting that patients can more easily see (cove lighting) and enjoy their personal possessions (Eshelman & Evans, 2002), and light-dimming controls facilitate relaxation by allowing patients to control their level of stimulation. Lockable cupboards and the use of familiar blankets, pillows, and personal grooming items (e.g., shaving or makeup mirrors) will go a long way toward easing patient stress and providing a sense of control. Features should be appropriate for the users' needs and abilities. For example, in acute care settings, patients may have telephones in their rooms; long-term care facilities can provide telephones or computers with Internet access in common areas.

It is important that resident living spaces for older adults and dementia sufferers be modified to compensate for the degenerative process. Dementia sufferers in particular often try to escape and could become lost or injured; therefore, it is important to control all exits (Zeisel, 2000). Designers, therefore, must select designs and materials that will reduce potential injuries, such as rounded walls that will prevent injuries that would result from impact with sharp corners and tempered safety glass in windows and doors in case they are bumped or walked into. Similarly, furnishings should utilize durable yet comfortable materials for spaces occupied by patients suffering from degenerative diseases. Such patients often require greater surveillance, but overly close monitoring can lead to perceived loss of autonomy; therefore, the use of too many cameras or observation windows can generate perceptions that one has lost control, which may lead to learned helplessness in long-term patients.

Practical Applications for Designers

Use these resources, activities, and discussion questions to help you identify, synthesize, and retain this chapter's core information. These tools are designed to complement the resources you'll find in this book's companion Study Guide.

Accessibility and safety are important considerations in every built environment, particularly for environments used by people whose abilities are impaired by age, disease, or genetic issues. Motor and cognitive limitations influence every aspect of an elderly person's daily life; therefore, the built environment must provide for his/her physical and mental well-being. Multiple factors contribute to successful aging, including a healthy diet, adequate sleep and exercise, a participatory social network, engaging in enjoyable activities and projects, and feeling as though one has a purpose. All manner of helpful design features should be in every space; these include handrails, frequent seating options, fixed furniture, and visual distractions (from pain).

Half a million Americans suffer from Parkinson's disease, a condition in which the neurons in the brain responsible for producing the neurotransmitter dopamine become impaired or die, thereby denying the people smooth muscle control and coordination. Alzheimer's patients need simple building configurations that provide smaller residentially scaled spaces such as kitchen areas, outdoor spaces, natural views, and landmarks. Designer must avoid the use of direct and concentrated light as well inadequate lighting of primary pathways.

It is more cost-effective to help people remain in their homes as they age.

One of the most challenging decisions for family members to make is when to place a loved one into an institution such as a nursing home or other type of long-term care facility. The transition from a familiar and private environment into a strange and crowded one can accelerate patient decline. Continuing care retirement communities provide independent-living apartments, assisted-living facilities, and skilled nursing facilities within campus-like environments. Healthcare facilities accommodate different patient populations with specific needs in separate Special Care Units (SCU). Healing gardens help to reduce stress by providing places for individual reflection and psychological restoration for both staff and patients.

You can also refer to this textbook's companion Study Guide for a comprehensive list of Summary Points.

When a Nursing Home Becomes Our Residence

Migette L. Kaup, M.Arch., IDEC, IIDA, Interior Design Program in the Department of ATID, Kansas State University

Home is a significant place in our lives, representing some of our deepest attachments (e.g., Dovey, 1993; Kumar, 1997; Lawrence, 1987; Tognoli, 1987). But what happens when a nursing home becomes our place of residence? Nursing homes are not often considered a domestic space or designed in a manner to supports home-like behaviors. More attention is often paid to the institutional practices that take place within the settings. Across the country, this is changing. More facilities are redesigning their buildings to support autonomy of resident life, and more attention is being paid to the quality of life that is lived by elders who call these settings their "home" (Lustbader, 2000). This re-conceptualization of the nursing home into a new place type returns us to the theoretical premises of home and domesticity. These concepts are often referred to as culture change, and these new forms of long-term care are often called households rather than nursing homes. The household creates different spatial boundaries that increase the residents' ability to identify with a family unit. Access to each of the households is sometimes provided through a unique residential front door with a doorbell that is used to request entrance to the semi-public social space within the household. The domains of public to private are more clearly defined in the household; therefore, like the private home, the household has a public side for guests within the private sphere for the intimate activities of the family. When a visitor is invited into these homes, they enter into an open social area. Doors to bedrooms and bathing areas are now located beyond the living room, down corridors that reflects a similar arrangement to a vernacular dwelling. These transition spaces between social areas and more private spaces are also architecturally defined in a way that supports privacy and territoriality (Rabig et al., 2006; Shields & Norton, 2006). Private spaces for residents and their invited guests are along this transitional space. Residents can go into bathing rooms or other private and semi-private spaces without having to cross over semi-public or public domains, thus increasing privacy and dignity in a way that more closely models traditional residential patterns. Circulation patterns through these households now follow a residential hierarchy of space. The community moves in and out of some of these spaces rather freely, while respecting the boundaries of the established domestic spaces that are now more clearly communicated through built form.

A significant example is the development of new stand-alone households that are beginning to dot the urban landscape across the country. The Green House® model is a current example of re-conceptualizing the nursing home by adopting the terminology of domesticity and designing physical space around these descriptors (Rabig et al., 2006). Founders of the Green House® acknowledge that it is through the household environment that residential behaviors become internalized and demonstrated. The role of the environment allows the organization to focus on doing the work in congruence with their stated values, creating a home for those who live there. This is the difference between making a place home-like versus making it a home.

Key Design Concepts

1. Scale is reduced. Smaller groups of elders live together and share common social spaces.

2. Spatial composition includes those rooms and places that are found in the home, and spatial patterns follow those that are congruent with domestic privacy.

3. Physical environment is designed to focus on the residents' needs and capabilities first, staff second.

References

Dovey, K. (1993). *Dwelling, archetype and ideology. Center, 8*: 9-21.

Kumar, K. I993. Home: The promise and predicament of private life at the end of the 20th century. In J. Weintraub & K. Kumar (Eds.), *Public and private in thought and practice: Perspectives on a grand dichotomy* (pp. 204-236). Chicago, IL: University of Chicago Press.

Lawrence, R. (1987). *Housing, dwellings, and home: Design theory, research, and practice.* New York: John Wiley & Sons.

Lustbader, W. (2000). The pioneer challenge: A radical change in the culture of nursing homes. In L. Noelker & Z. Harel (Eds.), *Qualities of caring: Impact on quality of life* (pp. 185-203). Rochester, NY: Springer.

Rabig, J., Thomas, W., Kane, R. A., Cutler, L. J., & McAlilly, S. (2006). Radical redesign of nursing homes: Applying the Green House concept in Tupelo, Mississippi. *The Gerontologist, 46*, 533–539.

Shields, S., & Norton, L. (2006). *In pursuit of the sunbeam: A practical guide to transformation from institution to household.* Milwaukee, WI: Action Pact Press.

Tognoli, J. (1987). Residential environments. In D. Stokels & I. Altman (Eds.), *Handbook of environmental psychology* (pp. 655-690). New York: Wiley.

For more about the writer, go to http://www.humec.k-state.edu/directory/listings/kaup/

KEY TERMS

- **Alzheimer's units**
- **behavioral health facilities**
- **hospices**
- **peripheral vision**
- **restorative environment**
- **special care units (SCUs)**
- **stalling**
- **visual cliffing**

WEB LINKS

The Center for Aging Services Technologies: (www.aahsa.org/cast.aspx)

The National Association of State Fire Marshals (www.firemarshals.org/mission/residential)

New York-Presbyterian Hospital, for an explanation and interactive graphic of brain changes within DAT patients (www.nyp.org/health/neuro-alzheim.html)

Senior Superstores (www.seniorssuperstores.com)

Valcucines, for an excellent example of a fully handicapped-accessible kitchen unit (www.valcucinena.com/pd_hb.html)

STUDIO ACTIVITY 8.1

Social Learning: Wandering for Alzheimer's Disease

Design Problem Statement

Your client is the caregiver for an Alzheimer's patient, but keep in mind that the end user will eventually be the patient. In the home of the Alzheimer's patient, arrange each room so that the patient is safe and understands where he/she is when he/she is in the room or where to go when he wants to go to another room.

Considerations

Here is a list of characteristics in an Alzheimer's patient:

65 years old.

On the brink of using a wheelchair, but is not reliant on it.

Brought up in the country where he/she did a lot of agricultural work. Now his/her family brought him/her back to the city, has designed a private home for him/her, and asks you to make this home livable for a 65 year old with Alzheimer's.

Moderate DAT (Dementia of the Alzheimer's Type), which includes some symptoms to watch out for:

- Changes in behavior and concern for appearance, hygiene, and sleep become more noticeable

- Readily confuses people's identities

- Poor judgment creates safety issues when left alone; may wander and risk exposure, poisoning, falls, getting lost, self-neglect, or exploitation

- Continuously repeats stories, favorite words, statements, or actions like tearing paper

- Has restless, repetitive movements in late afternoon or evening, such as pacing, trying doorknobs, or touching draperies

- Makes up stories to fill in gaps in memory; for example, a person might say, "Mama will come for me when she gets off work."

Directions

Step One: Arrange each room so that the client is safe and understands where he/she is when he/she is in the room or where to go when he/she wants to go to another room.

Keep in mind that there are only doorways, so add the appropriate lighting and navigation features for the client.

Step Two: Make things easy for the client. If you think the arrangement of the room is too difficult, then change it. Make the experience in the room like he/she has never left his/her original home.

Step Three: Show perspectives of each room. Have plans of all furniture and appliances shown. Also show any elevations that you find necessary to explain why a particular feature or aspect of your design would make life easier for the client.

Deliverables
Perspective drawing and elevations (as necessary)

DISCUSSION QUESTIONS

1. Describe the oldest old population, the youngest old, and their design needs. How can appropriate design alleviate this generation's aging needs?

2. Discuss what is meant by ADLs. What are some examples of daily activities you may take for granted that could pose a challenge for people with disabilities?

3. How can designers best serve physically challenged people and support their clients' feelings of autonomy? And why is it so important to address these issues with our aging population?

4. Discuss the psychological and physiological effects of aging, and compare those effects with how elderly individuals might view their surroundings.

5. How might emerging technology be used to help ensure the safety of dementia sufferers patients (particularly wanderers), while still affording them privacy?

LEARNING ACTIVITIES

1. How might the design of a space encourage healthy activities for independent oldest old people?

2. Design a room that promotes independence, physical health, and psychological health for an individual living alone.

3. Redesign the room where you live or study for a person who has lost the use of both legs. What factors do you need to consider? What aspects of standard design are no longer functional? Draw complete before-and-after floor plans, using the blueprint of your actual room.

4. Draw an elevation of a wall with a door, light switches, electrical outlets, exit signage, and a fire alarm. You are designing for five different disabled conditions: blindness, deafness, wheelchair-bound, amputation (prosthetic limb), and limited joint mobility. Ensure that an individual with any one or more of these impairments can access or utilize all items. Show dimensions and include comments about functionality or feasibility. (Some items may need to be duplicated in different locations on the wall to make them accessible to all parties.)

5. Design a garden that incorporates spaces for relaxation, stimulation, activity, social interaction, and rehabilitation. Keep in mind the need for patient safety and observation.

09 Persons with Disabilities

While they were saying among themselves
it cannot be done, it was done.

—Helen Keller

Many children question what it would be like to lose one their five senses. More often than not, what they really question is if they had to lose their ability to see or hear which sense would they rather live without? When Helen Keller, who was both deaf and blind (known as *deafblind*), was asked this question, she responded by saying that she believed being deaf would be worse than blind because blindness only isolates a person from things they can not see, but not being able to hear isolates a person from other people and the sounds of the world (Goldstein, 2002).

The ability to detect sensation is what allows us to thrive within a world that would otherwise be perilous. Among our different sense organs, many would agree that sight and sound are the most important sensations followed by touch. Regardless of the importance that we attribute to each of our sensory organs, the ability to detect a variety of sensations contributes to our ultimate health and safety. To illustrate, consider an immense amount of heat radiating from a closed interior door. Our ability to detect this heat will prompt us to call for help because we know something is wrong in the room behind the door. In essence, the detection of sensation is an ability that serves to warn us of dangerous situations or circumstances. When one or more of our abilities are compromised, we become vulnerable and thus require *methods of compensation*. The use of a tool (e.g., cane, wheelchair), the refinement of other sensory organs to detect stimulation, and the use of other animals (people included) are all methods of compensation.

During the nomadic hunter-gather phase of human history, a disability often meant a shorter life expectancy. Each person was expected to keep up with and contribute to the group, and there was little that others could do to help the disabled person. As we evolved, however, and settled into relatively permanent locations, the consequences of a disability became less imperative, and other members of the community could assist the impaired person with little threat to their own life. Consider a person who has lost his/her sight: In a nomadic society the person would be required to keep up with the group regardless of his/her inability to see the terrain as he/she moved from one settlement to another. When humans settled into relatively permanent villages, the person merely had to memorize the layout of the village, which made it easier for the person and the people who provided care.

DEFINING DISABILITIES

The current definition of disabilities in the United States as defined by the Americans with Disabilities Act (ADA) includes physical impairments such as limited mobility, sight, hearing, and intellectual impairments such as mental retardation, Alzheimer's disease, learning and behavioral disorders, and drug and alcohol addictions (Stencel, 1996). The 2000 U.S. Census Bureau cites almost 50 million residents as being disabled or as having a long-term condition that encumbers their daily lives. This represents approximately 20 percent of the U.S. population over the age of 5 and not institutionalized (e.g., prison, medical institutions; Kopec, 2006). We must, therefore, consider disabilities from a broad definition, which includes a multitude of conditions that hamper or make everyday life difficult. This includes limited mobility, vision, and hearing, as well as general conditions of mentality (e.g., cerebral palsy, dementia, obsessive-compulsive disorders), physicality (e.g., obesity, dwarfism, gigantism), and health (e.g., chronic fatigue syndrome, arthritis, HIV/AIDS). Understanding user needs within the built environment is crucial to meeting those needs.

All humans experience either partial or complete loss of one or more of their abilities as a result of the normal aging process. Among these losses include our ability to distinguish detail. In Western culture we have a catch phrase—over the hill—to categorize people who are in the last half of their life. The top of this proverbial hill is about age 45. After age 45 most people will experience a dulling in their sensory acuity. For example, by the age of 50 almost all adults will require the use of reading glasses (Zuger, 2000). Hearing and vision are often the senses most affected by age, but it's important to realize that all of the senses are diminished by aging including smell, taste (Fukunaga et al., 2005), and touch (Wickremaratchi & Llewelyn, 2006).

As we have seen throughout this book, our senses acquire information from the environment in the form of light, vibrations, pressure, and other stimuli. When the body detects stimuli, the sensation is converted to a nerve impulse and proceeds to the brain for interpretation. We all have a threshold, however, which is the lowest level of stimulation we are able to detect. As we age, this threshold increases, which means that we will continually need higher levels of the stimulus for detection. We rely on this process for our interactions with the material and social world. With age, however, our diminished ability to detect details in the world around us can negatively affect our quality of life by limiting our enjoyment of activities and social interactions, and even our overall safety by an inability to detect warning signals.

The effect of the built environment on an aging population is a significant factor in the overall design process. The U.S. Census Bureau (2008) projections state that by the year 2050, approximately 22 percent of the nation's population will be over 65 years of age. The last of the baby boomers born between 1946 and 1964 will reach the age of 85 by the year 2050 (U.S. Census, 2008), thereby increasing the percentage of older Americans by 125 percent from the year 1900. From this data, the living arrangements in 2050 have been forecast to be that of the 88 million elderly Americans, 50 percent will be living alone, 26 percent will be living with their spouse, 22 percent will be living with family members, and 2 percent are expected to be living with nonfamily members (U.S. Census, 2008). Depending on the severity and the manifestation of the disability, attempting to devise universal design solutions for these populations can pose creative challenges.

When we consider disabilities we must do so from multiple perspectives. In many cases, a disability will be congenital, which means that the person has been born without, or with a limitation to, a particular ability. In other cases the person will have lost a particular ability as a result of an accident or illness. These abilities are often related to sensation, mobility, and cognition. In many situations the impairment to one's sensation such as vision and cognition will impede one's mobility. However, mobility can also be affected by accidents that damage nerves, infections that lead to amputation or nerve damage, or diseases such as multiple sclerosis and amyotrophic lateral sclerosis (ALS), also known as Lou Gehrig's disease. Each person's disability and how that disability manifests will command a unique design.

Universal design practices are a set of principles that promote complete and unencumbered access by all people. The basic premise is that whether a person is in wheelchair, uses a walker, has a prosthetic leg, is blind, and so on, he/she will be able to use and interact with the environment without the assistance of another person. Its intent is to reduce the difficulty of performing **activities of daily living** (**ADLs**) as much as possible (Figure 9.1).

ISSUES WITH DISABILITIES

Construction of the built environment is based on the assumption that there is an *average* person. In the past, people dealt with problems of accessibility by using an itemized approach intended to reduce the disadvantages of specific groups by way of special features such as ramps and special doors, handrails, and Braille signage. Individuals with disabilities were incorrectly and unfairly perceived as exceptions to the norm and were, therefore, stigmatized and further disenfranchised. Most residential designs are based on the measurements of only a fraction of the population—a so-called average-size adult male—and guidelines and the regulations concerning housing design and accessibility do not apply to single- or two-family homes, which make up most residences (DeMerchant & Beamish, 1995).

The Americans with Disabilities Act (ADA), a federal civil law, was enacted in 1990 to end discrimination against people with disabilities. Title III of the ADA guarantees individuals with disabilities equal access to places of public accommodation. Today, more buildings incorporate universal design features (i.e., those that are accessible and useable for all people regardless of age or ability); however, social institutions and attitudes, as well as government legislation, often hamper further advancement toward universal accessibility. For example, trying to meet certain accessibility requirements may offset others (Mazumdar & Geis, 2002). Because users have a wide range of ability levels, meeting the needs of some individuals may compromise the needs of others (Osterberg, Davis, & Danielson, 1995). For example, installing hotel room light switches at heights that accommodate wheelchair-bound people can confuse and frustrate those hotel guests whose vision is limited. This is because the standard for where to place a light switch is not uniform.

Although well-intentioned, the ADA's accessibility guidelines are not well aligned with universal design principles. A study of a university campus that evaluated the adequacy of the guidelines from a user's perspective noted many areas where these requirements were found to be insufficient: entrances, lecture halls, libraries, **accessible routes**, doors, elevators, stairs, restrooms, tables and seating, computer workstations, and signage (Osterberg et al., 1995). When considering an accessible route we must regard it as a continuous, unobstructed path that connects all accessible elements and spaces of a building or facility. For example, interior accessible routes may include corridors, floors, ramps, elevators, lifts, and clear floor space

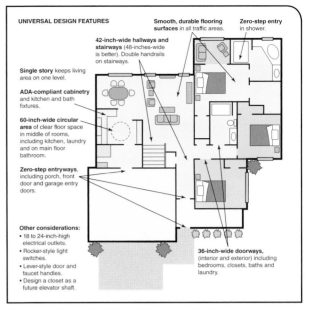

[**Figure 9.1**] For a building to be universally designed, it must contain many features and attributes that allow for mobility and for the sensory-impaired person to use the environment in the same way as a person who has no disabilities. Illustration by Precision Graphics

around fixtures and exterior accessible routes may include parking access aisles, curb ramps, crosswalks at vehicular ways, walks, ramps, and lifts. In the ADA's accessibility guidelines study, subjects gave highest priority to providing at least one universally accessible entrance to every building, followed by improving communication barriers (e.g., signage), replacing hard-to-use hardware, and modifying restrooms and classrooms. The researchers' recommendations included decreasing reach ranges by 6 to 12 inches on vending machines, photocopiers, shelves, coat hooks, and drinking fountains to improve access, and increasing knee space under tables from 27 inches deep to 29 to 30 inches to accommodate users of motorized wheelchairs.

Environments that are disability-compatible support the development and everyday functioning for all occupants; therefore, it is essential to determine during intake interviews if there is or will be a need for special or modified designs, construction, or materials. Many people may think "Why consider universal design features if I'm currently healthy and mobile?" However, incorporating features of universal design in a residence from conception can decrease long-term housing costs and make homes safer and more accessible for residents of all ages and abilities over time (Femia, Zarit, & Johansson, 1997). Table 9.1 provides examples of universal design solutions to common disability-related issues.

VISUAL IMPAIRMENTS

Nearly five million, or about 1 in 20 children ages 3 to 5, and 12.1 million, or 25 percent, of children ages 6 to 17 are affected with a visual impairment (Braille Institute, 2006). The term *visual impairment* can refer to total or partial blindness, a slow and progressive loss of eyesight due to age or degenerative disease, or even a difficulty in processing and decoding visual images (i.e., dyslexia). For these people, the world can pose a significant challenge because much of the built environment is designed for people with optimal vision and cognitive processes.

For sighted people, vision enables us to experience the world as a combination of forms, shapes, lighting, and shadows. Although all blind people adapt to their loss of vision by refining the acuity of their remaining sensations, better adaptation occurs for people who lose their vision at a younger age. Many of these people are better than sighted people at being able to interpret information derived from touch, smell, and sound. As a result of this increased sensory acuity, the visually impaired are able to develop and understand inferential spatial relationships (Adenzato, Cornoldi, Tamietto, & Tinti, 2006). Like dolphins who use echolocation, sounds enable the blind to be aware of spatial volume; and some blind can learn to locate objects in a room by selectively attending to higher audio frequencies (Hall, 1969). In this way the blind person experiences the world through shapes, textures, sounds, and temperatures. In short, the sighted person sees the world around him/her while the blind person feels and hears it.

For people who are blind or suffer from a visual disability, there are a number of unique concerns, especially within public environments. Predominating concerns include the random movement or temporary placement of objects such as furniture, boxes, or displays (Harkness & Groom, 1976; Wilcoff & Abed, 1994). Also, unexpected fixtures such as signs, lights, or architectural features that protrude into the path of movement can present the blind or visually disabled with a hazard or obstacle. Hence, these items should be designed to be flush with the wall. Likewise, for those who experience difficulties perceiving depth, the fear of tripping can be debilitating; therefore, area rugs must be securely attached to the floor, and high contrast color combinations such as blue and red should be avoided because of the three-dimensional illusion created (see Chapters 4 and 8). Also, because stairs and other elevation changes in flooring surfaces, and thresholds can pose a unique hazard (Harkness & Groom, 1976), there should be visual and textural indicators that signal an impending change in elevation. For example, an interior carpeted floor might switch to ceramic tile or some other covering prior to the first ascending or descending tread or incorporating different textures into exterior surface materials such as concrete curb cuts to alert the visually impaired to an open roadway (Wilcoff & Abed, 1994). These changes in textures within flooring surfaces can also be used to signify entrances/exits, restroom facilities, and stairways (Harkness & Groom, 1976).

Of the different causes of blindness, congenital conditions are the least frequent. Notwithstanding, *Leber Congenital Amaurosis* (LCA) is a condition that is passed from parent to child through heredity and affects newborns. This condition is a degenerative disease of the retina and is characterized by roving eye movements, deep-set eyes, sensitivity to bright light, and a severe loss of vision at birth (Diseases Database, 2006). Another congenital disorder effecting vision is called **retinitis pigmentosa**. This condition also affects the retina, and it is characterized by progressive peripheral vision loss and difficulties seeing at night. Currently there are fewer than 200,000 cases of this disorder in the United States (National Institutes of Health, 2006); however, just because a condition is rare doesn't mean that designers should neglect its possible presence.

The two leading causes of blindness among infants are **retinopathy** and **optic nerve hypoplasia** (Braille Institute,

[Table 9.1] Universal Design Solutions to Common Environmental Challenges of Disability

Issue	Environmental Challenge	Universal Design Solution
Mobility	Stairs create multiple challenges for people who use mobility assistive devices.	One-story living accommodations; stairless entryways; gradually inclined ramps with secure handrails; elevators.
	Threshold elevation changes often lead to trip-and-fall injuries.	Thresholds built flush with floors.
	People who use walkers and wheelchairs need sufficient room in entryways and hallways.	Pocket doors; doorway widths of at least 32–36 inches; hallways widths of at least 36–42 inches.
	People who use walkers and wheelchairs need sufficient room to move around furnishings.	Floor space of at least 32 inches around furnishings.
Stability	Smooth, wet surfaces are slippery.	Nonslip surfaces on floors, bathtubs, and ramps.
	People who experience dizziness need to feel like they are stabilized and not in danger of falling.	Grips or handrails in hallways and bathrooms.
	Dim lighting is problematic for people who have limited vision, and indirect lighting causes shadows that affect depth perception.	Bright direct lighting, particularly in stairways and entranceways.
Grip	Globe door handles pose a challenge for people who lack strength or dexterity.	Lever door handles.
	Toggle- and twist-type light switches require manual dexterity.	Rocker light switches.
Height	Fixed shelving may require the use of stepstools and reaching devices.	Adjustable shelving and brackets.
	Electrical outlets installed at standard heights are inconvenient for wheelchair-bound people and others who cannot bend or kneel.	Electrical outlets installed 2 to 3 feet above floor level.

2006). Retinopathy occurs when the retinas are damaged shortly after birth, usually the result of a premature infant being exposed to bright light.

The American Academy of Pediatrics recommends lighting levels between 0.5 and 60 footcandles in neonatal intensive care units (NICU; Floyd, 2005). Of particular note for designers are the direct and indirect lighting levels. For example, when a door is opened into the NICU, the light from a brighter room will flow into the dimmer lit room. Hence, the neonate can be exposed to brief bursts of light that can be just as damaging. As such, the designer will want to consider incorporating a transition zone between the regularly lit areas of the hospital and the dimly lit NICU.

Optic nerve hypoplasia is a condition in which the optic nerve never fully develops. In this situation, there is little designers can do to help mitigate the condition other than design techniques used to accommodate the blind at the early stages of development. This means that nurseries will need to contain a diverse array of sensory stimulating objects that include different types of sound, textures, temperatures, and scent. For example, a stuffed toy can be infused with a natural scent to make it easily locatable.

With the loss of vision, the sensation of touch becomes more acute. This increased sensation assists in the ability to read **Braille**. Researchers have found that people with severe visual disabilities often gain the ability to detect minute changes in air currents and thermal conditions from windows, doors, and ventilation ducts, which serve as a method for navigation and wayfinding (Hall, 1969). Similarly, the blind are often able to detect subtle differences among a group of objects with varying textures such as shells (Goldstein, 2002).

Braille and the ADA

In today's modern civilization, we have a host of devices that assist people in compensating for a loss of a sensation, and many of these people have positively contributed to society through a variety of ways. For example, Louis Braille, who was blinded as a child, developed the Braille system, which has assisted many visually impaired in learning to read.

The Braille system is composed of a series of six raised dots per letter or symbol, and it is currently produced in five major formats in the United States. The five formats are similar to Spanish, French, Italian, Portuguese, and Romanian languages. However, they are all different languages.

Through the use of raised dots, a person can process up to 125 words per minute (Hounshell, 2005). Recent studies have shown that reading Braille letters/symbols from top to bottom enable quicker comprehension than reading the symbols from right to left. This is because the touch sensors in the fingertips are better able to process information in a top-down direction (Ackerman, 1990). It is also interesting to note that because Braille letters consume approximately two and a half times more space than standard written letters, the Braille system relies on approximately 189 contractions and about 76 abbreviated words. This reduction in words and lettering is one reason that reading Braille is faster than reading raised letters (Hounshell, 2005).

Currently, Title III of the Americans with Disabilities Act (ADA) mandates the removal of architectural and communicational barriers that might interfere with a disabled person using retail or service facilities. This means that:

1. All signage in all common areas of mixed-use facilities must comply with ADA guidelines. (See Box 9.1, "ADA Guidelines for Interior and Exterior Signs.")
2. All permanent areas such as conference rooms, elevators, and restrooms must be identified by signs using internationally recognized symbols along with tactile and Braille lettering.

As of January 26, 1993, all newly constructed commercial buildings must comply with ADA mandates, and as of July 26, 1994, these mandates were extended to include businesses that employ 15 or more people. Included in these mandates is the use of Braille signage in all public facilities and amenities (elevators and ATM machines). Noncompliance of these mandates could lead to a $50,000 civil fine plus additional compensatory damages. As such, it's important for designers to consider the usability features such as:

1. Standardization of height
2. Lettering size and style
3. Ease of location
4. Materials

Ideally, firm and smooth surfaces such as hard-formed plastic should be used in the areas intended for Braille embossment. Be sure to take notice of the environmental conditions where the Braille placard may appear. For example, a metal placard on an outside elevator or ATM will be colder to the touch, and prone to rusting. Rusting metal results in the metal rising thus interfering with the Braille. It often produces jagged edges, thereby creating a source of potential injury.

CULTURAL CONNECTION 9.1

Within the blind culture there is a phenomena called *blindisms*. Blindisms are behaviors that serve a purpose to the blind person, but are hotly contested as to precisely what purpose they serve. Generally these behaviors are limited to blind children, but some adults still display any of the following: rocking, head bobbing, pressing the eyes, spinning, bouncing, and in rare cases, headbanging. The most commonly accepted reasons for these behaviors are that the blind are taking in audio information and stimulating their vestibular system. The vestibular system coordinates information from the senses to transcribe the location and interrelationship between the body and the world; in other words, balance. Imagine the world as a gyroscope and a person floating in the center; the vestibular system is the complex mechanics of the senses working together to keep the person upright and balanced regardless of the spinning, rotating, or wobbling of the world. The blind, without the appropriate visual component of the vestibular system, can feel like they are drifting or falling in the world; therefore, designers might accommodate this spatial disorientation need by either creating safe environments for these behaviors (i.e., no sharp edges or surfaces) or adding features to facilitate the activity (e.g., rocking chairs).

Aging Eyesight

The amount of information gathered by vision is greater than the information gathered by any of the other senses (Kunishima & Yanase, 1985), the fear of becoming blind ranks as the third greatest fear behind AIDS and cancer among the U.S. population (Braille Institute, 2006). The American Foundation for the Blind (AFB, 2006) states that every seven minutes someone in the United States will become blind or visually impaired, which translates to roughly 10 million people. Among these people include those who have no visual abilities to those who have limited visual abilities such as the elderly (65+) and to people who are legally blind (AFB, 2006).

In addition to blindness, many older people experience difficulties with depth perception, reduced visual field, sensitivity to glare, and difficulties adjusting from dark to light conditions. Many of these conditions are a result of the gradual loss of flexibility in the lenses of our eyes. Detection of color also becomes problematic for the older adult: discerning the differences between cooler colors such as blues and greens becomes increasingly difficult. This is because the lens of the eye becomes less flexible, slightly cloudy, and takes on a yellowish hue as carotene builds-up on the lens (Brabyn, Haegerström-Portnoy, Schneck & Lott, 2000).

Changes that occur with eyesight begin at about age 30 with reduced production of tears. As a result, many adults and particularly older people suffer from a condition called **dry eye**. Also, with age, the part of the eye known as the **cornea** loses sensitivity, which means that injuries to the eye may not be detected. Consider for a moment how often it seemed like things were getting into your eye as a child, but in adulthood this doesn't seem to be as much of a problem. This is because our eyes are not as sensitive as they were when we were younger. By the time we reach the age of 60 our eyes will have sunk back into the socket, and the supporting muscles will atrophy, prohibiting the eye from being able to fully rotate. Another biological change is a one-third

reduction in our pupil size, along with a reduced ability to respond to changes in lighting; including transition zones to aid the visual changes from very bright areas to more dimly lit areas will help the older person's eyes better adapt. Designers will also want to avoid shiny surfaces that create glare, particularly in brightly lit areas. Consider incorporating night-lights with a red bulb, as opposed to a regular incandescent bulb, because the red light produces less glare and makes it easier for the person to see. When selecting furnishings and surface materials, stick with the warmer contrasting colors of yellow, orange, and red to reduce the risk of accidents. Keep in mind that the combined use of some cool colors with warm colors (red and blue) can create an illusion of depth, which can result in someone falling.

Some of the conditions and disorders that also effect vision include **presbyopia** or difficulty focusing. Another condition results in visual "floaters." This is caused by changes in the eye's fluid composition and volume. Also, older people tend to experience a reduction in their peripheral vision, resulting in more accidental spills and greater probability of bumping into things. Among the more influential disorders of the older eye include cataracts, glaucoma, senile macular degeneration, diabetic and hypertensive retinopathy, and retinitis pigmentosa

Macular degeneration is another condition that affects the eyesight of the elderly. With this disease the central vision deteriorates. In advanced cases, the entire central vision is gone leaving only peripheral vision. Unfortunately, this can cause straight lines to appear wavy and thus cause disorientation. Approximately 1.75 million Americans currently have age-related macular degeneration (AMD), and this number is expected to reach nearly 3 million by the year 2020 (Friedman et al., 2004). Cheong, Legge, Lawrence, Cheung, & Ruff (2007) concluded that the visual span of people with AMD shrinks and that visual loss in the central field deteriorates, thus requiring the individual to rely upon peripheral vision. Visual patterns perceived through peripheral vision are processed more slowly (Cheong et al., 2007), thus causing a **Thorndike halo effect**. This halo effect results from a cognitive bias that causes the visual perception of a current object to be influenced by the perception of a former object in a sequence of interpretations (Schwartz, 2004). In other words, parts of the image seen directly before the present image will be added to the current image thus influencing current perceptions.

AMD is only one of the ocular motor deficits associated with aging. The other most common visual impairments among the elderly include **cataracts**, **glaucoma**, and **diabetic retinopathy** (Desai, Pratt, Lentzner, & Robinson, 2001). These conditions often result in either a loss of visual acuity, depth perception, sharpness, a loss of cognitive processing of visual cues such as those needed for reading, or any combination thereof. However, many of these symptoms can be improved with good design that begins with an in-depth analysis of the intended occupant's individual and unique needs.

Unilateral mydriasis is a condition characterized by prolonged abnormal dilatation of the pupil, which can result from corrective surgery. This condition is often associated with headaches and blurred vision (Hallett & Cogan, 1970). Many people with this condition complain of continuous glare within the affected eye, a sensitivity to light, and conflicting signals between the eye with a constricted pupil and the eye with the dilated pupil during bright lighting levels (Toy, Simpson, Pleitez, Rosenfield, & Tintner, 2008).

Ganglion cells located in the retina are used with **mesopic vision** (vision for low contrast conditions such as at dawn and dusk) and perhaps *unconscious sight* (Kanski, 2007), which is a phenomenon in which a blind person cannot see an object, yet when asked to guess the object, the object is identified most accurately (also called *blindsight*; Weiskrantz, 1995). In low-contrast environments, an elderly person with a visual impairment may register an object on an unconscious level but not be able to respond to it efficiently (Shepherd, 1994). Rods are extremely sensitive to light and will restrict excessive light from entering the eye by constricting the pupil. However, in conditions where the rods are damaged or lost, such as with macular degeneration, the message to constrict the pupil may be lost. This results in mydriasis or an over-exposure to high intensity light, subsequently causing periodic episodes of momentary blindness (Kanski, 2007; Schwartz, 2004). Therefore, washing an interior environment with excessive daylight or bright white walls can decrease visual sharpness and increase visual fatigue through the introduction of glare. One study showed that patients with photoreceptor rod dysfunction had decreased pupil response rates, thereby further supporting the connection between light, rod function, and pupil diameter (Kawasaki, Anderson, & Kardon, 2008). The effect of lighting on the visual perception of an illuminated environment requires much more research and special attention from the designer, particularly when designing for an aging population.

Contemporary studies show that excessive light causes great discomfort and cognitive impairments to people with age-related macular degeneration or other ocular motor deficits (Cheong et al., 2007). The reflections caused by direct light entering through the windows rebound off of various objects thereby leading to high levels of glare and **halo effects** (Ritschel et al., 2009). As already mentioned, a halo effect can result from a cognitive bias that influences visual perception. Or, a halo effect can result in a false

image that appears around brightly illuminated objects (Schwartz, 2004).

Overall, in the United States, age-related macular degeneration, glaucoma, diabetic retinopathy, and age-related cataracts are the foremost causes of blindness (Braille Institute, 2006). In the United States, glaucoma (a disease causing gradual degradation of peripheral vision) has taken the sight of about 120,000 people (Braille Institute, 2006), and there are approximately 12,000 to 24,000 new cases of blindness as a result of diabetic retinopathy every year (Centers for Disease Control, 2005). Current reports indicate that approximately 21 percent of all people age 65 and over have some form of vision impairment (Braille Institute, 2006), which means that the majority of people who suffer from loss of sight and other visual impairments are older.

Designer's Role

When designing for those who suffer from visual impairments, designers need to be knowledgeable about how the different visual deficits affect perception and interpretations of color schemes, lighting, and lettering (Kopec, 2006). Harkness and Groom (1976) suggest that designers do the following:

- Use an assortment of materials that vary in terms of color, shape, size, and texture within the environment.
- Include safeguards against movement such as fixtures and furnishings that are fastened to a surface, or weighted so that they cannot be easily knocked over.
- Develop a good space plan so that occupants will not need to rearrange the furniture.
- Avoid placing benches, statues, and water fountains in the center of a primary walkway.

Furthermore, pathways should be free from drainage grates where a cane or guide dogs' paws could slip into the holes (see Figure 9.2).

Designers should also be aware of wall-mounted objects that do not touch the ground and are higher than 27 inches, such as signs, mailboxes, and shelves. By bumping into these objects, a person using a cane can injure his/her arm, shoulder, or head (Wilcoff & Abed, 1994; see Figure 9.3). Likewise, signs and maps used for wayfinding should have raised lettering in combination with Braille and an auditory feature.

For those who have limited vision, consider the use of contrasting colors and appropriate lighting levels. Be aware, however, in some instances a visually impaired person may experience light sensitivity, which can be exacerbated by overly bright lighting and glare. Carefully considering the lighting levels to provide the greatest levels of ambi-

[**Figure 9.2**] Whether used for the interior or the exterior, drainage grates should contain opening that are small enough to keep a person's cane or a dog's paws from slipping into the hole. © John Norman / Alamy

[**Figure 9.3**] Objects should not protrude into any portion of the travel space. If they must, then to avoid potential injury they should not extend more than 101 mm (4 in) and they should maintain a vertical clearance of 2.44 m (8 ft). Within many modern buildings water fountains, such as the one shown here, are recessed into the wall, thereby clearing the walkway.© Roy Lawe / Alamy

ent light without glare or heavy shadowing should be of priority. Lighting levels in designs occupied by the elderly, for example, should be increased by 20 percent, and signage should use large lettering with strong contrast (Henry Dreyfuss Associates, 2002). Also, avoid the use of wavy or artistic substitutes for items such as handrails and edgings because they may cause visual confusion, particularly with the person who suffers from macular degeneration. Recall that straight lines may appear wavy to a person with AMD; therefore, the introduction of wavy lines might lead to cognitive confusion.

HEARING IMPAIRMENTS

It's widely accepted by the general populace that our ears enable us to detect sound, but what is less known about our ears is that they help us maintain balance. We are able to detect sound because vibrations cross the eardrum into the inner ear. These vibrations are converted into nerve impulses that travel to the brain via the auditory nerve. Balance, on the other hand, is obtained as a result of fluid and small hairs in the semicircular canal of the inner ear, which provides stimulation to nerves that help the brain maintain balance.

There are a host of conditions that lead to congenital hearing loss including: prenatal infections, illnesses, or exposure to toxins by the mother during pregnancy. The three primary causes of hearing loss in all humans are:

- Conductive
- Sensorineural
- A combination of conductive and sensorineural

In cases of **conductive hearing loss**, the condition is usually characterized by a reduced ability to detect low or faint sounds. In these situations sound is unable to effectively proceed from the outer ear canal to the eardrum and middle ear. In most cases, when diagnosed properly, this kind of hearing loss can be corrected. **Sensorineural hearing loss**, on the other hand, often results from damage to the inner ear or to the nerve pathways leading to, or within the brain. This type of hearing loss often limits a person's ability to hear faint sounds as well some of the different tones commonly associated with voice patterns. Unfortunately, hearing loss of this type tends to be permanent. In some instances, conductive hearing loss occurs in combination with sensorineural hearing loss. For example, severe and prolonged infection can damage the sensorineural pathways, thus making correctable hearing loss permanent. Whereas the majority of inherited hearing loss is conductive, most instances of acquired hearing loss are sensorineural.

Many people are born with normal hearing abilities, but because of disease or injury many lose complete or partial hearing ability. Some examples of conditions that can cause acquired hearing loss include:

- Chicken pox
- Ear infections
- Damage to the auditory system as a result of drug use
- Encephalitis
- Head injury
- Influenza
- Measles
- Meningitis
- Mumps
- Noise exposure

During the past 30 years the prevalence of people with hearing disorders aged 3 and older has doubled. To illustrate this trend, in 1971 there were an estimated 13.2 million people who suffered some form of hearing loss. This is fol-

lowed by 14.2 million in 1977, 20.3 million in 1991, and 24.2 million in 1993 (Benson & Marano, 1994; Ries, 1994). Reports from the year 2000 indicate that approximately 28.6 million Americans suffer from an auditory disorder (Kochkin, 2005), which shows a continuation of the trend recorded from the 1970s to the 1990s (Castrogiovanni, 2004). More current estimates suggest that approximately 738,000 U.S. residents are effected with severe to profound hearing loss. Of these people, approximately 8 percent are under the age of 18 (Blanchfield et al., 2001). Some estimates suggest that early-onset deafness is present in about six children per ten thousand. Fifty percent of these cases can be attributable to genetic causes (Marazita et al., 1993) such as **autosomal dominant**, **autosomal recessive**, or **X-linked** (one of the two sex chromosomes). Other estimates show a variance in the prevalence of newborns with congenital hearing loss at around 3 per 1,000 newborns (Cunningham & Cox, 2003 ; Kemper & Downs, 2000).

Hearing loss may be limited to a specific tone and/or frequency, and is thus labeled accordingly. For example, hearing loss that only affects the detection of high frequencies is described as a high-frequency loss. People with this type of hearing loss are able to hear low frequencies without issue. Likewise, people may exhibit low-frequency hearing loss. These people are able to hear high frequencies but not the low. Another category of hearing loss is called flat-hearing loss. For people with this condition, hearing loss is encountered at both high and low frequencies. In design, high-frequency sounds might be associated with the whistle of a teakettle, certain doorbell sounds, and smoke detectors. In these situations the designer will need to find alternatives that include low-frequency smoke detectors, different doorbell rings, and other audio alternatives. Also, visual mechanisms can be used for sound detection such as flashing lights for doorbells, and smoke detectors, and a mirror can be placed behind the stove so that it steams up when a teapot is hot.

According to Kryter (1996), noise can be defined as "acoustic signals, which can negatively affect the physiological or psychological well-being of an individual." In many cases, parents are not aware of the harmful effects of noise or the myriad of other noise sources their children encounter. For example, some baby rattles can produce sound at 103 decibels; sirens and some squeaky toys can produce sounds as high as 90 decibels (dB), which is comparable to the sound generated by snow blowers, lawnmowers, and leaf blowers. The danger with noise-producing toys becomes amplified when the toy is held directly to the ear, which produces sounds that can be as high as 120 dB (comparable to a jet plane during take-off).

[**Table 9.2**] Noise Sources and Design Solutions

Source	Design Solution
Noisy appliances	Install vibration mounts; isolate source in sound insulating enclosure.
Ventilation noise	Reduce blower speed; install acoustic lining and flexible connectors in ducts.
Reverberant noise	Install sound absorbing materials, e.g., carpets and pads, drapery, upholstered furniture, acoustical wall padding, ceiling. Total surface area of absorbent material should be at least one-fourth of total room surface area.
High-pitched sounds from ventilators, heating and refrigerant systems, high-velocity gas flow through furnaces and burners, or worn out or defective washers.	Reduce pressure in plumbing system, and isolate pipes and valves from supporting wall and floor structures with resilient sleeves or collars. Replace worn or defective faucet washers or valve seals. Wrap pipes.
Excessive noise from conversations (above 70 dB at 3 to 5 ft)	Install barriers and/or a prefabricated, sound-insulated booth or field office enclosure.
Neighboring conversations (sounds from transmission through a partition or ductwork, and ventilation ducts).	Caulk or seal all visible cracks at ceiling and floor edges of party wall. Remove cover plates of all electrical outlets in party walls to check for back-to-back installation; in such cases, pack cavities with foam mat or jute fiber wadding and then seal with a resilient caulk.
Noise from upper floors	Install a gypsum board ceiling mounted on resilient hangers, place foam mat blanket in void between ceilings. In some cases, wall-paneling w/foam backing mounted on resilient furring members may be required in addition.
Outdoor noise	Install window "plugs." Install gaskets around existing windows and doors, install storm windows and doors, replace hollow core or paneled entrance doors with solid core doors.

Source: Adapted from: www.soundproofing.org/infopages/solutions.htm

For people with hearing impairments, the ambient noise common to most public environments can pose a significant problem. Those who use hearing devices such as hearing aids often find it difficult to understand conversations when there is too much ambient noise. Likewise, studies of young children exposed to excessive noise revealed limitations in the acquisition of language (Dickens & Flynn, 2006) and the discrimination of different tones associated with language; therefore, designers should create sound barriers and use good quality sound-absorbing materials. Some of the common sources of noise include appliances, ventilation systems, and exterior sounds. Common methods to reduce noise include the minimization of vibration, instillation of sound barriers, and sealing cracks, holes and other places that sound can seep into an environment (see Table 9.2). For a more thorough list of noise sources and decibel ratings refer to Figure 9.4.

One environment where reverberation and outside noise are often found, and should be mitigated, is the classroom. Noise has been shown to interfere with the perception of speech, especially with children who suffer from mild hearing loss (Bess, 2000; Crandell & Smaldino, 2000). Research indicates that frequency-modulated (FM) systems may be of some benefit to those with mild **bilateral hearing loss** (Anderson & Goldstein, 2004; Flexer, 1990; Smaldino & Crandell, 2000), as well as those who suffer from **unilateral hearing loss** (Kenworthy, Klee, & Tharpe, 1990; McKay, 2002) when used in the classroom. These FM systems work similar to a small radio transmitter and receiver. The teacher wears a small FM transmitter with a lapel microphone, which sends a low-power FM radio signal to the receiver, which is attached to the bottom of a person's hearing aids. Although additional research is needed before concluding

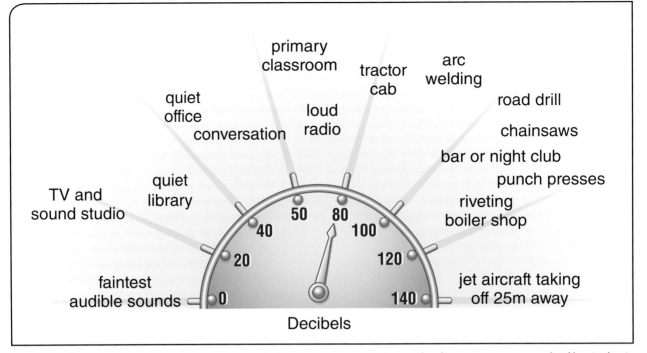

quiet office

quiet library

conversation

TV and sound studio

faintest audible sounds

primary classroom

loud radio

tractor cab

arc welding

road drill

chainsaws

bar or night club

punch presses

riveting boiler shop

jet aircraft taking off 25m away

0   20   40   50   80   100   120   140

Decibels

[**Figure 9.4**] Many common activities produce sound at levels that can damage hearing. As a result we're starting to see noise-related hearing loss in younger adults. Illustration by Precision Graphics

that the combined use of hearing aids and FM systems provide beneficial acoustical conditions, designers should still control sound reverberation. When a person's voice reverberates throughout a room the sounds get distorted thus making it harder to detect certain words.

Hearing and Aging

As mentioned earlier in this chapter, the United States has a growing elderly population, and with increased age come hearing problems. The three most common forms of age-related hearing disorders are *noise-induced*, *presbycusis*, and *tinnitus*. Among the three forms of hearing loss, tinnitus serves as a prelude to future and more severe hearing problems. Tinnitus is often described as a perpetual ringing, roaring, clicking, or hissing sounds. It is a common hearing loss associated with the natural aging process, but can also be caused by loud noises, certain medicines, allergies, or heart- and blood vessel-related problems. Tinnitus can also result in noise-induced hearing loss as a result of repeated exposures to loud sounds. However, noise-induced hearing loss may also result from a single exposure to one very loud sound (artillery, machinery, or blast). When sound is too loud, it kills the nerve endings or ruptures the membrane within the inner ear. Eventually, when enough nerve endings have been destroyed, the person will experience hearing loss. The other form of age-related hearing loss is called presbycusis.

This is a gradual diminishing of hearing commonly found in people over the age of 50. As part of the natural aging process, people with this condition often interpret sounds and words as being less clear and in lower tones.

With age, the structures within the ear begin to deteriorate, and the eardrum thickens. As a result, by about age 50 the majority of people will experience a decline in their ability to hear and thus the ability to maintain physical balance. Consider how easy it was as a child or young person to recover their balance after being on an amusement park ride. However, with age, the recovery time takes longer and longer. Reasons for this deterioration in balance and the detection of sound has been linked to impacted ear wax that increases with age, changes in the auditory nerve's ability to conduct impulses, or a reduced ability of the brain to process or translate sounds into meaningful information.

Age affects our abilities to understand spoken language in noisy environments. Many older adults experience difficulties recognizing words in noisy conditions because of age-related changes and our ability to hear words distinctly (Tun & Wingfield, 1999). Researchers have found that listening performance, particularly the ability to hear clearly in all directions, is also affected by age, and that age-related difference in language processing can be magnified due to distracting sounds (e.g., background music, competing speakers, white noise, or background babble).

One of the common sources of hearing loss in industrial societies is exposure to excessive noise. Current estimates state that the population with noise-induced hearing loss (NIHL) has grown to 31.5 million, and the population most affected are the baby boomers and elderly persons aged 75 and above (Kochkin, 2005). Because of the multitude of noise sources and the increased average levels of environmental noise, hearing loss is also showing up at younger ages. For the most part, *noise* is unwanted sound and is often referred to as the most pervasive form of pollution in the United States. The World Health Organization reported in the 2000 Global Burden of Disease study that the "years lost due to disability" (YLD) on the global scale counts hearing loss as the second-leading cause after depression for people 14 and older. Nearly 25 million people globally have hearing loss due to noise or age-induced circumstances. This global trend is larger than the combined effects of alcohol abuse, osteoarthritis, and schizophrenia.

Designer's Role

Title III of the ADA requires businesses and service agencies to provide auxiliary aids and services to enable deaf and the hard of hearing people to communicate effectively. Aids include devices such as a telecommunications device for the deaf (TDD); teletypewriters, commonly referred to as text telephones (TTY); as well as visible doorbells; flashing light smoke detectors; and captioning decoders (Dunlap, 1997). Services include interpreters or note takers and written informational materials. The ADA also requires the installation of flashing alarm systems, permanent signage, and adequate sound buffers, and the removal of structural communication barriers in existing facilities. Another important accommodation for the deaf is the use of visual information signs. Further issues pertinent to those who rely on the use of hearing aids are background noise and echoing. For these people it is important to reduce as many surrounding noises as possible through the use of sound buffers between spaces, and the incorporation of noise absorption materials. Ideally, environments should be designed so that people can easily understand one another without complete silence or excessive noise (Kopec, 2006). Restaurants, malls, airports, and similar such environments usually have many people all speaking at once, thus creating cacophony and reverberation.

Planners and designers must carefully consider structural and layout choices when designing interiors to accommodate hearing-impaired individuals. Interpreters, for example, must be clearly visible to those they serve whether they are in a courtroom, educational/lecture setting, theater, or community forum; therefore, seating arrangements and lighting systems must provide clear lines of sight for interpreters and the deaf (National Association of the Deaf Law Center). White noise (repetitive sound, i.e., machinery) should be eliminated or significantly reduced, and the environmental **acoustics** (quality of audibility) designed to enable people of all ages to comprehend, understand, and process language regardless of distracting sounds.

DEAF BLIND

In some rare cases people have been known to suffer the loss of more than one sense, in which case, the person is severely disadvantaged. Approximately more than 70,000 people are both deaf and blind (*deafblind*) in the United States (www. deafblindinfo.org). Perhaps the most famous deafblind person was Helen Keller, who dedicated her life to bringing the plight of the deafblind community to the public's attention. Helen Keller proved to the world that deafblind people are able to learn through the sensation of touch. In her case, she was able to mimic gestures and movements that she was able to feel with her hands and lips. Recall from Chapter 2 that humans' have high densities of nerve receptors in the hands and lips, which is why infants mouth so many objects.

TOUCH AND FEELING

A third level of sensation that is vital to our ability to experience the world are **somatic senses**, which include **tactician** (touch), **thermoception** (sense of heat), and **nociception** (perception of pain). Recall from Chapter 2 that we have specialized receptors in our skin that enable us to detect temperature, atmospheric conditions, and pressure. When these receptors are stimulated, electrical impulses are generated that then proceed to the brain for interpretation. We rely on these receptors to tell us where we are in relation to the rest of the world. However, research shows that older adults have difficulty interpreting touch sensation and in many cases have less acuity. Consider the insatiable laughter that often accompanies a child being tickled; but as an adult, the tickling has little or no effect. Likewise, after about age 50, many older adults will experience reduced sensitivity to pressure-related pain. The combined inability to detect pressure and pain thus leads many to experience difficulties detecting where their body is in relation to the floor or other items of potential harm, which can impair one's ability to walk. It is not completely understood why this happens, but some suggest that as part of the normal aging process, less blood flows to the touch receptors or to the brain and spinal cord, which reduces the excitatory response associated with touch. Others suggest that a diet low in thiamine (Vitamin B1) may cause changes in the touch receptors.

The inability to detect sensation can also be attributed to neurological disorders. Because neurological disorders affect an entire system that links communication between the body and brain, there are a host of conditions that can manifest in the ability to detect pressure (touch), temperature, or both. For example, nerve damage as a result of an accident can leave persons with the inability to feel sensation in certain parts of their body. This condition can have catastrophic consequences for them because they might accidentally burn their flesh on a hot stove, cut themselves with a knife, or close a door on their foot, hand, and so on, all of which would result in a severe injury. Injuries to areas where sensation has been lost often become infected and can result in the need for amputation.

For people who experience difficulties discerning the difference between warm and hot, or cool and cold, the risk increases for an unintentional injury resulting in a burn or frostbite. To accommodate this sensory decline or lack of sensation, designers will want to reduce the maximum water temperature delivered from the water heater and install thermometers outside of the kitchen window and main doors so that individuals can easily identify the outside temperature and dress appropriately.

Disease and Illness

Medications, brain surgery, problems in the brain, confusion, and nerve damage from trauma or chronic diseases such as diabetes can change the interpretation of *pain* without changing awareness of the sensation. For example, persons may feel and recognize a painful sensation, but it does not bother them. Some of the more common diseases that effect the detection of sensation included **multiple sclerosis** (MS) and **amyotrophic lateral sclerosis** (ALS; also known as Lou Gehrig's disease after the famous baseball player who died of the disorder in 1941). Multiple sclerosis occurs when the body's own defense system attacks the fatty substance that surrounds and protects the nerve fibers called the myelin sheath. The nerve fibers are then damaged and the myelin forms scar tissue called sclerosis; hence, the name multiple sclerosis. When the nerve fiber is damaged, nerve impulses traveling to and from the brain and spinal cord become distorted or interrupted, producing a variety of symptoms. The most common are:

- Fatigue
- Numbness
- Difficulty walking
- Issues with balance and coordination
- Dizziness and **vertigo**
- Vision problems
- Bowel and bladder dysfunction
- Sexual dysfunction
- Pain

- Cognitive dysfunction
- Emotional instability
- **Spasticity**

ALS is caused when certain neurons in the motor cortex and spinal cord die. Most of these neurons control voluntary muscles and the ability to move. It should be noted that with both multiple sclerosis and ALS, the primary impairment is mobility, not the loss of sensation.

Aside from accidental trauma, loss of tactition (ability to perceive *pressure*) can lead to issues of balance, particularly if the loss occurs in the feet or legs. This is because the inability to detect pressure in the feet or legs can result in conflicting messages being sent to the brain, which often causes overcompensation on the part of the limb that can detect pressure. This is similar to trying to walk when your foot falls asleep. People with a loss of feeling in one or both of their legs or feet will require the use of a cane or walker, which means that the flooring materials must facilitate a firm grasp between the surface and the rubber tips of a cane or walker (Henry Dreyfuss Associates, 2002). Side railings should also be included in the event that the person loses his/her balance, then he/she will have something to grab onto. If stairs are to be used, they should be designed with wide treads (minimum of 11 inches) and low risers (maximum of 7 inches). Also, items that need to be gripped such as handles should be large and easy to manipulate.

ISSUES OF MOBILITY

Mobility impairment can result from age, disease, genetics, injury, or amputation. More than 14.2 million Americans have physical impairments (Gray, Gould, & Bickenbach, 2003) that may call upon the use mobility aids or **assistive devices,** such as canes and walkers, yet they and their significant others often find the built environment to be problematic, particularly in the design of housing and transportation systems. Although design features that serve to maximize mobility are often implemented for wheelchair-bound people, disabled people who can walk tend to receive far less consideration. For example, stairs are obstacles that wheelchair users easily overcome with ramps. However, a ramp can be as challenging as stairs for individuals who require assistive devices that must be lifted higher to correspond with a ramp's incline; users may lack the strength, balance, or depth perception to do so. Ramps can also be problematic for visually impaired people.

Consider incorporating low and wide landings in the design of entrance stairways because people with poor depth perception will typically see the rise of a landing more clearly than the incline of a ramp. If a ramp is needed, a very gradual incline will minimize the height that a user will need to lift

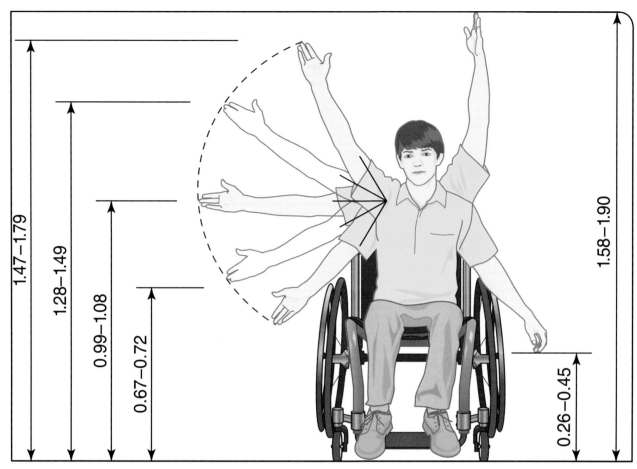

[**Figure 9.5**] Besides the increased width and required radiuses for a wheel chair, the person who is wheelchair bound is also encumbered by height both in terms of table height, which is slightly higher than standard, but also in terms of reaching height. Designers must accommodate all circumstances associated with the wheelchair user. Illustration by Precision Graphics

an assistive device as well as minimize slip-and-fall accidents. Either circumstance warrants a sturdy, easy-to-grip handrail parallel to the entrance path, which itself should be as easily navigable as possible. Designers should note that attractive landscaping from the street to the entrance is best savored by people who travel slowly.

In a survey of features available in homes designed for wheelchair-bound people many of these features were found deficient in basic needs such as maneuvering space in entryways, lower counter heights in kitchens and bathrooms, and easily operable windows and doors (Figure 9.5).

Designers must consider that this population requires wider doorways and doors that will not obstruct their access to spaces (ideally, pocket doors or doors that swing easily). Individuals with mobility issues need varying distances between pieces of furniture, furnishings, and walls. A wheelchair user will require more space, and an older adult not using a wheelchair will need less space. To utilize wall cabinetry and

closets, rods should be hung at lower than standard heights. Designers should be aware of accessibility features that will assist people in the bedroom and bathroom, such as grab bars and handrails, hydraulic or wheelchair lifts, built-in tub transfer seats, roll-in or transfer showers, and adequate space under sinks and counters (Connell & Sanford, 2001).

Researchers of a college campus study advocate providing approximately 60 inches between furnishings and structures—which will allow wheelchair users a clear turning space and allow blind people to walk next to a guide dog or another person comfortably—and replacing spherical door/window hardware (which requires wrist twisting) with lever hardware to allow people who have prosthetic devices or poor grip strength or coordination to open doors easily (Osterberg, Davis, & Danielson, 1995).

Interior spaces must provide not only for safety and ease of use but also for ease of cleaning and maintenance (Connell & Sanford, 2001; see Figure 9.6).

[**Figure 9.6**] A key factor when designing for people with certain conditions is to remember that they are people with aspirations and desires. The problem is that we often neglect them. In this figure we see a ping-pong table that has been lowered so that the wheelchair-bound person can enjoy a common recreational activity. © Directphoto.org / Alamy

Designers should avoid using flooring materials with inconsistent surfaces, such as slate, flagstone, and tile with dramatic grout lines, as well as high-piled, heavily textured, and sculptured carpeting. If disabled clients desire area rugs, then the rugs must be firmly affixed. Electrical outlets and light switches placed between three and four feet above floor level will allow people who require mobility assistive devices to access them easily.

COGNITIVE PROCESSING

Disabilities of any kind can be devastating, but the least understood and often dismissed are disabilities associated with cognitive processing. In such cases, a person's brain has either lost its ability to interpret incoming stimuli, or his/her brain interprets incoming stimuli differently than the majority of the population. Recall from Chapter 2 that there are two distinct processes for sensory perception. The first is a biological process in which our different sense organs are able to receive and transmit information to our brains. The second is our brain's ability to interpret and respond to information; also called sensory processing. As such, impairment can be biological or neurological. Designers, and the general populace, need to consider disabilities from the broader perspective of individual interpretation. For example, blindness is the inability to see; however, one's eyes may function perfectly, but the way in which the brain interprets information may be flawed. Oftentimes these disabilities are not discovered until school, when a child is placed in a learning environment. In this situation children with cognitive processing deficits struggle and are often thought of as "slow."

Within the array of cognitive disabilities include individuals who have learning disabilities such as dyslexia and dysgraphia, attention disorders like attention deficit hyperactivity disorder (ADHD), and developmental disabilities including autism, Down syndrome, fragile X, and cerebral palsy.

In addition to these, there are a host of neurological impairments that result from accidents and diseases. The challenge with designing for one with cognitive disabilities is that the needs of individual users are diverse. This is because it is common for individuals with cognitive disabilities to have deficits in one area but exhibit typical or even advanced skills in other areas. The primary issue of designing for a cognitive disability is that the disability cannot be mimicked in order to identify solutions. For example, a designer can easily put him/herself in a wheelchair and move about an environment; likewise, he/she can put on a blindfold or soundproof headset to gain some understanding of how a person who is blind or deaf interprets the world. With a cognitive disability, the manifestation and severity differs from person to person, and it is next to impossible to replicate the world as the effected person understands it. As such, it is the designer's responsibility to gain as thorough an understanding of the different cognitive disabilities as possible.

For many people with cognitive disabilities, the built environment rarely serves as a barrier (Wilcoff & Abed, 1994). What is of interest, however, is how the person perceives, processes, identifies, and then integrates environmental cues into meaningful information; however, with many cognitive disabilities, problems may arise when decoding individual words, comprehending literal or abstract language, and constructing responses when required.

Learning disabilities are defined by the *Statistical Manual of Mental Disorders-IV* (APA, 1994) as being lower achievement on standardized tests in reading, mathematics, or written expression. To accommodate persons with learning disabilities, consider placing a bank of glassed-in cubicles along one wall where the person with learning disabilities can listen to information orally or visually from a computer or tape recorder. Also, this quiet and distraction-free space allows the person to dictate information into voice processing software or into a recorder for transcription. Also consider using more pictographs instead of words and numbers to assist in wayfinding or other forms of directions.

Practical Applications for Designers

Use these resources, activities, and discussion questions to help you identify, synthesize, and retain this chapter's core information. These tools are designed to complement the resources you'll find in this book's companion Study Guide.

SUMMING IT UP

The current definition of disabilities in the United States as defined by the Americans with Disabilities Act includes physical impairments such as limited mobility, sight, hearing, and intellectual impairments such as mental retardation, Alzheimer's disease, learning and behavioral disorders, and drug and alcohol addictions. The Americans with Disabilities Act (ADA), a federal civil law, was enacted in 1990 to end discrimination against people with disabilities. Title III of the ADA guarantees individuals with disabilities equal access to places of public accommodation. The ADA's accessibility guidelines are not well aligned with universal design principles. For example, installing hotel room light switches at heights that accommodate wheelchair-bound people can confuse and frustrate those hotel guests whose vision is limited.

More than 14.2 million Americans have physical impairments that may call upon the use mobility aids or assistive devices, such as canes and walkers, yet they often find the built environment to be problematic, particularly in the design of housing and transportation systems.

You can also refer to this textbook's companion Study Guide for a comprehensive list of Summary Points.

EXPERT SPOTLIGHT 9.1

Importance of Designing for People With Various Disabilities

Richard Duncan,
RL Mace Universal Design Institute
(Executive Director)

Accessible and Universal Design
The accessibility field in the United States has been part of the civil rights movement for people with disabilities that began after World War II and was related to the larger worldwide human rights movement. The initial major push into accessible building design came after the publication of the American National Standards Institute's (ANSI)

A117.1 standard in 1961, the first U.S. accessibility design standard. The A117.1 standard has been revised many times since then. Federal law calling for accessibility features followed with the Architectural Barriers Act of 1968, the 1973 Rehabilitation Act, 1988's Fair Housing Amendments Act, and the Americans with Disabilities Act of 1990.

Although not uniformly applied or consistently rendered, by the mid-1980s accessible design was becoming more of a reality for the design and construction industry across the United States. By 1985 people with disabilities had begun to gain significant access to buildings, programs, and services. Unfortunately, the access was not always equal or appropriate.

The term *universal design* was coined in 1984 in part from the realization that many of the "specialty" design features characterized by accessible design turned out to improve life for others and have much broader beneficiaries than was presumed. It also arose because the specialty features were often rendered in a way that limited the availability of their broader benefits.

The disability movement is properly credited with creating the context from which greater attention to design for everyone could materialize in the last half of the 20th century. The world's altered demographics that now include the aging of many societies have strengthened the relevance of accessible, and now universal, design. Often cited as the reason for considering a universal design approach in recent years, the changing demographics instead offer the *occasion* for focusing on improved usability, safety, and inclusion. The aging of many societies and the increased numbers of people with disabilities creates an undeniably larger number of people who are obvious, immediate, and significant beneficiaries of a more supportive environment.

In its 25-year history in the United States, universal design has slowly gained acceptance but has seen an uneven adoption. Universal design still remains a strategy that has been implemented by different sectors of the private and public domains, selectively and for fairly narrowly framed purposes. From the perspective of more usable and supportive environments, the United States remains principally focused on accessibility: developing regulations, codes, standards, policies, and procedures to provide societal inclusion to people with disabilities.

Today, we take for granted the many accessibility and ease-of-use features that populate our environment. Step-free entrances into buildings, transportation facilities that allow us all to use our rolling luggage, and convenient door hardware and control locations are now used by all, but rarely associated with specific building code requirements. Without intentionally pushing it, we are evolving toward design for everyone, not just a few: neither for the "average" nor just for those with great differences.

Practical Solutions
In spite of the progress that has been made in the field of universal design, it must be remembered that this field is still young. Accessibility itself has only been practiced for 50 years. It has been 25 years since universal design emerged, and the universal design principles and guidelines only

came into being in 1997. Areas of potential remain relatively unexamined, much research is needed, the principles themselves are evolving, and practical implementation needs to be developed. By embracing universal design, policies, and design, planning practices will be better able to handle the demands of the 21st century demographic.

Collaborations

Connections and collaborations between public health, planning, and design professions are essential. Work must develop and disseminate validated, practical, environmental assessment tools and best practice designs.

Standards

Standards of performance should be based upon universal design standards for residential and non-residential environments.

Research

Research is needed to

- Determine individual reach ranges required for standing and seated adults, older individuals, and children.

- Understand and improve wayfinding methods in general and ground surface types specifically, where great variations in theory and practice make consistency and true usability difficult.

- Examine costs and benefits of universal housing, including health benefits.

- The relationship between universal features, higher physical activity levels, and increased community participation.

Source: Portions adapted from Duncan, R. (2007). *Universal Design Clarification and Development: A Report for the Ministry of the Environment.* Government of Norway.

References

Connell et al. (1997). Universal design principles, Version 2.0. North Carolina State University.

International Code Council. (2006). Chapter 11. Accessibility, in International Building Code.

Healthy People 2010: Understanding and Improving Health, 2nd ed. 2000, U.S. Department of Health and Human Services. The Centers for Disease Control and Prevention. Washington, DC: U.S. Government Printing Office.

Kochtitzky, C., & Duncan, R. (2006). Universal design: Community design, public health, and people with disabilities, in integrating planning and public health: Tools and strategies to create healthy places. American Planning Association, National Association of County and City Health Officials.

Lusher, R., & Mace, R. L. (1989). Design for physical and mental disabilities. In J. A. Wilkes & R. T. Packard (Eds.), *Encyclopedia of architecture, design, engineering and construction.* New York, NY: John Wiley.

United Nations. (1948). *Declaration of Human Rights*, 6.

Steinfeild, E. (2006). The future of universal design. Position paper presented at 2006 IDEA Center, Buffalo, NY: State University of New York, Buffalo.

Storey, M., Mace, R., & Mueller, J. (1998). *The universal design file: Designing for people of all ages and abilities.* Raleigh, NC: Center for Universal Design, North Carolina State University.

Storey, M., & Mueller, J. (2003). *A guide to evaluating universal design performance of products.* Raleigh, NC: Center for Universal Design, North Carolina State University.

Storey, M., & Mueller, J. (2002). Universal design: Product evaluation countdown. Raleigh, NC: Center for Universal Design, North Carolina State University.

KEY TERMS

- **accessible route**
- **acoustics**
- **activities of daily living (ADLs)**
- **amyotrophic lateral sclerosis (ALS)**
- **assistive device**
- **autosomal dominant**
- **autosomal recessive**
- **bilateral hearing loss**
- **Braille**
- **cataracts**
- **conductive hearing loss**
- **cornea**
- **diabetic retinopathy**
- **dry eye**
- **ganglion cells**
- **glaucoma**
- **halo effects**
- **macular degeneration**
- **mesopic vision**
- **multiple sclerosis (MS)**
- **nociception**
- **optic nerve hypoplasia**
- **presbyopia**
- **retinitis pigmentosa**
- **retinopathy**
- **sensorineural hearing loss**
- **somatic senses**
- **spasticity**
- **tactician**
- **thermoception**
- **Thorndike halo effect**
- **unilateral hearing loss**
- **unilateral mydriasis**
- **universal design**
- **vertigo**
- **x-linked**

Absorption coefficient chart
(www.sae.edu/reference_material/pages/
Coefficient%20Chart.htm)

Accessible Design for the Blind
(www.accessforblind.org)

The American Foundation for the Blind
(www.afb.org/Section.asp?SectionID=1)

The Center for Universal Design in the College of Design
at North Carolina State University
(www.design.ncsu.edu/cud/)

Medicinenet.com (www.medicinenet.com)

National Braille Press, for the Braille alphabet
(www.nbp.org/ic/nbp/braille/index.
html?id=PZoXeJDm)

Room reverberation calculator
(www.johnlsayers.com/Pages/Reverb_Calc.htm)

The United States Access Board
(www.access-board.gov)

U.S. Department of Housing and Urban Development's
*Residential Remodeling and Universal Design Making
Homes More Comfortable and Accessible* handbook
(http://www.huduser.org/Publications/PDF/remodel.
pdf)

STUDIO ACTIVITY 9.1

The World of Touch

Design Problem Statement
Without the ability to see, we begin to rely more on our other sensations. Although we often consider the loss of a sensory capability as a disability, others have argued that fully functioning sensations limit our complete awareness of what our senses can offer.

Issue: To develop an understanding of different sensations that we may otherwise be unaware of or take for granted.

Directions
Step One: Gather a bunch (10 to 15) of different shaped and different sized rocks. With a marker, assign each rock a number. Then analyze each rock, describing it in detail.

Step Two: Bring the rocks to class while keeping them concealed from your classmates. Identify a partner and blindfold him or her. Then spread your rocks out in front of him or her. As your partner picks up a rock and starts to describe it, make sure you note the number on the rock along with all of the words your partner used to describe that rock. Your partner should feel all the surfaces of the rock with his/her fingers, gently run them along his or her forearm and face. Then switch places, so that you get to be blindfolded and experience your partner's rocks.

Step Three: Note the similarities and differences that you used to describe your rocks and the description your blind folded partner gave. Which description was more detailed and accurate?

Step Four: Photograph each rock and then provide the full sensory description along with the blindfolded description.

Deliverable
A report with each rock photographed and a description comparison between you as a fully sighted person and your partner as blind person.

STUDIO ACTIVITY 9.2

Noise Pollution

Design Problem Statement
We are exposed to numerous sounds each day, many of which we simply ignore or screen out.

Issue: Because we are exposed to a multitude of sounds almost every minute of every day, we have learned to screen out some sounds while concentrating and accentuating different sounds.

Directions
Step One: In groups of four to six, identify a place on your campus where all of you can sit undisturbed for a period of five minutes.

Step Two: While one person watches the time, other group members must sit in silence and record all of the different sounds they hear. For each sound, the student must rank the intensity of the sound as well as the pleasurableness of the sound on a scale from 1 to 10. A score of 10 would indicate the greatest intensity or most pleasurable. For example, a bird chirping might command a level 5 in intensity but a level 10 for pleasurable.

Step Three: Have the group members compare notes and discuss their reasons for assigning the scores.

Step Four: Identify those sounds that everyone heard as well as those sounds that only a few people heard. Did one person in the group hear a host of sounds that others did not hear?

Step Five: As a group project, list the sounds they heard along with the score that they gave to those sounds. As a group, identify commonalities in the sounds, and then identify commonalities in the scoring of those sounds. Also indicate any discrepancies between the group members in both sounds heard and the scoring of sounds. Write this as a report to submit to your instructor.

Deliverable
Report described in Step Five.

1. Discuss the psychological impacts of aging. Consider the design issues mentioned in the chapter, but also investigate and consider the social consequences of aging. Consider ways that design may be used to help minimize the age stereotypes.

2. This chapter mentions many specific issues in which the ADA accessibility guidelines conflict with universal design principles. How does this knowledge inform and affect your future design decisions?

3. What design solutions should be implemented when designing for people who experience difficulties of the senses?

4. Describe design features that should be addressed in the design of spaces for the mobility impaired?

5. Because it is nearly impossible to replicate the world of a person with a cognitive disability, what is the designer's responsibility when designing a safe and comfortable environment?

1. Consider how a blind individual might navigate through a crowded retail space (e.g., a mall or grocery store), and what services might be made available to aid accessibility. Contact the manager of a local grocery store or mall and discuss the methods their establishment uses. What ideas were new to you? Did you have novel ideas? Present your data in a table that lists all comments and opinions next to each method.

2. Research the most common injuries to individuals who are 70 years or older. Write brief summaries of the top three injuries, and suggest methods by which design can lessen the severity or frequency of these injuries. Make note of any mention of the location where the accident occurred (e.g., home, office, car, retail setting). List all sources using proper bibliographic format. Use images only if necessary.

3. Design a room for a patient suffering from DAT, incorporating all of the information included in this chapter as well as any research you perform online or in the library. Present your design in a way that highlights any adjustments made specifically for a DAT patient and explain how these modifications are beneficial. Cite your research sources, including the specific pages in the chapter that informed your design decision.

Redesign the room where you live or study for a person who has lost the use of both legs. What factors do you need to consider? What aspects of standard design are no longer functional? Draw complete before-and-after floor plans, using the blueprint of your actual room.

10

The Environment Called Home

A comfortable house is a great source of happiness. It ranks immediately after health and a good conscience.

—Sydney Smith

Home is a set of conditions that when combined lead to a concept (Rapoport, 1995) that is then assigned an emotion. Notions of what constitutes the physical aspect of a home vary by culture, but the psychological components are fairly static: emotional attachment to place and perceived safety and security. The home environment can be considered in terms of its capacity to nurture and sustain psychological and social processes (Lawrence, 1987), but this need not be limited to a physical structure. The idea of home contains meanings that extend beyond the physical building (Easthope, 2004). Nomadic tribes in Tibet, Mongolia, and other parts of the world wander vast expanses of land, setting up their villages for periods of time only to disassemble and set them up someplace else. For these people, the notion of home is much larger than their immediate sleeping quarters; it consists of the vast plains they roam. Similarly, Romany (Gypsy) clans travel the European countryside in colorful caravans, RV dwellers roam North America, and many military families frequently relocate from one military base to another. From this perspective, home thus becomes a concept whereby individuals and groups experience a particular spatial, temporal, and sociocultural understanding, which adds to and reinforces a sense of the self, family, and community (Dovey, 1985).

In traditional Western culture, home is often regarded as a specific dwelling or building where we reside and one we travel away from with the intention of returning. To most of us the ideal home symbolizes stability, security, and safety. Popular films and books have long capitalized on these romanticized ideas of home by depicting characters who return to former houses and relive events ranging from heinous acts of violence to precious moments with family members. This theme illustrates how intense emotion can be inextricably woven into a physical place, thereby forming meaning or an identity. This is why places are so important to people: They provide paths to self-identity by way of memories and emotional attachment. However, when a house has been abandoned, or when great acts of violence have occurred there, the fondness that makes a house a home can be lost (Hockey, 1999); but the memories that formed the meaning and identity continue to linger.

CONCEPTS OF PLACE

Place identity is fundamentally formed by our experiences and is an important factor in our emotions and **self-regulation** (expression of pleasure, pain and the experience of the self; Korpela, 1992). For example, when a person visits a family home after being away for many years, old memories will likely surface and may even bring about old behavior patterns. These memories can hold such deep and meaningful significance that the psychological effect of the environment itself can evoke or alter a person's sense of time and space (Ganoe, 1999), meaning that a person may relive an experience or event through memory alone. Although places can provide feelings of privacy, control, and security, children or the elderly might identify specific places as being sources of fear and danger. This identification will likely foment negative feelings toward those environments (Matthews, 1992). To a child who associates positive feelings with Grandma's house, the mere mention of going there evokes happy feelings and behaviors; conversely, to a child who associates negative feelings with school, the mere mention of going to school will evoke fear and anxiety that may translate into negative feelings and behaviors. Other research findings show that people form *place attachments* to specific places that allow them to fulfill emotional needs (Korpela, Hartig, Kaiser & Fuhrer, 1996), thereby assigning meaning to those places. From the first perspective, the human–environment relationship is *transactional;* from the second, it is *interactional.*

People influence environments and vice versa: Imagine yourself as a small child at a doctor's office. In the waiting room, you become upset because other children are crying. Later, when the doctor gives you a shot, it hurts. When you go back to the waiting room, you are crying, which in turn upsets another child. These concepts of interaction and transaction are components of *integration theories,* which describe the way people see themselves in relation to their environments. A third component, the *organismic* perspective combines multiple contributing factors (e.g., the child's experiences that day, the child's health, and the parent's mood) with the memory of pain and other children crying in the waiting room.

Age, gender, and the effects of specific environments determine a child's environmental behavior and opin-

[**Figure 10.1**] People can form temporary or permanent attachments to certain places regardless of the event. Roadside memorials are an example where a tragic event occurred and people form an attachment to that space. © vario images GmbH & Co KG / Alamy

ions (Van Andel, 1990). Young boys prefer places where gratification and protection are readily available, whereas older children and adolescents tend to favor places that are comfortable, calm, relaxed, and beautiful (Malinowski & Thurber, 1996). Included within this notion of place is the meaning it is assigned along with one's attachment to it. Place meaning can be positive or negative, and place attachment can be based off of this positive or negative meaning. For example, one may develop an attachment even from a negative meaning; such as a parent's attachment to the place where their son or daughter died in a tragic accident (Figure 10.1).

MEANING OF PLACE

Concepts of *home* are often tied to *place meanings;* both terms identify a state of mind rather than a physical place. What a place means to someone (i.e., the feelings a person associates with a physical place) is an important concept related to the self, others, and environments. Some researchers believe that people's distinctions of place, *sense of place,* and *place identity* are becoming less clear due to increases in technology and globalization (Gustafson, 2001).

Place meanings change over time. Aspects of our experiences and personalities, as well as our relationships with others and the physical environment, interact to create and define the meanings that we attribute to places. Suppose that every time two friends visit the city of Tempe, Arizona, they also visit the Arizona State University (ASU) campus and drive past certain places because one of the two friends was a former ASU student. The university and surrounding area has meaning for him/her, and it has become so strong that it has been incorporated into his/her identity. Conversely, a person

[**Figure 10.2**] On the Flickr website (www.flickr.com) where it was originally posted, this photo was titled "Bad, Ugly, Communist Architecture." Did the photographer find the building ugly because it is Communist architecture, or is the title an opinion based on an emotional reaction to Communist ideology rather than design? © GeoPic / Alamy

who grew up feeling like an outsider and harassed by peers may deny any affiliation with the place where these events occurred once he/she has moved away. In the first example, the person exhibits a strong place attachment to ASU; in the second example, the individual has no attachment to the place. However, both examples illustrate how meaning can become attributed to a place, whether positive or negative.

One task of environmental psychologists is to help create a sense of place for people. An environment's distinct spatial features, how it compares with others, its connections to personal life paths, and its potential for change combine to affect the meanings places have for people. The person who developed place attachment to the ASU campus holds positive memories of past experiences; however, if this person were to move back to Tempe, the incongruity between past and present experiences could destroy the place meaning. Place meaning should precede place attachment, but just because a place means something to us does not guarantee that we will form an attachment to it. For example, a person who experiences physical and emotional pain may develop strong negative feelings for the place but not develop place attachment. Communist-style architecture, for example, is filled with meaning, but the people formed no attachment, and in some cases they actively seek the destruction of this architectural style (Figure 10.2)

CULTURAL CONNECTION 10.1

Since the 1970s, the prevalence of "home staging" is an ideal example for demonstrating the psychological aspects of home and the perception of self-actualization. Staging a home occurs when homeowners want to sell their house. The professional home stager will create design illusions to make the home appear larger, brighter, and generally more inviting to buyers. The stager does this by creating a *vignette* or a portrait of a lifestyle with furniture, plants, and other objects. To illustrate; by adding a bowl of juicy fresh fruit, several gourmet cookbooks, and a small bistro dining set to an otherwise uninspired kitchen creates a portrait in the minds of the buyers where they come to envision themselves eating healthy, cooking more, and having quaint intimate conversations within this kitchen; although they must buy the house to have that lifestyle. Now of course, not all people will think this way, which is why home stagers will attend to every room and yard with a specific person in mind. Quite a few real estate companies claim that staging a home sells the home faster and for more money than without staging. If the claims are accurate, it would seem to confirm people are willing to buy a house to realize a perception of self. Simply put—they hope the home will define them.

Place identity serves two basic functions: It defines who people are, and it defends or protects people from settings and properties that threaten who they are and what they want to be (Proshansky, Fabian, & Kaminoff, 1983). Three broad elements influence the attachments people form to places and their well-being:

1. Personal characteristics and behaviors
2. The availability of facilities, opportunities, and resources
3. A sense of belonging (Popay et al., 2003)

Memories are fundamental to the formation of meaning and may evolve through objects or artifacts. Many clients demonstrate this by walking designers through their homes and recounting when and where every artifact was obtained. For designers, the development of place meaning should precede discussions of aesthetics. A key question to ask clients before deciding on an architectural style, design scheme, or individual piece is, "What does this mean to you?" Because the person in the earlier ASU example developed place attachment to the university and still identifies with it, inclusion of a modest ASU artifact would help to extend this past emotional connection to his/her present-day surroundings, thereby giving it meaning.

Personalization often reflects self-identity; the manner in which people decorate their homes reflects their realistic or idealized self-images. The complexity of a residence's interior is analogous with the owner's materialistic values (Weisner & Weibel, 1981). In other words, greater interior complexity is directly associated with greater materialism, whereas less complexity is directly associated with lower material value. The material culture of Americans and Western societies as a whole belies an associated respect gained from our family, friends, and neighbors based on material possessions (Chapman & Hockey, 1999). When this association and perceived degree of respect falls short of expectations, the person's self esteem may be negatively affected (Chapman & Hockey, 1999). This pattern has reached new heights as competition and advancements in the commercial and technological sectors has brought about significant changes in the relationship and expectations that we have for our homes. For example, in the last two decades small theater systems with surround sound have been introduced into the home. This is an added expense and desire not required for safety or shelter. Commercial and technological advancements such as these have shifted the way we think about environment and the objects contained within them (Manzini, 1995). Rather than an object possessing great intrinsic or personal value, objects today carry great extrinsic value often related to status and prestige. This shift from an intrinsic to an extrin-

sic value for objects significantly dampens our relationship with individual objects (Manzini, 1995).

Meanings of place may be increased by the comfortable, "homey" feelings instilled by personalization (Becker & Coniglio, 1975); because women tend to engage in more personalization, it is theorized that they develop greater feelings of attachment to their homes than men (Sebba & Churchman, 1983; Tognoli, 1980). Conversely, the meaning of a place and identity may be stifled in environments where personalization of a home or workspace is restricted. In many housing developments, for example, the homeowner association (HOA) restricts the level of personalization that residents may display through landscape and architectural design. Residents in these developments are less likely to associate meaning with the place and as a result develop weaker (if any) place attachment to such homes than people who own homes that they may freely personalize. Homeowners in housing developments with HOAs and weak place attachment to their community are more likely to relocate.

The degree to which the neighborhood, exterior design, and interior décor reflect an occupant's sense of self (self-identity) is directly associated with the occupant's level of meaning and subsequent attachment. Within Western societies the home represents the interconnections that people form with each other inside of the house and the relationships formed with neighbors and friends outside of the house (Altman, Brown, Staples, & Werner, 1992). The physical features of a house and how people interpret and relate to those features can have a direct effect on the personal meaning that is conveyed (Zwartz & Coolen, 2006). Some have argued that Western societies are becoming more self-conscious of the values and messages their homes convey (Cooper-Marcus, 1995). This is supported through the connections made between property value and neighborhood conditions (Kauko, 2006).

PLACE ATTACHMENT

Place attachment refers to a person's bond with a social and physical environment (Brown & Perkins, 1992); and it is an attachment that develops over time. We form attachments to places that not only define or express who we are (i.e., support our self-images) or who we want to be seen as, but also give us a sense of belonging, freedom, or both (i.e., provide psychological security). Consider the case of a design team who, through blood, sweat, tears, fun, and laughter, turn a condemned building into a stunning home, which they then refused to sell. It could be that through the process of rehabilitation, the team developed an attachment to the structure because of the memories they took with them from the experience. Clearly, a person who is very attached to a home is less likely to move, thereby strengthening the neighborhood through stability.

Place attachment is an affiliation between a person and a place; it is a personal sense of connection that elicits feelings of comfort and security. It can be facilitated or destroyed by a person's level of control over household members, neighbors, or both—an important concept for both developers and designers, as many problems stemming from the lack of control can be mitigated by design. One study shows that greater place attachment is linked with greater ease in regulating privacy, an important part of identity (sense of self; Harris, Brown, & Werner, 1996). For instance, older teens are more likely to leave home if they have too little privacy, and tenants are more apt to leave apartments where they feel their personal freedoms are infringed upon (e.g., being blamed for or subjected to excessive noise). In such circumstances, doors, windows, and landscaping can be positioned to decrease visual exposure to other occupants, and shared walls can be constructed to dampen sounds and augmented with design elements such as carpeting, tapestries, or both.

We can use four perspectives to measure place attachment. The first relates to fulfilling *psychological needs* because the manner in which a person plans to use a home beyond a simple means of shelter, such as to escape stress, enhance social relations, or maintain identity, is key to developing attachment. The second perspective relates to *monetary value* (i.e., the structure for the occupant is primarily a means to acquire financial assets). For example, some people purchase homes in foreclosure during periods of economic strife and sell them when the real estate prices increase rather than live in them and become part of the community. The third perspective focuses on *amenities* or *attributes* (e.g., appliances, storage space, views). This third evaluation has traditionally been made by women as the primary occupants, but as homes are becoming more versatile from the standpoint of both working from home and equitable domestic roles, men are currently evaluating amenities as much as, if not more than, women. The fourth perspective relates to *specific functionality* (i.e., how well each room allows for its desired functions); for example, having the kitchen and dining room on opposite sides of the home would be problematic for occupants who enjoy cooking and entertaining guests. Western societies typically require both parents to work outside the home to support a household. As a result, designers are often asked to ensure that kitchens and living rooms are large enough to accommodate the entire family as they prepare meals and share activities for times when everyone is at home (Figure 10.3).

[**Figure 10.3**] The advent of the great room allows adults to multitask. They can prepare meals, watch the news, and help the children with their homework all at the same time. © InsideOutPix / Alamy

These four perspectives are not exclusive of one another but rather, are ranked according to relative importance; therefore, a woman may value her home for its ability to satisfy her psychological need for stress relief from her busy career, a businessman may view his home only in terms of the equity it can produce, and a stay-at-home parent may measure his/her home in terms of its amenities and its efficiency toward fulfilling various functions for child rearing. As mentioned, evaluations can also change over time. Thus, one person may measure his/her home in this sequence: monetary value, amenities, functionality, and psychological fulfillment. For this person, home is a means to increase wealth, which is why amenities (upgrades that tend to increase property value) are ranked second. Another person may view his/her home in the same way, but over time these priorities could change to the following: amenities, functionality, psychological fulfillment, and monetary value. The difference between these two people is perhaps that the former is younger and eager to acquire wealth; the latter is older and has no desire to leave the home where he/she intends to spend his/her retirement. Understanding how a client perceives his/her home will allow a designer to create the most appropriate design. The older person in the previous example will want creature comforts that increase the home's functionality and ability to satisfy needs; however, designers should keep in mind that people who want nice things to portray current status and that serve as reminders of former accomplishments may not want to spend excessive amounts of money on them.

Functionality

For most people, the meaning of home is analogous with its ability to satisfy their needs at a functional level. There are three classifications of functional space in a residence: primary, secondary, and tertiary (i.e., first, second, and third environments situated within larger territories). **Primary spaces** are communal or common areas where most of a resident's communication and social interaction take place (e.g., living and dining rooms). **Secondary spaces**, also communal, are where communication and social interaction migrate to and from (e.g., kitchens, porches). **Tertiary spaces** are private or personal areas (e.g., bathrooms, bedrooms) where a resident generally goes to be alone.

Five themes related to a pleasant atmosphere are also crucial to the functionality of successful home designs (Pennartz, 1986): communication, accessibility, freedom to do any desired activity, occupation, and relaxation.

Communication

Designers must first determine where and when most communication occurs within a residence; keep in mind it will vary among different families. Primary communal spaces tend to be in or around the kitchen during food preparation times and eventually shift to the dining and living rooms. Communication among primary, secondary, and tertiary spaces can be compromised by distance, closed doors, sleep schedules, and so on. The design of a home should allow for comfortable dialogue between primary and secondary spaces (kitchen and adjacent rooms or areas).

This can be accomplished with openings, partial walls, service bars, or islands along shared walls or dividing points and by adding features that will accommodate other common activities (e.g., a place to do pay bills, do homework or crafts, a small television, a comfortable seating area for reading) in the secondary space. An intercom system can help facilitate communication among primary, secondary, and tertiary spaces, while also allowing for the delivery of brief messages or for a parent to listen in on a sleeping infant. However, there are many who would rather have their infant or toddler closer to them.

Accessibility

Accessibility means having space and an ease of use for group interaction, sharing, and for ensuring adequate privacy. For designers this means not only developing primary communal spaces (e.g., great rooms), but also distancing them from secondary and tertiary spaces (e.g., home offices, gyms, bedrooms, bathrooms). Many features that enhance communication can also enhance access. Visual and acoustical privacy must be considered as part of accessibility. To achieve visual privacy, place bedrooms away from primary areas and use solid doors. Acoustical privacy can be achieved by building sound attenuating walls or using interior finishes that dampen sound. Hard rooms (bare floors, minimal decoration, modern or industrial furnishings) can act like echo chambers, whereas soft rooms (carpeting, canvas-based artwork, overstuffed furnishings) absorb sound. Low ceilings in hallways, carpet runners, and other creative sound-dampening items should be used between communal and private spaces. Designers should also consider designing better-spaced units to accommodate children within multifamily dwellings (Evans, Lercher, & Kofler, 2002). One suggestion is to place all closets and storage cupboards on walls that are shared between units.

Freedom

Many people view their homes as sanctuaries wherein they may do as they please, from watching a favorite television show whenever they want to walking around naked. Architectural, interior, and landscape design can all mitigate feelings of restriction. Minimizing visual access from the street by using appropriate window height, type and overhangs; selecting window tinting, blinds, and other window treatments indoors; and placing hedges or opaque fencing along the exterior space will ensure privacy for occupants (Figure 10.4).

Occupation

The manner in which we occupy our time influences our design styles. Home may be the primary location for work, recreation, social, or family relationships, or any combinations of these, with separate rooms serving as workshops, studios, home offices, gyms, and so on, and containing the various devices and equipment related to the activities (e.g., workbenches, computer systems, home theaters). The amount of space required for preferred activities within the home must be factored into the home's overall design. For example, if the occupants own a billiard table, provide enough space so they can play comfortably. Televisions can be visually distracting, so the current design trend is to conceal bulky equipment in armoires and hang flat-screen styles as if they were art.

[**Figure 10.4**] In high-density situations, people's personal freedoms can be compromised by a lack of privacy. In areas such as these, designers must consider using reflective glass and blinds that allow light in but prevent potential onlookers from watching without permission. © Caro / Alamy

---

CULTURAL CONNECTION 10.2

Many cultures require outdoor spaces to be treated the same as indoor spaces. Other cultures still separate genders; therefore, dual gathering areas would need to be factored into the space planning. Child rearing in some ethnic communities requires that young children never leave the caregiver's sight; therefore, every room should have an alcove or window seat for the child. Still other cultures have highly structured customs of foot apparel appropriate for entering and leaving a space; shoe storage and changing space must be supplied. These are but a few examples of cultural aspects that affect the occupation of a space of which designers must be cognizant.

Basements are often underutilized and tend to become haphazard storage areas; however, they can be ideal places for uses requiring larger spaces, cooler temperatures, or sound dampening. Louder-than-average sounds associated with media rooms, home gyms, and game rooms, which could disturb other occupants of a home or neighbors, can be dampened by locating them in basements. These underground spaces are also good for extra pantry storage, mechanical equipment, computer equipment, wine storage, or anything requiring an environment maintaining a consistently lower temperature.

Relaxation

The final theme gains greater importance as life becomes more complicated.

Home is where people expect to be able to de-stress after the day's activities, and designers must consider an environment's level of stimuli. Undesirable noise is the main source of stressful stimuli (followed by lighting levels and bad smells). Designers should strive to dampen noise as much as possible, even if it means adding sources of white noise (e.g., water fountains, fans, recordings of nature sounds). Efficient and unobtrusive lighting, artwork depicting scenes found in nature, and potted plants should also be incorporated into the design. Designs that enhance the ability to relax can encompass the entire home or be concentrated in an area or room, depending on the occupants' particular needs and how they use their homes.

THE MEANING OF HOME

Some notions of home correspond to basic human needs, as outlined by Maslow. For example, individuals who have limited economic means rank their residential concerns in order of priority: safety, health, familial needs, and aesthetics; wealthier individuals are more sensitive to their homes' aesthetic qualities, presumably because their more basic needs are not at risk (Salling & Harvey, 1981). In lower-income communities, design is often less of a concern than safety and finances. If we subscribe to Maslow's hierarchy of needs, we may conclude that as people become wealthier and reach higher levels of the hierarchy pyramid, they become more concerned with abstract concepts such as aesthetics and even self-actualization.

In some respects, the concept of home can be an abstract idea because it is not merely a physical place where people live, it is an idea created by how people think and interact with those physical places. This interaction can occur on one or more levels: personal, social, temporal, and physical (Kenyon, 1999). We often seek to personalize each of our environments (house, car, office) by extending our concept of self to include

[**Figure 10.5**] People have long personalized their individual environments. One's home, office, and car are among our primary environments. For some, the importance of expressing ourselves through our environments is so compelling that we are willing to seek out and pay for customized designs. © Ellen Isaacs / Alamy

that place. For example, we may have a specific preference for a color or a type of design.

As we imbue a house with our individual style, making it a *home*, the home in return serves a significant role in shaping our perceptions of life and self identity (Popay et al., 2003) People will often rely upon their house to communicate something about themselves to their neighbors (Chapman & Hockey, 1999). People further call upon smaller movable objects that can be used to personalize both interior and exterior spaces (Cooper-Marcus, 1995). In some cases these small objects will gain sacred or priceless meaning (Belk, 1992; Csikszentmihalyi & Rochberg-Halton, 1981) that reflect the occupant's identities more so than the home's architectural style (Cooper-Marcus, 1995; see Figure 10.5).

Establishing a connection with an environment is a process of *association* that is not limited to a house. The connection results from a series of events that occur in the past, present, and future (Altman, Brown, Staples, & Werner, 1992). Whether it is an individual or society as a whole, we progress through developmental stages that mark periods in time. These periods then get assigned meanings based on the temporal association, such as bringing a newborn infant home for the first time or the recollection of where one was during an important historical event. These events must hold great significance, such as the day two planes flew into the Twin Towers (negative) or when a child is born (positive). Emotions tied to temporal events related to developmental stages can be so important that many have made the statement, "It's the children who make a house a home." Presumably it is because children proceed through developmental stages fairly quickly and these different stages are often infused with intense emotions, that

the meaning and association with the physical environment become fused together. Perhaps it is this reason that has led some to suggest a home is rarely experienced without the companionship of others (Gibbs, 2007).

CULTURAL CONNECTION 10.3

Of all the factors that affect the satisfaction in one's home, the complex interplay between material culture (human artifacts) and the emotive signatures they carry is the most important. Material culture is addressed through anthropology and the study of domestic history. Furnishings, knick-knacks, personal memorabilia, and family heirlooms evoke strong emotions in people; therefore, designers must treat the belongings of clients with the utmost respect. Much like a photograph, these objects are infused with memories of past people and experiences which help to define a person's sense of self. There have been times in American history when people have struck out on long and arduous journeys in search of better lives, only to reach their destinations without many of their personal belongings. In these times of great population shifts, such as in the nineteenth century Manifest Destiny and the California Gold Rush and again in the twentieth-century Great Depression, many were unable to carry all of their possessions, and some had to leave them along the roadside. Even today, on some level, everyone has some objects that they physically *want* and others that they emotionally *need*. A poignant reminder of the connection people can have to the objects in their homes can be seen in Steinbeck's novel, *The Grapes of Wrath*: "How can we live without our lives? How will we know it's us without our past?" (Steinbeck, 1939, p. 112).

Through self-expression and personalization, the home thus comes to resemble and represent who we are; provide us with a sense of connection to other people, our pasts, and our futures; provide both physical and symbolic warmth and safety; and be physically suitable for our physical and psychological health. This may be why newly acquired homes tend to be remodeled or thoroughly cleaned. Remodeling or deep cleaning symbolizes the removal of the previous occupants' lives (Hockey, 1999) and enables the new occupants a fresh start—a clean slate.

From a design perspective, residential designers need to first understand a client's personal interests, lifestyle, preferences, familial arrangement, and cultural identity in order to develop a design the client will accept. Much of this information can be obtained by analyzing the client's existing surroundings. For example, a client may have a strong spiritual orientation and require artifacts, altars, crystals, candles, or inspirational/meditation spaces dispersed throughout the environment. As a designer, it is your choice to accept or reject the job; but as a professional, it is your ethical responsibility not to make value-based judgments regarding design preferences or desires. In addition, a successful designer's notion of design must expand beyond regional ideas and styles to include more cosmopolitan designs. It would behoove the person commissioned to design the home of the Southern Californian client who relocated to New England, mentioned in Chapter 1, to integrate meaningful artifacts and objects supporting the regional designs of Southern California with new items that reflect the regional designs of New England. A sensitive designer should be able to perform this integration as a means of retaining the client's emotional connection to his/her past in a way that supports adaptation and acceptance to the new environment.

CONCEPTS OF HOME

The concept of home can be thought of as an experience between an individual and a select environment (house, neighborhood, and community). Home within Western culture is often the meaning people attach to the house (Rapoport, 1995), but it is an evolving psychological-construct based on people's cultures, traditions, and personality traits. In a more global sense, we can say that the idea of home falls somewhere along each of the following five continuums (Altman & Chemers, 1980):

1. Permanent versus temporary
2. Homogeneous versus differentiated
3. Communal versus noncommunal
4. Identity versus commonality
5. Openness versus enclosure

People who have extroverted personalities tend to view their homes as being more temporary. Extroverts prefer a more homogeneous floor plan, have guests, possess more mainstream objects, and consider their homes to be very open both physically and socially. Conversely, people who have introverted personalities tend to view their homes as safe havens and as being more permanent. Introverts prefer a more differentiated floor plan that allows them to spend time in different environments, have few guests, and control who may visit or stay. Their homes will probably contain many artifacts that have strong personal meaning and reflect their individuality.

Although these two examples illustrate extremes within the five continuums, every person's perception of home will vary, and each person will view his/her position on each continuum differently. Some people may be at one extreme on one point, in the middle on another, and at the other extreme on a third. To get a better idea of these continuums, let us examine each of the categories in greater detail.

Permanent Versus Temporary

In older communities, residents typically occupy permanent dwellings that have been in their families for generations. These tend to be permanent structures tied to the land, as opposed to residential structures that can be disassembled and transported elsewhere at any time such as tents, mobile homes, manufactured homes, or recreational vehicles.

As a **psychological construct** (e.g., conceptual representation), *home* can be defined by a person's intentions. Young adults, for example, often live in temporary or transitional homes (e.g., college dorms, military barracks, small apartments) with the intention of moving to more permanent dwellings later in life. It is important to note that many people regard their current homes as being temporary and that this feeling can last for several years: Think of an apartment dweller who, in every conversation, talks about moving. Conversely, people who move from home to home, each time swearing it will be the last move, view their homes as permanent regardless of the number of times they relocate. Affluent people who find that their permanent residences don't meet all of their needs may augment their primary residence with a secondary or vacation home.

With this continuum from a design perspective, it's important to understand the expectations of and willingness for alterations. A person who views his/her home with *permanence* will have higher expectations of the structure's quality and function and will be more apt to use greater financial resources in the overall architecture, landscaping, and interior design. People who regard their homes as being *temporary* will not be worried about a structure's quality and function, will desire items that are easily moved to new homes, and will often not concern themselves with landscape or interior design.

Homogenous Versus Differentiated

Many of our ancestors occupied single-room dwellings (**homogenous homes**), and in some cases the farm animals stayed indoors with the family as well. A single large room would serve multiple uses: cooking, eating, sleeping, socializing, working, and recreating. When society and social rules became more complex, our homes did as well. We started to develop structures with multiple rooms (**differentiated homes**) with each serving a specific purpose. Many European buildings from the Victorian and Edwardian eras are highly segmented. This type of layout was preferred because it was easier and cheaper to keep small rooms warmer than large ones, and because in these

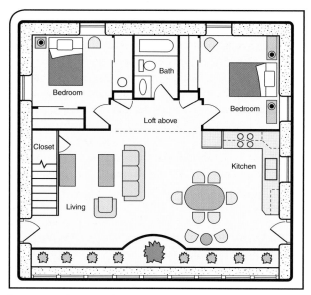

[**Figure 10.6**] Today's floor plans often call for the kitchen, dining, and living rooms to all be open to each other. In the past, floor plans were differentiated with the parlor, dining, and kitchens completely separate from each other. © Illustration by Precision Graphics

[**Figure 10.7**] Recreational vehicles are an example of homogeneous spaces that call upon furniture adaptability. For example, the dining table collapses to form a bed, and the commode and shower occupy a single space, allowing the commode to also serve as a shower bench. © imagebroker

socially complex eras the predominantly wealthy owners of the period had the services of many servants but found it undesirable to see their work in progress. This is also why many homes have a door between the kitchen and dining area.

Also, segmenting a home aided in isolating the activities of women from the activities of men, which can explain the dual seating rooms that typically flank the front foyer entries in these segmented homes.

There is often a positive correlation between the level of differentiation and wealth of the occupant. As an extreme example, a sharecropper's cabin is a homogeneous home, and a castle is a differentiated home. The manner in which occupants spend their leisure time within their homes is strongly affected by the size and degree of differentiation. Occupants of homogenous homes (e.g., studio apartments) may spend less time at home than occupants of differentiated homes (e.g., mansions) who have many rooms in which to wander. Although homogeneous homes are often associated with lower levels of wealth, an interesting trend seems to be challenging this concept. Many upper-middle-class people have opted for homogenous loft spaces in urban areas instead of the differentiated home in the suburbs. However, even in the suburban home, social interaction areas are becoming more homogeneous, whereas private spaces are becoming more differentiated. The "great room" (which usually encompasses the kitchen, dining, and living room) is becoming a popular trend as evidenced in homes built during the late 1990s and early 2000s (see Figure 10.6). Private areas in some larger homes, such as master bedroom suites, appear to be more differentiated with large walk-in closets, large bathrooms equipped with spas, reading areas, and even small kitchenettes. Some researchers contend that privacy, territoriality, and crowding are strongly affected by a home's degree of differentiation (Gifford, 2002).

It is essential for designers to both understand and design appropriately for spaces that serve multiple purposes. For example, in homogeneous spaces such as studio apartments, consider incorporating dual-purpose items, such as sofa beds. Recreational vehicles make excellent use of dual-use furnishings; for example, dining areas and quasi-living rooms convert to sleeping spaces (see Figure 10.7).

Communal Versus Noncommunal

Communal homes are shared by entire families or even communities; noncommunal homes are limited to the **nuclear family**. Communal spaces include religious monasteries, college dormitories, the kibbutzim of Israel, and the tenements of the former Soviet Union, where several families lived on one floor, sharing a common kitchen, bathroom, and living space.

For centuries, Western societies engaged in communal living: Commonly, a single property was shared by large extended families and sometimes employees. With mid-20th century affluence came the splitting up of the extended family: Most individual families were able to afford—and were, therefore, expected to have—their own homes, and communal living arrangements were limited to school, religious and military dormitory settings, or to groups of young people cohabitating to split costs. Today's economy has sparked a resurgence in communal living; it is no longer uncommon to find families pooling their resources to acquire a first property, hold it for several years, and use their equity to purchase separate homes.

The fundamental concept behind communal living is that each individual brings with him/her a particular talent or skill and utilizes it for the betterment of everyone in the community. Although the realities bring many challenges, the idea of communal living as a means of attaining a sense of belonging and happiness has periodically flourished in the United States. More than 600 "intentional communities," such as the Utopian Socialist Societies, arose and dissolved in the 1800s alone (Bedford, 2003). The latest U.S. communal living trend, however, takes a financially proactive stance in a market where the cost of living has increased faster than the average annual wage by almost 100 percent. Some families embrace the notion of developing compounds where several homes share one piece of property; others merge their resources to purchase smaller multifamily residences or very large homes for cohabitation. For example, many members of the Filipino community of National City, California, purchase properties with more than one residence. The parents typically reside in the main home and their adult children in one of the secondary dwellings; one family might have a house, a duplex in the back yard, and yet another unit over the garage. This close living arrangement maximizes financial resources and furthers the support system within the family.

Although designers probably will not be commissioned to design communal habitats in the strictest sense, they can contribute much to homeowners' association projects (planned communities, condominiums, and retirement villages), all of which entail negotiating among public forums and boards of directors, particularly when developing the budget. Designers working at this level must have strong presentation, communication, and facilitation skills. They must also have patience, well-developed listening skills, the ability to understand multiple points of view, and knowledge of the various issues, which are all vital when working with community members who may tend to focus on issues directly affecting them rather than on the project as a whole. To illustrate, an adjacent property owner to a new development may be concerned only with his/her parking situation rather than considering the value a new development may bring to the community. Hence, designers must be patient and willing to have a calm discussion when vocal residents push their own personal agendas. They must possess excellent listening skills to discern important concepts, exhibit the capacity to understand each person's point of view, and be able to propose alternatives that will best fulfill all their needs. Designers who lack these skills should hire a consultant who specializes in community participatory design facilitation.

Identity Versus Commonality

In this and subsequent discussions, a sense of individuality as opposed to commonality will be an issue of concern because a home's identity is partially formed when the physical construct depicts an occupant's specific interests and needs. For example, the exterior fencing at Graceland has musical notes and guitars incorporated into the design, and the palaces of European nobility are rich in architectural detail; the first home denotes an obvious interest in music, whereas the latter is obviously one of social prominence, wealth, and a desire for ornamentation. An example of commonality is a community of mass-developed homes that look alike, where residential associations keep tight control over what can be displayed in the front yard. In this community, people cannot deduce any particular attributes or characteristics of the inhabitant from the exterior architecture (Figure 10.8). Both identity and commonality can be examined on three different levels: physical, psychological, and individual.

Architecture, landscaping, and interior décor reveal a home's physical identity. In the past, a home's physical identity was highly valued, as were the creator's skills, craftsmanship, and painstaking attention to detail. In the United States, owners often sought to imitate the ornately detailed homes of the European aristocracy, and their basic social status could be implied simply by the level of detail of their homes. Today, economic efficiency often overshadows detail and innovation, in effect, shifting design from physical identity to physical commonality.

In the 1980s, large-scale developers began to attribute names and logos to developments (psychological notions of identity rather than physical identity) to create a sense of pride for the occupants. For example, Leisure World develops retirement communities internationally, and its logo is a

[**Figure 10.8**] Many mass developments in the past few decades have reduced costs by developing homes that lack distinguished features that lead to identity. In this way every person gets virtually the same home. Illustration by Precision Graphics

giant globe. Such names and logos also serve to **commodify** developments. The U.S. communities of Palm Springs, California; Palm Beach, Florida; and Newport, Rhode Island; all have brand-name recognition associated with wealth. (A home in these areas can cost four to five times more than an identical home in York, Pennsylvania.) Developers strive to elicit this kind of positive identification. Ideally, identity is expressed through design choices (physical identity), but it can be established, reinforced, or even made memorable simply by naming a property (psychological notions of identity). For example, Cornelius Vanderbilt II built his Newport mansion where he could watch the waves break on the shore; therefore, the mansion, referred to as *the Breakers,* is given identity with that name, which suggests an important attribute of the home. Likewise, William Randolph Hearst constructed and decorated his estate to resemble a European castle; his mansion is referred to as Hearst Castle, and that name clearly reflects the main attribute of the home. Psychological notions of identity are not reserved exclusively for the rich; it works the other way as well. For example, the general public often associates Watts in Los Angeles, Harlem in New York, and the South Side in Chicago with crime and violence. Negative identification is very difficult to change; cities will often rename these areas in the hopes of building positive identification associations. However, it should be noted that many residents of these neighborhoods often have just as much pride in and affiliation with their homes—especially in places with historic or cultural significance, such as Harlem—as do residents of Palm Springs, Palm Beach, and Newport (McAuley, 1998).

The idea of identity-commonality can also relate to how individuals choose to design their spaces. People who regard their homes as safe havens tend to adorn them with personal artifacts (objects that express their identities); their décor can range from traditional to eclectic, but the design style has a specific and satisfying personal meaning to them. For example, a person may choose to display a collection of ancient weaponry, which an outsider may perceive as a messy, mismatched array and a design faux pas. Another person may choose to display only items that complement a particular design theme and invest very little emotionally. The former ranks high on identity because we can gain insight into the weapons collector's personality; the latter ranks high on commonality because the style is too generic and makes it nearly impossible for anyone to learn anything about the occupant.

Although most people perceive their homes as extensions of themselves, self-expression through home identity is often limited to a home's interior in relation to strict association rules and codes of décor. Large-scale developers capitalize on the human need for positive identification through name recognition, place commodification, or both.

In effect, residents pay for the psychological construct of what it means to live in a particular development. Self-expression through architectural identity has all but vanished in modern home development and seems to be limited to the outrageous or kitsch. Architecturally, many new homes have shifted along the continuum from high identity to high commonality.

Openness Versus Enclosure

Both openness and enclosure can be perceived psychologically as well as physically. Many contemporary homes have open interiors; pillars, archways, and service bars used to separate floor space between rooms rather than floor-to-ceiling walls that conceal one room from another.

These types of physically open homes rely on social and psychological rules to prevent intrusion, such as keeping noise levels down so as to not disturb others.

Another concept of openness pertains to the degree in which the home is open to the natural world. In colder climates, homes are closed to the natural elements; but in warmer coastal temperate zones, desert climates, and island areas many homes are open so that they can benefit from the natural breezes, views, and light.

This is an important design for sustainability. When these homes are closed, they often become very warm and thus require air conditioners and purifiers. In Indonesia, where most homes are open to the natural elements, the culture enforces strict rules regarding access to private spaces.

Closed environments have physical or symbolic barriers that keep out the natural environment, animals/bugs, or other people, and thus signal an occupant's desire for privacy. Parallel with physical enclosure is the psychological perception that a place is uninviting or closed. Moats, drawbridges, and walls ensured the protective privacy of ancient castles, whereas today's barriers range from locked doors, metal grates, and dense vegetation, to security cameras and electrified fences. Many people have opted to live within gated or guarded communities, which are closed environments, as a means to thwart crime. Interestingly, people during Victorian times often fortified their homes against the social instability of the time (Hepworth, 1996). In the minds of many, the home was a place to escape and overcome the harsh realities of life (Hepworth, 1996). The same holds true today. Many people escape to the refuge of their home and use it for restoration from the harsh realities of the society. A closed environment presupposes safety and security, but when a burglar violates the home's barriers the inhabitants often feel a loss of security (Chapman, 1999) and feel vulnerable.

In many ways, the degree to which the occupants are willing to interact with their neighbors or other visitors will determine level of a home's openness or closeness. There are still many small towns across North America where people leave their doors unlocked and neighbors are free to enter and borrow a cup of sugar without the owner's permission; however, many residents of urban environments have multiple barricades to their homes. Understanding the occupants' desired levels of openness will assist in developing designs that complement their physical and psychological needs.

INFLUENTIAL FACTORS IN RESIDENTIAL SATISFACTION

Places can have many meanings, but satisfaction will determine how that meaning manifests and effects any subsequent formation of attachment. Residential satisfaction involves multiple contributing factors that include cultural identification, personality, values, expectations, and aspirations; social influences relating to independence, security, privacy, and neighbors; and physical factors that include the psychological attributes of the physical residence. Although often predictable, residential satisfaction is very personal. It tends to increase when we think that others around us share similar beliefs and values, when there is a balance between separateness and togetherness, and when our housing conditions are similar to those of people with whom we feel affiliated (i.e., people are encouraged to interact socially with their neighbors but avoid infringing upon their privacy and feel secure in the belief that they are more similar than dissimilar).

Many people in the West aspire to own their own homes, although many doubt they can actually do so. One study found that more than 85 percent of residents of all ages surveyed desire their own homes (Michelson, 1977). For designers, what the client expects in a home is a crucial consideration. Some people may dream of a mansion in the Ozarks, but to those who desire a penthouse in New York City, that mansion would be just a large box in the middle of nowhere. Residential satisfaction, therefore, may be measured by the difference between residential *preference* and residential *choice*.

Personal factors and housing attributes can help designers to predict their clients' residential preferences, and economic factors can help them to predict their clients' residential choices (Lindberg, Gärling, & Montgomery, 1986, 1989). If there is a large gap between a person's present residential conditions and expectations, chances are that the person will be dissatisfied. For example, a woman may dream of owning a geodesic dome nestled in the rolling foothills, but due to economic constraints she may have to settle for a boxy, late-1970s apartment near her workplace. However, this woman can make choices about her home's physical attributes and amenities and adapt the home to her desires; by incorporating natural elements, colors, and lighting, she can increase her residential satisfaction substantially yet incur minimal expense. We all have the ability to adapt to things we cannot change and modify those features we can, and we can use design to optimize our residences to satisfy our needs (Tognoli, 1987).

There are two cognitive processes related to overall residential satisfaction (Canter, 1983). The first is *purposive,* which means that the home is evaluated according to specific rooms and functions. This is an objective evaluation because the home is perceived according to its ability to function effectively and efficiently. The second process is *comparative,* which means an occupant or visitor compares the home with a past home or one that belongs to a friend, relative, or peer. Such highly subjective evaluations often lead to dissatisfaction unless the evaluator has the financial resources to replicate the desired attributes and features from the other homes.

Understanding how clients will view their homes and the features within them helps designers to make appropriate selections. For example, a man may not care what his furnishings look like, but he may be very demanding about how well the sound system can be heard throughout the home. The designer can deduce from this limited information that this man will desire optimal acoustics. Working with a client who makes comparisons can be both easy (the designer can view the desired effect) and difficult (an identical design will look different in another environment

[Table 10.1] Design Preferences According to Personality

Type	Design Preference
A	Embraces designs that are asymmetrical, eccentric, and less conventional. A mixture of modern designer furniture, tapestries, silk screens, and antiques will increase the type A person's affiliation with his or her environment.
B	Although similar to type A, the type B person tends to prefer less expensive, more functional objects; this person is not so affluent that he or she can view possessions from a purely aesthetic perspective.
C	The type C person possesses expensive art, prefers wooden floors, and displays antiques in a ritualistic or ostentatious way. This person tends to be affluent and likes to use possessions as status symbols.
D	Similar to the type C person, the type D person prefers less-expensive items and typically displays copies of original art. This person prefers more symmetrical arrangements.
E	The type E person has fewer objects of value and embraces very symmetrical ways of displaying possessions.

Adapted from: Amaturo, Costagliola, & Ragone (1987). Furnishing and status attributes: A sociological study of the living room, *Environment and Behavior, 19,* 228–249

because of room size, wall angles, and differences in lighting and geometric layout). Planners and designers must ascertain from which perspective their clients assess their homes. This requires a bit of deductive reasoning because most people will not admit to wanting to copy attributes of another person's home. Clients will, however, be happy to talk about past homes and divulge functional preferences and thereby provide the information that designers need.

Personal Disposition

The manner in which people evaluate homes is largely dependent upon their perceived social positions and status. One study identified five major types of living rooms ranked according to richness of furnishings and symmetry of arrangements, each of which is attributable to a type of preference relative to status and social mobility (Amaturo, Costagliola, & Ragone, 1987). Table 10.1 describes these types and the designs representative of each.

In short, type A and B people tend to dislike conspicuous consumption and prefer décor that is more artistic; they tend to be older, prefer recreational activities that are more intellectually based, and hold professional career positions. Type C and D people tend to be successful, older businesspeople who prefer objects that demonstrate their status, represent more traditional social norms of behavior, and represent a symbolic order of society. Type E people tend to have limited resources (e.g., retired, elderly, working-class individuals). It should be noted that whereas one person may fit perfectly into a personality stereotype with regard to the living room types, others are strongly influenced by other variables such as age, peer group, personal experiences, and life-altering experiences (see Figures 10.9a–d).

Age and Stage of Life

As we age, our needs, goals, purposes, and status change, all of which affects our levels of satisfaction. For example, many older people grow tired of large family homes that have become empty nests (after their offspring have grown up and moved away), especially when the winter months make daily activities and yard maintenance painful for those with arthritis and laborious for those who must shovel snow. As the satisfaction they once experienced in their large homes diminishes, they may opt to migrate to warmer regions and move into smaller communal homes that require less maintenance. Similarly, families with young children typically prefer suburbs, which provide more schools, outdoor spaces for play activities, and other people with young families to help watch the children. Older couples and single adults, in contrast, often prefer downtown residences (Gifford, 2002), which generally have better access to transportation and services. Not always, but typically, younger adults gravitate toward ornate dwelling styles whereas older adults prefer plain ones (Nasar, 1981b, 1983). This may be because younger people tend to have the energy to perform routine maintenance, whereas older people find such maintenance to be exhausting and a possible source of injury. Simplicity and clarity are preferred by elderly individuals who have difficulties with perception or mobility (Gifford, 2002). This, in combination with universal design principles, can help facilitate independence and freedom for the older person (Imrie, 2004). Young children can also benefit from universal design principles, but it should be known that children often lack their own notion of residential satisfaction and most often adopt their parents' viewpoints and preferences (Michelson, 1977).

[**Figures 10.9a–d**] Personality A and C often have an elevated sense of style and often reject traditional notional notions of symmetry. Personalities B and D have similar design preferences as A and C, respectively, but use less expensive materials and tend to incorporate more symmetry. a: Livedin Images/©Margot Hartford; b: Livedin Images/Jessie Walker/SHELTERED Images; c: Livedin Images/Marc Gerritsen; d: Livedin Images/Marc Gerritsen

Gender and Social Roles

Men in the United States often abdicate control over aesthetic factors in the home (Chapman, 1999), and women tend to be more social than men. One researcher suggests that for "men the world is a place to do things, while for women it is a place to relate to things (and others)" (Franck, 2002). Women still bear most of the burden for child, elder, and home care; not surprisingly, the integration of services into housing and neighborhoods is a predominant need among women (Peterson, 1987). When men and women were asked to construct model homes, women seem to prefer smaller homes that had more communal space, wall curvature, and design originality than men (Keeley & Edney, 1983), who tend to prefer homes with greater symmetry, simplicity, and space in both design and décor. One study showed that the men value objects of action (e.g., televisions, sports equipment), whereas women value objects of contemplation (e.g., photographs, artwork) (Csikszentmihalyi & Rochberg-Halton, 1981). For men owning the biggest house in the neighborhood projects the message that he is successful and a good provider (Belk, 1992). He often uses his house to measure his own position in the world (Caplan, 2005).

Corroborating much of what has been said above, a study of floor plan layouts reveals that both men and women tend to prefer kitchens that are open to the dining and family rooms (Hasell, Peatross, & Bono, 1993); however, this preference is stronger for women who work outside the home than for those who do not (Gifford, 2002). Individuals who work within the home tend to prefer greater **segmentation,** which allows them to experience different environments. Such gender- and work-related preferences may reflect primal behavior patterns and could explain why suburban women reported greater residential satisfaction in denser, more urban communities (Rothblatt, Garr, & Sprague, 1979). In sum, women are likely to prefer environments that have greater functionality, intimacy, and originality, while men are likely to prefer more simplicity and personal space in their environments.

Physical Influences

A residence's physical characteristics can be related to four kinds of physical features: housing form, architectural style, interior areas, and outdoor areas. Numerous studies have demonstrated that most North Americans prefer single-family, detached homes to town houses and condominiums; and mobile homes are the least popular form of housing.

People often, but not always, prefer architectural styles that reflect their cultural background, and style preferences can shift according to changes in fashion. A study of apartment preferences revealed that people tend to prefer older buildings over those that look like multifamily dwellings and highly detailed designs over plain and simple ones (Widmar, 1984), possibly due to higher quality of construction, greater aesthetic appeal, and perceived similarities to former homes. Most individuals prefer flat or sloping ceilings that are higher than the 8-foot average and walls that meet at 90-degree or greater angles (Baird, Cassidy, & Kurr, 1978); psychologically, this combination creates the greatest perception of space. When it comes to color, hue relates more to perceived warmth, saturation to elegance, and brightness to activity. Older people's preferences seem to relate more to locale than architectural features; seniors whose housing affords views of nature report the greatest residential satisfaction (Gifford, 1999).

EVOLUTION OF HOME

In the past, many people remained in one home or geographic area their entire lives. This trend is changing rapidly with approximately 43 million Americans moving each year (U.S. Census Bureau News, 2000). One international survey found that 96.4 percent, 74.5 percent and 42.9 percent of respondents from Ireland, the Middle East, and Australia respectively, indicated that they had relocated to a different country for employment opportunities (ManPower, 2008). When asked, 78 percent of the respondents throughout the world stated that they would consider relocating for work

in the future, 36.9 percent were willing to move anywhere in the world (ManPower, 2008). Interestingly, 40.5 percent said they were willing to permanently leave their home country (ManPower, 2008). These results indicate that there are a growing number of people willing to move away from their historical roots—to other counties, states, and even countries—often taking with them their ideas of beauty and design preferences.

Based on the average human lifespan of 77.8 years, westerners spend an estimated 70 years of their life inside a man-made structure. Most of this time is in a secure habitat with an average size of 2,000 square feet that we call home. Throughout human existence, shelter (or *home*) has taken many forms. Early homes included caves, huts, tepees, and yurts. As human societies evolved, their housing demands changed. Wood, earthen, or stone structures with only one room were slowly replaced by more complicated structures. The level of complexity or **segmentation** of indoor space along with the hierarchical ordering of rooms was often related to the socio-political complexity of the culture. The house thus became a framework from which people could build and organize conditions that express a predictable and complementary impression of core values and beliefs (Chapman, 1999).

As society gained in complexity; so did its structures. The Victorian era ranks among the most complicated and rigid societies in which elaborate codes of conduct were strictly enforced. During this time society saw the home as an expression of a family's values, and the person's moral character was reflected in the home's architecture (Hepworth, 1996). The interior environment was a place where social ideas of a "polite society" could be displayed while providing some relief to the rigidity of social rules (Hepworth, 1996). However, the level and degree of the home's segmentation for specialized uses of individual rooms reflected the Victorian culture of everything in its place and a place for everything.

Throughout history and around the globe, our dwellings mirror the complexity of our societies, and homeowners strive for architectural styling that best expresses the occupant's unique personality (Chapman, Hockey, & Wood, 1999). Homes of recent times have favored open floor plans that better suit a society with far fewer social restrictions and where everyone is expected to multitask. Today's changes in the housing market, economics, and technologies are changing our relationship with home. We no longer inhabit a single dwelling for multiple generations. It is not uncommon for parents and their adult offspring to live in different parts of the world, and the exportation of Western architecture has diluted the meaning of home (Gibbs, 2007; Sparke, 2004). Some have argued that home is no longer a physical location, but an understanding dependant upon time and space (Easthope, 2004). In a transient society, people create a sense of stability through the association of a home with a type of town, architecture, or possessions (Feldman, 1990). It has been further argued that like photographs, which are now rarely stored in a physical photo album that can be touched, smelled, and looked at, the idea of home is becoming an ethereal emotion no longer tied to a place but rather just a thought or concept. This conceptualization can be likened to one's appreciation for a table made of wood. Because most people have seen a lumberyard or a tree, the table has meaning in terms of its points of origin. Plastics and various composite laminates, on the other hand, have little to no relation in terms of their points of origin. This separation between a product and its point of origin thus makes it difficult for people to form meaningful bonds (Caplan, 2005). Whereas a house may still be made of wood, its design lacks substantial origins. Like plastic chairs that are mass produced, mass-produced houses lack *meaning*, thus the emotional construct called *home* is lost.

GREEN SPACES

Although many North Americans in the not-so-distant past prized concrete landscapes for their low maintenance, the importance of green landscaping in human settlements has and continues to receive a great deal of attention from both the public and official sectors, especially in urban environments. City planners, developers, architects, and designers in Europe, Asia, and the Americas recognize the importance of including greenscapes in our communities, public buildings (schools, hospitals, and governmental facilities), and housing developments and have begun to advocate for them.

The view afforded by a purchased or rented residence is directly related to the property's perceived economic value; therefore, developers try to maximize view potential, and communities adopt ordinances to prevent new developments from obscuring existing views. Natural views tend to be most favored, followed by distant views of downtown areas and urban views.

One research team, finding that people actually avoid outdoor spaces that are devoid of grass and trees, suggests that green spaces have the ability to promote social relationships (which are crucial for personal and communal well-being) and that groupings of trees planted in and around high-density residential spaces attract more people to the outdoors and thereby encourage social interactions (Levine-Coley, Kuo, & Sullivan, 1997; see Figure 10.10). The logic is simple: Trees provide oxygen, relief from heat and glare, and visual stimulation. Gardens are another form of green space where people can gain a connection to each other as well as the causality of life (Cooper-Marcus, 1995). Some have suggested that gardens can facilitate a past sense of meaning that can be applied to a modern environment without manipulating the architecture of a house (Cooper-Marcus, 1995).

Natural landscaping and green spaces provide both psychological benefits and positive functionality. Ancient strongholds were built on hard-to-reach land (e.g., along the face of a cliff, on an island) whenever possible; if not, defensive obstacles such as moats, berms (earthen mounds or walls), and pales (tall, spiked fences) were built around them, and additional protection was afforded by natural barriers such as bodies of water and thorny vegetation. People still employ natural elements to help them feel more secure in their homes; rocks, trees, and built-up soil levels are used to delineate boundaries and prevent unauthorized entry. However, in our quest for privacy and security, we often inadvertently create the very problem we seek to prevent. For example, although certain design elements ensure privacy, they also create a lack of visibility that is attractive to potential burglars (Ham-Rowbottom, Gifford, & Shaw, 1999).

SUSTAINABILITY CONNECTION 10.2

For many Western communities, residents tend to be extremely territorial and live by an unwritten code that each resident must remain on his/her property and not venture onto someone else's without invitation. In the United States, property owners purchase and install approximately 38,880 miles of chain link, 31,680 miles of wooden, and 1,440 miles of ornamental fencing annually. This roughly translates to enough fencing that we could encircle the earth almost three times. Because hedges and thick bushes can produce the same security affect, designers should consider plantings that also offer fruits, flowers, or unique textures to increase the productivity of the "fence." Some selections that have thorns and beauty include the edible—blackberry bushes and citrus trees—and the non-edible—hollies, agave, rose bushes, or pyracantha. Designers and owners should be prudent because although these plants will repel intruders, they may also injure a child or pet.

In addition to protection, green spaces provide positive health benefits. One study found that one-year-old children whose homes had no views of the outside had slower cognitive development (Taylor, Kuo, & Sullivan, 2001); according to another study, increased time spent in green outdoor settings can reduce overall symptoms related to attention deficit/hyperactivity disorder (ADHD) in children. Views of nature are fundamental to satisfaction and well-being, and windows provide opportunities for both *prospect-refuge* and *restorative experiences* (Kaplan, & Dana, 2001; Verderber, 1986). Voluminous research demonstrates that people prefer rooms with windows (Ullah, Kurniawan, Pho, Wai, & Tregenza, 2003).

[**Figure 10.10**] Green spaces, whether a park or a community garden, provide a place for people to go and be social with one another without the constant stream of stimulation common to highly dense environments. © Janine Wiedel Photolibrary / Alamy

Likewise, exterior landscaping not only helps to produce natural scenes, but also helps to reduce the amount of atmospheric pollutants that can infiltrate a home and build up on exterior surfaces (Lindberg, Hartig, Garvill, & Gärling, 1992). Leafy vegetation absorbs pollution by way of its natural cycle and provides additional surface area to which particulates will cling to instead of clinging to the home, thereby not only providing the opportunity for prospect-refuge and attention restoration, but also enhancing the indoor air quality.

Understanding that natural elements attract people to outdoor spaces can help designers create environments that promote well-being and social interaction. Developers and city planners should take active measures to maintain and preserve existing natural features in and around urban locations; and designers should create attractive landscapes by utilizing natural elements such as water, rocks, and trees in interior and exterior designs (Gottfried & Gottfried, 1984). Because not all homes can offer breathtaking views, measures can be implemented to ensure attractive and natural views for most residential properties.

There is currently no counterpart in primate evolution for a life lived almost entirely indoors, and hence many try to bring the outdoors inside. Designing better homes and outdoor gardens act as subtle reminders of the natural world beyond our walls, including its warmth, lighting, colors, vistas, textures, and plants; and we use windows to create that connection (Cooper-Marcus & Sarkissian, 1986).

Practical Applications for Designers

Use these resources, activities, and discussion questions to help you identify, synthesize, and retain this chapter's core information. These tools are designed to complement the resources you'll find in this book's companion Study Guide.

SUMMING IT UP

The primary purpose of sense organs is to protect. For people who have a diminished or complete failure of one or more senses, the world can be complicated place. This is because the world is meant to be seen, heard, felt, tasted, and smelled.

For those who were born with the absence of a sense, or lost the use of a sense early in life, the brain has the capacity to augment the loss. The elderly person loses abilities gradually, and this loss symbolizes a loss of independence. As designers of the built environment, we can mitigate some of the obstacles that are presented when one or more of the senses is either lost or compromised. Through environmental modification and the adoption of inclusive design practices, designers can either ameliorate or minimize the effects associated with the absence or reduction in our ability to detect sensation.

Design is the best source of practical solutions to environmental problems encountered by a wide range of people. Concerted efforts must be made to establish direct communication among challenged people, their significant others, healthcare providers, designers, planners, architects, and contractors early in the design process. When designing environments for impaired populations, strive to create spaces appropriate to their needs wherein they can enjoy as much comfort, personal control, and self-sufficiency—and therefore relative freedom—as possible.

You can also refer to this textbook's companion Study Guide for a comprehensive list of Summary Points.

Residential Satisfaction

Russell James III, J.D., Ph.D.,
University of Georgia, Athens

In 1966, Julian Rotter proposed a theory applicable to human satisfaction known as "locus of control." Researchers have since applied the model to many areas from job satisfaction to satisfaction with one's body. Applied to an environmental context, this theory suggests that when we feel we are in control of our environment, we will usually have greater satisfaction with the environment. This "internal" locus of control generates positive emotional responses. Conversely, when we feel that our environment is controlling us (an "external" locus of control), then we will tend to be less satisfied with our environment. This idea corresponds with research findings on residential satisfaction in a number of areas.

In general, homeowners have more control over their housing than do renters. Correspondingly, research in the United States and many Western European nations shows that homeowners are usually more satisfied with their residences than renters are, even when the residences are otherwise similar. However, for the oldest adults, the responsibility for maintenance and repairs that comes with homeownership can become especially burdensome, perhaps reversing this sense of control. This could explain why the satisfaction gap between homeowners and renters narrows after retirement age and eventually reverses at the oldest ages (James, 2008a).

In a study of renters' residential satisfaction, the most important issue was the relationship with the property manager. If renters felt the manager was responsive to their concerns, they tended to be satisfied with most other aspects of their residence. Conversely, if they felt that the managers were not professional or responsive, their residential satisfaction was much lower. Again, one might explain this as a difference in perceived control. If I cannot get the manager to fix the leaky faucet, then I cannot control my environment and I am more likely to be dissatisfied (James, Carswell, & Sweaney, 2009).

Physical environment can also enhance one's sense of control through design features. Although easy to overlook, the ready accessibility of bathrooms is a critical factor in one's sense of control in a residential space. Bathrooms not only provide important functionality but also are a socially acceptable zone of privacy. Statistical analysis of a national data set revealed that the number of bathrooms in a residence was the most important physical feature in predicting residential satisfaction (James, 2008b).

In an analysis of residential satisfaction in apartment dwellings, bathrooms were important; but so were other forms of separated space. For example, having a porch or balcony allows the resident to separate from the normal living environment without leaving the residence. In this study, features that created the potential for separated space such as an additional living room, bathroom, balcony, or patio, positively affected satisfaction, even when total floor area did not change (James, 2007).

Although there may be no single answer to achieving residential satisfaction, understanding how we can improve the residents' sense of control over their environment may be an important consideration in designing and managing towards this goal.

References

James, R. N., III. (2007). Multifamily housing characteristics and tenant satisfaction. *Journal of Performance of Constructed Facilities, 21*(6), 472–480.

James, R. N., III. (2008a). Residential satisfaction of elderly tenants in apartment housing. *Social Indicators Research, 89*, 421–437.

James, R. N., III. (2008b). Investing in housing characteristics that count: A cross-sectional and longitudinal analysis of bathrooms, bathroom additions, and residential satisfaction. *Housing & Society, 35*(2), 67–82.

James, R. N., III., Carswell, A. T., & Sweaney, A. L. (2009). Sources of discontent: Residential satisfaction of tenants from an Internet ratings site. *Environment & Behavior, 41*(1), 43–59.

Rotter, J. B. (1966). Generalized expectancies for internal versus external control of reinforcement. *Psychological Monographs, 80*(1), 1–28

KEY TERMS

- **commodify**
- **differentiated homes**
- **homogenous homes**
- **nuclear family**
- **primary spaces**
- **psychological construct**
- **secondary spaces**
- **segmentation**
- **self-regulation**
- **tertiary spaces**

WEB LINKS

InformeDesign (www.informedesign.umn.edu)

Journal of Scientific Exploration; read *The Archaeology of Consciousness* by Paul Devereaux for more on the discussion on the *meaning of place* (www.scientificexploration.org/journal/jse_11_4_devereux.pdf)

School Construction, for more on the benefits and challenges of participatory design (www.djc.com/news/co/12009245.html)

Sirkin and Associates, for more on group home ownership (www.andysirkin.com/HTMLArticle.cfm?Article=1)

U.S. Environmental Protection Agency, read about starting a greenscape for a residential project (http://www.epa.gov/epawaste/conserve/rrr/greenscapes/owners.htm)

Waymark, for more on semiotics and residential design (http://homepages.waymark.net/~bikechic/signs1.html)

STUDIO ACTIVITY 10.1

Meaning

Design Problem Statement

The world is composed of meaning. Some are obvious, whereas others are not; but when we see spaces consistently occupied by people, we can be assured that the place holds meaning. Your job is to try to identify that meaning.

Directions

Step One: Visit a popular hangout in your community. Photograph the places where people gather and the surrounding environment. Make sure to include a couple of panoramic photos. Analyze the photos in an effort to identify features or elements that lend themselves to meaning. These features usually stand out, being ornate, colorful, shiny/reflective, and having other qualities.

Step Two: Using one of the best panoramic photos, remove the popular hangout place with Photoshop. Then, using your list of features and elements, develop a new place for that spot. Make sure to diagram the new space to highlight the features that you will be including for meaning.

Step Three: Prepare a visual list of example pieces of furnishings, artwork, and other design elements that will be used for the interior spaces. Make sure to explain how each piece will contribute to one or more aspects that affect meaning.

STUDIO ACTIVITY 10.2

Communal Homes

Design Problem Statement

We live in a society where multiple families or generations share a single living space. Your job is to find an existing residential floor plan from the Internet; this must be an average, everyday floor plan for a middle-class family. Then reconfigure this floor plan to accommodate two families or two generations under one roof. The goal is to allow both families a sense of privacy, territoriality, and autonomy.

Rules

You cannot include more than one kitchen.

You cannot add additional bathrooms.

You cannot alter the original footprint.

Deliverables

Profile of the two families (e.g., elderly, presence of children, gay or lesbian).

The original floor plan including the author of the floor plan and the website from which it was downloaded.

The modified version of the floor plan.

Discussion of how privacy, territoriality, and autonomy have been achieved and to what degree.

DISCUSSION QUESTIONS

1. Discuss places to which you are attached. What characteristics evoke the emotional responses that lead to your *place attachment?* How would you design a bedroom to ensure calm and peace, relative to place attachment?

2. Using the five dimensions of home to define your space preferences, give examples from your life that support each choice.

3. Discuss U.S. culture in terms of living environments. Imagine having no knowledge of U.S. history, tradition, culture, beliefs, morals, or language. What would you infer about U.S. lifestyles based solely on residences?

4. Discuss how you would determine the design needs of a family of four plus a set of grandparents. What questions would you need to ask to design effectively?

5. Based on information in this chapter, discuss possible reasons for the current popularity of Asian-inspired architecture and design.

LEARNING ACTIVITIES

1. Poll 20 people outside of this class. Ask where they are from and record their answers, graphing the data according to category (e.g., city, state, region, country). Then ask the same subjects to list where they have lived, and graph the number of locations (e.g., bar graph: x-axis = locations, y-axis = individuals).

2. Draw a humorous sketch or write a story illustrating the imaginary encounter of a historical figure in a modern architectural structure (e.g., Marie Antoinette in the Guggenheim Bilbao).

3. Design a home for you and four other students to share, showing floor plans as well as circulation. What features are essential for communal living? What typical residential features can easily be excluded from your design?

4. Draw a sketch of your residence, focusing on *personalization*. Highlight areas that are highly personalized (e.g., a bookcase with a collection of photos) and those that are not (e.g., a bathroom). Repeat this exercise in a friend's residence; then compare and contrast the level of personalization with your personalities. How could this information aid your design process? What attributes about your residences would you consider when designing a new home?

5. Contact a realtor and ask if you can work together to poll prospective homebuyers. Create a short survey that gathers nonspecific background information: age range, occupation, number of residents, expected period of residence, and so on. Ask homebuyers to rank their prospective or ideal home according to amenities, functionality, monetary value, and psychological fulfillment. Share all data if the realtor desires, and ask if she or he already collects similar information or uses a similar technique for establishing clients' residential preferences.

11 The Community and Neighborhood

When was the last time you spent a quiet moment just doing nothing – just sitting and looking at the sea, or watching the wind blowing the tree limbs, or waves rippling on a pond, a flickering candle or children playing in the park?"

—Ralph Marston

It can be argued that community parks, playgrounds, and schools are the reflection of the larger community. Site selection for these environments should be based, in part, on an ability to afford a multitude of different experiences for developing young people and adults of all ages. These attributes should further mirror the cultural and developmental attributes found within the community. For example, if Latinos compose the primary cultural constituency, a soccer field would be more relevant than an American football field (Figure 11.1). Similarly, if the school or recreational center has a strong performing arts component, an outdoor stage or small amphitheater would be beneficial.

To examine design in relation to recreation environments, they must first be clustered according to common characteristics. **Parks**, for example, can include city parks, county parks, and even gated-community "pocket" playgrounds. A common shared element is that they are based on outdoor green spaces and most are *public* spaces, which mean that they are open to anyone. These environments are very important to communities because they provide opportunities for **unstructured play** for both children and adults. Accommodating activity spaces for these two populations can be another challenge. For example, a group of adults may want to play volleyball, but the space allowed for this activity is adjacent to the family picnicking area. Hence, the periodic wayward ball could result in it accidentally hitting a person, or landing on someone's barbecue.

[**Figure 11.1**] The activities and events found within a neighborhood or community are reflections of the predominant cultural values of the inhabitants. In a reciprocal symbiotic manner, humans influence their environments just as much as environments influence humans. ©Photo Resource Hawaii / Alamy

It is, therefore, important to understand the *uses* of parks, playgrounds, and schoolyards early in the design process, as well as all of the adjacencies of the activities (intended and unintended) that may occur within the spaces.

It is generally accepted that the physical environment influences a young person's behavior. As such, the schools, classrooms, and playgrounds should be regarded as a means for achieving desired socioemotional, cognitive, and motor development (Weinstein, 1987). For example, the socio-emotional outcomes that can be obtained through environmental design include self-esteem, security and comfort, self-control, peer interaction and pro-social behavior, and sex role identification. Cognitive development can be facilitated through environmental design by incorporating symbolic expressions that promote logical thought, creativity, problem-solving, increased attention span, and greater task involvement. Much like a stimulus response, symbolism is predicated on sensory stimuli. In essence, sensations are the translations ascribed to meaning or representation, which is referred to as symbolism. Visual recognition of shape, color, and size are the most common sources of symbolism, but taste and smell (chocolate or flowers [sweet] on valentines day), sounds

(sirens versus church bells), and touch (cotton is associated with comfort) also contains symbolic meanings. Symbolism as discussed in this chapter is the integration of multiple and sometimes competing systems of meaning into a single organized message. Symbolism is something that can be experienced with the senses and used to provide understanding. What is important to understand about symbolism is that it is learned and is not uniform throughout all cultures.

ROLE OF CHILDREN

Children select and compete with other children for places within their territorial ranges; however, social restrictions such as parental or physical restrictions such as traffic can limit the range of environments from which they can choose. Children's influence in the home is increasing (Rybczynski, 1986); however, their freedom may be limited to social interaction with little influence on environmental design (Cooper-Marcus, 1995). When permitted, children's evaluations and choices of places are affected by variables, including their prior exposure, upbringing (whether urban or rural), exploration restraints, portrayal of environments by the media, and peers' preferences (Malinowski & Thurber, 1996).

In the United States, understanding the human–environment relationship has been commonly regarded as unnecessary until recently. However, valuable research is coming from European, Mediterranean, and Asian countries. A study conducted on the island of Cyprus found that the concept of home differed between children and adults; the children's wants and needs for their homes matched or exceeded the general standards common to U.S. suburbs and included the desire for a grass lawn (Hadjiyanni, 2000). Other studies reveal housing preference among westerners for detached single-family dwellings over all other housing types (Booth, 1985; Cooper-Marcus & Sarkissian, 1986; Kenyon, 1999). Interestingly, studies show that children learn that they are not only related to people but also to various objects contained within the home (Proshansky & Fabian, 1987), and that children are aware of their housing condition in relation to societal norms. Research is accumulating on the human–environment experience, providing a better understanding of how the environment affects our behaviors. For example, according to one study (Evans, Saltzman, & Cooperman, 2001):

- Children, especially when young, spend a majority of their time at home, and housing quality has been shown to affect children's general psychological health and task persistence.
- As with noise and crowding, chronic exposure to poor-quality housing can decrease children's sense of control

over their environments and contribute to their sense of helplessness.

- Children living in higher-quality housing not only have fewer behavioral problems and lower incidences of anxiety, depression, misconduct, or deviant acts, but also score higher on tests designed to measure personal motivation.

OUTDOOR ENVIRONMENTS

Natural environments provide mental and physical restorative benefits. This seems especially true for young people: Children run, jump, and tumble in open spaces, which allows them to develop their gross motor skills. Children also develop their imaginations (e.g., pretending to be superheroes, inventing new games) and social skills (e.g., playing team sports). Studies on how children behave in outdoor spaces of public housing show that they engage in significantly more play—and more creative play—in high-vegetation areas than in barren spaces (Taylor, Wiley, Kuo, & Sullivan, 1998) and both teacher-led activities and pretend play in school yards concentrate in natural places (Lindholm, 1995) and not on manmade play equipment. Research has also determined that children who relocate to homes with improved natural views tend to have more attentional capacity (Wells, 2000); that children with attention deficit/hyperactivity disorder (ADHD) function better than usual following activities in green settings; and that the symptoms of ADHD are less severe in children who have access to natural play areas (Taylor, Kuo, & Sullivan, 2001). For these reasons, both indoor and outdoor natural spaces must be considered in the overall design process (Figure 11.2).

Children's exposure to natural environments is often through schoolyards, playgrounds, and community parks; however, the natural aspects of these environments are declining because of safety concerns, the time constraints of parents bringing their children to parks, and the loss of natural spaces as a result of urban sprawl and mass development. This reality is contrary to the research that demonstrates exposure to well-designed schoolyards, playgrounds, and community parks can enhance positive behavioral patterns and facilitate development of gross motor, cognitive, and social skills, which are linked to greater academic success. One important attribute of a well-designed outdoor space is the ample provision of natural topography and vegetative growth. These natural environments are a source of mental and physical restoration. Studies demonstrate that children engage in significantly more creative play in high-vegetation areas as opposed to barren spaces.

[**Figure 11.2**] We often over-plan play spaces for children, thereby impeding their imagination. Through the use of natural elements such as streams, small wooded areas, and patches of sand, children can use their imagination while exploring their environments. © Image Source/SuperStock

[**Figure 11.3**] Increased student population translates to more wear and tear on the turf, the natural vegetation, and the equipment on the playground. In addition, playground crowding can lead to competition for a turn on the equipment, thus promoting a hierarchy based on physical prowess. Notice in this figure that it is mostly bigger children occupying the equipment. © David Grossman/Alamy

Despite the research demonstrating the positive benefits of vegetation on attitude formation (Kaplan & Kaplan, 1989; Ulrich, 1984), many schoolyards, playgrounds, and community parks remain bleak and monotonous spaces; some of which have been completely hardscaped. Some researchers have suggested that schoolyards, playgrounds, and community parks within the United States are in such dire shape because of the significant increases in student population providing more wear and tear on facilities (Figure 11.3), diminished value of recreation and physical education resulting in the shortening of recess, fears of litigation prompting the removal of play equipment, and the growing incidences of bullying (Malone & Tranter, 2003).

Natural Settings

Exposure to outdoor natural settings has consistently been shown to benefit psychological and physical well-being of children and adults alike. Within these spaces people are exposed to a host of visual, auditory, tactile, and olfactory stimuli that work in unison to develop creativity, intellect, and social skills. Historically, natural settings were where most children played: canyons, meadows, forests, lakes, and fields. These settings help to facilitate experimental learning (Johnson & Hurley, 2002) and problem solving that occur as children touch, taste, climb, and interact with natural elements. Also, because of the greater complexity of the natural environment, children develop motor skills that are required for understanding and navigating their surroundings (Fjørtoft, 2004), which thus leads to greater sophistication of their developmental skills.

Outdoor play allows children to learn, discover, create, and interact with their environments; however, children of today are increasingly regimented in their daily activities and shuttled between child care centers, schools, after-school programs, and organized sports activities. Currently, more than 5 million U.S. children younger than 3 years of age are cared for by adults other than their parents during the workday. These are typically facilities outside the home, usually day-care centers and preschools for very young children and public and private schools for older children and teens. Often the care of these children is substandard (Carnegie Corporation of New York, 1994), and there is little time for unstructured play. When there is time, the only areas available for unstructured play for many children may be informal places, such as vacant lots, alleys, or construction sites. Although not terrible places, there is a greater possibility of danger, and supervision is insufficient or nonexistence; thus, the dangers at these locations may outweigh the benefits for them to be considered true outdoor recreational environments.

The benefits gained through outdoor natural settings can be documented by personal experience and by scientific research studies. Benefits span the distance of providing for cultural unity, community cohesion, and sustainability efforts, although the most profound benefit is how the environment affects *us*. The tactile sensations from the various textures and patterns found in nature inspire experiences and memories through *touch*. Learning through touch is one of the basic building blocks of human development; a large amount of physical information passes through the material to support cognitive function, memory, and language for-

---

BOX 11.1 PARKS AND DEVELOPMENTAL SKILLS

Elements of a park, playground, or schoolyard that promote necessary developmental skills in children include:

- Multiple spaces for diverse activities, such as team sports, solitary play, socializing, daydreaming, and playing with the raw materials of nature.

- A variation in levels, surface materials, seating options, foliage, artwork, colors, textures, and sources of shade.

- Spaces that promote adventure, inspire mystery, and support intrigue.

- Places children can use to create their own environments (i.e., building a fort).

- Items and areas that support different levels of difficulty yet still support attainable goals.

- Covered seating areas with tables to support socializing or quiet play activities.

- Regardless of the size of the playground or schoolyard, there should be at least one shade tree surrounded by a patch of grass to facilitate access to nature.

- Other important design considerations are the cultural, geographical, and socioeconomic aspects of a community (Dierkx, 2003).

Source: Project for Safe Space

---

mation (Pimenidis, 2009). Designers must therefore strive to provide **multisensory experiences** throughout their outdoor recreational projects. With this goal, designers will ultimately provide all users, on a very fundamental level, all that they need to activate *interest* and *stimulation*.

Sensory stimuli include taste, smell, sight, sound, and touch. The design of a space for human activity should include all five, with the addition to mental and motor stimulation. Consideration should be given to the diversity of experiences related to sounds; for example, trees with wind blowing through leaves and branches. A variety of sounds can be added to the design, such as water trickling over stones in a stream or splashing in a fountain. Offering opportunities for the interplay with light adds yet another dimension—visual stimulation. Because of the different patterns and textures associated with foliage, an assortment of shadows can be cast throughout the day. Likewise, sculptures, bridges, and other forms of art provide visual cues or motivation to explore; therefore, they should be peppered throughout the project.

Other suggestions to aid in sensory development and entertainment within parks include the provision for an array of mental and motor activities that include: contemplation, adventure seeking (such as a rock climbing), and suitable areas for sporting activities (tennis, lawn bowling, swimming). Designers are encouraged to utilize a variety of ground coverings such as grass, sand, woodchips, paving materials, and stones. Varying the heights, shapes, textures, and colors of seating and walls encourages interest and curiosity. Plants and trees of differing sizes and shapes can be used to encourage exploration and a variety of sensory experiences (Herrington, 1997).

When planning outdoor play areas, designers should involve the primary stakeholders: children, parents, caregivers, and teachers (Herrington, 1997). Although their input is important, stakeholders must first be educated about the affects of design on child development so that they can make well-informed decisions. Traditional playgrounds for children based on *adult* ideas and notions of what *should* be fun have been shown to promote social hierarchies based on *physical abilities* as opposed to intellectual and creative abilities (Malone & Tranter, 2003). To garner the best advice and ideas for the project, children should be consulted and included in the process from the beginning.

Playgrounds

A large part of a child's development depends on the condition and physical attributes of his/her environment (Lindholm, 1995). In many Western societies, outdoor recreation spaces and parks are the primary environments where children learn and develop skills such as balance, coordination, and self-confidence. Unfortunately, many of these environments contain only fixed play structures (e.g., swings, jungle gyms, slides) and green expanses. Not only is this insufficient, but research suggests that these types of playgrounds promote and establish social hierarchies based on physical prowess (i.e., gang turf wars; Ulrich, 1984), and may actually foster bullying behaviors. In contrast, schoolyards, playgrounds, and community parks that include many natural features and vegetation encourage the development of social hierarchies based on communication and creativity (hide and seek), thereby leading to greater academic performance (group projects; Malone & Tranter, 2003). This is not to say that fixed playground equipment should be eliminated; on the contrary, it should be improved upon so that it facilitates both physical and cognitive development (see Box 11.1, "Parks and Developmental Skills").

The years from age 2 to 5 according to Piaget are characterized by an increase in representational thought, particularly as a young person engages in pretend play and language acquisition. Some call for the inclusion of dramatic play areas within the playground, such as the incorporation of a pirate ship complete with various equipment into which the young children can climb or crawl (Figures 11.4a and b).

[**Figure 11.4a**] (*left*) Structured play areas include equipment and games that offer visual cues, rules, instructions, or adults who direct the activities or set parameters for the children on "how best to play." (This play ship may not inspire children to use/play with it in any different way other than to pretend to be sailing). © Kerry Dunstone / Alamy

[**Figure 11.4b**] (*below*) Unstructured play areas include natural elements that children can explore using their imagination and innate curiosity to develop an activity for themselves. © Hengleim and Steets/Media Bakery

Outdoor Amenities

Ideally the recreational attributes of an outdoor space for supporting the growth of children should include play equipment and an uncultivated natural area (to provide shade and opportunities to explore nature and to promote creativity and inventiveness) as well as hardened surfaces intermixed with other types of natural spaces to facilitate a variety of activities (Lindholm, 1995). For example, trees, grasses, edible plants, and nontoxic flowers afford a variety of subtle stimulation to each of the senses and are proven to promote restorative effects on people of all ages. Natural habitats such as ponds where children can witness frog eggs hatch into polliwogs that then transform weeks later into frogs provide an invaluable educational experience. Other benefits from natural areas include a distinct array of sensory stimulation derived from different interpretations of light and shadow and a diverse array of scents. Children can also benefit from more structured play areas that include fields of thick grass for various organized sports, colorful structures to be climbed on and explored, and covered structures such as open-air pavilions for shade

and shelter, or tree houses that enable children to see over large expanses and vistas (Johnson & Hurley, 2002). These different areas can be connected through pathways made of sand or wood chips to facilitate the total use of the play space (Herrington, 1997). It is important to note that separating the playground equipment reduces the total surface area of concrete or other material, thereby reducing costs as well as heat gain absorbed by the play area (Figures 11.5a and b).

To ensure optimal safety, recreational spaces should incorporate ideas related to space planning, safety technologies (fencing and rubber matting), and the inclusion of natural elements to serve as protective barriers. Landscaping features that provide shade or serve as a low, natural barrier are one such example. Because many features found within recreational spaces have important developmental capabilities, consider the use of contrasting color to draw attention to those items that might pose a threat to others. For example, low-level balance beams are excellent for developing skills related to balance and coordination, but they are easy to trip over for an adult. Painting the beam a contrasting

color from the ground cover will make it highly visible, and surrounding it with an "island" of loosely packed fill material (e.g., wood chips, mulch, sand) will help cushion most falls (see Figure 11.6). To maximize year-round uses, designers might develop favorable microclimates throughout the environment through the use of strategic site planning. A structure on the site, for example, can be positioned to block prevailing winds in colder climates.

In today's Western society, increased urbanization and suburban sprawl have led to the disappearance of many natural environments, which has led to a dramatic reduction in the number of complex and stimulating environments. This, along with a combination of social and economic pressures faced by both public and governmental agencies, has led to compromises in the amount, location, and maintenance of many public parks and playgrounds throughout the United States. Recently, however, joint-use agreements between public schools and municipal recreation departments are working to provide shared access to the fields and playgrounds (after school hours), thereby allowing for an income opportunity for the school districts and increasing outdoor activity space for the city's residents. The benefits of outdoor recreational space cannot be overstated, and the challenges designers face in accommodating all the activities and user groups must not be understated.

[**Figure 11.5a**] (*opposite*) For playgrounds to have an optimum influence on a young person's development it must stimulate all of the senses in new and exciting ways each time the young person uses the equipment. © Dale O'Dell / Alamy

[**Figure 11.5b**] Unfortunately, the fear of irresponsible lawsuits has lead to sterile and often uninspiring playgrounds that yield very little by way of sensory development or creative play. © ICP-UK / Alamy

Formal Recreation

Adults, old and young, gain from outdoor recreational environments through physical activity as well as the psychological and emotional therapeutic qualities stemming from natural settings and opportunities for socialization (Gies, 2006). On the other hand, the teen population requires regular physical activity, preferably in outdoor spaces to ward off the consequences of *inactivity*, which include type 2 diabetes, hypertension, and heart disease (Babey, Hastert, & Brown, 2007). The UCLA Center for Health Policy Research defines regular physical activity as, "performing at least 20 minutes of vigorous activity on three or more days of a week" (Babey et al., 2007).

Adults and teens may enjoy a fitness course around the perimeter of the park, complete with different exercise stations to improve strength and flexibility. There should also be large open green spaces where team sports or rough-and-tumble play, such as wrestling, dancing, and rolling around can be performed. The space allowed for physical

[**Figure 11.6**] Whenever low-lying playground equipment is used it can become a trip hazard. To help reduce the risk of accidental injury it is best to use a contrasting color that will make the item more visible. © Getty Images/Burazin

[**Figure 11.7a**] (*above*) Introducing challenging activities such as chess and backgammon into a playground environment allows opportunities for children and adults alike to exercise their mind as well as body. The social aspect and accessibility of the game cannot be overlooked because it allows for equality among the players and the spectators; also, the game does not discriminate based on physical ability. © Gale S. Hanratty / Alamy

[**Figure 11.7b**] (*left*) Structured park exercises aid in the fight against adult obesity and stress while unstructured open spaces allow for park visitors control over their environment to choose their activity. © Richard Levine / Alamy

activities should also be balanced with places for *mental* prowess such as ceramic-tiled chess or backgammon tables (Figures 11.7a and b).

Another aspect of parks to be considered is the ample provision for shaded areas. This is because children (Black, Grise, Heitmeyer, & Readdick, 2001) and older adults are vulnerable to the negative effects of overexposure to ultraviolet (UV) rays and their body's ability to protect itself from heat exhaustion. Skin cancer and eye damage are linked to high UV radiation levels, and children are most vulnerable to the negative effects of UV rays (Black et al, 2001) because their skin and eyes are more sensitive. As such, all parks, playgrounds, and schoolyards should include large canopy trees or shade structures for refuge from the hot summer sun and water fountains to re-hydrate.

PLAYGROUNDS AND SCHOOLYARDS

The most desirable types of playgrounds include designed play equipment areas as well as natural or "undesigned" areas. Gardens and informal play spaces not only help children to understand the world and connect with nature, but these spaces also cultivate creativity (Cobb, 1977) and self-confidence that will stay with the child long into adulthood. These outdoor places allow for unstructured play, also known as *free play*. Unstructured play emphasizes symbolic thought, inventiveness, and problem solving.

The play is initiated and engaged in by the children and is driven by their own creativity and not that of a teacher or parent. Undesigned (or unplanned) play spaces inspire creative use of existing materials found within nature such as sand, twigs, stones, leaves, and feathers. According to recent research, the inclusion of undesigned spaces helps to facilitate imaginative play and allows for children to practice their social skills (Johnson & Hurley, 2002). Thus, landscape design should include the use of trees, shrubbery, and flowering plants, all of which can produce edible fruits or berries. Designated spaces might also host gardening activities or include fruit trees or herbs, referred to as **edible spaces** (see Figure 11.8).

SUSTAINABILITY CONNECTION 11.1

Edible spaces (Lang, 2005) are particularly beneficial in schoolyards because they can serve the dual function of providing creative exploration or a snack, as well as an opportunity to teach a variety of subjects including horticulture, basic biology, life cycle, and entomology, just to name a few. In some spaces designers might want to consider not doing anything and leaving the space natural. This is not to say that designed playgrounds should be avoided; quite the contrary. Research shows that advanced social, cognitive, and motor skills necessary for successful maturation can be supported by carefully designed play areas (Legendre, 1999).

Because of limited budgets, playgrounds and schoolyards often fall into disrepair. There is often insufficient healthy foliage in or around the playgrounds, which not only hinders the air quality but also the developmental benefits that children gain from these environments. These play areas can be dangerous for young children because they are frequently neglected and limit adult or parental surveillance. This trend is taking its toll on our children by negatively impacting childhood development (Johnson & Hurley, 2002) with substandard climbing equipment positioned on hard surfaces such as concrete or packed dirt, not to mention all too often becoming the meeting grounds for less-than-reputable people.

Safety thus becomes a concern, and researchers stress the importance of creating environments that minimize the potential for children falling or running into things (Schwebel, Binder, & Plumert, 2002). A child who falls just 3 to 5 inches onto concrete or asphalt can sustain a 210 g-force impact, which is enough to cause a fatal injury (Ramsey & Preston, 1990). Surface mats made of safety-tested rubber or rubber-like materials may be utilized as long as its use is kept to a minimum. Such mats usually come in dark colors, and dark surfaces absorb the sun's ultraviolet (UV) rays, thereby increasing the ambient temperature, potential for heat-related illnesses, and probability of sunburn. Some of these mats produce the same effects as asphalt. In a study by the National Toxicology Program (NTP), asphalt has been shown to *out-gas* the deadly carcinogens benzo[a]pyrene and ethylbenzene, which cause tumors and cancer in humans (Surveillance, Evaluation and Research, 2007). Careful consideration must therefore be given to the placement of asphalt and petroleum-based rubber products in outdoor play spaces. To alleviate this concern, designers should use natural products in play areas such as sand, ground-cover plants (thyme strata, and so on) and allow those spaces to be as naturalistic as possible so they offer a stimulating setting complete with playground equipment and opportunities for socializing.

SUSTAINABILITY CONNECTION 11.2

Leaving areas of the landscape (park, playground, and schoolyard) in their natural state not only educates the community about the environment in which they live, but also allows for the biosphere to prosper without the introduction of invasive nonnative plant species. Nonnative plant species upset the balance of an ecosystem, from soil composition (Ehrenfeld, Kourtev, & Huang, 2001) to degrading habitats for native animals and transmitting foreign diseases. Ecotoxicology studies the toxins and stressors on an ecosystem from the standpoint of all organisms, and recent findings have shown that some native populations do not have a resistance to the foreign diseases introduced by nonnative plant species (Sakai et al., 2001).

Benefits of Play

Many playgrounds and schoolyards provide opportunities for children to build or play by eliciting change in the environment—such as planting areas, building blocks, and small movable apparatuses—all encourage physical and cognitive development, as well as provide sensory stimulation

[**Figure 11.8**] Nature provides a wealth of sensory stimulation and should be incorporated into play spaces in both planned and natural ways to encourage sensory exploration and develop sensory oriented experiences. Public farms are one means to provide these opportunities while helping to bring about a sense of community. © Ambient Images Inc. / Alamy

[**Figure 11.9**] Many early childhood educators believe that bright contrasting colors such as the ones shown here are not good for child development. However the reconfigurable nature of this kind of play equipment will allow for the development of creativity and gross motor skills while providing diverse interactions between the children and the environment. © PhotoStock-Israel / Alamy

and entertainment (see Figure 11.9). As such, activities should provide diverse interactions between the children and the environment. Current research into participatory play and cognitively stimulating activities show that varied and engaging environments help children to develop emotional connections (Johnson & Hurley, 2002) as well as positive behaviors. Also, children prefer the look and feel of natural environments, and tend to engage in more vigorous play (Fjørtoft, 2004) and cooperative problem-solving behaviors (Malone & Tranter, 2003).

The complexity of the playground environment should reflect the developmental abilities of the children using it (Read, Sugawara, & Brandt, 1999) and should foster and promote physical, cognitive, and social skills (Project for Public Spaces, 2005). Improving playgrounds to better suit the needs of children can help their physical and social development while promoting diverse, safe outdoor play and teaching activities. Included in these areas should be unique equipment (see Box 11.2, "Unique Playground Equipment"; Malone & Tranter, 2003) that fosters problem-solving, cause and effect, geospatial problems, and explanations.

CULTURAL CONNECTION 11.1

When designing parks, playgrounds, and schoolyards, consider the inclusion of the various user groups by age, physical ability, culture, gender, and multisensory stimulation because these settings also serve as social spaces. These environments should reflect the ways in which people behave in group settings and offer places conducive for people of all proximity ranges. To illustrate, women often like to be closer when speaking to one another than do men, and Latinos often stand in closer proximity when conversing with a stranger than do their Northern European counterparts. A variety of spaces will be required to serve as informal spaces for imagination and free-play, semi-formal spaces for venders or performers, and formal venues for celebrations or concerts.

BOX 11.2   UNIQUE PLAYGROUND EQUIPMENT

This simple playground drum set is a fun way for children to develop in all these areas:

- Language: By "pounding out" syllables to the words of a song

- Analytical: By reproducing patterns in sounds, tone, tempo, and movement

- Physical science: By describing and feeling the properties of acoustics

- Social: By playing with others and collaborating skills to make music together

- Motor: By using both gross and fine motor and sensory skills

- Art: By developing an appreciation of music

[**Box Figure 11.2**] Unique playground equipment—boys playing calypso drums. © Eric Fowke / Alamy

TEEN CENTERS

As young people enter preadolescence and adolescence, green spaces can be just as valuable as they are for younger children. When children leave elementary school for junior high, they transition from activities and events intended to develop motor skills to activities and events intended to refine cognitive skills; however, excessive concentration, prolonged exposure to cognitive activities. and heightened use of one or more of the senses can lead to mental fatigue. This reduction in concentration abilities is called **directed attention fatigue**. To restore children's attention capacities, they will need access to outdoor natural settings where they can engage in activities that require *undirected* attention (Kaplan & Kaplan, 1989). These natural environments allow for attention restoration because the child does not have to focus on any one stimulus, but rather can enjoy the varied natural stimuli without conscious thought.

Teenagers are a unique population because they undergo dramatic physical, cognitive, and social developmental changes concurrently and within a relatively short period of time. This often leads to emotional confusion and internal conflict, which can be resolved through the formation of peer bonds. Sadly, most public spaces incorporate design measures intended to *detour* teenagers from gathering in those spaces (Owens, 2002). It is, therefore, important for designers and policymakers to allocate and develop spaces that promote healthy social interaction among teenagers. Positive social relationships support the formation of self-identity and self-esteem and promote the transition from teenager into adult (Owens, 2002). An interesting study by the Carnegie Council on Adolescent Development found that on average, teens reported having 14 hours per week unaccounted for—especially older youth (16–19). The annual breakdown of hours per activity according to the study was as follows:

- 3,232 hours for sleeping
- 1,660 hours for productive (school, studying and jobs)
- 1,922 hours for maintenance with supervision/structured
- 1,922 hours for maintenance *without* supervision/unstructured

Thus, the question might be, "where were they and what were these young adults doing?" In 2006, the U.S. Census Bureau projected that teens and adults will spend nearly 3,518 hours "watching television, surfing the Internet, reading daily newspapers, and listening to personal music devices." Within 14 years, American teens went from having a good deal of unaccounted time on their hands to spending the accumulation of nearly 5 months time indoors being entertained—mostly alone.

When developing teen spaces, designers must take into consideration the multitude of activities that teens enjoy, their many modes of communicating, and their desire for diversity. Young girls, for example, tend to prefer quiet comfortable spaces where they can relax and share thoughts and feelings with one another (James, 2001). Boys, on the other hand, tend to communicate with each other more while engaged in activities. Hence, spaces for boys need to provide a variety of options that range from soft living-room type environments to areas that support activities such as pool tables, ping-pong tables, and air hockey tables. Another important environmental component and provision that teens seek out are places where they can participate together and/or just watch from the sidelines.

One venue that lends itself nicely to a teen center project is the ever-increasing vacant malls and shopping centers (Anderson, Burns, & Reid, 2003). Some estimates state that over 300 malls have closed since the mid-1990s (Greene, 2001), and their overall popularity is declining. Rather than letting these large facilities close, municipalities might consider leasing and converting them into safe recreational places for teens. These spaces could then be a centralized location where teens could engage in recreational activities. In addition, the center could offer tutoring services, research library, a free clinic, art studio, and other such amenities germane to teenagers. As a unique population, teens require areas of socialization, recreation, and a *cause* or community involvement unique to them. Designers have an opportunity to coalesce recreation and community service into one space for a dynamic population that is being underutilized and underserved in many communities.

CULTURAL CONNECTION 11.2

The not-quite-child, not-quite-adult is a position in life sometimes full of uncertainty and angst. The teen who straddles two cultures can have additional difficulties that need to be considered by the designers of any young adult environment. A phenomena exists within the teen psyche; reflect on these scenarios: the smart kid who lives in a poor neighborhood, the successful Black kid who is told he/she is acting "White," the new-to-America kid who begins to reject his/her cultural heritage—all these teens will likely experience an identity crisis that they will have to navigate in addition to the unique conditions experienced by all teens. Economic, academic, racial, citizenship, gender, and sexual orientation status are all cultural identifiers in the world of teenagers. Many bicultural teens assimilate into the dominant culture much quicker than their parents who are often strongly tied to their native cultures (Smokowski, Buchanan, & Bacallao. 2009).

Designers can add symbolic cues throughout the building to send the message of inclusion and ownership, a sense that everyone is welcome and *belongs*. Visual symbolic cues include culturally appropriate colors, artwork, and space planning. The design and materials of the center should not be outwardly pretentious or showy, so that teens from lower economies feel that they do not fit in or are unworthy of participating. Getting design feedback and ideas from the teens themselves is the best way to know if the project is *culturally* going in the right direction for the teens and the community.

Spaces for teenagers need a wide variety of activities, including a music room with soundproofing and a media room for television or movies. Larger spaces can be adapted by segmenting according to activities, such as a sitting area for talking, a game area with a pool table, ping-pong or air-hockey tables, and perhaps a "gaming" corner for video and computer games (see Figure 11.10).

An important component of a teen center is surveillance. Because the media and music rooms require the lighting and sound quality to support the "experience," these rooms could also promote inappropriate behaviors related to substance abuse, sexual activity, or vandalism; therefore, for the safety of the teens, maintain total visual access throughout the common areas and install security cameras and one-way reflective glass throughout the facility.

Teenagers are known to read and study while listening to music or watching a movie or doing all three simultaneously; therefore, room lighting can be supplemented with the strategic placement of several dimmable nonglare task lights. Although recreation and safety are key components of a teen center, the "whole" teen must be served; therefore, spaces should be conducive to:

- *Health.* Gardens, counselor and nurse offices, and exercise equipment
- *Wealth.* Skills training, resume help, or job boards
- *Academic endeavors.* Computer labs, a research library, and literacy classrooms
- *Social interaction.* Talking spaces, playing spaces, and relaxing spaces
- *Artistic endeavors.* Studios, tools to create things, indoor and outdoor spaces
- *Productive endeavors.* A kitchen, lockers for ongoing projects, easily maintained spaces
- *Neighborhood stewartship.* Meeting rooms, central city location
- *Multisensory experiences.* Recreational environments create a diversity that supports improved cognitive function and development of memories and learning
- *Sensory stimuli.* Taste, smell, sight, hearing and touch; the design of a space for human occupation should include all five with the addition of mental and motor stimulation
- *Parks, playgrounds, schoolyards, and teen centers.* Physical activities, mental stimulation, and opportunities for socialization
- *Edible spaces.* Herbs, plants, and fruit-bearing bushes and trees for nutrition, biodiversity, stewardship, and education

[**Figure 11.10**] Teen centers need to be designed and developed to host a wide variety of activities. Segmentation of larger spaces according to behavioral zones can help provide delineation between different activities. © Jeff Greenberg/Alamy

SCHOOLS AND THE COMMUNITY

More and more people recognize that schools are an important component of all communities and should be designed to fit the individual neighborhoods in which they are to serve. Within schools there are often auditorium spaces, dance and performance rooms, gymnasiums, laboratories, and classrooms. These diverse arrays of spaces allow for the school to be used for various community activities, such as community theater, adult and student sporting events, community and town hall meetings, and dances.

In many communities, schools also serve as centers for adult learning. To be perceived as *a part of a community*, the building's design should use features that are prevalent to the immediate area; for example, if the predominate construction type in the area is brick, a school should respect and adhere to that material. The purpose here is to reinforce the identity of the school as one with the neighborhood, friendly, "home-like," and consistent with the material culture of the area and people. Home-like characteristics might include creating smaller spaces for more intimate grouping of students, adding more outside seating areas, providing friendly and welcoming entry sequences, incorporating residential type sloping roofs, and including operable windows.

A school environment should be developed for optimal growth and development because it represents a system of complex relationships among the physical structure (size and arrangement of a room), a teacher, and a student (Martin, 2002; Rivlin, Leanne, & Rothenberg, 1976). The physical aspects of a learning environment can have a direct influence on learning, behavior, and productivity (McAfee, 1987). The ideal learning environment contains appropriate and comfortable furnishings, provides a variety of tools for learning, facilitates individual learning styles, and contains design features that are interesting and novel (Maxwell, 2003). Also included in the physical environment are ambient features such as color, noise, lighting, temperature, textures, and odors. These ambient features tend to influence mood, emotion, behavior, interaction, and learning (McAndrew, 1993).

A significant part of student and community development depends on the physical environment (Lindholm, 1995). Schools, therefore need to support development by providing a variety of stimuli, accommodating many activities, and providing opportunities for privacy. Young people, in particular, receive enormous amounts of complicated information on a regular basis within the educational environment. How they interpret and aggregate that information will affect their learning and subsequent behaviors (Gibson, 1996). Researchers confirm that the design of physical environments will affect a young person's perception, learning, and behavior (Read et al., 1999). Experts have also found that early development of motor, cognitive, and social skills can be supported by the design of play spaces (Legendre, 1999). Understanding which characteristics of the physical environment affect a young person's behavior will help designers create more developmentally appropriate environments (Read et al., 1999).

The design of schools should begin with the site selection, scope of the project, and community integration (see Figure 11.11).

Some of the considerations when developing the site include the location of moving cars as well as parked vehicles, the building's location, and the availability of

[**Figure 11.11**] Schools and communities function best when the school is at the center of a community and serves the community in multiple and integrative ways. © David R. Frazier Photolibrary, Inc. / Alamy

natural elements (see Figure 11.12). Smaller children, particularly those in preschools, kindergartens, or elementary schools, lack sufficient appreciation for the dangers associated with automobiles. Likewise, because of a young person's diminutive stature, drivers of automobiles may not see a child who has wandered into the roadway until it is too late. Designers have the ability to help prevent these kinds of accidents through the use of barriers. The most obvious barriers are walls and fences, but landscape design can serve as a more effective barrier. For example, drawing upon the idea of surrounding the castles of ancient times with a moat of water or a manmade brook could be constructed with gated walking bridges as a means to separate areas of human activity from automobile traffic. By using this type of barrier we can incorporate another element (water) into the design while retaining visual access and building aesthetics.

It is true that the populations utilizing our schools and community centers are growing. Prekindergarten enrollment through the eighth grade, for example, increased from 29.9 million in the fall 1990 to 34.1 million in the fall of 2002. Likewise, high school enrollment has increased from 11.3 million in 1990 to 14.1 million in 2002, and it is anticipated that the population within U.S. schools will continue to increase well into the next decade (U.S. Department of Education, National Center for Education Statistics, 2005). With greater population come larger facilities, and many current public high schools already resemble the size and complexity of some college campuses.

One consideration for the design of schools and recreation centers is the interconnectivity between buildings. In the Sun Belt states, many elementary and high schools are arranged on campus by dispersing multiple buildings around a core plaza. In the northern states where inclement

[**Figure 11.12**] School sites should be designed similar to parks in that the exterior environment should provide passive learning opportunities as well as ample means to promote attention restoration. © Skyscan Photography / Alamy

weather is a factor, elementary and high schools are often contained within one or two large buildings with limited dedicated outdoor spaces. Throughout the country generally, all schools are structured according to student age ranges. Students are divided by age and grade level and then clustered according to grade because of the discrepancy between physical and emotional development. Consider a third grader (7–9 years old) compared to a sixth grader (11–13 years old): Not only is there a substantial discrepancy between physical height and coordination, but there are also considerable differences in the young person's emotional capacity and social skills. Schools and recreations centers, therefore, are often arranged so that first and second graders, third and fourth, and fifth and sixth graders are clustered into similar parts of a building or campus. Likewise, similar clustering occurs at the junior and high school levels.

Practical Applications for Designers

Use these resources, activities, and discussion questions to help you identify, synthesize, and retain this chapter's core information. These tools are designed to complement the resources you'll find in this book's companion Study Guide.

SUMMING IT UP

Community parks, playgrounds, and schools are the reflection of the larger community. A common shared element is that outdoor green spaces, parks, and schools are *public* spaces, which means that they are open to anyone. Children spend a majority of their time at home; therefore, outdoor activities are crucial to developing a balance between interior and exterior worlds. Teens and adults gain from outdoor recreational environments through physical activity as well as the psychological and emotional therapeutic qualities stemming from natural settings and opportunities for socialization

Outdoor spaces for physical activities should also be balanced with places for mental prowess, such as ceramic tiled chess or backgammon tables. Teenagers are a unique population because they undergo dramatic physical, cognitive, and social developmental changes concurrently and within a relatively short period of time. As a unique population, teens require areas of socialization, recreation, and a *cause* or community involvement unique to them.

With a greater population come larger facilities, and many schools already resemble the size and complexity of some college campuses. Thus, the designer of schools must regard the interconnectivity between buildings as opportunities to use those transitions to incorporate outdoor or greenhouse type spaces based on the local climate as well as a way in which to segment age and grade groups.

You can also refer to this textbook's companion Study Guide for a comprehensive list of Summary Points.

EXPERT SPOTLIGHT 11.1

Environmental Psychology's Contribution to Urbanism

Joongsub Kim, Ph.D., RA, AIA, AICP,
Lawrence Technological University

In recent decades, a number of new urban paradigms have emerged in response to suburbanization and urban ailments. New urbanism, smart growth, landscape urbanism, and critical regionalism are among the most popular urbanisms (Garde, 2008; Larice & Macdonald, 2007). Proponents of some of these urbanisms have claimed that their urbanism is more effective than others in addressing contemporary urban problems (Kelbaugh & Krankel McCullough, 2008; Krieger & Saunders, 2009). However, literature that assesses the effectiveness of these urbanisms is scant. Environmental psychology can contribute to the urbanisms in many areas, and one of these is community (Churchman, 2002; Kim, 2009a). Scholars have speculated that a critical trend running through the various urban ailments is the decline of sense of community in suburban and urban developments (Kim & Kaplan, 2004). Although literature generally identifies two types of community (a community of place and a community of interest; Nasar & Julian, 1995), these contemporary urbanisms have focused on a community of place such as a neighborhood.

Some of these urbanisms have enjoyed some success in addressing lack of sense of community and other community concerns; however, perspectives of environmental psychology, particularly on privacy, social interaction, density, environmental perception, and spatial cognition, can give us rich insights into understanding residential environment. Studies suggest that some residents prefer suburban developments for the level of privacy that is afforded, whereas others favor new urbanist developments to seek opportunities for social interaction (Kim, 2007). However, lessons from environmental psychology suggest that residents desire both privacy and social interaction in their neighborhoods (Lawrence, 2002). Whereas the literature somewhat remains unsettled on whether or not new urbanist developments foster a sense of community, scholars have reported that high-density housing, various open spaces, and a pedestrian-friendly environment, among other things in new urbanist developments, are likely to promote social interaction among residents (Talen, 2005). Others have speculated that cookie-cutter houses, cul-de-sacs, curvilinear streets, lack of intersections, and the like, which are ubiquitous symbols of suburban development, undermine people's spatial cognition ability in the community. Yet rigorous empirical evidences to support such claims or alternative development models that facilitate effective wayfinding or spatial cognition seem difficult to find.

Although proponents of some of the urbanisms have claimed that their urbanisms promote sustainability in community development, they have arguably neglected underserved communities (Kim, 2009b). Despite the fact that disenfranchised communities have challenging environmental problems in their own backyards, they have not received much attention, even though a sustainable development movement is sweeping the world (Parr, 2009). Studies report that polluted sites are often found in or near the poor urban communities. Some residents in such neighborhoods get so used to pollution that they no longer feel the danger of it; that is, they become apathetic, which is the phenomenon sometimes known as environmental numbness (Gifford, 2002). Environmental psychology offers tools such as environmental assessments to address environmental justice, environmental numbness, or other environmental concerns faced by disadvantaged communities (Gifford, 2002).

Today we face more threats especially in dense urban areas. Catastrophic natural or man-made disasters, a sick city phenomenon, and a shrinking city syndrome are among the new challenges (Moor & Rowland, 2006). The shrinking city phenomenon, a challenge to many major cities around the world, has recently received much attention (Oswalt, 2005). Shrinking populations, the decline of manufacturing, and the vacant land crisis are among the phenomena of shrinking city. Landscape urbanism (Waldheim, 2006), smart growth, and a number of other emerging urbanisms have begun to address that phenomenon. These urbanisms advocate development of green infrastructure, preservation, adaptive reuse, and sustainable strategies to address a shrinking city syndrome (Ritchie & Thomas, 2009). Although the benefits of nature have been extensively documented in the environmental psychology literature, recent attention to urban agriculture and other cutting edge responses to the shrinking city syndrome would require more empirical studies based in environmental psychology. That is among the next steps for environmental psychologists.

References

Churchman, A. (2002). Environmental psychology and urban planning: Where can the twain meet? In R. Bechtel & A. Churchman, (Eds.), *Handbook of environmental psychology* (pp. 191–200). New York: John Wiley.

Garde, A. (2008). Innovations in urban design and urban form: The making of paradigms and the implications for public policy. *Journal of Planning Education and Research, 28*(1), 61–72.

Gifford, R. (2002). *Environmental psychology: Principles and practice.* Colville, WA: Optimal Books.

Kelbaugh, D., & Krankel McCullough, K. (Eds.). (2008). *Writing urbanism: A design reader.* New York: Routledge.

Kim, J. (2007). Perceiving and valuing sense of community in a New Urbanist development: A case study of Kentlands. *Journal of Urban Design, 12*(2), 203–230.

Kim, J. (2009a). Urban design as a catalyst for advancing architectural education. *ARCC (Architectural Research Centers Consortium) Journal, 6*(1), 38–48.

Kim, J. (2009b). *Contemporary urbanisms and their roles in sustainable urban revitalization.* The Proceedings of the International Conference on Green Tech., Eco Life and Sustainable Architecture for Cities of Tomorrow 2009 (pp. 209–222). Korea Institute of Ecological Architecture and Environment & Yonsei University, Seoul, Korea.

Kim, J., & Kaplan, R. (2004). Physical and psychological factors in sense of community: New Urbanist Kentlands and nearby Orchard Village. *Environment & Behavior, 36*(3), 313–340.

Krieger, A., & Saunders, W. S. (Eds.). (2009). *Urban design.* Minneapolis, MN: University of Minnesota Press.

Larice, M., & Macdonald, E. (2007). *The urban design reader.* New York: Routledge

Lawrence, R. (2002). Healthy residential environments. In R. Bechtel & A. Churchman, (Eds.), *Handbook of environmental psychology* (pp. 394–412). New York: John Wiley.

Moor, M., & Rowland, J. (2006). *Urban design futures.* New York: Routledge.

Nasar, J. L., & Julian, D. A. (1995). The psychological sense of community in the neighborhood. *Journal of American Planning Association, 61*, 178-184.

Oswalt, P. (Ed.). (2005). *Shrinking cities.* Ostfildern-Ruit [Germany]: Hatje Cantz; New York : D.A.P. (Distributed Art Publishers).

Parr, A. (2009). *Hijacking sustainability.* Cambridge, MA: MIT Press.

Ritchie, A., & Thomas, R. (Eds.). (2009). *Sustainable urban design: An environmental approach.* New York: Taylor & Francis.

Talen, E. (2005). *New urbanism and American planning: The conflict of cultures.* New York: Routledge.

Waldheim, C. (Ed.). (2006). *The landscape urbanism reader.* New York: Princeton Architectural Press.

KEY TERMS

- **directed attention fatigue**
- **edible spaces**
- **multisensory experiences**
- **parks**
- **sensory stimuli**
- **unstructured play**

DeadMalls.com, on vacant malls of America and the cultural impact on their communities (www.deadmalls.com)

Dull Olson Weekes Architects, on the mixed-use, sustainable, community-oriented Rosa Parks School (www.dowa.com)

National Environmental Education Week (www.eeweek.org)

National Park Service (www.nature.nps.gov/biology)

Plants for a Future (www.pfaf.org)

Play England, on the importance of childhood development through *free play* (www.playengland.org.uk)

Thousand Oaks Teen Center (www.thousandoaksteencenter.com)

The Trust for Public Land (www.tpl.org)

DISCUSSION QUESTIONS

1. Explain how cognitive development can be facilitated throughout environmental design.

2. Based on research findings, why is it so important to integrate more indoor and outdoor natural spaces, and how do these spaces impact children?

3. What should designers strive to provide throughout their outdoor recreational projects?

4. Describe the needs of an adult and teen recreational area, and describe the benefits of outdoor spaces for adults of all ages, and teens.

5. How can improving playgrounds to better suit the needs of children benefit their development, and what should be included in the design?

STUDIO ACTIVITY 11.1

Childcare

Design Problem Statement
Develop a facility that would only be used during the late spring, summer, and early fall.

Issues: In an economy that requires both parents to work outside of the home, more and more families require childcare services. Children have special needs pertaining to environmental stimuli, and they need access to natural features within the environment.

Directions
Be sure to follow these parameters:

- Develop an interior environment with only three walls and a roof. The interior environment must look as if it were completely enclosed; this is not a shed or covered patio. It is an interior space.

- Be sure to include all amenities that would be included within an interior play space.

- The open wall should allow the children free access to a natural landscape.

- Within this landscape should be recreational opportunities.

- The landscaping and recreational opportunities must blend with each other so that the scene appears natural and not man-made. For example, if you include a pool, it might take on an irregular shape (like a pond) or the decking might be a brown cool deck that wraps around trees and shrubbery so that the deck blends into the natural environment.

Deliverable
Presentation board.

STUDIO ACTIVITY 11.2

A Place for Teenagers

Design Problem Statement
With parents spending more time at work, many teens are left to fend for themselves. Likewise, the places for teens to hang out continue to decline. Conversely, many indoor and strip malls have been abandoned leaving vacant spaces.

Directions
Adapt one of these dead buildings into a membership-type "village" for teens. This means that memberships can be revoked for illegal activities or acts of violence. As you redevelop this space, you must consider:

- Safety from weapons and bullying

- Different developmental stages 13–19

- Prevention of illegal activity including drug and alcohol use

Deliverable
Presentation board

LEARNING ACTIVITIES

1. Discuss two possible scenarios, one in which there is a large housing complex with little to no outside gathering space or park and another that incorporates green spaces within the living quarters and has a shared community park. Evaluate how the people of each community would cognitively respond to the lack of green open space versus having a space in which to be active and interact with others.

2. Evaluate a child at play. Go with a friend or family member who has children to the park and observe the child at play. The next day, go back to visit your friend or family member and again observe the child at play inside his/her home. Take note of your observations, and describe the differences between the child's interactions in both environments.

3. Design an ideal natural-setting community park for your neighborhood. Describe the benefits the community would be able to enjoy and how it would improve the community's cognitive development.

4. Compare two different playgrounds for children in your neighborhood. Describe the environments of both, including the positive and negative descriptions of the design. Explain what you think should be changed and/or added to the design to update the environment to optimal cognitive developmental standards.

5. Research an empty shopping mall in your city. Redesign the mall as a teen center. What amenities would you include, and what services would be provided to attract the teen population?

12 Learning and Education

According to this conception, the sole function of education was to open the way to thinking and knowing, and the school, as the outstanding organ for the people's education, must serve that end exclusively.

—Albert Einstein

There is an interactive relationship between humans and the environment (Kyttä, 2003; Wachs, 1989). When developing learning or educational environments, it behooves a designer to understand the different developmental stages of youth along with the fundamental purposes of different environments that promote learning and education. This can be a complex endeavor because young people are clustered into averages based upon age. Most young people around the same age progress through developmental stages at different rates. As such, it is important to note that the term "average" is highly subjective. Still, with thoughtful, groundbreaking, and inventive designs, professionals can help young people develop to their fullest potential.

Of the different environments occupied by youth, many will remain stationary as a young person progresses through each of the developmental stages. For example, a preschool will remain a preschool for many years until it is either converted into something else or is torn down. But the preschool child will continue to develop and progress to the elementary school, junior high, and high school levels. Other types of stationary environments accommodate a wide range of ages and developmental stages. These include children's hospitals, pediatricians' waiting rooms, and various recreational venues. The challenge for the designer in these types of environments is to help the young person feel safe and secure without offending the older child's sense of developmental accomplishments.

Arguably, some experts contend that environments should be developed in accordance to the unique developmental stage of each individual rather than a single standard. This means that, for example, restrooms should be equipped with varying size commodes in order to accommodate the different heights of young persons as they grow from toddlers to preadolescents to adulthood.

Others argue that unless every aspect of all environments (homes, schools, recreation centers, etc.) provides the same accommodations throughout, the designers would be doing a disservice to the users. One environment that is less stationary and should evolve with the young person's development is the individual's home.

For young users of the built environment, the discrepancy between their physical and mental abilities can pose significant issues, such as the appearance of a facility being viewed as imposing or unwelcoming, which can lead to undesirable behaviors such as aggression, hyperactivity, or boredom (White, 2004). Consider the school-age individual who cannot see what the instructor is doing on a counter because the counter top is too high. Because the young person's line of vision is obstructed, he/she cannot participate in the class and is, therefore, likely to seek out other forms of entertainment until the lesson is complete. Likewise, because young people view the world from their smaller stature and limited perspective, studies have shown that facilities that appear massive or give off an "institutional" image inspire discomfort whereas smaller structures and those resembling residential homes tend to be perceived as being more welcoming (White, 2004), thereby encouraging exploration and growth. The unique stature of a young person along with his/her rudimentary skills of decoding environmental stimuli combine to create a distinctive response and reaction to the way in which the environment is perceived.

BRAIN DEVELOPMENT AND LEARNING

Giving credence to Piaget's ideas of child development, neuroscience research has since proved:

- 25 percent of the brain is developed at birth and 90 percent is developed by age three.
- Experiences gained throughout ones' youth will affect the structure and performance of the brain.
- The brain's resilience enables young people to effectively cope with most negative experiences.
- The brain continually forms new neural connections (also called *neural plasticity*).
- Experiences obtained throughout life will continue to shape the brain's structure and function (Healy, 2004).

What this means is that despite notions of *individualism*, from a much larger perspective, all humans are fundamentally the same. It is the environmental conditions, both socially and physically, and through direct and indirect experiences that combine to promote cognitive development and the interpretation of sensation, which then influences our worldviews and perspectives. This assertion is further supported by neuroscience research, which contends that as infants mature, the earliest form of memory is **object memory**. Object memory means that infants will remember specific objects previously encountered. **Event memory** is the second developmental stage, in which infants gain the ability to remember specific events. The third memory stage is **contextual memory**; this form of memory merges objects and events together to create a larger framework that works during memory recall. It is this stage of memory that enables the young person to develop cues for the recall of prior events and activities. What is amazing is that these three developmental stages are thought to occur all during the first year of life. The contextual memory, which is the stage that dominates much of young person's early memory, is eventually replaced with source memories that enable the young person to separate inherent feelings from those conscious feelings that are influenced by particular events and activities. Therefore, a young person in persistent and prolonged contact with various sensations within different environments will shape the way he/she understands and relates to the environment as an adult.

Modes of Learning

The primary purpose of a learning environment is to support the acquisition of new skills through three modes: visual, auditory, and kinesthetic.

- **Visual learners** process information from what they see and think in terms of pictures.
- **Auditory learners** process information from what they hear; they listen carefully and reason through discussion.
- **Kinesthetic learners** process information by experiencing, doing, and touching. They are more inclined to try things out and manipulate them.

Most people learn through all three modes to a certain degree; however, each person has a preferred mode that he/she uses more than the other two. Approximately 35 percent of the population learns visually, 25 percent are auditory learners, and the remaining 40 percent learn kinesthetically (Ngee Ann Polytechnic, 2001). By understanding how people learn, designers can customize environments to optimize the particular learning process (see Table 12.1).

The first learning environment that young people will be exposed to is their nursery or bedroom. It is important to understand that young people develop extremely fast during their first years of life, and it is very important to provide the individual with ample and appropriate tools to help facilitate that development (see Table 12.2).

[Table 12.1] Design Strategies Based on Modes of Learning

Learning Activity	Modality	Implication for Design
Reading and hearing words	Auditory	Use semicircular seating arrangements, and include features that facilitate small group discussions such as alcoves or niches. Ensure noise control from distracting exterior noises, but include sound system for low background music without words.
Looking at pictures or watching a demonstration, movie, or exhibit	Visual	Ensure noise control from distracting exterior noises with proper classroom acoustics. Provide multimedia, posters, paintings, and drawings of significance and visual penetration. Use natural daylight, as fluorescent lights are distracting. Refrain from using drab wall colors.
Participation in a discussion	Kinesthetic	Provide alternative flexible seating: extra floor padding in a "group" area, window seats, rocking chairs, or wide steps to a small stage in the classroom.
Replicating a real thing	Mixed	Provide open laboratory space and large flat work surfaces for model-making and experimental learning opportunities to facilitate students' need to move around.

Adapted from: Haroun and Royce, 2004, and Cuyamaca College Faculty Handbook at http://www.cuyamaca.edu/eops/DSPS/dspsresources.asp

[Table 12.2] Basic Design Considerations for Developmental Stages

Age	Visual Acuity	Design Initiative	Possible Objects
One month	High contrast	Black and white	Panda bears or door/window molding
Four months	Object separation	Shapes floating in space	Mobiles or ceiling articulation
Five months	Figure ground	Patterns	Wall paper or carpeting pattern

CHILD CARE CENTERS AND PRESCHOOLS

Infants become mobile at around 12 months, at which time they enter the toddler stage of development. Most will spend the majority of the day at home, in school, or in day care centers (Lang, 1996). In the 1950s, 1960s, and into the 1970s, one parent would often remain at home to care for the child; however, by 1998 as many as 59 percent of mothers with children younger than 3 years, and 60 percent of mothers with children ages 1 to 5 re-entered the workforce (Maxwell, 1996). Current estimates suggest that 48 percent of children ages 5 or younger whose mothers are employed

outside the home receive care in either a family-based or center setting (U.S. Bureau of the Census, 2001). Day care and preschool settings can be found in private residences, workplaces, campuses, community parks, and recreation centers such as YMCAs, JCCs, and religious organizations throughout the United States. Settings vary significantly according to financial resources, as do size and social density. In many lower-income communities, inadequate public resources for day care centers and schools have resulted in increasingly crowded classrooms (Capizzano, Adams, & Sonen-Stein, 2000), especially in communities where parents cannot afford private care.

[**Figure 12.1**] Children can be quite content under a box or in a tent made from blankets. These provisions help children to create their own separate spaces. © Michael Hitoshi / Getty Images

The behaviors and emotional well-being of toddlers are influenced by their social and physical environments. Their interaction with peers in day care centers helps them develop their sociocognitive skills, but when such interaction is too demanding, it becomes stressful (Maxwell, 1996). Crowding in these settings can have many negative implications for a child's emotional, psychological, and cognitive development (Maxwell, 1996), which can manifest as increased aggression, lower task performance, poor memory, anxious feelings, physiological responses related to high blood pressure, ulcers, and nervous habits (such as nail biting, hair pulling, skin picking, and other symptoms of stress).

The combination of crowded day care and residential settings has been shown to increase a child's propensity for behavior problems (Legendre, 2003). A well-designed day care setting is divided according to homogenous age groups and has at least five square meters or 16.4 feet of play space (not total floor space) per child (Maxwell, 1996). Facilities that operate at these density levels have fewer incidences of negative behaviors resulting from crowding and stress. Lower social density levels in day care and school settings may provide the additional benefit of easing the effects of crowding at home (Maxwell, 1996) because the detrimental effects of crowding carry over from one environment to the other. Day care and preschool settings should contain safe, small spaces in which children can seclude themselves if they require it. Children value such intimate environments because they fulfill needs for both privacy and exploration (Capizzano et al., 2000). Several studies have shown that children's psychological development can be affected by how much control they have over their environments. They will often take the initiative to explore their surroundings and engage in more social interaction when they feel they have some control. Portable private spaces within open-plan

settings enable young persons to self-regulate their privacy needs, thus giving them more control over their emotions and environments.

Open play areas within preschools and child care settings allow caregivers to maintain supervision no matter how close or far away from the child (Boschetti, 1987). Open spaces, however, are not conducive to educational activities related to counting or reading; therefore, designers should incorporate a variety of smaller spaces within open environments (Legendre, 1995). These smaller spaces do not require fixed walls; for example, children can be quite content under a box or in a tent (Figure 12.1). Spaces can also be separated visually by lowered or differentiated ceiling heights and contrasting wall colors and textures.

Other ideas include the use paint, fabric, or netting on walls and ceilings to help differentiate spaces (Friedmann & Thompson, 1995). These methods help to facilitate cooperative behavior in young person; however, using both wall and ceiling strategies within a single space may be overwhelming to the child and thus defeat the designer's purpose (Legendre, 1999). When a child feels overwhelmed he or she tends to become less cooperative and withdrawn (Read, Sugawara, & Brandt, 1999). If designers implement the size-reducing and segmenting method of ceiling and wall treatments, they will want to reduce any color contrast as a way to help avoid sensory overload. Overall, interior surfaces should appear warm, soft, and friendly; and they should be easy to clean, nonabrasive, nontoxic, nonflammable, and nonhazardous (Olds, 2001). Also, because of associations created through media, designers will want to exercise caution when using materials such as metal, concrete, chain link, and other materials commonly associated with institutions. This is because young people may perceive the facility negatively, which could inspire fear and anxiety.

In practice, the Montessori schools have, with great success, long predicated their curriculum on the importance of ordered environments for optimal learning styles (Rathunde, 2001).

For young children, cognitive development and the formation of memories is strongly dependent on the people and physical spaces that immediately surround them, which is why a quality preschool can enhance and support the overall development of a young person as early as age 3 (Kirp, 2004). The design of preschools and child care settings throughout the past few decades relied heavily upon the predictable stages of development. The dominating paradigm on development has been based on Jean Piaget's universal stage theories of cognitive development. Despite Piaget's notions that all young people proceed through developmental stages at approximately the same times, designers still have a great deal of latitude when designing environments for youngsters.

Another way to ensure uniqueness in the design of a preschool or child care facility is to incorporate the components found within the **Kaplan and Kaplan Preference Model**, a theoretical framework used to organize environmental preferences according to four elements:

- Coherence (making sense)
- Legibility (the promise of making sense)
- Complexity (involvement)
- Mystery (the promise of involvement; Kaplan & Kaplan, 1982a)

When utilizing these elements, keep in mind that the environment must remain diverse and flexible, easy to maintain, and perhaps most importantly inspire feelings of safety and friendliness.

The Facility

The first image of a day care or preschool will be the exterior of the building. As such it is paramount that designers make these buildings as welcoming and exciting as possible. Methods used to accomplish this include the use of bright colors incorporated into the building's accessories (awnings, window treatments, and signage), the creative use of landscaping (see Figures 12.2a and b), and playful caricatures incorporated into the sidewalks and entryways. Children often find these features reassuring, and they provide visual cues for orientation (Read, 2003).

Children often perceive the world larger than adults do, and, as such, something appearing large can be foreboding to a child. When children are first exposed to preschools or day care environments they often are experiencing feelings of apprehension and separation anxiety from their parents for the first time. Facilities with large and imposing entries such as over-sized doors, tall columns, and huge foyers can intensify these feelings and cause the young person to feel overwhelmed. It is, therefore, best to design child care centers and preschools to be smaller in scale (see Figures 12.3a and b).

Designers will also want to use shorter walkways and find creative ways to break up long corridors. With long walkways, the designer can employ methods of segmentation into the design through the incorporation of small nodes with interesting features as well as varying the materials. Other techniques used for creating an illusion that a building is smaller than it actually is are to use fewer but larger residential-style windows, along with planting larger

[**Figures 12.2a and b**] Designed in similar colors and patterns, this (*left*) tree could be perceived by a child as something from the book Dr. Seuss's *The Cat in the Hat*, whereas the (*above*) lion could be representative of Aslan, the protective lion in C. S. Lewis's book *The Lion, the Witch, and the Wardrobe*. a: © mediasculp / Getty images; b: © Steven Widoff / Alamy

[**Figures 12.3a and b**] The image on the left shows two over-sized doors, which can appear ominous to a small child. Compare this image with the image above. In this figure, the door has been effectively "removed" by incorporating it with a wall of glass. The visual access created by this large transparent door helps to reduce stress among smaller children. a (*left*): © Getty Images/Greg Dale; b (*right*): ©VIEW Pictures Ltd/Alamy

[**Figure 12.4**] Children often require unique features to serve as landmarks. The features in this figure provide fun points of reference. Similar design concepts can be applied to child care facilities and preschools. Children will feel more comfortable and safe within such an environment because they will "know where they are." © John Eik III/ Alamy

trees and bushes adjacent to the building. By *visually* breaking up the building's facade with these simple techniques it can be seen only in segments, therefore reducing the perceived size of the building.

To reduce the perception of size within the building's interior, consider lowering the ceiling heights and using sculptures, wall murals, and pictures along the walls, or nodes that might contain interesting objects or seating to segment long hallways and thus reduce the perception of distance. Also, the interior spaces should incorporate the use of bright and differentiated colors to help parents and young people find their way around the facility (Read, 2003), as well as one central area containing a readily identifiable landmark, such as a significantly different lobby area with a large statue or a distinctive feature (see Figure 12.4). This area will help parents and children to find, easily recognize, and orient themselves; however, this space should not only serve as a landmark, but it should also visually and symbolically reinforce that the school will be a safe and fun place to learn and play.

The entranceways and thresholds into the classroom setting should be similar in scale to those found in residential environments; and as such, designers should avoid the use of large institutional-type doors. Instead, the goal for classroom entranceways and thresholds should be a design that appears familiar, friendly, and inviting. This is because young people need reassurance that the activities within the room will be safe, fun, and within the boundaries of their confidence level. Hence, the entranceway and threshold can provide the young person with a glimpse of the activities that occur within the room. For example, the doors to each of the classrooms could be different shapes (arched, squared, and/or rounded corners) and colors. Likewise, the thresholds could be set within a mural depicting popular characters engaging in activities that the young person will encounter while in the room

Classrooms

When planning the classrooms or recreational areas for children, consider the incorporation of viewing rooms so that the child can maintain visual contact with his/her caregiver from multiple locations. This will help the child to feel more secure in the environment, thereby promoting greater exploration (Legendre, 1995). Without this visual connection, the child may feel at risk thereby causing him/her to withdraw, become anxious or bored, and/or engage in undesirable behaviors (White, 2006). This viewing room should be on the same elevation as the class or recreational room and allow for visual access for both the caregiver and the young person.

Within classrooms young people need ample opportunities to experience a variety of stimuli that include soft environments that are responsive to touch, such as beanbags, stuffed couches, carpeting, sand, dirt, furry animals, sling swings, clay, paint, and water. These kinds of attributes tend to promote comfort and help to relieve stress (Jones & Prescott, 1978). Also, there should be numerous display spaces for items such as plants, fish, and birds. The presence of life, other than human, will help the young person to reflect on the *aliveness* of an environment that is much more convincing than a few over-sized stuffed toys (Olds, 2001; see Figures 12.5a and b). Finally, designers will want to create rooms that accommodate a logical organization of common classroom items in order to enhance a young person's understanding of that space. To illustrate this point, consider the description given by a 4-year old with regard to his environment (Nash, 1981):

> Over here we make lots of things, and here, we find things out. This is where we pretend, and build, and be as grown up as anything. And this is a nice quiet place where the puzzles and books are—you can't ride a trike or play balls or bring sand in here. This is a good place to be (p. 155).

For designers planning the spaces of preschools and child care facilities, careful consideration must be given to the purpose and location of the different spaces used within the classroom or found throughout the facility. For example, most preschools and child care facilities contain areas for play, crafts, naps, and snacks. Hence, when space planning, consider locating the places where food is consumed far from sleeping areas; this will minimize disruptions during naptime (Maxwell & Evans, 2000). In most layouts, the ideal location for rest areas is on the northern side of the building where it tends to be darker and cooler. Designers should also consider the use of darker or muted colors in areas where calmer activities are to be conducted. More specifically, the colors black, purple, blue, and deep yellow attract the least amount of attention when used as a background color and thus tend to have a calming effect (Camgöz, Yener, & Güvenç, 2004). The use of a subdued color palette, sound-controlled environment and a darker and cooler room will help to reduce stimulation levels within the space and help the child to relax (Figure 12.6).

For space planning purposes, activities involving high energy should be placed on the southern side of the building where it tends to be brighter and warmer. High energy space should utilize brighter colors (Mahnke 1996; Moore, 1987; Olds, 2001) because they can help invigorate the child as well as attract attention (Camgöz et al., 2004). Bright color combinations can include cyan on a red or yellow background, or red or magenta on a cyan background.

[**Figures 12.5a and b**] The addition of small animals in classroom settings supports responsibility and encourages pro-social feelings through caregiving experiences with the animals. a: © Picture Partners / Alamy: b: © Steve Skjold / Alamy

However, it's important to remember that this attraction leads to greater stimulation, thereby inspiring greater activity (see Figure 12.7).

SCHOOLS

Schools are where young people spend most of their time from preschool, kindergarten, elementary, and to high school. Many young people in the United States begin preschool as early as one year old and remain there through age 4. At age 5, most children in Western countries are required to attend kindergarten, and then progress one grade per year until they are about 17 or 18, at which time they are expected to graduate from high school.

Much of contemporary school design and education practices within the United States are based on design and education reform concepts that marked the culturally creative period of Germany's Weimar Republic (1919–1933); however, much of the original intent and scope has been lost over time (Read et al., 1999). According to these reforms, buildings were to be limited to one or two stories in order to improve air circulation and increase natural light, thereby promoting

health (Wu & Ng, 2003). The Weimar design philosophy viewed design as a collaborative extension of the community, such as the Bauhaus school developed through collaboration among professionals of various specialties (Henderson, 1997). These professionals studied the effect of environmental factors such as natural lighting and air circulation on a young person's ability to learn.

During most of the early twentieth century, school buildings were designed to admit as much fresh air and direct sunlight as possible (Read et al., 1999). Unfortunately, by the 1970s, many of these reform principles had been lost, due in part to a decade-long energy crisis, which resulted in attempts to reduce building heating and cooling costs. Windowless classrooms became the norm, as windows were perceived to be sources of excess heat loss and distraction (Henderson, 1997). This, in conjunction with larger facilities, especially in secondary schools, all but eradicated natural light and fresh air circulating within classrooms. Today's trend in school design has moved toward *consolidation*: larger, more centralized schools that accommodate more students. This trend is driven primarily by costs; with only one structure, money that would have been spent on main-

[**Figure 12.6**] The goal for designing sleeping areas is to minimize disruptions and distractions during naptime, such as excessive light, sounds, colors, or toys. © Ingram Publishing / Alamy

[**Figure 12.7**] Areas of high energy stimulate and attract children to move, explore, and learn by "doing." This image shows a play space that highlights different areas through the use of bright colors and varying levels of attention. © Corbis Flint / Alamy

taining several buildings can be reallocated to education. As a result, the student populations of many urban middle and high schools rival those of some larger universities; however, some studies indicate that what is saved in financial resources is lost in social development (Yamamoto & Ishii, 1995) and transportation costs.

FACILITY DESIGN

There are several considerations when designing a building that affects *learning*. For example, when and where sunlight enters a building can effect visual perception, acuity, and thermal conditions. Room conditions depend upon the global location, the time of year, quality of insulation, and east/west orientation, and the amount of heat gain; sunlight entering into a classroom can raise the ambient temperature about five to ten degrees. Likewise, noise can be a source of student distraction, which will impair learning outcomes (Guski, 1999); and scent can be either distracting when the scent is repugnant or soothing when it is pleasing. Designers of schools therefore need to consider these and many other variables when developing the program for a successful school design. For example, while including natural light is important, designers will want to avoid incorporating openings that allow direct sunlight into the building because glare can effect visual perception (Dubois, 2003). Designers may want to consider placing science labs and computer labs on the north side of buildings where illumination can be controlled while reducing the risk of excess heat gain. The south side of a building can then be reserved for endeavors requiring greater visual activity such as reading or eating.

Circulation

Hallways and corridors can double as active learning spaces. Meandering pathways increase opportunities for positive social interaction and create gentle transitions between spaces. Turns and bends can also be configured to create unique areas for studying and a brief getaway for students. The facility's interior circulation will need to conform to local safety codes, and Universal Design and ADA Accessibility guidelines; but it should also provide unique and interesting activity nodes that promote social contact. Beware of long corridors, which are a costly percentage of a school building. Within these corridors, consider diversifying the levels of illumination along with the incorporation of seating and bookshelves. These materials will help to add a lighter dimension to a space that is often stark and unimpressive. Also, these areas might be designed to highlight various student works as well as to contain a variety of indoor foliage and play structures; however, caution should be exercised not to create niches conducive to acts of bullying. Design components could include flaring out walls to minimize niche depth or increasing visibility with cut-outs (windows) within the side walls. Consider incorporating windows that open along the length of the corridor so that they can be opened during good weather thereby establishing contact with the outdoors.

Reducing visual boundaries through the creation of partially open/partially closed space with adjacent, smaller, enclosed spaces (Lackney, 2001) helps to prevent behavioral problems in schools. These open spaces along with a greater number of windows allow for "passive surveillance" (teachers can supervise their students in a less intrusive or overt manner), which increases the sense of community and reduces the frequency of negative behaviors.

Flexibility of Use

Spaces such as an auditorium or gymnasium that may be used or rented by the community should have a separate and aesthetically pleasing entry. These entries should be appropriately designed to meet the expectations of a patron who might want to enjoy a theater performance or watch a sporting event without having to walk through the school. These separate entries might contain a small lobby area with informal seating, public restrooms, and display of various awards and trophies. The idea behind this is to allow for auditoriums and gymnasiums to serve the school by day, and by night become a recreation destination where adults are comfortable enjoying a performance or sporting event.

Though it may be counterintuitive, the location of the buildings on the site should be placed in the least noteworthy (in topographic terms) locations (Olds, 2001). This will allow the more interesting parts of the site to be preserved or reserved for landscaped pathways, planned play spaces, and unplanned natural areas where students and visitors can experience nature.

Student Ownership

A *sense of place* and *place attachment* are goals that many school boards and administrators strive to inspire in the student body because they are predominantly associated with profound feelings and a deep emotional connection to a certain physical locality. Schools can better solidify this affiliation by creating associations through the stimulation of one or more of the senses. One way to do this is to incorporate designs that allow for the permanent display of student artwork (Killeen, Evans, & Danko, 2003), graduating class photos, and accomplishments. Young children and adolescents who are allowed to participate in the personalization of their spaces are more likely to develop a sense of ownership and thus become more active in the learning process (Killeen et al., 2003). This participation might take

the form of liberally dispersed display cases throughout the facility. Some of these display cases might feature student artwork; others might display a collage depicting various scenes in a theatrical production; and still others might display trophies won by the school's sports, academic, or drama teams.

Encouraging students to develop ownership, territoriality, and school pride can help prevent negative behaviors such as bullying, which is a significant problem in most schools. Incorporating the students and their works into the school's décor also increases a student 's sense of ownership (Osterberg, Davis, & Danielson, 1995). In addition to display cases, a school's hallways should showcase student academic accomplishments. Another idea might be the placement of small concrete slabs bearing different students' names and accomplishments within walkways that lead to entries (resembling the Hollywood Walk of Fame). This demonstrates the school 's pride in its students and encourages students to develop a sense of ownership in the learning process and the development of their learning environment (Sommer & Olsen, 1990).

Incorporating school achievements into the facility must be done with forethought simply because display spaces are finite and thousands of students may progress through a school during its lifetime. Hence, developing a hierarchy of accomplishments and their display must be carefully considered. For example if a student wins a national spelling competition he/she can get a name plate in "Concrete Square" in the school's walk of fame. If a sports team wins a regional championship, they get their trophies placed in a display case located in another prominent area. The student who wins the top prize at a local science fair can get his/her award placed in a display case located in the science wing, and an actor who was featured in the local newspaper can get that photo and article hung in the auditorium foyer.

For many, a sense of place is deeply tied to cultural identity and is expressed in art, literature, music, or history shared by the memories of an individual or group.

Wayfinding

Wayfinding comprises navigational techniques such as signage and architectural and spatial cues that orient people and help them travel from place to place confidently. As populations continue to grow, many educational campuses are also growing in size. This means that elementary, high school, and college campuses are very large, thereby creating wayfinding difficulties when maneuvering through large buildings or grounds (Erin & Koenig, 1997). Large, well-designed facilities and complexes accommodate the various ways humans cognitively interpret an environment. Whether a campus is made up of several buildings or a single large structure, designers should proactively implement optimum wayfinding strategies.

The ability to navigate through an educational campus depends upon a person's experience within an environment; new students will naturally experience greater feelings of confusion and vulnerability. However, all students can have difficulties reaching various destinations quickly and efficiently unless good wayfinding measures are built into the design (Henderson, 1997). Wayfinding increases in importance as campuses increase in size and student population. Minimizing spatial complexity and varying the size, form, color, or architectural style of buildings enhance wayfinding (Abu-Ghazzeh, 1996). Educational campuses can become more "legible" and facilitate human circulation when a variety of visual cues, including color (Read, 2003), are used as identifiers.

In a row of buildings, for example, each could be painted a different color or simply have a different accent stripe. Key areas within building groupings on large campuses should be named, and the signage for each unit or group should be painted a different color. Another example for the interior spaces is the use of tile mosaics or wall lettering indicating the predominate use of a given area (i.e., "Freshman Class," or "Science Wing"). It is also useful to incorporate wayfinding cues in the floors and sidewalks because many students walk with their eyes directed down at the floor. Wayfinding of this type can be as simple as a restroom symbol embedded into the walkway near the restroom's entry, arrows in the direction of exits, or icons to depict the student's current location ("you are here" map). The signs or symbols should be in a contrasting color and/or with a differently textured surface. Research shows that the use of color along with other landmark features such as sculptured walls; murals; and pathways with an array of imprinted patterns, metal inlays, or tile mosaics incorporated into the pathway help to facilitate better wayfinding (Read, 2003; Figure 12.8).

Wayfinding maps that combine pictorial representations of architecturally diverse buildings with diagrams, name lists, and color keys will accommodate people who rely on either *scenographic* iconography or *abstract representations,* which are understood codes consisting of letters or numbers. People who prefer pictures will quickly discern visual differences in architectural style, and people who prefer maps will be able to pinpoint named areas or structures easily. Color coding supports wayfinding for both types of people but is often useless for the 10 percent of the male population who are colorblind.

Many educational facilities are composed of several buildings, which means that gardens and courtyards might be used to link spaces throughout the campus. For example, one area might be a fruit tree orchard, another might be a sculpture garden, and still another could be a rose garden. When including these gardens and courtyards into the site plan, however, take measures to ensure that they are not only accessible from the building but that there are also options for shelter against the elements of nature. In areas with inclement weather patterns, walkways can be shortened and covered by exaggerated eaves, transparent roofs, or trellises covered with vines. These measures will enable students to experience the changes in nature, while offering protection against wind, rain, and snow. It should be noted, however, that courtyards do not have to encompass large areas; instead they can be a series of small niches such as an arboretum with a small reflection pool with turtles or fish.

CLASSROOM DESIGN

The physical structure of the learning environment includes the arrangement of space, furniture, and materials used in it (McAndrew, 1993). The physical structure also includes the size, shape, and scale of the actual classrooms. In most circumstances, larger more spacious rooms are more flexible and accommodate more uses; however, smaller classrooms allow for more class participation and group discussion. Research shows that rectangular-shaped rooms afford more interactive visibility, L-shaped rooms or rooms that have alcoves better accommodate privacy needs, and rooms that have movable wall partitions within the classroom enable

[**Figure 12.8**] A wayfinding landmark can be a three-dimensional statue or it could be a mosaic relief placed within the pathway. Because blind people rely on smell and touch to augment their inability to see, the relief also provides wayfinding information for them (much like a tactile address). © DigitalVues / Alamy

teachers to reconfigure rooms into many different shapes depending upon the tasks at hand (Lang, 1996). When designing classrooms, whenever possible, consideration must be given to the intended course to be taught in that room (i.e., science vs. music). Likewise, designers should consider the room's size and location as well as the presence and location of windows, furniture, and storage elements.

The goal for the design of individual classrooms should be the development of age-appropriate and inspiring environments that are not over- or understimulating. However, it's important to remember that young people neither understand nor respond to spatial references in the same way as adults. For example, a shiny-waxed hallway floor may indicate a place to walk for an adult; but to young people it is the perfect place to practice running, skidding, sliding, or making funny squeaky noises with their shoes. The allure of creating echoes or of making loud clattering sounds while running on a hard surface is irresistible to most children. Likewise, low pony walls indicate a division of space for an adult; but for a young person they are often seen as something to be jumped over, climbed on, or a place to practice one's balancing skills. To avoid undesirable or potentially dangerous behaviors, designers must consider the perspectives of the young person when designing classrooms (White, 2004).

The future of the learning environment is one that seems to be evolving almost as fast as the health care environment. The advent and advancement of online technologies are driving new ways to deliver information. Some of the new researchers advocate that traditional visual and auditory learning methods to be placed online so that the classroom time can be dedicated to kinesthetic learning opportunities along with analytical group discussions. With this new paradigm schools will need more "studio" or laboratory spaces from which they can explore ideas and concepts. With this kind of participatory learning, however, students will also need places where they can safely store personal equipment and projects, as well as spaces for individual, small group, and larger group activities. Some smaller learning centers might include lofts or small alcoves, whereas larger activities might take place in traditionally arranged classrooms or lecture pits.

Classroom Configuration

Young people receive a considerable amount of complicated information from their environments, all of which affect learning, behavior (Gibson, 1986), and perception (Read et al., 1999). One of the environments where young people spend a considerable amount of time is in the classroom. This is a unique environment because it must func-

tion for two types of end users. On one hand, this is a place for student's to engage in learning activities, but on the other, it's a place where an adult teacher must maintain control and authority while disseminating the course information to an ever-increasing number of students. It is the instructor's responsibility to teach the students a given subject matter and effectively convey important concepts, as well as to monitor and maintain order within the classroom. As such, classrooms that are designed to be teacher-centered are often associated with fewer disruptions, but they have been criticized for limiting student engagement and overall educational quality (McFarland, 2001). Zandvliet and Straker (2001) suggest that a classroom layout should enable instructors to freely move about, particularly in classrooms where computers are utilized. The idea is to allow maximum visual access to student work; particularly the computer screens.

Rectangular rooms are often seen as being teacher-centered, more unified, traditional, structured, and typically preferred in classrooms requiring time-structured and focused learning (Amedeo & Dyck, 2003). The advantage of a rectangular room is that the instructor can maintain greater eye contact with the students because they will be in the instructor's primary visual field. (i.e., instructors will not have to continually turn their heads from side to side as they would have to in a square or round room). Instructors experience more visual and kinetic distractions from children in large rooms with high ceilings, most likely because there is simply more space to supervise and the larger space reduces focused attention. Paradoxically, students tend to experience more kinetic (*movement*) distractions but fewer visual distractions in rooms with lower ceilings, presumably a result of focusing attention on one person at the front of the room. Overall positive classroom satisfaction is associated with greater space, ceiling height, and more square footage per person.

A ceiling that it is higher in the front of the classroom and slopes gradually toward the back will not only reduce the teacher's visual distraction but also increase the students' perceptions of the space in front of the room while decreasing their feelings of crowding. This design will also have a positive effect on ambient temperature. Instructors, who are located in the front of a room, tend to move around and be closer to electronic equipment. This often leads to an instructor feeling warmer than the students. Research has shown that classrooms made uncomfortable because of temperature, noise, or inadequate lighting can negatively affect a young person's learning comprehension (Bernardi & Kowaltowski, 2006). With a sloped ceiling more heat can rise up and away from the instructor and audio/visual equipment in the front of a room. Also, this design can help focus the instructor's voice toward the students while dispersing the instructor's exposure to the clamor associated with students fidgeting at their desks. If a rectangular room is not possible, consideration should be given to how an instructor will monitor student behavior (Amedeo & Dyck, 2003) and maximize the comfort of the students to negate disruptive behaviors.

When considering the interior design of classrooms, the design of walls and what is displayed on them will affect learning (Creekmore, 1987). The walls within a classroom should accomplish one of three functions:

1. The acquisition of new knowledge
2. The maintenance of learned knowledge
3. An announcement and celebration (i.e., a *dynamic wall*; Creekmore, 1987; Figure 12.9)

Each function should be situated in a particular location within the classroom. The acquisition wall should be located in the front of the room and contain only a chalk or white-board and cork board to display materials related to new or difficult concepts. The maintenance walls provide quick reference materials that can be easily seen; they are best located on the sidewalls so as to not be the focus of the room. Materials placed on the maintenance walls should be reserved for those items that reinforce previously learned material and provide a venue to review material that students already know: for example, maps, class outlines, additional reading lists, related articles or artifacts relative to the class. The back wall should contain examples of student work, important school notices, and seasonal/holiday decorations. The idea of using a classroom's walls in this way focuses attention on new learning materials while reinforcing materials already learned, honoring students and their work, along with holidays, events, and so on—but not allowing those distractions to be prevalent during classroom time.

Taking this system a step further, the acquisition wall should be painted in the color ranges of yellow-green, green, and cyan to attract more attention; or use red in front and blue in the background, which will also attract attention (Camgöz et al., 2004). However, keep in mind that color selection should be based on each individual classroom and be contingent upon size and average ambient temperature. This is because color is known to influence the perception of space, size, temperature, comfort, and excitement level.

User Groups

A **user group** is a defined set of individuals who will be utilizing the space for a predetermined function; for example,

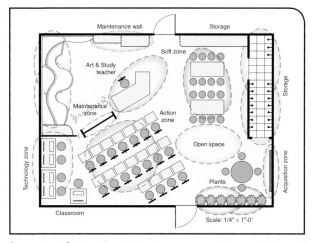

[**Figure 12.9**] The walls within a classroom should accomplish one of three functions: (1) the acquisition of new knowledge, (2) the maintenance of learned knowledge, and (3) an announcement and celebration (i.e., a *dynamic wall*). Illustration by Precision Graphics

students use a classroom to learn, teachers use a classroom to teach, and administrators use a classroom to monitor the teachers. Of all the educational settings, the primary school classroom requires the greatest diversity in terms of its physical environment with regard to the user group—students. Most are set up with the traditional row of desks facing the front of the room; some have open settings with movable partitions for separating spaces and smaller class groups; and some are soft classrooms complete with carpeting, incandescent lighting, sofas and tables (instead of desks), and potted plants. Soft classrooms have also been effective in post-secondary educational settings and in smaller courses that involve discussion and philosophical reasoning. Primary schools should be designed to enhance gross motor skills, with facilities for grades five and higher that promote concentration as well as tactile learning.

As young people mature, their ability to learn from their environments increases (Read et al., 1999). Adolescents and early teens require less stimulation and more private spaces and a sense of personal control. For example, we often encounter young teens wearing headphones and similar devices in an attempt to achieve privacy and autonomy. For this age group we should provide spaces where the adolescent can be alone or gather with small groups to express himself/herself. It is also helpful for designers of high school classrooms to consider the effects of color on behavior. For example, soft greens, pale blues, and creamy yellows have a soothing effect on people (Kopec, 2006), which is why they are often used in schools and other institutions where behavioral controls are necessary. When appropriate, consider the use of soft furnishings for classrooms intended for discussion or self-disclosure because research has shown that "soft classrooms" facilitate greater student-instructor communication and increases student classroom participation (Kopec, 2006). Horseshoe or circular seating arrangements provide many benefits, including increased student visibility, attentiveness, participation, and performance (Zandvliet & Straker, 2001). Likewise, social areas should have a variety of soft furnishings for informal or spontaneous gatherings. Some suggest that furniture layout include a variety of positions including *centripetal* (inward facing) for group work and *centrifugal* (outward facing) for individual work (Lackney, 2001).

Overall, classrooms should be designed for specific uses (e.g., science laboratories) and equipped with furnishings and other components that promote and facilitate those uses (Henderson, 1997). For example, the increasing use of technology in classrooms has far outpaced the design of workstations and furnishings (i.e., chairs that aren't adjustable and inadequate desk space for laptops) that cause distractions and discomfort—both of which are detrimental to learning (Read et al., 1999) and often uncomfortable, thereby becoming a source of fidgeting in students. Deficiencies in the physical environment can have a negative effect on students' task orientations, class cohesiveness, and feelings of autonomy. Likewise, the size of a classroom can have a direct relationship to density levels and students feeling crowded. Unfortunately, many classrooms that were already too small are becoming intolerable with the consolidation of schools and increased enrollment (McAndrew, 1993). Higher densities in classrooms result in limited spatial arrangements, more aggressive behavior, and greater demands for resources (McAndrew, 1993).

Furnishings

Classroom seating is a design component based on the considerations of comfort, safety, learning and teaching (Henderson, 1997). Furnishings and ergonomics are an important aspect of design. The poor ergonomic design of the chairs, coupled with the length of time students are expected to remain seated, can lead to lower back pain, which has become a major health concern in industrialized nations (Troussier et al., 1999). Research indicates that the types of classroom furnishings relate to the young person's health, behavior and education (Zandvliet & Straker, 2001). Researchers state that young people who sit for long periods of time accumulate stress to their back muscles, ligaments, and discs, and that the incidence of back pain correlates to increased sitting time (Knight & Noyes, 1999). Musculoskeletal fatigue and pain can cause students to focus more on easing their discomfort than on the subjects they are learning because the human brain is configured to satisfy *physiological* needs before *cognitive* needs. Students who move around in their seats are often attempting to find comfort and not paying attention to the instructor.

Furnishings should support students comfortably in their two main seated positions: leaning forward to write, read, or draw and leaning back to listen or watch (Troussier et al., 1999). School furniture should allow for natural body positions (e.g., trunk and thighs at 120° angle) (Henderson, 1997); a seat that tilts forward will help alleviate strain on the spine by increasing the trunk-thigh angle (Troussier et al., 1999). Furnishings should be moveable and scaled for students of different ages and needs (Zandvliet & Straker, 2001). Chair seat height should not exceed a student's popliteal height, which is measured from the back of the knee to the floor (Troussier et al., 1999). When integrating seating at the front and back of lecture halls and other locations for students who use wheelchairs, ensure that the seating surface is flat and out of the path of travel (Henderson, 1997). Experts recommend round tables be used in lunchrooms instead of the standard long rectangular tables because they promote more collaboration as opposed to a hierarchy. They also reduce the need for students to yell across large distances to one another.

AMBIENT CONDITIONS

The ambient conditions in a school environment are the nonvisual qualities that influence the moods and memories of people (McAndrew, 1993). These qualities include color, noise, lighting, and temperature. Color and noise, in particular, have a distinctive impact on individuals. Some of the other issues that affect the physical environment include crowding, density, and personal space. Crowding and density are closely related and often occur together: High-density situations typically promote feelings of crowding, and feelings of crowding are usually, but not always, related to high density. Perhaps the most notable effects of crowding are people demonstrating aggressive behaviors, lower task performances, poor memory, and feelings of anxiousness (McAndrew, 1993); however, during times of competition (which include the classroom environment) feelings of crowding lead to exhibiting behaviors associated with social and psychological withdrawal (McAndrew, 1993). Both crowding and density will have a direct impact on students emotionally and behaviorally (McAndrew, 1993). Students who feel crowded will be less likely to develop relationships and may not perform as well in school (Cooper et al., 1984).

Personal space zones are highly individual because they stretch and shrink depending on many factors, including culture, gender, and age. Most people will react on some level when personal space is violated (McAndrew, 1993). Research suggests that the personal space requirements of a young person increase as they get older and until they reach puberty. Females tend to use smaller personal space zones when they are interacting with familiar individuals, whereas males tend to be more sensitive and reactive to invasions of their personal space (McAndrew, 1993).

Lighting

The human need and desire for natural sunlight and for views to adjoining spaces (for orientation) requires a balance of natural and artificial sources of illumination (Lang, 1996). The lighting conditions within a classroom can affect learning and behavior, and are an important consideration when designing an educational environment (Dunn, Krimsky, Murray, & Quinn, 1985). The illumination provided by sunlight varies with the season, time of day, weather, and glazing of windows; therefore, designers must consider measures to control its entry into classrooms. Such measures may include the use of longer roof overhangs, window tinting, retractable awnings, and adjustable blinds.

Young people spend a significant portion of their day inside educational buildings, so it is important to expose them to high-quality, full-spectrum lighting as a means of enhancing their general well-being (Hathaway & Fielder, 1986), and to counter symptoms related to light deprivation (e.g., fatigue, irritability, general malaise). Researchers report that schools using full-spectrum lighting and ultraviolet enhancements (Hathaway, 1994; Lexingtron, 1989) have experienced increases in student attendance, academic achievement, and physical and cognitive growth and development. Full-spectrum lighting is also associated with a decrease in the incidences of hyperactivity (King & Marans, 1979). An early study of fifth- and sixth-grade students showed that test scores were higher for students who were taught in well-lit classrooms (Luckiesh & Moss, 1940). Likewise, students demonstrated better concentration levels in rooms with better quality and greater quantity of lighting (Horton, 1972). Therefore, we can say that the quality and quantity of lighting directly impacts a student's performance, but we must be careful to avoid glare that bounces off reflective surfaces (e.g., marker boards, computer monitors) and glare that is caused by the imbalance of light sources. The reflectivity of surface finishes, arrangement and location of light sources, and their methods for diffusion within the classroom all influence the comfort of students and instructors (Lang, 1996).

Color

The use of color within schools and other learning environments has been shown to influence students' attitudes, behaviors, and learning comprehension by affecting their level of attention and the instructors' perceptions of time (Sinofsky & Knirck, 1981). It can transform a dull and drab environment into one that is pleasing, exciting, and stimulating, which has been implicated in the reduction of absenteeism and promotion of greater school affiliation (Papadotas, 1973). In most cases, bright rooms with light colors are preferred over rooms with dark colors (McAndrew, 1993).

In addition to preferences, physiological and emotional reactions have been linked to room color, including respiratory rate and blood pressure (McAndrew, 1993), as well as the release of hormones within the brain and hypothalamus (Engelbrecht, 2003), which in turn affects mood, mental clarity, and energy levels. The transmission of light energy to the brain also affects the functioning of the cerebral cortex (where thought occurs) and the central nervous system (responsible for muscle control, eyesight, breathing, and memory; Birren, 1997). Although the use of warm colors in classroom environments appears to stimulate the optic nerve (and when combined with bright lighting, people have increases in blood pressure, heart and respiratory rates, muscle tension, and brain activity; Wohlfarth, 1986), the reverse physiological response is associated with the use of cool colors and dim lighting (Failey, Bursor, & Musemeche, 1979; Hathaway, 1988). Interestingly, white and off-white decrease human efficiency by an average of 25 percent (Birren, 1997).

Based on their own research, Frank Mahnke and Rudolf Mahnke offer the following guidelines for how to integrate color into learning environments:

- Preschool and primary school: warm, bright color scheme
- Secondary school: cool colors
- Hallways: diverse color range
- Libraries: pale or light green (Lang, 1996)

In addition to these guidelines, designers should use colors in middle range (not light or dark) for the walls and floors in order to minimize glare and brightness, and use contrast between workstations and the rest of the room to create appropriate focal points. Objects of bright light colors tend to advance and objects of dim or dark colors tend to recede (Mahnke, 1996). In classrooms designed for young people, consider using stronger colors with warm tones.

[Table 12.3] Cultural Meaning Behind the Color Red

Culture	Meaning
Celtic	Death, afterlife
China	Good luck, celebration, summoning
Native American	Success, triumph
Hebrew	Sacrifice, sin
India	Purity
South Africa	Color of mourning
Russia	Bolsheviks and communism
Latin	Excitement, danger, love, passion

Adapted from: http://webdesign.about.com/od/colorcharts/l/bl_colorculture.htm

CULTURAL CONNECTION 12.2

Other environments in a school include gymnasiums, auditoriums, and lunchrooms; designers should use warmer colors with lighter tones for each of these environments. Hallways, doors, and stairwells should be painted in a variety of colors to enhance stimulation (Pile, 1997). In cultural enclaves, however, it may behoove the designer to first research color symbolism to avoid a cultural faux pas. Studies indicate that one-fourth of the population views or perceives color differently from the general populace (Lang, 1996). This finding has important implications for designers: People's perceptions and reactions to color are linked to cultural style and often have historic and symbolic references (Lang, 1996). For example, consider the color red. Among Celtic cultures the color symbolizes death and the afterlife, whereas Chinese cultures view red as being good luck and celebration (see Table 12.3).

Acoustics and Noise

Excess noise has been shown to negatively affect the acquisition of language as well as a young person's ability to read (Maxwell & Evans, 2000). External noise typically derives from machines: cars, trucks, buses, trains, airplanes, lawn mowers, leaf blowers, and mechanical equipment. Buildings should therefore be placed well away from areas of heavy traffic, airplane flight paths, and rail lines. Designers should use heavy vegetation between the primary areas of the school and sources of noise/air pollution. Vegetation can help to absorb noise and particulate matter as well as provide an additional source of visual stimulation.

Schools must be constructed with these concerns in mind, and sound-dampening zones should be incorporated into the walls and ceilings; double- and triple-paned windows should be used along walls where noise levels are highest; and tall greenery can help to reduce external noise pollution, but will not eliminate it. Thick walls with sound insulation will prevent exterior noise transfer only if constructed properly (i.e., walls insulated only to the bottom of a suspended ceiling will not be effective; Lang, 1996). Scheduling of groundskeeping activities such as lawn mowing and tree trimming can also reduce noise; this includes prohibiting the use of leaf blowers and lawn mowers to before or after school hours.

The effects of noise in learning environments are controversial. Some researchers believe that noise causes distraction and interferes with learning, whereas others insist that becoming distracted can be traced to gender, age, and academic ability (McAndrew, 1993). The effects of noise in educational settings can range from impairment of psychomotor performance (Hambrick-Dixon, 1986), language acquisition and understanding (Maxwell & Evans, 2000), reading skills (Bronzaft, 1981; Maxwell & Evans, 2000), and, to a greater likelihood, elevated blood pressure (Evans & Lepore, 1993); however, many researchers agree that learning is compromised when students cannot hear clearly (Evans & Lepore, 1993).

The three most common sources of classroom noise are reverberation, internal noise, and external noise. Reverberation (also termed *acoustical liveliness*) occurs when sound waves rebound or reflect off of hard flat surfaces. Imagine throwing a tennis ball; it will bounce off a wall but not off a pillow. Hard surfaces reflect sound, and soft surfaces absorb or diffuse it. Reverberation reduces audio (i.e., hearing) perception because it creates extra noise, which students must filter out. To illustrate this, tennis players devote all their energy to the ball in play; but if additional balls keep coming at them, eventually there will be too many bouncing around for players to be able to focus on just one of them (Figure 12.10).

Reverberation is a product of:

- Room configuration (parallel walls)
- Surface finishes (hard or soft)
- Material density (solid or hollow)
- Air tightness (sound transfer; Lang, 1996)

Reverberation can be either enhanced or reduced by changes to room size, internal surface dimensions (walls, ceilings, floors, and windows), and surface materials (chairs, desks, flooring, wall coverings, and ceiling treatments). Angling walls at least 5 degrees out from their original parallel plane can help reduce reverberation (Lang, 1996). Flooring should be composed of soft material (e.g., cork, linoleum, or carpeting) to minimize noise caused by foot traffic, dropped objects, and the movement of chairs and tables; at the very least, designers can incorporate carpet strips into their design schemes. Carpet on floors and acoustical ceilings can also cut down on reverberation.

Within the interior spaces, sound absorbent panels should be installed throughout the building. The instillation of these panels has been shown to reduce noise levels by as much as 5 dBA (Maxwell & Evans, 2000). With the incorporation of sound-reducing measures, students not only scored higher on letter-number-word recognition, but they also scored higher on language tests and showed less vulnerability to the effects of learned helplessness (Maxwell & Evans, 2000). Lower noise levels also aid in facilitating student attention to the instructor, and reduce the amount of fidgeting.

Internal noise is harder to mitigate because much of it comes from human actions. Sources of classroom noise include dozens of voices; the movement of chairs and desks on hard floors as students fidget in their seats; the tapping of pens or pencils against desks; mechanical devices such as computers, printers, copiers, and cell phones; older lighting fixtures; and heaters or air conditioners. To compensate, place pads on the feet of chairs and tables, and affix rubber strips to desks (thick rubber absorbs sound better). Rooms where group activities are more prevalent should be designed

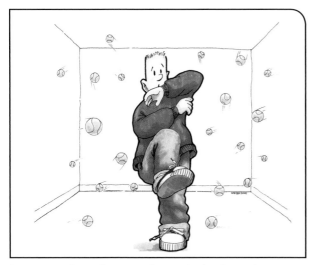

[**Figure 12.10**] Reverberation reduces audio (i.e., hearing) perception because it creates extra noise, which students must filter out. Illustration by Paul Norman Reyes

to absorb more sound (Lang, 1996). Generally speaking, lower frequencies are louder than the high frequencies.

Where necessary, designers should mask low-frequency sound with what is sometimes called white or pink noise, such as a recording of a distant ocean or a gentle rain to mask mechanical or conversational noises.

Temperature, Humidity, and Ventilation

The results of several studies show that temperature fluctuations within classrooms affect teachers more so than students. Early studies of classroom temperature found that when learning environments included air conditioning, the incidences of classroom annoyances were reduced (Lang, 1996; and attitudes, performance, and student behavior improved McDonald, 1960). One study found that at temperatures higher or lower than 72 degrees Fahrenheit, students showed decreases in memory, suggesting that the optimum temperature for learning is 72 degrees (Stuart & Curtis, 1964). When temperatures exceed 80 degrees, there is a significant decrease in students' work efficiency and productivity levels (Pilman, 2001). Likewise, human beings work most efficiently at psychomotor tasks when the environment is at a comfortable temperature (Herrington, 1952), and The New York State Commission on Ventilation found that temperatures higher than 75 degrees produced harmful effects such as increased respiration, decreased amount of physical work, and conditions conducive to the spread of disease (Canter, 1976). Designers must consider and allow for the regulation and maintenance of temperature because of its role as a contributor to the ambient environment in classroom settings.

One of the main issues with temperature is the lack of adequate ventilation and/or air movement, which interferes with the body's ability to dissipate heat. Temperature, humidity, and ventilation depend on a number of factors, including the configuration and materials in a building, amount of glazing on windows, size and volume of the space, and the number of occupants and their activity (New York State Commission on Ventilation, 1931). To ensure the comfort of occupants, flexibility in manipulating this system is extremely important, and designers should consider including independent controls for each room that are simple to operate (Lang, 1996).

OTHER EDUCATIONAL ENVIRONMENTS

Other educational environments include libraries and residential dormitories.

Libraries

To promote active participation in a building with a vast array of user groups, designers must utilize flexible features. Features that include aspects compatible for all:

- ages
- genders
- learning styles
- cultural leanings
- group sizes and dynamics
- special needs groups
- user group—staff
- user group—visitors

For example, a library could have a series of "music rooms" where students who prefer to study with music can bring a small handheld device and plug it into a sound system. Some research suggests that older children (girls in particular) find the library environment (Bagot, 2004) fascinating and restorative. Other studies find that providing both open and private areas accommodates people working on different tasks. Private spaces support people who are focusing on complex tasks, whereas open areas sustain an environment conducive for less challenging activities and group interactions (Osterberg, Davis, & Danielson, 1995; Stone, 2001).

It can be observed, however, that most students work alone in libraries; therefore, designers must consider many personality variables when developing library designs, including differences between individuals who are *screeners* and those who are *nonscreeners*. Screeners (people who can screen or block out distractions) are able to concentrate while people are moving or talking around them; therefore, an open library plan neither enhances nor impedes their learning. For nonscreeners, however, the stimulation of people walking by or sitting close by can be extremely distracting. For these individuals, small private rooms with reflective film on the interior glass would minimize both visual and audile distractions while still allowing the library staff to supervise them.

SUSTAINABILITY CONNECTION 12.1

Because nonscreeners tend to be more introverted, they will also benefit from green spaces as a means of attention restoration; therefore, the private rooms should also have windows that face green spaces. These design techniques also have sustainable benefits given that natural light reduces the constant need for artificial light and operable windows reduce the requirement for mechanical ventilation. Such rooms are ideal places for visually impaired students to listen to recorded textbooks and lectures. Research suggests that reading conducted in environments painted blue or pale green yields greater comprehension and retention than in environments painted red (DesignCouncil.org 2005; Stone, 2001).

The design features for a library include (but are not limited to) features such as a large open space with large potted plants dispersed throughout. Furthermore, sound-dampening ceiling, floor, and window treatments will minimize noise, and operable skylights will allow natural light and air into the space. All west-facing windows should have either exterior shading devices and/or tinted film to reduce direct sunlight, glare, and associated heat. Rooms of various sizes should accommodate both individual and group study. The floor should be carpeted, and the recommended color schemes should be composed of shades of blues or pale greens. The central open space should include both individual desks with privacy barriers (study carrels) and large tables for groups. Designers should be cognizant of and allow for the behaviors of human proximity. For example, studies report that men seated at a table alone will negatively view those people who take the seat *opposite* to them, whereas women negatively view those who sit *beside* or flanking them (Fisher & Byrne 1975). Round tables may work better in libraries because they reduce the consequences of proximity conflicts.

Library study areas should contain a study (task) lamp, as well as the ability to dim the light source, which allows people to control their lighting and thus their visual attention to materials (Osterberg et al., 1995). Knee space under tables and desks should also be increased from the standard 27 inches to 29 or 30 inches deep to accommodate wheelchairs (Mahnke & Mahnke, 1996).

Residential Dormitories

Residential facilities within an educational environment include day schools, boarding schools, and dormitories. By and large, the majority of students will encounter their first residential educational facility at the college level, but there are a host of residential facilities that can begin much earlier. These are commonly referred to as boarding schools. Within residential educational facilities, dormitories are of special concern for designers. Understanding the unique behaviors and emotions associated with life away from home for the transitional years of a teenager is crucial. Occupants' perceptions of room size combined with their feelings of crowdedness can affect their senses of privacy and satisfaction as well as the quality of their social interactions (Erin & Koenig, 1997). Residential crowding significantly affects psychological well-being by causing residents to withdraw from their supportive relationships with other residents (Henderson, 1997). Neither gender nor race appears to influence the relationship between crowding and psychological well-being. Age appears to be a considerable factor, such as teenage and adult men who seem to be more affected by perceptions of crowding than young boys, who are not as bothered by crowding (Kaya & Erkip, 2001). Dormitory residents frequently desire private time alone and the ability to control their personal interactions with others (Evans, Lepore, & Schroeder, 1996).

Dormitory residents who occupy the upper levels of a building report more satisfaction with their individual rooms, perceive the dormitories as less crowded, and believe they have more privacy and better views than residents of the lower levels (Henderson, 1997). All of these positive effects may be due to the absence of a neighboring building of the same height, an exceptional scene of a vast landscape or horizon viewed out their windows, combined with the reduced flow of people walking by, past, or through "their spaces."

Designers can take the following measures to reproduce these conditions toward supporting resident satisfaction. Tall greenery or trees planted between structures will limit views of adjacent buildings from upper floors and create a park-like retreat for residents at the ground level. **Green walls** or cascading planters with automatic irrigation systems can be incorporated into the design of high-rises dormitory buildings to create vistas of natural greenery for residents.

SUSTAINABILITY CONNECTION 12.2

The sustainable benefits include reducing building heat gain/loss through shading and increasing air quality through the filtration process of vegetation. Cultural or social benefits of green walls also include being a deterrent to graffiti and having the ability to absorb excessive environmental noise.

Within the building, elevators and stairs placed at entry and exit points will minimize pedestrian traffic. Designers should consider providing a common area, mail room, or informal gathering niche between the main corridor and the entry point into the dorm rooms, rather than a single-loaded corridor that leads directly to the dorm rooms (Erin & Koenig, 1997).

SAFETY AND SECURITY

There is an increasing emphasis on the design of safety and security measures for educational campuses. Most schools are conveniently accessible *public territories* that have relatively uncontrolled access by students and the community at large. This degree of accessibility has often left the campus open to theft, damage, or destruction. The safety and security principles include access-control doors, shrubs, fences, gates, and other physical elements to discourage access to an area by all but its intended users. This includes the strategic placement of windows that allow users to see or be seen ("eyes on the street theory") while monitoring the activities of strangers. A provision required for proper surveillance is adequate lighting,

transparent glass, and proper landscaping to maintain sight lines—high branches and low ground cover. Low-level shrubs should not grow over three feet in height and tall trees should be clear of branches to five feet above the ground.

Criminals prefer locations that afford them visual control (i.e., allow them to see and remain concealed; Archea, 1985), and robbers are most attracted to facilities that have large amounts of cash on hand, obstructed views, poor outdoor lighting, and easy escape routes (Athena Research Corporation 1981; Crow & Bull, 1975; Jeffery, Hunter, & Griswald, 1987). These attributes have been named in numerous studies, and experienced criminals have confirmed these environmental factors when selecting a target (Brantingham, 1997; Newman, 1972).

Ideally teacher offices should be located near or inside of their classrooms. Some experts suggest that teacher offices should be clustered together (Lackney, 2001). But given the recent tragedy of high school and college shootings, it may be more advantageous to disperse teachers' and administrators' offices throughout the facility to increase surveillance. Each of these offices should have one-way mirrors from which the teacher can see out, but people cannot see in. Should a shooting occur, the teacher or administrator would then be able to:

- Detect the occurrence much quicker
- Notify the police undetected
- Lock the door, thereby increasing the chances of survival

Administrative offices, however, should be visible from all public areas of the school and not on the periphery of the school or hidden from view. Moving the instructors' lunch areas closer to the students' cafeterias (Crawford, 2002) also helps to maintain surveillance. In these changing times, however, designers will need to be acutely aware of a multitude of defensible space measures that can be utilized to protect students, teachers, and the community.

The theoretical concept of **territory development** states that after a certain amount of time, the members of a perceived "community" will band together to protect or defend their area and the resources on it from others that they view as not "belonging." Attributes that will help to establish this bond include sidewalks, plenty of street lights, and attractive landscaping elements that establish the boundaries and denote a school or specific building's *territory*. Such attributes also increase the desire or motivation for the members to stroll, circulate, or otherwise populate the property at all hours. The cultural, social, and architectural aspects of the campus should work in unison to convey the message of a safe and secure environment to all of the members and residents of the campus community.

Practical Applications for Designers

Use these resources, activities, and discussion questions to help you identify, synthesize, and retain this chapter's core information. These tools are designed to complement the resources you'll find in this book's companion Study Guide.

SUMMING IT UP

stages of youth along with the fundamental purposes of different environments that promote learning and education. The primary purpose of a learning environment is to support the acquisition of new skills through three modes: visual, auditory, and kinesthetic.

A school should embody the character of the area's neighborhood and natural terrain as a means of fostering a sense of place. Many educational facilities are comprised of several buildings, which means that gardens and courtyards might be used to link spaces throughout the campus. The physical structure of an educational facility also includes the size, shape, and scale of the actual classrooms. The goal for the design of individual classrooms should be the development of age-appropriate and inspiring environments that are not over- or understimulating.

The ambient conditions in a school environment are the nonvisual qualities that influence the moods and memories of people, such as color, noise, lighting, and temperature. The lighting conditions within a classroom can affect learning and behavior, and they are important considerations when designing an educational environment. Color is known to influence the perception of space, size, temperature, comfort, and excitement level; therefore, color selection must be thoroughly researched prior to installation within a classroom setting. The effects of noise in educational settings can range from impairment of psychomotor performance, language acquisition and understanding.

Residential facilities within an educational environment include day-schools, boarding schools, and dormitories. Most schools are conveniently accessible *public territories* that have relatively uncontrolled access by students and the community at large. This degree of accessibility has often left the campus open to theft, damage, or destruction. The cultural, social, and architectural aspects of the campus should work in unison to convey the message of a safe and secure environment to all of the members and residents of the campus community.

You can also refer to this textbook's companion Study Guide for a comprehensive list of Summary Points.

EXPERT SPOTLIGHT 12.1

Interior Design of Schools: Culture and Community

Stephanie A. Clemons, Ph.D., FIDEC, FASID, Colorado State College

Many schools, at both the elementary and secondary level, are remodeling or in phases of new construction throughout the United States. Proper design of the interior spaces has elevated in importance due to research indicating that the physical qualities of the classroom, such as furniture, temperature, and lighting are all clearly linked to enhanced student learning. Uncomfortable temperatures, ergonomically incorrect furniture, poor aesthetics, and low lighting bring uneasiness to the student and a sense of helplessness. The design of learning environments can impact motivation, concentration, and performance, thereby impacting student's comfort, control, attention, access, and enjoyment. In addition, case studies reveal a trend that if the school is designed from the inside out (beginning with design of the classroom), rather than the outside in, a more efficient, healthy environment for learning will result (*Rebuild Colorado,* 2003).

Although good design of the classrooms is critical for student learning, it is important to realize that the school itself serves as focal point of its community and should, therefore, reflect its specific culture in the exterior, interior, and playground facilities. A community culture may be identified as a common thread among the majority of the residents or reflect an entire region where there are well-established, even historical, cultural communities of new immigrant populations.

Culturally sensitive school design offers benefits of beauty, an increase in student and staff identity resulting in increased comfort level, and an opportunity for teachers to engage students who have experienced neglect due to their cultural differences (Kollie, 2008). The interiors should reflect the culture of the people who create it. This should be evident in the selection of functional and pleasing furnishings, colors on the walls, daylight streaming through large windows, and entry level flooring materials that communicate executable art from the community. The exterior of the school may also reflect the culture through walls that illustrate brickwork in beautiful patterns, natural colors of the earth, the shape of the building or the orientation of doors to the outside. An attention to details should be evident in everything from the regional touches in the materials selected to the interior displays of student work (Edwards et al., 1998; Goddard, 2007).

Physical spaces offer the opportunity for expression of multiple perceptions and messages as well as a peculiar mix of styles and cultural levels. Staff, students and families bring and leave distinct traces in each school they inhabit. Today's schools should reflect the diversified cultures that make up their student and staff populations with their cultural identity clearly communicated through design— particularly in the interior spaces.

References

Brook, D. (2009). *Designing learning spaces for 21st century learners*, 1–9. Retrieved from http://center.uoregon.edu/ISTE/uploads/NECC2009/KEY_43175395/Brook_DesigningLearning SpacesforContemporaryLearning16.6.09.pdf

Edwards, C., Gandini, L., & Forman, G. (1998). *The hundred languages of children: The Reggio Emilia approach—Advanced reflections* (2nd. ed.). Greenwich, CT: Ablex.

Goddard, T. (2007). *Learning journeys, Moving towards designs for new learning spaces: Two truths and a suggestion.* British Council for Schools Environments, London, England.

Kollie, E. (2008, March). Cultural connections. *Schooldesigner. com, 19,* 1–5.

Rebuild Colorado. (2003). A high performance design success story. Governor's Office of Energy Management.

KEY TERMS

- **auditory learners**
- **contextual memory**
- **event memory**
- **green walls**
- **Kaplan and Kaplan Preference Model**
- **kinesthetic learners**
- **object memory**
- **territory development**
- **user group**
- **visual learners**

WEB LINKS

Acoustical Surfaces, on acoustical analysis (www.acousticalsurfaces.com/acoustic_IOI/101_6.htm)

Classroom Architect software (http://classroom.4teachers.org)

DesignShare.com, for an example of a school following the Montessori philosophy (www.designshare.com/index.php/projects/montessori-school-maui/narratives)

Education Information Resource Center, Designing space for sports and arts: Design guidelines for sports and arts facilities in primary schools for dual community and school use (www.eric.ed.gov/ERICDocs/data/ericdocs2sql/content_storage_01/0000019b/80/19/cf/90.pdf)

flexDorm (http://graphics.boston.com/multimedia/2007/09/02dorm/dorm.pdf)

Herbert Schenk Elementary School courtyard project, Madison, Wisconsin (www.youtube.com/watch?v=5x7XJCBh7TY)

National Association for the Education of Young Children (NAEYC) (www.naeyc.org)

Noiseaddicts.com, on low-frequency sound (www.noiseaddicts.com/2009/03/can-you-hear-this-hearing-test)

The Lighting Research Center at Rensselaer Polytechnic Institute (www.lrc.rpi.edu)

The National Clearinghouse for Educational Facilities, on color theory (www.edfacilities.org/rl/color.cfm)

STUDIO ACTIVITY 12.1

Inner School for Fourth, Fifth, and Sixth Graders

Project Design Problem

You have been asked to design an inner school for fourth, fifth, and sixth graders. The school has a significant autistic and attention deficit hyperactivity disorder (ADHD) population. Your job is to develop a school complete with playground, classrooms, hallways, bathrooms, lunchroom, and gymnasium.

Challenge One: The location is in the inner city, and ambient noise will be a problem for children using the playground. Another issue will be security to prevent children from wandering out and in. A third concern will be the adequate provisions to support the Kaplan and Kaplan attention restoration model both inside and outside.

Challenge Two: The needs of the population constituency are at odds. Autistic children can easily need lots of stimulation to keep their attention. How can a single design accommodate both needs simultaneously?

Challenge Three: Cafeterias and gymnasiums can be loud environments because they are large open spaces that promote noise reverberation. These spaces can be overstimulating to many people, including those with ADHD. The large space also means that many different people will be moving at different times and in different ways, thereby increasing the visual stimulation. All of this stimulation will not be good for the autistic child, so how will you address this issue?

Challenge Four: Classrooms are a place to concentrate and learn new things. Children with ADHD have a hard time sitting for extended periods of time. How can a classroom be designed to keep the attention of the ADHD child?

As you develop your design, please identify the purpose of each feature and how it addresses the unique needs of the population constituency.

Deliverables
Presentation board

STUDIO ACTIVITY 12.2

Mall City

Design Problem

All of the adults in the world have died from a devastating disease that claims its victims at age 21. Teenagers are the only humans left inhabiting world. Teens within the United States have gravitated to malls and have created micro-cities within these malls. Each store space has become the home of a small village. Your job as the designer is to anticipate and demonstrate what these mall cities will look like.

Step One: From literature discussing teen development and information gained from other cluster communities (nursing homes, prisons, dormitories, etc.) identify and describe how you think the mall people will divide themselves into the different villages (i.e. Nordstrom Village, Gap Village, Foot Locker Village, Apple Village, etc.). Will each village be formed by age? Ethnicity? Gender? Interests?

Step Two: From the literature and case studies identify leadership styles and roles.

Step Three: Imagine how each village will look, where the leader will reside, and how the central trading posts would be formed. Also, consider the individual safety and security of each village, and the mall city as a whole.

Deliverables

1. Research a minimum of five sources that have led to the deductions contained within your design.

2. Rendered and labeled (what is where) plan view of the mall city.

3. Two cone view perspectives of two villages contained within mall city.

4. One cone view perspective of the leadership space. Is this a space that shows an autocratic leadership style? Does it show a democratic leadership style? Does the space reflect military power? Does the space reflect monetary power? You decide, but your decision must be defended.

5. One rendered and detailed plane view of the trading center.

6. Aggregate the research and diagramed images and assemble into an 8 to 10 minute narrated video that tells the story of how mall city came about and what daily life is like. You may supplement your renderings with other images, just be sure to cite the sources of those images.

DISCUSSION QUESTIONS

1. Based on the information presented in this chapter, how might the average school day for elementary and middle school children be altered? How would you design an environment where elementary school children can relax?

2. Discuss ways to evaluate a client's home for potential dangers relating to children. How would you approach subjects that may be personal? How would you evaluate the risks for a particular child? How would you work with the family to rid the home of potential allergens, if necessary? Keep in mind that many people have a difficult time differentiating between needs and wants and are not aware of the many options available.

3. How might you design a playground based on the research presented in the chapter? What elements make a playground soothing and calming to adolescent youths? How would you incorporate these features without increasing any hazards?

4. How would you change your design techniques to deal with a preadolescent compared with a young child? What questions would you ask, and what role would the older child play in the design process? What materials and illustrations would you use to keep the preadolescent involved and engaged?

5. How can you apply the information in this chapter about stress, environmental agents, and green spaces to your current life? What aspects about your living space can you alter to better suit your stress and health levels?

LEARNING ACTIVITIES

1. Research the clinical diagnosis for attention deficit/hyperactivity disorder (ADHD), and develop a plan for creating a study and play space that would help to minimize negative stimuli for a child diagnosed with ADHD.

2. Spend 30 minutes pretending you are a child who is 7 years old or younger. Spend time at the average 7-year-old's height, and minimize your physical characteristics to approximate those of an average child. What dangers do you find in your living space? What temptations exist? Sketch your living space and highlight areas of potential danger, and overlay adaptations to make your living space child-friendly.

3. You have been hired to design an addition to an existing family home that will accommodate the family's two children (ages 7 and 10) as well as future newborn twins. Devise a step-by-step approach to evaluating the children's current needs and wants as well as planning for their future needs. Consider information learned in previous chapters about territoriality as well as the stress expected from a major change in family structure. Devise methods for ensuring privacy for the older children and for allowing the twins to develop as individuals.

4. Visit a local playground, and sketch the layout accurately. Create a new drawing that shows adjustments to improve the use of the facility for all potential users. Write a brief description of your modifications and reasons for those changes.

5. Design a playroom that is appropriate for both a toddler and a child. Consider intellectual stimulation, safety, shared space, spaces with multiple functions, and so on. Describe the key features of the room, and explain how they are appropriate for each age.

13 Office Environments

Corporations no longer try to fit square pegs into round holes; they just fit them into square cubicles.

—Robert Brault

Every environment in which work of any kind is carried out is a workplace; therefore, a kitchen is a workplace whether it is located in a restaurant or residence, or on a catering truck or cruise ship. Every occupation has its workplace: teachers, doctors, librarians, housekeepers, pilots, clerks, and hundreds of other specialists who perform their specific function in a myriad of interior and exterior environments. The office environment must be taken into special consideration, as it becomes a microcosm in and of itself. A potentially large and diverse group of people, in relatively close quarters, work for many hours toward a common goal; the environment in which all this takes place can either help or hurt the unity, productivity, and "bottom line."

Around the world, today's workforce consists of men and women of varying ages, cultures, and physical abilities whose environments require many special considerations. Perceptual and physical differences based on gender, age, culture, and skill levels on the many types of office equipment available are creating workplace issues and circumstances yet to be resolved. For example, because increasing numbers of older people are either postponing retirement or returning to the workforce, workplace design now needs to accommodate the special issues that affect older workers (Kupritz, 2001; see Figure 13.1).

The workplace has been evolving for centuries, and during the past three centuries, the evolution has been fueled by historic revolutions: political, industrial, sexual, and, most recently, technological. During the past 50 years, the office environment has evolved much faster than ever. This is because computer and communication technology has exploded during the past 20 years; word processing software, scanners, cell phones, and Smart Phones have replaced typewriters, photocopiers, pagers, and calendars.

[**Figure 13.1**] Many elderly people have no choice but to join or even re-enter the workforce in order to meet their monthly expenses. © Jose Luis Pelaez Inc / Blend Images / Corbis

In today's technological era, however, the **hierarchical structure** has been losing favor as new corporate structuring strategies are being explored. These include integrative, democratic, and self-managing team structures—what we will refer to here as **a collaborative structure**. In models of this nature, employees with varying skill sets work together in groups. Although this type of social structure within the work environment is being encouraged, it is not as common as the hierarchical model. In addition, because it is still in the experimental stages, long-term studies examining the effects of this type of structure on employee satisfaction, morale, and productivity are minimal at best.

A predominant feature of an office, regardless of its size, location, or year it was built, has been the hierarchical *organizational structure*, identified by the *chain of command*. This type of structure relies on linked and ranked (i.e., joined and separated) groups of individuals working together toward a common goal and can be identified throughout history and across species. (Consider that every wolf pack has its alpha leader and every beehive, its queen bee.) A growing field called biomimicry looks to the natural environment as way to develop a more sustainable lifestyle. Biomimicry may also be extended to the social constructs of behavior and then analyzed in terms of social ranks and subsequent environmental needs. For example, discovering the role of the omega wolf in the pack along with his/her needs may tell us something about line workers in a company.

Given these changes, it is clear that the office environment must be as flexible as possible if it is going to accommodate a future with endless technological possibilities.

Today, more than ever before, the rules of the workplace environment are evolving before our eyes. Differences in gender expectations and working styles, employer demands and compensation, the Internet and global expansion, and a market-driven economy have all combined to create a set of situations that are unique to human civilization. Consider for a moment how people lived only a few hundred years ago.

In addition to the technological and social changes, we have many age-old psychological dysfunctions that have likely been with us since the dawn of time. Nonetheless, there are concerns that need to be addressed here that include, but are not limited to, racism, sexism (including homophobia), issues of power and control, and people who integrate their jobs into their personas and become workaholics.

ORGANIZATIONAL STRUCTURES

The traditional office environment developed at the beginning of the industrial era is seen as a bureaucracy consisting of hierarchical tiers of employees ranging from general workers through managers to corporate heads. The number of levels within the hierarchy is dependent on the size, structure, and goals of the company. This model was and has been the standard in corporations throughout Western societies for over a century.

SUSTAINABILITY CONNECTION 13.1

For millennia humans have imitated nature for design inspiration—birds for aerodynamics, spiders for weaving, floating leafs for boats, and more recently termite mounds for ventilation systems. Perhaps the time has come for this method to be used on office environment organization. Social structure comes in many forms: presocial, subsocial, semisocial, parasocial, and quasisocial; however, the highest level of social order is called *eusociality*. Bees, ants, and termites are natural examples of a eusociality organization. This is not to say that human office workers should aspire to become "worker drones," although this discussion utilizes the spatial characteristics of their *place of work:* the hive, hill, or mound. There are many spatial forms based on species and location, though all share these features: multiple exits yet one main entry, galleries, and halls and passages leading to common areas and nodes. The most interesting feature found in nearly every colony (which office designers can imitate) is the many alcoves and niches along every path of circulation. This design feature would support the micro-communication needed to complete a task, as well as a specific outlet or place for personal contact—perhaps this is their version of "meeting at the water cooler."

Hierarchical Structure

In many respects we can equate modern corporations to the many medieval kingdoms of Europe. Many of our corporations are currently so large that their cadre of employees rivals some of the past mighty kingdoms. For example Wal-Mart is estimated to have 1,900,000 employees (Fortune500, 2007). To give this perspective, think about the different points in medieval Europe; all of Great Britain, with its English, Irish, Scottish, and Welsh kingdoms, had a total population that was only slightly more (Backman, 2002) than Wal-Mart's entire employee base. Many of these companies also run according to the kingdom model, which places the CEO/president as the king or queen of his/her domain. From this viewpoint we have princes and princesses (COO et al., vice presidents), lords and ladies (directors); and down the list the titles go.

This top-down structure of power can be conceptualized as a pyramid with one or more decision makers at the top, the least influential group members at the bottom, and the workload distributed throughout the hierarchy of directors, organizers, or overseers (i.e., managers and supervisors) and producers (subordinate workers). This structure has been the backbone of nearly every religion, civilization, government, militia, school, club, and team in human history.

In 1911, Frederick Taylor identified pivotal principles of management that would serve as the basis for the American corporation in the 20th century. His influential text, *Principles of Scientific Management,* advocated a hierarchical structure and the segmentation of jobs into tasks assigned to specific workers as a means of achieving maximum productivity and profit (Taylor, 1911/1985). This approach, referred to as *Taylorism,* served as the basis for the traditional American corporation and is still used today. In short, Taylorism is the transfer of power from the people doing the work to the managerial elite. In a free and democratic society, many may regard managerial duties as requiring subordinates to become mindless automatons in the tradition of the master-slave relationship (Belasco & Stayer, 1993).

Various permutations of the hierarchical model have been advanced over the years, including democratic and autocratic hierarchies (Rehm, 2000). The understanding in hierarchical structures of either sort, however, is that individual employees have very specific work requirements and are accountable to a person next in rank superior to themselves (McHugh, O'Brien, & Ramondt, 2001; Williamson, 2001), with the most important decisions being made by the highest-ranking employees (Williamson, 2001). The power of people in lower tiers of the corporate structure is diminished by their lower rank within the company and is visible in their physical separation from higher-level employees (see Figure 13.2).

This type of corporate structure is most easily visible in the traditional factory environment, where workers on the

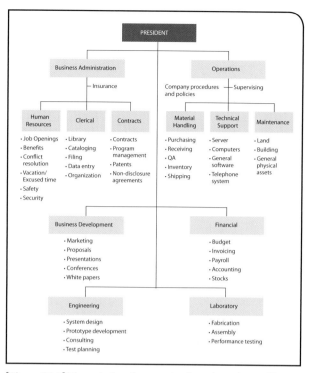

[**Figure 13.2**] The majority of companies throughout the world operate as a hierarchy in which a single entity commands a cadre of people. Orders are thus funneled through communication channels in which any person at any point can serve as a gatekeeper, or fail to receive or relay a message accurately. Illustration by Precision Graphics

production line have almost no say in company policy and are accountable to a supervisor. The supervisor, in turn, has limited participation in company policies and is accountable to a middle manager. This middle manager in turn has slightly more power and must report to a manager of higher rank than himself/herself, and so forth. Although this type of structure is fairly stable, it tends to be inflexible (McHugh et al., 2001). However it demonstrates and facilitates poor intercompany communication (similar to the "telephone" game played by many children—the message becomes more lost with each transfer; Figure 13.3). It is, however, a proven system of maintaining tight control (Williamson, 2001).

OFFICE CULTURE

Office politics can be thought of as tribes or an adult version of high school cliques. Based on notions of superiority, office politics is a complex stew of power, ambition, control, and ego (Fabian, 2009). Office culture is the rules of conduct, general understanding of one's role within the office environment, the social dynamics that take place within a company, and a set of collective beliefs and values—all of which contribute to the office culture and, ultimately, to employee behaviors. The

[**Figure 13.3**] In preschool and kindergarten we learned that communication passed from one person to the next becomes distorted, and often results in an entirely different message; however, many corporate structures insist on this form of communication, thus leading to a disconnect between line staff and those in power to make decisions. © Anderson Ross / www.fotosearch.com

social structure of an office is built gradually over time and can result in job satisfaction for employees who feel a personal connection with fellow workers. Often, when a company undergoes restructuring, such as downsizing or a corporate takeover, the resulting damage to, or destruction of, the office culture can lead to employee dissatisfaction, absenteeism, poor work quality, and poor customer relations.

An office culture can be one of support and encouragement, friendly competition and collaboration; or it can be a culture of fear, jealousy, and inequality. When an office culture turns sour, it is extremely hard to make it positive. Some of the elements that contribute to a positive **workplace culture** include (Levering, 1995):

- Fair treatment of employees, which is often reflected through the provision of resources. For example, does everyone have the same quality of equipment and furnishings?
- Keep up with environmental design trends. For example, is the décor up-to-date, or old and pieced together?
- A high degree of employee responsibility to make important choices. For example, what mechanisms are in place to promote those employees who take initiative?
- Well-publicized employee recognition. For example, is there a system to publicly recognize employees, such as their photos displayed in a highly visible place?

- Promote employee personal growth. For example, a wall of fame might be incorporated where employee accomplishments and personal growth activities can be displayed.
- Social experiences in which everyone can partake. For example, a company may sponsor a summer retreat where only employees engage in team-building activities, such as white water rafting, hiking, or rock climbing. Pictures of these events can then be displayed in the primary work space.

It is important for designers to make provisions for a variety of ways that employees can be celebrated. This might mean a built-in space to host or display a corporate mascot, the provision for displaying photographs taken from a company retreat, and maybe an entire wall in the employee lounge where employees can tack up photos or notifications of some personal news.

Some people require more from their places of employment than others. The level of compatibility with the corporate culture and an individual's personality traits determine the degree of compatibility between an employee and an organization. It is generally assumed that a successful relationship between an individual and an organization is based on shared beliefs and behavioral expectations. Inspiring a positive office culture and showing appreciation for employees has a direct relationship to employee loyalty and retention. This is important because it costs a company a lot of money to replace an employee, which is why the old saying "everyone is replaceable" may be true, but at a high cost.

The majority of office workplaces are semipublic spaces that make up both social systems and physical environments (*behavior settings*). The social workplace operates by a strict set of rules that depend on the office culture. To identify the culture of a workplace, consider the following questions:

1. Does the company promote empowerment of employees through a "hands-off" managerial style, or does it subscribe to a micromanagement style?
2. To what degree does the company enforce predetermined processes to complete a task? Is it the end goal that is prized or the ability to follow rules and procedures?
3. Does the company allow employee freedoms such as flextime or remote work programs?
4. Does the organization's administration show distrust of its employees through formal accounting measures such as time clocks and e-mail monitoring?
5. Do managers work in the same area and environmental conditions as their employees, or are they separated from their employees?

The best ways to learn about an organization's culture is to listen to what employees say about the working conditions, listen to what the general populace says about the company, and observe and analyze the physical workplaces. Important physical indicators of an organization's culture include lighting levels and access to natural views, aesthetics, levels of privacy, and quality of furnishings. These attributes of the physical environment serve as symbolic representations of the working conditions and the office culture. For example, when managers and staff share similar physical environmental features, this represents equality within the office culture.

When a designer has determined a current office culture and whether or not a company wants to retain or change a given office culture, he/she can begin the design process. For example, the design of a highly competitive sales office might use designs that promote a high degree of formality and allow the employees to overhear each other and provide situations for overt rewards that serve as constant reminders to other employees of what they need to strive for. In other situations a management team may want to promote more collaboration among the employees and, as such, the designer will want to make the environment much more casual and provide informal spaces for employees to gather for impromptu discussions and brainstorming. These spaces of *collaborative creativity* do not require much in the way of square footage, but they will need resources such as pin-up wall space, white boards, large round or oval tables, informal comfortable furniture, and good lighting.

Racism and Sexism

An unfortunate reality within human civilizations is that racism and sexism are ubiquitous. At the heart of the matter; these are spatial systems and the "segregation" of minorities, women, and others deemed unworthy in the past, was accomplished by creating *physically* different places for each group or caste to use. Discrimination based on race tends to be more overt because we can see the common features associated with a race.

Discrimination based on religion, family disposition, or sexual orientation, on the other hand, can be hidden or an unspoken rule for management in the company to not hire people belonging to particular religions, women of child-bearing age, single parents, or homosexual individuals. This is because they may see a worker as able to fit in with the corporate culture during working hours but have a lifestyle that may interfere with the work place. For example, a person who is Islamic may not have his/her faith brought into question until he/she requests a time and space to pray. Likewise, many Latinos or homosexuals might "pass" for the dominant European heterosexual until they bring their Spanish-speaking spouse or same-sex partners to the company picnic. Single parents (or parents in general), although attempting to balance work, children's school schedules, and home management, often find office environments restrictive as they try to find places at work for private "family matters" and day care. When personal factors are revealed, they can bring about discriminatory practices.

Within the office environments of the United States, strides to eliminate and remedy discrimination in any form have given rise to words such as *reverse racism, reverse discrimination,* and *reverse sexism.* Specifically, reverse discrimination is defined as "discrimination against whites or males (as in employment or education)" (Merriam-Webster Online Dictionary, 2010). These terms are more often used when speaking about affirmative action. Reverse discrimination comprises the ideas of "undoing" past wrongs of racism and sexism, as well as equal opportunity principles, and sets out to *overprotect* based on race, sex, and so on. The basic purpose is to provide access and opportunity to education, financing, and jobs. In many cases, the minority group member is the most qualified and the best candidate for the job, grant, or scholarship; however, the issue opponents have is that in some cases, the "best" candidate is denied, so that the organization can "fill its quota" for diversity. These terms often underscore the real problem— that anyone can be a racist or sexist, or engage in discriminatory practices, simply by helping or hurting—based on race, sex, or anything other than the person's experience and merit alone. Therefore, the modern office or workplace now has two forms of discrimination to deal with.

There is little designers can do to rectify racism and discrimination in the world; but in the workplace, they can promote diversity through environmental design. This can be accomplished by incorporating diverse ethic patterns, colors, and tasteful gender symbology into artwork, statues, carpets, vases, and pots for plants. Enclosed, small, private spaces can be built into employee lounges to accommodate prayer and to give breastfeeding mothers a place to pump and store milk. Daycare centers can be designed into the workplace environment to assist working parents and promote a more stress-free environment. A plethora of research has shown that when persons are exposed to or hear children or other people laughing, their stress levels drop dramatically, they achieve higher learning and task productivity, and their morale is lifted, just to name a few (Bennett & Lengacher, 2006; Cueva, 2010; Seaward, 1992). If designers were to position the day care center playground adjacent to the outdoor area of the employee lounge, not only could parents check on their children briefly but everyone wanting to hear a bit of laughter could partake in the restorative properties of children at play by stepping outside.

The Office Environment

For humans who roamed Africa only yesterday from an evolutionary perspective, the workplace environment was an estimated 440 square miles. Today, many people work in approximately 260 square feet, many of which have been subdivided into approximately 80 square feet of cubicle space. Employees thus claim these cubicles as their primary territory. As an interesting comparison, the average prison cell is approximately 70 square feet (Ford & Kerle, 1981).

The first large-scale office spaces appeared in the United States in the late nineteenth century within the Northeast and Midwest industrial cities of Boston, New York, Cleveland, Detroit, and Chicago. Technologies such as electric lighting, the typewriter, and the use of calculating machines allowed for faster and more efficient processing; and in many respects the employees became a component in the larger corporate machine. Chicago, the home of the American skyscraper, was among the first to use steel-frame buildings in conjunction with elevators to bring about the vertical growth of the office building. With large open expanses and increased square footage, this profit-driven development became the hallmark of the 20th century office building.

In the 1920s, a group of researchers theorized that improved environmental conditions would positively correlate to increased worker productivity (e.g., the Hawthorne studies). Although this theory was never proved, the study did reveal that social factors influence employee satisfaction and efficiency (Cairns, 2002). The physical environment is a place for social interactions (Goodsell, 1993), but whereas physical design of the workplace has historically been used to establish social control over employees, recent studies have been examining the workplace as a means of promoting employee empowerment (Cairns, 2002). From this perspective, the ideal work environment supports high levels of performance and job satisfaction by enabling employees to conduct their work in distraction-free environments, receive support from unplanned interactions, and engage in uninterrupted meetings and group projects (Brill, Weidemann, Alard, Olson, & Keable, 2001); however, the traditional office environment is only one type of workplace environment. Today's workplace options support popular trends in computer-aided work decentralization such as **nonterritorial offices**, **telecommuting**, **virtual offices**, **satellite offices**, and **neighborhood work centers**, each of which has demonstrated varying degrees of success (Becker, 1986; McCoy, 2002).

Since the formation of governments and business, there has been a need for people to perform clerical duties. These duties were often performed in a room shared by one or more people. As society and businesses grew, more people were added to the single space. By the 19th century, nearly 100,000 Americans worked within an office environment in various capacities. When we consider that carpeting wasn't yet mass produced, typewriters were the dominant business tools, lighting technology was still relatively young, and the average worker was expected to work 60 hours per week— 10 hours per day for 6 days—we can only image their quality of life. Noisy, crowded, dimly lit echo chambers are probably the best description (Figure 13.4).

The chair and desk symbolized the office environment in the past, and thus they were the objects of design. The goal of past designers was to make better desks and chairs. At the 1876 Centennial Exposition in Philadelphia, the first rolltop desk was introduced (Smithsonian, 1998). The rolltop could be locked in the closed position, thereby protecting the contents of the desk from territorial invasion or contamination. This is an important event because it established a person's desk as his/her private primary territory. However, the rolltop desk didn't last because of the typewriter; it was simply too bulky for the rolltop. So although employees lost some of their privacy, the desk had been firmly established as the employee's primary territory.

The Cubicle

By the 1960s the cubicle replaced the desk and chair as the dominating symbol of the office environment. The first

[**Figure 13.4**] Early workplace environments had numerous hard surfaces that reverberated the noise generated from typewriters, and no employee had any sense of personal space or territorial control. © thislife pictures / Alamy

incarnation of the cubicle appeared in 1964. Robert Propst and George Nelson introduced what they called the "Action Office." The concept was simple; use freestanding units such as bookcases and credenzas as space dividers. The idea behind the concept expanded the employee's primary territory and, thereby, afforded the employee more personal space. Unfortunately the idea didn't catch on, but Propst knew he was onto something. Then, in 1968, while working for Herman Miller, he created the first Action Office, and the cubicle replaced the desk and chair as the symbol of the office environment (Schlosser, 2006). Since the first commercial installation in 1969, the cubicle has evolved into many incarnations and is likely to continue evolving.

Modern cubicles attempt to promote a degree of privacy through the use of the modular panels. Although if a person is facing a wall working on a computer, his/her back to the opening, the screen can be seen from the cubicle's opening, thus creating a potential for a violation informational privacy from passersby. Notwithstanding, the cubicle does have the ability to limit visual distraction that was once a common problem within open bullpens. Distraction comes from peripheral vision, which means that no matter how focused we are on a task, we can still detect the movement of others through peripheral vision. Movement within our periphery causes excitatory responses related to the ancient *fight-or-flight*

behavior. While many can control this instinctual behavior, these peripheral images continue to affect our stimulation levels and serve as a distraction for many employees. Keep in mind that these peripheral distractions can be direct or indirect (i.e., resulting from reflections or shadows).

In the late 1980s there was a small social revolution with regard to the role employees played in the workplace environment. Because the cubicle had become the symbol of the workplace environment, it became fodder for popular media, by way of comedy and science fiction metaphor. On April 16, 1989, Scott Adam's popular comic strip *Dilbert*, which is a parody of workplace idiocy and life within a cubicle, was launched. Interestingly, less than a month later (May 8, 1989) the popular science fiction television show *Star Trek: The Next Generation* introduced its newest villain who traveled in a cube-shaped spaceship. These alien beings (called "the Borg" for cyBORGnetic creatures) worked in their cube and were described as drones with zombie-like qualities. Both Dilbert and the Borg resonated with the populace so much so that Dilbert became a television show in the 1990s, and the Borg became the main story line in the next Star Trek series called *Voyager*.

While cubicles replaced the more exposed "pool" of desks, which had lined the floors of early cavernous workrooms, they also became a symbol of corporate oppression that mandated conformity. Rather than direct attention to the corporate structure, which created the oppression and mandated the conformity, design became the focal point. By the late 1990s Herman Miller unveiled its Resolve series. The intention was to get people out of "the box" and divert the evolution of the office cubicle. By 2004 many companies moved away from the cubicle, and Robert Propst expressed grief over his contribution (the Action Office) to what he called "monolithic insanity" before he died in 2000. Despite being maligned in popular culture, the cubicle brought to the workplace environment a degree of privacy and sense of territorial control, which employees did not have in earlier workplace environments.

Office Layout

Many organizations use open office plans, which are based on the concept that, due to the minimization of physical barriers, employees will be more likely to increase communication and collaborative efforts. Open office plans can provide both financial and spatial conservation (i.e., portable, modular furnishings are less expensive and occupy less floor space than fixed partitions) and are popular with organizations that are highly dependent on creativity; walls and work spaces can be easily reconfigured. The use of open office spaces allows flexibility in office layout, which can easily meet the changing needs of an organization, and is often associated with increased teamwork; however, research findings are mixed (COPE Project, 2003). Open office designs are insufficient to meet privacy needs, and visual and auditory distractions, thereby decreasing worker productivity and increasing the frequency of errors (Kupritz, 1998). Although open office plans were promoted as being a cheaper way to build, they have been scientifically demonstrated to have inherent costs that counteract these initial savings.

People associate psychological privacy with architectural privacy (i.e., physical barriers), and common complaints from employees regarding open offices are related to disturbances and lack of privacy (Brennan, Chugh & Kline, 2002). Because of the greater *social density* and the lack of modifiers (i.e., walls), employees' moods are more likely to affect others; however, shared feelings can lead either to positive outcomes, such as a strong team spirit, or negative outcomes, such as low employee morale (Totterdell, Kellett, Teuchmann, & Briner, 1998). Studies of open plan offices have shown increases in worker interaction and problem solving, but also more instances of interruptions and privacy violations (Vithhayathawornwong, Danko, & Tolbert, 2003).

Limited visual and aural privacy can cause employees to limit their communication with other employees, which reduces overall communication; therefore, consider providing break or conference rooms for private conversations, telephone calls, meetings, and specific tasks requiring concentration (Brennan, Chugh, & Kline, 2002). Privacy needs within the workplace vary depending on the work and the needs of the individual (Kupritz, 1998); therefore, before opting for an open office plan, consider the privacy needs of the employees (Brennan et al., 2002).

Personalization

Workplace personalization serves to signify identity, mark territories, and regulate social interactions, and has been shown to promote a positive workplace culture, higher employee morale, and less employee turnover (Wells, 2000b). Some employers believe that office "clutter" is a mark of inefficiency and chaos; therefore, their company policies prohibit employees from personalizing their workstations. Others allow or even encourage personalization as an expression of individuality and a symbol of the corporation's commitment to the contribution of the employees (Figure 13.5). Unfortunately, the ability to work more efficiently in an apparently haphazard work space is of little concern to many employers who gladly opt for reduced production in exchange for the illusion of a better organization and a stronger public image.

CULTURAL CONNECTION 13.2

Ethnic identity is shown in choices of clothing, music, artwork, jewelry, and food. Office employees with the ability to define and display their cultural identity and ethnic pride have shown a reduction in symptoms of depression and anxiety (Mandara, Gaylord-Harden, Richards, & Ragsdale, 2009). Spaces and places dedicated for multicultural expressions such as desk/wall displays, office cultural fairs, and ethnic potlucks can promote interest in, awareness of, and tolerance for different ethnic, cultural, and racial backgrounds.

Personalization can positively affect the individual's environmental satisfaction, well-being, and overall job satisfaction, as well as the corporate culture (Wells, 2000b). Women often personalize their work spaces more than men. Men often personalize their work spaces with items associated with status (diplomas, awards, and trophies). Women tend to personalize their workplaces in ways that are more associated with relationships (photos of friends, pets, and family members; Wells, 2000b). This difference in office personalization represents a shift from competition to relationships. In whatever way the personalization of office work

[**Figure 13.5**] Currently, there are several designers who help their clients develop designs that best reflect their personal identities. The ability of an employee to design his or her space is dependant upon the policies of the organization that he or she works for. © Getty Images/ Thomas Barwick

space is perceived, employee satisfaction with the physical environment correlates to how much employees are *allowed to* personalize, in relation to, how much they would *like to* personalize and to what extent they can influence their work space (Wells, 2000b).

Personal satisfaction within the work environment is directly related to job satisfaction and indirectly related to productivity (Carlopio, 1996) and is influenced by perceived levels of privacy, freedom, and control. Although personal territories are an important aspect of all environments, the workplace engenders many ambiguities related to territorial control. On the one hand, the employer controls the territory; therefore, some supervisors might believe this gives them the right to enter a subordinate's territory at will (i.e., commit territorial violation). On the other hand, employees often feel free not only to utilize work spaces that are temporarily unoccupied, but also to leave behind vestiges of their occupation, called territorial contamination (coffee cups, trash, or project remnants). Not surprisingly, doors and locks provide the greatest degree of territorial control, whereas cubicles and open office designs afford the greatest opportunities for territorial infringement. In cubicle layouts, employees often establish their spaces through décor and the treatment of boundaries, signs, colors, and artwork. These items serve as territorial markers

that provide a sense of identity, control, and purpose among workplace occupants (Becker & Steele, 1995). If employees cannot make their environment their own, they are less likely to "bond" with the company and more likely to seek employment elsewhere.

Research demonstrates that people are more comfortable in interior spaces that are decorated than in those that are not (Campbell, 1979). Employees in work spaces with little or no attention to architectural detail feel deprived and compensate for feelings of embarrassment, loss of prestige, and vulnerability with behaviors ranging from social withdrawal to quitting (Mazumdar, 1992). The result can manifest as apathy, withdrawal, or rage; however, through good environmental design, we have the ability to promote empowerment and facilitate one's notion of equality and fairness (see Table 13.1).

Incorporating details, such as privacy spaces, can facilitate employee feelings of "being special," which typically translate into higher morale and job satisfaction. Even a low level of visual stimulation, provided by variation in table and desk shapes, is vital to worker satisfaction. In one study, researchers showed that aesthetics, privacy, furniture, communication, temperature control, and lighting were related to job performance, quality communication, and satisfaction with the environment (McCoy, 2002).

Design professionals must understand the nature of work to be conducted (e.g., creative development versus repetitive tasks) before they can develop supportive workplace designs. One group of researchers asserts that a physical work environment can promote creativity when it facilitates positive social-psychological conditions such as freedom, sharing, trust, support, and respect. Contending that dynamic environments facilitate creativity, these researchers suggest creating environments that inspire intensity and vigor (Vithayathawornwong et al., 2003). Another research team concluded that more stimuli (e.g., brighter or warmer colors, increased visual and aural stimuli) should be incorporated into work spaces in which routine or low-demand tasks are performed, and fewer stimuli (e.g., cooler or darker colors, artwork depicting nature scenes) for those environments in which creative or high-demand tasks are performed (Stone & English, 1998). Their study found that the beat of music or repetitive sounds (aquarium or fountain) can help to establish a rhythm and may increase productivity levels for routine tasks; participants whose work spaces were designed in blue appeared calmer, perceived more privacy and lower temperatures, and were more focused on their tasks.

To facilitate work space privacy, incorporate conference rooms that will accommodate worker interaction without distracting others, as well as floor-to-ceiling walls,

[Table 13.1] Emotional Responses to Workplace Oppression

Condition	Description	Design
Apathy	Decrease in motivation, initiation, interest. This person responds with indifference and lacks commitment to his or her job duties.	Provide methods for employee empowerment by allowing individuals to lock their personal spaces (desks and lockers), providing spaces for relaxation, and allowing employees to personalize and individualize their work spaces.
Withdrawal	The person who withdraws from the workforce to work for himself or herself, or decides to live off social services. Every year people leave the workforce either voluntarily or involuntarily, leaving a gap in the entrepreneurial talent pool.	Many companies have come to realize that it is often these people who enable a company to be cutting edge. Again, empowerment and respect can reduce the incidences of withdrawal. Design can help through equitable design. This means that the corner office might get views, but it is not closed in; an office now with windows gets walls for increased privacy. Hence, all work spaces have positive and negative attributes.
Rage	The person who decides to join a militia group, or decides to commit acts of violence on his or her own.	Design needs to protect all employees. Managers and executives are often the primary targets of violence. One way to ensure their security is to place them in the middle of the work space so that there is no easy ingress or egress to the individual.

solid doors, and sidelights (e.g., partition windows) with window treatments. Be aware that five-foot partitions provide limited visual privacy whereas seven-foot partitions are better in providing both visual and audial privacy (Kupritz, 1998). Consider providing attractive, comfortable, nonwork related areas within the work facility (Vithhayathawornwong et al., 2003). An ideal work space will have provisions for people who cycle or jog to work; a place where meals can be stored, prepared, eaten, and shared (parties); and quiet, relaxing places where people can escape the stressors associated with the job. Locker rooms, shower facilities, sitting rooms, kitchenettes, and cafeterias go a long way toward increasing job satisfaction and reducing job-related stress. Planners and designers can help to increase workers' perceptions of spaces by incorporating large, unobstructed windows to bring in more natural light; enhancing artificial lighting with full-spectrum, diffused ceiling lighting, which will enable people to move about the room safely; incorporating task lamps at each desk; and using lighter and brighter colors as well as furnishings with smooth, simple lines. Also consider the use of indoor atriums around which offices may be organized.

THE HOME OFFICE

Perhaps the most predominating alternative to the contemporary workplace environment is the **home office**. Since the

dawn of time people have "worked from home," although over the centuries along with industrialization, technological advances, and mandated zoning laws, the *workplace* has moved further and further from "home." Currently we are seeing a revival of home occupation for financial gain. Many of these individuals are entrepreneurs; others balance work and family life by occasionally working remotely from home; and still others live at work (live/work lofts) or homes built atop businesses (mixed-use). The U.S. Department of Labor estimates that as of 2005, 25.4 million people work at home as part of their primary job (U.S. Bureau of Labor Statistics Division of Information Services, 2005). In the United Kingdom over 25 percent of the total workforce works from home on occasion, and nearly 2.5 percent do so regularly. This represents nearly double the number of people who worked from home back in 1981 (Felstead, Jewson, Phizacklea, & Walters, n.d.). Thanks to the relative ease of Internet access, laptop computers, and cellular telephones, work can be done in a hotel, on an airplane, in a public park—just about anywhere a person happens to be.

For many, the idea of working from home equates to freedom. Many workplace environments understandably curtail personal freedoms simply by virtue of the function—work spaces are for places for work. A typical restriction within a workplace is that many people with many different working-styles typically share a single space. For example some people perform best in the early mornings whereas others do their best work late at night—although the typical workplace hours are from 8 to 5. Also, some people work best with background music whereas others prefer absolute silence. Still others find that movements, sounds, or even aromas can easily distract them. Working from a home-based office allows the individual more control over his/her environment, thereby offering potential for a more conducive workplace environment for that person. A home office or working remotely from a company a few days a week is not for everyone, however.

Telecommuters, small business owners, independent contractors, freelance consultants, and artists make up the home-based workforce; and a growing number of people are opting to work from home (Magee, 2000). Benefits include increased job satisfaction related to greater flexibility and control over the work itself, as well as freedom from the constraints of corporate life (e.g., commuting issues, standard work hours, dress codes, office politics).

[**Figure 13.6**] Home offices can bring about an assortment of issues ranging from a discrepancy in privacy expectations between an employer and employee (i.e., does an employer have the right to enter a home office at will?) to the psychological delineation between home and work. An ideal situation is an external office on the property but separate from the main living quarters. © Tom Merton / Alamy

SUSTAINABILITY CONNECTION 13.2

Corporations are also looking at remote work programs because of the increased retention of valued employees, increased production rates and work quality, as well as a reduced need for new or larger facilities (Karnowski & White, 2002). From a sustainability perspective working from home means fewer automobiles on the road, which means less demand for cars, less need for petroleum-based rubber for tires, and less need for gasoline. This amounts to reduced commuter congestion and improved air quality. In addition the companies can expect reduced energy consumption because the employee pays for the heating, cooling, and lighting by working from home.

Working from home allows for a high degree of freedom, but this has the potential of leading to other personal side effects. For example, many people lack the self-discipline to engage in self-directed work. For these people, supervision or co-worker competition provides motivation. With the home office, the employee is likely to spend the day by him/herself. This can lead to the Electronic Cottage Syndrome. This euphemism of home offices (Holland & Hogan, 1998) is not a recognized disorder within *Diagnostic and Statistical Manual of Mental Disorders* (DSM-IV, 1994); however, it can be used to describe a set of experiences and behaviors that result from *social isolation* experienced by those who work from home. The effects of isolation can include anxiety, increased arousal, and increased stress (House, 2001).

Conversely, many people experience decreased stress by being allowed to work from home. The office environment can be a source of stress from some people, arising from competing personal and employee-related demands: With the home office, one can negotiate these demands. An additional source of stress derived from workplace environments comes from office politics and inter-colleague disputes. (This is discussed in the Office Culture section later in this chapter).

Other issues that arise from working from home include conflict between employer and family demands, as well as the separation between work and leisure. The home office will also affect spatial and personal relationships within the household, which will lead to necessary changes in social and physical configurations of territorial boundaries (Magee, 2000). It is important, therefore, to design the residential environment to support both professional and personal activities without sacrificing either. One researcher, noting that spatial boundaries seem to be more effective than temporal boundaries in delineating home-work environments, recommends both the physical separation of work space from the rest of the home and the restriction of work-related equipment and materials to the work space (Magee, 2000). The greater the distance of the home office from the residence, the fewer distractions for the worker (Figure 13.6).

One team's study revealed that home-based creative writers most commonly worked in home offices, kitchens, basements, bedrooms, and dining and living rooms. This team also noted that women used nature, memorabilia, and color more within their work spaces, whereas men used their desk area, privacy features, and size to create theirs (Zavotka & Timmons, 1996). Another study of home-based workers found that work space selection was based on availability (90 percent), seclusion and separation (84 percent), overall size (40 percent), and views and the presence of natural light (27 percent; Magee, 2000). Depending upon the type of occupation, home-based workers might also require a location closest to data, cable, and electrical ports. This means that designers must work with clients to identify the best locations for home office space, particularly in smaller residences.

A home office housed in a separate building outside of the house or in a designated area of a separate space (e.g., in the garage, basement, attic) is ideal. If this is not feasible, place the home office as far as possible from central living spaces and provide doors that will ensure privacy. For those who live in apartments, condominiums, or other smaller residences, consider the use of rolltop desks, computer armoires, or tri-fold screens that serve as temporal boundaries by concealing the work area when the office is "closed." For those who have the luxury of a dedicated office in a separate area of the home, provide spaces in which memorabilia and natural objects can be displayed, add a couch or easy chair to provide an alternative work position that can enhance cognitive stimulation, and incorporate general and task lighting to enhance the overall work environment (Zavotka & Timmons, 1996).

WORKPLACE HEALTH AND SAFETY

A workplace environment is a place where many people spend the majority of their life. Many people find satisfaction and happiness in their career accomplishments, friendships with co-workers, and camaraderie with like-mind individuals. Unfortunately, an office can also be a source of many health issues related to physical design and emotional well being. These factors by themselves or in combination can affect persons' levels of satisfaction with their job and oftentimes their life. Although stress is a significant indicator of future physical and psychological illnesses, other more recent concerns are sick building syndrome and ergonomics. Our modern built environment contains many chemical combinations and emissions, whether from the formaldehyde in the carpeting, glues in fake wood products, or the ozone emitted from copy machines that are continually recirculated throughout the modern office building with mechanical heating and cooling. Office staff must remain in these environments for many hours performing repetitive tasks, often without fresh air.

Occupational Safety and Health Act

The Occupational Safety and Health Act of 1970 was enacted to protect workers from harm while performing their job duties. Its intent was to reduce the high numbers of individuals dying or becoming disabled while performing their job duties. The Secretary of Labor, James Hodgson, helped draft the law and called it "the most significant legislative achievement" for workers in a decade (MacLaury, 2009). When enacted, the first order of business was to establish an oversight agency, the Occupational Safety and Health Administration (OSHA) to administer the Act (MacLaury, 2009). As a federal regulating body, OSHA has the authority to perform inspections and conduct investigations. If they identify areas of noncompliance at a workplace, they have the authority to issue citations and impose penalties.

Penalties imposed by OSHA often arise from failure to immediately eliminate or remove a potential hazard from the workplace environment. Depending upon the level and seriousness of the threat, an OSHA officer can petition the court for legal action. OSHA tends to look at safety and health in terms of seriousness or threat to physical harm that an employer should have known about. In these situations OSHA will initiate penalties. In some cases where an employer is truly unaware of a situation or event and the risk is not too serious, OSHA may or may not impose penalties; however, willful repetition of such a violation will result in penalties. This is important to designers because many aspects of the built environment, either during the design installation or as part of the routine intended use of the environment, are issues that affect safety and health and, therefore, fall under the jurisdiction of OSHA. There are many standards and areas of compliance required by OSHA, and it behooves a designer to become aware of these standards and regulations. For example, OSHA does not allow for the use of extension cords as permanent wiring; extension cords cannot be used for longer than 90 days. It is permissible to use appropriate extension cords for remodeling and maintenance or repair of structures or equipment, or for light holiday decorations. Caution should be used to prevent overloading power capabilities of the cord during temporary use; and daisy chaining is not permissible (plugging one extension cord into another and another, and so on), nor is plugging one surge protector/power strip to power another (Office of Compliance: Safety and Health Fast Fact, 2004).

The workplace environments have a host of other equipment and tools that often require cords and other trip hazards. Researchers at Boston University, Smart Lighting Engineering Research Center are developing an innovative network system in which low-powered LED light transmits data to other data equipment (see Figure 13.7; Portnoy, 2008). Essentially this new communication technology transmits data that could potentially eliminate the need for the data cord from computers to printers, or PDAs to laptops, or even the thermostats to the main heating and cooling systems. This technology might mean that we will have to rethink the office cubicle, however, simply because light cannot penetrate opaque surfaces, which

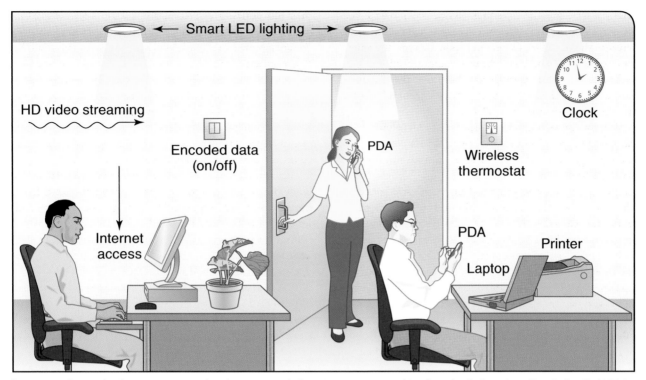

[**Figure 13.7**] From this diagram we can see that the smart LED lighting is powering everything from the clock on the wall to the handheld PDAs. This technology allows for greater flexibility in the office arrangement and helps to minimize the potential for overloading an electrical source. Illustration by Precision Graphics

means that equipment will need unobstructed access to these special light sources. We will have time to reconcile these and any other potential issues because the center doesn't anticipate the availability of this technology for another ten years (Portnoy, 2008).

OSHA places limits on the length of time employees can be exposed to noise according to their decibels. Match the maximum amount of exposure time to the decibel level. Occupational noise exposure is harmful when employees are subjected to sound levels exceeding:

- 8 hours 90 decibels
- 6 hours 92 decibels
- 4 hours 95 decibels
- 3 hours 97 decibels
- 2 hours 100 decibels
- 1.5 hours 102 decibels
- 1 hour 105 decibels
- .5 hour 110 decibels
- .25 hour 115 decibels

It is anticipated that feasible administrative or engineering controls will be implemented (United States Department of Labor: Occupational Safety and Health Administration, n.d.).

Ergonomics

Ergonomics is the study of the relationship between people and their working environment. This relationship can be in terms of how the physical environment conforms to an individual's body size and movement patterns, or how the environment affects one's mental and emotional state. In recent years the main focus of ergonomics in the workplace environment has been directed to computer use and associated injuries. A fundamental premise of ergonomics is that the work place design be adaptable to meet the individual needs of the employee as opposed to forcing the employee to work within the constrains of a given workplace design. The benefit of good ergonomics in the workplace is more effective and efficient performance levels. This translates to increased productivity and quality of work, reduced staff turnover and absenteeism, and a general increase in employee morale.

Ergonomics is an important design consideration. When workers are uncomfortable or in pain, their productivity and

[**Table 13.2**] Office Space Profiling

The Office	Individual Workstations	Individual Employee
Lighting	Desk and cabinets	Gender
Noise	Task lighting	Height and weight
Temperature	Chair	Arm span
Dress code	Computer hardware	Visual capacities
Pathways	Monitor type and size	Unique characteristics
Workstation layout	Speakers	Physical disabilities
Adjacencies	Mouse	Mental disabilities
Copy room	Computer software	
Receptionist		

[**Figure 13.8**] Ergonomics is an important health concern. In our mechanized society many of us perform repetitive tasks. The human body was not designed for this kind of activity; and as such we must remain vigilant to ensure proper posture, body alignments, and movements so that we do not cause undue injury. Illustration by Precision Graphics

morale decline; or worse, an acute discomfort can lead to a chronic or permanent affliction that negatively affects a worker's overall quality of life. Employers pay millions annually in worker's compensation benefits (including rehabilitative training) for employees who have sustained injuries as a result of poor ergonomics. As greater numbers of employees work with computers, the ergonomic design of office workstations, including proper distance and placement of computer monitors and keyboards, becomes increasingly important.

When developing a design for a work place environment, employers will expect the design to be ergonomically appropriate for that business. To do this, the designer will need to identify and analyze the overall space, the assortment of tasks that an employee will be expected to perform, and the different styles and accommodations available for individual workstations (Table 13.2; Figure 13.8).

SICK BUILDING SYNDROME

According to the U.S. Environmental Protection Agency (EPA), sick building syndrome (SBS) is exhibited by people experiencing severe yet unidentifiable health problems that present symptoms only in specific environments or buildings (U.S. Environmental Protection Agency, 1991). Sick buildings contain airborne substances (contaminants) that are health threatening (Gifford, 2002). Poor air quality resulting from polyvinyl chloride (PVC) emissions and other indoor contaminants often leads to this condition. Researchers have determined that two different sick building syndromes exist: Type 1 and Type 2 (Hedge, Sterling, & Sterling, 1986).

The term **building-related illness** describes symptoms of diagnosable illnesses that are found to some degree in occupants of all office buildings; the term **building-specific illness** refers to symptoms that occur only in air-conditioned buildings. SBS symptoms include headaches; fatigue; dry or itchy eyes; sore or dry throats; coughs; cold and flu symptoms; irritability; skin rashes; and neck, shoulder, and back pain. These physical afflictions often lead to the manifestation of stress and other psychological ailments. The EPA cites inadequate ventilation, chemical contaminants from indoor and outdoor sources, and biological contaminants (organic pollutants) as causes of or contributing factors to SBS.

Sick building syndrome is a serious health problem. Thousands of people each year report a host of illnesses related to respiratory problems, headaches, and fatigue; chronic coughing and overactive sinuses; and chronic eye, nose, and throat irritations (Apte, Fisk, & Daisey, 2000). Many workplace environments display attributes that cause SBS. Poor indoor air quality results from air-conditioned rooms, sealed windows, limited ventilation, and lack of natural light and these conditions seem to promote symptoms related to SBS (Brasche, Bullinger, Morfeld, Gebhardt, & Bischof, 2001). Research indicates that carbon dioxide (CO_2) levels, in combination with other indoor pollutants—such as volatile organic compounds (VOCs) released by building materials, office machines, and cleaning products; human **bioeffluents;** formaldehyde found in carpets and furniture; and dust—are responsible for symptoms related to SBS (Apte et al., 2000).

One research team noted that a tendency for women to report SBS-related symptoms more often than men may be related to differences in biology, work patterns, specific job duties, or a combination of these factors (Brasche et al., 2001). In their study, three types of employees were more likely to complain of SBS-related symptoms:

- Professional, educated women who shared office space with many other people, experienced allergy-related symptoms, and smoked
- Men who had an *external locus of control*, were younger than 31 or older than 50 years of age, and suffered from an acute illness
- Employees who had less education, suffered from an acute illness or allergies, and had low job satisfaction

Some symptoms associated with SBS can be attributed to psychological rather than physiological factors. Such cases tend to be related to low job satisfaction, high job-related stress, and beliefs or expectations that some environmental factor will make the individual sick. For example, many people believe that they will get sick from air conditioning. This notion is supported by a research team whose test subjects experienced more symptoms related to poor indoor air quality when they were stressed from work than when engaged in nonwork-related activities (Pejtersen et al., 2001). Thus, the question remains: Is it the air conditioning that is making them sick, or is it their belief that they will get sick from air conditioning?

Research supports the idea that more SBS symptoms occur in air-conditioned buildings than in those that are naturally ventilated (Seppanen & Fisk, 2002). The problem lies not with air conditioning, per se, but rather with the mechanical systems and the air itself, especially in buildings that are tightly sealed. When we breathe, we take in oxygen and release CO_2, and oxygen levels cannot be replenished by recirculated air. Increased CO_2 levels are associated with sore throats, nasal irritation, inflamed sinuses, tight chests, wheezing, and decreased oxygen levels, all of which can cause higher levels of fatigue (Apte et al., 2000). Air-conditioning systems recirculate indoor air that is already contaminated by various pollutants, thereby worsening indoor air quality by adding dust and bacteria from dirty ducts (Seppanen & Fisk, 2002; Figure 13.9).

STRESS AND SATISFACTION

Stress can be a psychological or physiological response to a stimulus or *stressor*. Our daily stress levels derive from a variety of situations including social (e.g., an employer's unrealistic demands), physical (e.g., manual labor required of the employee), or biological and chemical (e.g., carpet or equipment fumes that cause nausea, headaches, and fatigue), all of which affect our responses (Donald & Siu, 2001). Stress can also be thought of in terms of internal or external (Marion, 2003). **Internal stressors** include interpersonal conflict or violence, or disorganized daily life. **External stressors** include variables from the physical environment, such as noise, temperature, crowding, and over- or understimulation. Stress is rarely derived solely from internal or external sources, but rather stems from a combination of both. All stressors can build over time and manifest into physical ailments.

Designers have the ability of minimizing some of the affects of stress after they determine if the stressor is acute or chronic. An **acute stressor** is sudden, intense, and short-lived; a **chronic stressor** is ongoing or recurring and has the most significant and detrimental effects (Gunnar &

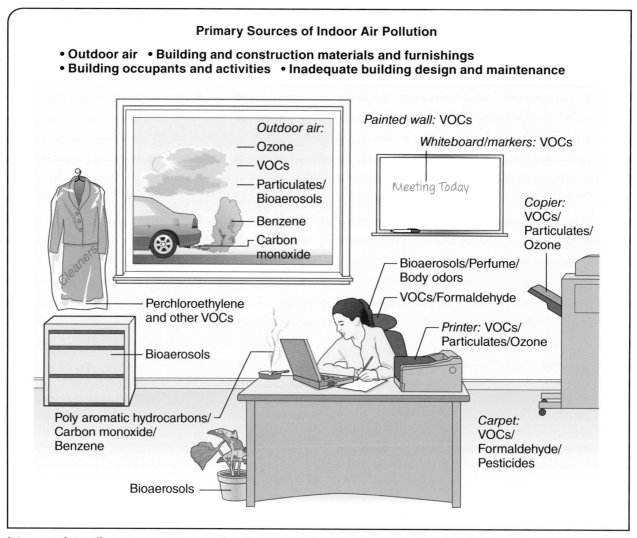

Primary Sources of Indoor Air Pollution

- **Outdoor air** • **Building and construction materials and furnishings**
- **Building occupants and activities** • **Inadequate building design and maintenance**

Outdoor air:
— Ozone
— VOCs
— Particulates/ Bioaerosols
— Benzene
— Carbon monoxide

Painted wall: VOCs

Whiteboard/markers: VOCs

Meeting Today

Copier: VOCs/ Particulates/ Ozone

Bioaerosols/Perfume/ Body odors
VOCs/Formaldehyde

Printer: VOCs/ Particulates/Ozone

Perchloroethylene and other VOCs

Cleaners

Bioaerosols

Poly aromatic hydrocarbons/ Carbon monoxide/ Benzene

Carpet: VOCs/ Formaldehyde/ Pesticides

Bioaerosols

[**Figure 13.9**] The office environment contains and produces many pollutants that become recirculated by air conditioning systems. With HVAC systems, pollutants can be dispersed and thus accumulate throughout the environment. Illustration by Precision Graphics

Barr, 1998; Lombroso and Sapolsky, 1998). Because an acute stressor occurs randomly, the designer can do little to minimize its effects. Chronic external stressors, on the other hand, can be addressed by using sound-dampening materials to reduce noise; employing varying ceiling heights to control heat; and incorporating large windows, mirrors, or paintings for moments of mental "escape." Designers can also help to minimize some chronic internal stressors by incorporating ample storage areas and providing adequate spacing between workstations, customer service counters, and seating, as well as get-away alcoves within employee lounges.

Stressors such as odors, heat, noise, and crowding are often referred to as **ambient stressors** (Campbell, 1983) because they are chronic, nonurgent, physically perceptible, and limited to a particular environment. Chronic environ-

mental stressors (e.g., feeling unsafe, at risk) slowly wear away our abilities to cope. A stressor's ambience or chronicity is determined by its frequency and its impact on a person. For example, one person may find perfumes to be a perpetual annoyance (chronic stressor), whereas others may not be bothered as long as they can put some distance between themselves and the fragrance (ambient stressors).

Stress itself does not cause injury or illness, but how we respond to it can, especially over time. Bioemotional reactions to stressful environments can result in a wide range of physiological responses including increased activity in the heart, stomach, intestines, and endocrine glands, which can result in stress-related illnesses such as increased heart rate, high blood pressure, ulcers, and migraine headaches. Behavioral responses to stress include aggression, withdrawal, and compulsion, and in extreme cases violence, delusions, or psychosis. The effects of stress "outlive" the stressor: Our physical and psychological responses continue even after the stressful event or experience has ended (Baum, Cohen, & Hall, 1993). Medical experts declare that if the body must continually cope with particular stressors over a long period of time, the circulatory, cardiovascular, gastrointestinal, and hormonal (glandular) systems may suffer permanent damage.

The consequences of physical and psychological workplace stress cost millions of dollars annually in insurance payments deriving from company-funded workers' compensation and government-funded disability programs. Employers and government agencies around the world are concerned about the growth in workplace stress and the decrease in worker satisfaction (Donald & Siu, 2001) and are taking proactive measures to overcome these challenges—many of which can be alleviated by design.

Satisfaction

Job satisfaction is determined by how well people's jobs meet their work expectations (Heslop, Smith, Metcalfe, Macleod, & Hart, 2002). A person's satisfaction with his/her physical work environment is positively associated with job satisfaction, which is positively correlated with life expectancy and employee well-being and negatively associated with stress, anxiety, depression, and low self-esteem (Wells, 2000b). Although every job and every workplace has stressful elements, people who are dissatisfied with their jobs experience higher levels of negative stress, which may be related to the early onset of cardiovascular disease (Heslop et al., 2002) and depression.

Computer technology has been a mixed blessing for job satisfaction. More work can be done by fewer people, which can increase production levels as well as reduce the need for new or expanded facilities for people or archives. However, when we work with computers, we do it sitting down, and decreased physical activity contributes to the decline of our overall health status—as do a range of other computer-related worker ailments (e.g., strained eyes, necks, shoulders, and backs; headaches; carpal tunnel syndrome) that result in thousands of disability and workers' compensation insurance claims around the world each year.

Workplace culture is also a source of job satisfaction, and people are strongly affected by the moods of the individuals with whom they work closely. We naturally compare our moods with those of others around us, which we unconsciously assess through many modes (e.g., "reading" facial expressions, body postures, gestures, levels of eye contact) and consistently bad moods negatively affect others' overall satisfaction and stress levels (Totterdell et al., 1998). People who have a need for absolute control are usually highly stressed

and often frustrated; their constant dissatisfaction can easily spread up or down the corporate structure until it affects an entire office, department, or company. To illustrate, a clerk's chronic bad mood irritates a secretary, who is then rude to the manager, who then argues with the owner, who then decides to cancel the company picnic.

ENVIRONMENTAL ANALYSIS

Designers should begin with the design of an office environment by examining the location of where the office is to be located. This examination should include source, quantity and quality of natural light; location of ventilation ducting; sources of noise and decibel ratings; and quantity and location of electrical outlets.

Lighting

The provision of natural lighting is important because it is proven to have many health and attitudinal benefits (Küller, Ballal, Laike, Midellides, & Tonello, 2006). When natural lighting patterns have been established, the illumination levels will likely require supplementation with artificial lighting. This should be done by calculating the level of natural light entering into the space throughout the day and at different times of the year (Figure 13.10). The artificial lighting should then be specified and strategically placed to provide the maximum illumination benefits possible. Using individual task lighting for each employee is another effective strategy from two standpoints: control over the location and amount of light is given to the worker; and whole room lighting may not be used as much if the light is turned on only where and when it is needed.

Keep in mind that lighting technology is evolving quickly, and there are some systems that can now be programmed to maintain a predetermined number of foot-candles. This means that when natural lighting levels are at their peak on the south facing side of the building that the artificial lighting will automatically dim. Although this is an excellent system for energy conservation, the interplay between lighting and surfaces changes, thus either forming or changing glare and shadow patterns.

Windows

Views of nature and sunlight are fundamental to human satisfaction and well-being, and windows can be beneficial to humans by providing opportunities for *prospect-refuge* (Kaplan & Dana, 2001). Workers increasingly are being housed in artificially illuminated workplaces where they spend a significant amount of time using computers, televisions, and other video display screens, all of which have been shown to cause mental and physical fatigue (McCoy, 2002).

Mental fatigue can lead to other negative side effects, including irritability, anxiety, depression, and obesity (i.e., if a person is mentally exhausted, he/she is less likely to exercise and more likely to slip into bouts of depression).

Mental fatigue caused by excessive *directed attention* can be reduced or eliminated via methods based on *attention restoration theory* (ART; Kaplan and Dana, 2001). Copious research has determined that window views of nature positively affect the health and well-being of building occu-

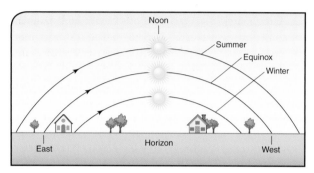

[**Figure 13.10**] Natural lighting is one of the hallmarks of good design; however lighting levels, intensities, and positioning change throughout the day and year. Designers need to consider these differences when developing the designs of buildings. Illustration by Precision Graphics

[**Figure 13.11**] Not every office can have views of nature, but the ability of an employee to mentally escape a given task even for a few moments along with the presence of natural light will have a therapeutic effect. © Cultura RM / Alamy

pants, and views have restorative value in relation to stress at work; one research team contends that it is primarily the presence of windows and the penetration of sunlight into the workplace that lead to increased worker satisfaction and well-being (Kaplan & Dana, 2001; McCoy, 2002; Ulrich, 1984; Figure 13.11).

Access to natural light is highly desirable for office workers and positively influences worker satisfaction (Kupritz, 2001; Leather, Pyrgas, Beale, & Lawrence, 1998; Wineman, 1982). Designers must consider the quality and amount of sun exposure, as well as the ability to reduce or enhance sunlight penetration when developing designs that provide views of natural environments (Leather et al., 1998). Design initiatives that incorporate sunlight and views of nature can provide brief *restorative experiences* that, if accumulated over time, can forestall the need for long breaks and reduce emotional and mental fatigue (Kaplan & Dana, 2001).

Illumination

Illumination is simply a measure of visible light striking a surface. The purpose of lighting systems is to place light where it is needed, and to avoid glare and shadowing where it can interfere with a given task. High-quality lighting will respond to its space and provide good visibility, comfort, and safety (COPE Project, 2003). **Luminance** is the brightness of an object, whereas **illuminance** is the amount of light seen on a surface (Veitch & McColl, 2001). *Ordered* lighting results when the layout of the light source is proportional to that of the space. *Coherent* lighting produces equally distributed modeling or shading across the space (Jay, 2002). Every interior space is unique, and every lighting system should meet the requirements of not only the owner and the occupants, but also the space itself; systems that provide too much or too little light are wasteful, and our understanding of a space and the appearance of it can be diminished if the lighting conflicts with the architectural structure (COPE Project, 2003).

Lighting affects our well-being on many levels—visibility, activity, communication, mood and comfort, health and safety, and aesthetic judgment—and interior lighting design, utilizing natural or artificial lighting, must respond to all of these needs (COPE Project, 2003). Although sunlight has greater beneficial effects than does artificial illumination, the general level of interior sunlight is less important than the size of the sunlit interior area (Leather et al., 1998).

Overhead fluorescent fixtures are the most common sources of workplace lighting. The component of a fluorescent **luminaire** (light fixture) that provides the starting voltage and operating current is called the *ballast*. Whereas high-frequency ballasts supply current electronically, conventional ballasts supply current electromagnetically and usually cause light flicker and an audible hum. Fluorescent-light flicker is not always visible to the human eye, but even at very low levels, it can be detected by the central nervous system and lead to physiological arousal; it has a greater impact on people who suffer from headaches, stress, and visual discomfort, and can become especially stressful in spaces that lack natural light (Kuller & Laike, 1998). This flicker frequency has been known to negatively affect women and children, in particular

In one study, the light from fluorescent lamps powered by high-frequency ballasts was perceived as more pleasant than light powered by the electronic type; and subjects who were sensitive to flicker exhibited a sharp contraction of EEG-alpha waves (an indication of arousal), increased performance speed, and decreased performance accuracy when exposed to the conventional-ballast condition (Kuller & Laike, 1998). Other researchers have cited numerous early studies that demonstrated that luminous flickering affects neural activity, visual performance (including reading ability), and headaches; their findings reveal that the use of high-frequency ballasts reduces the negative effects of fluorescent light flicker on performance and physiological arousal (McCoy, 2002; Veitch & McColl, 2001).

Manufacturers of full-spectrum fluorescent lamps (i.e., those that mimic daylight) assert that their use improves people's performance, vision, and mood; but existing research only confirms improved accuracy in distinguishing colors. Reports of beneficial effects on performance and mood are likely influenced by personal beliefs and expectations rather than the lamps' actual characteristics (Veitch, 1997). Consider designing lighting systems so that indirect lighting accounts for 60 percent or more of total horizontal illuminance because direct (down-light) illumination casts more shadows and makes rooms seem smaller and less spacious than does indirect (up-light) illumination; and direct-to-indirect lighting ratios affect brightness, shadowing, visual comfort, uniformity of light distribution, perceptions of spaciousness, and overall workplace satisfaction (Houser, Tiller, Becker, & Mistrick, 2002). Inadequate or improper lighting can result in glare or shadows; light from general, ambient, and indirect lighting is often more suitable for working horizontally with paper documents than for working vertically with computers; and glare can cause eyestrain and headaches as well as contribute to accidents and stress (McCoy, 2002). It is important to note that computer monitors and other video display terminals (VDTs) or screens produce glare and also reflect light from other sources.

Ventilation

Another factor that needs to be considered when planning the design of a workplace environment is the location of ventilation ducts (if natural ventilation is not an option) and level of force from which the air is expelled from those ducts. In spaces with higher ceilings and ceiling-based ventilation, this force will need to be greater in order to adequately circulate the air. Keep in mind that too much force can lead to noticeable air movement, which can adversely affect the employee (Melikov, Pitchurov, Naydenov, & Langkilde, 2005). Also gender-based discrepancies affect how men and women perceive, interact, communicate (i.e., connect and share), and dress. Men often wear much more clothing than women in the workplace environment. Men also tend to experience heat to a greater degree because the average man has more muscle mass and a slightly higher body temperature and heart rate than the average woman. Although modern fashion trends are allowing for more casual attire, office dress codes consistently require more coverage for men than for women. In office environments, these conditions result in situations wherein temperature controlled by men creates a cold environment for women, and temperature control by women creates a hot, sweaty environment for men. Designers should specify thermal controls for each office or cubicle space, such that if a smaller, individual system could be moderated (under desk system; closing a vent or turn up the fan speed) by the individual, then each would have his/her own thermal comfort zone. Smaller independently controlled systems decrease the energy consumption of the building and increase worker satisfaction.

Noise

Sound levels in interior environments can be decreased via architectural variations and the strategic use of interior materials. Research indicates that noise can be controlled by a combination of floor plan layout, interior finishes, and equipment selection and placement (Bame & Wells, 1995). Ceiling angles and materials have the most potential for acoustical control; and designers can use suspended ceilings, partitions, and specific insulating materials to reduce noise (Banbury, Tremblay, Macken, & Jones, 2001). Extraneous noise can be inexpensively masked in workspaces simply by providing a continuous noise stream of music (pink noise) at about 45 to 50 dB; this increases the pitch baseline, which decreases the perceived impact of the original source of noise. To reduce noise in large open spaces, consider focusing on the shape of the room, varying ceiling heights, and limiting the amount of hard smooth surfaces (Maxwell & Evans, 2000).

Space Planning

When the environment has been addressed, the next step is to assess each of the individual workstations. One way to plan for the diversity of workers intended to occupy a space is through the analysis of the different job descriptions.

This should provide a generic look at many of the intended functions that an employee will be responsible for within a given job. An example of how this information may help with the space planning might be the frequency at which a particular job function requires photocopying. Often receptionists are charged with greeting people entering the office space, answering telephones, and making copies. With this knowledge it makes sense to place the copy room close to the receptionist and with a view (reflected or direct) to the front door. Because many employers will not want visitors to see inside a copy room, a one-way mirror can be installed so that the receptionist can monitor the front desk while making copies. If possible, it is also a good idea to speak directly to and observe employees to find out which jobs require more repetitive movements, static loading (such as carrying stacks of copies or other equipment), or awkward postures (such as spending a great deal of time on the telephone). Simply speaking to an employee may not yield accurate results because many people are unaware of the harmful effects that can arise from poor ergonomics.

Within the workstation analysis it may behoove the designer to develop a floor plan depicting zones relative to ventilation ducting and windows. Employees may then select a cooler zone versus one that is warmer, or a zone with more natural light versus one that is dimmer. Some people will prefer a cooler environment to the presence of natural light, and some will prefer natural light to cooler temperatures. Workstations should also be designed according to the intended task. Accountants and drafters, for example, will require larger and sometimes multiple computer monitors. Attorneys and editors will require ample lighting, but it must be soft so that glare isn't produced from the light hitting white paper. Keep in mind that there are different weights and degrees of gloss used for paper. For example, the book you are reading right now is a heavier weight of paper with a gloss finish, which means that it has higher light reflecting qualities.

Also consider that there will be different people occupying the different work spaces, and that the needs of six-foot-two-inch man with broad shoulders will be very different from those of a five-foot petite woman. Not only will the distance between the back of the knee to the bottom of the foot (important while sitting) be different, but so too will be the arm span reach. We do not want the woman to be reaching or having to constantly get up from her chair to retrieve items, and likewise we do not want the man to be cramped up or be constantly bending over in his space. This means that we need adjustable chairs, cabinets, computer monitor stands, and keyboard trays that raise and lower according to the individual's body.

Practical Applications for Designers

Use these resources, activities, and discussion questions to help you identify, synthesize, and retain this chapter's core information. These tools are designed to complement the resources you'll find in this book's companion Study Guide.

SUMMING IT UP

The office environment must be taken into special consideration, as it becomes a microcosm in and of itself with a potentially large and diverse group of people in relatively close quarters working for many hours toward a common goal. The office environment must be as flexible as possible if it is going to accommodate a future with endless technological possibilities.

The traditional office environment developed at the beginning of the industrial era is seen as a bureaucracy consisting of hierarchical tiers of employees ranging from general workers through managers to corporate heads. New corporate structuring strategies are being explored, including integrative, democratic, and self-managing team structures—which are collaborative structures. A predominant feature of an office is its hierarchical organizational structure. Workplace designs provide not only opportunities to build allegiances between workers and the organization, but also a way for outsiders to glimpse the values of the organization. This greater accountability leads to a sense of ownership, which in turn leads to pride in the work, better interpersonal and customer relations, and improved quality of the product or service.

You can also refer to this textbook's companion Study Guide for a comprehensive list of Summary Points.

Global Workplace: Conducting Business and Workplace Design

Ruth Beals, IDEC, ASID,
Converse College

Diverse cultures across the world are changing the way they work and conduct business. The global marketplace has exposed people to many types of business relationships and technologies. Knowledge-based workers transcend business relationships with their need for both collaborative environments and flexible worksites.

Westerners conduct business following rules and regulations; in contrast, Easterners typically conduct business based on relationships (Hooker, 2003, 2007). Rule-based business cultures adhere to employment laws and equal opportunity, executives are of a wide age range and both genders, and corporations often utilize flattened hierarchies. Relationship-based business cultures are staffed by loyal relatives and friends of the owners and/or top administrators, age commands respects due to its implied higher status, women are often marginalized (Hooker, 2008), and corporations follow a highly disciplined hierarchy ruled by an elder.

Corporate interiors reflect these practices, which are based on cultural beliefs. The rule-based cultures may have open office settings with management and staff in the same or similar size workstations with a consistency in the finishes. Highest level administrators may still reside in private offices, yet these are typically located for the best communication efficiency and designed to reflect the company's image. Coffee-shop-type meeting spaces encourage spontaneous conversations among all positions, which result in a vertical sharing of ideas.

Relationship-based businesses can be found in buildings with traditional, sumptuous private offices. Entry and elevator lobbies and corridors to the private offices have higher-quality materials, thus providing a regal path to the top executives. Staff areas are often surrounded by management offices along window walls, providing a supervisory atmosphere. Multiple floors of these office types faced with nondescript materials support staff feeling unimportant and uninspired.

The increase in knowledge based workers needed for creative strategies and product development is establishing new requirements within both rule-based and relationship-based business cultures. New types of workplace environments are needed to support these employees' ability to "engage in the more cognitive and collaborative patterns of knowledge work" (Myerson and Ross, 2006). Knowledge-based workers tend to consider their office a destination for collaboration within their professional community. These effective and efficient workers need fluid exchanges of information without the constraints of dated furniture and interiors.

Rule-based cultures are better able to integrate knowledge-based workers due to established levels of trust and responsibility, and flattened hierarchies. These corporations and institutions recognize and accept that their staff is not physically or psychologically tied to the equipment of the past generation. Office hoteling—the system of impermanent, flexible workstations and storage for those workers not needing a day-to-day work space—began in the 1990s. Now, employees can work from virtually anywhere because all records and information needed are available through laptops and cell phones with wireless Internet access.

The new generations of young employees will challenge relationship-based cultures. Knowledge workers define themselves within their professions rather than by their corporate culture; they will find inflexible and hierarchal environments out of date and inefficient (Myerson & Ross, 2006). To retain a competitive work force, relationship-based corporations and institutions will be forced to embrace integrated levels of responsive work environments.

References

Hooker, J. N. (2007). *Cross-cultural issues in business ethics.* Retrieved from http://web.tepper.cmu.edu/jnh/aib.pdf

Hooker, J. N. (2003). *Working across cultures.* Stanford, CA: Stanford University Press.

Myerson, J., & Ross, P. (2006). *Space to work: New office design.* London: Laurence King Publishing Ltd., p. 8.

KEY TERMS

- **acute stressor**
- **ambient stressors**
- **bioeffluents**
- **building-related illness**
- **building-specific illness**
- **chronic stressors**
- **collaborative structure**
- **ergonomics**
- **external stressors**
- **hierarchical structure**
- **home office**
- **illuminance**
- **illumination**
- **internal stressors**
- **luminaire**
- **luminance**
- **neighborhood work center**
- **nonterritorial office**
- **satellite office**
- **telecommuting**
- **virtual office**
- **workplace culture**

WEB LINKS

Architects H. Hendy Associates, featuring the Pacific Sunwear corporate office (www.hhendy.com/portfolio/corporate/corporate_09.htm)

Biomimicry Institute (www.biomimicryinstitute.org)

Environmental Protection Agency on the types of sick building syndrome (www.epa.gov/iaq/pubs/hpguide.html)

Ergonomics.org (www.ergonomics.org)

HGTV, on home office space (www.hgtv.com/designers-portfolio/home-offices/index.html)

Metromedia.com on day care, wellness centers, and other creative spaces (www.metromodemedia.com/features/Balance0047.aspx)

Occupational Health & Safety Administration (www.osha.gov)

OWP/P | Cannon Design, featuring Metropolitan Capital Bank design (www.owpp.com/content.cfm/metropolitan_bank)

Popular Science, on the future of work (www.popsci.com/archive-viewer?id=eVMLO1GM9uQC&pg=44&query=employee+lounge)

Smart Lighting (http://smartlighting.rpi.edu)

STUDIO ACTIVITY 13.1

Office Layout

Design Problem Statement
Facilities managers or other nondesign professions often design many current office environments. Your job is to analyze an existing office and identify ways to improve its layout.

Directions
Step One: Contact a local design firm and ask to meet with the office manager. Have the office manager give you a tour of the workplace environment. Be sure to take notes on all of the different duties different employees are expected to perform. Also take note of the environmental conditions in which they perform their duties.

Step Two: Sketch out the floor plan of that office from memory. Be sure to include where certain job functions are and identify if they are clustered; i.e., do the accountants, contract reviewers (attorneys), and so on?

Step Three: Develop a floor plan for this office space that not only clusters similar job functions, but provides adequate environmental provisions for specific functions (i.e., walls for sound proofing, ventilation for copy machines and printers, and so on).

Deliverables
Two rendered plan views: one of the existing office layout and one of the modified versions you develop. Be sure to diagram both drawings to identify the problem (and why) and the solution (and why). Include two perspective drawings of design improvements to the two worst areas in the office.

DISCUSSION QUESTIONS

1. Describe the way the workplace environment has evolved more than ever before. Provide your own examples.

2. What is Taylorism, and when was it established? Do you think that it should be applied in our modern day 21st-century society, or do you find it to be primitive?

3. What is important for a designer to research before redesigning a working environment, and what aspects of the work should be considered?

4. Describe the benefits and the drawbacks from open office designs.

5. What are some design methods that can be used in the design fields to dampen noise?

LEARNING ACTIVITIES

1. Research biomimicry, and describe ways in which we can apply this technology to the way businesses of any kind can be run. Provide your own examples.

2. Design a modern 21st-century ideal working environment; what important elements would you include in your design to make it successful, and why?

3. Design a solution to the office environment–office cubicle dilemma; how would you solve the design problems that face this working environment?

4. Create a layout of an office that promotes a healthy working environment, encourages dialog among employees, and allows for sufficient privacy for employees to work comfortably and in optimal conditions.

5. Design a stress relief area in a working office for employees to use on their breaks and lunches to de-stress. What amenities would you provide and how would having this space accessible in a working environment increase employee satisfaction and productivity?

14 Health Care Environments

Hospitals are places that you have to stay in for a long time, even if you are a visitor. Time doesn't seem to pass in the same way in hospitals as it does in other places. Time seems to almost not exist in the same way as it does in other places.

—Pedro Almodovar

When the United States entered the 21st century, we saw a 10-year increase in the average human life expectancy (U.S. Census Bureau, 2008). Prior to this time many people died during childhood, and few lived to old age. Within early human civilizations the practice of medicine and religion were intertwined, thus much of health and healing was attributed to the supernatural. These early civilizations relied upon specific temples dedicated to a healer-god to meet their health needs (Goldin, 1983). The unfortunate truth was that most of the people who entered these "hospitals" ultimately died.

Between ancient times and the 19th century, the design of hospitals evolved very little. In the United States, many hospitals served as *death houses* for the poor (Risse, 1999). These facilities were usually composed of large, open spaces, housing many beds arranged in long rows. Patients not only had to endure a lack of sanitation and privacy, but the practices and protocols within the hospital often led to the dehumanization of patients and their loved ones (Figure 14.1).

Throughout the 20th century, the design of health care facilities changed significantly (Risse, 1999). Many of these changes were in response to social and political influences. In recent decades, changes in the design of health care facilities can be attributed to the many advances in medical technology; for example, the 1950s ushered in an era of germ phobia. Antiseptics and antibacterial agents gripped American

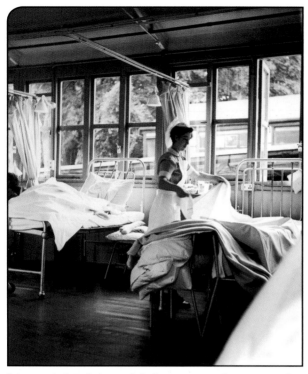

[**Figure 14.1**] Early hospitals had no provision for privacy, and in many cases, they were overcrowded, with conditions that were less than humane. © Mary Evans Picture Library / Alamy

culture, and most hospitals reeked of disinfectant. Germ phobia brought rise to sterile designs that called upon the extensive use of plastic, vinyl, and latex. In addition, bright harsh lighting and the color white provided the illusion of, and subsequent association to, cleanliness; however, these design styles made the environment appear cold, austere, and impersonal, which disaffected many of the patients and even the caregivers. These uniform appearances also led to a set of beliefs about one's role as a patient in the health care environment. Termed a *behavior setting* by Gibson, the subsequent behaviors were what Talcott Parsons called the **sick role**. Developed in the 1950s, Parsons' sick role theory outlined two rights and two obligations of individuals who become sick:

- **Rights**
  1. The sick person is exempt from normal social roles.
  2. The sick person is not responsible for his/her condition.

- **Obligations**
  1. The sick person should try to get well.
  2. The sick person should seek out and cooperate with the health care provider.

The resulting behavior from the patient includes passivity in health care decisions, the surrendering of one's belief to a person of power, and behaviors related to learned helplessness (Holton, 1986). The *behavior setting* and the *sick role* continue to be issues of significance in some of today's health care settings.

Communicable diseases were major health problems in the past, and sanitation or cleanliness was, and continues to be, the main combatant to infection. Many people believed if something looked clean and smelled clean, then it must be clean; however, modern associations and notions of cleanliness with the color white and the smell of antiseptic are disappearing. Many now realize that an environment can be comfortable and have color while also being clean. Likewise, many experts and the general populace have embraced the idea that inviting, easily understood, and nonthreatening environments can play a pivotal role in patient recovery, although this shift in sociocultural values has occurred slowly.

Birthing centers of the middle and late 1970s began the trend of making hospitals warmer and more inviting (Sloane, 1994), as well as models for scientific and medical excellence.

This model adopted a holistic approach to promote healing by simultaneously addressing a patient's physical, psychological, emotional, spiritual, and social well-being (World Health Organization, 2007). Consistent with this model is the development of a more inviting, home-like environment, with softer furnishings, warmer colors, and barrier-free designs that maintain the patient's dignity and promote family participation in care.

Of particular importance to designers is the *Planetree's* focus on architectural and environmental design as a co-variable in the healing process. This importance has been revealed in numerous studies (van den Berg, 2005). More specifically, the *Planetree* model advocates for facility design that is conducive to the healing process through the use of efficient layouts that support patient dignity; warm, home-like, noninstitutional designs; and the removal of unnecessary architectural barriers. In addition, art, aesthetics, and elements that connect patients with nature are emphasized (Planetree, 2009).

Increasingly, health care facilities have incorporated similar features into their design, and the present-day hospital often includes patient suites, gift shops, community meeting rooms, and greenscaping. This new look inspires perceptual impressions that are very different from the facilities endured by our great-grandparents. As designers consider various plans for the health care environment, they will need to develop designs that help reduce stress and anxiety; foster place attachment; facilitate patients', caretakers', and visitors' abilities to find their way around the facility; and be aware of the symptom manifestations for various diseases in order to use design as a proactive measure for health and safety. Some of the specific issues that designers should consider include natural and artificial lighting levels and lighting transitions (lighting levels from indoors to outdoors); facility layout (corridors and intersections); surface materials; themes; and the relationship of nature to human health and satisfaction. Today's health care environment is no longer the sterile environment of our not-so-distant past; instead, it is a complex environment involving people, nature, and technology, and designs that bring them together.

PERCEPTIONS OF THE HEALTH CARE INSTITUTION

Although the designs of health care facilities are evolving, the unfortunate truth is that they continue to effect behaviors through our perceptions. Recall from Chapter 2 that Roger Barker's behavior-setting theory is a set of behaviors that result from common sensory elements that occur throughout environments that share similar purposes. Unfortunately, many hospitals in the past shared common attributes with other federally funded institutions of the day, such as schools and prisons. Each of these institutions shared common physical attributes, such as large concrete or brick buildings, long corridors, and lobbies that echoed—all environmental factors that led to a perceptual belief about those institutions.

Common institutional attributes, combined with popular media, such as the 1975 movie *One Flew Over the Cuckoo's Nest,* to symbolize an inhabitant's lack of personal autonomy or control over our person within the health care, educational, or correctional institutions. This symbolization fostered an unequal distribution of power in which the institution's employees had near absolute authority over the occupant (patient, student, and prisoner).

Scale

To counter the effects of the sick role, designs for health care facilities should strive to minimize institutional perceptions. Exterior elements affecting homeyness include supportive protection (i.e., elements that evoke familiarity, enclosure, and care), **human-scale elements** (elements that are neither oversized nor undersized), and those that promote qualities of naturalness. Designers should avoid massive buildings with long uninterrupted façades, and instead utilize elements found in single-family homes (e.g., covered entries protected from the weather, detailed window treatments, differentiated roof lines, diversity in building materials) and generous landscaping with elements such as benches to suggest human presence (Marsden, 1999; Figure 14.2). Additionally, many may find low-rise buildings more comfortable because they are perceived as being easier to enter and exit. Vital institutional elements, such as security systems and areas of rescue

[**Figure 14.2**] Note the varying rooflines, coupled with changes in elevation. These elements combine to create the illusion that the environment is smaller than it actually is and help make it a more inviting place. © Arcaid Images

assistance (spaces that have direct access to an exit, utilized during evacuations), should be blended into the environment and made easily accessible to staff and emergency workers but should not detract from the overall ambience.

Layout Issues

Layout is integral to successful design within any large facility; therefore, design layouts must be consistent and easily understandable. If a person is disoriented within a community, he/she can look for cues from street signs, landmarks, or sounds. Within institutional environments, however, orientation cues are usually smaller and much less familiar; this can lead to difficulties in wayfinding. Creating architecturally diverse environments within the larger facility—with clear sight lines between different areas, visually distinctive features, and recognizable furniture—provides reference points that serve to improve patient wayfinding (Passini, Pigot, Rainville, & Tetreault, 2000). As discussed in Chapter 1, Lynch's elements of the city can be used as a way to enhance environmental legibility. Each floor or department (Intensive Care, Surgery, Emergency Room, and so on) can be thought of as a district; nursing stations might serve as nodes from which people travel to and from; the hallways are paths and the walls serve as edges. This leaves landmarks. It behooves designers to develop landmarks that are not only appropriate for the area that they serve, but they should also be a source of inspiration with special meaning (Passini, Rainville, Marchand, & Joanette, 1998; see Figure 14.3).

A health care facility's overall design should attempt to evoke a more residential feel, with flexible spaces (i.e., those used for recreational and other social activities) that

[**Figure 14.3**] Inspirational statues commissioned from local artists can serve as landmarks if they are strategically placed throughout the health care facility. © Daily Mail/Rex / Alamy

are centrally located (Passini et al., 2000). Facilities serving a Catholic constituency might contain a large cross in the lobby or a different "station of the cross" for each floor; in a Buddhist community, the statues could be one of the different Buddhas or Bodhisattvas. Through these kinds of such special considerations, design can help compensate for the physical and mental losses of the various patients (Zeisel, 2000).

Security

Security in the health care environment is an issue that can command its own chapter or an entire book dedicated to the subject. As is the case with all sections in this chapter, the discussion of security is brief, and by no means comprehensive. One of the more prominent safety concerns is the control of pharmaceuticals. Because drug abuse now spans all segments of society including physicians, nurses, and patients, the careful monitoring of pharmaceutical dispensaries and administration of medication are priorities. An innovative approach to this issue is dispensaries similar

to vending machines that dispense appropriate medication to the health care worker depending upon each patient's medical needs. Of course each health care worker would have to log into the machine, thus providing a record of who received, what medication, how much was administered, and for which patient.

Another significant concern is related to patient outbursts. Many illnesses and medications can alter a person's behavior and in some cases cause that person to become violent toward the medical staff, other patients, and to himself/herself. This requires security measures that might include environmental restraints such as restricting access of patients to certain parts of the facility, physical restraints such as straps that hold patients to their beds, or chemical restraints such pharmaceuticals. Although there are many laws pertaining to the use of restraints by medical staff, the health care designer's role is to simply ensure the least invasive provisions for environmental and physical restraints, as well as spaces and furnishings that would not hurt a patient who has temporarily lost self-control.

More recently the health care environment has been identified as a viable source for terrorist attacks. Today's notion of terrorism is largely associated with extremist foreign groups who despise the United States and other Western countries. Clearly this is a concern that should not be diminished in any way; however, health care designers need to also consider the activities of homegrown terrorists such as the mass shootings of recent years. Inner-city hospitals, located in the more socially disadvantaged communities, are at particular risk of terrorist activities; and emergency rooms are the most vulnerable. Designers need to make provisions for these situations. One idea to help control the effects of a possible terrorist attack might be a waiting room that is detached from the main hospital. This waiting room could be reinforced to contain the damage of a potential explosive devise, and to withstand the potential of a person trying to drive a vehicle through the wall. When the medical staff is ready to see the patient, he/she would then need to pass through a built-in metal detector prior to entering the actual hospital. This is only one idea; health care designers need to think out-of-the-box in order to ensure the safety and security of patients and medical staff.

ISSUES IN HEALTH CARE ENVIRONMENTS

Patients and their families, as well as health care providers who participated in focus groups pertaining to the design of health care environments, identified wayfinding, privacy, and accommodations for family members as the three most important features (Leventhal-Stern et al., 2003). Other more endemic issues of concern include stress and place attachment. Stress is a biological reaction to adverse stimulus—physical, mental, or emotional, internal or external—that can affect a person's normal state of well-being. For most people, illness is a source of stress that is elevated when they are placed into a health care setting. The bonds of place attachment can also be a source of stress when abruptly severed. These bonds are an affective connection between people and a particular place or setting (Tuan, 1974). In many ways, a person's place attachment involves an interpretive and cognitive perspective toward an environment and his/her subsequent emotional reaction to it (Hummon, 1992). Stress brought about by the severing of place attachment bonds usually arises when a person is forced to leave his/her home and enter an institution such as a health care facility.

CULTURAL CONNECTION 14.1

For a hospital to be considered truly "patient-centered," the designers, staff, and administration must reflect a high degree of *cultural competency* (Guadagnino, 2008). This concept of cultural competency speaks to issues of the sociocultural factors or differences being reflected in the quality of care received upon a clinical encounter. Patients come to the medical facilities not only with health issues but also with their culturally based expectations, beliefs, and behaviors. Because many health care professionals are no longer taught *Medical Anthropology,* a once-valuable tool for the medical arts has become something akin to folk remedies. The cultural belief that medicinal benefits can be had in methods other than modern Western medicine have been forgotten and abandoned; and oftentimes doctors are the ones left at a disadvantage for understanding their patients. Designers can aid in this by adding in some fashion ethnographic details and symbols into surfaces. Symbols or pictographs could be representative of holistic healing beliefs and other ethnic or cultural information medical staff might need. For example, were an individual to come into an emergency room with chest pain and could not speak English well, pictographs containing well-known culturally specific art engraved into the admissions desk top could be used to expedite the admitting process. If the individual were to select the image or symbol best representing his/her culture, the appropriate staff member could be summoned to facilitate language and cultural health barriers. The goal is, as quickly as possible, to provide a bridge between patient and staff through a design feature. Recent research shows racial and ethnic inequality in health care as being pervasive throughout the United States (Guadagnino, 2008). Therefore, as a reminder to those who design health care environments: The doctors' creed of "First, do no harm" is near identical to the architects' solemn oath to "protect the health, safety, and welfare of the public." Thus, cultural or ethnic prejudice and bias have no place in the design of health care environments.

Stress and Anxiety

Providing environments that help mitigate stress should be a primary concern when developing health care institutions. Many people experience strong emotions related to fear and anxiety when they are required to stay in a health care environment. People who are admitted to health care facilities often experience a profound sense of loss, particularly in long-term care facilities and rehabilitation hospitals. For many, when hospitalized, nearly everything about the person, with the exception of their illness, becomes invisible; and the psychological loss of control that results from not being allowed to make decisions about their lives and the activities that they can partake in, reduces the patients' desire to be proactive about their health (Brannon & Feist, 1997). Much of a patient's stress derives from feelings generated by negative experiences—losing control of privacy and normal routines, feeling vulnerable because their condition diminishes their sense of mastery, fearing an unknown outcome—and is exacerbated by the separation from home. High levels of stress, especially when sustained over time, can have devastating psychological and physical effects, which include depression.

Views of Nature

Stress reduces the efficiency of the human immune system. When under stress, older adults (who require the services of health care facilities most) are particularly vulnerable to decreased **immunocompetency**, the ability or capacity for the immune system to respond or function adequately (Lutgendorf et al., 2001). Incorporating aspects of nature within health care environments can help establish a semblance of familiarity and evoke feelings of relaxation (Kaplan & Kaplan, 1989), as can allowing patients to personalize their rooms. The use of natural settings within institutions helps to reduce the anxiety many patients experience (see Figure 14.4). Research has shown that gardens and green spaces that promote privacy also promote healing for all patients (Sherman, Varni, Ulrich, & Malcarne, 2005).

In long-term care facilities, rehabilitation facilities, and behavioral health settings, a garden incorporated into the overall design helps to increase participation in future-oriented exercises (e.g., planning, planting, tending). Stress levels encountered by family members have also been mitigated by exposure to natural settings, and access to nature and gardens has been shown to be a beneficial distraction as well as a mood enhancer (Whitehouse et al., 2001). It has also been shown to alleviate stress and anxiety, improve psychological function, increase identification with an environment (Larsen, Adams, Deal, Kweon, & Tyler, 1998), and promote psychological restoration for both patients and health care workers. For example, tending and nurturing plants can have

[**Figure 14.4**] Views of nature have been shown to bring about a calming effect on people who experience stress. The access to nature can be incorporated into the interior design or into the landscape design. © Robert Daly / Alamy

many psychologically and physically therapeutic qualities; such activities help to restore patients' sense of control, give patients a sense of purpose and meaning, and keep patients mentally active. Researchers recommend garden features that can be viewed or touched as a means to promote interaction among patients and health care workers. Some suggest that these natural spaces may be appropriate for areas where medical consultations and some treatments occur (Sherman et al., 2005). Roger Ulrich's (1984a) findings indicate that psychologically appropriate artwork, such as nature scenes (especially those of water and trees), can also positively affect patient outcomes in an acute care setting by reducing blood pressure, anxiety, intake of pain medication, length of patients' hospital stays (Friedrich, 1999), and sadness and depression. Gardens and other similar amenities tend to work best, however, when they allow for socialization or afford comfortable seating near views and sounds of nature (Sherman et al., 2005). Features might include fountains, shaded seating, garden paths, and secluded sitting areas. Patients in hospitals who have a view of pleasant landscapes outside their hospital room also have shorter postoperative stays, require lower doses of painkillers, and experience lower levels of stress. Conversely, nursing reports revealed more negative outcomes from patients whose

hospital room had a view of a brick wall (Ulrich, 1984a). Consider the following scenario:

> A young man who suffered a brain injury in a traffic accident is now in a rehabilitation facility. His higher cognitive functions are not affected, but his ability to speak is impaired. This patient is experiencing tremendous stress as a result of the trauma and pain of the injury itself; intrusive thoughts about permanent brain damage and immobility; and the unfamiliar sights, sounds, smells, and activities of his surroundings. If he were healthy, his feelings of anxiety and helplessness would likely cause him to seek the refuge of his home, but his condition prevents that option.

Design can serve to increase this patient's feelings of comfort and control, as well as his rate of recovery, by providing the following features in this new environment:

- A private room with colors, materials, and features typical of a home or hotel

- Comfortable accommodations for visitors
- Various sources of distraction (e.g., TV, DVD, radio, reading materials, natural elements, a view)
- Areas in which to mingle with other patients, as well as a garden he can visit or tend when he is able

As part of the overall facility design, it is important to include visual access to surrounding garden spaces through the use of tinted windows or small private patio areas. Also sitting areas that allow an individual to view green spaces from both inside and outside the facility should be part of the design's programming. In the **long-term care facility**, designers will want to develop flexible designs that allow patients to bring with them personal items, such as a bed and dresser. Attributes such as these convey familiarity with the space and evoke personal, often happy memories, thus helping patients feel more comfortable in their new surroundings. Also, designs should provide opportunities for occupants to control their environment by being able to open or shut blinds, make their beds, and display items that reflect their personal tastes.

Patient Control

Patient rooms accommodating multiple roommates often evoke feelings associated with being overwhelmed by unwanted noise and social interaction; resident physicians and family members indicate that private rooms allow for more control over unwanted interaction, and therefore facilitate visits with family and friends (Morgan & Stewart, 1998).

CULTURAL CONNECTION 14.2

Many individuals from Western cultures value privacy, especially when they feel vulnerable; but members of large families or other cultures may prefer shared rooms over private ones (Day & Cohen, 2000). This inconsistency between cultural and individual preferences requires that both designers and caregivers gain an intimate knowledge of current and potential patient populations. It should be noted that the HIPAA (Health Insurance Portability and Accessibility Act of 1996) regulations address security and privacy of "protected health information" (PHI; Gostin, 2001). These regulations put an emphasis on acoustic and visual privacy. This means that shared rooms where a nurse or other health care provider verbally discusses a patient's condition, medications, or treatment options should not be overheard; or they could be found in violation. Although HIPAA does not regulate facility design per se, the act calls into question the affects of location and layout of workstations that handle medical records and other patient information, paper and electronic transmissions (e.g. placement of computer monitors, copy machines, fax machines), as well as patient accommodations (see Figure 14.5).

Following admission to a health care facility, other factors contribute to patients' stress. People tend to conceptualize illnesses as being temporary rather than permanent (which helps us maintain a sense of control), and when we are (or believe we are) sick or injured, we assume the "role" of patient (Brannon & Feist, 1997). The sick role, as discussed earlier in this chapter, is based on *operant conditioning,* and does not realistically apply to chronic conditions. Instead, being diagnosed as having a chronic illness changes our self-perception and our coping strategies according to our understanding of both the disease and the outcome (Brannon & Feist, 1997). This role can lead patients, especially the elderly, to adopt a passive or defeatist attitude toward both their immediate circumstances and their overall lives.

Intrusive negative thoughts, which can remain with patients for months, can interfere with patients' successful adaptation, contributing to anxiety, depression, and physical symptoms (Lutgendorf et al., 2001). These thoughts may derive from the patient's own concerns or from overheard conversations among relatives or caregivers. Intrusive thoughts can be kept to a minimum by pleasant distractions, such as those afforded by a private room in which a person may speak freely, enjoy a favorite TV show, or read a book with little interference.

Designers can provide specific living components that give residents greater control over their lives, such as layouts that allow them to move easily and freely throughout the environment. Feelings of autonomy can be increased by homey, inviting environments that provide various means for residents to increase physical strength, decrease mental stressors, and maintain social connections (Martin, 2002; Young & Brewer, 2001). Researchers recommend creating a noninstitutional atmosphere that includes outdoor spaces (Passini et al., 2000), and advocate using rich colors to enhance social areas. In long-term care facilities, designers should consider incorporating residents' personal objects into public spaces, providing opportunities for residents to enjoy agreeable aromas (from sources such as cooking, flowers, and herbs), and designing workspaces that enable residents to be involved in the facility's daily operations (e.g., answering telephones) to give them a sense of inclusion and control (Martin, 2002).

Designers should strive to minimize the negative feelings typically associated with institutional environments, which include lack of control (i.e., feelings of powerlessness or helplessness) resulting from perceived financial, physical, and psychological constraints and social factors (e.g., sick role, stereotyping, power or status levels; Martin, 2002; Young & Brewer, 2001).

[**Figure 14.5**] This nurse's station not only serves as a landmark and is easily identified as a place to acquire information, but it also helps protect patient privacy by keeping the computer monitors low and behind the counter. Note, too, that there is no visible fax machine where an unattended document might accidentally sit in public view, nor a photocopier where prying eyes might observe private content on a page. © Thomas Photography LLC / Alamy

SUSTAINABILITY CONNECTION 14.1

Hospitals are where sick people go, and they are also where many germs hang out. There is a specific issue that needs to be addressed regarding surviving or maintaining health—while in the hospital. Decades of Americans overusing antibiotics and antibacterial soaps have given one bug the opportunity to learn how to beat all human precautionary medicines/soaps. It's called the "Superbug" because this *staph* bacterium can resist and thrive even with antibiotic treatment—almost nothing can kill it. Health care-associated Methicillin Resistant *Staphylococcus aureus* or more commonly referred to as MRSA (pronounced *mur-sa*) has been categorized separately because all cases have been found contracted in hospitals by patients with weakened immunity. MRSA enters the body through a cut, catheter, or breathing tube via the equipment or the hands of personnel. Designers can, therefore, create health care environments that support and bring focus to proper sanitary procedures. Sanitary items such as Personal Protective Equipment (PPE) "face masks," folded gowns, towels, and bedding could be integrated into the design. Perhaps shelving wraps around every column in a ward to display and promote the use of these hygiene items. Laundry capabilities, trash chutes, hand washing stations, proper equipment disposal or cleaning areas (autoclave), easily accessible gloves and gowns; none of these sanitary features needs to be ugly or institutional—merely easily cleaned.

PATIENT POPULATIONS

Of the populations served within health care environments, children and teenagers are especially vulnerable and experience a great deal of stress. Children depend upon the safety of their home and the security of knowing that their family is near; therefore, when children are removed from their home and separated from their parents, the result will be increased stress. An equally important population is teenagers. Not quite children anymore but also not an adult, this group can appear and sound mature but often have the stress-coping abilities of children. Their cognitive abilities also allow them to fear for their future, which inspires high levels of stress. Within this population, many struggle with their identity and thus try to disassociate themselves from their younger counterparts. This natural inner conflict becomes exacerbated with the fear of one's future, which often accompanies an illness. A third vulnerable population is the elderly. This population is the predominant population served by health care facilities. Once masters of their world, many elderly experience myriad of emotions related to declining health, which must be considered as part of the health care regime.

Children

Young people in the health care environment can range from infants to adolescent teens. Within this range there are a wide degree of developmental capabilities and needs that must be considered. Premature infants, for example, require diaper changing and assistance with feeding. Eight-year-olds, on the other hand, may desire books, crafts, and games to help them pass the time. For these populations the health care environment can be a terrifying place because it separates them from their families, friends, and home. Studies have shown that the presence of family members in the health care environment provides many benefits for the sick child (Dudley & Carr, 2004). As a result, hospital administrators have recognized the need for family-centered health care, thus fueling design trends that help facilitate parental involvement in a child's overall treatment plan. This forward thinking wasn't always part of health care practices (Figure 14.6).

Prior to the mid-19th century, there were no facilities dedicated to the care of sick children in the United States. Instead, when a child became ill, he/she often ended up in municipal almshouses, also known as poorhouses where the majority perished (Connolly, 2005). It wasn't until 1821 when a group of physicians in Dublin, Ireland who were concerned at the lack of medical services available to sick children founded the National Children's Hospital of Dublin (NACHRI, 2003). This hospital was among the first in the English-speaking world to provide services specifically to infants, toddlers, and children. In 1855, the first hospital dedicated to the health of children opened in the United States in the city of Philadelphia (NACHRI, 2003). The advent of specific hospitals for children was a necessity because many of the general hospitals during that time denied care to children (Connolly, 2005). It is interesting to note, however, children who were hospitalized throughout the 1800s and early 1900s often remained so for several months, which deprived the child of fresh air and fresh food. Additionally, during these times it was common for the hospital staff to discourage, or made it difficult, for parents to visit a sick child. The intent of this action was to prolong the child's contact with the hospital staff so that the child, who was often of immigrant parents, would be exposed to American middle-class values, behaviors, and health practices (Connolly, 2005). It was thought that this prolonged exposure would foster better overall health and hygiene practices of the foreign-born child (Figure 14.7).

Throughout the years, hospital care and design has made significant strides for all populations. Today, much research goes into the design of health care facilities, particularly for special populations such as infants and children. Some of this research has revealed a need for private patient rooms even within hospitals dedicated to children (Dudley & Carr, 2004). Private rooms are important because they help to control unintentional eavesdropping and protect

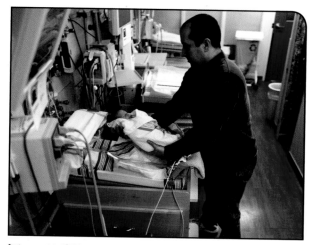

[**Figure 14.6**] This neonatal intensive care unit has many home-like features intended to make the mother and father more comfortable while visiting their infant. Numerous studies have shown that infants and children often pick up on the stress and anxiety experienced by their parents. These designs go a long way to alleviating some of that stress. © MCT via Getty Images

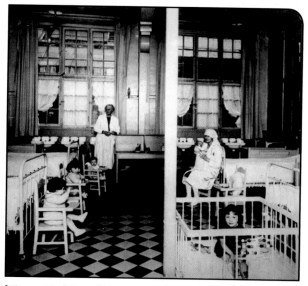

[**Figure 14.7**] In early hospitals, children were often inpatients for several months. It was believed that prolonged contact with hospital staff would inculcate a child, who was often of immigrant parents, with American middle-class values, behaviors, and health practices. © Mary Evans Picture Library / Alamy

privacy. Another advancement was related to the formation of associations. Research found that children created associations between a negative event such as an injection with the environment where the injection was given. The result was that medical procedures could no longer occur in the child's hospital room. Conversely, other recent research suggests that it may be beneficial for children to have certain

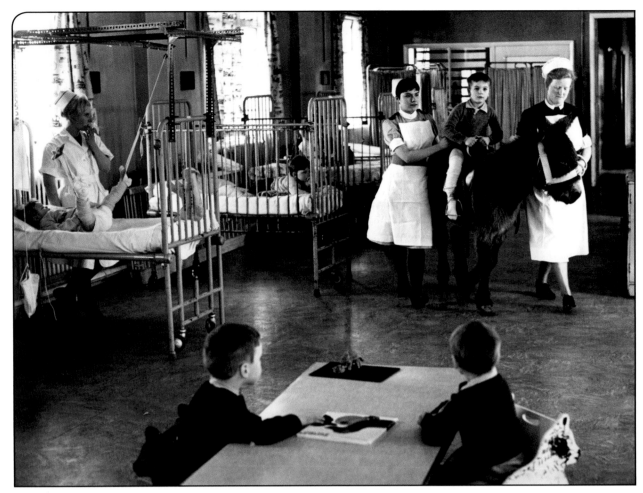

[**Figure 14.8**] Within patient rooms for children it is important to conceal medical equipment behind cupboards and drawers so that the child is not constantly reminded of his or her condition or a traumatic or painful medical procedure. Such relatively simple design solutions would also reduce the need for more inventive diversions. © Trinity Mirror / Mirrorpix / Alamy

procedures (usually those that take a significant amount of time such as dialysis) performed in their rooms (Fanurik et al., 2000) because the child is less likely to experience anxiety. In these situations, it is important that proper accommodations be made to allow for those procedures and the associated equipment. After the procedure is completed, provisions and space must be made to mask or hide the equipment. Without such provisions an association between the illness, procedure and the environment may remain at the forefront of thought, which would likely result in higher levels of stress for the patient (Figure 14.8).

Within today's health care environments for children, it is important to ensure that the child's needs are considered along with those of the parents. This might include multiuse comfortable furnishings, such as sofas that convert to a bed, adjustable and movable bedside and end tables, along with task lighting. Many parents encourage young children to share their bed, particularly when the child is frightened or feels vulnerable; therefore, designers might want to include larger beds so that the child can snuggle with mom or dad during the night. Also, consider that the family member may have to work while staying with the child. To accommodate such needs, desks with Internet access (data transmission must not interfere with hospital communication systems) should also be made available.

Adolescent Patients

Adolescence is a period of time that is relatively short, but extremely intense within the human lifespan. During this period, individuals tend to experience extreme thoughts and beliefs (Blumberg & Devlin, 2006), and they understand the world in profound ways. Likewise, as a teen's body develops into its adult form, he/she may become insecure about its appearance (Hutton, 2005). For these reasons, privacy is often an absolute need of this population.

Designing spaces in the health care environment for teenagers means that design consideration must be made to delineate this group from younger children and adults (Blumberg & Devlin, 2006). In many current hospitals and rehabilitation facilities, the adolescent patient is placed in either pediatric or adult wards. Unfortunately, neither of these places fully supports the unique social and emotional needs of the adolescent such as personal privacy and peer interaction (Hutton, 2005). Some research suggests that it may be beneficial to cluster adolescent patients within a separate unit in the hospital (Blumberg & Devlin 2006).

However, because teens are highly suggestive and self-conscious about their appearance and associations, they are highly influenced by styles and trends. Designers will, therefore, want to consult with teenage representatives either through focus groups or interviews in order to identify key attributes within the overall design style that will help foster feelings of familiarity and promote the teenage patient to be more comfortable. Among some of the important qualities of a patient room intended for a teenager is the provision for personalization and self-expression.

Despite most teenagers' claims of self-reliance and desire for independence, when faced with a frightening situation, most will seek emotional support from their family and friends. Included in the design of patient rooms should be sofas that can be easily pulled out into a bed (Blumberg & Devlin, 2006). Also additional activity spaces should be provided to encourage peer interaction without the presence of hospital staff (Hutton, 2005). Such spaces might include a game room, lounge, or fitness facility.

Be sure to include spaces where a teen can display posters, photographs of friends and family, or some memorabilia such as a football jersey. This provision will help accommodate the need for personalization or self-expression. Also, because privacy is so important to the teen, be sure to include locks on doors for patient rooms and bathrooms (Hutton, 2005). An override system can be implemented for those times when the health care worker is needed and a teen is unable to respond. Another possible solution to provide privacy is the use of curtains that are hung just inside the door. In this way, a person who enters the teen's room would have to pass through a second visual barrier (Kopec and Han, 2008). Teens are also likely to desire access to various forms of media and communication devices including telephones, computers, televisions, and DVD players (Blumberg & Devlin, 2006). As such, the designer will want to make provisions for the use of such devices.

The Elderly

As designers continue to pursue evidence-based design, the overall look and practice of health care facilities are expected to undergo radical changes. A catalyst for these changes is an aging Baby Boomer population, which are people who were born between 1943 and 1960 (Strauss & Howe, 1991). This population is unique in many ways from their predecessors in that many have a strong internal locus of control, as well as higher expectations. They are also technologically savvy and independent, and they also have the dubious distinction of having one of the highest divorce rates. This means that the aging Baby Boomers are more likely to be single but maintain close social bonds with friends and family who are dispersed throughout the world (Kopec, 2007).

Additionally, many within the Baby Boomer generation desire clearly defined social and physical boundaries between social interaction and privacy. This means that designers will need to strive toward greater segmentation within the floor plan to allow clear delineation among primary, secondary, and tertiary spaces. Alternatives will also have to be made to accommodate visual and auditory privacy.

When designing patient rooms for the Baby Boomer population, consider making provisions for the use of cellular phone, email, video chat rooms, and other emerging technologies. Also, a generational trend is the Baby Boomer's desire for daily showers. To accommodate this desire, designers will need to include universally designed shower stalls that allow for a mobility device to easily roll into the shower stall, as well as a bathroom large enough to accommodate various medical devices, including but not limited to rolling intravenous (IV) stands and wheelchairs.

OVERVIEW OF HEALTH CARE FACILITIES

Health care facilities are rapidly evolving in response to new technologies, treatment methods, shifts from acute to chronic diseases, and changes within the demands of the patient population. These changes have had a direct impact on the practice and design of health care facilities. For example, inpatient care is being replaced by outpatient services, which generates the need for special-care units and smaller satellite facilities. The modern health care facility thus takes many forms that range from small community clinics, urgent care centers, and out-patient surgery centers to small community hospitals, level-one trauma centers, and large teaching and research institutions, some of which occupy several acres. The key to successful health care design, however, is flexibility. Because health care is evolving quickly, it is imperative that health care facilities be designed so that they do not become obsolete.

The current economic state of the U.S. health care system on a whole poses another hurdle for health care designers. The high cost of doing business coupled with low and sometimes no reimbursement force many hospital administrators to wrestle with the *where* and *how* to allocate resources. For example, a single piece of medical technology can run into the hundreds of thousands to millions of dollars. The Stephens County Hospital in Georgia plans to purchase and have an MRI machine installed at a total cost of $2 million (Bauder, 2009). Designers are thus asked to find ways to cut the design and construction budget while still ensuring high quality. This is a conundrum that has yet to be resolved to the satisfaction of the patients, medical staff, health care insurance companies, and health care administrators.

At the time of this writing, H.R.4872 Health Care and Education Affordability Reconciliation Act of 2010 had been signed into law, thereby amending H.R.3590 Patient Protection and Affordable Care Act and becoming U.S. Public Law No. 111-148. It is as yet unknown how these legislative measures will come to affect the financing, form, and design of health care facilities; therefore, designers must be vigilant in remaining knowledgeable of the subsequent changes of health care mandates. One way hospital administrators have cut costs is to furnish and design the facility as a workplace environment; however, this is counterproductive to the patients occupying the hospital or other care centers. These places are their temporary homes.

Attracting and maintaining good physicians and nurses is one cornerstone of all successful hospitals. Another cornerstone is patient and family satisfaction with a health care facility. The architecture and interior design of hospitals can be an important tool in attracting and retaining the quality medical staff, successful HMOs and insurance plans, as well

as patients and their families (Carr, 2009). Achieving this level of satisfaction with design can be a challenge because the health care environment is unique from many other environments. It must accommodate myriad of end-users that include day-to-day patients who periodically come in for a treatment, patients who require one or more overnight stays, clinical employees, administrative employees, guests and visitors, and an assortment of venders, just to name a few. Designers can find it challenging to meet the unique needs of each user group with one design.

One's perceived level of power and control are important to the psychological health of patient populations (Martin, 2002); therefore, facilities should be designed with both patient populations and health care staff members (e.g., caregivers, administrators, maintenance workers) in mind. In many situations, staff discord and negative attitudes often transfer to patient-residents, (Martin, 2002). Likewise, the safety and comfort of visitors and guests must be ensured. It is an understanding of the patient populations and subsequent designs for the intended constituency of the health care facility that are the first steps in a successful environment.

For many, an aesthetically pleasing facility conveys the associative meaning that the facility provides high quality care. The logic is simple: "If the administrators care about the facility, then they will care for me." Designers, therefore, must consider each aspect of the patient, visitor, and venders' experience as he/she interacts with the environment. In many respects this interaction will begin with the approach to the facility, the wayfinding signs, the drop-off area, and the parking lots (Figure 14.9).

The ideal design will convey the message that the environment is inviting, caring, compassionate, and comfort-

[Figure 14.9] In many respects a patient and visitor's first impression of a health care facility is the physical attractiveness and ease with which a patient can be dropped off and then picked up. This means that designers must concern themselves with issues of automobile congestion and associated noise, as well as the inviting ambience of the entrance. © Leonard F. Wilcox / Alamy

able, but most of all, committed to patient safety and well-being. This is a tall order considering that many people (patients and visitors) often enter a health care facility with high levels of stress and anxiety.

Designs should be calming and convey the message that people have entered a safe refuge where competent people are ready to provide assistance in any way possible. This can be accomplished with symbolism such as wall murals depicting recovery, the use of color that symbolizes health and healing, and inspirational artwork (statues and painting). Kopec (2007), when discussing cultural diversity, suggests embedding inspiration proverbs into the flooring because most people will look down when they feel vulnerable and insecure.

Types of Health Care Environments

Current trends toward specialization within the field of health care have resulted in numerous types of health care environments with different needs. Among these environments are acute care, rehabilitation, psychiatric, long-term care, assisted living, outpatient care, hospices, congregate housing, adult daycare, and many more. The health care environment can be further divided according to the acceptance of public and private insurance.

Emergency rooms are typically found in the **acute care hospitals**. They are equipped to deal with emergencies, life-threatening illnesses and injuries, and to provide surgical operations; stays in these facilities tend to be relatively short, ranging from a few hours to a week or more. Within Western countries health conditions stemming from chronic (long-term) diseases are far more common than acute illnesses (short-term), such as infection (Brannon & Feist, 1997). This means that the problems many face when entering an acute care facility are complicated and require sophisticated technologies. A large number of patients who enter acute care facilities may do so through emergency rooms; however, the average emergency room is overcrowded, lacks privacy, personal space, and personal control. All of this can lead to a dehumanizing experience for the patient.

When designing emergency rooms consider the following:

- *Many windows.* When people have a nonthreatening scene to look at, they can lose themselves in their thoughts, thus bringing down their anxiety levels; however, the designer should be aware of issues such as glare and solar gain, and make the necessary shading provisions.
- *Televisions.* Window space in any building is limited and, therefore television screens can be added to the waiting room to augment limited window space.
- *Private spaces.* Many people who go to emergency rooms have high levels of anxiety and can benefit from private spaces.

- *Waterproof upholstery.* Oftentimes people who visit emergency rooms are bleeding, vomiting, or incontinent; therefore, flooring and upholstery materials should inhibit absorption and be easily cleaned.
- *Chairs.* Chairs with wide seats and solid arms or occasional small sofas maximize personal space and allow for a sick person to lean on and be comforted by a loved one.
- *Sound system.* Provide a system to bring in soft soothing sounds that will help to take the patient's mind off of his/her condition.
- *Sustainability connection.* A note of caution to designers on finishes and upholstery: The scientific community has known vinyl and rubber products to contain highly toxic carcinogenic compounds (phosphorous, arsenic, and antimony) since the 1960s, although the mainstream media and general population continue to behave as if they are unaware of the significant health hazards of these products (cancer, liver failure, and endometriosis; Thornton, 2002), that are typically found covering our baby cribs, sofas, car seats, and entire football fields. Designers must therefore refrain from adding these materials into any health care environment because patients are more at risk due to longer exposure times to the chemical offgassing of vinyl or rubber. If in the event these products are already in the space and cannot be replaced, heat and sunlight must be kept from hitting the material (with curtains, blinds or exterior shading devices) because heat and light accelerate the toxins permeating the surrounding air.

Evidence-based designers are being asked to justify design decisions with credible research in order to maximize patient outcomes and reduce unnecessary burdens (clinical, economic, productivity, and satisfaction) on the health care institution. A fundamental goal of evidence-based health care design is to create safe and therapeutic environments for patient care and to encourage family participation in the health care process (Harris, et al., 2008). Equally important is the promotion of efficient performance and restoration of medical staff who experience high levels of stress every work day.

In many ways the acute care facility was designed to meet the needs of the adult patient; however, of all populations, the adult is the least likely to require the services of a health care facility. Children often sustain injury while exploring their environment with natural reckless abandon, which often places them in harm's way; particularly within the built environment, which is riddled with manmade hazards. By the same token, teenagers and young adults often think they are indestructible and participate in sports that have the potential of causing serious injury. At the other end of the spectrum are the elderly who desperately try to stay one step ahead of

[**Figure 14.10**] Staff lounges are an important aspect of a health care facility because they allow the medical staff person to escape the high-stress conditions associated with people who are ill. Also, because many medical staff personnel are required to work long shifts, these lounges should accommodate the ability to take a short nap should one desire. © Getty Images / ERproductions Ltd.

the natural aging process but often succumb to age-related degeneration. It is these populations that require and utilize health care much more than the typical adult population.

Notwithstanding adults are found in the health care environment in great numbers: They are often the staff running the facility. The average staff member spends more than a third of a 24-hour period in the facility, which is why designers need to make provisions for this population as well. Considerations might include flat panel computer monitors with larger screens, ergonomically designed chairs and desks, adequate lighting levels, reduction in glare and air purification systems to reduce the inhalation of chemical cleansers and disinfectants, and flooring materials that provide some cushion for those who are on their feet all day (see Box 14.1, "Rubber Flooring"). Other considerations include the availability of quiet and secluded spaces that are well maintained, where the staff member can take his/her break, catch up on personal tasks, or exercise some stress away.

A unique facet of the medical profession is the frequent demand to work extended hours. In many facilities it is expected for a doctor or nurse to work 12 or more consecutive hours. Long hours equate to mental fatigue from continuous directed attention and physical fatigue from continuous standing or repetitive movements. Also, excessive fatigue increases the likelihood of mistakes (Ramsay, 2000) such as technical or judgment errors regarding medications or surgical procedures. It is, therefore, important to include places where the medical practitioner can take a quick nap or a place where he/she can simply relax for a short period of time (Figure 14.10). Research indicates that even short naps can have positive effects on mental restoration (Meltzer & Arora, 2006).

If a patient is required to remain in a health care environment for a prolonged period of time, he/she will move from an acute care setting to a **rehabilitation hospital**. These facilities provide care for extended stays that can last weeks or months. During a patient's stay in a rehabilitation hospital, he/she will often work to regain health following an accident, amputation, and/or stroke. Common constituents of rehabilitation hospitals are young men who have been injured while engaging in an extreme sport or in an auto accident, and senior citizens who have suffered a stroke or heart attack. Of course there are other populations found in the rehabilitation hospital that range from young adult to the elderly.

The medical staff of the rehabilitation hospital, however, is primarily composed of physicians who specialize in rehabilitation, and physical and occupational therapists. The therapist helps the patients either to regain physical mobility or to learn methods for coping with a change to his/her body. When designing a rehabilitation hospital, designers will need to consider a wide variety of circumstances and conditions affecting the patients. Some of the more unique needs of patients in these facilities are the acclimation of assistive devices as well as possible anxiety and depression. A person learning how to use a prosthetic leg for the first time will likely experience difficulties with coordination, and he/she may feel depressed or angry at the loss of the leg (Figure 14.11).

In this situation, the designer will want to avoid high stimulus colors such as red, and to include grab bars (see Box 14.2, "Grab Bars") throughout the facility.

Exercise rooms are integral to rehabilitation facilities. Inclusion of a sound system is a key design feature in these rooms because music plays an important role in stimulation and motivation. Patients in rehabilitation facilities often suf-

BOX 14.2 GRAB BARS

Within all health care environments, the provision for grab bars throughout the facility is highly recommended. Grab bars of today come in an assortment of colors and designs so they do not have to detract from the overall design of the facility. Instead, they can be used to enhance the overall environment.

The diameter or width of the gripping surface of a grab bar should be 1-1/4 inches to 1-1/2 inches. The shape of the bar can deviate from the standard cylindrical shape, but the gripping surface should still be between 1-1/4 in to 1-1/2 inches. When grab bars are mounted adjacent to a wall, the grab bar must be at least 1-1/2 inches. Also, the grip bar can be located in a recess, as long as the recess is a maximum of 3 inches deep and extends at least 18 inches above the top of the rail.

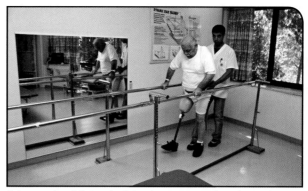

[**Figure 14.11**]] Our bodies can sometime adapt faster than our psyche. Rehabilitation hospitals should be both physically and psychologically supportive. © Tony Watson / Alamy

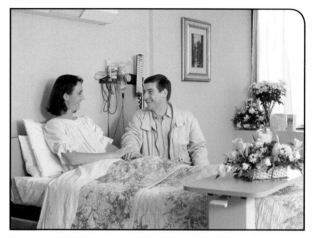

[**Figure 14.12**] The interior of health care facilities needs to appear inviting and supportive to the patient, family, and the health care provider. © Horizon International Images Limited / Alamy

fer from insecurity about the future, and the use of warm colors can promote feelings of safety and security. A mural can be a source of inspiration; plants provide soothing natural elements; and a mirror enables patients to observe their progressive improvement. Provide multiple opportunities for the person to think through his/her condition. Some ideas include gardens with ample spaces to be alone, a media room where one can get lost in a movie, community recreation rooms where people can discuss their conditions with others experiencing similar feelings while engaging in an activity, and personal computers with wireless Internet connections.

DESIGN FEATURES OF THE HEALTH CARE SETTING

The interior design features of the health care setting must promote a therapeutic atmosphere and should be sustainable. Because of the length of time we spend inside of the built environment, the design of the interior spaces is critical to patients, families, and health care providers. As mentioned, the design communicates and reflects the institutions attention to detail and quality of services, and it must support the unique needs of its employees in order to ensure that consistent quality care. Maslow's hierarchy of needs provides a useful perspective: When lower-level needs of physiology and safety are met, higher-level needs of belongingness and self-esteem can be addressed (Eshelman & Evans, 2002; Maslow, 1970). Smells, sights, sounds, and tactile sensations influence aesthetic assessment, (Martin, 2002) along with supportive elements that communicate, acknowledge, and accommodate the psychosocial needs of the patient, family, and caregivers (see Figure 14.12).

Therapeutic Environment

A therapeutic health care environment can be defined as an environment that contains and provides superior clinical services. This means that the facility should have and be willing to use up-to-date equipment and treatment options. For example, robots are being introduced into operating rooms. Robotic surgery has many benefits, including the reduction in the number of people in the operating room. Under current conditions, there can be as many as a dozen people in the operating room at any given time. With robotic technologies this number can be reduced to three or four. When we consider the old proverb, "Too many cooks spoil the soup," we can appreciate how fewer people in the operating room can reduce the possibility of error. Also, with the robotic arms conducting the invasive part of the surgery, we can be assured of greater sterilization. This is because it is easier and more effective to sterilize a machine than it is to sterilize human hair and skin cells. This, coupled with the enhanced precision, reduced trauma to the patient because the robotic arms do not require as much space as a surgeon's hands to manipulate tools and work in the afflicted area, and decreased potential for infection, all of which translate to less pain, trauma and bleeding, which translates to a faster recovery (Brown University, 2008).

From a design perspective, using robotics in the operating rooms can save the facility in square footage and cooling costs. The current operating room must be large enough to accommodate a dozen or so people who must be able to freely move about. When the number of people in the room is reduced to three or four, the physical size of the room can also be reduced thus allowing for more surgical bays, or the reallocation of space. Smaller spaces also allow for the room to be cooled off more quickly and remain cool with less energy expenditure. The preferred temperature of an operating room by surgeons is 65 to 70 degrees Fahrenheit (18 to 21 C) and about 75 degrees when operating on infants (Brock, 2005). Surgeons prefer cooler operating rooms because it helps them remain comfortable under the bright lights that are needed to perform surgery; however, if a surgeon can control the robotic arms from a small room within the operating room he/she can keep that area cooler while the actual surgical bay is kept warmer thus decreasing the risk of infection. Decreased body temperature from ambient conditions, along with an opened body cavity and vasoconstriction increases chance of infection (Craven & Hirnle, 2008).

Another aspect of a therapeutic environment is the level and degree of facility support and staff effectiveness. As mentioned in this chapter, the medical staff is often expected to work many hours at a single time. This causes physical and mental fatigue. Oftentimes the health care worker is subjected to high levels of stress. It is important that medical staff be given spacious and comfortable lounges where they can converse with colleagues, read a book, speak with a friend on the phone, and so on. This should be done without the fear of invasion from a patient or a patient's family member. The goal is to provide the employee with a refuge from the stressors associated within his/her job. Within this sanctuary could be a library with Internet access to major medical journals and other publications. Libraries where employees can look up answers to questions they are unsure of contribute to the overall professionalism of the employee and the institution. Another consideration is the provision of a secluded outdoor patio where staff can enjoy fresh air and sunlight, as well as the provision of food and dining areas for groups and small secluded single tables for a staff member to enjoy his/her meal in private.

A patient should be assured of the health care facility's relevance with regard to technologies as well as be assured that the staff members' needs are accommodated so that they can provide the best care possible. In addition, attention to the physical, psychosocial, and spiritual needs of the patient and his/her family should be addressed. More often than not, patients experience high levels of stress related to the fear and uncertainty of their condition. In many cases, a large complicated facility can contribute to this stress. As mentioned, stress can impede the effective functioning of the immune system and negatively effect a person's emotional perspective, thus contributing to feelings of melancholy.

Noise

An effective therapeutic environment will also consider issues of noise. The health care environment can be an extremely busy and noisy environment. Sound decibel (dB) ratings have increases from 57 in 1960 to 72 dB in 2005, between the continual movements and communication between the medical staff; the noise of various equipment including telephones, copy machines, heart monitors, and so on, and the movements of support staff such as cleaning and maintenance, dietary, and vendors (Busch-Vishniac et al., 2005). Background noise is often the main culprit of high dB ratings. The World Health Organization (WHO) recommended dB ratings for patient rooms to be no greater than 35 dBA during the day, 30 dBA at night, with peaks no higher than 40 dBA (WHO, 2001). A major design issue that contributes to high noise levels within the health care environment is the numerous hard surfaces and right angles. These attributes cause noise to reverberate or reflect (Busch-Vishniac et al., 2005). Unfortunately, many soft surfaces such as carpeting act as microorganism sinks (they get embedded and accumulate in the material), which can compromise the health care environment. Designers will want to consider cork as one possible flooring option because it is a good noise dampener, easy to clean, and can be assembled in a variety of decorative patterns.

Noise has been shown to increase heartburn in patients with gastroesophageal reflux disorder (Fass et al., 2008) as well as to induce secretion of cortisol (a stress hormone) (Hebert & Lupien, 2008), and increased noise has been associated with hypertension, ischemic heart disease, and the onset of aggressive behavior and psychiatric symptoms (WHO, 2001). However, the direct affect of noise in patient healing has not yet been quantified scientifically. The studies that have been done thus far have shown noise has negative outcomes for patients who have had surgery. Moore et al., (1998) note that there is a connection between the request for pain medication and the levels of noise, and WHO (2001) states that noise is a significant factor in the rates of patient rehospitalization. Patients who have been hospitalized state that noise is among the most significant irritants as they are healing (Moore et al., 1998).

Duke University Medical Center has taken proactive initiatives to reduce levels of noise. One initiative is to install sound meters around the nurses' stations. When the meter hits 70 dB, a red light turns on. In addition to this, the intercom was turned off, communication was relayed through individual phones set to vibrate, and signs were strategically placed around the facility reminding visitors to speak softly. The initial self-report data from the patients has been favorable thus far (Gowan, 2009; Figure 14.13).

Lighting

Lighting can be an influential factor of one's perceptions of the spaces within the health care environment. Light affects human health and performance by enabling us to perform visual tasks, helping to regulate our circadian rhythms, influencing our perceptions and mood, and regulating neurochemicals and hormones (serotonin and melatonin; Boyce, Hunter, & Howlett, 2003; Veitch & McColl, 1993).

When designing health care environments, designers must consider the building's orientation along with its elevation and relationship to other buildings around it throughout a 24-hour cycle and a 365-day calendar year. This is because the sun's relationship to the building will change with the seasons and throughout the day. There is evidence that morning sunlight is twice as effective as evening light when treating some forms of depression such as Seasonal Affective Disorder (SAD; Lewy et al., 1998). Overall, the goal is to increase the amount of natural daylight throughout the facility because natural daylight has been found to be superior for tasks involving fine color discrimination (Boyce, Hunter, & Howlett, 2003), and increased satisfaction among health care workers (Mroczek, Mikitarian, Vieira, and Rotarius, 2005); however, the color, angle, and intensity of light will change throughout the day, and these changes can affect mood. La Garce (2002) states that disruptive behaviors among dementia sufferers are most often associated with mid- to late afternoon (around 2:00 p.m. to 4:00 p.m.); and by controlling lighting levels we can decrease disruptive behaviors such as wandering, repetitive statements, and pilfering among dementia patients by 11 percent during the spring months and 41 percent in the winter months when there is much less natural daylight.

Sunlight is brightest from the south, weakest from the north, most invigorating from the east, and most intense from the west. One interesting study showed that patients with bipolar disorder stayed in the hospital an average of 3.67 days longer when their room had a western exposure (Benedetti, Colombo, Barbini, Campori, & Smeraldi, 2001). The patients on the eastern-facing side were able to leave 3.67 days sooner, thereby supporting the notion that eastern sunlight has more therapeutic qualities. In one study done by Walch et al., (2005), patients who had undergone elective cervical and lumbar spinal surgeries were postoperatively admitted to a bright or dim side of the same hospital unit. Patients staying on the bright side of the hospital were exposed to approximately 46 percent higher-intensity level of sunlight. These

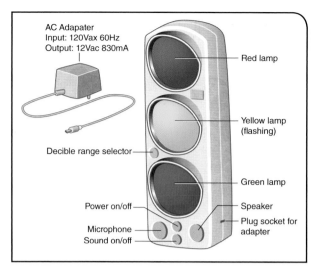

[**Figure 14.13**] Used predominately in schools to help children discern between an indoor and outdoor voice, the Yacker Tracker can measure sound decibels and indicate with a red or yellow light when those decibels reach unsatisfactory levels. Illustration by Precision Graphics

patients on average experienced less perceived stress and took 22 percent less pain medication per hour (Walch et al., 2005). A similar retrospective study of patients in a cardiac intensive care unit found that female patients stayed in the hospital an average of one day less when they recovered in rooms that received more sunlight (Beauchemin & Hays, 1998).

Studies of institutionalized older adults, who are generally confined to their rooms with very little exposure to sunlight, suggest that several changes occur in brain chemistry and circadian rhythms, leading to depression (Sumaya, Rienzi, Deegan, & Moss, 2001). When researchers exposed depressed institutionalized adults to bright light treatment for 30 minutes per day for five consecutive days, they found that the patients' became less depressed and began to resume activities levels similar to that of their peers.

Surface Materials

Another design challenge lies in the selection of surface materials. Materials and adhesives that peel, flake, or crack creates maintenance issues as well as potential for harm (Sloane et al., 2002). All finishes should be durable and functional for the space. Details such as door frames, casework, and finish transitions must be designed and installed to avoid the potential for dirt accumulation. Areas with hard-to-clean crevices and joints should be avoided, and new antimicrobial surfaces might be considered for appropriate locations; however, it should be noted that antimicrobial surfaces by themselves are not a solution to infections rates.

Floor finishes, wall coverings, and cabinet sheathing and their colors, patterns, or textures may be appropriate for one facility but may cause confusion or hazardous conditions in another (Passini et al., 2000). This inconsistency results from differences in light and shadow along with individual perceptions generated as one interacts with the design features. Although the fully functioning brain can screen out extrasensory information and maintain fairly uniform cognitive perceptions, people with a cognitive impairment either caused by high levels of stress or dementia have a decreased capacity to recognize and understand sensory experiences. This can cause them to be hypersensitive to various environmental conditions (Sloane et al., 2002) and possibly perceive subtleties that fully functioning people might not. Designers need to be aware of different light patterns generated by the sun throughout the course of the day, the moon throughout the night, as well as artificial lighting within a given space before selecting surface materials. Because many health care facilities opt for easy-to-clean surfaces, which tend to be glossy, the designer must be equally aware of the degree and patterning of glare. For example, glare has the potential of "washing out" colors and patterns, causing temporary blindness and pain, or generating optical illusions related to elevation changes.

All surface materials must be carefully evaluated to ensure their appropriateness for each facility, unit, and individual space. Recognizable cues such as signs and colors for people to rely on while wayfinding (Martin, 2002) should be selected with care. When using color to decorate social spaces, use enough to promote interest but not so much as to reduce environmental comprehension (i.e., a color scheme that is too dull, too bright, or too busy; Martin, 2002; Zeisel, 2000).

In many environments the risk of injury from falling is a serious problem. Even nonslip flooring can be hazardous to patients if it has a strong or raised pattern or a monochromatic color scheme. For example, bright colors against dark backgrounds can create the illusion of three-dimensionality, which can lead to disorientation and falls among patients who suffer from cognitive degeneration; therefore, avoid the use of highly contrasting colors (e.g., black and yellow). Similarly, the use of monochromatic colors in areas that change elevation (e.g., stairs and landings, sunken rooms) can be problematic for those whose brains cannot recognize or interpret elevation changes. Varying rich colors between elevations will help to minimize this perceptual problem. Incorporate handrails, nonslip flooring, and high-rise toilets into spaces to both encourage and enable patients to function independently (Zeisel, 2000). Note, however, that even safety devices can be sources of risk to elderly people with canes and others who have poor depth perception; handrails and grab bars often blend into the background, which is especially problematic in bathing areas. A contrasting background accent (e.g., a gold accent behind brushed steel) will focus attention on the rail.

Practical Applications for Designers

Use these resources, activities, and discussion questions to help you identify, synthesize, and retain this chapter's core information. These tools are designed to complement the resources you'll find in this book's companion Study Guide.

SUMMING IT UP

Many experts and the general populace have embraced the idea that inviting, easily understood, and non-threatening environments can play a pivotal role in patient recovery. To counter the effects of the sick role, designs for health care facilities should strive to minimize institutional perceptions. The biggest issues within hospital settings pertain to wayfinding, privacy, and accommodations for family members. Health care design focuses on dispelling patient stress which derives from feelings generated by negative experiences—losing control of privacy and normal routines, feeling vulnerable because their condition diminishes their sense of mastery, fearing an unknown outcome—all of which are exacerbated by the separation from home. Designers can provide specific living components that give residents greater control over their lives, such as layouts that allow them to move easily and freely throughout the environment.

You can also refer to this textbook's companion Study Guide for a comprehensive list of Summary Points.

EXPERT SPOTLIGHT 14.1

Health Care Environment

Debra D. Harris, Ph.D., RID, AAHID,
RAD Consultants (CEO)

Over the past 15 years, there have been many challenges and changes in the design of health care facilities along with culture changes in health care institutions. A shift toward (1) patient-centered care, (2) sustainability, and (3) evidence-based design suggests that there is a demand for a holistic evidence-based approach that includes the physical environment as a partner of care.

Patient-centered care is health care that respects and honors patients' individual wants, needs, and preferences, and that assures that individual patients' values guide all decisions. One of the recognized leaders in patient-centered care is Planetree, an organization that develops and promotes a model of care that focuses on healing and nurturing the body, mind, and spirit. Environments designed to support this mission provide health care facilities where patients can receive care in a healing environment that also provides access to information needed to become active participants in their own care and well-being. Today, informed patients are maintaining decision-making authority and increasingly seeking a collaborative relationship with providers, becoming more responsible for their own health.

A patient-centered care model focuses on the patient, family, and staff experience based on respect for patients, coordination of care, patient education, physical comfort, emotional support, and involvement with family and friends (Stone, 2008). Architecture and interior design is an important element of the patient-centered model of care, providing an environment that supports collaboration of the patient and his/her medical team and creates the physical space that humanizes, personalizes, and demystifies the health care experience. By connecting the patient, family, and staff to the building, gardens, and grounds around the facility in a meaningful way, the physical environment supports the other components of the Planetree model of patient-centered care—human interaction, food and nutrition, patient and family education, family involvement, spirituality, human touch, healing arts, complementary/alternative therapy, and healthy communities (Frampton, Gilpin, & Charmel, 2002).

Sustainable design is the philosophy of designing physical objects, the built environment, and services to comply with the principles of economic, social, and ecological sustainability. According to the Sustainable Design Program at the U.S. General Services Administration (GSA), sustainable design principles include the ability to optimize site potential, minimize nonrenewable energy consumption, use environmentally preferred products, protect and conserve water, enhance indoor environmental quality (IEQ), and optimize operational and maintenance practices (USGBC, 2010). The U.S. Green Building Council (USGBC) Leadership in Energy and Environmental Design (LEED) green building certification system provides the framework for identifying and implementing green building design, construction, operations, and maintenance solutions. The LEED rating system for health care was developed specifically to meet the unique requirements of health care facility design. Projected outcomes suggest that sustainable health care facilities minimize ecological harm and increase patient healing and staff satisfaction.

The research related to high-performance green building practices, technologies, and techniques that minimize environmental and human health impacts is very limited. As more health care facilities pursue LEED certification, the demand for justification based on measurable outcomes will continue to grow, including return on investment, an expectation for decreased operating costs, and increased occupant health and productivity.

Evidence-based design (EBD) is defined as design decisions based on the best available information from credible research and evaluation of existing projects. An essential factor in the process is critical thinking by the design professional to synthesize the available evidence and expertise to fit the design problem. Though the shift toward the use of evidence to support the design of health care environments has been emerging over the past 30 years, a growing body of research shows that design of the built environment contributes to key outcomes for both patients and health care staff: (1) encouraging patient healing, (2) increasing patient and staff safety, (3) reducing stress, (4) improving patient and family satisfaction, (5) increasing staff effectiveness, (6) reducing staff turnover, and (7) reducing operating costs.

When we look back, we see great progress in the environmental design of health care facilities—Patient-centered care is the norm, not the alternative. Currently, we are shifting toward evidence-driven analysis of outcomes to inform design. As we look toward the future, we see new research and environmental technologies that will demonstrate a value to the pursuit of increased patient quality of care.

References

Frampton, S., Gilpin, L., & Charmel, P. (Eds.), (2003). *Putting patients first: Designing and practicing patient centered care.* San Francisco: Jossey-Bass.

Stone, S. (2008). A retrospective evaluation of the impact of the Planetree patient-centered model of care on inpatient quality outcomes. *Health Environments Research & Design Journal, 1*(4) 55–69.

USGBC .(2010). What LEED is. U. S. Green Building Council. Retrieved from http://www.usgbc.org/DisplayPage.aspx?CMSPageID=1988

KEY TERMS

- **acute care hospital**
- **birthing centers**
- **human-scale elements**
- **immunocompetency**
- **long-term care facility**
- **rehabilitation facility**
- **sick role**

WEB LINKS

Environmental Protection Agency, on the toxicity of vinyl and rubber products (www.epa.gov/ttn/atw/hlthef/vinylchl.html)

Federal Emergency Management Agency (www.fema.gov/plan/prevent/rms/)

Generation Model (www.generationmodel.eu)

OR Design and Constrution (http://ordesignandconstruction.com)

PCV Free Fabrics (www.pvcfreefabrics.com)

Planetree (www.planetree.org)

Rady Children's Hospital, San Diego (www.rchsd.org/aboutus/healingenvironment)

St. Elizabeth East Hospital's Women's Center
(http://ste.org/DesktopDefault.aspx?tabid=1106)

U.S. Department of Health and Human Services, on provisions of the security rule
(www.hhs.gov/ocr/privacy/index.html)

Victorious Foundation, on teen lounges
(www.victoriousfoundation.org)

STUDIO ACTIVITY 14.1

Views of Nature

Design Problem Statement
Research has shown that patients heal faster and become released from hospitals faster when they have access to nature. The question is how does a designer ensure views of nature from every window within a hospital?

Directions
Develop a mock up (drawings or models) of creative ways that nature can be incorporated outside of windows within a hospital without blocking the natural light.

You will be graded on:

- Creativity
- Innovation
- Level of naturalness the person is able to view
- Ability for natural light to enter Into the room
- Quality of drawing or model

Deliverable
Mock up (drawings or models)

STUDIO ACTIVITY 14.2

Children's Hospital Room

Design Problem Statement
Children are a special population within the health care environment. Among the more significant concerns are the strong formations of associations. For example, a large machine being rolled into a room may become associated with pain; therefore, the mere sight of that machine will inspire fear.

Your job is to design a hospital room for a five-year-old boy who requires regular dialysis.

Directions
Step One: Develop an understanding of what dialysis machines look like, their purpose, and what a child experiences while hooked up to such a machine.

Step Two: Develop a way in which the dialysis machine can be camouflaged and/or reduce the visual access to the machine by the child.

Step Three: Develop methods that will help the child refocus his attention from the procedure to something more pleasurable.

Step Four: Develop a drawing or model that demonstrates how you would design this room, along with a diagram discussing the element or feature and its purpose in relation to the child who must receive dialysis.

Deliverables
Drawing or model

DISCUSSION QUESTIONS

1. Discuss the design and layout of a health care facility from a healthy visitor's point of view. What psychological effect does entering the facility have on healthy people? How might the facility's design change their behavior and responses?

2. Discuss programs that could help to reduce patient stress in health care facilities.

3. How do you recover from stressful events? How might that knowledge be used to inform your design decisions for health care facilities? What role does the natural environment play in your recuperation?

4. What design elements can help control lighting for patients? What technology is available for maintaining a regular lighting schedule to help minimize the effects of the winter and summer solstices?

5. What materials are most effective for ensuring the safety of patients? How can they be used to make patients feel comfortable and secure without overwhelming them with restraints or other equipment?

LEARNING ACTIVITIES

1. Divide into groups of five. Each group member will visit a different health care environment. Take notes on the design of these different environments, and report your observations to your group and then the class.

2. Design the lobby of a hospital, paying particular attention to wayfinding mechanisms. Discuss the reasons why you chose certain mechanisms.

3. Contact a local health care facility and arrange to meet with staff members when they are off duty or on break. Discuss the facility's design, and determine if the layout of the hospital is conducive to an effective and satisfactory work environment. Are design issues interfering with patient care? Does the facility itself hamper or improve the staff's emotional responses to daily situations?

4. Research interior surfacing and upholstery materials created by new technologies. How might they be used to improve appearances and comfort levels for patients? Keep in mind that because decreased immunocompetency affects almost all patients, antibacterial and nontoxic materials are particularly effective. Provide proper citations for all articles and papers referenced.

15 Resorts and Recreation

I've always thought a hotel ought to offer optional small animals. I mean a cat to sleep on your bed at night, or a dog of some kind to act pleased when you come in. You ever notice how a hotel room feels so lifeless?

—Anne Tyler

Recreation is an important part of the human condition because it allows us to escape and regenerate from our daily routines and stressors. In today's world there are a multitude of **recreational environments** and hospitality settings that include outdoor places, indoor spaces, and a combination of the two. Outdoor examples include:

- Parks
- Playgrounds

Indoor recreational environments and hospitality settings include:

- Motels
- Hotels

Places that offer a combination of indoor and outdoor experiences include:

- Bed-and-breakfasts
- Resorts
- Cruise ships

Within all of these environments, greater demands are being placed upon designers to accommodate a vast array of recreational desires and user groups. Recreational desires can range from an exhilarating sport, to leisurely activities, to profound learning experiences. Providing a balance between rest and adventure can be a challenge for designers of recreational environments. Similarly, designers may find it difficult to offer enough recreational variety to satisfy the interests of many different people. For example, consider the cruise ship industry. Some of these floating "cities" are equipped with water slides and rock-climbing walls, and some even have bungee jumping. In addition, there are numerous opportunities for rest by the pool or conversations in a semiprivate lounge.

Another category of recreational environments are primarily indoor places, but they can include a combination of indoor and outdoor spaces, which are clustered under the broad term of **hospitality.** These are places that can take many different forms. The most well-understood form is the room-and-board facility, such as hotels, motels, and bed-and-breakfasts. By definition, hospitality is a way to characterize the act of a guest being received and entertained by a host. Within the design industry, hospitality environments are expected to be one of the fastest growing markets worldwide. Among the expected market growth within the hospitality sector includes hotels, motels, resorts, cruise ships, timeshares, and private residence clubs.

An important part of the success associated with hospitality environments is the belief by the patrons that they *belong*. This has led many resorts and cruise ships to incorporate themes or population-specific environments. Examples include **ecological (eco) resorts** that promise a degree of communal living and profound experiences with nature and **agricultural (agri) resorts** that offer patrons an opportunity to experience farm life and sustainable practices. In addition, there are population-specific resorts that

have been designed for certain segments, such as couples with young children, senior citizens, singles, and members of the gay and lesbian community. Within all of these population groups, *physical ability* is a factor that designers must legally and ethically consider. With regard to all of the recreational environments this chapter will cover, special consideration must be given to include design elements that respond to a large segment of our population—the visually impaired.

CONSIDERATIONS FOR THE VISUALLY IMPAIRED

Blind and **visually impaired**, also referred to as *partially sighted*, children and adults have different needs from people who have other physical impairments. In one study, 21 million Americans reported having vision problems or eye conditions that compromised their vision (Pleis & Lethbridge-Çejku, 2007); and as a result, they limited their time outside of their homes for fear of injury. Wayfinding and navigating within unfamiliar spaces is a labor-intensive task for the visually impaired. To successfully navigate an environment, people must continually reassess and respond to different stimuli and objects. Blind people in particular require suitable strategies for acquiring, processing, and recalling spatial information that promotes safety and independence and minimizes wayfinding time and effort (Espinosa, Ungar, Ochaita, Blades, & Spencer, 1998). To illustrate the difference between the blind and the partially sighted, designing hotel rooms according to principles that comply with the Americans with Disabilities Act (ADA) for the blind can be problematic. Many visually impaired people are partially sighted, whereas other visual limitation might be confined to limitations in color and depth perception. Hence, a change in the position of a light switch on a wall to better accommodate a wheelchair-bound person might cause confusion for the partially blind person who relies on consistency to know where important attributes are located within the built environment. In addition, when designing recreational spaces, consideration must be given to the blind and partially sighted person who may require the assistance of a guide dog (Figure 15.1; Baker, Stephens, & Hill, 2002). Another example of this is that people who are partially sighted prefer deeper counters (to avoid spilling), whereas those with mobility problems prefer shallower ones (to limit the distance required to reach something; Boschetti, 2002). Restricted vision also serves to limit locomotion, such that the mobility of older adults can be further hindered by their decreased depth of perception and peripheral vision (Brabyn, Haegerström-Portnoy, Schneck, & Lott, 2000).

Specific design goals for the visually impaired within recreational settings include incorporating easily accessible routes

[**Figure 15.1**] Dogs are assisting greater numbers of people with a variety of physical, cognitive, and psychological disabilities. A principle in universal design is the use of lever style handles for doors. Dogs can be trained to open doors that have lever handles, thus affording the individual greater accessibility. © Arterra Picture Library / Alamy

to enhance the mobility of the visually impaired, their service dogs and perhaps their wheelchairs (Baker et al, 2002). Also included are tactile maps to help people navigate unfamiliar public environments (Espinosa et al., 1998), and/or directional signage with raised letters for people who cannot read Braille (Osterberg, Davis, & Danielson, 1995). These simple additions to the park, hospitality, or recreational facility will go a long way toward providing the accommodations necessary for all community members to use and enjoy the space.

HOSPITALITY ENVIRONMENTS

The largest segment of the recreational environment is the hospitality industry. This form of recreation is one of the fastest-growing markets (Hobson, 2002) within the United States and throughout the world. Hotels, motels, bed-and-breakfasts, resorts, cruise ships, and more recently timeshares, private residence clubs, adventure excursions, ecotourism, and agri-tourism are among the many strategies used to entice travelers. These environments are designed to capitalize on *environmental meaning,* which in hospitality settings, is most often related to a fantasy, an ideal, or an expectation and must be supported and enhanced by architectural and design elements. As an example, consider the city of Las Vegas, Nevada, which is composed of many themed resorts that resemble notable city skylines and landmarks throughout the world.

The hospitality environments must elicit positive associations and feelings from guests and visitors in order to endure and prosper. To evoke positive feelings, the hospitality environment must provide a "home away from home." Travelers bring with them expectations pertaining to privacy, territoriality, and access to features and amenities such as television sets, toiletries, telephones, and Internet access. Today's travelers include people from all walks of life, including elderly and disabled persons, who require special features from their environments (e.g., roll-in showers, grip bars in bathrooms, places for companion pets and service animals to relieve themselves). In addition, because many hospitality environments, particularly themed resorts and cruise ships, are so large, designers need to be creative in developing and incorporating wayfinding methods into the environment. This is important not only for elderly and disabled populations, but also for fully functioning patrons to easily locate themselves in relation to their rooms.

The hospitality environment consists of many varied forms that attract their own unique clientele. The specificity of each environment enables patrons to select from a variety of environments that support their needs. Recently, because of a desire on the part of many people to reconnect with nature, a new category of hospitality environment has emerged:

[**Figure 15.2**] For many people, reconnecting with nature is about an ideal rather than a reality. With this in mind, many "nature" resorts create the illusion of this reconnection but still provide the comforts and luxuries that many people demand from a resort. © Danita Delimont / Alamy

the nature resort (Figure 15.2). These environments, which include ecotourism and agri-tourism, range from settings that provide a total connection with nature to those that offer an environmentally friendly facility and experience.

Timeshares and private residence clubs are another form of hospitality environment. These facilities are open to people who become members, thus enabling them to have access to that environment during specified times of the year. The main feature that separates this type of environment from other hospitality settings is the removal of the fantasy element. People who seek these kinds of environments often seek ownership, and these facilities are more likely to be viewed as a second home and serve as a place for escape and stress reduction.

HOSPITALITY PATRONS

Tourists have more travel and destination options than ever before, and as the global population increases, so do the possibilities for new and different experiences. Some individuals seek restorative destinations or refuges where they can "get away from it all"; some crave the stimulation of the unusual, adventurous, or even dangerous settings; others may indulge in a once-in-a-lifetime extravagance or simply drive their home-like settings to new locations; and still others focus on exploring or preserving foreign cultures and landscapes. Business travelers, however, share virtually universal needs: convenience, reliability, connectedness, and specific services relative to the necessities of both the work and the person. Design can easily support and enhance each of these purposes.

Patrons' perception of value is often influenced by the purpose of their visit (Mattila, 1999) or reason for the travel. Thus, a working knowledge of the target population will enhance the design of any environment. Couples, families, and groups utilize hospitality settings for a variety of personal and professional reasons, including cultural or family celebrations (i.e., holiday, honeymoon, anniversary, reunion, vacation, and school break), business meetings and conventions, and pure entertainment according to their interests and finances. A recent phenomenon within the travel industry directly linked to the hospitality industry is the singular traveler, not that they are unmarried or otherwise committed: It is that they prefer to travel alone. They are referred to as **FITs**, the Free Independent Traveler. From an economic standpoint the FIT demographic spends more money while traveling to more places than any other group, thereby making FITs the largest population segment of concentrated effort on the part of tourist boards and travel agents to attract them to their country, resorts, and destinations. The Internet has played a vital role in the rise and relative popularity of traveling alone. FITs often can access social-networking sites and travel/reservation sites from virtually anywhere around the world. The ease and flow of information guarantees a level of comfort and confidence among solo travelers as other fellow FITs can post real-time specifics and details such as "the best hotel in this town was . . .", "the bus is always early in this city . . .", "this region does not recognize the document . . . as valid." The plethora of useful information that can be had at a moment's notice gives this demographic a competitive edge; therefore, when designing hospitality settings, it is critical to know the market—who is the design catering to?

Travelers' requirements for convenience, image, services, and amenities vary according to their needs. For example, business travelers seek convenient environments that provide separate working and living areas, dry-cleaning services, transportation, dining facilities, fax, computer, and Internet connections or secretarial services (Mattila, 1999). Vacationing families need child-friendly settings that include care and activity facilities and age-appropriate, in-room movie, and

video game options, whereas newlyweds require little more than ensured privacy, a pleasant outdoor view, and discreet room service. Younger adult (30s) travelers seem to have a greater regard for luxury items and amenities, whereas older travelers appear to focus on accessible convenience (Bernstein, 1999). People who travel for pleasure are more likely to select hotels based on prior personal experience or the recommendations of others, whereas business travelers tend to base their selections almost entirely on previous travel experiences, location and the hotel's amenities and reputation for customer service (Chan, 1998; Figures 15.3 and 15.4).

Recently the Swiss company SGS, which specializes in management systems, audits, and certifications, has developed

[**Figure 15.3**] Most people who travel for business require wireless high-speed Internet, good cellular phone reception, printing, and dry cleaning services. Other desired amenities include easy access to food and drink, quick and direct transportation services, and reliable concierge services. © Corbis Flirt / Alamy

[**Figure 15.4**] Many hotels have opted to incorporate rooftop gardens and cafés into their hotel as one method to help address "the heat island effect." These gardens or cafes add a nice amenity to the hotel because of the views afforded. © TurkeyShoot / Alamy

a set of guidelines for six- and seven-star ratings. Comprehending the relationship between luxury hotel attributes and business travelers' personal values, as well as the role of culture in defining service, will help planners and designers to better meet the needs of global customers, maintain a competitive edge (Mattila, 1999), and incorporate design elements that will meet the distinct needs of all travelers (Chan, 1998).

DESIGN ISSUES IN HOSPITALITY SETTINGS

When designing hospitality settings, the totality of the environment—purpose and function, patrons, location and climate, style and theme, services and amenities, and so on—must be considered. Careful attention must be paid to all design components from the architecture, landscaping, and layout, to finishes, furnishings, and amenities (Hobson, 2002). For example, luxury hotels are patronized to a greater extent by international clients (Mattila, 1999) and require not only superior services and amenities, but also décor and signage appropriate to their clientele's tastes and languages. The physical environment influences the perception of value, but different cultures have different notions of beauty and value and, therefore, different design expectations. Architects and designers must understand cultural attributes that affect viewers' perceptions of design. For instance, in most Western cultures, the color white symbolizes new beginnings and purity, but in most Asian cultures, it symbolizes death and mourning. Addressing each of the variables associated with preferences and design of hospitality environments can positively affect the overall image and subsequent success of that environment (Kandampully & Suhartanto, 2003).

Resorts, cruise ships, and some large hotels are micro-communities; they contain restaurants, nightclubs, theaters, shops, art galleries, libraries, emergency care facilities, and other amenities common to cities and towns. Like communities, they consist of multiple settings that require the careful consideration of transitional zones during the space-planning process. For example, many cruise ships have libraries and Internet stations, and placing a bar or dance club in close proximity would clearly be a result of poor planning because a "quiet activity" must be segregated from a "loud activity." Understanding Roger Barker's notion of **synomorphy** and his **behavior settings** are, therefore, important concepts for planners and designers of the hospitality environment. The word synomorphy is the combination of several Greek forms (prefix, root and suffix): "syn" meaning "together with," "morph" meaning "form," and "y" meaning "quality." Together the word synomorphy can be thought of as together with the quality of form. Essentially the environment creates a setting, which in turn promotes certain behaviors that are compatible with the activ-

ity (Barker, 1968). To illustrate this, consider in a library people are generally quiet, in a church people are generally reflective, and at a basketball game people are generally gregarious, thus—environment-setting-activity-behavior.

In many instances resorts and cruise ships host a variety of amenities and are often target-population specific. For example, The Disney Cruise Line™ is intended for families with small children, and RSVP Vacations™ are intended for the gay and lesbian population. This ability for any hospitality environment to target a specific segment of the population is important because most vacationers would rather fit into his/her social surroundings rather than stick out as an anomaly.

"Home Away from Home"

Motels, hotels, resorts, bed-and-breakfasts, and cruise ships are temporary, often high-density residences and social communities—"a home away from home" for guests—architects and interior designers must creatively mitigate negative perceptions of certain inherent design components. For example, long corridors serve to maximize the use of space, yet research has demonstrated that long residential corridors increase negative feelings of crowding and anxiety (Baum, & Valins, 1977; Baum, Aiello, & Calesnick, 1978; Baum, Davis, & Valins, 1979), whereas greater architectural depth (i.e., more spaces to pass through when going from room to room) results in less psychological distress and social withdrawal (Evans, Lepore, & Schroeder, 1996). Designers can lessen the negative psychological effects of long hallways by placing lounges, seating alcoves or cluster suites intermittently along corridors, changing color schemes, or modifying hallway widths; these measures encourage **segmentation bias,** the process of mentally breaking a route into separate segments that alters the perception of excessive distance (Tlauka & Wilson, 1996). Guests can use these segments to "count down" the distance to their rooms (i.e., "Only two more alcoves to go").

Generally speaking, guest room designs should be distinctive enough to delineate them from other guest rooms yet not excessively complex (Siguaw & Enz, 1999b). Windows positively influence perceptions of spatial density: Rooms with windows have more appeal (Kaye & Murray, 1982), and people tend to prefer windows in smaller rooms to be proportionally larger (Butler & Steuerwald, 1991). Ceilings that are higher than usual are also preferred (Baird, Cassidy & Kurr, 1978), as are rooms that are square rather than rectangular (Nasar, 1981a). These design elements contribute to perceptions of greater spaciousness and minimize feelings of being crowded. Many guests experience a *sense of place* better when residential elements common to the location's cultural heritage are used within the design; but whether those elements are down comforters, bamboo chairs, or hand-woven rugs, they should be durable enough to withstand heavy use (Siguaw & Enz, 1999b).

TYPES OF HOSPITALITY ENVIRONMENTS

There are several different types of hospitality environments designed to meet the diverse needs of a wide range of patrons. For example, the *motel* is designed to meet the needs of the road warrior who travels from destination to destination by automobile. On the other hand, there are two types of *hotel* guests: They typically are the business traveler and the vacationer. At *bed-and-breakfast* establishments the clientele tend to be travelers in search of a personal connection with local inhabitants and a quiet get-away. Tourists coming to a *resort* setting will have the expectation that all their needs will be seen to, such as food, lodging, entertainment, transportation, shopping, and more. *Cruise ships* are nearly identical to resorts, albeit on water. Passengers have all the amenities of a small town with one benefit; they arrive at a different location than the one from which they departed. Hospitality environments require special design considerations to meet the unique needs, expectations, and desires of the clientele who visit them.

Motels

In 1925, Arthur Heinman, a Los Angeles architect, decided to capitalize on the growing connection between San Francisco and Los Angeles by erecting the first "mo-tel" (a hybrid of the words *motor* and *hotel*) between the two cities. Unlike hotels, which were predominantly located in urban areas, motels were specifically designed to be automobile friendly. The idea gained popularity for two reasons—America's growing love affair with the automobile (Witzel, 2000), and the reluctance of many travelers to walk through the elegant lobbies of hotels after spending long hours traveling in a car. Motels appealed to the weary motorists as they could park their cars next to their rooms and would not have to be seen in public in their oftentimes-disheveled state.

Although motels offered convenience for cross-country travelers, they had unique design needs. To attract travelers, they needed to be located near popular roadways and surrounded by complementary services such as gas stations, repair shops, and diners. The original layout of motels contributed to their uniqueness in the hospitality environment. Many took the form of a single-story building often in the shape of an "I," "L," or "U" configuration with connected rooms and doors that faced the parking lot (Figure 15.5).

By the 1960s and 1970s, the uniqueness of motels began to vanish when large chain franchises gained dominance, replacing mom-and-pop operations. Many motels began to resemble hotels: multistoried and with a homogeneous exterior and interior designs. By the 1980s, many of these franchises began replacing the word *motel* with terms such as *roadside inn, suites,* and *lodge.*

The expectations of today's motel patrons do not differ much from the patrons in the early to mid-20th century. Most are not interested in fancy décor; they simply want a clean, comfortable bed, and a hot shower. Privacy, peace, and quiet are other key characteristics of a motel because many weary drivers may need to sleep and get back on the road (truck drivers are a good example). Although the original design features of motels have all but vanished among the big-chain franchises, the original one-story facility has experienced resurgence among those seeking the nostalgia of a bygone era. Many of these travelers spend their leisure time motel hopping across the United States. For these people, the enduring symbols of the motel are an important part of the American cultural experience.

SUSTAINABILITY CONNECTION 15.1

Sustainability in the hospitality industry includes but is not limited to employing energy and water conservation measures, utilizing local food and beverage sources (Sloan, Legrand, & Chen, 2009), using efficient waste management practices (recycling and limiting waste), using "green" building materials and methods, and reducing **heat island effect** and vehicular smog through landscaping and a central location (or a connection to mass transit). The **urban heat island effect** is defined by the EPA as "a measurable increase in ambient urban air temperatures resulting primarily from the replacement of vegetation with buildings, roads, and other heat-absorbing infrastructure. The heat island effect can result in significant temperature differences between rural and urban areas" (U.S. Environmental Protection Agency, 2009).

[**Figure 15.5**] A motel's signature attributes are the doors that lead directly to the exterior of the building and the close proximity of parking. This design allowed travelers to enter their rooms without being seen by other guests in the disheveled state that often accompanies long road trips. © Stuart Kelly / Alamy

[**Figure 15.6**] This business center offers computers and printers. A flaw with this design is that there is no protection from others seeing what is on the monitor. This can be problematic for the stockbroker, attorney, or medical doctor who is often required to review confidential materials. © Jeff Greenberg / Alamy

When designing motels, consider layouts that utilize the bathroom, closets and double-walls as buffers between each room. Heavy window treatments will not only block out light, but also insulate against sound and outdoor temperatures. The interior design should be comfortable and accessorized with warmer colored fabrics, which can better endure wear and tear. Unlike hotels, motel rooms are usually accessed directly from the outside, meaning that rain, snow, dirt, and debris will be tracked directly into the room; therefore, flooring finishes should be able to withstand this abuse.

Hotels

Hotels, in one form or another, have been part of human civilization for millennia. Although they once simply offered the traveler a place to stay on a short-term basis, hotels have evolved to provide the short-term guest with a variety of services such dining, recreation, fitness, and child care. To attract business travelers, many hotels offer facilities that can accommodate large and small conferences, along with business services centers that provide printing, copying, and other business-related devices (Figure 15.6).

Many people have preconceived expectations about hotel settings. The most basic of these expectations is the provision of a room with a bed, closet space, and bathroom facilities. In hotels touting more luxurious accommodations, other items such as a television, telephone, Internet capabilities, coffee maker, alarm clock, iron, and blow dryer are often expected. Because patrons' expectations of a hotel can vary, systems for ranking hotels have been implemented. The most well known is the star system, which associates specific characteristics with a designated number of stars. A similar ranking system, developed by the American Automotive

Association (AAA), uses a five-point system of diamonds instead of stars (see Table 15.1).

The design of a hotel differs based on its location and adjacencies to other types of businesses. For example, a facility's accommodations and services will vary greatly if it is located next to an interstate highway opposed to across the street from a large convention center (Piotrowski & Rogers, 2007). Type and configuration (conceptual design) of the individual guest rooms and the services to be provided will need to be accommodative and supportive to the type of guest and their reason for the travel. Predesign and market research should include but not be limited to: a *needs assessment*, which is an evaluation of the clients and their needs. The basic design considerations are:

- private guest space (rooms)
- lobby or functional gathering space (meeting room)
- circulation for staff and guests (halls and corridors)
- support space (mechanical or janitorial rooms)

Space allocated for private guest use can be up to 90 percent for some hotels; although regardless of the size, all hotel circulation must be factored for safety and staff efficiency (Piotrowski & Rogers, 2007). Accessory spaces such as, gift shops, laundry facilities and dining must be decided on a case-by-case basis.

Wayfinding

The ease in which people can navigate a space or structure influences their overall perceptions of that space, and greater **environmental legibility** facilitates greater exploration. Environmental legibility has cognitive indicators and

[**Table 15.1**] Five-Star Hotel Rating System (Hotel Star Rating Guide)

Star Rating	Accommodations and Services
One star (Economy)	Accommodates the basic needs of budget travelers.
	Tends to be located near major attractions or thoroughfares.
	Usually located within walking distance of dining establishments.
Two stars (Moderate)	Offers moderate aesthetic enhancements in the property grounds, room décor, and quality of furnishings.
	May offer limited restaurant services with no provisions for room service.
Three stars (First class)	Provides a high level of service with basic amenities, features, and facilities.
	Décor emulates a sense of style and class.
	Contains restaurants serving breakfast, lunch, and dinner.
	Offers room service, valet parking, pool, and fitness center.
Four stars (Superior)	Offers a high level and wide variety of amenities.
	Comfort and convenience are the primary concerns of staff.
	Facilities are upscale and with a highly stylized décor.
	High-end restaurant facilities are available.
	Grounds are well landscaped and manicured.
Five stars (Deluxe)	Luxurious property with original design styles and elegant room décor.
	Provides an exceptionally high degree of service by meeting all conceivable needs for visitor comfort and convenience.
	Offers outstanding dining facilities.
	Grounds are meticulously kept.

behavioral dimensions that in a given setting offer people information and *tell* people how to act and move (Moughtin, Cuesta, Sarris, & Signoretta, 2003). There are spatial relationship indicators, which are made clear through shape, size, hierarchy, or proximity (i.e., private space vs. public space). Symbolic cues or visual indicators based in sociocultural circles such as historic references, religious iconography, or graphic representations known and meaningful to specific groups (i.e., municipal buildings and churches) are generally the tallest and most ornate structures to convey "importance, social strength and to serve as a landmark." *Behavior legibility* or the ability to comprehend what to *do* or *how to move* through a place (i.e., at a restaurant, a path clear of tables would be where guests are to walk or indicate how to leave the dining area). Environmental legibility in hospitality environments can positively affect guests' level of satisfaction with the overall environment.

Orientation or *reference points* common to hospitality settings include lobbies, landmarks, particular amenities, and décor elements such as floor and wall treatments. Tall, multistoried structures such as cruise ships can seldom use ceiling and landmark height to support wayfinding and must rely on signs, wall artwork; varying the colors, patterns, or materials used for flooring and wall coverings; and perhaps wall niches to display information or *objects d'art*.

The psychological process of wayfinding is facilitated by spatial organization (Figure 15.7): The more intricate the layout, the more problems people will have finding their way.

[**Figure 15.7**] Large spaces can be be segmented without the use of walls. When the space is too large, as is often the case with airports and convention centers, disorientation can occur. Using alternative segmentation methods such as the one depicted in this figure whereby delineation of an area within the larger space is achieved through the change in flooring color. This area thus becomes the landmark, or reference point, from which one can orient themselves. © Barak Brudo / Dreamstime.com

Increasing visual access to an environment enhances wayfinding within it. For example, if a large hotel were to host a product convention in its grand ballroom, wayfinding would be well facilitated via numbered or color-coded vendor booths delineated by four-foot-high partitions, directional signage with arrows located at the entrance, clearly visible booth signage atop the partitions or suspended from ceilings, and printed reference maps handed out to vendors and attendees.

Features and Amenities

The entrance and lobby are two of the most influential spaces in a hospitality setting. Their design is critical for visitors who are unfamiliar with the environment; they must not only be functional but the layout must be coherent in order for patrons to easily locate their destinations (e.g., exits, guest rooms, elevators, restaurants, gift shops; Bitgood & Tisdal, 1996). The lobby is a **strategic junction node** (a point where activity converges for different purposes) in that it is the point of entrance and departure. It also serves as a dual **concentration node** (an area in which people gather for a common purpose). The lobby is the center of

guest travel and activity, and as the first space a person experiences upon entering, its characteristics establish the environment's image (e.g., luxurious, rugged, fantastic; see Box 15.1, "Sophisticated Lobby" and Box 15.2, "Rustic Lobby").

Creating a positive image can be a challenge for designers because the judgments people have regarding "beauty" are highly subjective and change according to trends, culture, and personal experiences (Bourassa, 1990). One way to influence patrons' perceptions is to design the public spaces within the hospitality environment using interesting and significant pieces of artwork with descriptions (Bernstein, 1999). Early museum studies reveal that the lower right corner of artwork is the best location for placards and descriptions because humans tend to have a **right-side bias**; people will better see and remember those items placed on the right side (Melton, 1935). Later studies of exhibitions indicated that the addition of sound, smell, or touch to art displays helps to attract attention to them and can add another dimension of stimulation for memory enhancement (Melton, 1972). Rather than having only written placards to describe the work, a button could be pressed to initiate a recorded description and a hint of a scent could also be released.

A restaurant located within the hospitality environment is an important amenity that can strongly affect guest preferences, but it can suffer economically if its only clientele comes from the hotel, especially in smaller settings with shorter tourist seasons. Placing the restaurant close to the entrance, or perhaps having both a street and lobby entrance, enables it to attract patrons from both the hospitality environment and the local community (Elson & Muller, 2002) Consider giving guests a choice of different ambiences and food selection by providing two dining areas (Siguaw & Enz, 1999a). Be aware, however, that most people will perceive the restaurant and the hospitality environment as one entity, and dissatisfaction with the restaurant's food or service will lower overall satisfaction levels and may deter guests from returning to the hospitality setting (Nield et al., 2000). Alternatively, "name-brand" restaurants (i.e., chain, franchise, or chef-owned eateries with corporate financing and geographical or epicurean renown) can provide stabilizing elements—an independent image with positive associations, a sense of familiarity for guests, and consistency in food, service, and customer attraction—that can increase overall customer satisfaction and reduce capital costs (Siguaw & Enz, 1999a).

Special Accommodations

More families are engaging in a variety of recreational opportunities, including fine dining, cruises, and trips to foreign countries. Individuals with physical disabilities are engaging in mainstream types of recreation. Although these trends are positive steps toward the consideration of diverse needs and restrictions among the population, an unintended consequence may have a negative response on the part of other patrons (e.g., some people are offended by hearing a baby cry in an elegant restaurant, seeing a service dog defecate on a private beach, being in close proximity to people who are disabled or deformed).

Design can correct the first scenario by incorporating dedicated space for children within guest rooms and utilizing solid concrete and precast materials for sound reduction (Siguaw & Enz, 1999b). Hotels and resorts welcoming or catering to the child and family markets will want to create interesting and interactive spaces to delight and inspire.

The other scenarios can only be minimized, by incorporating *behavioral zoning,* a concept that is related to *behavior setting* in that it restricts behaviors to certain locations. Many hotels already implement a basic form of "zoning" by reserving certain rooms for wheelchair users, families with children, or smokers. Expanding this concept to include the designation of specific zones (e.g., for young families or persons with service dogs) will not only provide spaces that can accommodate specific needs and accoutre-

BOX 15.2 RUSTIC LOBBY

This rustic lodge lobby area, inspired by the multifaceted layering found in nature, can impart to guests a hearty wholesome welcome. The informal quality of the rough-hewn log furniture yet finished with intricate patterned cloth cushions can be interpreted by guests as a place with an unpretentious comfortable atmosphere in which guests should come to for rest and relaxation. The vertical expanse of the lobby affords guests views to multiple levels, circulation paths, outdoor views, and the gift shop tucked under the second floor dining area. The uniform color palette of dark earth tones is in contrast to the seating area; from the sprinkling of light from the pendant chandelier, the golden glow of the table lamps, the daylight streaming from a high window, to the light colored carpeting. These cues are consistent with a *strategic junction node* that the hotel designers do not want to specifically

[**Box Figure 15.2**] An example of rustic design where the designers do not want to control activities in the space. © Chuck Pefley / Alamy

designate or control what will happen in this particular area; guests must decide what activity will take place (read a paper, wait to check in or out, meet up with friends, take a nap, have a cup of coffee, and so on). This further supports the home-like quality imparted through the architecture, craftsmanship, color palette, materials and finishes.

ments (e.g., high chairs and playpens or food and water bowls), but also give other patrons the opportunity to distance themselves if they so desire.

The senior tourist population, with more discretionary income and free time, represents a significant force within the hospitality market (Marvel, 1999), especially during off-season times (Wuest, Emenheiser, & Tas, 2001). The relative convenience and sense of security provided by hotels may have advantages for senior or disabled guest populations (Marvel, 1999); however, it is important to develop environments that support autonomy and increase self-esteem and trust for these individuals (Deci & Ryan, 1987).

Special population travelers have unique desires and needs that include safety and security relative not only to potential invaders, but also to the environment itself (Marvel, 1999). The Americans with Disabilities Act (ADA) addresses many of these concerns as issues of *universal design*; however, as previously noted, trying to meet all ADA requirements can be problematic but necessary because over 18 percent of the U.S. population is disabled in some fashion (Steinmetz, 2003).

When designing spaces for public use, consider the various circumstances that could arise. For example, a ballroom or restaurant may be used for award ceremonies or events in which one person may rise to offer a toast or the audience may

be moved to a standing ovation. The ADA guidelines require that wheelchair seating be liberally dispersed throughout public arenas to allow for appropriate seating and that locations provide unobstructed lines of sight comparable to those provided for the general public, regardless of whether others are seated or standing (Mazumdar & Geis, 2002).

Guest rooms can accommodate visitors with impaired vision by providing ample lighting, contrasting color schemes that minimize glare, and room accessories (e.g., telephones, TV/CD remote controls, alarm clocks) with large-character display panels, as well as Braille signage (Baker et al., 2002; Marvel, 1999). Directional and location signs should have large lettering in sharp contrast to the background, along with Braille markers. Provide pedestrian-friendly throughways in public spaces to enhance mobility and accessibility, and consider the use of auditory navigation aids, such as elevators that automatically announce floor stops and floor panels that trigger recorded announcements (e.g., "Welcome to the lobby; the front desk is located to your right"; Baker et al., 2002).

Design must not only serve to compensate for various human limitations but also make provisions for different means of disability support staff and animals. For example, all types of service animals require both living spaces and exercise facilities.

Themes

Although many hospitality settings employ unique themes related to environmental meaning, many of the larger hotel chains pursue a level of standardization in their designs, and some utilize the same design throughout the chain with only mild changes to exterior finish.

Homogeneous design rationales include the development of brand recognition and cost savings; however, such consistency may alienate guests who desire a unique experience (Siguaw & Enz, 1999b), and uniformity among luxury hotels can lead to a loss of potential patrons (Bernstein, 1999). For example, if someone was to visit Budapest, he/she might rather stay in an environment that looks the same as it would in any other part of the world (comfort in familiarity) or in one that is distinctly Hungarian (excitement in the new). As much as a hospitality business must know its market base, so too must the designers know the demographic and give the experience that would be most appropriate.

Themes work well for many bed-and-breakfasts, resorts, and cruise lines. The primary purpose of a theme is to create an illusion or fantasy experience, which can range from childhood dreams, to a former era, to a pampered life of luxury. Many people visit themed hospitality environments to relieve the stress associated with everyday life and to form life-long memories. Take a moment to examine these ideas. As society becomes more structured, people will desire a method of escapism through items such as fantasy books, games, and movies (Gilsdorf, 2004), and through other contrived experiences such as themed hospitality environments. Although the traditional hospitality environment fulfills this desire to some extent, in recent years there have been significant increases in the numbers of themed resorts, cruise ships, and adventure resorts that promise fantasy. The intent of these fantasy experiences is to instill long-lasting memories in patrons that will prompt a return visit or a recommendation (*word-of-mouth advertising*) to others. Patrons tend to have pre-conceived ideas of what the experience will be like; therefore, if these expectations are either not met or are surpassed, there is a high probability that these encounters will be encoded into long-term memory (Reisberg & Hertel, 2004).

Some cruise themes are based on popular amusement parks, others on guest commonalities such as age (e.g., senior citizens, 35 and under, young families), and shared interests (e.g., film, music, and sports). Popular resort themes include dude ranches, ski lodges, and island getaways. Fantasy theme settings can range from life in Colonial America (depicted by authentic/replicated designs and period costumes) to a modern ski lodge where comfortable shelter is provided.

The premise of themes within hospitality environments is to create an emotional experience for the guests, a total immersion into a flight of the imagination, an adventure or a lifestyle visitors wish they had. Bear in mind that designers do not necessarily create a *place* as create a *scene,* much like a movie set. Props and facades, sights, textures, lights and smells all work together to produce a show in which the guests will play the part of the actors. When designing themed resorts, be aware of the implications and associations of different architectural styles to avoid applying them in an incorrect way (Hertz, 2002). In addition, in order to "sell" the show, designers must do their research into the theme and portray all the elements as authentically as possible. Every detail must be considered because tourists will remember every detail.

Bed-and-Breakfasts

Country travelers in Colonial America often spent the night at private houses or small inns. This custom continued into the 1800s and today lives on in the form of the bed-and-breakfast. The typical bed-and-breakfast serves as temporary housing for travelers and is usually operated out of large, single-family residence. Guests have private bedrooms, which may or may not include a private bathroom. As indicated by the name, the principal amenity of a bed-and-breakfast is the provision of a homemade breakfast, which is often based on regional flavors and produce or a particular theme. Many bed-and-breakfast establishments consciously seek to recreate a historical atmosphere; one based on nostalgic recreation of a once idyllic and "simpler time."

Travelers who choose a bed-and-breakfast are generally seeking *an experience*; whether it is motivated by romance, history or a desire for a cultural immersion. They will require a fully realized and thoughtful set of activities; settings and sensations that will allow them direct participation. Guests may desire sampling the local cuisine, sleeping in authentic environments, perusing local shops and galleries, and establishing a personal connection with local inhabitants.

The *atmosphere* which the designer creates will generally attract the clientele to the bed-and-breakfast; therefore, in contrast to the design of a hotel or motel, the bed-and-breakfast designs its own image. If the conceptual design involves an authentic renovation of a historic home along with furnishings and décor, the designer may want to complement and connect it to the regional heritage. When possible, try to accommodate guests by providing them with their own bathrooms and private entry into the main building. The most important aspect that a bed-and-breakfast should provide is a home-like atmosphere so that the guest feels as if he/she is experiencing the local life or perhaps even being part of it.

Resorts

The word *resort* can be used to describe towns in which tourism accounts for a significant portion of the local industry (e.g., Aspen and Vail, Colorado) as well as large properties owned by a single company that usually incorporate some type of theme (e.g., Disney themed resorts). These hospitality environments are generally high in quality and strive to fulfill all of their patrons' wants and needs so that they feel as if they never have to leave the resort. As such, a common denominator between resort towns and single-owner resorts is that they tend to be all-inclusive, providing a host of dining opportunities, lodging, entertainment, recreation and shopping within their confines.

The challenges that come with resort design are simply the sheer size and scope of the project. These challenges can be summed up with only a few of the many design considerations:

- Main entry and exiting
- Pattern and flow of guests
- Activities and resting points
- Maintenance and safety needs
- Restroom and medical facilities
- Commerce and surveillance issues
- Large group accommodations and family needs
- Lodging and dining services

- Inventory delivery and trash collection
- Landscaping and peripheral environmental

Megaresorts are, in fact, much like designing small cities. And, in that way, the designers of a resort environment can work through many of the factors that they must design and coordinate into the project—consider the resort a city.

A resort can fall into one of two categories: a destination or a nondestination resort (Mill, 2008). Destination resorts tend to be extremely far away from their main market. The Atlantis Resort, for example, has two locations—one in the Bahamas and the other in Dubai; this is an example of a themed destination resort (Figure 15.8; Mill, 2008). These resorts are typically more upscale and more expensive than nondestination resorts, and guests generally stay between 5 to 7 days.

Many people will select Las Vegas as a destination, but most will not go there for a single resort. Hence, Las Vegas, Monte Carlo, and Atlantic City are destination cities, thereby rendering their resorts as nondestination resorts. Some of the trends in the resort industry that specialists report are spas and health-related resorts and casino-type gaming resorts (Mill, 2008).

[**Figure 15.8**] The Atlantis on Paradise Island is a resort in the Bahamas that covers over 600 acres and includes water parks, aquariums, casinos, shopping, dining, a spa, golf course, museum, children's learning center, and so on. The theme of "the lost city of Atlantis" permeates every aspect of the environment. © CuboImages art / Alamy

[**Figure 15.9**] The MS Freedom of the Seas is a Royal Caribbean International cruise ship, and the "main street" takes advantage of an atrium skylight, larger amounts of glass throughout, and the expansive sightlines. Conversely, luxury staterooms promote calm with muted earthen colors and windows with a view. In both environments, the heavy use of natural illumination supports the illusion of spaciousness. © Ramona Settle / Alamy

Cruise Ships

Cruise ships began as a form of transportation; however, with the advent of the jet plane, the appeal of cruise ships as a mode of travel declined. Today, cruise ships are essentially floating resorts where people go to have an *experience*. Many cruise ships provide unique experiences but most simply pamper their guests.

In 1998, 7.8 million people took their vacations on a cruise ship (Cartwright & Baird, 1999); and in 2008, 16.8 million people worldwide went on a cruise (Moody, 2008). A larger ship can accommodate up to 3,000 passengers. One of the reported benefits cruise passengers state as their motivation for cruise ship travel is that they are more comfortable in exotic locations when they know that they have their "comfort zone," their "home away from home" with them the whole time (Cartwright & Baird, 1999).

The profit margin for cruise ships derives mostly from onboard purchases, which include alcoholic beverages, poolside snacks, and duty-free shops, as well as special events such as art auctions. To maximize these expenditures, cruise ships open a running tab for each patron upon boarding the ship, and that tab remains open until the patron is ready to leave. Without conscious thought of the flow of money, people are more apt to spend; therefore, a well thought-out spacing of income opportunities for the cruise line owners and entertainment possibilities for the passengers must be attained.

Similar to resorts, cruise ships rely on their ability to create fantasies as a means of attracting and satisfying patrons; thus, the balance remains in creating spaces with props and stimulating settings within main areas (i.e., bright and high contrast spaces) and the private suites as areas of retreat for the passengers (i.e., muted and neutral colors). Another important consideration in design for cruise ship interiors is the limitation of space. Designers must enhance the illusion of more spacious environments. This includes increasing the sightlines through spaces, maximizing mirrors and glazing to allow as much natural light into an area as possible, making spaces appear both brighter and larger (see Figure 15.9). Overall, however, the main objective is to design for a specific demographic group or theme and to take into account the aspects of efficiency and safety.

BACK TO NATURE

An increasingly popular international tourism trend serves those environmentally conscientious travelers who wish to experience, explore, or simply enjoy a site or region's natural or cultural resources. **Nature tourism** in its most basic form allows tourists to restore their relationship with nature. It encompasses an eclectic range of recreational and cultural activities and experiences, from bird and whale watching to

[**Figure 15.10**] This image is of an ecoresort in Jordan within the Dana Nature Reserve. Jordan's Royal Society for the Conservation of Nature operates the "Guest House," which is perched on a cliff with spectacular views of the Wadi Dana Valley below. This remote destination offers tourists peace and quiet, access to archeological sites, traditional Arab food, and access to the work of regional artisans. The Guest House was built with local materials and in the traditional vernacular. Tourists often help the local community by adding to the economy through employment opportunities and education of the village residents, as well as through the promotion and conservation of the natural preserve. © Ron Buskirk / Alamy

mountain trekking, to *artesian* produced crafts, to surfing, cycling, climbing, diving, and driving adventures. Whereas traditional resorts are frequently luxurious and generally self-contained, nature tourism ranges from communal lodges and one-room cabins to primitive survivalist camps; and the pursuit of leisure and exploration activities usually involves travel into the surrounding environment.

Ecotourism

Ecotourism can be considered a specialized segment of the nature tourism market. It also has been called by many terms, such as *environmentally friendly, ecological, sustainable, eco-social, nature-, culture-,* or *community-based tourism.* Ecotourism supports and conserves indigenous cultures, economies, traditions, and landscapes while promoting ecologically sustainable development (Ayala, 1996). The International Ecotourism Society (TIES, 2004) defines ecotourism as "responsible travel to natural areas that conserves the environment and improves the well-being of local

people," noting that those who implement and participate in ecotourism activities should follow these principles:

- Minimize impact
- Build environmental and cultural awareness and respect
- Provide positive experiences for both visitors and hosts
- Provide direct financial benefits for conservation efforts
- Provide financial benefits and empowerment for the local people
- Raise sensitivity to host countries' political, environmental, and social climate
- Support international human rights and labor agreements

Although no standards currently exist for certifying the environmental friendliness and sustainability of ecoresorts, the resort must provide meaningful participation from the host community and be profitable for themselves (Mader, 2004; see Figure 15.10). Unfortunately, the smaller the setting often equates to a smaller profit margin.

Ecotourism settings and experiences range from the primitive to the luxurious, depending on location and visitors demands. Some ecotourists relish in "the simple life" (i.e., sleeping on dirt floors in huts or tents, sharing traditional meals with the indigenous people, bathing in streams or lakes), whereas others demand all the amenities and services of a grand hotel.

Given the current trends in environmentalism, many companies and resorts narrowly define the eco-friendly so that they can fit the definition. There are, however, some establishments that are truly sustainable such as the 92-acre Spring House Farm in North Carolina, which provides only six guest cottages. These sanctuaries are carefully designed, constructed, and maintained to preserve and protect the natural environmental balance while providing ample opportunities for leisure, recreation, and solitude for guests who seek a peaceful refuge in quiet, secluded settings.

What all ecotourism destinations offer is hospitality with a more sustainable attitude and they attempt to provide a profound connection to the systems of ecology and the surrounding environments.

An *authentic experience* is what most ecotourists are seeking; therefore, designers have the opportunity to create an environment that celebrates a region, with the location of the resort, the architectural form, the interior materials and layout, the adjacencies to the town or village center, and the activities that could occur on or near the resort. Designers can expedite the design process by imagining the journey the tourists will take from arrival through to departure. Where will they sleep? Where will they eat? How will they get around? What amenities will they require? How and where will they best see and experience the "flavor or vibe of the region"?

Agri-tourism

Agri-tourism's earliest forms began with working ranches (dude ranches), farms, orchards, and vineyards. To generate additional income, many farmers invited and visitors and provided entertainment. The entertainment generally included hands-on experiences for visitors that allowed them to experience some portion of the agricultural business. Visitors might assist ranching, pick apples, or care for the livestock in an effort to learn and reconnect with a rural lifestyle. It is also sometimes called *rural tourism*, which has come to include resorts, markets, tours, and other hospitality businesses that attract visitors to the countryside. The primary goal of agri-tourism is to preserve the traditional way of farming while conserving rural historic buildings through the education and exposure of tourists and day visitors.

For many travelers, agri-tourism provides a necessary educational bridge between urban and rural lifestyles. It is in essence a form of nature tourism that offers outdoor recreation opportunities, educational experiences, access to rural forms of entertainment (e.g., harvest balls, winter festivals, barn dances), and direct sales of agricultural products (fresh produce, artisan cheeses, or other homemade products; Williams, Paridaen, Dossa, & Dumais, 2001). The main feature of an agri-tourist destination is that the owners are farmers, the primary source of their income is derived from authentic farming, and guest accommodations account for no more than 50 percent of the total farm.

The typical agri-tourist shares an interest and curiosity in rural and natural environments, and wishes to escape overcrowded urban and suburban areas to the peace and tranquility of the countryside (Williams et al., 2001). Accommodations at agricultural destinations are diverse and can range from simple rustic campgrounds to four-star luxury accommodations; however, the majority are restored historic country farmhouses or cabins that function as bed-and-breakfasts or private getaways (Williams et al., 2001).

People who are attracted to agricultural destinations are looking for an experience beyond what they are used to. When adding an accommodation component to an existing farm, the daily activities of the farm must be safely integrated into the entertainment venue. Also, lodging and gathering spaces for the guests should be within close proximity of the actual farm or ranch. Designs for agri-tourist destinations should evoke an authentic image of an agrarian life that includes a level of communal living. Specific design aspects must be inspired by the local heritage and customs of the farming family to create a thoughtful connection with the visitors. Typically, simple rustic furnishings, flooring, and wall coverings, combined with hand-sewn or embroidered quilts, can promote and enhance the interior ambiance, as well as exhibiting the work of local artists (see Figure 15.11). The farm or ranch specifically should be simply clean, easily maintained, and a safe environment for guests.

SHARED REAL ESTATE

Shared real estate is an alternative to a vacation. It attracts a group of people who are often well-educated couples who enjoy luxury items. Two predominant forms of shared-ownership real estate are **timeshares** and **private residence clubs**. Whereas these two forms of vacation ownership are fundamentally the same, public residence clubs tend to be larger units with more floor space, have many more services available to guests, and require substantially higher annual maintenance fees (Rezak, 2003). Timeshares, however, tend to be more popular with middle-income vacationers who are looking for a less-expensive place to go on vacation and relax (Elson & Muller, 2002 Hobson, 2002). Consumers who invest in timeshares and public residence clubs consider

[**Figure 15.11**] A key element in the design of agri-tourism accommodations is a rustic ambience. Many allow guests to assist in the daily chores, enjoy seasonal recreation, or simply enjoy the tranquil surroundings all within a rustic ambience. Courtesy of Liberty Hill Farm Inn

these properties their second homes and may feel safer in fully self-contained exclusive complexes and neighborhoods.

Timeshares are a piece of real estate in which many people share ownership in the property. The owners pay to stay at the property for typically one specific week every year. The majority of timeshares are condo-type dwellings with fully equipped kitchens and furnished rooms. Some timeshares are hotel rooms or suites within large resort settings.

A private residence club (also called a *luxury fractional property*) is generally a luxury or custom home in an exclusive area in a highly sought after location. Owners pay an initial fee of several hundred thousand dollars and a lesser annual maintenance fee to own a faction of the home. (For example, a one-sixth share of a $2 million luxury home is purchased for $300,000.) Each owner receives a specified amount of time during a prime season (i.e., 6 to 12 weeks). The main motivation for these affluent vacationers is that

they do not want to own or be responsible for a second or third home (Hobson, 2002).

As the shared real estate industry grows in response to a sophisticated and demanding consumer market, it must consider additional amenities to enhance "resident guest" experiences and establish a competitive market edge (Siguaw & Enz, 1999b). More vacationers are looking for home-like elements in their hospitality environments (Williams et al., 2001); shared ownership properties require a much greater investment yet without the responsibility for maintenance or care. Designs for shared real estate facilities should include dining and entertaining options: interior dining and entertaining spaces as well as exterior ones. Another aspect of design is the inclusion of casual spaces with opportunities for play to accommodate families with small children, as well as formal spaces for the socialization and the enjoyment of the adult group. The design of shared real estate should satisfy the unique needs of its users—people who seek a more familiar environment but still want to experience the sense of being on vacation. Design professionals must ensure that their designs are in accordance with the image that the consumer is attracted to and respectful to the local vernacular.

SUSTAINABILITY CONNECTION 15.2

About 50 percent of a typical hotel and motel's waste comes from not recycling paper, glass, and plastic materials (food can also be recycled in the form of composting; City of Los Angeles Waste Generation Study, 1993). Therefore, if recycling could start in the rooms by designing dual trash receptacles and/or by offering washable glass and mugs rather than plastic or polystyrene foam, this one effort would go a long way to solving this immediate problem. The facility should be outfitted with water-saving devices throughout. Filtering grey water from showers, sinks, and laundry to the irrigation system for landscaping is another way to recycle and conserve water simultaneously.

Practical Applications for Designers

Use these resources, activities, and discussion questions to help you identify, synthesize, and retain this chapter's core information. These tools are designed to complement the resources you'll find in this book's companion Study Guide.

SUMMING IT UP

Recreation is an important part of the human condition because it allows us to escape from our daily routines and stressors and regenerate. In today's world there are a multitude of recreational environments, also referred to as hospitality settings. Hospitality is a way to characterize the relationship between a guest and a host that includes reception and entertainment. Today's travelers include people from all walks of life, including elderly and disabled persons who require special features from their environments.

The word synomorphy can be thought of as *together with the quality of form*. Essentially the environment creates a setting, which in turn promotes certain behaviors that are compatible with the activity.

You can also refer to this textbook's companion Study Guide for a comprehensive list of Summary Points.

EXPERT SPOTLIGHT 15.1

The Symbiotic Nature of Hotel, Restaurant, and Gift/Convenience Store Design

Holly L. Cline, Ph.D., LEED AP, IDEC, NCIDQ, Radford University

Symbiotic hospitality design is a mutually beneficial relationship with two or more groups of businesses contained within the hotel design. A common example of a mixed-use complex in hospitality design is the gift shop contained within the hotel lobby. The gift shop can be (or is usually) an independent retailer who is renting space within the hotel environment and is providing the hotel guest with a variety of convenience items such as toiletries, beverages, and snacks. The gift shop retailer benefits because he/she has a captive audience in the hotel patron, and these patrons are willing to pay a higher price for the added convenience of proximity. In turn, the hotel is perceived as providing a higher degree of service.

Within all hotels and resorts are public spaces. Many hotels lease portions of this space to outside services. But caution must be exercised to ensure a high level of quality and service because the hotel guest will associate a bad experience from the outside service to the service of the hotel. For example, during the past decade, coffee houses/shops have been integrated into hotel environments; however, most hotels prefer to lease to nationally recognized franchises because large franchises are better able to provide assurances of reliability and predictability of product and service. Another reason that hotels and resorts prefer national franchises is because of brand identity. Starbucks, for example, has strong branding, which means that if the guest receives bad service, the guest will be more likely to blame Starbucks and not the hotel.

Developments in hospitality/resort design have been maximized by the success of the symbiotic retail/hotel arrangements. The advantages of built-in market demand with predefined lifestyle demographics promote the success of these types of mixed-use design. One element contributing to this success is the notion that everything can be provided within a secure complex. Leasing space to a variety of retailers and service providers allows the hotel to strengthen its brand's message and lifestyle without the product cost and upkeep. And, it brings a level of safety and convenience often embraced by the clientele. Consider a business convention where groups are able to meet at a bar or restaurant located in the hotel. This convenience allows people to have more time for the meeting because there is no travel; people are able to reduce travel-related costs because taxis are not needed and should one or two people consume too much alcohol, they can easily and safely return to their room.

From these discussions, we can then say that there are three key components to a mixed-use environment's success:

1. Preliminary development and planning considerations

2. Market research

3. Lobby design

Carefully designed developments are critical to the overall success of the space. Maximizing combined services and energy management are essential for sustained success. Predesign market research provides the basis for decision making and determining the right mix of retail/services/hotel guests ratios. The lobby design is key to the fluidity of movement and the information the patron receives about the space. Shared spaces within the lobby must provide for a variety of activities and communicate to the patron the formality and atmosphere of the entire complex. The lobby "sets the stage" for the entire experience thereafter. One can then state with some certainty that whether we are designing for a small scale boutique hotel or a large mix-use resort complex, the symbiotic nature of combined environment types cannot be ignored. When mixed-use spaces are designed in a harmony, a synergy of activity occurs. The end result is a gestalt in the environment where the whole is greater than the sum of its parts.

KEY TERMS

- **agricultural (agri) resorts**
- **agri-tourism**
- **behavior settings**
- **concentration node**
- **ecological (eco) resorts**
- **ecotourism**
- **environmental legibility**
- **FIT (free independent traveler)**
- **heat island effect**
- **hospitality**
- **nature tourism**
- **private residence clubs**
- **recreational environments**
- **right-side bias**
- **segmentation bias**
- **shared real estate**
- **strategic junction node**
- **synomorphy**
- **timeshares**
- **urban heat island effect**
- **visually impaired**

WEB LINKS

American Foundation for the Blind, select "Information for Professionals," then "Creating an Accessible Environment" for design-related suggestions for the visually impaired. (www.afb.org)

Blogabond (www.blogabond.com)

Bushmans Kloof Wilderness Reserve (www.bushmanskloof.co.za)

Eco-Tropic Resorts (www.eco-tropicalresorts.com)

Exploritas, on Elderhostel (www.exploritas.org)

Govtrack.us, on tracking Congressional bills (www.govtrack.us)

Priestmangoode, on re-design of Motel 6 (www.priestmangoode.com/environment)

Sherpareport, on shared investment properties (www.sherpareport.com)

Travel + Leisure magazine, "World's Best" hotels and motels awards (www.travelandleisure.com)

Treehouse.com, on interactive family-friendly resort design (www.treehouses.com)

Walt Disney Imagineering (http://disney.go.com/disneycareers/internships/walt_disney_imagineering.html)

STUDIO ACTIVITY 15.1

Luxury Resort

Design Problem Statement
You are asked to design and build a five-star luxury resort, located on the site of your choice. The idea of this project is to provide deluxe accommodations for vacation travelers. It should be luxurious with great views and elegant room decor. There should be an assortment of services to satisfy an array of needs that may be required of guests. These services should be easily findable and the decor of these spaces should be consistent with the service being provided and also should exude luxury. Similarly the resort should have many amenities that should be included within the interior and exterior portions of the resort.

Directions
Step One: Choose a site anywhere in the world, paying close attention to the local culture, traditions, residents, and/or art. Also, pay close attention to your choice of color and building materials. How do people from other countries perceive luxury?

Step Two: Incorporate original design styles or elements into your design.

Step Three: Provide a minimum of three high-end restaurants for guests and one nightclub or lounge. Pay close attention to what services, activities, and entertainment you want to provide for your guests.

Step Four: Provide a one-page typed paper on the location of your project and your site analysis.

Step Five: Provide at least one large pool and great landscaped grounds. Pay close attention to native plants and their use. The resort must be able to handle and accommodate handicapped guests.

Step Six: Provide all relevant drawings or sketches that convey your ideas and concepts of your design (sections, sketches, elevations).

Deliverables
Your design (drawing or sketches) along with the one page paper.

STUDIO ACTIVITY 15.2

Going Green Resort

Design Problem Statement
You have been commissioned to design and build a 100 percent recyclable resort that will be located in Costa Rica. Explore ways to build using only those items found in a recycled trashcan.

Directions
Step One: Determine if you want your eco resort to be urban, suburban, or rural.

Step Two: Print out common features of the environment that you will want your eco resort to contain. You could have many photos; these should all be taped together to form a place mat, with your model on top of it.

Step Three: Empty out your trash from home and sort through it for items that could be used to build your model.

Step Four: Clean all of the items you pulled from your trash.

Step Five: Catalogue (list all of your items on a sheet of paper) and plan out how you will use the items.

Step Six: Assemble your model for an eco resort.

Step Seven: Bring model to class; place it on your environmental context place mat. Place some blank sheets of paper next to your model so that classmates can write down some of their perceptual notions pertaining to your eco resort.

Deliverables
Model, environmental context place mat, extra blank sheets of paper

DISCUSSION QUESTIONS

1. Describe the specific design goals for the visually impaired within recreational settings.

2. Compare examples of travelers who prefer unique culinary and lodging experiences based on locale with those who opt for a homogenous experience irrespective of geography.

3. Discuss what makes a community. What features of a resort setting are necessary to make guests feel they need not leave the resort community?

4. Discuss the importance of food and mealtime in different cultures. How might this knowledge affect your design of a hotel or resort in different areas of the world? Considering that smell is the sense most strongly tied to memory, how might a hotel or resort exploit this fact and utilize an eating establishment to increase patron satisfaction?

5. Discuss the ramifications of over-zoning a built environment. What happens if too many spaces are set aside for specific groups? Discuss the positive and negative aspects of providing secluded settings that may isolate parts of the guest population

LEARNING ACTIVITIES

1. Research market trends over the last five years to determine the top five trends in hospitality and leisure. Pick one trend, select a property associated with that type of market, and explain how environmental psychology concepts are exhibited through the marketing, interior and exterior design, and the concept of the property. Draw sketches and diagrams to illustrate your findings.

2. Design an experiment to prove or disprove the theory that humans have a right-side bias. Remember to cite all sources and use an experimental control.

3. Visit a large local hotel and obtain permission to enter the guest room area. Sketch the view of the corridor from the elevator on at least three floors. What, if any, methods are used to differentiate the floors? What effect does this have on you, the temporary guest? Are there any aspects of the design that invite you farther into the building or encourage exploration?

4. Pick a resort or hotel that interests you and write a brief description of what intrigues you about it. Contact the business office and request information regarding the facility's clientele. Gather specific, current information regarding the following: clients' average age, gender, marital status, socioeconomic status, and number in party (adults or children); how these data have changed over the last decade; how the management uses the information to predict future trends; and how this information affects both the design philosophy and the amenities offered.

5. Research examples of hospitality design being altered to reflect the clientele's desires or needs. Look for large-scale examples and try to find before-and-after images. Investigate and explain the basis for the changes and the effect these changes have had on the clientele. (For example, the MGM Grand in Las Vegas originally had a large statue of an open-mouthed lion in its lobby, which was altered to mitigate the superstitious fears of numerous Asian tourists.)

16 Retail and Service Environments

Whoever said money can't buy happiness simply didn't know where to go shopping.

—Bo Derek

The experience people have with a **retail** or **service environment** begins long before they step inside a building. The experience begins with a desire or a need for a particular product or function (the objective); it involves the amount of time, effort, and expense required to achieve it (the process); and it results in the feelings evoked before, during, and after the fact (the outcome).

Retail and service environments include, but are not limited to, convenience stores, gas and service stations, banks, restaurants, bars and clubs, specialty shops, department stores and emporiums, shopping malls, bulk warehouses, booths, kiosks, and vending carts. These establishments all sell products or services and have a need for customers. They are *public territories,* open to the community at large and, therefore, subject to the specific perceptions of individuals. These perceptions are based on individual personalities, ages, gender, status, and life experiences. Each environment is affected by periodic *crowding,* which is contingent on the time of day, season, weather, and events such as sales, specials, and holidays. And they are at constant risk for criminal activity.

A service might include *tangible* objects such as food or drink, or *intangible* ideas or concepts such as a consultant who provides knowledge to a client. All service-oriented businesses that serve the general public must ensure the satisfaction of their customers and their employees because many services lack physical (tangible) properties to which people can relate. Service industries are beginning to value their physical spaces as sources for positive affects on customer behavior and satisfaction.

The retail and service environment, or **servicescape**, can be viewed according to three predominate factors—ambience, layout, and signage— each of which can influence customers' satisfaction or dissatisfaction with

[**Figure 16.1**] The mannequin on the left is part of a line of fashion displays for size 20 and larger, whereas the mannequin on the right (sizes 2-6) is representative of what is typically displayed in stores. © Newspix via Getty Images / Alamy

[**Figure 16.2**] Color can be used with branding. The color is often intertwined so deeply with a brand that the product and color become indistinguishable. © Steve Stock / Alamy

the service or product (Ang, Leong, & Lim, 1997). For instance, using plus-size mannequins in a plus-sized clothing store will ingratiate the target market population to the store more than using thin mannequins (Figure 16.1). The same can be said of utilizing multiethnic mannequins rather than exclusively white European representations.

This chapter discusses the effects of these variables on the retail and service industry. It examines designs that mitigate undesirable behaviors and foster desirable ones. It discusses crowding and density as they relate to public spaces and applies those concepts to banks and convenience stores, restaurants and cafés, retail facilities, and malls.

ASSOCIATION

Color can often set the tone of a space as being practical, whimsical, sophisticated, or playful. Because of the strength color has with *association*, many Western retail and service industries try to capitalize on its associative qualities to form **brand identity**. The Coca-Cola label with its distinctive red background and white script shows how a product and color can be linked together to form an association. The text may

have changed over the years, but the color combination is recognizable in all countries where it is sold regardless of language (see Figure 16.2).

Color is the first and most important consideration when deciding whether or not to purchase an item (Pegler, 1998). If there are no suitable colors from which to select, then the size, shape, or price will be irrelevant (see Box 16.1, "Color: What's in a Name?").

The careful use of color schemes can be considered a subtle messaging technique because of the mood altering effects induced by color (Birren, 1978; Malnar & Vodvarka, 2004; Mahnke, 1996). In design, a carefully selected color can be used to evoke a desired mood. For example, natural wood in "homey" brown tones creates a welcoming atmosphere and makes a large space seem warmer and more intimate. Creating an atmosphere of this kind through the use of subtle environmental cues including color, ambient temperature, and aroma, tends to inspire more communication and facilitates feelings of relaxation. Although research demonstrates a relationship between color and human behavior, cultural backgrounds can be a mitigating variable to the effects of color. This is because color often possesses cultural significance and symbolism that is not uniform throughout the world (Mahnke, 1996).

An **association** within the retail environment is about the connection between a stimulus and a meaning. In many ways color serves as an associative quality between a place or item and the different feelings elicited in different people (Bell & Ternus, 2006). The popular home improvement store Home Depot capitalized on the association between neon orange and construction activities and thus adopted the color for its logo. In the fashion world, wearing similar colors as one's peers or social sect suggests social ties, such as shared membership in a club, gang, school, sorority, team, or tribe. An example of an association between color and a brand, fashion designer Giorgio Armani developed his signature color "greige" by mixing gray and beige (Showalter, 2001).

Branding

The use of color combinations, scent, slogans, and imagery are ways in which businesses can create "brand identity." Some businesses have been so successful at branding that the product becomes quite literally etched into memory. Then, at some future date, when a person is exposed to a certain color, **logo**, or catch phrase (also known as a slogan), the product is immediately recalled. To illustrate, if someone were to ask about, "that store with the red bull's-eye sign," most Americans would instantly recognize it as the retail store Target. And, if someone were to say, "good to the last drop," Maxwell House coffee might be the first association made. Some examples of brand images and logos include:

- The famous "swoosh" of Nike brand sportswear
- The bright yellow shell with red trim of Shell gasoline
- The golden arches of McDonald's
- The four rings of Audi automobiles

Many specialty stores such as FAO Schwartz make great efforts to develop brand identity and associations with their products and services. According to FAO Schwartz (Berkowitz et al., 2003), "It is important to leave people with a memorable image of your store. Disneyland has Cinderella's castle. For us, it's the clock."

Brand identity isn't limited to colors and color combinations, logos and slogans; it can also occur as a result of a particular interior design or architecture. The Transamerica tower in San Francisco is an example of a building whose image is protected by a United States trademark because the building's shape is intrinsically tied to the identity of Transamerica Corporation. Not only do businesses use branding techniques to generate instant associations between the gen-

---

BOX 16.1 COLOR: WHAT'S IN A NAME?

Crayola® LLC has been in the business of "color" since 1885. Originally the founders were manufacturers of pigments; although in 1903, Binney & Smith (as they were known then) introduced the first set of crayons in only eight colors: black, brown, orange, violet, blue, green, red, and yellow. Today, there are more than 120 colors with interesting and descriptive names. Some color names have changed along with society, for example:

1. 1958—Prussian Blue was renamed Midnight Blue
2. 1962—Flesh was renamed Peach

Flesh was renamed partially because of the U.S. Civil Rights Movement (Givens, 1986). Also, teachers recommended the company change Prussian Blue because the children no longer related to Prussian history because the country was abolished after Germany's defeat in World War I.

Another example of the importance of color and its name is with the automobile industry. Color creates linkages with a product or service, so the name given to a color can hold positive or negative associations. For example, one of the colors offered for the Ford Taurus, a car that appealed to older customers, was called Silver Frost. However, when the same color was targeted for the Generation-X population (1960–1979), Ford changed the color's name to CD Silver—and requests for that color doubled (Givens, 1986). Hence, the name given to a product's color can hold strong associative meaning and either contribute to or detour sales.

For example:

- Ford Motors changed Silver Frost to CD Silver
- Toyota changed Lavender Steel to Cool Steel

Both names were changed because of their associations with age. The word Lavender also appeals more to females and Cool Steel appeals to males.

---

eral population and some products or services, cities often create a brand association between themselves and some attribute within the city. Examples include the Space Needle of Seattle, the Art Deco buildings of South Beach Miami, and the Petronas Towers of Kuala Lumpur (Malaysia).

It is generally understood that the brand identity of an establishment can be enhanced by signage within and outside of a store or business. Often the style of the signage, be it sophisticated, delicate, or sporty, can tell the consumer a great deal about what the store has inside (Bell & Ternus, 2006; Pegler, 1998). Such distinctive design features serve as cues to the kind of setting they can expect. Successful branding methods are often imitated through the use of similar concepts as a means of capitalizing off another company's

[**Figure 16.3**] Irish-themed pub and grill-type restaurants draw upon the base colors of green and gold, which have strong associations with the country of Ireland; however, notice the use of the symbolic American Eagle under the words "Irish American" in the Bennigan's logo. This is a particular distinction from other Irish-themed restaurants because Bennigan's is extending and differentiating itself as an Irish-American establishment. © MCT via Getty Images

[**Figure 16.4**] The facades differ from store location to store location, but the font and color of the signage remain stable. Another relatively staple feature of all stores is the use of a continuous glass front for the Gap, the use of three window panels for Abercrombie & Fitch, and the department store look for the front of Old Navy stores. © F1online digitale Bildagentur GmbH / Alamy

brand identity. For example, there are many independently owned "Irish bar and grill" type restaurants that use similar associative cues (see Figure 16.3).

This is because humans often fail to remember details, but instead cluster similar pieces of information together to create a holistic message: a conclusion. To avoid confusion resulting from possible similarities, many shops located in large shopping malls will use their design footprint, entry threshold, or external façade as a common attribute for all of their stores (Figure 16.4). Examples of such stores include Old Navy, The Gap, and Abercrombie & Fitch. Common design styles used throughout a chain of stores and restaurants makes is easier for a customer to locate a particular store when shopping, and the person can feel relatively confident that the quality of service or product will be the similar to a past experience regardless of location.

IMAGE AND SETTING

Many factors contribute to the design of a successful retail or service facility. Each establishment has an image to project. One of the industries that has studied this relationship at great length is the commercial world. The automobile industry, for example, once delineated the brand of automobiles by the accessories available. In this way it was clear to the consumer why a Cadillac, with its power windows and seats, was more expensive than a Chevrolet, which did not offer these amenities. In today's market a person can purchase a Chevrolet with the same amenities available as in a Cadillac, thus making the two cars virtually indistinguishable. Nonetheless, the name "Cadillac" commands a greater price and is thus regarded as a higher caliber automobile. This perception of value extends to physical environments, and thus the location of retail or service environments can indicate a baseline for price markup. Consider that a boutique in Beverly Hills can offer the same items as a store on Chicago's South Side; however, the boutique in Beverly Hills can charge substantially higher prices simply because many consumers associate Beverly Hills with having perceived higher value. Likewise, the facility's design also affects consumers' environmental perceptions; the architecture, exterior design elements (e.g., façade, entryway, window displays, & signage), and interior design elements (e.g., layout, color scheme, & materials) contribute to the perceived value of the items or services offered.

Atmospherics

A store's image—its appearance and ambience—is an intangible commodity that has both a physical and a psychological impact on the consumer. In a department store, **atmospherics,** which are environmental cues, contribute to an overall ambience. These cues include the sensory stimuli of human environmental information transfer of taste, smell, sight, hearing, and touch. Within a department store this may come in the form of scents from perfume samples, the smells of new fabrics and leathers, to odors emanating from the shoppers themselves. Visual stimuli may include lighting that is neither too bright nor too dim, to reflected light from various surfaces. Audio cues might be intentional sounds such as background music, or unintentional sounds such as the clamor of many people talking at once or heavy traffic noise outside. Climatic or signals *felt* by people can range from stores that are perceived as too hot, cold, dry, or damp. Atmospherics serve to differentiate one store from another, including the competition, but also to attract and keep consumers who may rely on the image to communicate information about the quality and value of products and services, especially those unfamiliar to the customer (Bell, 1999). The external physical attributes of a retail or service setting—the structure itself plus the street and sidewalk conditions—landscaping, doors and windows, signage, displays, decoration, and so on—provide *external stimuli* that can trigger the consumer's behavior process (Schlosser, 1998). For example, some shops use constant streams of fragrance outside the door as a means to entice customers inside. Think of cinnamon roll shops. An interesting fact is that a potential customer may not consciously notice a pleasant environment, but a poor atmosphere can quickly and easily create a negative impression (Jones, 1999). This is why it is important for designers to remain attentive to the details.

Atmospherics is the design of an environment through various modes of sensory stimuli. The purpose of atmospherics is to stimulate people's perceptual and emotional responses, thereby affecting behavior (Levy & Weitz, 2003), and to conjure a positive mental image for the customer (see Figure 16.5). By many accounts the atmosphere of a retail environment is composed of several layers of sensory stimuli that create the overall ambiance (Bell & Ternus, 2006; Kopec 2006). The incorporation of atmospherics is commonly regarded as contributing to an enhanced environmental experience because it engages each of the senses simultaneously (Bell & Ternus, 2006). When properly incorporated into the design, atmospherics will immerse people into the overall environment. The result often leads to a person losing his/her sense of time and feeling less inhibited with money (Bell & Ternus, 2006).

The Victoria's Secret chain store selling women's lingerie uses atmospherics by incorporating visions of beautiful feminine décor in natural, almost residential, lighting; using sounds of classical music; and providing numerous opportunities to touch soft, lacy fabrics. Feminine scents are also incorporated and available for purchase through the company's cosmetic line (Bell & Ternus, 2006). Further enhancing the vibrancy of these stores are the soft warm color palettes, which are often selected and rotated in accordance with seasonal changes; an abundance of mirrors for viewing gar-

ments next to one's body; and large, well-lit dressing rooms for comfort and ease of changing.

Another establishment that excels in its atmospherics is Eatzi's, a small national specialty grocery store. What makes Eatzi's such a fine example in atmospherics is that they have included professional chefs cooking on site and samples of the foods they have prepared are provided to the patrons. These samples are available at every counter, which helps to promote an ambience similar to old-fashioned market-style displays. Eatzi's also includes piped-in opera music and quaint hand-written chalkboard signs throughout the store, and keeps bins of fresh fruits and vegetables out in the open (Bell & Ternus, 2006). What Eatzi's reflects as a business model utilizing atmospherics is that an *atmosphere* cannot be supported by design alone; it also requires the inclusion of people who support the image and occupy the environment to fully stimulate the "experience" for consumers.

[**Figure 16.5**] Dark mahogany wood combined with low lighting creates the atmosphere of elegance and sophistication that often is needed to attract business-oriented males. The atmosphere represents an image that the male wants to project. © Chuck Pefley / Alamy

It is possible, however, that retailers could be doing themselves a disservice by trying to create brand identity through the uniformity of atmospherics within a retail environment and not take into consideration the community in which the store is located. The Italian fashion retailer, Miss Sixty, has taken a very unique approach in merchandising through the use of their more-expensive-than-mass-produced fixtures, which has proven highly successful with their patrons. Each of the Miss Sixty shops is independently designed to stimulate each of the five senses, but within the location and context of the community where the store is located (Bell & Ternus, 2006). The Miss Sixty on Melrose Avenue in Hollywood, for example, fits the area's predisposition for sparkle and glamour. It has slick hard-surface flooring with a color scheme of bright sunny yellows, oranges and reds. The fixtures in the store include modern furnishings with high-lacquer shelving that both excite and tantalize the customers as they peruse the glamorous line of clothing. Likewise, the high-luster finishes and unusual exterior are not only appealing to shoppers, but provide information to would-be customers. Very often cues in the overall design—such as textures, lighting, sounds, and scents—will influence a person's perception of price, which means that designers will want to avoid the perception that the products or services are too expensive or too cheap. For high-end service and retail environments, the use of an attractive and unusual image can draw a more affluent clientele to imply higher quality and unique merchandise (Ailawadi & Keller, 2004). Likewise, if a person perceives a retail atmosphere to be appealing, then he/she is more likely to stay longer and establish a preference for that environment (Ailawadi & Keller, 2004).

SHOPPERS AND CONSUMERS

People often shop as a social or recreational activity and are more likely to become consumers if a setting's external attributes are compatible with their personal beliefs and values and stimulate the consumer behavior process by arousing potential shoppers' interests, curiosity, or desires (Thang & Tan, 2003). Recreational shoppers seek *entertainment*, whereas utilitarian shoppers seek *accomplishment*; therefore, the design should focus on enticement for the former and convenience for the latter, and it should provide an attractive, spacious setting for both (Jones, 1999). When products are intangible, as is the case in many service environments, the physical environment becomes more influential; thus, pleasant surroundings diffuse negative reactions when mistakes are made or accidents occur (Leong, Ang, & Low, 1997). In other words, when we are satisfied and comfortable within an environment, we will be less critical of the services delivered.

One way to mitigate negative environmental associations is to lower the setting's level of stimulation. For example, in a restaurant, elements designed to reduce noise levels may include variations in ceiling height and the use of wall partitions that provide more surface area to diffuse sound as well as increase privacy for diners at tables. Other elements might include soft materials on the chairs to absorb sound, with the addition of soft lighting and a muted color scheme, which will help to relax. Soft, soothing background music also helps patrons to pass the time pleasantly while they await their orders.

Throughout the world, people use fragrances as a means to evoke certain feelings or represent symbolic gestures. Within Western cultures cleanliness is oftentimes determined by the scent of fragrances commonly found in soaps, air fresheners and cleaning supplies. Burning incense during religious ceremonies and cultural rituals has been done since before written history, although this practice has its origins based more on the medicinal qualities of the plants rather than for use as a perfume (Moussaieff, & Mechoulam, 2009). Based on *social learning theory*, certain scents and aromas become associated with people, places, or ideas. Research has shown that smell is strongly tied to the retrieval of memories (Goldstein, 2002). After a person has smelled a particular aroma it is highly unlikely that he/she will forget the scent. Because of the strong association between scent and memory, it is not surprising that scent would also be strongly connected with emotion. One study examined the effects of pleasant fragrances in relation to effective task performance with an interesting outcome (Baron & Thomley, 1994). The results of the study showed that people performed better, showed improved alertness and demeanor, and that pleasant memory recall was also improved (Malnar & Vodvarka, 2004) when pleasant aromas were introduced to the work environment. As such, we can say with confidence that scent is strongly associated with some of our favorite places and events. In time, an association between a scent and an emotion can become so strong that the mere remembrance of a smell can evoke strong memories and emotions. One example of a strong association between scent and emotion is the "new car" smell. This smell is so strongly associated with feelings of excitement that many pre-owned automobile dealers try to replicate the scent in order to increase sales. Likewise, homeowners trying to sell their property are frequently advised by their realtors to flood a home with the scent of fresh-baked cookies or a pot of coffee as a means of facilitating an association between a wholesome lifestyle, happiness, and the purchase of the house (Malnar & Vodvarka, 2004). Thus, designers can use *scent* within the built environment to evoke positive feelings and memories.

Similarly, candle and beauty stores often allow the scents of their products to drift out through their open doors, enticing customers into the store. Some infant clothing shops in the United Kingdom have been known to infuse the air within the store with the sweet smell of baby powder (Underhill, 1999) as a method to inspire the purchase of more items. This technique of using **olfaction** to entice shoppers and elicit emotions is not always subtle, but it does send clear messages. Through the manipulation of scent in conjunction with other sensory stimuli, designers can create the illusion that a space is larger, fresher, cleaner, and brighter than it is in actuality (Malnar & Vodvarka, 2004). In one study, people comparing *identical* rooms declared the room with a low fragrance level to be more pleasant (Clifford, 1985). It is interesting to note, however, that none of the study participants acknowledged the scent in the room that they preferred. In this way, the use of scent can make an environment distinctive from other similar environments (Malnar & Vodvarka, 2004).

PERSONAL EXPERIENCE

The entertaining or pleasure-seeking shopping experience is most enjoyable when the shopper gains intrinsic satisfaction, perceived freedom, and involvement (Jones, 1999). Utilitarian shoppers share the first two needs, but prefer simplicity to involvement; they desire convenient, coherent, well-organized settings in which they can complete their tasks as quickly as possible. One study, which noted two main merchandise categories—social identity products (e.g., jewelry, fine china, gourmet foods) and utilitarian products (e.g., toothbrushes, duct tape, groceries)—found that subjects who evaluated social identity products were significantly affected by store atmosphere, whereas those who evaluated utilitarian products were not. The study also found that a more prestigious store atmosphere created an impression of higher-quality products (Schlosser, 1998).

Even after we have left an environment, our behavior affects that of others by way of **implicit cues** we leave behind that indicate what we have done. This is an essential concept for planners and designers of servicescapes to understand because shoppers are often influenced by the buying behaviors of other shoppers, especially regarding products with which they are unfamiliar. For example, shoppers often take the items they want from shelves and leave gaps or incomplete stacks of merchandise that imply their behavior (i.e., someone bought those items because they are valuable). Incomplete product displays can lead other shoppers to make positive assumptions about missing items and, therefore, purchase the same items. One research team found that customer purchases can be stimulated by **virtual modeling** (i.e., the use of implicit cues

[**Figure 16.6**] This store lacks diversity in its selection of items, and it shows limited quantities. The message is that each item is unique and there are only a limited number of them. © Chuck Pefley / Alamy

to modify behavior) even though retailers assume near-empty shelves discourage sales. By maintaining incomplete product displays, especially for new and slow-moving items and for private-label brands retailers encourage customers to purchase (Razzouk, Seitz, & Kumar, (2002). Despite this, customers who are repeatedly denied the products they seek will eventually take their business elsewhere. Conversely, many high-end retail stores have adopted a modified interpretation of virtual modeling and implicit cues by keeping their displays sparse. The implicit cue is that the person is buying a limited edition or one of a kind (Figure 16.6). The economic principle of supply and demand then comes into play. If there is a limited supply, the demand increases—which is the justification for the inflated prices.

The personal experiences of consumers can be affected by design. How can we modify the environment to elicit feelings related to these concepts without redesigning the entire facility? One possible way is to introduce comfortable seating areas in each department. Because most stores have no such areas, patrons may view the change as an improvement. They may consider it a *privilege* to relax in a pleasant setting with nice furniture and if more than one person uses the space, there is bound to be social interaction. The secondary outcome is that patrons may spend more time in the store, which will likely lead to more sales. As these patrons discuss the merchandise, they may help to reassure others that their purchases are good ones and, therefore, reinforce positive perceptions about the store.

Another way in which to develop a retail environment conducive to supporting the consumers' experience is to ask their opinion on the setting. As stakeholders in the success of the environment, customers and employees can and should be involved in the design process. As an illustration of this, in the 1920s, the Western Electric company undertook an investigation at their Hawthorne plant just outside of Chicago, Illinois. This investigation later became known as the *Hawthorne study*. The goal of the study was to analyze the effects of indoor lighting on workers' performance, although it resulted in additional environmental and experimenter information—the *experimenter effect* and the *social effect*. These unintentional consequences can be summarized into three important concepts:

1. The physical environment affects and influences humanity yet is buffered by perceptions, beliefs, preferences, experiences, and personality.
2. Study participants will see their involvement in a scientific study as an indication of their being *special*. (By focusing on one group of employees, researchers inadvertently promoted this belief among the participants.)
3. The physical environment created a change in social dynamics, and the increased social contact had a positive effect on performance.

For the benefit of the customer, employee, and management of the retail establishment, the design team should interview and implement features that these users groups state they need, require, or would like to see instituted.

[**Figure 16.7**] Retail facilities need to plan for and accommodate varying degrees of crowding. The facilities need to adapt to those seasons when there are few shoppers so that the place doesn't look empty, as well as accommodate the seasons when there are many shoppers so that people do not feel crowded. © Caro / Alamy

Crowding and Density

Crowding is subjective, whereas *density* (the number of individuals per unit area) is objective. Conditions of crowding are affected by other people, objects, and structures (Machleit, Eroglu, & Mantel, 2000), whereas feelings of crowding are mitigated by a person's perception of personal control (Schmidt & Keating, 1979), as well as the levels of *stimulation* and *arousal* that person experiences (Figure 16.7). Many retail environments try to display as many products as possible, which often results in narrow aisles that limit distances between merchandise displays. Issues such as temperature, odor, noise, and density can also exacerbate or alleviate feelings of crowding.

If people believe that they have options or that they can control a given situation, they are less likely to experience stress related to crowding. For example, if you want to go to a popular restaurant that you know is always busy, you can exert some control by making a reservation. People's perceptions of control are also influenced by the amount and quality of information available to them. Large department stores have cash registers dispersed throughout the individual departments, and busy salespeople are responsible for many duties besides customer service. When customers are rushed and cannot locate a register or salesperson, they become stressed by just trying to make a purchase. The use of ceiling-suspended signs to indicate open registers and hand bells for customers to ring when they are ready to make a purchase can greatly reduce checkout confusion, stress, and potential feelings of crowding for both customers and employees.

Crowding, a source of psychological stimulation and arousal, can be related to stimuli other than density, including unpleasant situations or people. **Density-intensity theory,** as it relates to urban versus suburban areas, suggests that density itself is not harmful, but that it can be amplified by co-variables. If a clothing store is having a sale and many people are rifling through the merchandise, the competition for a certain size and color is a co-variable that can lead to positive arousal (excitement) or negative arousal (crowding). These environmentally based co-variables influence people's experiences and subsequent judgment of the environment.

Gender

Most men shop for utilitarian rather than entertainment purposes, whereas most women do both. Men tend to respond more negatively to high-density situations than women (Aiello, Thompson, & Brodzinsky, 1983), who tend to approach high-density more cooperatively (Karlin, Epstein, & Aiello, 1978; Taylor, 1988). Numerous studies have demonstrated that men generally require more personal space than women (Barnard & Bell, 1982; Bell, Kline, & Barnard, 1988; Gifford, 1982). Women choose more complex routes (Hill, 1984), and men require more personal space when ceilings are lower

(Savinar, 1975). Apparently, men are more susceptible than women to feelings of crowding in environments where spatial density is high; however, their feelings of cognitive control can be easily enhanced with information and organization.

Planners and designers can optimize the male shopping experience by creating simple, well-organized floor plans and large open spaces that offer maximum visual range and minimal clutter in environments where men are the market base. For example, position clothing racks far apart in men's departments; provide wide aisles at hardware, automotive and home improvement stores; and ensure ample open spaces at sporting equipment and convenience stores (Figures 16.8a and b). One research team noted that most men prefer shopping for clothing in department stores (although

[**Figures 16.8a and b**] The retail environment on the right is an example of optimizing the male shopping experience by creating simple, well-organized, and large open spaces that offer maximum visual range and minimal clutter. The image below, however, illustrates an environment that would be more appealing to women. a: © Alex Serge / Alamy; b: © Marmaduke St. John / Alamy

their age influences their expectations and needs) and recommended the use of display kiosks in department stores to provide information about and directions to the merchandise (Torres, Summers, & Belleau, 2001). This information can be encoded with numbers, symbols, colors, or any combination of these; however, encoding by color alone is not recommended, as approximately 10 percent of the male population has some form of colorblindness.

Men and women experience and respond to crowds and crowding differently, as do members of different cultures; therefore, physical layouts and merchandise displays should be designed to accommodate these variables. Small sitting areas in women's departments can enhance the shopping experience for couples; they serve not only as resting places for people who aren't shopping at the moment (i.e., they afford *refuge*), but also as vantage points from which to contemplate purchases (i.e., they afford *prospect*). By anticipating the constituency of the shopping population and expected levels of consumer traffic, designers can instigate many proactive initiatives to help minimize stress and maximize consumer satisfaction in retail and service environments.

SERVICE DELIVERY

Citing the original *pleasure–arousal–dominance theory,* which holds that emotion is a mediator between people's environments, personalities, and behaviors, one research team demonstrated that positive shopping behaviors resulted when store designs induced pleasure and arousal (Donovan & Rossiter, 1982). Other researchers noted that all three emotional states can be used to predict and modify customer behavior and that meeting the needs of all three will result in customer satisfaction (Ang et al., 1997). These pleasurable emotions can be stimulated by the business itself and aroused by an integrated servicescape (i.e., consumers may first be interested by the goods or services offered, and subsequently drawn into the store by its image; Ang et al., 1997). The reverse is also true; a physical image can induce shoppers to investigate an unknown business. In other words, both the business and the building can attract customers and even more so when they function in a cohesive, coherent combination. A clean and attractive store draws more customers (Patricios, 1979), but high densities can lead to negative perceptions and ideas (Harrell, Hutt & Anderson, 1980; Machleit, Eroglu, & Mantel, 2000). In short, a visually appealing facility can stimulate consumer interest and ensure continued patronage (Bell, 1999).

Image
Using design and décor to communicate and reinforce a store's image, improving the store atmosphere instead of relying on promotional techniques to attract customers, and matching the merchandise's functions to the store's atmosphere will create an effective sales environment (Schlosser, 1998).

Quality and product displays are crucial image setters and selling factors; therefore, consider the perceived differences of two products placed adjacent to each other (Razzouk, Seitz, & Kumar, 2002). Because lighting is most important when visual acuity and color discrimination are needed (Galer, 1987), designers should ensure they get the most natural illumination possible in establishments where color and texture are important (e.g., art stores galleries). Although one researcher noted that there are several contradictory studies regarding the effects of lighting on mood, cognition, and social relationships (Knez, 1995), the work of other teams (Butler & Biner, 1987; Gergen, Gergen, & Barton, 1973) supports earlier studies that equate lower lighting with greater intimacy. Therefore, a business that provides a service based on a personal relationship (e.g., physical therapy) or a location for a personal encounter (e.g., an intimate restaurant) will be enhanced by dimmer lighting.

Flexibility
Service delivery was once limited to face-to-face interaction, but technology now allows service industries to interface with consumers in many ways. Banking transactions can be conducted at drop-boxes; by telephone, computer, or automated teller machines; or with human tellers at branch offices and drive-through windows. Many eateries offer in-house or take-out dining, curbside and home delivery, and even catering services. Environments that allow flexibility in the delivery of services can accommodate a wider range of individual preferences (Ang et al., 1997); greater appeal to more potential consumers can easily translate into greater sales. We all are drawn to stimulating environments, and we all enjoy places that make us feel good; however, we mostly want to be in places that are very pleasurable and moderately arousing (Mehrabian & Russell, 1974). The proliferation of catalog and Internet shopping options has made the question "Is it worth the trip?" important for many consumers.

Location, Location, Location
More than ever, an establishment risks losing customers if it is hard to find or get to or if parking is problematic. As the old business and real estate adage goes, "location, location, location." A business's location is essential to its success, and design professionals can assist those in the service and retail industries to meet their sales goals by first establishing appropriate site evaluation criteria. A team of researchers who conducted a study of restaurants in Taiwan (Tzeng,

Teng, Chen, & Opricovic, 2002) recommend using the following criteria to determine site selection:

1. Availability of transportation
2. Compatibility of the commercial area
3. Comparable economic climate
4. Limited direct competition
5. A suitable environment

The researchers also advocate including input from prospective patrons, marketing professionals, and city planners, among others, noting that customers' internal and external proceedings will affect their perceptions of a location. *Internal proceedings* include factors such as a person's background and decision-making processes; *external proceedings* include cost, neighborhood quality, availability of parking, and ease of locating the business.

Visual Stimuli

Like our hunter-gatherer ancestors, humans are attracted to sparkly things, loud sounds, soft textures, and sweet smells (Kopec, 2006). Because we are visually attracted to sparkly and flashing things, we tend slow down when we see reflective surfaces (Underhill, 1999) or blinking lights. This includes reflective glass used on buildings, mirrors on walls, and reflective foils used with art. This, coupled with our innate curiosity, can be used to attract us to different locations and entice us to interact with various components within the environment. Many in the retail industry capitalize on this to "activate" areas of a store. Research has shown that displays with moving lights are noticed by 46 percent of shoppers as compared to the 6 percent of shoppers who noticed the same display with nonmoving lights (Underhill, 1999). The Kmart "blue-light special" epitomized this concept. In 1965 a Kmart store manager introduced a roving flashing blue light at the site of special discounts. This flashing light along with the auditory announcement "Attention, Kmart shoppers" became a successful method to facilitate the purchase of slow-moving merchandise. Ultimately, the blue-light special became part of the American lexicon and has become synonymous with Kmart.

Casinos have also used sensory stimuli to attract people and entice them to linger at the various slot machines. Flashing lights combined with a multitude of exciting sounds combine to activate the environment and entice patrons, while atmospherics such as the blue-light special can affect consumer spending patterns (Turley & Milliman, 2000). Atmospherics, however, are much more than *operant conditioning*. Both the physical environment and the service quality affect customers' tendencies toward pleasure or avoidance, but research into the aggregated affects

of both variables occurring concurrently has been limited (Ang et al., 1997).

Audio Stimuli

Research emphasizes the importance of engaging multiple senses within the retail environment, contending that sound and music in particular can motivate customers to make purchases (Fulberg, 2003). In retail environments, low levels of white noise (also called pink noise) can be used to create ambient sound that will keep people comfortable and able to communicate easily without the discomfort of silence. In the past, slow music was played in elevators as a means of alleviating the stress associated with sharing a small and confined space with strangers. As a result, an association was spawned between slow music and elevators, which thus gave way to the classification of some music as "elevator music." Although there is no such genre of music, the title and classification is widely known and understood by the population.

Music influences our perceptions and behaviors; a fast rhythm and tempo increases psychological arousal (Mattila & Wirtz, 2001), and the tempo of background affects the speed at which shoppers move through supermarkets (Milliman, 1982). Music can facilitate a comfortable atmosphere by masking unpleasant background noises, reducing the negative effects of silence, and promoting social interaction; however, be aware that background music should not attract attention, but rather should entice customers to linger (Areni, 2003). Highly complex music causes high levels of activity in the displeasure centers of the brain, which can neutralize positive activity in the pleasure centers, whereas music of moderate complexity will produce the maximum level of pleasurable arousal (North & Hargreaves, 1999). One researcher noted that retailers do not take advantage of positive associations that can be formed between products and people through the use of background music, which can serve as a "brand trigger" (i.e., facilitate consumer recall of an experience with a particular product or brand; Fulberg, 2003). It should be noted, however, that some genres of music appeal to specific populations; for example, teens generally find classical music unappealing.

Greater consumer approachability, more impulse buying, and a more positive evaluation of the environment may be achieved through the congruent use of music and scent (Mattila & Wirtz, 2001). For instance, a woman who shops for pajamas may instead buy a negligee because the soft music and delicate perfume-scented air make her feel sexy; feeling good about her experience will increase the likelihood of her returning to that store. Negative effects will occur, however, if the scent does not relate to the merchandise (Mattila & Wirtz, 2001), and it must be noted that individuals vary greatly in their responses to scent.

DESIGN CONCERNS

The servicescape exterior is made up of the building façade, means of entry and exit, window displays, and parking accommodations. The building itself can serve as a form of branding or name recognition; consider the golden arches of McDonald's and the dark brown sign with red star of Macy's. Although this use of branding is easily recognizable to passersby and sometimes even foreign visitors, a visual menagerie of façades in a confined area can appear disorganized. Some communities have ordinances mandating or restricting the use of specific designs within designated zones to create coherence and a sense of order in the community. For example, Santa Barbara, California, allows only Spanish colonial designs in certain areas (Easton & McCall, 1995). Clearly, a designer's challenge is to incorporate designs associated with branding and name recognition with appropriate styles that complement *community branding*.

Window Displays

R. H. Macy devised a plan in the 1870s to attract customers to his Manhattan department store. He used window displays as an advertising medium. Because of the quality and friendly competition among New York's emporiums, such window displays not only provided advertising to passersby but also generated free publicity because of media coverage. Unobstructed window displays should always be used along pedestrian routes, not only to provide a positive first impression and visual entertainment for those passing by but also to entice pedestrians inside.

Flaws common to many servicescapes include excessive exterior window bars and excessive window signage. The proprietors of many small boutiques and salons who subscribe to the belief that "the more advertising, the better" often have an array of competing signs, many in neon, in their windows. This *environmental load* precludes many potential customers from seeing any one message; instead, they often see only a chaotic mass of color and shape. For storefronts to be effective advertising mediums, messages must be kept simple and to the point, and displays should be changed and updated regularly. Heavily barred windows indicate risk and danger; a profusion of messages cannot be comprehended by the average person in the time it takes to pass by; and dust, cobwebs, and outdated goods imply lack of quality and care. Window displays should be coherent and colorful, on the cutting edge of fashion, not too busy, and above all, updated regularly.

Access and Parking

Transportation access should be as accommodating as possible: wide roads, few barriers to navigation, limited funneling of traffic, and multiple entrances and exits. Suburban consumers often must walk considerable distances from their cars or homes to shopping areas, whether along a boulevard or through a large parking lot. Ideally, parking lots and structures should be designed along with the main building. Placing pedestrian paths strategically throughout parking areas not only facilitates navigation but also sets the mood for incoming consumers (van Asperdt, 1999). Parking structures, although often intrinsic to large commercial centers and undeniably convenient, can also be problematic: Being relatively isolated while surrounded by stark concrete walls and columns can evoke feelings of anxiety and apprehension, especially for women, elderly or disabled people. These structures also tend to be drab places with many dark areas that inspire fear. Incorporating well-lit displays throughout adds light and makes the overall setting more inviting, affords merchants additional advertising space, and affords all users opportunities for *attention restoration*.

Designers can help to reduce feelings of anxiety by providing adequate lighting and visually appealing attributes, such as artwork, nature displays (e.g., aquariums, terrariums, arboretums), and raised cobblestone or slate walkways lined with indigenous, shade-tolerant vegetation. When designing the exteriors of servicescapes, particularly those that are accessible from parking lots or structures, consider developing causeways lined with native landscaping, statuary, and display kiosks that highlight the products or services offered and are constructed to complement the façade of the main structure. Such kiosks afford retailers additional display venues, which can increase consumer interest and profits.

BANKS AND CONVENIENCE STORES

The primary functions of, and the design issues relevant to, convenience stores and banks are not dissimilar. Efficiency is intrinsic to their success, as they each compete for a customer base that prefers to complete their transactions as quickly as possible—with or without human interaction, since we can now obtain cash, pump gas, and make purchases with just the swipe of a card. Perhaps the most profound commonality between banks and convenience stores is their vulnerability to crime; both are known to contain large quantities of cash, and many are ideally located for quick criminal getaways.

Convenience Stores

Convenience stores with smaller parking lots and those that do not sell gas are more susceptible to robbery because their interiors are less visible to a passerby, including the police (D'Allesio, & Stolzenberg, 1990). Businesses in disorganized locations or extremely busy corners, which offer easy escape (e.g., on a corner, in a high-traffic area, near a freeway *on-ramp*) are particularly susceptible to criminal activities. When selecting a site for a convenience store, consider placing it close to a freeway, but not next to an on-ramp. An optimal site would be about a block away from the off-ramp and situated so that traffic would have to be crossed to get back onto the freeway. Ensure maximum visibility of the interior from the exterior, provide ample lighting both inside and out, and install visible video surveillance equipment in the parking lot and inside of the store. Thus, the least attractive environments to criminals are those that provide the occupants with full surveillance capabilities throughout their premises.

[**Figure 16.9**] Using mostly glass, the convenience store has made ample provisions for visibility while also allowing for sufficient space for advertising. Note how the advertising doesn't compete with visual surveillance. © Chris Pearsall / Alamy

---

CULTURAL CONNECTION 16.1

"Convenience stores are part of our culture, both positive and negative. The negative is: most don't act like a corner store any more. They don't care who the customer base is. The positive is: you can learn to be part of consumer society and, obviously, the convenience" (Mackey, 2007). In many ways, "convenience stores are our landmarks, our meeting places, a part of our cultural heritage" (Mackey, 2007). Along with these observations, perhaps design professionals can take inspiration and create convenience stores that are more in line with the needs of the local citizen, as well as remaining convenient. Consider adding window displays for exhibiting local fresh produce, providing bulletin boards dedicated for advertising posters, and small kiosks inside the store offered for lease to local restaurants, caterers, or bakeries. Any of these design features have the potential to solidify the convenience store into the neighborhood culture while increasing consumer activity, which leads to more "eyes on the street" (Jacobs, 1961) and less crime.

Convenience stores require a high degree of visibility, ample natural lighting, and organization to deter criminals and offer patrons with a convenient, pleasant shopping experience. The goal of the convenience store owner is to make a profit, not unlike all business purveyors—although it can be readily observed in the majority of convenience stores that lack of dedicated "advertising space" is available, such that many business owners must use a large percentage (if not all) of the storefront to entice shoppers. This reduced visibility makes the business vulnerable to crime. The designer would be wise to explore ways to provide a proper venue for the sheer volume of advertising necessary for the industry while maintaining clear views throughout the entire environment. The outcome will support environmental legibility and sales (see Figure 16.9).

Banking

Banking is a service industry that has changed tremendously since the early 1900s, when transactions were conducted through holes lined with bars that were set into solid walls. This design maximized the separation between tellers and customers. Later, high countertops with niches denoted individual teller stations; the counters prevented surveillance by those nearby, and the niches provided customers with usable counter space and privacy for their transactions. Some of the banks replaced the bar.

The interior design of banks has changed very little until recently; much of the elegant dark wood and leather that symbolized stability and prosperity has been replaced with cost-effective vinyl furnishings and applied décor. Today, however, some banks are opting to place individual teller stations throughout the bank; in these designs, the teller and the customer can stand side-by-side throughout the transaction. We can assume that removing the traditional barrier between teller and customer will facilitate warmer social interaction and subsequently strengthen customer loyalty. This approach may further dissuade would-be criminals because customers and employees are dispersed throughout the facility as opposed to clustered in one location (Figure 16.10).

Convenience is a top priority for most bank customers. Drive-through teller windows were popular until the mid-1970s, when they were replaced by automated teller machines (ATMs). Interestingly, the first ATM, located outside of New York City's Chemical Bank in 1971 was situated with little concern for weather and sustainability of the design; as such, the machine was often damaged by the area's diverse weather patterns. Today, ATMs are found just about everywhere, and financial transactions can be completed without human interaction in most cases. ATMs today are part of the servicescape,

[**Figure 16.10**] Recent innovations within the design of the banking environment have been the "teller pod" and video tellers. Placing the bank teller stations in the center of the bank not only increases safety levels, but also increases social interaction and, thereby, customer loyalty. The video teller concept is another safety design protocol; tellers take care of the customers' needs from somewhere else in the building while conversing over a video feed as customers wait within an ATM-like niche. Losing the physical teller-customer contact may reduce customer loyalty from those who value traditional face-to-face customer service. © AP Images / Mary Altaffer

and, as such, deserve the same attention to location, convenience of use, and safety as larger settings.

The safety of patrons and employees in all public territories must be ensured. Banks with smaller, compact, square lobbies are more likely to be robbed than those with larger, rectangular lobbies with bank clerks situated farther apart (Wise & Wise, 1985). The development of a safe and convenient banking environment is dependent on factors that include the site, neighborhood, physical design, landscaping, and security measures. The principles of **Crime Prevention through Environmental Design** (**CPTED**) can help banks remain safe while thwarting potential crimes. CPTED principles include the following recommendations (Crowe, 2000):

- Allow for natural surveillance and observation points from inside and outside the bank.
- Avoid placing furnishings and promotional signs in areas that obstruct visibility.
- Locate exterior signs in places where important sight lines are not compromised.
- Use a uniform white light source that minimizes glare inside and out.
- Select and arrange landscaping so that visual surveillance is not compromised. Examples include trees with high branches and low ground cover.
- Install surveillance cameras on the interior and exterior.
  - Be sure to orient cameras so they are not aimed at the rising or setting sun.

- Strategically place signs around the perimeter of the property advising visitors that the property is under video surveillance.
- Include large windows with clear and nonreflective glazing.
- Avoid window treatments, blinds, or window covers. In certain situations, a window awning or tint may be used to help shade the upper third of the window
- Avoid the inclusion of formal or informal seating areas or other types of public amenities (e.g., information kiosks) *outside* of the bank.

In both the banking and convenience store setting, greater surveillance equates to less vulnerability for clients and employees.

SUSTAINABILITY CONNECTION 16.1

Worldwide banking facilities consume and dispose of the most computers, software, hardware, printing equipment, and electricity (United Nations, Economic Commission for Europe [UNECE], 2002); therefore the sustainability issues that need to be resolved with the design of banking institutions are energy consumption and **electronic waste** (**e-waste**). **Information and communication technologies** (**ICT**) is the term for processing and exchanging digital information with computers. ICTs are mainly used for monitoring and controlling the energy usage of a building. Designs should include onsite power generation such as solar and wind technologies and be regulated with ICTs connected to all of the building's main electrical components. Recent advances in this area include building skin systems that moderate the internal temperatures of the building by maneuvering shading devices to either warm or cool the building before any internal system would need to be used. With regard to e-waste, banks should be designed and specified only with electronic devices in which the manufacturers take full "life-cycle responsibility" for their products and, as such, reuses, recycles, or disposes of their old devices. To expedite the process of locating environmentally friendly products, the *Electronic Product Environmental Assessment Tool* (EPEAT) was created. According to the U.S. Environmental Protection Agency (EPA), "EPEAT was developed using a grant by the EPA and is managed by the Green Electronics Council (GEC)." It is dedicated to reporting to consumers of the environmental conditions of electronic products.

Bank architecture or bank design has evolved from massive structures symbolizing strength and trust into anonymous commercial buildings (Belfoure, 2005). In an effort to maximize customer convenience, some financial institutions are moving away from freestanding buildings and into more symbiotic relationships within grocery stores and retail centers. The features of banking, therefore, will be reduced to the core concepts of business's function and the requirements of the *users*. From a *functional* standpoint, designs should incorporate:

- Customer privacy for filling out sensitive information/paperwork
- Excellent lighting and total visual access throughout the lobby
- Surveillance equipment and security features
- Multiple points of service (live teller, ATM, online banking stations or video teller)
- Sustainable equipment, building materials and an onsite power generation source

From the perspective of the *users*, designs should include:

- A comfortable and safe environment inside and outside of the bank
- Quality furnishing and finishes consistent with the company's image or mission
- Robust technologies to accommodate cultural factors and physical needs
- Convenient location and efficient service layout

THIRD PLACES

Third places are environments beyond home (first place) and work (second place), which people select for relaxation and socialization (Oldenburg, 2001). In many respects, the third place can be regarded as an essential component for community development because it affords continual visual surveillance of the community; a term called "eyes on the street" (Jacobs, 1961). Additionally, third places facilitate community activity along with broader and more creative forms of interaction. In the past, hair salons provided for the ideal third place because it was a gathering point for women who would have their hair done on a weekly basis. The counterpart to the hair salon was the local pub, which is where men gathered. These environments were replaced with coffee shops in the 1990s, which afforded destinations that men and women could share. In order for a third place to become adopted by the local community it must:

- Be free or inexpensive
- Offer food and drink (although not essential)
- Be very accessible
- Be located within walking distance
- Have a core group of people who regularly frequent the place
- Be welcoming and inspire comfort

[**Figure 16.11**] This local neighborhood coffee lounge is a good example of a third place. The home-like setting, furniture arrangement, tables in the loft, outdoor area, and soft music draw clientele as much as the friendly staff and good food. © Sarah Hadley / Alamy

- Involve making new friends while visiting with an old friend (Oldenburg, 2001; see Figure 16.11)

In a modern world, third places have less to do with social interaction and community surveillance, and are more about being a stranger among others. For many, the third place has become de facto offices; and for others they simply provide a different environment to study, chat on the Internet or phone, or a place to congregate with close friends.

The applicability of third place theory to the design of interior spaces is that they serve as gathering places (Waxman, 2006), particularly when they include:

- Convenience
- Human scale
- Functional design to support human interaction
- A pleasing aesthetic design
- A way to communicate diversity and accessibility
- Internet accessibility (Oldenburg, 2001)

Many local economies are finding value in the food service industry as families struggle to balance their domestic and professional duties. More people are eating out (Dermody, 2002). As such, restaurants and casual eateries serve as places for people to conduct business or recreational meetings (Satler, 2003) and are playing an increasingly important role in the economy (Leong et al., 1997). Restaurants prosper in part because of customer loyalty; and attaining that loyalty involves attitudinal, emotional, and behavioral commitments on the part of all staff members (Mattila, 2001).

[**Figures 16.12a and b**] From a purely functional perspective, both places in this pair of photos offer a table, seating, and utensils, and both serve food. It is the ambience that changes our expectations. The image on the top suggests that our meal choices will be limited to a selection of fried foods. The image on the bottom suggests a higher quality of food, as well as a significantly higher price. a: © Chuck Pefley / Alamy; b: © SERDAR / Alamy

RESTAURANTS AND CAFÉS

Service, atmosphere, and the quality of food are the main reasons for selecting a food service setting; expense and location are important only to those customers who have not bonded to a particular restaurant through personal recognition, feelings of familiarity, or memorable experiences (Mattila, 2001). If customers favor an eatery because of its overall service, or that of a particular staff member, employee turnover can result in customer loss; therefore, an enjoyable work environment is critical for employee happiness, and thus customer happiness (Satler, 2003). Sociologists have classified bars, restaurants, and many stores into three different levels, by differing clientele:

- The smallest with a constant local clientele who, in bars or restaurants, usually have their own seats
- Weekenders that have a local clientele during the week but draw outside customers on the weekend
- Large establishments that always appeal to an outside crowd of travelers and visitors to the area

The quality of a restaurant's physical space is as important to overall customer satisfaction as that of the food and service (Satler, 2003). The amalgamation of environmental features (e.g., shapes, colors, noises, odors, & temperature) influences consumers' perceptions of service quality and performance (Leong et al., 1997). It is important to enhance a restaurant's environment to give customers an enjoyable experience and create a *sense of place*. Consider incorporating unique features, handmade or signature objects, nostalgic features, and opportunities to dine alone (Satler, 2003).

An environment's overall design facilitates the social atmosphere within it by affecting the occupants' expectations and their expected and actual behaviors. Therefore, an elegantly appointed restaurant (e.g., dark woods, subtle illumination, music, rich fabrics, deep colors, table settings, artwork) becomes a *behavior setting* in which customers expect a more sophisticated level of fare and service than that of an eatery incorporating bright lights, bold colors, inexpensive place-settings, and louder, faster-paced music. Although, in general, if a restaurant is not as clean as patrons expect, then no matter how good the food or service is, the environment will foster negative perceptions (Figures 16.12a and b).

Customer loyalty can be destroyed, constant continual dissatisfaction, which might include having to wait for a table. In such a situation, customers with service complaints may simply take their business elsewhere (Wildes & Seo, 2001). Having a combination of table sizes can decrease wait time for customers and maximize seating capacity, but combining tables leads to a decrease in overall available seating (Thompson, 2002). For example, three tables seating four people at each will lose four seats when combined. Business losses can also result when tables are not available to accommodate larger groups (Thompson, 2003). One research team, finding that the tolerance for waiting is highly dependent on age and culture (e.g., individuals ages 25 and younger are more tolerant of longer waiting periods than older people), advocates including space for predining activities to modify customers' perceptions of waiting times and prevent their leaving in frustration (Becker & Murrmann, 1999). Of course, ensuring comfortable seating is an obvious way to increase positive perceptions and satisfaction among customers.

The food-service industry provides much more than just places to eat. Restaurants afford us the privilege of being catered to amid pleasant surroundings wherein we may relax and socialize, consume culturally specific or diverse foods, experience a different lifestyle, and hold parties or meetings. Successful eateries occupy settings that promote satisfaction and enjoyment for all parties concerned. Restaurants and cafés are another place where teenagers and adults often choose as a place to hang out, which makes them a recreational environment and a *third place*. In addition, restaurants are a very important part of tourism. Tourists spend approximately 25 percent of their vacation budget on food (Nield, Kozak, & LeGrys, 2000); it is therefore important to understand the factors that contribute to customer satisfaction and repeat business. These factors include:

- Wait time
- Comfort level of waiting areas
- Degree of politeness and attentiveness by employees
- Quality of seating and overall ambiance
- Food quality (Sulek & Hensley, 2004)

Another important factor of customer satisfaction is the congruence between the external façade and signage with the clientele served. For example, there should be design clues to indicate if the restaurant targets small families, or if it supports fine dining. Larger restaurants may want to take advantage of behavioral zoning techniques in order to increase target population ranges. For example, one restaurant may cater to families with small children, as well as adults without children by clustering the different populations into different portions of the restaurant. To support this endeavor, it is important to design recognizable boundaries between the different spaces; but keep in mind that the overall continuity of the atmosphere must remain intact (Erickson, 2004).

Other design considerations include seating arrangements. One study found that corner and wall tables are occupied first (Eibl-Eibesfeldt, 1970) indicating a preference for these *peripheral* locations. Another consideration is the design and layout of the menu. Previous research suggests that gaze motion, item placement (e.g., sequence in a list, placement in most viewed areas of menus), color, and pricing strategy (e.g., visually de-emphasizing prices) influence consumer decisions (Reynolds, Merritt, & Pinckney, 2005).

Some methods designers have used to increase spending at restaurants include de-emphasizing menu prices and optimizing items with photos or other graphic elements; however, these methods have not been proven to increase spending or selecting those items (Reynolds et al., 2005). To the contrary, research indicates that sophisticated patrons are not influenced by these methods at all (Reynolds et al., 2005). This is not to say that menu design is not important; clearly indicated categorization (i.e., salads, pastas, etc.)

along with short concise descriptions and clear pricing will go a long way in supporting customer satisfaction.

Recycling is a component underutilized in the food service industry. Discarded food can be an excellent source for composting, although necessary containers must be designed into the plan of the restaurant. Food establishments also consume a large amount of water and energy to maintain a clean environment, heat and refrigerate foods, and comply with local health department standards. By the year 2030, world consumption of energy is projected to increase by 44 percent (Energy Information Administration, 2009), and the food service industry takes up one-third of the U.S. commercial sector's energy use. It is imperative that onsite power generation, passive design techniques, and conservation/efficiency measures be employed as part of the initial design of the restaurants or cafés.

Toxic chemicals are prevalent in the food service industry, mostly in the form of cleaning products. Chlorine, sodium hydroxide (lye), and other hazardous substances are commonly used as degreasers and cleansers. These chemicals are highly **exothermic**, which means they release energy in the form of heat (i.e., chemical burns) and with extended use are released into our environment and contaminate soil, water, and ultimately our food sources. Unfortunately, there has been little testing to determine the long-term human health and reproductive implications of these chemicals; therefore, to err on the side of caution, eliminating their use immediately and using only safe nontoxic products, is highly recommended. Designers can mitigate these ecological issues by designing easy to clean, energy-efficient, and recycle-ready environments

Design professionals can ensure unique and memorable experiences by creating supportive environments that provide owners and managers with appropriate images and good locations that are easily accessible and perceived as being both safe and attractive. Designers can also provide employees with pleasant, efficient, and safe workstations and restorative break areas; and afford customers enjoyable settings that minimize negative variables and distractions (e.g., *ambient stressors* such as noise, odor, and temperature and *environmental pollutants* such as vehicular traffic noises and emissions). Such environments promote the development of *place meaning* and *place attachment* for management, staff, and patrons. When designing a restaurant or a café, consider that patrons do not like to feel crowded while they are eating or while waiting for a table. When space planning, designers should make sure to provide wide aisles, and incorporate privacy shields between tables where they are clustered. In addition, make ample use of wall, window, and corner spaces for seating, as patrons tend to prefer these spaces. Also, consider the seating types and arrangements; whereas booths provide a higher level of intimacy, larger people tend to prefer chairs. Lastly, make sure that the environment and ambiance is appropriate for the type and caliber of food being served.

RETAIL SPACES

In the past few decades retailers have begun to value environmental psychology as a means of enhancing sales, developing store loyalty, and creating pleasing environments (Donovan & Rossiter, 1982). Specific environmental features serve as **descriptors** that help us to understand and connect with or respond to our environments; these features, which include sights, sounds, and scents (individually or in combination), can provide us with instant information or stand out in our minds after we have left an environment. Descriptors affect consumer perceptions and preferences, but because overall appeal is created by a combination of elements—overall design, appearance, ambience, circulation, and parking areas—it can be difficult to determine the influence of each (Oppewal & Timmermans, 1999).

From a proprietor's perspective, the primary purpose of retail and service design is to increase sales. Customers are unlikely to return to an environment that they perceived negatively; therefore, enhancing shoppers' experiences with the environment will increase both customer satisfaction and company profits. One way to increase the odds of a positive perception is through the use of caricatures. Many retail and service environments have adopted likable caricatures such as Jack from Jack in the Box fast foods, the roaming gnome of Travelocity, and Geoffrey the Giraffe of Toys R Us.

Some design principles, however, are contrary to increasing sales. For example, good wayfinding mechanisms ensure that consumers will be able to locate products with relative ease, but they decrease impulse buying. Poor wayfinding mechanisms may increase impulse buying, but they will not induce shoppers to return. It is a fine line between increased sales through impulse buying and good wayfinding that helps establish personal control for the buyer. Recreational and social shoppers engage in more leisurely and impulsive buying than purposive or utilitarian shoppers (consumers having specific needs and goals); therefore, designers of retail establishments must understand the primary source of sales (e.g., tourists, locals, trade and businesspeople, & students).

A popular mall in downtown San Diego, located near the convention center and other tourist destinations, has been historically more popular with tourists than with the local population. Whereas many locals (purposive shoppers) seldom come downtown to shop (they contend that the mall is confusing and that they routinely get lost), tourists (recreational shoppers) tend to comment on the mall's beauty, uniqueness, and convenient access. Much of the local population complains about the design of this mall because of its seemingly poor wayfinding mechanisms; however, unique pathways and one-way elevators inspire mystery and surprise for many tourists who enjoy visiting the mall (Figure 16.13). By understanding a retail or service environment's primary constituency, the designer should then use that information to improve the environmental designs (Oppewal & Timmermans, 1999).

SHOPPING MALLS

The proliferation of **megastores** (or *hypermarkets*) has changed the retail industry almost as dramatically as the supermarket did in the 1930s. These huge facilities offer consumers an expansive variety of goods and services that were once limited to specific retail outlets (pharmacies, groceries, clothing and shoe stores, and so on). Because many communities lack the population to support these megastores, and small retailers cannot match their prices or product ranges, these larger facilities attract and serve populations from outside of the community. And as a result, some populations may cease using their local retailers, thereby negatively affecting the local economy (Moreno-Jimenez, 2001). The largest retail facility in the United States, the Mall of America in Bloomington, Minnesota, (Berger, 2005) houses more than 500 stores as well as a small indoor amusement park. Many other shopping malls offer consumers a wide range of recreational, dining, and shopping opportunities. Planners and designers of such large public spaces must consider initiatives that were once the sole domain of city planning, such as monitoring the flow of traffic to keep it moving steadily and to minimize bottlenecks wherever possible. One difficulty in designing attractive shopping malls lies in the need for spaces that allow for adequate circulation (vehicular and pedestrian) during peak hours and seasons but that don't feel empty during off times (Oppewal & Timmermans, 1999).

Enclosed or open-air mall environments provide reasonably safe places for people to shop, browse, socialize, dine, relax, or take in some entertainment in relative freedom. Bargains are usually available, as are one-of-a-kind specialty items. In some malls, people can pay bills, get haircuts, or see doctors or dentists. Many malls serve as both early-morning walking tracks for seniors and after-school hangouts for teens, in effect functioning as centers of social and cultural interaction. Therefore, malls by their very nature meet the needs of the recreational shopper: intrinsic satisfaction, perceived freedom, and involvement (Jones, 1999).

[**Figure 16.13**] Poor wayfinding can be an asset when it inspires feelings of mystery and surprise. These attributes also promote greater sales for the businesses via impulse buying; however, the benefits of these features are location-specific. Because they often frustrate shoppers, they are useful only in areas that satisfy the needs of temporary nonrepeat business. © SERDAR / Alamy

For young people, malls often serve as a **fourth environment** (i.e., a place to hang out that is not their home, playground, or other site developed specifically for them; van Vliet, 1983). Teens have a strong impact on the economy and retail market; because this group makes up a large population segment and has disposable income, designers and marketers should understand what motivates and satisfies this population (Kim, Kim, & Kang, 2003). Although the stereotypical "mall rat" is a teen with plenty of spare time and disposable income, one study of two large malls counted more elderly men than teens hanging out (relative to overall population percentages; Brown, Sijpkes, & MacLean, 1986). One reason may be users' perceptions of greater security among more people in a public place. Youngsters usually hang around malls after school and on weekends, whereas older people often gather at malls during early mornings and afternoons to exercise or to meet for socializing and "people watching." When designing malls, designers should consider both the primary purpose of retail sales and the secondary functions of exercising and socializing, all of which serve to enhance the community.

One research team's study explored earlier findings that consumers' shopping mall preferences are affected by overall design, circulation, parking areas, appearance, and atmosphere, and revealed that people prefer shopping centers that are well maintained, have attractive window displays, and offer more greenery and street activities (Oppewal & Timmermans, 1999). Another researcher noted that people tend to prefer building façades with ornate or elaborate surfaces that seem to invite touch and exploration and that express a sense of the past more than the future (Frewald, 1990).

Environmental legibility is critical within shopping malls, which are extremely complicated public environments. Both the overall design plan and individual design elements play important roles in a facility's legibility, but it is important to note that design elements can oftentimes *reduce* wayfinding, even for those with experience in an environment (Dogu & Erkip, 2002). One example of this reduction in environmental legibility would be the overuse of signage. When people are bombarded with excessive signs, arrows, and lights all attempting to "direct" them all over the mall, this can cause *information overload* and ultimately serve to confuse people rather than help. Wayfinding design techniques should therefore be simple, consistent, and have a succinct hierarchy of information. Planners and designers of mall environments must consider the needs of a diverse clientele in striving to create simplicity, organization, and convenience to meet shoppers' needs (Jones, 1999); rest areas for adults and play areas for young children; and stimulation for adolescent and young adult consumers (Kim et al., 2003).

With the different uses of the mall, the facility program would benefit from the inclusion of community centers that host programs for teens and seniors (e.g., fashion shows, stage performances, exhibits). Additional programming should include food courts that facilitate social gatherings, events and "people watching" (Kim et al., 2003). Provide logical and consistent organization within mall directories ("you-are-here" maps, etc.); include *pictographs* for people who speak other languages or who have reading disabilities; and incorporate clear store numbering systems using a logical sequence that corresponds accurately to the various stores and levels (Weisman, 1981).

SUSTAINABILITY CONNECTION 16.2

The four Rs of sustainability are reduce, reuse, recycle, and regenerate. The ubiquitous suburban *shopping mall* built over the last 30 years essentially defies each of these principles. Although sustainable opportunities abound with the recent recession, some estimates claim that nearly 20 percent of all U.S. malls have "died" in the last several years (Hudson & O'Connell, 2009). The official term is *dead malls*. With upwards of 500,000+ square feet of usage space, parking lots, and accessibility to transit routes, developers, urban planners, and designers are attempting to reuse and renovate them into what is being called *lifestyle centers*. This process reconfigures the internally focused structure by either quite literally turning the building inside out or opening up the center and creating boulevards, streets, and green spaces out of the corridors and hallways (mini-malls). The huge footprint of the parking lots can become sporting fields and tree-lined green spaces. It is recommended that designers go a step further in their sustainable efforts by including residential units (for students and seniors), medical clinics, offices, and education components, along with integrating water reclamation and onsite power generation systems. By increasing connectivity to the surrounding environs with transit options and bike paths, designers will not only increase the location efficiency (Yudelson, 2010) but in the process regenerate or *re-urbanize* an entire district for other smaller neighboring enterprises.

CULTURAL CONNECTION 16.2

The culture of malls: the old conspicuous consumption, consumerism, and see-and-be-seen social aspect and entertainment diversion (Berger, 2005) has given way to the *virtual world*, online social networking and discount big-box centers. The way in which people use malls has changed. Designers should prepare themselves as much as possible by creating an inventory of what the local citizens would want or desire in a mall design. As Americans contract financially from a massive recession, they have nearly cocooned themselves indoors in their homes and places of employment (if they are so lucky) riding out the storm. It is, therefore, difficult to know how people will come to use malls in the future. One can speculate that people will no longer desire to be indoors because people have a physiological and psychological need for nature and natural elements; therefore, giving the illusion of being outdoors (Berger, 2005) is the best approach for designers when access to nature or natural views is impossible.

SAFETY AND SECURITY

Both workers and customers must be protected in retail and service environments. Security systems, devices, and signage may deter criminals; but they will also inform customers that they are at risk. Planners and designers must not only consider the unintended causes of their designs, but also devise creative strategies for employing defensible space measures without making the general public feel they are at risk (i.e. security bars on windows). The U.S. Occupational Safety and Health Administration (OSHA) cites the following statistics:

- Robbery and other crimes motivated 80 percent of workplace homicides across all industries in 1996.
- A large proportion of retail sector homicides are associated with robberies and attempted robberies.
- The largest share of such homicides occurred in convenience and other grocery stores, eating and drinking places, and gas stations.
- The risk of sexual assault for women is equal to or greater than the risk of homicide for retail employees in general (OSHA, 1998).

Locations that provide the occupants with full surveillance capabilities throughout their premises are more likely never to fall victim to criminals. OSHA provides the following design recommendations for the late-night retail industry, many of which can be applied to other servicescapes, especially those located in areas with high crime rates (Crow & Bull, 1975):

- *Improve visibility* so that employees have an unobstructed view of the street and passersby can see inside. Minimize window signage. Design work areas to prevent entrapment of employees and to minimize the potential for assault incidents. The interior layout should ensure that both clerk and cash register are visible from outside of the establishment, employees have two or more clear escape routes, and the area behind the counter is slightly elevated, affording employees greater visual range of the premises.
- *Maintain adequate lighting* inside and outside the establishment after dark. Interior lighting at floor level will cast shadows high onto walls, allowing for easy detection of criminal behavior by police or passersby.
- *Use fences* and other structures to control and direct ingress and egress of customer traffic to areas of greater visibility. Wrought iron fences, for example, allow for surveillance of the store from inside and limit possible escape routes for criminals—and they are harder to climb than chain-link fences.
- *Use drop safes* to minimize available cash, and use signage that indicates that little cash is kept on hand.
- *Install video surveillance equipment* and a closed-circuit TV to maintain surveillance of interior and exterior activities. Post signs indicating the use of such equipment at front doors and cash registers.
- *Install self-locking doors* or door buzzers so that entrances can be controlled, but always ensure unimpeded egress in case of emergency. For banks and convenience stores, consider the use of metal-detection systems to identify possible weapons.
- *Use door detectors* to alert employees when persons enter the store. Consider that hi-tech electronic movement detectors can be disabled by a power loss (accidental or deliberate), whereas glass or metal chimes or bells hung just above door height will sound at the slightest breeze, and cannot be disabled silently.
- *Height markers on exit doors* will help witnesses provide more accurate descriptions of assailants.
- *Use silent and personal alarms* to notify police or management in the event of a problem.
- *Install physical barriers* such as bullet-resistant enclosures with pass-through windows to protect employees from customer assaults.

Practical Applications for Designers

Use these resources, activities, and discussion questions to help you identify, synthesize, and retain this chapter's core information. These tools are designed to complement the resources you'll find in this book's companion Study Guide.

SUMMING IT UP

Retail and service environments include, but are not limited to convenience stores, gas and service stations, banks, restaurants, bars and clubs, specialty shops, department stores and emporiums, shopping malls, bulk warehouses, booths, kiosks, and vending carts. The retail and service environment, or servicescape, can be viewed according to three predominant factors—ambience, layout, and signage—each of which can influence customers' satisfaction or dissatisfaction with the service or product.

Planners and designers must not only consider the unintended effects of their designs, but also devise creative strategies for employing defensible space measures without making the general public feel they are at risk.

You can also refer to this textbook's companion Study Guide for a comprehensive list of Summary Points.

EXPERT SPOTLIGHT 16.1

Third Places

Lisa K. Waxman, Ph.D., LEED-AP, NCIDQ, Florida State University

The experience of place is unique to each individual and is directly related to his or her lived experiences (Waxman, 2006). Understanding the concept of place provides an important framework for understanding the way people form relationships with places. Third places are those places other than home or work that offer informal opportunities for people to gather and connect with others in their community. Oldenburg (1999) suggests there are eight characteristics of third places. Third places must be neutral ground where people can easily join and depart another's company and where no one has to play host. These places also welcome people from all walks of life, and neither rank nor status is important. For many, the third place offers opportunity for conversation and is accessible almost any time of day. These spaces often have "regulars," those familiar faces who frequent the third place and contribute to the atmosphere. Often the physical structure is plain and low profile and the atmosphere of the third place is usually playful. The final characteristic is that it serves as a "home away from home." Oldenburg (1999) said, "If an individual has a third place, the place also has him."

My research on coffee shops, which often serve as third places, found several key themes that contribute to the success of these places. Some of these themes are social in nature, whereas others relate to the design features.

Third Place Themes

1. *Opportunities to Linger.* This is influenced by the attitude of the management and friendliness of the staff and patrons, and the ability to linger after a meal or beverage has been consumed.

2. *Pleasant Ambient Conditions.* Features include cleanliness, adequate lighting, good acoustics, background music that still allows for conversation, pleasant aroma, natural light, views, and pleasing decor.

3. *Seating.* Design should include a variety of comfortable seating types and seating that can easily be moved to accommodate conversations or groups.

4. *Feelings of Prospect and Refuge.* Patrons often preferred seats against walls, half walls, or windows, which provide feelings of being sheltered while still having a view of the space.

5. *Feelings of Ownership and Territoriality.* Patrons may exhibit territorial feelings toward various areas, such as a favorite seat or place at the bar.

6. *Social Beings and Familiar Strangers.* A person's presence in the third place seems to validate or confirm his/her existence as a social member of the community. For many people, conversation is the main activity, but for others the third place provides an opportunity to watch the action and see "familiar strangers" who enrich the lives of patrons in indirect ways.

7. *Climate of Trust and Respect.* When a climate of trust and respect is established, people feel welcome and able to relax and be themselves.

8. *Support.* Part of the social climate of the third place is the support provided by the staff to other staff, the staff to the patrons, and the patrons to each other.

9. *Place Attachment.* A well-designed and managed third place often results in feelings of place attachment, a bonding of people to these special places.

References
Oldenburg, R. (1999). *The great good place.* New York: Marlowe & Company.

Waxman, L. (2006). The coffee shop: Social and physical factors influencing place attachment. *Journal of Interior Design, 31*(3), 35–53.

For more about the author, go to http://interiordesign.fsu.edu/pages/people/faculty/waxman.shtml

KEY TERMS

- **association**
- **atmospherics**
- **brand identity**
- **Crime Prevention through Environmental Design (CPTED)**
- **density-intensity theory**
- **descriptor**
- **electronic waste (e-waste)**
- **exothermic**
- **fourth environment**
- **implicit cue**
- **information and communication technologies (ICTS)**
- **logo**
- **megastore**
- **olfaction**
- **retail or service environment**
- **servicescape**
- **third place**
- **virtual modeling**

WEB LINKS

Consumer Psychologist (www.consumerpsychologist.com)

CPTED Association (www.cpted.net)

Dead Malls, on the decline of the American postal system: (www.deadmalls.com)

The Electronic Product Environmental Assessment Tool (www.epeat.net)

Freewebs.com (www.freewebs.com/chuckd23/index.htm)

Green Restaurant Association (www.dinegreen.com)

Higher Logic, on the retail environment industry (www.nasfm.org)

Logobird, go to the blog section (www.logobird.com.au)

Metropolis Magazine, on spaces designed for the five senses (www.metropolismag.com/pov/20091218/architecture-for-the-five-senses)

MIT Media Lab (http://cfb.media.mit.edu/)

Profumo, on scent in relation to marketing and mental stenography (www.profumo.it/perfume/olfactory_communication/olfactory_psychology.htm)

The Sustainable Table (www.sustainabletable.org)

STUDIO ACTIVITY 16.1

A Welcoming Environment for Children

Design Problem Statement
The Magic toy store has just bought the site next door to an important downtown mall and is looking for a design that is a welcoming environment to children. Using your knowledge about child development, create a design that will facilitate sidewalk interaction within the store's exterior. This design should be geared to each of the different end users:

1. Infants (ages 0–2)

2. Toddlers (ages 2–5)

3. Children (ages 5–12)

4. Teenagers (13–18)

Task: Design weatherproof interaction devices within the building's façade that showcase the diverse array of toys found inside. Your challenge is that you cannot isolate any age group away from the other.

Directions
Step One: Design the space that can show the progression of development within the four primary stages of development.

Step Two: Facilitate interaction between different age groups.

Step Three: Identify skill levels and what constitutes entertainment for the different age groups.

Step Four: Formulate ways to prevent the exterior spaces from becoming occupied by homeless people, thereby precluding pedestrians from interacting with the building.

Deliverables
- Four mock-ups of to-scale activities that would be incorporated into the exterior building façade of the toy store.

- Four written explanations (one for each activity) of what the activity does, what age group it targets, and why this activity would inspire someone to go inside.

- One model of the building showing the positioning of the different activities (this model should include adjacencies). The model should also show a viable design solution to prevent homeless people from obstructing the activity centers

STUDIO ACTIVITY 16.2

The Success of Cafés

Design Problem Statement
Discern the design differences and relative effects of atmospherics on the success of cafés.

Directions
Step One: Survey several similar style cafés to find one that appears to be doing very little business and one that is bustling with activity.

Step Two: Identify subtle and overt differences in the design and layout of each café.

Step Three: List possible reasons related to design that could be negatively affecting the success of the slow café while identifying the design attributes that may be contributing to the success of the busy café.

Step Four: List design measures that could contribute to increased business for the slow café.

Deliverables
Presentation boards

DISCUSSION QUESTIONS

1. Discuss the effects of store appearance (e.g., cluttered, dirty, bright, organized, and well stocked) on your interest in a store's merchandise.

2. Discuss the relevance of store location in an Internet economy. Is location still important to a retail store's success? Why or why not?

3. Discuss the types of music played in different types of stores. What does the music tell you about the target clientele?

4. Discuss important design characteristics of a restaurant known for exceptional service. What features support the efficiency and quality of customer service?

5. Discuss ways in which urban planning is affecting the layout and traffic flow of new malls. What methods are being used to encourage exploration and increase universal comfort in large shopping centers?

1. Design a window display along a community sidewalk, noting any special circumstances to be considered (e.g., window breakage, socioeconomic status).

2. Design parking facilities that are supportive of both vehicles and pedestrians, and analyze your designs with your classmates.

3. Visit a local grocery store during a busy shopping period and, in an aisle displaying similar products with different brand names, spend time observing how individuals choose between the products. How do one shopper's selections influence those of another? Gather data regarding the quantity of each brand selected over a set period of time. Next, manipulate the setting: Remove a noticeable number of slower-selling products from the shelf (be sure to replace or purchase them after this experiment). Does this change alter shoppers' selection patterns?

4. Visit three different kinds of convenience stores and make quick sketches of the locations and surroundings. What similarities and differences are there relative to the defensibility of the spaces? How are the employees protected? How is theft deterred?

With the traditional town square designs of smaller towns in mind, design a mall floor plan that incorporates many features of a town square. Be sure to consider activities that appeal to people of many age ranges and ways to allow several activities to occur simultaneously.

Glossary

absolute threshold The lowest level of stimulation that a person can detect 50 percent of the time.

abstract representation Data-based communication.

accessible route Continuous, unobstructed path connecting all accessible elements and spaces of a building or facility; interior accessible routes may include corridors, floors, ramps, elevators, lifts, and clear floor space at fixtures, and exterior accessible routes may include parking access aisles, curb ramps, crosswalks at vehicular ways, walks, ramps, and lifts.

acetylcholine A chemical stimulant found in the brain and throughout the entire nervous system.

acoustics Increased sound qualities of an environment; design elements that affect the sound characteristics of a space through transmission, absorption, and reflection.

activities of daily living (ADLs) Routine functional activities such as bathing, grooming, dressing, dining, cooking, light housekeeping, and taking medication.

actual Existing in fact; typically as contrasted with what was intended, expected, or believed.

acute care hospital Health care environment equipped to deal with emergencies, life-threatening illnesses and injuries, and surgical operations.

acute stressor Sudden and intense burst of stress.

adaptation The process of adjustment to environmental conditions.

adaptation level theory Premise that individuals adapt to certain levels of stimulation in certain contexts.

adaptive reuse The recycling of a structure and the adaptation of an old building for a new purpose.

attention deficit hyperactivity disorder (ADHD) A behavior disorder characterized by impulsivity, an inability to pay attention, and in some cases hyperactivity.

adrenaline A hormone and neurotransmitter that increases heart rate, contracts blood vessels and dilates air passages and participates in the "fight-or-flight" response.

aesthetics The values and expressions that the physical environment can embody and represent.

affect A person's emotional reaction to the environment.

affiliative-conflict theory A theory that suggests that we simultaneously want to be closer to and farther from others and that we use interpersonal distance to balance these conflicting desires.

agricultural (agri) resorts Resorts that offer patrons an opportunity to experience farm life.

agri-tourism A specialized division of tourism dedicated to providing travelers with exposure to organic and environmentally friendly farms, ranches, orchards, and vineyards.

allergen Substance frequently airborne that compromises the human immune system; source of allergic reactions.

Alzheimer's units Specialized unit equipped to deal with specific behaviors and problems associated with the disease.

ambient Something that envelops or surrounds.

ambient stressors Stressors that come from the surrounding environment.

amygdala An almond-shaped neural structure in the anterior part of the temporal lobe of the cerebrum associated with feeling emotions.

amyotrophic lateral sclerosis (ALS) A progressive degeneration of the motor neurons of the central nervous system, leading to a wasting away of the muscles and paralysis. Also known as Lou Gehrig's disease.

anecdotal evidence Personal accounts not based on verified facts.

angular gyrus The cerebral gyrus of the posterior part of the external surface of the parietal lobe that arches over the posterior end of the sulcus between the superior and middle gyri of the temporal lobe—called also *angular convolution*.

anthropomorphizing Attributing human qualities to nonhuman items.

architectural determinism theory A theory that there is a direct relationship between the built environment and a particular behavior.

area of rescue Assistance space that has direct access to an exit where people who are unable to use stairs may remain temporarily in safety and await instructions or assistance during emergency evacuation.

arousal Excitement or stimulation to action or physiological readiness for activity.

arousal perspective theory A theory that much of human behavior and experience is related to arousal levels.

assistive device Physical mobility aid that assists users' movements, such as a brace, cane, crutch, walking frame, wheelchair (standard or motorized), prosthetic limb, or service animal.

association The process of forming mental connections or bonds between sensations, ideas, or memories. A connection between the stimulus and a meaning.

atmospherics Sights, sounds, or scents that contribute to the over-all ambience of an environment.

attention deficit hyperactivity disorder (ADHD) A chronic condition that includes some combination of problems, such as difficulty sustaining attention, hyperactivity, and impulsive behavior.

attention restoration theory (ART) The premise that mental fatigue is caused by excessive directed attention and that attentional capacity and mental balance can be restored by engaging in effortless attention.

attentional deficit The inability to focus or concentrate; also, inadequate attentional capacity caused by mental fatigue due to excessive directed attention; can be ameliorated by restorative experiences.

attitude A belief that tends to follow the values of an era and vice versa; predisposition.

auditory learners People who process information by what they hear and reason through discussion.

autism spectrum disorder (ASD) A group of developmental disabilities that can cause significant social, communication, and behavioral challenges.

autosomal dominant A pattern of inheritance in which an affected individual has one copy of a mutant gene and one normal gene on a pair of autosomal chromosomes.

autosomal recessive A genetic condition that appears only in individuals who have received two copies of an autosomal gene, one copy from each parent.

basal ganglia A group of structures linked to the thalamus in the base of the brain and involved in coordination of movement.

behavioral controls Physical or psychological elements that serve to restrict or encourage specific behaviors

behavioral health facilities Specialized facilities that ensure positive and meaningful opportunities for persons with various mental illness.

behavior setting physical or psychological environment A place or occasion that elicits or supports certain patterns of behavior that are based on the environmental design and learned as a result of operant conditioning.

best-bet theory Stacking the odds in our favor.

Big Five inventory (BFI) Statistical analyses that show how different personality traits can be linked together to define certain human qualities.

bilateral hearing loss Partial hearing loss in both ears.

bioeffluent Organic body waste such as carbon dioxide, skin cells, hairs, and microbes (bacteria, germs, and viruses).

birthing center Facility that allows women to give birth in a home-like setting.

Braille Language developed for the blind.

brand identity The associations connected with a company, service, name, logo, color or visual appearance of the building.

building-related illness Symptoms of diagnosable illnesses that are found in occupants of all office buildings to some degree.

building-specific illness Symptoms that occur only in air-conditioned buildings.

cardinal directions The compass directions of north, south, east, and west.

cataracts A medical condition in which the lens of the eye becomes progressively opaque, resulting in blurred vision.

catastrophic reactions Commonly seen as sudden and extreme emotional or physical outbursts.

catecholamines A group of neurochemicals composed of naturally occurring compounds, serve as hormones, neurotransmitters.

caudate nucleus In each hemisphere of the brain, the most medial of the four basal ganglia; responsible for regulating and organizing information being sent to the frontal lobes from other areas of the brain and is responsible for body movement and coordination. Impaired caudate function is related to Parkinson's and Huntington's diseases.

charette A collaborative design session which includes designers, planners, stakeholders, and users with the goal of creating an initial design that will address the many issues brought to the table.

chronic stressor Constant or recurring source of stress that slowly erodes our abilities to cope.

cognition Mental analysis or how information is interpreted, stored, and recalled; second phase in overall thought process.

cognition mental analysis A method that shows how information is interpreted, stored, and recalled; second phase in overall thought process.

cognitive map, pictorial and semantic (language) A mental image of an environment or setting.

cognitive truth Belief that may not necessarily be factual but is held to be true.

collaborative structure Environment team roles, goals, and operating principles are an important part of the joint problem-solving and innovative ideas.

comfort theory Comfort is found in a world that is reminiscent of us.

command and control theory Humans view themselves as superior to everything else on the planet.

commodify to commercialize Turning an intrinsic value into a commodity (i.e., a recognizable unit of economic production).

complex cells Cells that coordinate information from a group of simple cells.

concentration node An area in which people gather for a common purpose.

conductive hearing loss Reduced ability to detect low or faint sounds.

cones Aspect of the human eye that enables us to see color.

contextual memory Third developmental stage of memory; child can merge objects and events together to create a situation or context.

continuing care retirement communities (CCRC) Campus-like environment that allows residents to "age in place" as their health deteriorates.

cornea The transparent layer forming the front of the eye.

Crime Prevention through Environmental Design (CPTED) A multidisciplinary approach to deterring criminal behavior through environmental design.

crowding Subjective term that refers to a psychologically or emotionally based feeling that we perceive ourselves as being physically constrained in some way or that other people are interfering with us.

crowds Large, temporary groups of often-emotional individuals.

culture the values, norms, and artifacts of a group of people.

decay theory Theory that memory fades with the passage of time.

declarative memory Recall that uses semantic representations as related to facts, rules, and concepts.

density Mathematic ratio of individuals to a specific area.

density-intensity theory Premise that density itself is not harmful but rather that it amplifies everything else.

descriptor Environmental feature that helps us to understand and respond to a place.

determinism theory Premise that acts of will, occurrences in nature, or social or psychological phenomena are causally determined by preceding events or natural laws

deterministic behaviors Acting on the notion that preceding events and conditions determine every succeeding event.

diabetic retinopathy A complication of diabetes that results from damage to the blood vessels of the light-sensitive tissue at the back of the eye.

dichromacy Color vision defect in which one of the three basic color mechanisms is absent or not functioning.

difference threshold The smallest change in stimulation that a person can detect without the use of equipment.

differentiated homes Structures with multiple rooms each serving a specific purpose.

directed attention fatigue A neurological condition caused by intense and prolonged concentration while in the midst of multiple distractions from external and/or internal sources.

directed attention intention or goal-based attention Requires focused mental effort and can cause attentional deficit; also called voluntary attention.

dopamine A chemical substance found in the brain that regulates movement, balance, and walking.

dry eye A deficiency of tears.

dysgraphia A language disorder that affects a person's mechanical ability to write.

dyslexia Impaired ability to comprehend written words usually associated with a neurologic disorder.

ecological perception A theory that much environmental information is conveyed by perceptual patterns that do not require higher-brain processing.

ecological (eco) resorts Resorts that offer travelers a degree of communal living with nature.

ecotourism (also known as ecological tourism) Travel to fragile, pristine, and usually protected areas that strives to be low impact and (often) small scale. It helps educate the traveler, provides funds for conservation, directly benefits the economic development and political empowerment of local communities, and fosters respect for different cultures and for human rights.

edible spaces Spaces found in parks and school yards where the landscape consists of plants, trees, and bushes that are either consumable or produce consumable foods.

effect Resulting state or condition.

effortless attention Interest-based attention that can serve to restore attentional capacity; also called automatic and involuntary attention.

electronic waste (e-waste) No longer useful electrical or electronic devices.

embodied energy The combination of energy, raw materials, and transportation required to make a building.

endogenous cannabinoids Neuromodulators that influence the activity of a sending neuron.

environmental cognition analysis How we understand, diagnose, and interact within the environment.

environmental load State of excessive arousal; also called overstimulation.

environmental legibility The ability for people to "read" their surroundings and "know" where they are, what can be done there, and who belongs.

environmental numbness State of being unaware of one's environment until it or something in it changes.

environmental perception Interpretation of the world around us as influenced by our experiences and sensations.

epinephrine A hormone produced by the adrenal glands in response to stress, exercise, or fear that increases heart rate.

ergonomics Applied science concerned with designing and arranging the things we use so as to ensure both efficiency and safety; also called human engineering or human factors psychology.

ethic of care theory Theory that it is in a woman's nature to focus on sustaining relationships and taking care of others' needs.

event memory Second developmental stage of memory; child remembers specific events.

exothermic Occurs when a chemical releases energy in the form of heat (i.e., chemical burns).

external locus of control (ELOC) The belief that lives are controlled by external forces (e.g., fate, luck, chance, or powerful otherworldly beings).

external stressor Sources of stress that derive from variables in the physical environment, such as noise, temperature, crowding, and over- or understimulation.

familiarity theory Theory based on a cognitive motivation to understand the world, but we must do it from a point of reference that we already know and understand.

fight-or-flight response An automatic response to stress that is perceived to be a survival threat.

formal aesthetics Assessment based on color, material, shape, space, and texture.

fourth environment Place where individuals congregate other than their primary, secondary, and tertiary territories or spaces (i.e., not their residences or sites specifically developed for them).

free independent traveler (FIT) A solo traveler.

functionalist People who theorize that the environment contains an abundance of cues and that perceivers (people) must be able to make sense of the most important ones if they are to function effectively.

ganglion cells A nerve cell whose body is outside the central nervous system.

glaucoma A condition of increased pressure within the eyeball, causing gradual loss of sight.

green walls An external architectural wall or façade system incorporating vegetation into the structure.

habituate To get used to one's environment.

halo effects Reflections caused by direct light entering through the windows and rebounding off various objects, thereby leading to high levels of glare.

haptic realm Exclusively related to the sensation of touch.

hard room A room decorated with bare floors, minimal wall and standing artwork, and modern or industrial furnishings.

hard science Natural and physical sciences that use the scientific method and experiments to test theories.

heat island effect The urban environment having persistently higher than rural air temperatures due to a lack of vegetation; an excess of heat producing buildings; and heat-absorbing structures such as roads and pavement.

hierarchical structure Traditional imperial organizational structure, characterized by bureaucracy and a chain of command of power and control.

high power distance Ascribes superiority to those with a certain social status.

hippocampus The elongated ridges on the floor of each lateral ventricle of the brain, thought to be the center of emotion, memory, and the autonomic nervous system.

home office Designated space in a private residence that can support either household record keeping or a home-based business or can serve as a telecommuting site.

homogenous homes Structures with one single large room that serves multiple uses.

hormones Chemical substances produced by our glands and act as neuromodulators.

hospices A type of care and philosophy that focuses on the care of a terminally ill patient's symptoms.

hospitality Reception and entertainment: hotels, motels, resorts, cruise ships, theme parks, timeshares, and private residence clubs.

human-scale element Design element that is neither oversized nor undersized.

hypercomplex cells Cells that respond to complex stimulus features.

illuminance Lighting level or amount of illumination; measured in lux.

illumination Quantity of light striking a surface, which is measured in foot-candles.

immunocompetency Ability or capacity for the immune system to respond or function adequately.

implicit cue Indicator of our behavior that we leave behind when we leave an environment.

information and communication technologies (ICTs) Term for processing and exchanging digital information with computers.

integration (integral) theories Theoretical models intended to encompass the complex range of human–environment relations.

interactional territories Temporarily controlled by a group of interacting individuals.

interactional theory Simplest form of integration theory; maintains that people and the environment are separate but interacting entities.

interference theory The belief that information held in our short-term memory gets forgotten because we get additional information that interferes with the memory.

internal locus of control (ILOC) Belief that their actions, choices, and pursuits control their destiny.

internal stressors Sources of stress that derive from interpersonal conflict or violence, disorganized daily life, or a combination of these factors.

ions Particles that are electrically charged.

Kaplan and Kaplan Preference Model A theoretical framework used to organize environmental preferences according to four elements: coherence, legibility, complexity, and mystery.

kinesthetic Result of the sensation of bodily position, presence, or movement.

kinesthetic learners People who process information by experiencing, doing, and touching.

lateral inhibition Capacity of an excited neuron to reduce activity of its neighbors.

limbic system A system of functionally related neural structures in the brain that are involved in emotional behavior.

logo A company symbol or graphic which acts as a trademark.

long-term care facility A residential environment for individuals (usually elderly) who require routine medical care and assistance with activities of daily living; also called nursing or convalescent home.

looming A phenomena in which objects enlarge quickly so they fill the retina and are perceived as moving toward the viewer.

low power distance Distance required to assume equality among people, and focus more on earned status than ascribed status.

luminaire Complete lighting unit: fixture, light source, electrical hookup, and parts that help control the light.

luminance Brightness of an object, which is measured in lumens.

macular degeneration A condition where the rods are damaged or lost.

magic bullet approach The approach of easing the symptom of a problem instead of finding the main cause of it (e.g., A + B = C; taking a pill for a headache instead of looking at the social conditions or physical environment to prevent the headache to begin with).

megastore Large retail facility that offers consumers an expansive variety of goods and services; also called hypermarket.

melatonin A naturally occurring hormone associated with sleep.

mesopic vision Vision for low contrast conditions such as at dawn and dusk.

monochromatism Color blindness.

mores Societal practices rather than laws.

multiple sclerosis (MS) A disease that affects the brain and spinal cord resulting in loss of muscle control, vision, balance, and sensation (such as numbness).

multisensory experiences Ambient conditions that stimulate more than one of our sensations.

music stream Constant flow or stream of pleasurable, musical background noise.

Myers-Briggs Type Indicator (MBTI) A personality inventory or test developed by Katharine Briggs and Isabel Briggs Myers that expands on personality types developed by Carl Jung to include a judging-perceiving function resulting in four primary personality dichotomies converged to create sixteen possible personality profiles.

nature tourism The division of the travel industry relating to environmental recreational and cultural experiences related to the nature.

navigational space The space we move through and explore, which usually cannot be seen all at once.

needs assessment A survey conducted prior to construction or occupancy to determine environmental conditions and user needs.

neighborhood work center Fully furnished and equipped cooperative facility shared by employees of different companies and/or by entrepreneurs.

neurochemicals Any organic substance that occurs in neural activity.

neuromodulators Modulators that alter the effect of neurotransmitters.

neuroscience The study of the entire nervous system including the brain, spinal cord, and networks of sensory nerve cells, or neurons.

neurotransmitter Chemical substance that transmits nerve impulses across synapses.

nociception Perception of pain.

nonspatial environmental cognition A mental model of how we conceptualize ideas and concepts (e.g., categorizing local restaurants according to food, price, location and so on).

nonterritorial office Work spaces are not dedicated (assigned) but are available as needed for employees who work part-time or spend most of their time out in the field.

noradrenaline A hormone and neurotransmitter produced by the adrenal gland and involved in arousal.

norepinephrine Chemical substance important in sympathetic arousal and vasoconstriction.

nuclear family A family group that consists only of father, mother, and children.

objective Undistorted by emotion or personal bias.

object memory First developmental stage of memory; child remembers specific objects.

object-subject interchangeability People attribute meaning to other people and objects in the construction, adaptation, and maintenance of the self.

occupancy evaluation Survey of a planned development conducted during the formative stages to determine the needs of the intended users.

olfaction The sensory experience of the nose, mouth, and throat.

operant conditioning Social process that teaches and reinforces acceptable/desirable behaviors; a form of behavior modification.

optic nerve hypoplasia A medical condition present at birth, in which the optic nerve is underdeveloped, so that adequate visual information is not carried from the eye to the brain; affects people in a broad range from little of no visual impairment to near-total blindness.

organismic theory Form of integration theory that focuses on the complex interaction of social, societal, and individual factors.

organizers Mutually acceptable ground rules for the transaction of social behaviors.

overload The negative mental state that results when a person experiences excessive information, stimulation, and arousal.

ozone A colorless gas that can be produced by electrical discharges in oxygen.

paradigm Philosophical or theoretical conceptual framework.

park A piece of open land for recreational use.

pediatric hospital Specialized hospital dedicated exclusively to the care of infants and children.

perceived To attain awareness or understanding of.

perception The process of attaining awareness or understanding.

perception of sensation Becoming aware of something via the senses.

perceptual consistency Objects appear to remain stable even as our eyes move.

perceptual expectancies Perceptions that depend on a previous experience and relate to a context.

perceptual set The sum of one's assumptions and beliefs about people, places, or things.

peripheral vision The outer part of our field of vision.

personal control The ability to control the environment or situation.

personalization Ways that represent some aspect of their identities.

phobia An intense and persistent fear of certain situations or activities.

picking A fixation to remove small items, bit by bit.

pineal gland Cone-shaped organ that secretes the hormone melatonin.

plasticity Neural condition in which the brain is highly adaptive.

pleasure–arousal–dominance hypothesis Premise that people have three primary emotional responses to an environment: positive feelings, excitement, and a sense of control.

postoccupancy evaluation (POE) Survey conducted after a space is occupied to determine if user needs were met.

power distance Term used to describe the degree of difference and acceptance of unequal power between people.

predesign research (PDR) See *needs assessment*. Survey conducted prior to construction or occupancy to determine environmental conditions.

presbyopia Farsightedness caused by loss of elasticity of the lens of the eye, occurring typically in the middle and old age.

primary spaces Common areas in territories such as residences and workplaces where communication and social interaction take place (e.g., living rooms and conference rooms).

primary territories Spaces that are generally owned by individuals or primary groups and are controlled on a relatively permanent basis.

private residence clubs High-end private homes or suites that a portion or fraction of the property interest is sold for the vacationing purposes of the partial owners for a predetermined amount of annual weeks (9–13 weeks typically).

probabilism A concept in which environmental cues have only a certain probability of being useful.

procedural memory Recall based on performance, actions, and skills (see declarative memory).

prospect-refuge theory Suggests that humans prefer edge settings between open and closed areas such as plains and forests.

prospect visual range Distance required for detecting food or danger.

pruning A process in which the brain severs neural connections that it no longer uses.

psychological construct A conceptual representation of an environment or idea; a way of thinking about or conceiving of a place or idea.

psychological reactance An attempt to regain one's freedom within or control over an environment stemming from feelings of lack or loss of control; also called reactance.

public territories Open to anyone in good standing within the community and occupants cannot expect to have much control.

reciprocal determinism Theory that a person's behavior both influences and is influenced by personal factors.

recreational environments Areas such as parks, resorts, cruise ships, and other hospitality settings.

reflections The potential of seeing oneself or another's reflection can be very disturbing to the dementia patient.

refuge A safe haven or shelter.

rehabilitation facility An extended-stay environment that provides multidisciplinary physical restorative services in which patients work to regain their health after accidents and strokes.

restorative environment A place where we can function without conscious thought and where we find relaxation.

restorative experience An episode that allows a person to function primarily in the effortless attention mode as a means of restoring attentional capacity and, therefore, relaxing.

retail environment A business that sells tangible goods and materials.

retinitis pigmentosa A condition that affects the retina and is characterized by progressive peripheral vision loss and difficulties seeing at night.

retinopathy Occurs when the retinas are damaged shortly after birth, usually the result of a premature infant being exposed to bright light.

right-side bias The human tendency to locate faster and remember information (names and dates) placed on the right side of an object (e.g., painting or sculpture).

rods Part of the eye that facilitates vision in low light.

rummaging An insatiable need to search.

satellite office A remote workplace location controlled by an organization; a form of telecommuting.

scenographic representations Picture-based communication.

schema A structured framework or plan, or cognitive way of perception.

secondary spaces Common areas in territories such as residences and workplaces to and from which communication and social interaction migrate (e.g., kitchens and reception desks).

secondary territories Usually not owned by the occupants, and possess only moderate significance.

segmentation Division of a whole space or structure by separation or partition into smaller areas/sections.

segmentation bias Cognitive process of breaking a route into smaller segments that alters our perception of distance (distance estimates).

selective attention Ability to focus on select stimuli and screen out others.

self-regulation Behavioral limitations or boundaries that people set for themselves in either physical or social environments.

sensation A physical feeling or perception from something that comes into contact with the body and causes interest, curiosity, or emotion.

sensorimotor Functioning in both sensory and motor aspects of bodily activity.

sensorineural hearing loss Results from damages to the inner ear of to the nerve pathways leading to, or within the brain. This often limits a person's ability to hear faint sounds as well as some of the different tones commonly associated with voice patterns.

sensory stimuli Elements within an environment that provoke an acknowledgment or reaction.

separatism Belief system that one entity must dominate the other in the human–environment relationship.

Serial Position Effect The tendency to recall information that is presented first and last (like in a list) better than information presented in the middle.

service environment A business that sells intangible assistance or specialized help.

servicescapes Conveniently accessible public territories that contain money, goods, or both and have open, relatively uncontrolled contact with the general populace.

shared real estate Vacation property owned/shared by many individuals.

sick role Role we assume when we are sick or injured that affects our cognitive processes, behaviors, and medical outcomes.

simple cells Cells that respond to a line presented only at a certain angle or orientation.

social density Varied number of individuals occupying a fixed amount of space.

social theory A means to explain psychological discussions of attributing value and social consequence.

social or observational learning theory A construct that explains human behavior in terms of continuous reciprocal interaction among cognitive, behavioral, and environmental influences.

sociofugal seating arrangements Physical arrangements where people sit facing away from each other.

sociopetal seating arrangement Physical arrangements where individuals face each other.

soft room A room decorated with carpeting, canvas-based artwork, and overstuffed furnishings.

somatic senses A level of sensation that is vital to our ability to experience the world which includes tactician (touch), thermoception (sense of heat), and nociception (perception of pain).

spasticity A state of increased muscle tone, or stiffness, which leads to uncontrolled, awkward movements.

spatial cognition Specialized thinking process used to navigate environment.

spatial density A fixed number of individuals occupying different sized spaces.

special care units (SCUs) Patient populations with specific needs in separate units.

stalling Sudden stopping often results in falls.

stimulus association Memory of some prior event based on a current sensation.

stimulus response A response or action based on memory or learned response rather than current conditions.

stimulation theory A concept that explains the environment as a source of sensory information (stimuli) that leads to arousal.

strategic junction node A point where activity converges for different purposes (such as a lobby).

subjective Something that takes place within the mind and modified by individual bias.

sundowning A phenomenon that manifests in agitation, heightened confusion or unusual behavior during later afternoon or early evening.

supports and constraints Environmental elements that facilitate and restrict human actions.

supraliminal Existing above the threshold of conciousness.

supra-marginal gyrus A gyrus of the inferior part of the parietal lobe that is continuous in front with the postcentral gyrus and posteriorly and inferiorly with the superior temporal gyrus.

sustainable land management The practice of managing the site and land surrounding a project, prior and during construction, without harming ecological processes or biological diversity.

symbolic aesthetics Visual notions of beauty and meaning based on a set of values and beliefs.

sympathetic nervous system The branch of the autonomic nervous system that is responsible for breathing, circulation, and digestion.

synomorphy The principle that an environment's physical and social aspects should fit well together; also, congruity among the physical, psychological, and social aspects of an environment.

tactician Sense of touch.

telecommuting Working for a company as an employee, but away from the company's organizational workplace (does not apply to independent contractors and consultants); use of computer technology to transfer information from remote locations to the "main office."

teratogens Agents that can be inhaled or absorbed by the mother and thus circulated through her bloodstream to the developing fetus.

territorial contamination Intentional fouling of someone else's territory.

territorial invasion Situation when an outsider physically enters a territory with the intention of taking control of it.

territorial violation A temporary incursion into someone else's territory.

territory development A theoretical concept that states the members of a perceived "community" will socially organize themselves and protect or defend the area and the resources on it from others that they deem not to belong.

tertiary spaces Private or personal spaces or areas where people go to be alone.

thermoception Sense of heat.

threshold Point at which too much or too little stimulation has been received.

third place An environment beyond home (first place) and work (second place) where people select for relaxation and conversation.

Thorndike halo effect A cognitive bias caused by the visual perception of current object being influenced by the perception of a former object in a sequence of interpretations, i.e., parts of the image seen directly before the present image will be added to the current image, thus influencing current perceptions.

timeshares Shared form of real estate ownership.

tracking The process of following a moving object with one's eyes.

tradition A custom or practice that has been passed down from generation to generation.

transactional theory Belief that the human–environment relationship is mutually supportive.

trichromacy The ability to see color.

unilateral hearing loss Hearing impairment where there is normal hearing in one ear and impaired hearing in the other ear.

unilateral mydriasis A condition characterized by prolonged abnormal dilatation of the pupil, which can result from corrective surgery. This condition is often associated with headaches and blurred vision.

universal design An approach to the design of products and spaces that emphasizes usability by people with a wide range of needs; intended to enable people of all ability levels to achieve maximum environmental independence.

unstructured play A type of play that develops organically and from the imaginations of children without planning.

urban heat island effect A measurable increase in ambient urban air temperatures resulting primarily from the replacement of vegetation with buildings, roads, and other heat-absorbing infrastructure which can result in significant temperature differences between rural and urban areas.

user group A defined set of individuals who will be utilizing the space for a predetermined function.

vertigo A sensation of whirling and loss of balance, associated particularly with looking down from a great height, or caused by a disease affecting the inner ear or vestibular nerve.

vestibular Sensation, spatial perception, and orientation.

virtual modeling Practice of using implicit cues to modify behavior.

virtual office Mobile workplace supported by a portable computer and telephone; form of telecommuting.

visual cliffing An inability to differentiate between colors and textures.

visual learners People who process information by what they see and think in terms of pictures.

visually impaired Having greatly reduced vision also referred to as partially sighted or blind.

Weber Fechner Law A theory that attempts to describe the relationship between the physical magnitudes of stimuli and the perceived intensity of the stimuli.

workplace culture Social climate within a business organization; the way in which personnel interact.

worldview Perspective or philosophy incorporating a general belief; may be held by an entire culture or generation.

x-linked A gene on the X chromosome that expresses itself only when there is no different gene present at the locus (spot on the chromosome).

References

AARP Foundation. (October 2007). *State fact sheets for grandparents and other relatives raising children.* Retrieved from www.grandfactsheets.org/state_fact_sheets.cfm

Abramov, I., et al. (1982). The retina of the newborn human infant. *Science,* 265–267.

Abu-Ghazzeh, T. M. (1996). Movement and wayfinding in the King Saud University built environment: A look at freshman orientation and environmental information. *Journal of Environmental Psychology, 16,* 303–319.

Abu-Obeid, N. (1998). Abstract and scenographic imagery: The effect of environmental form on wayfinding. *Journal of Environmental Psychology, 18,* 159–173.

Ackerman, D. (1990). *A natural history of the senses.* New York: Random House.

Adams, L., & Zuckerman, D. (1991). The effect of lighting conditions on personal space requirements. *Journal of General Psychology, 118,* 335–340.

Adenzato, M., Cornoldi, C., Tamietto, M., & Tinti, C., (2006). Visual experience is not necessary for efficient survey spatial cognition: Evidence from blindness. *Quarterly Journal of Experimental Psychology, 59,* 1306–1328.

Adgate, J. L., et al. (1998). Chemical mass balance source apportionment of lead in house dust. *Environmental Science Technology, 32,* 108–114.

Aging in the Know: Your Gateway to Health and Aging Resources on the Web (March 15, 2005). Trends in the elderly population. Retrieved February 6, 2009 from www.healthinaging.org/agingintheknow/chapters_ch_trial.asp?ch=2

Aiello, J. R., Epstein, Y. M., & Karlin, R. A. (1975). Field experimental research on human crowding. *Journal of Applied Social Psychology, 5,* 34–53.

Aiello, J. R., Thompson, D. E., & Brodzinsky, D. M. (1983). How funny is crowding anyway? Effects of room size, group size and the introduction of humor. *Basic and Applied Social Psychology, 4,* 193–207.

Ailawadi, K., & Keller, K. (2004). Understanding retail branding: Conceptual insights and research priorities. *Journal of Retailing, 80*(4), 331–342.

Allen, G. L., & Kirasic, K. C. (1985). Effects of the cognitive organization of route knowledge on judgments of macrospatial distance. *Memory and Cognition, 13,* 218–227.

Allen, K. E., & Marotz, L. R. (2003). *Developmental profiles* (4th ed.). Albany, NY: Delmar.

Allport, G. W. (1961*). Pattern and growth in personality.* New York: Holt, Rinehart and Winston.

Altman. J., & Das, G.D. (1964) Autoradiographic examination of the effects of enriched environment on the rate of glial multiplication in the adult rat brain. *Nature, 204,* 1161–1163

Altman, I. (1975). *The environment and social behavior: Privacy, personal space, territoriality and crowding.* Monterey, CA: Brooks/Cole.

Altman, I., Brown, B. B., Staples, B., & Werner, C. M. (1992). A transactional approach to close relationships: Courtship, weddings, and placemaking. In W. B. Walsh, K. H. Craik, & R. H. Price (Eds.), *Person–environment psychology: Models and perspectives* (pp. 193-241). Hillsdale, NJ: Lawrence Erlbaum..

Altman, I., & Chemers, M. (1980). *Culture and environment.* Monterey, CA: Brooks/Cole.

Alzheimer's Association. (2004). *Statistics fact sheet.* Retrieved from www.alz.org

Amato, P. R. (1981). The effects of environmental complexity and pleasantness on prosocial behaviour: A field study. *Australian Journal of Psychology, 33,* 297–303.

Amaturo, E., Costagliola, S., & Ragone, G. (1987). Furnishing and status attributes: A sociological study of the living room. *Environment and Behavior, 19,* 228–249.

Amedeo, D. A., & Dyck, J. A., (2003). Activity-enhancing arenas of designs: A case-study of the classroom layout. *Journal of Architectural and Planning Research, 20,* 323–343.

American Foundation for The Blind (AFB). (n.d.). *Louis Braille biography.* Retrieved from www.afb.org/braillebug/louis_braille_bio.asp

American Psychiatric Association. (1994). Diagnostic and statistical manual of mental disorders (4th ed.). Washington, DC: Author.

American Psychological Association. (2003). *Division 34, Population and Environment.* Retrieved from http://web.uvic.ca/~apadiv34

American Psychological Association, (n.d). *APA divisions: Division 6 - Behavioral neuroscience and comparative psychology.* Retrieved from www.apa.org/about/division/div6.html

Americans With Disabilities (n.d.). *Americans With Disabilities Home.* Retrieved from www.ada.gov

Anderson, C. E., Burns, D. J., & Reid, J. S. (2003). The next evolutionary step for regional shopping malls: A measure of acceptance of new retail concepts as identified by different age groups of shoppers. *Journal of Shopping Center Research, 10*(2), 27–59.

Anderson, K. L., & Goldstein, H. (2004). Speech perception benefits of FM and infrared devices to children with hearing aids in a typical classroom. *Language, Speech, and Hearing Services in the Schools, 35,* 169–184.

Ang, S. H., Leong, S. M., & Lim, J. (1997). The mediating influence of pleasure and arousal on layout and signage effects. *Journal of Retailing and Consumer Services, 4*(1), 13–24.

Apte, M. G., Fisk, W. J., & Daisey, J. M. (2000). Associations between indoor air and CO2 concentrations and sick building syndrome symptoms in US office buildings: An analysis of the 1994 BASE study data. *Indoor Air, 10*(4), 246–257.

Archea, J. C. (1985). The use of architectural props in the conduct of criminal acts. *Journal of Architecture and Planning Research, 2,* 245–259.

Areni, C. S. (2003). Examining managers' theories of how atmospheric music affects perception, behaviour and financial performance. *Journal of Retailing and Consumer Services, 10,* 263–274.

Arnsten, A. F. T. (1998). The biology of being frazzled. *Science, 280,* 1711–1712.

Ashton, N. L., Shaw, M. E., & Worsham, A. P. (1980). Affective reactions to interpersonal distance by friends and strangers. *Bulletin of the Psychonomic Society, 15,* 306–308.

Aslin, R. N. (1981). Development of smooth pursuit in human infants. In D. F. Fisher, R. A. Monty, & J. W. Senders (Eds.), *Eye movements: Cognition and visual perception* (pp. 31–51). Hillsdale, NJ: Lawrence Erlbaum Associates, Inc.

Athena Research Corporation. (1981). *Robber Interview Report.* Presented to the Crime Committee of the Southland Corporation, Dallas, TX.

Atkinson, J., (2000). *The developing visual brain.* Oxford: Oxford University Press.

Autism Society of America. (Last updated: 21 January 2008). *About autism.* Retrieved from www.autismsociety.org/site/PageServer?pagename=about_home

Averill, J. R. (1973). Personal control over aversive stimuli and its relationship to stress. *Psychological Bulletin, 80,* 286–303

Avicena (n.d.). Disease Targets. retrieved June 20, 2005 from www.avicenagroup.com/disease_targets/neurology/parkinsons.php#2.

Ayala, H. (1996). Resort ecotourism: A master plan for experience management. *Cornell Hotel and Restaurant Administration Quarterly, 37*(5), 54–61.

Babey, S. H., Hastert, T. A., & Brown, E. R. (2007). *Teens living in disadvantaged neighborhoods lack access to parks and get less physical activity.* Los Angeles, CA: UCLA Center for Health Policy Research.

Backman, C. R. (2002). *The worlds of medieval Europe.* London, England: Oxford University Press.

Bagot, K. (2004). Perceived restorative components: A scale for children. *Children, youth and environments, 14*(1), 107–129.

Baird, J. C., Cassidy, B., & Kurr, J. (1978). Room preference as a function of architectural features and user activities. *Journal of Applied Psychology, 63,* 719–727.

Baker, S. M., Stephens, D. L., & Hill, R. P. (2002). How can retailers enhance accessibility: Giving consumers with visual impairments a voice in the marketplace. *Journal of Retailing and Consumer Services, 9,* 227–239.

Bame, S. I., & Wells, W. (1995). Acoustical design features associated with noise level in health facilities: The case of dialysis facilities. *Journal of Interior Design, 21*(2), 1–14.

Banbury, S. P., Tremblay, S., Macken, W. J., & Jones, D. M. (2001). Auditory distraction and short-term memory: Phenomena and practical implications. *Human Factors, 43*(1), 12–29.

Bandura, A. (1977). *Social learning theory.* New York: General Learning Press.

Bandura, A. (1986). *Social foundations of thought and action: A social cognitive theory.* Englewood Cliffs, NJ: Prentice-Hall.

Banich, M. T. (2004). *Cognitive neuroscience and neuropsychology.* Boston, MA: Houghton Mifflin.

Banks, M. S., & Salapatek, P. (1978). Acuity and contrast sensitivity in 1-, 2-, and 3-month-old human infants. *Investigative Ophthalmology & Visual Science, 17,* 361–365.

Barañano, D. E., et al. (2000). A mammalian iron ATPase induced by iron. *Journal of Biological Chemistry, 275,* 15166–15173.

Bargh, J. A., Lombardi, W., & Higgins, E. T. (1988). Automaticity in person X: Situation effects on person perception: It's just a matter of time. *Journal of Personality and Social Psychology, 55,* 599–605.

Barnard, W. A., & Bell, P. A. (1982). An unobtrusive apparatus for measuring interpersonal distances. *Journal of General Psychology, 107,* 85–90.

Barker, R. G. (1968). *Ecological psychology: Concepts and methods for studying the environment of human behavior.* Stanford, CA: Stanford University Press.

Baron, R. A., & Thomley, J. (1994). A whiff of reality: Positive affect as a potential mediator of the effects of pleasant fragrances on task performance and helping. *Environment and Behavior, 26,* 766–784.

Bauder, C. (2009, May, 20). *New MRI machine coming to Stephens County Hospital.* Retrieved from http://www.independentmail.com/news/2009/may/20/new-mri-machine-coming-stephens-county-hospital/

Baum, A., Aiello, J. R., & Calesnick, L. E. (1978). Crowding and perceived control: Social density and the development of learned helplessness. *Journal of Personality and Social Psychology, 36,* 1000–1011.

Baum, A., Cohen, L., & Hall, M. (1993). Control and intrusive memories as possible determinants of chronic stress. *Psychosomatic Medicine, 55,* 274–286.

Baum, A., & Davis, G. E. (1976). Spatial and social aspects of crowding perception. *Environment and Behavior, 8,* 527–545.

Baum, A., Davis, G. E., & Valins, S. (1979). Generating behavioral data for the design process. In J. R. Aiello and A. Baum (Eds.), *Residential crowding and design.* New York: Plenum Press.

Baum, A., & Valins, S. (1977). *Architectural and social behavior: Psychological studies of social density.* Hillsdale, NJ: Erlbaum.

Baxter, J. C. (1970). Interpersonal spacing in natural settings. *Sociometry, 33,* 444–456.

Beaglehole, R., & Jackson, R. (1991). Alcohol, cardiovascular diseases and total mortality: the epidemiological evidence. *The New Zealand Medical Journal, 104*(914), 249–51.

Bear, M. F., Connors, B. W., & Paradiso, M. A. (2002). *Neuroscience: Exploring the brain,* (2d ed.). Hagerstown, MD: Lippincott Williams & Wilkins.

Beauchamp, G. K., & Mason, J. R. (1991). In R. C. Bolles (Ed.) (1999). *The hedonics of taste.* Hillsdale, NJ: Lawrence Erlbaum.

Beauchemin, K. M., & Hays, P. (1998). Dying in the dark: Sunshine, gender and outcomes in myocardial infarction. *Journal of the Royal Society of Medicine, 91,* 352–354.

Becker, C., & Murrmann, S. K. (1999). The effect of cultural orientation on the service timing preferences of customers in casual dining operations: An exploratory study. *International Journal of Hospitality Management, 18*(1), 59–65.

Becker, F. D. (1986). Loosely coupled settings: A strategy for computer-aided work decentralization. In B. Staw & L. L. Cumming (Eds.), *Research in Organizational Behavior.* Greenwich, CT: JAI Press.

Becker, F. D., & Coniglio, C. (1975). Environmental messages: Personalization and territory. *Humanities, 11,* 55–74.

Becker, F., & Steele, F. (1995). *Workplace by Design.* San Francisco: Jossey-Bass.

Bedford, G. (2003). *Women's roles and the presence of gender equity in utopian societies.* Retrieved from http://athena.louisville.edu/a-s/english/subcultures/colors/red/g0bedf01

Bee, H. L., & Boyd, D. R. (2003). *Lifespan development.* Boston, MA: Pearson/Allyn & Bacon.

Belasco, J. A., & Stayer, R. C. (1993). *Flight of the buffalo: Soaring to excellence, learning to let employees lead.* New York: Warner Books.

Belfoure, C. (2005). *Monuments to money: The architecture of American banks.* Jefferson, NC: McFarland & Company.

Belk, R. W. (1992), Moving possessions: An analysis based on personal documents from the 1847–1869 Mormon migration. *Journal of Consumer Research, 19,* 339–361.

Bell, S. (1999). Image and consumer attraction to intraurban retail areas: An environmental psychology approach. *Journal of Retailing and Consumer Services, 6(2),* 67–78.

Bell, J., & Ternus, K. (2006). *Silent selling: Best practices and effective strategies in visual merchandising* (3rd ed.). New York, NY: Fairchild Publications, Inc.

Bell, P. A., Greene, T. C., Fisher, J. D., & Baum, A. (2001). *Environmental psychology* (5th ed.). Orlando, FL: Harcourt College Publishers.

Bell, P. A., Kline, L. M., & Barnard, W. A. (1988). Friendship and freedom of movement as moderators of sex differences in interpersonal distancing. *Journal of Social Psychology, 128,* 305-310.

Belsky, J. (2007). *Experiencing the Lifespan.* New York: Worth.

Benedetti, F., Colombo, C., Barbini, B., Campori, E., & Smeraldi, E. (2001). Morning sunlight reduces length of hospitalization in bipolar depression. *Journal of Affective Disorders, 62*(3), 221–223.

Bennett, E. L., Diamond, M. L., Krech, D., & Rosenzweig, M. R. (1964). Chemical and anatomical plasticity of brain. *Science, 146,* 610–619.

Bennett, M., & Lengacher, C. (2006). Humor and laughter may Influence health. I. History and background. *Evidenced Based Complement & Alternative Medicine, 3*(1), 61–63.

Benson, V., & Marano, M. A. (1994). Current estimates from the National health interview survey, 1993. National Center for Health Statistics. *Vital and Health Statistics, 10*(190). Hyattsville, MD: Department of Health and Human Services, Public Health Service Publication No. 95–1518.

Berger, A. A. (2005). *Shop 'til you drop: Consumer behavior and American culture.* Oxford, UK: Rowman & Littlefield Publishers, Inc.

Berger, K. S. (2006). *The developing person: Through childhood and adolescence.* New York: Worth.

Berk, L. E. (2006). *Child development* (7th ed). Boston, MA: Pearson/Allyn and Bacon.

Berkowitz, E. N., Hartley, S. W., Rudelius, W., & Kerin, R. A. (2003). *Marketing* (7th ed.).Columbus, OH: McGraw Hill.

Berlyne, D. E. (1960). *Conflict, arousal, and curiosity.* New York: McGraw-Hill.

Berlyne, D. E. (1971). *Aesthetics and psychobiology.* New York: Appleton-Century-Crofts.

Berlyne, D. E. (1974). *Studies in the new experimental aesthetics: Steps toward an objective psychology of aesthetic appreciation.* New York: Halsted Press.

Bernardi, N., & Kowaltowski, D. (2006). Environmental comfort in school buildings: A case study of awareness and participation of users. *Environment and Behavior, 38*(2), 155–172.

Bernstein, L. (1999). Luxury and the hotel brand: Art, science, or fiction? *Cornell Hotel and Restaurant Administration Quarterly, 40*(1), 47–53.

Bess, F. (2000). Classroom acoustics: An overview. *Volta Review, 101,* 1–14.

Bihrle, A. M., Brownell, H. H., Powelson, J. A., & Gardner, H. (1986). Comprehension of humorous and nonhumorous materials by left and right brain-damaged patients. *Brain Cognition, 5,* 399–411.

Bilich, K. A. (2006). Baby's developing senses: Find out how your new baby learns to see, hear, smell, touch, and taste. *American Baby.* Retrieved from http://health.discovery.com/centers/pregnancy/americanbaby/senses.html

Birren, F. (1978). *Color and human response.* Hoboken, NJ: John Wiley & Sons.

Birren, F., (1997). *The power of color.* Secaucus, NJ: Carol Publishing Group.

Bitgood, S., & Tisdal, C. (1996). Does lobby orientation influence visitor satisfaction? *Visitor Behavior, 11*(3), 13–16.

Bixler, R. D., & Floyd, M. F. (1997). Nature is scary, disgusting, and uncomfortable. *Environment and Behavior, 29,* 443–467.

Black, C., Grise, K., Heitmeyer, J., & Readdick, C. A. (2001). Sun protection: Knowledge, attitude, and perceived behavior of parents and observed dress of preschool children. *Family and Consumer Sciences Research Journal, 30*(1), 93–109.

Blanchfield, B. B., et al. (2001). The severely to profoundly hearing-impaired population in the United States: Prevalence estimates and demographics. *Journal of the American Academy of Audiology, 12,* 183–189.

Bloomer, K. C., & Moore, C. (1977). *Body, memory and architecture*. New Haven, CT: Yale University Press.

Blum, M. D. (1988). *The silent speech of politicians: Body language in government*. San Diego, CA: Brenner Information Group.

Blumberg, R., & Devlin, A. S. (2006). Design issues in hospitals: The adolescent client. *Environment and Behavior, 38*(3), 293–317.

Boeree, C. G. (1998–2004). *The history of psychology*. Retrieved from www.ship.edu/~cgboeree/historyofpsych.html

Booth, T. (1985). *Home truths: Old people's homes and the outcome of care*. Aldershot, Hants, UK: Gower.

Boschetti, M. A. (1987). Memories of childhood homes: Some contributions of environmental autobiography to interior design education and research. *Journal of Interior Design, 13*(2), 27–36.

Boschetti, M. A. (1995). Attachment to personal possessions: An interpretive study of the older person's experience. *Journal of Interior Design, 21*, 1–12.

Boschetti, M.A. (2002). An observational study of older people's use of standard U.S. kitchens. *Housing and Society, 29*(1/2), 1–12.

Bourassa, S. C. (1990). A paradigm for landscape aesthetics. *Environment and Behavior, 22*, 787–812.

Boyce, P., Hunter, C., & Howlett, O. (2003). *The benefits of daylight through windows*. Troy, NY: Rensselaer Polytechnic Institute.

Brabyn, J. A., Haegerström-Portnoy, G., Schneck, M. E., & Lott, L. A. (2000). Visual impairments in elderly people under everyday viewing conditions. *Journal of Visual Impairments and Blindness, 94*, 741–755.

Braille Institute of America, Inc. (2006). *General Statistics on Blindness*. Retrieved from www.brailleinstitute.org

Brannon, L., & Feist, J. (1997). *Health psychology: An introduction to behavior and health* (3rd ed.). Pacific Grove, CA: Brooks/Cole.

Brantingham, P. (1997). Understanding and controlling crime and fear of crime: Conflicts and trade-offs in crime prevention planning. In S. P. Lab (Ed.), *Crime Prevention at a Crossroads* (pp. 4–60). Cincinnati, OH: Anderson.

Brasche, S., Bullinger, M., Morfeld, M., Gebhardt, H. J., & Bischof, W. (2001). Why do women suffer from sick building syndrome more often than men? Subjective higher sensitivity versus objective causes. *Indoor Air, 11*, 217–222.

Brehm, J. W. (1966). *A theory of psychological resistance*. New York: Academic Press.

Brennan, A., Chugh, J. S., & Kline, T. (2002). Traditional versus open office design: A longitudinal field study. *Environment and Behavior, 34*, 279–299.

Brill, M., Weidemann, S., Alard, L., Olson, J., & Keable, E. (2001). *Disproving widespread myths about workplace design*. Jasper, IN: Kimball International.

Brock, L. (2005). The importance of environmental conditions, especially temperature, in the operating room and intensive care ward. *British Journal of Surgery, 62*, 253–258.

Bronzaft, A. L., Ahern, K. D, McGinn, R. O'Connor, J., & Savino, B. (1998). Aircraft noise: A potential health hazard. *Environment and Behavior, 30*, 101–113.

Brown University. (2008, April, 22). *Methods for improving outcomes in surgical procedures. Biology 1080 - organ replacement*. Retrieved from http://biomed.brown.edu/Courses/BI108/BI108_2008_Groups/group12/Roboticsurgery.html

Brown, B. B., & Perkins, D. D. (1992). Disruptions in place attachment. In I. Altman & S. M. Low (Eds.), *Place attachment: Human behavior and the environment* (Vol. 12, pp. 279–304). New York: Plenum Press.

Brown, D., Sijpkes, P., & MacLean, M. (1986). The community role of public indoor space. *Journal of Architecture and Planning Research, 3*, 161–172.

Brownell, H. H., Michel, D., Powelson, J., & Gardner, H. (1983). Surprise but not coherence: sensitivity to verbal humor in right-hemisphere patients. *Brain Language, 18*, 20–27.

Brunswik, E. (1942). Organismic achievement and environmental probability. *Psychological Review, 50*, 255–272.

Brunswik, E. (1956). *Perception and the representative design of psychological experiments*. Berkeley: University of California Press.

Burns, P. C. (1998). Wayfinding errors while driving. *Journal of Environmental Psychology, 18*, 209–217.

Busch-Vishniac, I. J., West, J. E., Barnhill, C., Hunter, T., Orellana, D., & Chivukula, R. (2005). Noise levels in Johns Hopkins Hospital. *Journal of the Acoustical Society of America, 118*, 3629–3645.

Butler, D. L., & Biner, P. M. (1987). Preferred lighting levels: Variability among settings, behaviors and individuals. *Environment and Behavior, 19*, 695–721.

Butler, D. L., & Steuerwald, B. L. (1991). Effects of view and room size on window size preferences made in models. *Environment and Behavior, 23*, 334–358.

Cahill, L., & McGaugh, J. (1998). Mechanisms of emotional arousal and lasting declarative memory. *Trends in Neuroscience, 21,* 294–299.

Cairns, G. (2002). Aesthetics, morality and power: Design as espoused freedom and implicit control. *Human Relations, 55,* 799–820.

Camgöz, N., Yener, C., & Güvenç, D. (2004). Effects of hue, saturation, and brightness: Part 2: Attention. *Color Research and Application, 29*(1), 20–28.

Campbell, D. E. (1979). Interior office design and visitor response. *Journal of Applied Psychology, 64,* 648-653.

Campbell, J. M. (1983). Ambient stressors. *Environment and Behavior, 15,* 355–380.

Candland, D. K. (1995). *Feral children and clever animals: Reflections on human nature.* New York: Oxford University Press.

Canter, D. (1983). The purposive evaluation of places: A facet approach. *Environment and Behavior, 15,* 659–698.

Canter, D. (1997). The facets of place. In G. T. Moore & R. W. Marans (Eds.). *Advances in environment, behavior, and cesign* (Vol. 4, pp. 109–147). New York: Plenum Press.

Canter, D. V. (1976). *Environmental interaction psychological approaches to our physical surroundings.* New York: International University Press.

Capizzano, J., Adams, G., & Sonenstein, F. L. (2000). *Childcare arrangements for children under five.* Washington, D.C.: Urban Institute.

Caplan, L. (2005). *American Academy of Neurology Press Quality of Life Guide Series.* St. Paul, MN: AAN Press.

Carlopio, J. R. (1996). Construct validity of a physical work environment satisfaction questionnaire. *Journal of Occupational Health Psychology, 1,* 330-334, C1, 11.

Carnegie Corporation of New York. (1994). *The quiet crisis. Starting points: Meeting the needs of our youngest children (abridged text).* New York: Carnegie Corporation.

Carnegie Council on Adolescent Development. (n.d.). Retrieved from http://cyd.aed.org/cost/time.html

Carr, R. F. (2009, June 2). *Health care facilities, WBDG Health Care Subcommittee.* Retrieved from http://www.wbdg.org/design/health_care.php

Cartwright, R., & Baird, C. (1999). *The development and growth of the cruise industry.* Oxford, UK: Butterworth-Heinemann.

Castrogiovanni, A. (2004, May 4). *Incidence and prevalence of hearing loss and hearing aid use in the U.S.* (2004 ed.). Retrieved from www.asha.org/members/research/reports/hearing.htm

Centers for Disease Control. (2006). *National Diabetes Fact Sheet.* Retrieved from www.CDC.gov

Center for Inclusive Design and Environmental Access. (2001). *Universal design New York.* New York: A City of New York Office of the Mayor Publication.

Chan, R. Y. K. (1998). Choice processes of luxury hotels in China: Application of the Fishbein–Ajzen model. *Journal of Hospitality & Leisure Marketing, 5*(4), 5–21.

Chapman, A. (2000). The difference it has made: The impact of the women's movement on education. *Independent School, 60*(1), 20–30.

Chapman, T., & Hockey, J. (Eds.). 1999. *Ideal homes? Social change and domestic life.* New York: Routledge.

Chappell, N. L., & Reid, R. C. (2000). Dimensions of care for dementia sufferers in long-term care institutions: Are they related to outcomes? *Journal of Gerontology: Social Sciences, 55B-4,* S234-S244.

Chawla, L. (1991). Homes for children in a changing society. In E. H. Zube & G. T. Moore (Eds.), *Advances in environment, behavior, and design* (Vol. 3, pp. 187–228). New York: Plenum Press.

Chein, I. (1954). The environment as a determinant of behavior. *Journal of Social Psychology, 39,* 115–137.

Chen, H. C., et al. (1996). Stepping over obstacles: Dividing attention impairs performance of old more than young adults. *Journal of Gerontology, 51A*(3), M116–M122.

Cheong, A. M. Y., Legge, G., Lawrence, M., Cheung, S., & Ruff, M. (2007). Relationship between slow visual processing and reading speed in people with macular degeneration. *Vision Research, 47,* 2943-2955.

Children's Hospital Boston. (2005). *Newborns: Senses.* Retrieved from www.childrenshospital.org/az/Site1356/mainpageS1356P0.html

Chong, R. K. Y., Horak, F. B., Frank, J., & Kaye, J. (1999). Sensory organization for balance: Specific deficits in Alzheimer's but not in Parkinson's disease. *Journal of Gerontology: Medical Sciences, 54A-3,* M122–M128.

Chrea, C., et al. (2004). Culture and odor categorization: Agreement between cultures depends upon the odors. *Food Quality and Preference, 15,* 669–679.

City of Los Angeles Waste Generation Study. (1993). *City of Los Angeles waste generation study.* Los Angeles: The City of Los Angeles Department of Public Works Bureau of Sanitation.

Clark, R., & Quinn, J. (2002, Summer). New patterns of work and retirement at the beginning of the twenty-first century. *Generations,* 17–24.

ClassRoomTools. (2002). *Sex and death among the ice cubes: Subliminal messages in advertising.* Retrieved from www.classroomtools.com/sublimad.htm

Clifford, C. (December, 1985). New scent wave. *Self,* 115–117.

Cobb, E. (1977). *The ecology of imagination in childhood.* New York: Columbia University Press.

Cochran, C. D., Hale, W. D., & Hissam, C. P. (1984). Personal space requirements in indoor versus outdoor locations. *Journal of Psychology, 117,* 121–123.

Cohen, D. J., & Volkmar, F. R. (1997). *Handbook of autism and pervasive developmental disorders.* New York: John Wiley & Sons.

Cognitive Atlas (n.d.) Prejudice. Retrieved from http://www.cognitiveatlas.org/term/prejudice

Cohen, S., & Trostle, S. L. (1990). Young children's preferences for school-related physical-environment setting characteristics. *Environment and Behavior, 22,* 753–766.

Cohen, U., & Weisman G., (1991). *Holding on to home: Designing environments for people with Alzheimer's.* Baltimore, MD: Johns Hopkins University Press.

Cole, M., Cole, S. R., & Lightfoot, C. (2005). *The development of children* (5th ed.). New York: Worth.

Comery, T. A., Shah R., & Greenough, W. T. (1995). Differential rearing alters spine density on medium-sized spiny neurons in the rat corpus striatum: Evidence for association of morphological plasticity with early response gene expression. *Neurobiology of Learning and Memory 63,* 217–219.

Confino-Rehder, S. (2008). Cost/benefit of visit-ability and universal design for single family homes: A USA comparison. Building Comfortable and Liveable Environments for All. International Meeting on Economic Issues Of Accessibility. Atlanta, GA: Georgia Institute of Technology. Retrieved from http://www.irbdirekt.de/daten/iconda/CIB8885.pdf.

Connell, B. R., & Sanford, J. A. (2001). Difficulty, dependence, and housing accessibility for people aging with a disability. *Journal of Architectural and Planning Research, 18*(3), 234–242.

Connolly, C., (2005). Growth and development of a specialty: The professionalization of child healthcare. *Pediatric Nursing 31,* 309–311.

Cooper-Marcus, C. (1995). *House as a mirror of self.* Newburyport, MA: Red Wheel/Conari Press.

Cooper-Marcus, C., & Sarkissian, W. (1986). *Housing as if people mattered: Site design guidelines for the planning of medium-density family housing (California Series in Urban Development).* Berkeley, CA: University of California Press.

Cooper, J., et al. (1984) *Cooperative learning and college instruction: Effective use of student learning teams.* California State University Foundation publication.

COPE Project. (2003). *Open-plan office lighting environment.* Ottawa, Canada: Institute for Research in Construction/National Research Council (IRC/NRC). Retrieved from http://irc.nrc-cnrc.gc.ca/ie/cope/04-Lighting.html

Courage, M. L., Edison, S. C., & Howe, M. L. (2004). Variability in the early development of visual self-recognition. *Infant, Behavior, and Development, 27,* 509–532.

Cowan, W. M., Fawcett, J. W., O'Leary, D. D. M., & Stanfield, B. B. (1984). Regressive events in neurogenesis. *Science, 225,* 1258–1265.

Cox, V. C., Paulus, P. B., & McCain, G. (1984). Prison crowding research: The relevance of prison housing standards and a general approach regarding crowding phenomena. *American Psychologist, 39,* 1148–1160.

Crandell, C. C., & Smaldino J. J. (2000). Classroom acoustics for children with normal hearing and with hearing impairment. *Language, Speech, and Hearing Services in the Schools, 31,* 362–370.

Craven, R. F., & Hirnle, C. J. (2008). *Fundamentals of nursing: Human health and function* (6th ed.). Philadelphia, PA: Lippincott Williams & Wilkins.

Crawford, M., & Unger, R. (2000). *Women and gender: A feminist ssychology* (3rd ed.). New York: McGraw Hill.

Crawford, N. (2002). New ways to stop bullying. *APA Monitor On Psychology, 33.* Retrieved from http://www.apa.org/monitor/oct02/bullying.html

Creekmore, W. N. (1987). Effective use of classroom walls. *Academic Therapy, 22,* 341–348.

Crow, W. J., & Bull, J. L. (1975). *Robbery deterrence: An applied behavioral science demonstration.* La Jolla, CA: Western Behavioral Sciences Institute.

Crowe, T. D. (2000). *Crime prevention through environmental design: Applications of architectural design and space management concepts* (2nd ed.). Stoneham, MA: Butterworth-Heinemann.

Csikszentmihalyi, M., & Rochberg-Halton, E. (1981). *The meaning of things.* Cambridge: Cambridge University Press.

Cueva, M. (2010). A living spiral of understanding: Community-based adult education. *New Directions for Adult and Continuing Education, 125,* 79–90.

Cunningham, M., & Cox, E. O. (2003). Hearing assessment in infants and children: Recommendations beyond neonatal screening. *Pediatrics, 111,* 436–440.

Curtiss, S. (1977). *Genie: A psycholinguistic study of a modern-day wild child.* St. Louis, MO: Academic Press.

Cutting, J. E. (1996). Wayfinding from multiple sources of local information in retinal flow. *Journal of Experimental Psychology: Human Perception and Performance, 22,* 1299–1313.

Dacey, J. S., & Fiore, L. B. (2000). *Your anxious child.* San Francisco: Jossey-Bass.

D'Allesio, S., & Stolzenberg, L. (1990). A crime of convenience: The environment and convenience store robbery. *Environment and Behavior, 22,* 255–271.

Dandridge, T. C., Mitroff, I., & Joyce, W. F. (1980). Organizational symbolism: A topic to expand organizational analysis. *The Academy of Management Review, 5*(1), 77–82.

Dark-Freudeman, A., West, R. L., & Viverito, K. (2006). Future selves and aging: Older adults' fears about memory. *Educational Gerontology, 32,* 85-109.

Day, K., & Calkins, M. P. (2002). Design and dementia. In R. B. Bechtel & A. Churchman (Eds.), *Handbook of Environmental Psychology* (pp. 374-393). New York: John Wiley & Sons.

Day, K., & Cohen, U. (2000). The role of culture in designing environments for people with dementia: A study of Russian Jewish immigrants. *Environment and Behavior, 32,* 361–399.

Deaux, K. K., & LaFrance, M. (1998). Gender. In D. T. Gilbert, S. Fiske & G. Lindzey (Eds.). *The handbook of social psychology* (4th ed.). New York: McGraw

DeCasper A., & Spence, M. J. (1986). Prenatal maternal speech influences newborn's perception of speech sounds. *Infant Behavior and Development, 9,* 133–150.

Deci, E. L., & Ryan, R. M. (1987). The support of autonomy and the control of behavior. *Journal of Personality and Social Psychology, 53,* 1024–1037.

DeMerchant, E. A., & Beamish, J. O. (1995). Universal design in residential spaces. *Housing and Society, 22(1/2),* 77–91.

Dennis, W. (1973) *Children of the creche.* New York: Appleton-Century-Crofts.

Dermody, M. B. (2002). Recruitment and retention practices in independent and chain restaurants. *International Journal of Hospitality and Tourism Administration, 3*(1), 107–117.

Desai, M., Pratt, L. A., Lentzner, H., & Robinson, K. N. (2001). Trends in vision and hearing among older Americans. *Aging Trends, 2,* 1-8.

Desor, J. A. (1972). Toward a psychological theory of crowding. *Journal of Personality and Social Psychology, 21,* 79–83.

Diamond, I., McDonagh, A. F., Wilson, C. B., Granelli, S. G., Nielsen, S., & Jaenicke, R. (1972). Photodynamic therapy of malignant tumours. *Lancet, ii,* 1175.

Diamond, M. C., & Hopson, J. (1998). *Magic trees of the mind: How to nurture your child's intelligence, creativity, and healthy emotions from birth through adolescence.* New York: Dutton.

Dickens, W. T., & Flynn, J. R. (2006) Black Americans reduce the racial IQ gap: evidence from standardization samples. *Psychological Science, 17,* 913–920.

Dickinson, J., & McLain-Kark, J. (1996). Wandering behavior associated with Alzheimer's disease and related dementias: Implications for designers. *Journal of Interior Design, 22*(1), 32–38.

Dierkx, R. J. (2003). Toward community-based architectural programming and development of inclusive learning environments in Nairobi's slums. *Children, Youth, and Environments, 13*(1). Retrieved from http://colorado.edu/journals/cye

DiSalvo, C., & Gemperlem, F. (2003). *From seduction to fulfillment: The uses of anthropomorphic form in design: Designing pleasurable products and interfaces.* Pittsburgh, PA: ACM Press.

Diseases Database, (2006). Retinitis Pigmentosa. Retrieved September 4, 2006 from www.DiseasesDatatbase.com.

Dobson, V., & Teller, D. Y. (1978). Visual acuity in human infants: A review and comparison of behavioral and electrophysiological studies. *Vision Research, 18,* 1469–1483.

Dogu, U., & Erkip, F. (2002). Spatial factors affecting wayfinding and orientation: A case study in a shopping mall. *Environment and Behavior, 32,* 731–755.

Donald, I., & Siu, O. L. (2001). Moderating the stress of environmental conditions: The effect of organizational commitment in Hong Kong and China. *Journal of Environmental Psychology, 21,* 353–368.

Donovan, R. J., & Rossiter, J. R. (1982). Store atmosphere: An environmental psychology approach. *Journal of Retailing, 58,* 34–57.

Dorward, F. M. C., & Day, R. H. (1997). Loss of 3-D shape constancy in interior spaces: The basis of the Ames-room illusion. *Perception, 26,* 707–718.

Dovey, K. (1985). The quest for authenticity and the replication of environmental meaning. In D. Seamon, & R. Mugerauer (Eds.), *Dwelling, place and environment: Towards a phenomenology of person and word* (pp. 33–50). Dordrecht: Martinus Nijhoff.

Dovey, K. (1993). Dwelling, archetype and ideology. *Center, 8,* 9–21.

Dubois, M., (2003). Shading devices and daylight quality: An evaluation based on simple performance indicators. *Lighting Research and Technology, 35*(1), 61–76.

Dudley, S. K., & Carr, J. M. (2004). Vigilance: The experience of parents staying at the bedside of hospitalized children. *Journal of Pediatric Nursing, 19,* 267–275.

Dunlap, D. W. (1997, June 1). Architecture in the age of accessibility. *The New York Times.* Retrieved from http://nclive.lib.unc.edu:2074/pqdweb?did=12172079&sid=1&Fmt=3&clientId=15094&RQT=309&VName=PQD

Dunn, R., Krimsky, J. S., Murray, J. B., & Quinn, P. J. (1985). Light up their lives: A research on the effects of lighting on children's achievement and behavior. *The Reading Teacher, 38,* 863–869.

Du Plessis, E. (2005). *The advertised mind: Ground-breaking insights into how our brains respond to advertising.* London, UK: Millward Brown.

Dyl, J., & Wapner, S. (1996). Age and gender differences in the nature, meaning, and function of cherished possessions for children and adolescents. *Journal of Experimental Child Psychology, 6,* 340–377.

Easthope, H. (2004). A place called home. *Housing, Theory and Society, 21,* 128–138.

Easton, R., & McCall, W. (Eds.) (1995). *Santa Barbara architecture.* Santa Barbara, CA: Capra Press.

Eccles, J. S., Jacobs, J. E., & Harold, R. D. (1990). Gender roles stereotypes, expectancy effects, and parents' socialization of gender differences. *Journal of Social Issues, 46,* 186–201.

Edney, J. J. (1974) Human territoriality. *Psychological Bulletin, 81,* 959–975.

Edwards, L., & Torcellini, P. (2002). *A literature review of the effects of natural light on building occupants (Technical report).* Golden, CO: National Renewable Energy Laboratory.

Ehrenfeld, J., Kourtev, P., & Huang, W. (2001). Changes in soil functions following invasions of exotic understory plants in deciduous forests. *Ecological Applications, 11,* 1287–1300.

Eibl-Eibesfeldt, I. (1970). *Ethology. The biology of behavior.* New York: Holt, Rinehart and Winston.

Elson, J. M., & Muller, C.C. (2002). Including the "restaurant mix" in vacation ownership and resort development planning. *International Journal of Hospitality Management, 21,* 277–284.

Energy Information Administration. (2009). International Energy Outlook 2009 (IEO2009) [Report #:DOE/EIA-0484(2009)] Retrieved from www.eia.doe.gov/oiaf/ieo/world.html

Engelbrecht, K. (2003). *Impact of color on learning.* (W305). Chicago: NeoCon.

Erickson, K. (2004). Bodies at work: Performing service in American restaurants. *Space and Culture, 7*(1), 76–89.

Erin, J. N., & Koenig, A. J. (1997). The student with a visual and a learning disability. *Journal of Learning Disabilities, 30,* 309–320.

Eshelman, P. E., & Evans, G. W. (2002). Home again: Environmental predictors of place attachment and self-esteem for new retirement community residents. *Journal of Interior Design, 28*(1), 3–9.

Espinosa, M. A., Ungar, S., Ochaita, E., Blades, M., & Spencer, C. (1998). Comparing methods for introducing blind and visually impaired people to unfamiliar urban environments. *Journal of Environmental Psychology, 18,* 277–287.

Evans, G. W. (2004). The environment of childhood poverty. *American Psychologist, 59*(2), 77–92.

Evans, G. W., & Lepore, S. J. (1993). Nonauditory effects of noise on children: A critical review. *Children's Environments, 10*(1), 31–51.

Evans, G. W., Lepore, S. J., & Schroeder, A. (1996). The role of interior design elements in human responses to crowding. *Journal of Personality and Social Psychology, 70*(1), 41–46.

Evans, G. W., Maxwell, L. E., & Hart, B. (1999). Parental language and verbal responsiveness to children in crowded homes. *Developmental Psychology, 35,* 1020–1023.

Evans, G. W., Saegert, S., & Harris, R. (2001). Residential density and psychological health among children in low-income families. *Environment and Behavior, 33*(2), 165–180.

Evans, G. W., Saltzman, H., & Cooperman, J. (2001). Housing quality and children's socioemotional health. *Environment and Behavior, 33,* 389–399.

Evans, G. W., Lercher, P., & Kofler, W. W. (2002). Crowding and children's mental health: The role of house type. *Journal of Environmental Psychology, 22*(3), 221–231.

Ewer, R. F. (1968). *Ethology of mammals.* New York: Plenum Press.

Fabian, J. (2009). Office Politics. *Job circle.* Retrieved from http://jobcircle.com/career/coach/jf_2003_04.html

Fagan, J. F. (1976). Infant's recognition of invariant features of faces. *Child Development, 47,* 627–638.

Failey, A., Bursor, D. E., & Musemeche, R. A. (1979). The impact of color and lighting in schools. *Council of Educational Facility Planners Journal,* 16–18.

Fallin, K., Wallinga, C., & Coleman, M. (2001). Helping children cope with stress in the classroom setting. *Childhood Education, 78*(1), 17–24.

Fanurik, D., et al. (2000). Hospital room or treatment room: Where should inpatient pediatric procedures be performed? *Children's Health Care. 29*(2), 103–111.

Fass, R., et al. (2008). The effect of auditory stress on perception of intraesophageal acid in patients with gastroesophageal reflux disease. *Gastroenterology, 134,* 696–705.

Fehrman, K. R. (1987). The effects of interior pigment color on school task performance mediated by arousal. *Dissertation Abstracts International, 48*(4A), 819.

Feldman, R. M. (1990). Settlement identity: psychological bonds with home places in a mobile society. *Environment and Behavior, 22,* 183-229.

Feldman, R. S. (2007). *Child Development* (4th ed.). Upper Saddle River, NJ: Pearson Prentice Hall.

Felstead, A., Jewson, N., Phizacklea, A., & Walters, S. (n.d.). *A statistical portrait of working at home in the UK: Evidence from the labour force survey. ESRC Future of Work Working Paper no. 4.* Retrieved from http://www.flexibility.co.uk/flexwork/location/leicester.htm

Femia, E., Zarit, S. H., & Johansson, B. (1997). Predicting change in activities of daily living: A longitudinal study of the oldest old. *Journal of Gerontology: Psychological Sciences, 52B,* P292–P304.

Fernald, A. (2001). Hearing, listening, and understanding: Auditory development in infantcy. In G. Bremner & A. Fogel, (Eds.), *Blackwell handbook of infant development* (pp. 35–70). Malden, MA: Blackwell.

Fiore, C. (1999). Awakening the tech bug in girls. *Learning and leading with technology, 26*(5), 10–17.

Fisher, J. D., & Byrne, D. (1975). Sex differences in response to invasions of personal space. *Journal of Personality and Social Psychology, 32,* 15–21.

Fjørtoft, I. (2004). Landscape as playscape: The effects of natural environments on young child's play and motor development. *Young Child, Youth and Environments,* 14(2), 21–44.

Flexer, C. (1990). Audiological rehabilitation in the schools. *ASHA, 32,* 44–45.

Floyd, A. M. D. (2005). Challenging designs of neonatal intensive care units. *Critical Care Nurse, 25,* 59–66.

Flynn, J. R. (2006). First days in school. *School Planning and Management, 45*(2), 30–33.

Ford, D., & Kerle, K. (1981). Jail standards—A different perspective. *The Prison Journal, 16*(1), 23–35.

Fortune500. (2007). *Our annual ranking of America's largest corporations.* Retrieved from http://money.cnn.com/magazines/fortune/fortune500/2007/performers/companies/by_employees/index.html

Franck, K. A. (2002). Women and environment. In R. B. Bechtel & A. Churchman (Eds.), *Handbook of environmental psychology* (p. 349). New York: John Wiley & Sons.

Freedman, J. L., Levy, A. S., Buchanan, R. W., & Price, J. (1972). Crowding and human aggressiveness. *Journal of Experimental Social Psychology, 8,* 528–548.

Frewald, D. B. (1990). Preferences for older buildings: A psychological approach to architectural design. *Dissertation Abstracts International, 51*(1B), 414–415.

Friedman, D. S., et al. (2004). Prevalence of age-related macular degeneration in the United States. *Archives of Ophthalmology. 122,* 564–572.

Friedmann, S., & Thompson, J. A. (1995). Intimate space issues in preschool environments. *Journal of Interior Design, 21*(1), 13–20.

Friedrich, M. J. (1999). The arts of healing. *JAMA Medical News & Perspectives, 281, 19,* 1779–1781.

Fukunaga, A., Uematsu, H., & Sugimoto, K. (2005). Influences of aging on taste perception and oral somatic sensation. *The Journals of Gerontology Series A: Biological Sciences and Medical Sciences, 60,* 109–113.

Fulberg, P. (2003). Using sonic branding in the retail environment–An easy and effective way to create consumer brand loyalty while enhancing the in-store experience. *Journal of Consumer Behaviour, 3*(2), 193–198.

Galer, I. A. R., Ed. (1987). *Applied ergonomics handbook.* London: Butterworths.

Ganchrow, J.R. (1995). Ontogeny of human taste perception. In R. L. Doty (Ed.). *Handbook of Olfaction and Gustation* (pp. 715–729). New York: Dekker.

Ganoe, C. J. (1999). Design as narrative: A theory of inhabiting interior space. *Journal of Interior Design, 25*(2), 1-15.

Gärling, T., Lindberg, E., & Mantyla, T. (1983). Orientation in buildings: Effects of familiarity, visual access, and orientation aids. Journal of Applied Psychology, *68*, 177–186.

Georgia Tech (2008, November 20). *Brain reorganizes to adjust for loss of vision*. Press Release. Retrieved from www.gatech.edu/newsroom/release.html?id=2312

Gergen, K. J., Gergen, M. K., & Barton, W. H. (1973). Deviance in the dark. *Psychology Today, 7*, 129–130.

Gibbs, A. (2007). Horrified: Embodied vision, media affect and the images from Abu Gharib. In D. Staines (Ed.), Interrogating the war on terror: *Interdisciplinary perspectives*. Newcastle, UK: Cambridge Scholars.

Gibson, J. J. (1976). *The theory of affordances and the design of the environment*. Paper presented at the annual meetings of the American Society for Aesthetics, Toronto.

Gibson, J. J. (1979). *An ecological approach to visual perception*. Boston: Houghton Mifflin.

Gibson, J. J. (1986). *The ecological approach to visual perception*. Hillsdale, NJ: Lawrence Erlbaum.

Gibson, J. J. (1986). *The ecological approach to visual perception*. Hillsdale, NJ: Lawrence Erlbaum.

Gibson, J. J. (1996). *The ecological approach to visual perception*. Hillsdale, NJ: Lawrence Erlbaum.

Gies, E. (2006). *The health benefits of parks: How parks help keep Americans and their communities fit and healthy*. San Francisco, CA: The Trust for Public Land.

Gifford, R. (1976). Environmental numbness in the classroom. *Journal of Experimental Education, 44*(3), 4–7.

Gifford, R. (1982). Projected interpersonal distances and orientation choices: Personality, sex, and social situation. *Social Psychology Quarterly, 45,* 145-152.

Gifford, R. (1983) The experience of personal space: Perception of interpersonal distance. *Journal of Nonverbal Behavior, 7,* 170–178.

Gifford, R. (1999). *The adjustment of the elderly to congregate care housing*. Report to the Canada Mortgage and Housing Corporation.

Gifford, R. (2002). *Environmental psychology: Practice and principles* (3rd ed.). Colville, WA: Optimal Books.

Gifford, R., & Ng, C. F. (1983). The relative contribution of visual and auditory cues to environmental perception. *Journal of Environmental Psychology, 3,* 375–384.

Gifford, R., & Price, J. (1979). Personal space in nursery school children. *Canadian Journal of Behavioral Science, 11,* 318–326.

Gillie, O. (2004). Sunlight robbery. *Health Research Forum*. Health Research Forum Occasional Reports: No 1.

Gignac, M. A. M., Cott, C., & Badley, E. M. (2000). Adaptation to chronic illness and disability and its relationship to perceptions of independence and dependence. *Journal of Gerontology Series B: Psychological Sciences and Social Sciences, 55B-6,* P362–P372.

Gilsdorf, E. (2004, September 1). Suburban warrior syndrome. *Psychology Today, 37.*

Givens, D. B. (1986). The big and the small: Toward a paleontology of gesture. *Sign Language Studies, 51,* 145–167.

Goldin, G. (1983). *Historic hospitals of Europe, 1200-1981*. Washington, DC: Department of Health and Human Services; Public Health Service; National Institutes of Health.

Goldstein, B. E. (2002). *Sensation and Perception* (6th ed.). Pacific Grove, CA: Wadsworth Group.

Goodsell, C. T. (1993). Architecture as a setting for governance: Introduction. *Journal of Architectural and Planning Research, 10,* 271–272.

Gosling, S. D., Ko, S. J., Mannarelli, T., & Morris, M. E. (2003). A room with a cue: Personality judgments based on offices and bedrooms. *Journal of Personality and Social Psychology, 83,* 379–398.

Gostin, L. O. (2001). National health information privacy: Regulations under the Health Insurance Portability Act. *JAMA, 285,* 3015–3021.

Gottfried, A. W., & Gottfried, A. E. (1984). Home environment and cognitive development in young children of middle-socioeconomic-status families. In A. W. Gottfried (Ed.), *Home environment and early cognitive development*. Orlando, FL: Academic Press.

Gould, E., Reeves, A. J., Graziano, M. S. A., & Gross, C. G., (1999). Neurogenesis in the neocortex of adult primates. *Science, 286,* 548–552.

Gowan, M. (2009, May, 12). SHHH! Keeps noise down, promotes healing. *Health Articles.* Retrieved from http://www.dukehealth.org/HealthLibrary/HealthArticles/shhh_keeps_noise_down_promotes_healing

Gray, D. B., Gould, M., & Bickenbach, J. E. (2003). Environmental barriers and disability. *Journal of Architectural and Planning Research*, 20(1), 29–37.

Greene, (2001). In Anderson, C. E., Burns, D. J., & Reid, J. S. (2003). The next evolutionary step for regional shopping malls: A measure of acceptance of new retail concepts as identified by different age groups of shoppers. *Journal of Shopping Center Research*, 10(2), 27-59.

Greenough W. T., & Chang F. L. F. (1988). Plasticity of synapse structure and pattern in the cerebral cortex. In A. Peters & E. G. Jones (Eds.), *Cerebral cortex: Development and maturation of cerebral cortex.* (Vol. 7, pp. 391–440). New York: Plenum Press.

Griffith, C. R. (1929). A comment upon the psychology of the audience. *Psychological Monographs, 30*(136), 36-47.

Guadagnino, C. (2008, June). Cultural competency for patient-centered care. *Physician's News Digest.* Retrieved from www.physiciansnews.com/spotlight/608.html

Gulian, E., & Thomas, J. R. (1986). The effects of noise, cognitive set and gender on mental arithmetic performance. *British Journal of Psychology, 77,* 503-511.

Gunier R. B., Hertz A., von Behren J., & Reynolds P. (2003). Traffic density in California: Socioeconomic and ethnic differences among potentially exposed children. *Journal of Exposure Analysis Environment Epidemiology, 13,* 240-246.

Gunnar, M. R., & Barr, R. G. (1998). Stress, early brain development, and behavior. *Infants and Young Children, 21*(1), 1-14.

Guski, R. (1999). Measuring retrospective annoyance in field studies: prerequisites, procedures and problems. *International Journal on Acoustic,* 85(Suppl. 1), S 293.

Gustafson, P. (2001). Meanings of place: Everyday experience and theoretical conceptualizations. *Journal of Environmental Psychology, 21,* 5–16.

Guthrie, S. E. (1997). Anthropomorphism: A definition and a theory. In R. W. Mitchell, N. S. Thompson, and H. L. Miles (Eds.). *Anthropomorphism, anecdotes, and animals* (pp. 50–58). Albany, NY: State University of New York Press.

Haber, G. M. (1980). Territorial invasion in the classroom: Invadee response. *Environment and Behavior, 12,* 17–31.

Hadjiyanni, T. (2000). Children and their housing: Insights from the island of Cyprus. *Housing and Society, 27*(2), 19–30.

Haines, D. (2003). *Neuroanatomy: An atlas of structures, sections, and systems* (6th ed.). Hagerstown, MD: Lippincott Williams & Wilkins.

Hall, E. T. (1969) *The Hidden Dimension.* Garden City, NY: Anchor Books.

Hallett, M., & Cogan, D. G. (1970). Episodic Unilateral Mydriasis in otherwise normal patients. *Archives of Ophthalmology, 84*(2), 130-136.

Ham-Rowbottom, K. A., Gifford, R., & Shaw, K. T. (1999). Defensible space theory and the police: Assessing the vulnerability of residences to burglary. *Journal of Environmental Psychology, 19*(2), 117–129.

Hambrick-Dixon, P. J. (1986). Effects of experimentally imposed noise on task performance of Black children attending day care centers near elevated subway trains. *Developmental Psychology, 22,* 259-264.

Hardy, M. (2002). Florida's aging population: Critical issues for Florida's future. Florida State University.

Harkness, S. P., & Groom, J. N. (1976). *Building without barriers for the disabled.* New York: Whitney Library of Design.

Harms, R. W. (May 2006). *Mayo Clinic guide to a healthy pregnancy.* New York: Harper Collins e-books.

Haroun, L., & Royce, L. (2003). *Teaching ideas and classroom activities for health care.* San Diego, CA: Delmar Cengage Learning.

Harrell, G., Hutt, M., & Anderson, J. (1980). Path analysis of buyer behavior under conditions of crowding. *Journal of Marketing Research, 17,* 45-51.

Harris, D. D., et al. (2008). *A practitioner's guide to evidence-based design.* Concord, CA: Center for Health Design.

Harris, J. R. (1998). *The nurture assumption: Why children turn out the way they do.* New York: Free Press.

Harris, L. R., Jenkin, M., & Zikovitz, D. C. (2000). Visual and non-visual cues in the perception of linear self motion. *Experimental Brain Research, 135,* 12–21.

Harris, P. B., Brown, B. B., & Werner, C. M. (1996). Privacy regulation and place attachment: Predicting attachments to a student family housing facility. *Journal of Environmental Psychology, 16,* 287-301.

Hasell, M. J., Peatross, F. D., & Bono, C. A. (1993). Gender choice and domestic space: Preferences for kitchens in married households. *Journal of Architectural and Planning Research, 10,* 1–22.

Hathaway, W. E. (1988). Educational facilities: Neutral with respect to learning and human performance. *CEFPI Journal, 26*(4), 8-12.

Hathaway, W. E. (1994). Non-visual effects of classroom lighting on children. *Educational Facility Planner, 32*(3), 12–16.

Hathaway, W. E., & Fielder, D. R. (1986). *A window on the future: A view of education and educational facilities.* Columbus, Ohio: Paper presented at the meeting of the Council of Educational Facility Planners.

Hayduk, L. A. (1985). Personal space: The conceptual and measurement implications of structural equation models. *Canadian Journal of Behavioral Science, 17,* 140–149.

Haynes, R., Reading, R., & Gale, S. (2003). Household and neighborhood risks for injury to 5- to 14-year-old children. *Social Science and Medicine, 57,* 625–636.

Healy, J. (2004). *Your child's growing mind: Brain development and learning from birth to adolescence* (3rd ed.). New York: Broadway Books.

Hebert S., & Lupien S. J. (2008). Salivary cortisol levels, subjective stress, and tinnitus intensity in tinnitus sufferers during noise exposure in the laboratory. *International Journal of Hygiene and Environmental Health, 212*(1), 37–44.

Heckel, R. V., & Hiers, J. M. (1977). Social distance and locus of control. *Journal of Clinical Psychology, 33,* 469–474.

Hedge, A., Sterling, E. M., & Sterling, T. D. (1986). *Building illness indices based on questionnaire responses.* Proceedings of the IAQ/86 ASHRAE Comference Managing Indoor Air for Health and Energy Conservation, 31–43, Atlanta, Georgia.

Hellige, J. B. (1993). *Hemispheric asymmetry: What's right and what's left.* Cambridge, MA: Harvard University Press.

Hellige, J. B., & Michimata, C. (1989). Categorization versus distance: Hemispheric differences for processing spatial information. *Memory and Cognition, 17,* 770–776.

Henderson, S. R. (1997). "New buildings create new people": The Pavillion schools of Weimar Frankfurt as a model of pedagogical reform. *Design Issues, 13*(1), 27–9.

Henry Dreyfuss Associates. (2002). *The elderly.* In *The measure of man and woman: Human factors in design* (pp. 33–43). New York: John Wiley & Sons.

Hepworth, M. (1996). Consumer culture and Social *Gerontology. Education and Ageing, 11,* 19–30.

Herrington, L. P. (1952). Effects of thermal environment on human action. *American School and University, 24,* 367–376.

Herrington, S. (1997). The received view of play and the subculture of infants. *Landscape Journal, 16*(2), 149–159.

Hertz, J. B. (2002). Authenticity, colonialism, and the struggle with modernity. *Journal of Architectural Education, 55*(4), 220–227.

Heslop, P., Smith, G. D., Metcalfe, C., Macleod, J., & Hart, C. (2002). Change in job satisfaction, and its association with self-reported stress, cardiovascular risk factors and mortality. *Social Science and Medicine, 54,* 1589–1599.

Hewitt, J., & Henley, R. (1987). Sex differences in reaction to spatial invasion. *Perception and Motor Skills, 64,* 809–810.

Hill, M. R. (1984). Walking, crossing streets, and choosing pedestrian routes: A survey of recent insights from the social/behavioral sciences. *University of Nebraska Studies, 66,* 1984.

Hobson, W. (2002). A research report on private residence clubs: A new concept for second home ownership. *International Journal of Hospitality Management, 21*(3), 285–300.

Hofstede, G. (2001). *Culture's consequences, comparing values, behaviors, institutions, and organizations across nations.* Thousand Oaks, CA: Sage Publications.

Holland, B., & Hogan, R. (1998). Remodeling the electronic cottage. *The Industrial-Organizational Psychologists, 36*(2), 21–22.

Holton, R. J. (1986). *Talcott Parsons on economy and society.* London: Routledge & Kegan Paul.

Horton, C. D. (1972). *Humanization of the learning environment.* Arlington, VA. Retrieved from ERIC database (ED066929)

Hounshell, M. (2005). *Braille.* Center for Disability Information & Referral. Retrieved from www.iidc.indiana.edu/cedir/kidsWeb/

House, J. S. (2001). Social isolation kills, but how and why? *Psychosomatic Medicine, 63,* 273–274.

Houser, K. W., Tiller, D. K., Becker, C. A., & Mistrick, R. G. (2002). The subjective response to linear fluorescent direct/indirect lighting systems. *Lighting Research and Technology, 34*(3), 243–263.

Hudson, K., & O'Connell, V. (2009, May 22). Recession turns malls into ghost towns. *The Wall Street Journal.* Retrieved from http://online.wsj.com/article/SB124294047987244803.html

Huitt, W., & Hummel, J. (2003). Piaget's theory of cognitive development. *Educational psychology interactive.* Valdosta, GA: Valdosta State University. Retrieved from http://www.edpsycinteractive.org/topics/cogsys/piaget.html

Hummon, D. M. (1992). Community attachment: Local sentiment and sense of place. In I. Altman & S. M. Low (Eds.), *Human behavior and environment; Advances in theory and research: Place attachment* (pp. 253–278). New York: Plenum.

Huttenlocher, P. R. (2002). *Neural plasticity: The effects of the environment on the development of the cerebral cortex*. Cambridge, MA: Harvard University Press.

Hutton, A. (2005). Consumer perspectives in adolescent ward design. *Journal of Clinical Nursing, 14*, 537–545.

Imrie, R. (2004). Urban geography, relevance and resistance to the 'poliy turn. *Urban Geography, 25,* 697–708.

Ivry, R., & Robertson, L. C. (1998). *The two sides of perception*. Cambridge, MA: MIT Press.

Jackson, M. (2002). Familiar and foreign bodies, a phenomenological exploration of the human-technology interface. *Journal of The Royal Anthropology Institute, 8,* 333–346.

Jacobs, G. H. (2 Jun 2005). Variations in primate color vision: Mechanisms and utility. *Evolutionary Anthropology: Issues, News, and Reviews, 3*(6), 196–205.

Jacobs, J. (1961). *The death and life of great American cities*. New York: Random House.

James, K. (2001). "I just gotta have my own room!": The bedroom as a leisure site for adolescent girls. *Journal of Leisure Research, 33*(1), 71–90.

Jans, L., Stoddard, S., & Kraus, L. (2004). *Chartbook on mental health and disability in the United States*. An Info Use Report. Washington, D.C.: U.S. Department of Education, National Institute on Disability and Rehabilitation Research. Retrieved from www.infouse.com/disabilitydata/mentalhealth/

Jay, P. (2002). Subjective criteria for lighting design. *Lighting Research and Technology, 34*(2), 87–99.

Jeffery, C. R., Hunter, R. D. & Griswald, J. (1987). Crime prevention and computer analysis of convenience store robberies in Tallahassee, Florida. *Security Systems, 1–4.*

Jewett, J., & Peterson, K. (1997). Stress and young children. Champaign, IL: Educational Resources Information Center (ERIC) Clearinghouse on Elementary and Early Childhood Education (EECE). Retrieved from http://ceep.crc.uiuc.edu/

John, O.vP., & Srivastava, S. (1999). The Big Five trait taxonomy: History, measurement, and theoretical perspectives. In L. A. Pervin & O. P. John (Eds.), *Handbook of personality: Theory and research* (2nd ed., pp. 102–138). New York: Guilford.

Johnson, J. M., & Hurley, J. (2002). A future ecology of urban parks: Reconnecting nature and community in the landscape of young children. *Landscape Journal, 21*(1-2_, 110–115.

Johnson, M. H., & Morton, J. (1991). *Biology and cognitive development: The case of face recognition*. Blackwell, Cambridge, MA: Blackwell.

Jones, E., & Prescott, E. (1978). *Dimensions of teaching learning environments II: Focus on day care*. Pasadena, CA: Pacific Oaks College

Jones, M. A. (1999). Entertaining shopping experiences: An exploratory investigation. *Journal of Retailing and Consumer Services, 6*(3), 129–139.

Jones T. A., & Greenough W. T. (1996). Ultrastructural evidence for increased contact between astrocytes and synapses in rats reared in a complex environment. *Neurobiology of Learning and Memory. 65,* 48–56.

Jones, W., & Pfau, P. (1987). *Either OR/igins*. Pamphlet Architecture #12: Building machines. New York: Princeton Architectural Press.

Jorgensen, K. M. (1999). Pain assessment and management in the newborn infant. *Journal of PeriAnesthesia Nursing,* 14(6), 349–356.

Juhasz, J. B., & Paxson, L. (1978). Personality and preference for architectural style. *Perceptual and Motor Skills, 47,* 341–343.

Kaiser, F. G., & Fuhrer, U. (1996). Dwelling: Speaking of an unnoticed universal language. *New Ideas in Psychology, 14,* 225–236.

Kandampully, J., & Suhartanto, D. (2003). The role of customer satisfaction and image in gaining customer loyalty in the hotel industry. *Journal of Hospitality and Leisure Marketing, 10*(1/2), 3–25.

Kanski, J. J. (2007). *Clinical ophthalmology: A systematic approach* (6th ed.). Woburn, MA: Butterworth-Heinemann.

Kaplan, R., & Dana, S. T. (2001). The nature of the view from home: Psychological benefits. *Environment and Behavior, 33*(4), 507–542.

Kaplan, S., & Kaplan, R. (1982a). *Cognition and environment: Functioning in an uncertain world*. New York: Praeger.

Kaplan, S., & Kaplan, R. (1982b). Cognition and environment: Functioning in an uncertain world. In Kopec, D. (2006). *Environmental Psychology for Design*. New York: Fairchild Books.

Kaplan, S., & Kaplan, R. (1989). *The experience of nature*. Cambridge, UK: Cambridge University Press.

Karlin, R. A., Epstein, Y., & Aiello, J. (1978). Strategies for the investigation of crowding. In A. Esser & B. Greenbie (Eds.), *Design for Communality and Privacy* (pp. 71–88). New York: Plenum.

Kauko, T. (2006). *Urban housing patterns in a tide of change.* Amsterdam, Netherlands: TuDelft.

Kawasaki, A., Anderson, S. C., & Kardon, R. H. (2008). Pupil light reflexes mediated by outer retinal versus inner retinal photoreceptors in normal subjects and patients with neuroretinal visual loss. *Acta Ophthalmologica 86,* s243 [Supplement]. Retrieved from http://dx.doi.org/10.1111/j.1755-3768.2008.432.x

Karnowski, S., & White, B. J. (2002). The role of facility managers in the diffusion of organizational telecommuting. *Environment and Behavior, 34,* 322–334.

Kaya, K., & Erkip, F. (2001). Satisfaction in a dormitory building: The effects of floor height on the perception of room size and crowding. *Environment and Behavior, 33*(1), 35–53.

Kaye, S. M., & Murray, M. A. (1982). Evaluations of an architectural space as a function of variations in furniture arrangement, furniture density, and windows. *Human Factors, 24,* 609–618.

Kazdin, A. E. (Ed.) (2000). *Encyclopedia of psychology,* (Vol. 7). New York: Oxford University Press.

Kearsley, G. (1998). *Explorations in learning and instruction: The theory into practice database: Gestalt theory.* George Washington University On-line. Retrieved from http://www.gwu.edu/~tip/wertheim.html

Keeley, R. M., & Edney, J. J. (1983). Model house designs for privacy, security, and social interaction. *Journal of Social Psychology, 119,* 219–228.

Kemper, A. R., & Downs, S. M. (2000). A cost-effectiveness analysis of newborn hearing screening strategies. *Archives of Pediatric and Adolescent Medicine, 154*(5), 484–488.

Kempler, D. (2005). *Neurocognitive disorders in aging.* Thousand Oaks, CA: Sage Publications.

Kenworthy, O. T., Klee, T., & Tharpe, A. M. (1990). Speech recognition ability of children with unilateral sensorineural hearing loss as a function of amplification, speech stimuli and listening condition. *Ear and Hearing, 11,* 264–270.

Kenyon, L. (1999). A home from home: Students' transitional experience of home. In T. Chapman & J. Hockey (Eds.), *Ideal homes? Social change and domestic life* (pp. 84–95). New York: Routledge.

Kern J. K., et al. (2006). The pattern of sensory processing abnormalities in autism. *Autism, 10,* 480–494.

Kettunen, J., et al. (2007). Associations of fine and ultrafine particulate air pollution with stroke mortality in an area of low air pollution levels. *Stroke, 38,* 918–922.

Killeen, J. F., Evans, G. W., & Danko, S. (2003). The role of permanent student artwork in students' sense of ownership in an elementary school. *Environment and Behavior, 35,* 250–263.

Kim, Y. K., Kim, E. Y., & Kang, J. (2003). Teens' mall shopping motivations: Functions of loneliness and media usage. *Family and Consumer Sciences Research Journal, 32*(2), 140–167.

King, J., & Marans, R. W. (1979). *The physical environment and the learning process.* (Report No. 320-ST2). Ann Arbor: University of Michigan Architectural Research Laboratory.

Kinsella K., & Velkoff V. A. (2001) An aging world: 2001. U.S. Government Printing Office, Washington, DC

Kirp, D. L. (2004, November 21). Life way after head start. *The New York Times Magazine,* Section 6, 32–38.

Kitchen, M. (2001). *Kaspar Hauser: Europe's child.* New York: Palgrave Macmillan, Ltd.

Knez, I. (1995). Effects of indoor lighting on mood and cognition. *Journal of Environmental Psychology, 15,* 39–51.

Knight, G., & Noyes, J. (1999). Children's behavior and the design of school furniture. *Ergonomics, 42,* 747–760.

Knowles, E. S. (1983). Social physics and the effects of others: Tests of the effects of audience size and distance on social judgments and behavior. *Journal of Personality and Social Psychology, 45,* 1263–1279.

Kochenderfer-Ladd, B., & Skinner, K. (2002). Children's coping strategies: Moderators of the effects of peer victimization? *Developmental Psychology, 38,* 267–278.

Kochkin, S., (2005). Marke Trak VII: Hearing loss population tops 31 million people. *The Hearing Review, 12*(7), 16–29.

Koger, S. M., & Scott, B. A. (2007). Psychology and environmental sustainability: A call for integration. *Teaching of Psychology, 34,* 10–18.

Kopec, D. (2007). *Designs that protect: Culturally sensitive designs for long term care facilities.* Washington, DC: National Council for Interior Design Qualification monograph series.

Kopec, D. (2006). Designing public schools. *ASID ICON, Fall,* 32–37.

Kopec, D. (2006). *Environmental psychology for design.* New York, NY: Fairchild Books.

Kopec, D. (2006). *Designing for the elderly population: The relationship between the elderly and the Americans with disabilities act.* Washington, DC: ASID Monograph Series.

Kopec, D., & LaCapra, D. (2008). Designing cognitive stimulating environments for infants and toddlers. *Journal of Interior Design, 33*(3), 50–62.

Kopec, D., & Han, L. (2008). Islam and the healthcare environment: Designing patient rooms. *Health Environments Research & Design Journal, 1*(4), 111–121.

Kopun, J. G., Stelmachowicz, P. G., Carney, E., & Schulte, L. (1992). Coupling of FM systems to individuals with unilateral hearing loss. *Journal of Speech and Hearing Research, 35,* 201–207.

Korpela, K. M. (1992). Adolescent's favorite places and environmental self-regulation. *Journal of Environmental Psychology, 12,* 249–258.

Korpela, K., Hartig, T., Kaiser, F., & Fuhrer, U. (2001). Restorative experience and self-regulation in favorite places. *Environment & Behavior, 33,* 572–589.

Kosslyn, S. M., & Rosenberg, R. S. (2005). *Fundamentals of psychology: The brain, the person, the world* (2nd ed.). Boston, MA: Pearson Allyn & Bacon.

Kreitzer, A. C., & Regehr, W. G. (2001) Cerebellar depolarization-induced suppression of inhibition is mediated by endogenous cannabinoids. *Journal of Neurosciences, RC174,* 1–5.

Kryter, K. D. (1996). *Handbook of hearing and the effects of noise.* New York: New York Academic Press.

Kuller, R., & Laike, T. (1998). The impact of flicker from fluorescent lighting on well-being, performance, and physiological arousal. *Ergonomics 41,* 433–447.

Küller, R., Ballal, S., Laike, T., Mikellides, B., & Tonello, G. (2006). The impact of light and colour on psychological mood: A cross-cultural study of indoor work environments. *Ergonomics, 49,* 1496–1507.

Kunishima, M., & Yanase, T. (1985). Visual effects of wall colors in living rooms. *Ergonomics, 28,* 869–882.

Kupritz, V. W. (1998). Privacy in the work place: The impact of building design. *Journal of Environmental Psychology, 18*(4), 341–356.

Kupritz, V. W. (2001). Aging worker perceptions about design and privacy needs for work. *Journal of Architectural and Planning Research, 18*(1), 13–22.

Kyttä, M. (2003). *Young child in outdoor contexts: Affordances and independent mobility in the assessment of environmental young child friendliness.* Helsinki University of Technology, Finland: Dissertation for the degree of Doctor of Philosophy, Department of Architecture.

Lachman, M. E., Howland, J., Tennstedt, S., Jette, A., Assman, S., & Peterson, E. W. (1998). Fear of falling and activity restriction: The survey of activities and fear of falling in the elderly (SAFE). *Journal of Gerontology: Psychological Sciences, 53B-1,* P43–P50.

La Garce, M. (2002). Control of environmental lighting and its effects on behaviors of the Alzheimer's type. *Journal of Interior Design, 28*(2), 15–25.

Lackney, J. A. (2001, Fall). School design: An architect's view. *Horace: The Journal of the Coalition of Essential Schools, 18*(1), 15–18.

Lambert, G. W., Reid, C., Kay, D. M., Jennings, G.L., & Esler, M. D. (2003). Effect of sunlight and season on serotonin turnover in the brain. *Lancet, 360,* 1840–1843.

Lang, D. (1996). *Essential criteria for an ideal learning environment.* Seattle, WA: New Horizons for Learning. Available at http://www.newhorizons.org

Lang, J. (1987). *Creating architectural theory: The role of the behavioral sciences in environmental design.* New York: Van Nostrand Reinhold.

Lang, T. (2005). Food control or food democracy? Re-engaging nutrition with society and the environment. *Public Health Nutrition, 8,* 730–737.

Langer, E. J., & Rodin, J. (1976). The effects of choice and personal responsibility for the aged: A field experiment in an institutional setting. *Journal of Personality and Social Psychology, 34,* 191–198.

Larner, M. B., Behrman, R. E., Young, M., & Reich, K. (Spring/ Summer 2001). Caring for Infants and Toddlers. *The Future of Children, 11*(1), 5–18.

Larsen, L., Adams, J., Deal, B., Kweon, B., & Tyler, E. (1998) Plants in the workplace: The effects of plant density on productivity, attitudes, and perceptions. *Environment and Behavior 30,* 261–281.

Laufer, R., & Wolfe, M. (1976). The interpersonal and environmental context of privacy invasion and response. In P. Korosec-Serfaty (Ed.), *Appropriation of space* (pp. 516–535). Strasbourg, France: Institut Louis Pasteur.

Lawrence, R. (1987). *Housing, dwellings, and homes: Design theory, research, and practice.* Chichester, England: Wiley.

Lawson, B. (2001). *The language of space.* Woburn, MA: Architectural Press.

Lawton, C. A. (1996). Strategies for indoor wayfinding: The role of orientation. *Journal of Environmental Psychology, 16,* 137–145.

Lawton, C. A., Charleston, S. I., & Zieles, A. S. (1996). Individual- and gender-related differences in indoor wayfinding. *Environment and Behavior, 28*(2), 204–219.

Leather, P., Pyrgas, M., Beale, D., & Lawrence, C. (1998). Windows in the workplace: Sunlight, view, and occupational stress. *Environment and Behavior, 30*(6), 739–762.

Legendre, A. (1995). The effects of environmentally modulated visual accessibility to care givers on early peer interactions. *International Journal of Behavioral Development, 19,* 297–313.

Legendre, A. (1999). Interindividual relationships in groups on young children and susceptibility to an environmental constraint. *Environment and Behavior, 31,* 463–496.

Legendre, A. (2003). Environmental features influencing toddlers' bioemotional reactions in day care centers. *Environment and Behavior, 35*(4), 523–549.

Leong, S. M., Ang, S. H., & Low, L. H. L. (1997). Effects of physical environment and locus of control on service evaluation: A replication and extension. *Journal of Retailing and Consumer Services, 4*(4), 231–237.

Lepore, S. J., Evans, G. W., & Schneider, M. L. (1992). Role of control and social support in explaining the stress of hassles and crowding. *Environment and Behavior, 24,* 795–811.

Leventhal-Stern, A., et al. (2003). Understanding the consumer perspective to improve design quality. *Journal of Architectural and Planning Research, 20*(1), 16–28.

Levering, R. (1995). *A great place to work.* New York: Random House.

Levine-Coley, R., Kuo, F. E., & Sullivan, W. C. (1997). Where does community grow? The social context created by nature in urban public housing. *Environment and Behavior, 29,* 468–494.

Levy, M., & Weitz, B. A. (2003). *Retailing Management* (5th ed.). Columbus, OH: McGraw-Hill.

Lewin, K. (1943). Defining the "field at a given time." *Psychological Review, 50,* 292–310.

Lewy, A.J., Bauer, V. K., Cutler, N. L., Sack, R. L., Ahmed, S., Thomas, K. H… , & Latham Jackson, J. M. (1998). Morning vs. evening light treatment of patients with winter depression. *Archives of General Psychiatry, 55,* 890–896.

Lexingtron, A. (1989). Healthy offices: Hard to define, but we need them. *The Office,* 73–75.

Lieberg, M. (1994). Appropriating the city: Teenagers' use of public space. In S. J. Neary, M. S. Symes, & F. E. Brown (Eds.). *The urban experience: A people-environment perspective* (pp. 321–333). London: Spon.

Lindberg, E., Gärling, T., & Montgomery, H. (1986). Beliefs and values as determinants of residential preferences and choices. *Umea Psychological Reports,* Number 194.

Lindberg, E., Gärling, T., & Montgomery, H. (1989). Preferences for and choices between verbally and numerically described housing alternatives. *Umea Psychological Reports,* Number 189.

Lindberg, E., Hartig, T., Garvill, J., & Gärling, T. (1992). Residential-location preferences across the life span. *Journal of Environmental Psychology, 12,* 187–198.

Lindholm, G. (1995). Schoolyards: the significance of place properties to outdoor activities in schools. *Environment and Behavior, 27,* 259–293.

Logsdon, R. G., Teri, L., McCurry, S. M., Gibbons, L. E., Kukull, W. A., & Larson, E. B. (1998). Wandering: A significant problem among community-residing individuals with Alzheimer's disease. *Journal of Gerontology: Psychological Sciences, 53B-5,* P294–P299.

Lombroso, P. J., & Sapolsky, R. (1998). Development of the cerebral cortex: XII. Stress and brain development. I. *Journal of the American Academy of Child and Adolescent Psychiatry, 37,* 1337–1339.

Lomranz, J., Shapiro, A., Choresk, N., & Gilat, Y. (1975). Children's personal space as a function of age and sex. *Developmental Psychology, 11,* 541–545.

Loveland, K. A. (1986). Discovering the affordances of a reflecting surface. *Developmental Review, 6*(1), 1–24.

Luckiesh, M., & Moss, F.K. (1940). Effects of classroom lighting upon the educational progress and visual welfare of school children. *Illuminating Engineering, 35,* 915–938.

Lutgendorf, S. K., et al. (2001). Effects of housing relocation on immunocompetence and psychosocial functioning in older adults. *Journal of Gerontology: Medical Sciences, 56A*(2), M97–M105.

Lynch, K. (1960). *The image of the city.* Cambridge, MA: MIT Press.

Machleit, K. A., Eroglu, S. A., & Mantel, S. P. (2000). Perceived retail crowding and shopping satisfaction: What modifies this relationship? *Journal of Consumer Psychology, 9*(1), 29–42.

Mackey, J. W., & Mackey, W. H. (2007). *A field guide to the convenience stores of the city of Tucson, Arizona.* Tucson, AZ: Neighborhood Residents Resources Ethnography Studies Unit.

MacLaury, J. (2009, August 27). *The Occupational Safety and Health Administration: A history of its first thirteen years, 1971–1984.* U.S. Department of Labor: Office of The Assistant Secretary for The Administration and Management. Retrieved from http://www.dol.gov/oasam/programs/history/mono-osha13introtoc.htm

Mader, R. (2004). *"Defining Ecotourism."* Retrieved from www.planeta.com.

Magee, J. (2000). Home as an alternative workplace: Negotiating the spatial and behavioral boundaries between home and work. *Journal of Interior Design*, *26*(1), 35–47.

Maguire, E. A., et al. (2000) Navigation-related structural changes in the hippocampi of taxi drivers. *Proceedings National Academy of Science, 97,* 4398–4403.

Mahnke, F. H. (1996). *Color, environment, and human response.* Hoboken, NJ: John Wiley and Sons.

Mahnke, F. H., & Mahnke, R. H., (1996). *Color, environment and human response.* New York: Van Nostrand Reinhold.

Malinowski, J. C., & Thurber, C. A. (1996). Developmental shifts in the place preference of boys aged 8–16 years. *Journal of Environmental Psychology, 16,* 45–54.

Malnar, J. M., & Vodvarka, F. (2004). *Sensory design.* Minneapolis, MN: University of Minnesota Press.

Malone, K., & Tranter, P. (2003). Children's environmental learning and the use, design and management of schoolgrounds. *Children, Youth and Environments, 13*(2) online. Available at www.colorado.edu/journals/cye/13_2/Malone_Tranter/ChildrensEnvLearning.htm

Mandara, J., Gaylord-Harden, N., Richards, M., & Ragsdale, B. (2009). The effects of changes in racial identity and self-esteem on changes in African American adolescents' mental health. *Child Development, 80,* 1660–1675.

Mandel, D. R., Baron, R. M., & Fisher, J. D. (1980). Room utilization and dimensions of density: Effects of height and view. *Environment and Behavior, 12,* 308–319.

Manning, R. E. (1985) Crowding norms in backcountry settings: A review and synthesis. *Journal of Leisure Research, 17,* 75–89.

ManPower. (2008, June). *Relocating for work: Global results.* Available online from www.manpower.com/research

Manzini, E. (1995). Prometheus of the everyday: The ecology of the artificial and the designer's responsibility. In R. Buchanan and W. Margolin (Eds.), *Discovering design: Explanation in design studies.* Chicago: University of Chicago Press.

Marazita, M. L., et al. (1993). Genetic epidemiological studies of early-onset deafness in the U.S. school-age population. *American Journal of Medical Genetics, 46,* 486–491.

Marion, M. (2003). *Guidance of young children* (6th ed.). Upper Saddle River, NJ: Prentice Hall.

Marlier, L., Schaal B., & Soussignan, R. (1998). Neonatal responsiveness to the odor of amniotic and lacteal fluids: A test of perinatal chemosensory continuity. *Child Development, 64,* 611–623.

Marsden, J. P. (1999). Older persons' and family members' perceptions of homeyness in assisted living. *Environment and Behavior, 31*(1), 84–106.

Martin, P. Y. (2002). Sensations, bodies, and the "spirit of a place": Aesthetics in residential organizations for the elderly. *Human Relations, 56,* 861–885.

Marvel, M. (1999). Competing in hotel services for seniors. *International Journal of Hospitality Management, 18,* 235–243.

Maslow, A. H. (1970). *Motivation and personality* (2nd ed.). New York: Harper & Row.

Maslow, A. H., & Mintz, N. L. (1956). Effects of aesthetic surroundings: Initial effects of three aesthetic conditions upon perceiving "energy" and "well-being" in faces. *Journal of Psychology, 41,* 247–254.

Matthews, M. H. (1986a). Gender, graphicacy and geography. *Educational Review, 38,* 259–271.

Matthews, M. H. (1986b). The influence of gender on the environmental cognition of young boys and girls. *Journal of Genetic Psychology, 14,* 295–302.

Matthews, M. H. (1992). *Making sense of place: Children's understanding of large-scale environments.* London: Harvester Wheatsheaf.

Mattila, A. S. (1999). Consumers' value judgments: How business travelers evaluate luxury-hotel services. *Cornell Hotel and Restaurant Administration Quarterly, 40*(1), 40–46.

Mattila, A. S. (2001). Emotional bonding and restaurant loyalty. *Cornell Hotel and Restaurant Administration Quarterly, 42*(6), 73–79.

Mattila, A. S., & Wirtz, J. (2001). Congruency of scent and music as a driver of in-store evaluations and behavior. *Journal of Retailing, 77,* 273–289.

Maxwell, L. E. (1996). Multiple effects of home and day care crowding. *Environment and Behavior*, 29, 494–511.

Maxwell, L. E. (2003). Home and school density effects on elementary school children: The role of spatial density. *Environment and Behavior*, 35, 566–578.

Maxwell, L. E., & Evans, G. W. (2000). The effects of noise on pre-school children's pre-reading skills. *Journal of Environmental Psychology*, 20(1), 91–97.

Mazumdar, S. (1992). Sir, please do not take away my cubicle: The phenomenon of environmental deprivation. *Environment and Behavior*, 24, 691–722.

Mazumdar, S., & Geis, G. (2002). Accessible buildings, architects, and the ADA law: The MCI Center Sports Arena case. *Journal of Architectural and Planning Research*, 19, 195–217.

McAfee, J. K. (1987). Classroom density and the aggressive behavior of handicapped children. *Education and Treatment of Children*, 10, 2.

McAndrew, F. T. (1993). *Environmental psychology*. Brooks/Cole Publishing Company: Pacific Grove, CA.

McAuley, W. J. (1998). History, race, and attachment to place among elders in the rural all-Black towns of Oklahoma. *Journal of Gerontology: Social Sciences*, 53B(1), S35–S45.

McCoy, J. M. (2002). Work environments. In R. Bechtel & I. Churchman (Eds.), *Handbook of environmental psychology* (pp. 443–460). New York: Wiley.

McCrae, R. R., & Costa, P. T. Jr. (1999). A five-factor theory of personality. In L. A. Pervin & O. P. John (Eds.), *Handbook of personality theory and research* (pp. 139–153). New York: Guilford Press.

McDonald, E. G. (1960). Effect of school environment on teacher and student performance. *Air conditioning, Heating, and Ventilation*, 57, 78–79.

McFarland, D. A. (2001). Student resistance: How the formal and informal organization of classrooms facilitate everyday forms of student defiance. *American Journal of Sociology*, 107, 612–678.

McHugh, M., O'Brien, G., & Ramondt, J. (2001). Finding an alternative to bureaucratic models of organization in the public sector. *Public Money & Management*, 21, 35–43. Retrieved from http://search.epnet.com/login.aspx?direct=true&db=bsh&an=4325388

McKay, S. (2002). To aid or not to aid: Children with unilateral hearing loss. *Healthy Hearing* [online newsletter]. Retrieved from www.healthyhearing.com

McLoyd, V. C. (1998). Socioeconomic disadvantage and child development. *American Psychologist*, 53, 185–204.

Meaney, M. J., Aitken, D. H., van Berkal, C., Bhatnagar, S., & Sapolsky, R. M. (1988). Effect of neonatal handling on age-related impairments associated with the hippocampus. *Science*, 239, 766–768.

Mehrabian, A., & Russell, J. A. (1974). *An approach to environmental ssychology*. Cambridge, MA: MIT Press.

Melikov, A., Pitchurov, G., Naydenov, K., & Langkilde, G. (2005). Field study on occupant comfort and the office thermal environment in rooms with displacement ventilation. *Indoor Air*, 15, 205–214.

Melton, A. (1935). *Problems of installation in museums (New Series No. 14)*. Washington, DC: American Association of Museums.

Melton, A. (1972). Visitor behaviors in museums: Some early research in environmental design. *Human Factors*, 14, 393–403.

Meltzer, D. O., & Arora, V. (2006). The effects of on-duty napping on intern sleep time and fatigue. *Annals of Internal Medicine 144*, 792–798.

Merchant, C. (1993). *Radical ecology: The search for a livable world*. New York: Routledge.

Michelson, W. (1977). *Environmental choice, Human behavior and residential satisfaction*. New York: Oxford University Press.

Milgram, S. (1970). The experience of living in cities. *Science*, 167, 1461–1468.

Mill, R. C. (2008). *Resorts: Management and operation* (2nd ed.). Hoboken, NJ: John Wiley & Sons.

Milliman, R. E. (1982). Using background music to affect the behavior of supermarket shoppers. *Journal of Marketing*, 46, 86–91.

Moeser, S. D. (1988). Cognitive mapping in a complex building. *Environment and Behavior*, 20, 21–49.

Mondak, P. (2000). The Americans With Disabilities Act and information technology access. *Focus on Autism & Other Developmental Disabilities*, 15(1), 43–51.

Monk, C. F., et al. (2000). Maternal stress responses and anxiety during pregnancy: Effects on fetal heart rate. *Developmental Psychology*, 36(1), 67–77.

Montano, D., & Adamopoulos, J. (1984). The perception of crowding in interpersonal situations: Affective and behavioral responses. *Environment and Behavior*, 16, 643–666.

Moody, A. (2008). Executive summary: *The contribution of the North American cruise industry to the U.S. economy in 2008*. Prepared by Business Research & Economic Advisors, Exton, PA. Accessed from http://www.cruising.org/Press/research/index.cfm

Moore, G. T. (1987). The physical environment and cognitive development in young child care centers. In C. S. Weinstein & T. J. David (Eds.), *Spaces for children: The built environment and child development* (pp. 41–72). New York: Plenum.

Moore M. M., et al. (1998). Interventions to reduce decibel levels in patient care units. *The American Surgeon, 64,* 894–899.

Moore, M. G. (1993). Theory of transactional distance. In D. Keegan (Ed.), *Theoretical principles of distance education.* New York: Routledge.

Moore, P., & Fitz, C. (1993). Gestalt Theory and Instructional Design. *Journal of Technical Writing and Communication, 23,* 137–157.

Moreno-Jimenez, A. (2001). Interurban shopping, new town planning and local development in Madrid metropolitan area. *Journal of Retailing and Consumer Services, 8,* 291–298.

Morgan, D. G., & Stewart, N. J. (1998). Multiple occupancy versus private rooms on dementia care units. *Environment and Behavior, 30,* 487–503.

Morgan, J. J. (1916). The overcoming of distraction and other resistances. *Archives of Psychology, 35*(24), 1–84.

Morris, C. G., & Maistro, A. A. (2006) *Understanding psychology* (9th ed.). Prentice Hall.

Morris, D. (1994). *Bodytalk: The meaning of human gestures.* New York: Crown.

Mostafa M. (2008). An architecture for autism: Concepts of design intervention for the autistic user. *International Journal of Architectural Research, 2*(1), 189–211.

MotorTrend. (2008, July 28). *What are the Top Ten "Chick Cars" you can buy today?* Retrieved from http://wot.motortrend.com/6268393/miscellaneous/what-are-the-top-ten-chick-cars-you-can-buy-today/index.html

Moughtin, J., Cuesta, R., Sarris, C., & Signoretta, P. (2003). *Urban design: method and techniques* (2nd ed). Oxford, England:Butterworth-Heinemann.

Moussaieff, A., & Mechoulam, R. (2009). Boswellia resin: From religious ceremonies to medical uses; A review of in-vitro, in-vivo and clinical trials. *Journal of Pharmacy and Pharmacology, 61,* 1281–1293.

Mroczek, J., Mikitarian, G., Vieira, E. K., & Rotarius, T. (2005). Hospital design and staff perceptions: An exploratoryanalysis. *Health Care Manager, 24,* 233–244

Mueller, C. W. (1984). The effects of mood and type and timing of influence on the perception of crowding. *Journal of Psychology, 116,* 155–158.

Murray, D. (1997). Autism and information technology: Therapy with computers. In S. Powell & R. Jordan (Eds.), *Autism and learning: A guide to good practice.* London England: David Fulton.

Myers, D. G. (2003). *Psychology.* New York: Worth.

NACHRI. (2003). *History of children's hospitals.* Retrieved from http://www.childrenshospitals.net

Nasar, J. L. (1981a). Responses to different spatial configurations. *Human Factors, 23,* 439–446.

Nasar, J. L. (1981b). Visual preferences of elderly public housing residents: Residential street scenes. *Journal of Environmental Psychology, 1,* 303–313.

Nasar, J. L. (1983). Adult viewers' preferences in residential scenes: A study of the relationship of environmental attributes to preference. *Environment and Behavior, 15,* 589–614.

Nasar, J. L. (1994). Urban design aesthetics: The evaluative qualities of building exteriors. *Environment and Behavior, 26,* 377–401.

Nasar, J. L., & Min, M. S. (1984). *Modifiers of perceived spaciousness and crowding. A cross-cultural study.* Toronto, ON: American Psychological Association.

Nash, B. C. (1981). The effects of classroom spatial organization on four- and five-year old children's learning. *British Journal of Educational Psychology, 51*(2), 144–155.

National Association of Realtors. (February 18, 2010). *Adding universal design features to your bathroom.* Retrieved from http://www.houselogic.com/articles/adding-universal-design-features-your-bathroom/

National Center for Health Statistics, (2006). *National Center for Health Statistics health, United States, 2006 with chartbook on trends in the health of Americans.* Hyattsville, MD: DHHS Publication No. 2006-1232.

National Institute of Environmental Health Sciences. (July 1997). Asthma and its environmental triggers: Scientists take a practical new look at a familiar illness. In *NIEHS Fact Sheet #9: Asthma.* Retrieved from www.niehs/nih/gov

National Institutes of Health. (July 19, 2006). *Genetic and rare diseases information center.* http://rarediseases.info.nih.gov/asp/resources/rardis_info.asp: National Institutes of Health: Office of Rare Diseases.

National SAFE KIDS Campaign. (2003). Washington, DC. Retrieved from www.safekids.org

Neddermeyer, D. M. (Nov, 2005). *What the bleep do we know?—The movie—An analysis.* Online: Genesis Consultants, Inc. Retrieved from www.gen-assist.com/features/articles/a1105.asp

Nelson. A. C. (1999). Comparing states with and without growth management: Analysis based on indicators with policy implications. *Land Use Policy, 16,* 121–127.

Nelson, C. A., & Horowitz, F. D. (1987). Visual motion perception in infancy: A review and synthesis. In P. Salapatek & L. B. Cohen (Eds.), *Handbook of infant perception: From perception to cognition.* New York: Academic Press.

New York State Commission on Ventilation. (1931). *School ventilation and practices.* New York: Teachers College, Columbia University.

Newell, P. B. (1994). A systems model of privacy. *Journal of Environmental Psychology, 14,* 65–78.

Newell, P. B. (1995). Perspectives on privacy. *Journal of Environmental Psychology, 15,* 87–104.

Newman, O. (1972). *Defensible space.* New York: Macmillan.

Ngee Ann Polytechnic. (2001). *Sensory learning styles.* Produced by Ngee Ann Polytechnic. Retrieved from http://tlcweb.np.edu.sg/esprit/tb-lc-eAudience-VAK-learning-styles.htm

Nield, K., Kozak, M., & LeGrys, G. (2000). The role of food service in tourist satisfaction. *International Journal of Hospitality Management, 19,* 375–384.

North, A. C., & Hargreaves, D. J. (1999). Can music move people? The effects of musical complexity and silence on waiting time. *Environment and Behavior, 31,* 136–149.

O'Neil, M. J. (1991). Effects of signage and floor plan configuration on wayfinding accuracy. *Environment and Behavior, 23,* 553–574.

Oelschlaeger, M. (1991). *The idea of wilderness: From prehistory to the age of ecology.* New Haven, CT: Yale University Press.

Office of Compliance: Safety and Health Fast Fact. (2004). *Extension cords & power strips.* Retrieved from www.compliance.gov

Oldenburg, R. (2001). *Celebrating the third place.* New York: Marlowe & Company.

Olds, A. R. (2001). *Child care design guide.* New York: McGraw Hill.

Olendorf, D., Jeryan, C., & Boyden, K. (Eds). (1999). *The Gale encyclopedia of medicine.* Farmington Hills, MI: Thomson Gale.

Oliver, M. B. (2002). Individual differences in media effects. In J. Bryant & D. Zillmann (Eds). *Media effects: Advances in theory and research (2nd ed.)* (pp. 507-24). Mahwah, NJ: Lawrence Erlbaum.

Oppewal, H., & Timmermans, H. (1999). Modeling consumer perception of public space in shopping centers. *Environment and Behavior, 31*(1), 45–65.

Ortiz, J. (2004, Mar 1). The human body: A sensing machine. *Welcome to the wonderful world of neuroscience,* Available at www.macalester.edu/psychology/whathap/diaries/diariess04/josh/diary_entry6.html

OSHA (1998). *Recommendations for workplace violence prevention programs in late-night retail establishments* (OSHA #3153).Washington, DC: U.S. Department of Labor: Occupation Health and Safety Administration.

Osterberg, A. E., Davis, A. M., & Danielson, L. D. (1995). Universal design: The users' perspective. *Housing and Society, 22*(1/2), 92–113.

Owens, P. E. (1988). Natural landscapes, gathering places, and prospect refuges: Characteristics of outdoor places valued by teens. *Children's Environmental Quarterly, 5,* 17–24.

Owens, P. E. (1994). Teen places in Sunshine, Australia: Then and now. *Children's Environments, 11,* 292–299.

Owens, P. E. (2002). No teens allowed: The exclusion of adolescents from public spaces. *Landscape Journal, 21*(1/2), 156–163.

Pallasmaa, J. (2005). *The eyes of the skin.* West Sussex, England: Wiley-Academy.

Papadotas, S. P. (1973). Color them motivated—Color's psychological effects on students. *National Association of Secondary School Principals Bulletin, 57,* 92–94.

Pardo, P. J., Pérez, A. L., & Suero, M. I. (2007). An example of sex-linked color vision differences. *Color Research and Application, 32,* 433–439.

Park, M. A. (1999). *Biological anthropology* (2nd ed.). Mountain View, CA: Mayfield Publishing Company.

Parkinson's Disease Foundation, (n.d.). Symptoms. Retrieved June 20, 2005 from www.pdf.org

Paron-Wildes, A. J. (2008). Sensory stimulation and autistic children. *Implications, 6.* Retrieved from www.informedesign.umn.edu

Passini, R., Pigot, H., Rainville, C., & Tetreault, M. (2000). Wayfinding in a nursing home for advanced dementia of the Alzheimer's type. *Environment & Behavior, 32,* 684–710.

Passini, R., Rainville, C., Marchand, N., & Joanette, Y. (1998). Wayfinding and dementia: Some research findings and a new look at design. *Journal of Architectural and Planning Research, 15,* 133–151.

Patricios, N. N. (1979). Human aspects of planning shopping centers. *Environment and Behavior, 11,* 511–538.

Pedersen, D. M. (1982) Cross-validation of privacy factors. *Perceptual and Motor Skills, 55,* 57–58.

Pegler, M. M. (1998). *Visual merchandising and display* (4th ed.).New York, NY: Fairchild Publications.

Pejtersen, J., et al. (2001). Effect of renovating an office building on occupants' comfort and health. *Indoor Air, 11*(1), 10–25.

Pelligrini, A. D. (1985). Social-cognitive aspects of children's play: The effects of age, gender, and activity centers. *Journal of Applied Developmental Psychology, 6,* 129–140.

Pennartz, P. J. J. (1986). Atmosphere at home: A qualitative approach. *Journal of Environmental Psychology, 6,* 135–153.

Persad, C.C., et al. (1995). Neuropsychological predictors of complex obstacle avoidance in healthy older adults. *Journal of Gerontology: Psychological Sciences, 50B,* P272–P277.

Peterson, R. (1987). Gender issues in the home and urban environment. In E. H. Zube & G. T. Moore (Eds.), *Advances in environment, behavior and design* (Vol. 1, pp. 187–220). New York: Plenum.

Piaget, J. (1963). *The origin of intelligence in children.* New York: Norton.

Piaget, J. (1969). *The theory of stages in cognitive development.* New York: McGraw-Hill.

Piaget, J. (1973). *The psychology of intelligence.* Totowa, NJ: Littlefield, Adams & Co.

Pile, J. (1997). *Color in interior design.* New York: McGraw-Hill.

Pilman, M. S. (Dec 15, 2001). *The effects of air temperature variance on memory ability.* Missouri Western State College. Retrieved from http://clearinghouse.mwsc.edu/manuscripts/306.asp

Pimenidis, M. Z. (2009). *The neurobiology of orthodontics: treatment of malocclusion through neuroplasticity.* New York: Springer.

Piotrowski, C., & Rogers, E. (2007). *Designing commercial Interiors* (2nd ed.). Hoboken, NJ: John Wiley & Sons.

Planetree. (2009). *About Plane Tree.* Retrieved from www.planetree.org

Pleis J. R, & Lethbridge-Cejku, M. (2007). Summary health statistics for U.S. adults: National Health Interview Survey, 2005. *Vital Health Statistics, 10, 232.*

Plotsky, P. M., & Meaney, M. J. (1993). Early, postnatal experience alters hypothalamic corticotropin releasing factor (CRF) mRNA, median eminence CRF content and stress-induced release in adult rats. *Molecular Brain Research, 18,* 195–200.

Pondy, L. R., Frost, P. J., Morgan, G., & Dandridge, T. C. (Eds.). (1983). *Organizational symbolism.* Greenwich, CT: Jai Press.

Popay, J., et al. (2003). A proper place to live: Health inequalities, agency and the normative dimensions of space. *Social Science & Medicine, 57,* 55–69.

Portnoy, S. (2008, October 7). *Future wireless networks could be powered by "smart lighting."* ZDNet News & Blogs. Retrieved from http://blogs.zdnet.com/soho-networking/?p=284

Project For Public Spaces. (2005). *What makes a great playground? Elements of a successful play space: Enhancing physical, cognitive and social experience.* Developed by urban parks. Retrieved from www.pps.org

Proshansky, H. M., & Fabian, A. K. (1987). The development of place identity in the child. In C. S. Weinstein & T. G. David (Eds.), *Spaces for children, the built environment and child development.* New York: Putman.

Proshansky, H. M., Fabian, A. K., & Kaminoff, R. (1983). Place-identity: Physical world socialization of the self. *Journal of Environmental Psychology, 3,* 57–83.

Rabins, P. V. (1989). Behavior problems in the demented. In E. Light & B. D. Lebowitz (Eds.), *Alzheimer's disease treatment and family stress: Directions for research* (pp. 322–339). (DHHS Publication No. ADM 89-1569). Washington, DC: U.S. Government Printing Office.

Ramachandran, V., & Rogers-Ramachandran, D. (2008). Sensations referred to a patient's phantom arm from another subjects intact arm: Perceptual correlates of mirror neurons. *Medical Hypotheses, 70,* 1233–1234.

Ramsay, M. A. E. (2000). Physician fatigue. *Baylor University Medical Center Proceedings. 13,* 148–150

Ramsey, L. F., & Preston, J. D. (1990). *Impact attenuation performance of playground surfacing materials.* Washington, DC: U.S. Consumer Product Safety Commission.

Rapoport, A. (1975). Toward a redefinition of density. *Environment and Behavior, 7,* 133–158.

Rapoport, A. (1995). Individual strategies in a market entry game. *Group Decision and Negotiation, 4,* 117–133.

Rathunde, K. (2001). Montessori education and optimal experience: A framework for new research. *The NAMTA Journal, 26*(1), 11–43.

Razzouk, N. Y., Seitz, V., & Kumar, V. (2002). The impact of perceived display completeness/incompleteness on shoppers' in-store selection of merchandise: An empirical study. *Journal of Retailing and Consumer Services, 9*(1), 31–35.

Read, M. A. (2003). Use of color in child care environments: Application of color for wayfinding and space definition in Alabama child care environments. *Early Childhood Education Journal, 30,* 233–239.

Read, M. A., Sugawara, A. I., & Brandt, J. A. (1999). Impact of space and color in the physical environment on preschool children's cooperative behavior. *Environment and Behavior, 31,* 413–428.

Rehm, R. (2000). *Workplace design paradigms. People in charge.* Retrieved from www.peopleincharge.og/paradigms.htm

Reisberg, D., & Hertel, P. (Eds.). (2004). *Memory and emotion.* New York: Oxford University Press. Retrieved from www www..nj.go gov/v/dep/opsc

Reynolds, D., Merritt, E. A., & Pinckney, S. (2005). Understanding menu psychology: An empirical investigation of menu design and consumer response. *International Journal of Hospitality & Tourism Administration, 6*(1), 1–10.

Rezak, S. B. (2003). *Timeshares versus fractionals: Naming by the numbers.* In Susan Green (Copywriter), CondoHotelCenter.com: www.condohotelcenter.com/News/timesharesvsfractionals.html

Rhawn, J. (2002). *Neuropsychology, clinical neuroscience* (3rd ed.). New York: Academic Press.

Ries, P. W. (1994). Prevalence and characteristics of persons with hearing trouble: United States, 1990-91. National Center for Health Statistics. *Vital Health Statistics, 10,* 188.

Risse, G. B. (1999). *Mending bodies, saving souls: A history of hospitals.* New York: Oxford University Press.

Ritschel, T., Ihrke, M., Frisvad, J. R., Coppens, J., Myszkowski, K., & Seidel, H. P. (2009). Temporal glare: Real-time dynamic simulation of the scattering in the human eye. *Proceedings Eurographics.*

Ritvo, E. (2005). *Understanding the nature of autism and Asperger's disorder: Forty years of clinical practice and pioneering research.* London: Jessica Kingsley.

Rivlin, L. G. (1990). Home and homelessness in the lives of children. *Child and Youth Services, 14,* 5–17.

Rivlin, L. G., & Rothenberg, M. (1976). *The use of space in open classrooms.* New York: Holt, Rinehart, Winston.

Rodin, J., & Langer, E. J. (1977). Long-term effects of a control relevant intervention with the institutionalized aged. *Journal of Personality and Social Psychology, 35,* 897–902.

Rogers, W. A., Meyer, B., Walker, N., & Fisk, A. D. (1998). Functional limitations to daily living tasks in the aged: A focus group analysis. *Human Factors, 40*(1), 111–125.

Rossano, M. J. (2003). *Evolutionary psychology: The science of human behavior and evolution.* Hoboken, NJ: John Wiley and Sons.

Rosser, S. (1985). The feminist perspective on science: Is re-conceptualization possible? *Journal of the National Association of Women Deans, Administrators, and Counselors, 49*(1), 29–35.

Rothblatt, D. N., Garr, D. J., & Sprague, J. (1979). *The suburban environment and women.* New York: Praeger.

Rotter, J. B. (1982). *The development and application of social learning theory.* New York: Praeger.

Rotter, J. B., Chance, J. E., & Phares, E. J. (1972). *Applications of a social learning theory of personality.* New York: Holt, Rinehart & Winston.

Rotton, J. (1987). Hemmed in and hating it: Effects of shape of room on tolerance for crowding. *Perceptual and Motor Skills, 64,* 285–286.

Rovee-Collier C. (2000). Memory in infancy and early childhood. In E. Tulving & F. I. M. Craik (Eds.), *The Oxford handbook of memory.* New York: Oxford University Press.

Ruback, R. B., & Juieng, D. (1997). Territorial defense in parking lots: Retaliation against waiting drivers. *Journal of Applied Social Psychology, 27,* 821–834.

Ruback, R. B., & Pandey, J. (1992). Very hot and really crowded: Quasi-experimental investigations of Indian "tempos." *Environment and Behavior, 24,* 527–554.

Ruff, H. A. (1989). The infant's use of visual and haptic information in the perception and recognition of objects. *Canadian Journal of Psychology, 43,* 302–319.

Russell, J. A., Ward, L. M., & Pratt, G. (1981). Affective quality attributed to environments: A factor analytic study. *Environment and Behavior, 12,* 259–288.

Rutter, M., and the English and Romanian Adoptees (ERA) Study Team. (1998). Developmental catch-up, and deficit, following adoption after severe early privation. *Journal of Child Psychology and Psychiatry, 39,* 465–476.

Rutter, M., et al. (1999) Quasi-autistic patterns following severe early global privation. *Journal of Child Psychology and Psychiatry, 40,* 537–549.

Rybczynski, W. (1986). *Home: A history of an idea.* New York: Penguin Group.

Sagmiller, G. J. (2000). *Dyslexia my life: One man's story of his life with a learning disability* (3rd ed.). Lee's Summit, MO: DT Publishing.

Sakai, H., et al. (2001). ARR1, a transcription factor for genes immediately responsive to cytokinins. *Science. 16,* 1519–1521.

Sakr, W., Knudsen, H. N., Gunnarsen, L., & Haghighat, F. (2003). Impact of varying area of polluting surface materials on perceived air quality. *Indoor Air, 13,* 86–91.

Salling, M., & Harvey, M. E. (1981). Poverty, personality, and sensitivity to residential stressors. *Environment and Behavior, 13,* 131–163.

Samovar, L., & Baldner, C. (1998). *Understanding intercultural communication in the health care setting.* Prepared for Vista Community Clinic with funds from The Office of Minority Health, U.S. Department of Health and Human Services, Grant #D56MP95012 01. Vista, CA.

Samovar, L. A., & Porter, R. E. (1994). *Intercultural communication: A reader* (7th ed.). Belmont, CA: Wadsworth Publishing Company.

Sanders, J., Koch, J., & Urso, J. (1997). *Gender equity right from the start: Instructional activities for teacher educators in mathematics, science and technology.* Mahwah, NJ: Lawrence Erlbaum Associates.

Sañudo-Pena M. C., Romero J., Seale G. E., Fernandez-Ruiz, J. J., & Walker J. M. (2000). Activational role of cannabinoids on movement. *European Journal of Pharmacology, 391,* 269–274.

Sapolsky, R. M. (1997). The importance of a well-groomed child. Science, *277,* 1620–1621.

Satler, G. (2003). New York City restaurants: Vernaculars of global designing. *Journal of Architectural Education, 56*(3), 27–39.

Savinar, J. (1975). The effect of ceiling height on personal space. *Man-Environment Systems, 5,* 321–324.

Scarre, C. (1993). *Smithsonian timelines of the ancient world.* New York: Dorling Kindersley.

Scarre, C., & Renfrew, C. (1995). *Cognition and material culture: The archaeology of symbolic storage.* Cambridge England: McDonald Institute.

Schaeffer, G. H., & Patterson, M. L. (1980). Intimacy, arousal and small group crowding. *Journal of Personal and Social Psychology, 38,* 283–290.

Schaeffer, M. A., Baum, A., Paulus, P. B., & Gaes, G. G. (1988). Architecturally mediated effects of social density in prison. *Environment and Behavior, 20,* 3–19.

Schein, E. H. (1990). Organizational culture. *American Psychologist, 45,* 109–119.

Schiffenbauer, A. I. (1979). Designing for high-density living. In J. R. Aiello & A. Baum (Eds.), *Residential crowding and design.* New York: Plenum Press.

Schlosser, A. E. (1998). Applying the functional theory of attitudes to understanding the influence of store atmosphere on store inferences. *Journal of Consumer Psychology, 7,* 345–369.

Schlosser, J. (2006). The great escape. *Fortune Magazine.* Retrieved from http://money.cnn.com/popups/2006/fortune/cubicles/frameset.exclude.html

Schmidt, D. E., & Keating, J. P. (1979). Human crowding and personal control: An integration of the research. *Psychological Bulletin, 86,* 680–700.

Schwartz, S. (2004). *Visual perception: A clinical orientation* (3rd ed.) New York: McGraw-Hill Medical.

Schwarz, B. (1997). Nursing home design: A misguided architectural model. *Journal of Architectural and Planning Research, 14*(4), 343–359.

Schwebel, D. C., Binder, S. C., & Plumert, J. M. (2002). Using an injury diary to describe the ecology of children's daily injuries. *Journal of Safety Research, 33,* 301–319.

Scott, J. (July 15, 2000). When child's play is too simple; Experts criticize safety-conscious recreation as boring. *Arts & Ideas/Cultural Desk.*

Scott, J. A. (1984). Comfort and seating distance in living rooms: The relationship of interactants and topic of conversation. *Environment and Behavior, 16,* 35–54.

Seaward, B. L. (1992) Humor's healing potential. *Health Progress, 73*(3), 66–70.

Sebba, R., & Churchman, A. (1983). Territories and territoriality in the home. *Environment and Behavior,* 15, 2, 191–210

Seligman, M. E. P. (1992). *Helplessness: On depression development, and death* (2nd ed.). New York: W. H. Freeman and Company.

Seppanen, O., & Fisk, W. J. (2002). Association of ventilation system type with SBS symptoms in office workers. *Indoor Air, 12*(2), 98–112.

Severy, L. J. Forsyth, D. R., & Wagner, P. J. (1979). A multimethod assessment of personal space development in female and male, Black and White children. *Journal of Nonverbal Behavior, 4,* 68–86.

Shaffer, D. R., & Sadowski, C. (1975). This table is mine: Respect for marked barroom tables as a function of gender, spatial marker and desirability of locale. *Sociometry, 38,* 408–419.

Shepherd, G. M. (1994). *Neurobiology* (3rd ed.). New York: Oxford University Press.

Sherman, S. A., Varni, J. W., Ulrich, R. S., & Malcarne, V. L., (2005). Post-occupancy evaluation of healing gardens in a pediatric cancer center. *Landscape and Urban Planning. 73*(2-3), 167–183.

Sholl, M. J., Acacio, J. C., Makar, R. O., & Leon, C. (2000). The relation of sex and sense of direction to spatial orientation in an unfamiliar environment. *Journal of Environmental Psychology, 20*(1), 17–28.

Showalter, E. (2001). Fade to greige. *London Review of Books, 23*(1), retrieved July 22, 2008, from www.lrb.co.uk/v23/n01/contents.html.

Shyue, S. K., Hewett-Emmett, D., Sperling, H. G., Hunt, D. M., Bowmaker, J. K., Mollon, J.D., & Li, W. H. (1995). Adaptive evolution of color vision genes in higher primates. *Science, 269,* 1265–1267.

Siegler, R., Deloache, J., & Eisenberg, N., (2006). *How children develop* (2nd ed.). New York: Worth.

Siguaw, J. A., & Enz, C. A. (1999a). Best practices in food and beverage management. *Cornell Hotel and Restaurant Administration Quarterly,* 40(5), 50–57.

Siguaw, J. A., & Enz, C. A. (1999b). Best practices in hotel architecture. *Cornell Hotel and Restaurant Administration Quarterly, 40*(5), 44–49.

Simion, F., Valenza, E., Cassia, V. M., Turati, C., & Umiltà, C. (2002). Newborns' preference for up-down asymmetrical configurations. *Developmental Science, 5,* 427–434.

Simons, S. H. P, et al. (2003). Do we still hurt babies: A prospective study of procedural pain and analgesia in neonates. *Archives of Pediatrics & Adolescent Medicine, 157,* 1058–1064.

Sinha, S. P., Nayyar, P., & Mukherjee, N. (1995). Perception of crowding among children and adolescents. *Journal of Social Psychology, 135,* 263–268.

Sinofsky, E. R., & Knirck, F. G. (1981). Choose the right color for your learning style. *Instructional Innovator, 26*(3), 17–19.

Slater, A., Morison, V., & Rose, D. (1983). Perception of shape by the new-born baby. *British Journal of Developmental Psychology, 1,* 135–142.

Sloan, P., Legrand, W., & Chen, J. (2009). *Sustainability in the hospitality industry.* Oxford, UK: Butterworth-Heinemann.

Sloane, D. C. (1994). Scientific paragon to hospital mall: The evolving design of the hospital, 1885–1994. *Journal of Architectural Education, 48*(2), 82–98.

Sloane, P. D., et al. (2002). The Therapeutic Environment Screening Survey for Nursing Homes (TESS-NH): An observational instrument for assessing the physical environment of institutional settings for persons with dementia. *Journal of Gerontology: Social Sciences, 57B*(2), S69–S78.

Smaldino, J. J., & Crandell, C. C. (2000). Classroom amplification technology: Theory and practice. *Language, Speech, and Hearing Services in the Schools, 31,* 371–375.

Smith, D. (2003). Environmental colouration and the design process. *Color Research and Application, 28,* 360–365.

Smithsonian. (1998). *Carbons to Computers.* Retrieved from http://www.smithsonianeducation.org/scitech/carbons/text/equip.html

Smokowski, P. R., Buchanan, R., & Bacallo, M. (2009, April). *Acculturation and adjustment in Latino adolescents: How risk factors and cultural assets influence mental health.* Presented at the Society for Research on Child Development conference, Denver, CO.

Snow, C. E. (1927). Research on industrial illumination. *The Tech Engineering News, 8,* 257-282.

Sobel, D. (1990). A place in the world: Adults' memories of childhood special places. *Children's Environments Quarterly, 7*(4), 5–12.

Society for Neuroscience. (2006). *About neuroscience.* Retrieved from www.sfn.org

Sommer, R. (1973). *Design awareness.* New York: Holt, Rinehart and Winston.

Sommer, R., & Olsen, H. (1990). The soft classroom. *Environment and Behavior, 12,* 3–16.

Soussignan R., Schaal B., Marlier L., & Jiang T. (1997). Facial and autonomic responses to biological and artificial olfactory stimuli in human neonates: Re-examining early hedonic discrimination of odors. *Physiology & Behavior, 62,* 745–758.

Sparke, M. (2004). Political geographies of globalization: Dominance. *Progress in Human Geography, 28,* 777–794.

Stansbury, K., & Harris, M. L. (2000). Individual differences in stress reactions during a peer entry episode: Effects of age, temperament, approach behavior, and self-perceived peer competence. *Journal of Experimental Child Psychology, 76*(1), 50–63.

Steinbeck, J. (1939). *The grapes of wrath.* New York: The Viking Press.

Steinmetz, E. (2003). Americans with Disabilities: 2002 Household Economic Studies. U.S. Census Bureau, Retrieved November 2, 2009 from: http:// www.census. gov/prod/2006pubs/p70–107.pdf.

Steiner, J. E. (1979). Human Facial Expressions in response to taste and smell stimulations. *Advanced Child Development and Behavior, 13,* 257–295.

Stern, D. N., & Bender, E. P. (1974). An ethological study of children approaching a strange adult: Sex differences. In R. C. Friedman, et al. (Eds.), *Sex differences in behavior.* New York: Wiley.

Stoecklin, V. L. (1999). *Designing for all children.* Kansas City, MO: White Hutchinson Leisure & Learning Group. http://www.whitehutchinson.com/children/articles/ designforall.shtml

Stone, N. J. (2001). Designing effective study environments. *Journal of Environmental Psychology, 21,* 179–190.

Stone, N. J., & English, A. J. (1998). [Effects of] Task type, posters, and work space color on mood, satisfaction, and performance. *Journal of Environmental Psychology, 18,* 175–185.

Stratton, G. (2000). Promoting children's physical activity in primary school: An intervention study using playground markings. *Ergonomics, 43,* 1538–1546.

Strauss, W., & Howe, N. (1991). *Generations: The history of America's future: 1584 to 2069.* New York: William Morrow.

Stuart, F., & Curtis, H. A. (1964). Climate controlled and non-climate controlled schools. Clearwater, Florida: The Pinellas County Board of Education. *Air conditioning, Heating, and Ventilation, 57,* 78–79.

Sulek, J., & Hensley, R. (2004). The relative importance of food, atmosphere, and fairness of wait. *Cornell Hotel and Restaurant Administration Quarterly, 45*(3), 235–47.

Sumaya, I. C., Rienzi, B. M., Deegan II, J. F., & Moss, D. E. (2001). Bright light treatment decreases depression in institutionalized older adults: A placebo-controlled crossover study. *Journal of Gerontology: Medical Sciences, 56A,* M356–M360.

Sun, H.-J., Campos, J. L., Young, M., Chan, G. S. W., & Ellard, C. G. (2004). The contributions of static visual cues, non-visual cues, and optic flow in distance estimation. *Perception. 33*(1), 49–65.

Sundermier, L., Woollacott, M. H., Jensen, J. L., & Moore, S. (1996).Postural sensitivity to visual flow in aging adults with and without balance problems. *Journal of Gerontology: Medical Sciences, 51A–2,* M45–M52.

Surveillance, Evaluation, and Research (2007). Knox County, Tennessee Environmental Health Status Report. Knoxville, TN: Knox County Health Department.

Tannis, G. H., & Dabbs, J. M. (1975). Sex, setting and personal space: First grade through college. *Sociometry, 38,* 385–394.

Taylor, A. F., Kuo, F. E., & Sullivan, W. C. (2001). Coping with ADD: The surprising connection to green play settings. *Environment and Behavior, 33*(1), 54–77.

Taylor, A. F., Wiley, A., Kuo, F. E., & Sullivan, W. C. (1998). Growing up in the inner city: Green spaces as places to grow. *Environment and Behavior, 30*(1), 3–27.

Taylor, F. W. (1985). *The principles of scientific management.* Easton, Md: Hive Publishing. (original work published in 1911)

Taylor, R. B. (1988). *Human territorial functioning: An empirical, evolutionary perspective on individual and small group territorial cognitions, behaviors, and consequences.* Cambridge, MA: Cambridge University Press.

Taylor, S. E., et al. (2000). Biobehavioral responses to stress in females: Tend-and-befriend, not fight-or-flight. *Psychological Review, 107,* 411–429.

Teller, D. Y. (1998). Spatial and temporal aspects of infant color vision. *Vision Research, 38,* 3275–3282.

Thang, D. C. L., & Tan, B. L. B. (2003) Linking consumer perception to preference of retail stores: An empirical assessment of the multi-attributes of store image. *Journal of Retailing and Consumer Services, 10,* 193–200.

Tharpe, A. M., & Ashmead, D. H. (2001). A longitudinal investigation of infant auditory sensitivity. *Journal of the American Academy of Audiology, 10,* 104–112.

Tharpe, A. M., Ricketts T., & Sladen D. P. (2003). FM systems for children with minimal to mild hearing loss. *ACCESS: Achieving Clear Communication Employing Sound Solutions.* Proceedings of Chicago conference, Chapter 20: 191, Nov. 2003.

The Sense of Smell Institute. (1996). *Living with your sense of smell.* New York, NY: Author.

Thompson, G. M. (2002). Optimizing a restaurant's seating capacity. *Cornell Hotel and Restaurant Administration Quarterly, 43*(4), 48–57.

Thompson, G. M. (2003). Optimizing restaurant-table configuration: Specifying combinable tables. *Cornell Hotel and Restaurant Administration Quarterly, 44*(1), 53–60.

Thornton, J. (2002). *Environmental Impacts of polyvinyl chloride building materials.* Washington, DC: Healthy Building Network.

Tlauka, M., & Wilson, P. N. (1996). Orientation-free representations from navigation through a computer-simulated environment. *Environment and Behavior, 28,* 647–664.

Tognoli, J. (1980). Differences in women's and men's responses to domestic space. *Sex Roles, 66,* 833–842.

Tognoli, J. (1987). Residential environments. In I. Altman & D. Stokols (Eds.), *Handbook of environmental psychology.* New York: J. Wiley & Sons.

Torres, I. M., Summers, T. A., & Belleau, B. D., (2001). Men's shopping satisfaction and store preferences. *Journal of Retailing and Consumer Services, 8,* 205–212.

Totterdell, P., Kellett, S., Teuchmann, K., & Briner, R. B. (1998). Evidence of mood linkage in work groups. *Journal of Personality and Social Psychology, 74,* 1504–1515.

Toy, E. C., Simpson, E., Pleitez, M., Rosenfield, D., & Tintner, R. (2008). *Case files: Neurology.* New York: McGraw Hill Medical.

Trainor, L. J., & Heinmiller, B. M. (1998). The development of evaluative responses to music: Infants prefer to listen to consonance over dissonance. *Infant Behavior and Development, 21,* 77–88.

Trehub, S. E., & Schellenberg, E. G. (1995). Music: Its relevance to infants. *Annals of Child Development, 11,* 1–24.

Troussier, B., et al. (1999). Comparative study of two different kinds of school furniture among children. *Ergonomics, 42,* 516–526.

Tuan, Y. F. (1974). *Topophilia: a study of environmental perception, attitudes, and values.* Englewood Cliffs: Prentice-Hall.

Tun, P. A., & Wingfield, A. (1999). One voice too many: Adult age differences in language processing with different types of distracting sounds. *Journal of Gerontology: Psychological Sciences, 54B,* P317–P327.

Turley, L. W., & Milliman, R. E. (2000). Atmospheric effects on shopping behavior: A review of the experi-mental evidence. *Journal of Business Research, 49,* 193–211.

Turner, A. M., & Greenough, W. T. (1985). Differential rearing effects on rat visual cortex synapses. I. Synaptic and neuronal density and synapses per neuron. *Brain Research, 329,* 195–203.

Tversky, B. (2003). Structures of mental spaces: How people think about space. *Environment and Behavior, 35*(1), 66–80.

Tzeng, G. H., Teng, M. H., Chen, J. J., & Opricovic, S. (2002). Multicriteria selection for a restaurant location in Taipei. *International Journal of Hospitality Management, 21*(1), 171–187.

U.S. Bureau of the Census. (2001). *Record share of new mothers in labor force (data from the June 1998 supplement to the Current Population Survey).* Washington, DC: U.S. Department of Commerce News.

U.S. Bureau of Labor Statistics, Division of Information Services. (2005, September 30). *Frequency of working at home in 2004.* Retrieved from http://www.bls.gov/opub/ted/2005/sept/wk4/art05.htm

U.S. Census Bureau (as reported in the online publication *Relocation Journal & Real Estate News,* January 24, 2000). *Newsbreak 6–4: Moving from here to there.* Retrieved from www.relojournal.com/nbarchive/nbn216.htm

U.S. Census Bureau News. (2000). *Moving rate among Americans declines, census bureau says.* Retrieved from www.census.gov/Press-Release/www/releases/archives/population/000420.html

U.S. Census Bureau (2006, December 15). Nearly half of our lives spent with TV, radio, internet, newspapers, according to Census Bureau Publication. Retrieved from http://www.census.gov/newsroom/releases/archives/miscellaneous/cb06-184.html

U.S. Census Bureau, Population Division. (2008, August 8). *Projections of the population by selected age groups and sex for the United States: 2010 to 2050* (NP2008-T2). Retrieved from www.census.gov/population/www/projections/files/nation/summary/np2008-t2.xls

U.S. Consumer Product Safety Commission, Office of Information and Public Affairs. (2003). *Consumer Product Safety Improvement Act.* Washington, DC. Retrieved from www.cpsc.gov

U.S. Department of Labor, Occupational Safety and Health Administration. (n.d.). *Regulations (Standards - 29 CFR): Occupational noise exposure. - 1926.52.* Retrieved from http://www.osha.gov/pls/oshaweb/owadisp.show_document?p_table=standards&p_id=9735

U.S. Department of Education, National Center for Education Statistics. (2005). *Projections of education statistics to 2014* (NCES 2005-074). Washington, DC.

U.S. Environmental Protection Agency. (April 1991). *Indoor Air Facts No. 4 (revised): Sick building syndrome (SBS).* Available at: http://www.epa.gov/iaq/pubs/sbs.html

Ullah, M. B., Kurniawan, J. T., Pho, L. K., Wai, T. K., & Tregenza, P. R. (2003). Attenuation of diffuse daylight due to dust deposition on glazing in a tropical urban environment. *Lighting Research and Technology, 35*(1), 19–29.

Ulrich, R. S. (1979). Visual landscapes and psychological well-being. *Landscape Research, 4,* 17–22.

Ulrich, R. S. (1984a). The psychological benefits of plants. *Garden, 8*(6), 16–21.

Ulrich, R. S. (1984b). View through a window may influence recovery from surgery. *Science, 224,* 420–421

Ulrich, R. S. (1986). Human responses to vegetation and landscapes. *Landscape and Urban Planning, 12,* 29–44.

Ulrich, R. S. (1987). Improving medical outcomes with environmental design. *Journal of Healthcare Design, IX,* 2–7.

Ulrich, R.S., et al. (1991). Stress recovery during exposure to natural and urban environments. *Journal of Environmental Psychology, 11,* 201–220.

Underhill, P. (1999). *Why we buy: The xcience of shopping.* New York, NY: Simon & Schuster.

United Nations, Economic Commission for Europe (2002). Towards a knowledge-based economy: Russian Federation – Country readiness assessment report. Business & economics. Retrieved from https://unp.un.org/details.aspx?entry=E03070.

University of Virginia Library. (Last Modified May 1, 2003). *The dictionary of the history of ideas.* Retrieved from http://etext.virginia.edu/cgi-local/DHI/dhi.cgi?id=dv2-26

Uno, H., et al. (1989). Hippocampal damage associated with prolonged and fatal stress in primates. *Journal of Neuroscience, 9,* 1705–1711.

Updike, C. D., (1994). Comparison of FM auditory trainers, CROS aids, and personal amplification in unilaterally hearing impaired children. *Journal of the American Academy of Audiology, 5,* 204–209.

Valdez, P., & Mehrabian, A. (1994). Effects of color on emotions. *Journal of Experimental Psychology: General, 123,* 394–409.

Valle, R. (1989). The emergence of transpersonal psychology. In E. Light and B. D. Lebowitz (Eds.). *Alzheimer's disease treatment and family stress: Directions for research* (pp. 322–339). (DHHS Publication No. ADM 89–1569). Washington, DC: U.S. Government Printing Office.

Van Andel, J. (1990). Places children like, dislike, and fear. *Children's Environments Quarterly, 7*(4), 24–31.

Van Asperdt, A. (1999). BOOGIE-WOOGIE: The suburban commercial strip and its neighborhood. *Landscape Journal, 18*(1), 41–53.

van den Berg, A. E. (2005). *Health impacts of healing environments: A review of evidence for benefits of nature, daylight, fresh air, and quiet in healthcare settings.* Groningen, Netherlands: University Hospital Groningen.

Van Houtven, G., Honeycutt, A., Gilman, B., McCall, N., Throneburg, W., & Sykes, K. (2008). Costs of illness among older adults: An analysis of six major health conditions with significant environmental risk factors. RTI Press publication No. RR-0002-0809. Research Triangle Park, NC: RTI International. Retrieved from http://www.rti.org/rtipress.

van Rijn, H., & Stappers, J. J. (2008). The puzzling life of autistic toddlers: Design guidelines from the LINKX Project. *Advances in Human-Computer Interaction, 10,* 1–8. doi:10.1155/2008/639435.

van Vliet, W. (1983). Exploring the fourth environment: An examination of the home range of city and suburban teenagers. *Environment and Behavior, 15*(5), 567–588.

Veitch, J. A. (1997). Revisiting the performance and mood effects of information about lighting and fluorescent lamp type. *Journal of Environmental Psychology, 17*(1), 253–262.

Veitch, J. A., & McColl, S. L. (1993). *Full spectrum fluorescent lighting effects on people: A critical review (No. 659).* Ottawa, Canada: Institute for Research in Construction.

Veitch, J. A., & McColl, S. L. (2001). A critical examination of perceptual and cognitive effects attributed to full-spectrum fluorescent lighting. *Ergonomics, 44*(3), 255–279.

Velmans, M. (Ed.). (1996). *The science of consciousness: Psychological, neuropsychological, and clinical reviews.* London: Routledge.

Verbrugge, L. M., & Taylor, R. B. (1980). Consequences of population density and size. *Urban Affairs Quarterly, 16*(3), 135–160.

Verderber, S. F. (1986). Dimensions of person window transactions in the hospital environment. *Environment and Behavior,1 8*(4), 450–466.

Vernon, H. M. (1919). *The influences of hours of work and of ventilation on output in tinplate manufacture.* Publisher unknown.

Vithhayathawornwong, S., Danko, S., & Tolbert, P. (2003). The role of the physical environment in supporting organizational creativity. *Journal of Interior Design, 29*(1/2), 1–16.

Vrugt, A. J., & Kerkstra, A. (1984). Sex differences in nonverbal communication, *Journal Semiotica, 61*(1/2), 1–40.

Wachs, M. (1989). When planners lie with numbers. *Journal of the American Planning Association, 55*(4), 476–479.

Wade, N., & Swanston, M. (1991). *An introduction to visual perception,* London: Routledge.

Walsh, D. W., Christen, H. T., Miller, G. T., Callsen, C. E., Cilluffo, F. J., & Maniscalco, P. M. (2005). *National incident management system principles and practices.* Sudbury, MA: Jones and Bartlett.

Wapner, S. (1981). Transactions of persons-in-environments: Some critical transitions. *Journal of Environmental Psychology, 18,* 102–112.

Warnock, F. F., & Sandrin, D. (2004). Comprehensive description of newborn distress related pain behavior (newborn male circumcision). *Pain, 107,* 242–255.

Watson, J. B. (1925). Psychology as the behaviorist views it. *Behaviorism.* New York: People's Institute.

Waxman, L. (2006). The coffee shop: Social and physical factors influencing place attachment. *Journal of Interior Design, 31,* 35–53.

Weinstein, C. S. (1987). *Spaces for children: The built environment and child development.* New York: Plenum Press.

Weir, E. (2005). Stroke prevention. *Canadian Medical Association Journal, 173,* 363.

Weiskrantz, L. (1995). Blindsight – Not an island unto itself. *Current Directions in Psychological Science, 4,* 146–151.

Weisman, J. (1981). Evaluating architectural legibility: Way-finding in the built environment. *Environment and Behavior, 13*(2), 189–204.

Weisner, T. S., & Weibel, J. C. (1981). Home environments and family lifestyles in California. *Environment and Behavior, 13*(4), 417–460.

Weisz, J. R., Rothbaum, F. M., & Blackburn, T. C. (1984). Standing in and standing out: The psychology of control in America and Japan. *American Psychologist, 39,* 955–969.

Weller, M. P. (1985). Crowds, mobs, and riots. *Medicine, Science, and the Law, 25,* 295–303.

Wells, N. M. (2000a). At home with nature: Effects of "greenness" on children's cognitive functioning. *Environment and Behavior, 32*(6), 775–795.

Wells, N. M. (2000b). Office clutter or meaningful personal displays: The role of office personalization in employee and organizational well-being. *Journal of Environmental Psychology, 20,* 239–255.

Welty, K., & Puck, B. (2001). *Modeling Athena: Preparing young women for work and citizenship in a technological society.* Madison; WI: Department of Public Instruction.

Wener, R. (1977). Non-density factors in the perception of crowding. *Dissertation Abstracts International, 37D,* 3560–3570.

Wener, R., & Kaminoff, R. D. (1983). Improving environmental information: Effects of signs on perceived crowding and behavior. *Environment and Behavior, 15,* 3–20.

Werner, L. A., & Bargones, J. Y. (1992). Psychoacoustic development of human infants. In C. Rovee-Collier & L. Lipsitt (Eds.), Advances in infancy research (pp. 103–145). Norwood, NJ: Ablex.

Westin, A. F. (1967). *Privacy and freedom.* New York: Atheneum.

White, R. (2004). *Adults are from Earth; Young children are from the Moon—Designing for children: A complex challenge.* Kansas City, MO: White Hutchinson Leisure & Learning Group.

Whitehouse, S., et al. (2001). Evaluating a children's hospital garden environment: Utilization and consumer satisfaction. *Journal of Environmental Psychology, 21,* 301–314.

Whyte, A. V. T. (1977). *Field methods in guidelines for field studies in environmental perception, MAB.* Technical Notes. Paris, France: UNESCO.

Wicker, A. W. (1987). Behavior settings reconsidered: Temporal stages, resources, internal dynamics, context. In D. Stokols & I. Altman (Eds.), *Handbook of environmental psychology* (Vol. 2, pp. 612–652). New York: Wiley.

Wickremaratchi, M. M., & Llewelyn, J. G. (2006). Effects of ageing on touch. *Postgraduate Medical Journal, 82,* 301–304.

Widmar, R. (1984). Preferences for multi-family housing: Some implications for public participation. *Journal of Architectural and Planning Research, 1,* 245–260.

Wilcoff, W. L., & Abed, L. W., (1994). *Practicing universal design: An interpretation of the ADA.* New York, NY: Van Nostrand Reinhold.

Wildes, V. J., & Seo, W. (2001). Customers vote with their forks: Consumer complaining behavior in the restaurant industry. *International Journal of Hospitality and Tourism Administration, 2*(2), 21–34.

Wilkoff, W. L., & Abed, L. W. (1994). *Practicing universal design.* New York, NY: Van Nostrand Reinhold.

Williams, P., Paridaen, M., Dossa, K., & Dumais, M. (2001). *Agritourism market and product development status report.* Centre for Tourism Policy and Research, Simon Fraser University: Burnaby, BC, Canada.

Williamson, S. (2001). Design principles for engaged workplaces. *The Nonprofit Quarterly, 7.* Retrieved from www.nonprofitquarterly.org/section/1773.html

Wilson, R. I., & Nicoll, R. A. (2002). Endocannabinoid signaling in the brain. *Science, 296,* 678-682.

Wineman, J. (1982). The office environments as a source of stress. In G. W. Evans (Ed.), *Environmental stress* (pp. 256-285). New York: Cambridge University Press.

Wise, J. A., & Wise, B. K. (ca. 1985). *Bank interiors and bank robberies: A design approach to environmental security.* Rolling Meadows, IL: Bank Administration Institute.

Witt, S. D. (1997). Parental influence of children's socialization to gender roles. *Adolescence, 32,* 253-259.

Witzel, M. (2000). *The American motel.* Osceola, WI: Motorbooks International.

Wohlfarth, H. (1986). *Color and light effects on students' achievement, behavior and physiology.* Edmonton, Alberta: Planning Services Branch, Alberta Education.

Wohlwill, J. F. (1966). The physical environment: A problem for a psychology of stimulation. *Journal of Social Issues, 22*(4), 29-28.

Womble, P., & Studebaker, S. (1981). Crowding in a national park campground: Katmai National Monument in Alaska. *Environment and Behavior, 13,* 557-573.

Worchel, S., & Teddlie, C. (1976). The experience of crowding: A two-factor theory. *Journal of Personality and Social Psychology, 34,* 36-40.

World Health Organization. (2000). *Occupational and community noise.* Retrieved from http://www.who.int/mediacentre/factsheets/fs258/en/

World Health Organization. (2007). *Harmonizing mind and body, people and systems: People at the Centre of Health Care.* Geneva, Switzerland: WHO Press.

Wu, W., & Ng, E. (2003). A review of the development of daylighting in schools. *Lighting Research and Technology, 35*(2), 111-125.

Wuest, B., Emenheiser, D., & Tas, R. (2001). Is the lodging industry serving the needs of mature consumers? A comparison of mature travelers' and lodging managers' perceptions of service needs. *Journal of Hospitality & Leisure Marketing, 8*(3/4), 85-96.

Xerri, C., Merzenich, M. M., Jenkins, W., & Santucci, S. (1999). Representational plasticity in cortical area 3b paralleling tactual-motor skill acquisition in adult monkeys. *Cereb. Cortex, 9*(3), 264-276.

Yamamoto, T., & Ishii, S. (1995). Developmental and environmental psychology: A microgenetic developmental approach to transition from a small elementary school to a big junior high school. *Environment and Behavior, 27*(1), 33-42.

Yavorcik, C. (2008, December 30). Make a Change Today! Retrieved from http://support. autism-society.org/site/News2?page=NewsArticle&id=12477.

Young, C. A., & Brewer, K. P. (2001). Marketing continuing care retirement communities: A model of residents' perceptions of quality. *Journal of Hospitality & Leisure Marketing, 9*(1/2), 133-151.

Yudelson, J. (2010). *Sustainable retail development: New success strategies.* Springer, New York, NY

Yussen, S. R., & Santrock, J. W., (1982). *Child Development* (2nd ed.). Dubuque, IA: Wm. C. Brown Company.

Zandvliet, D. B., & Straker, L. M. (2001). Physical and psychosocial aspects of the learning environment in information technology rich classrooms. *Ergonomics, 44,* 838-857.

Zavotka, S. L., & Timmons, M. A. (1996). Creative writers' psychological and environmental needs in their home interior writing environments. *Housing and Society, 23*(3), 1-25.

Zeisel, J. (2000). Environmental design effects on Alzheimer symptoms in long-term care residences. *World Hospitals and Health Services, 36*(3), 27-31.

Zentner, M., & Kagan, J. (1996). Perception of music by infants. Nature, *383,* 29.

Zubek, J. P. (Ed.) (1969). *Sensory deprivation: Fifteen years of research.* New York: Appleton-Century-Crofts.

Zuger, A. (August 8, 2000). Reading glasses, as inevitable as death and taxes. Or are they? *New York Times; Health Section.*

Zuravin, S. J. (1986). Residential density and urban child mistreatment: An aggregate analysis. *Journal of Family Violence, 1,* 307-322.

Zwarts, A. & Coolen, H. (2006). *The meaning of preferences for residential environment features: A case study among apartment dwellers in the Netherlands.* Chicago: Locke Science Publishing Company, Inc.

Index